AMERICAN
NEGRO SLAVERY

ULRICH BONNELL PHILLIPS

AMERICAN NEGRO SLAVERY

A Survey of the Supply,
Employment and Control
Of Negro Labor
As Determined by the Plantation Regime

LOUISIANA STATE UNIVERSITY PRESS
BATON ROUGE AND LONDON

Louisiana Paperback Edition, 1966
05 04 03 02 01 00 99 98 97 96   12 11 10 9 8

by arrangement with Appleton-Century-Crofts, Inc.
Copyright 1918 by D. Appleton and Company
Foreword copyright 1966, 1994 by Louisiana State University Press
All rights reserved
Manufactured in the United States of America
ISBN 0-8071-0109-5 (pbk.)

TO
MY WIFE

FOREWORD

ULRICH BONNELL PHILLIPS & HIS CRITICS

Eugene D. Genovese

Since World War II increasing numbers of American historians have been reading Ulrich Bonnell Phillips with hostility, suspicion, and even contempt; worse, they have not been encouraging their students to read him at all. This negative reaction is not difficult to account for, although it stands in the starkest contrast to Phillips' enviable reputation in his own day. David M. Potter spoke for the historical profession when, at the time of Phillips' death in 1934, he wrote of "his conciseness, his remarkable accuracy of expression, his avoidance of the trite and inane, and his profusion of fruitful suggestions" and then added, "He never set pen to paper without expressing cogent ideas." [1] Times have changed. Racism and a patronizing attitude toward the Negro have gone out of style since they began to embarrass United States foreign policy. What could be more natural than that Ulrich Phillips, a Georgian who loved the Old South and never could take the Negro seriously, should have gone out of style too?

Phillips came close to greatness as a historian, perhaps as close as any historian this country has yet produced. We may leave to those who live in the world of absolute good and evil the task of explaining how a man with such primitive views on fundamental social questions could write such splendid history. Let there be no mistake about it: Phillips was a racist, however benign and paternalistic. Some historians have argued that he was gradually moving away from racist doctrines as he began to catch up with the new anthropological and biological researches making their

[1] David M. Potter, "A Bibliography of the Printed Writings of Ulrich Bonnell Phillips," *Georgia Historical Quarterly,* XVIII (September, 1934), 271.

appearance in the last decade or two of his life. Between *American Negro Slavery* (1918) and *Life and Labor in the Old South* (1929) he is supposed to have shifted away from a view holding the Negro to be biologically inferior to one holding him to be culturally backward. The shift, in my judgment, was merely one of emphasis, for Phillips held both views simultaneously. But, in any case, it is difficult to become enthusiastic about a shift from a less to a more sophisticated racism that could not have stood critical examination even in his day.[2] If we dwell on this weakness now, it is neither to establish our own superior virtue (it is not especially difficult to be verbally an integrationist in 1966, especially if one lives in New York City), nor even to try to provide a balanced estimate in deference to the academic niceties. It is rather to suggest that his racism cost him dearly and alone accounts for his lapse from greatness as a historian. It blinded him; it inhibited him from developing fully his own extraordinary insights; it prevented him from knowing many things he in fact knew very well.

We may begin with Chapter I, "The Early Exploitation of Guinea," which is easily the worst in the book and is close to being worthless. The kindest thing that could be done with it would be to burn it, for its discussion of African society was foolish and incompetent when written and is embarrassing to have to read today. The student who wishes to learn anything about the range of problems discussed must begin elsewhere—with J. D. Fage's *Introduction to the History of West Africa*, J. Spencer Trimingham's studies of African Islam, Basil Davidson's *Black Mother* and *Lost Cities of Africa*, or with the researches of R. S. Rattray and other anthropologists, especially the British. I doubt that there is an important point made in Phillips' opening chapter that

[2]See the criticism of Phillips' racial views in Melville J. Herskovits, *The Myth of the Negro Past* (New York, 1941), Chapters I and II; Kenneth M. Stampp, *The Peculiar Institution* (New York, 1956), Chapter I; and Eugene D. Genovese, *The Political Economy of Slavery* (New York, 1965), Chapter III.

could stand critical examination. We may hurry past this clumsy beginning, but the bias which led him so far astray will return to plague him elsewhere.

In Chapter II we meet Phillips the historian. Much work has been done on the African slave trade since Phillips wrote, and no advanced student could be content with this sketch, but it stands up surprisingly well as an introduction to such important questions as the rise of the trade within the context of European rivalries or even the corrupting effects of European penetration on African culture. The most remarkable part of the discussion, however, concerns tribal differences. Phillips was apparently convinced that these differences somehow affected life in the New World. His discussion is halting, unsure, speculative, but it does mark the way forward. Unfortunately, his insight has not been developed by his successors, apart from some discussions of doubtful value in the work of Melville J. Herskovits. Here as elsewhere, Phillips grasped the complexity of his subject and indicated the need to probe on many fronts.

Chapter III, "The Sugar Islands," again confronts us with a tantalizing collection of insights and hypotheses that ought to make us wonder what historians have been doing for the last half century. Long before Frank Tannenbaum, not to mention Stanley M. Elkins, Phillips drew attention to the different kinds of New World slavery, to the importance of divergent cultural traditions, and to the separate developments of the ruling classes. His remarks on the bourgeois quality of the British West Indian slaveholders, in contrast to the American, still need to be pursued and extended. In short, even in his background explorations, if we leave aside those which succumbed completely to his racist bias, he asked more and better questions than many of us still are willing to admit, and he carried on his investigations with consistent freshness and critical intelligence.

The chapters on the tobacco colonies, rice coast, Northern colonies, and many others, remain peerless introductions to their subjects. His treatment of the revolutionary era will still stand up. The appearance of Robert McColley's *Slavery and Jeffersonian Virginia* (1964), for example, deepens and complements much more in Phillips than it upsets. The account of the closing of the African slave trade, the westward movement, and the domestic slave trade, however much they need to be qualified, corrected, or supplemented by the work of later historians, may still be read with the assurance that they are rarely wide of the mark. I find it incredible that Kenneth M. Stampp should write: "It may be that his most durable monument will be the vast amount of new source material which he uncovered." [3]

I have so far not discussed the heart of the book, Chapters XII-XXIII, against which his critics have struck their most telling blows. Since Richard Hofstadter and Stampp have led the attack we shall have to examine their arguments in some detail. We may quickly dispose of the attack on Phillips as an economic historian. Chapters XVIII and XIX of this book are still worth reading after decades of the most severe criticism. Undoubtedly, they suffer from some confusion and hasty generalization; undoubtedly they contain mistakes. [4] Their central notions retain force and value: that slavery "was less a business than a life"; that its economics cannot be understood apart from politics, social structure, and prevailing values; that the system struggled against a tendency toward unprofitability in the narrow sense of the term; and that even when it was profitable in that narrow sense for the slaveholders it seriously retarded regional development. Not everyone agrees with these and other conclusions; the debate has been unusually vigorous and will continue. What is astonishing is how well Phillips presented his case and how much of it remains respectable interpretation worthy of continued ex-

---

[3]Kenneth M. Stampp, "The Historian and Southern Negro Slavery," *American Historical Review*, LVII (April, 1952), 613.

[4]For example, in his discussion of the profitability of slavery Phillips makes much of the relationship between slave and cotton prices but fails to consider labor productivity. As a result, he neglects the factor that might have offset the unfavorable spread between the two sets of price data.

ploration and discussion. Harold D. Woodman has demonstrated
Phillips' continued relevance for the debate on the economics of
slavery and not surprisingly has given Phillips unusual attention
and space in his anthology *Slavery and the Southern Economy*.[5]
To appreciate Phillips as an economic historian one needs to go
beyond the impressive discussions in this book. His groundbreak-
ing work in the formation of the black belts (1906) stressed the
concentration of wealth and economic power and laid the basis
for a social history of the constituent classes. His study of the
plantation under slave and free labor (1925) developed several
of the themes presented here and is still useful as an introduction
to antebellum and postbellum Southern society.[6] These and
many other specialized articles deserve to be studied with the
greatest care; much of the analysis they contain has yet to be
surpassed. This side of Phillips' work received considerable
praise at one time but no longer receives the attention it deserves.
Perhaps the most striking illustration of how easy it is to slight
his accomplishment may be found in a generally appreciative
and sympathetic essay by Wood Gray. He evaluates *A History
of Transportation in the Eastern Cotton Belt to 1860* (1908) as
"essentially a straight forward factual narrative . . . ."[7] On the
contrary, the book is an impressive contribution to political economy and economic history. Phillips carefully traces the development of a quasi-colonial transportation system, which arose in
response to special kinds of economic needs and then reinforced
not merely a particular economy but an entire structure of political
and social power. Phillips' modesty, unwillingness to resort to an

[5]Harold D. Woodman, "The Profitability of Slavery: A Historical Perennial," *Journal of Southern History*, XXIX (August, 1963), 303-25;
Woodman (ed.), *Slavery and the Southern Economy*.
[6]Ulrich Bonnell Phillips, "The Origin and Growth of the Southern Black
Belts," *American Historical Review*, XI (July, 1906), 798-816; "Plantations with Slave Labor and Free," *American Historical Review*, XXX
(July, 1925), 738-53.
[7]Wood Gray, "Ulrich Bonnell Phillips," in *The Marcus Jernegan Essays
in American Historiography*, ed. William T. Hutchinson (Chicago,
1937), 361.

unnecessarily technical vocabulary, and cautious presentation of generalizations ought not to cause us to underestimate his achievement. That book like this one and the whole body of his lifetime's work might well serve as required reading for students of colonialism—or as we politely call it today, "the economics of underdevelopment."

Hofstadter's critique pertains, as he himself cautions us, to four chapters: XII, "The Cotton Regime"; XIII, "Types of Large Plantations"; XIV, "Plantation Management"; and XV, "Plantation Labor." It consists of two main points: Phillips' data are inadequate and misleading, for they are drawn only from plantation-sized estates; and they are not even a good sample of plantation-sized estates, for they are overwhelmingly drawn from the largest. Hofstadter adds a third point, which is, however, a corollary of these, that the vast majority of slaves did not live on large plantations. He adds that Phillips nowhere made a serious effort to compare large and small plantations or plantations and farms but observes, "The precise importance of this failure . . . cannot be stated until much more investigation has been done in the great realm that Phillips chose to ignore. . . ." [8]

Hofstadter recognizes the paucity of data for small units but says that we should at least suspect generalizations based only on larger units. He shows that Phillips cited manuscript material pertaining to units averaging two hundred slaves—virtually a handful of estates and certainly only those forming the extreme top of society. The states of Maryland, Missouri, Kentucky, and Tennessee, with a small-slaveholders' economy embracing 18 percent of all Southern slaves, virtually went unnoticed by Phillips. Hofstadter notes that the task of studying the Deep South absorbed Phillips' energies but properly adds that consideration of the border states might force important revisions in his findings.

Hofstadter raises fair questions but hardly touches the value of Phillips' work. Phillips drew his illustrations from the largest

[8] Richard Hofstadter, "U. B. Phillips and the Plantation Legend," *Journal of Negro History*, XXIX (April, 1944), 110.

plantations because they provided the fullest accounts, but his lifelong researches undoubtedly brought him into contact with the records of smaller units. He clearly believed that in certain essential respects the largest plantations did not vary significantly from the "average" ones. The real question concerns the units below the plantation rank. There is no evidence that treatment of slaves, for example, varied dramatically between units of twenty and two hundred. Since half the slaves lived on plantations (units of twenty or more) Phillips work would be of great importance even if it could be shown that conditions did vary dramatically on the farms.

As a matter of fact, there is no reason to believe that data from small farms would upset Phillips' generalizations. Hofstadter admits that Phillips might have used Olmsted's work to advantage, for he thought slaves better treated on the smaller units. Stampp, in *The Peculiar Institution*, argues strongly for this view, although on little evidence. In short, after fifty years we still could not demonstrate that a consideration of smaller units would in itself shake Phillips' main contentions. Similarly, the work of specialists on slavery in the border states has not supported the common assumption that treatment there varied much from Deep South patterns. When, therefore, Hofstadter tells us that Olmsted offers us "a fuller and more accurate knowledge of the late antebellum South" [9] than Phillips, he is well wide of the mark.

All of this "scientific" and statistical refutation of Phillips does not get us anywhere, but we soon do get to the heart of the matter. At the beginning we note the charge that Phillips slights the smallholder in favor of the great planter. Thus appears his class bias. Later, we note that he could not take the Negro seriously and that he hardly did him justice. Thus appears his race bias. The two together provide us with the perfect white Southerner: "The way of thinking which underlay Phillips' work

[9]*Ibid.,* 121.

needs no elaboration here. He was a native of Georgia, to whom the Southern past always appeared in a haze of romance . . . . His books cannot best be placed in the course of our intellectual history when it is realized that they represent a latter-day phase of the pro-slavery argument." [10] I do not find these *ad hominem* thrusts helpful. Phillips' concern with the small ruling class of slaveholders was altogether proper: that class dominated the economy, politics, and social life of the South; it imposed its visions and values on the humbler men in society; it in fact ruled more completely than many other ruling classes in modern times. Even its notions of master-slave relationships set the tone for society, and for that reason alone an emphasis on its practices has been justified. Thus, Hofstadter even misses the point when he attacks Phillips for stressing "ideal rules" of treatment, instead of actual practice. Phillips did look closely at practice, but did not err by considering carefully those "ideal rules," for the standards men publicly set for themselves tell us much of the quality of the men and tell us something of the practice.

We are finally brought to the last complaint: Phillips' race bias made him a prisoner of the slaveholders' viewpoint and blinded him to much of the record. Hofstadter scores heavily when he remarks with barely restrained sarcasm that Phillips' "great powers of intellectual resistance" are attested to by the avoidance of the enormous problem of miscegenation. The charge is unanswerable, but the conclusion of Hofstadter's argument is another matter: "Let the study of the Old South be undertaken by other scholars who have absorbed the viewpoint of modern cultural anthropology, who have a feeling for social psychology . . . and who will realize that any history of slavery must be written in large part from the standpoint of the slave . . . ." [11] Since there is no "viewpoint of modern cultural anthropology"— only contending schools of thought, as in every discipline—the

[10]*Ibid.*, 121-22.
[11]*Ibid.*, 124.

criticism is hard to take. Most anthropologists today reject racism, but we might reflect on the development of this rejection, for Adolf Hitler probably had more to do with it than Franz Boas. A theory of racial inferiority could no more be debated calmly and tested scientifically today than could the virtues of communism under the watchful eye of the late Senator McCarthy. Phillips had an anthropological view of his own. It was certainly primitive, but it is not certain that his neo-abolitionist critics today defend views that will stand up forever or that have been more objectively arrived at. Phillips' racism needs to be rejected firmly, for it condemns a people to inferior status without evidence of inherent inferiority, but the task facing us is to evaluate its effects on his work, rather than to assume that it automatically ruined everything by its pervasive sinfulness.

The stage has been set for a reevaluation of Phillips' view of slavery by the publication of Stanley M. Elkins' *Slavery: A Problem in American Institutional and Intellectual Life* (1959), which was originally prepared as a dissertation under Hofstadter's direction. Elkins pays handsome tribute to Phillips in his excellent survey of the literature on slavery and then identifies and criticizes Phillips' view of the Negro. Elkins argues that Phillips' work has been surpassed by Stampp's *The Peculiar Institution*: "There is now little that Phillips did with the plantation regime that has not been done with greater thoroughness by his Northern successor." Elkins hails Stampp's greater scholarship and wider research. He is entitled to his opinion, just as we are entitled to dissent on each count without denying the immense value of Stampp's work, which permanently and positively destroyed some of the worst features of the older scholarship. The irony in Elkins' enthusiasm for Stampp, as he himself at least once seems to glimpse (p. 83), is that Phillips' view of the Negro slave, with its racist underpinnings, comes out close to the Sambo whom Elkins seeks to explain. His views of slavery present a firmer basis for Elkins' social-psychological analysis than do those of Stampp, whose emphasis on brutality fits into Elkins' controversial and dubious concentration-camp analogy. Phillips' view of a patriarchal plantation dominated by a spirit of paternalism, which of course may be either benign or cruel, should be taken into full account by any theory of infantilization of the dependents.

Stampp published his critique of Phillips in 1952 and presented his alternative account in 1956. If we examine his 1952 effort in relation to that of 1956 we get a clearer notion of the difficulties inherent in the subject, for Stampp was not able to do in his own book much that he, like Hofstadter, had criticized Phillips for not doing. When, for example, Stampp wrote that we still awaited "the first scientific and completely objective study of the institution which is based upon no assumptions whose validity cannot be thoroughly proved," [12] he might have known that we would still be waiting in 1966. He wrote hopefully that the subject was becoming "less and less an emotional issue between scholarly descendants of the northern abolitionists and of the southern proslavery school." [13] That the present generation of writers on slavery, so many of whom display a blind hostility toward slavery and slaveholders, may qualify as more objective and "scientific" than their predecessors remains to be demonstrated.

Stampp agreed with Hofstadter that Phillips erred in sampling only the largest estates and insisted that travelers' accounts, which Phillips used sparingly, and the manuscript census returns and court records uncovered by Frank L. Owsley and his students could provide a satisfactory picture of slavery on small units. Stampp himself noted that the results of such investigations would be unpredictable since logic suggested that slaves on small units would be treated better than those on large in some respects and worse in others. When Stampp faces these problems in *The Peculiar Institution,* he insists that small slaveholders generally demonstrated greater paternalism and treated their slaves better

[12]Stampp, "The Historian and Southern Negro Slavery," 613.
[13]*Ibid.,* 614.

than did large slaveholders. This conclusion hardly does violence
to Phillips' main contentions, but the more interesting feature of
Stampp's argument is that it is thinly documented and consists of
little more than vague impressions. The difficulties of arriving at
a more precise view of difference between large and small units
plagued Stampp quite as much as they plagued Phillips.

Stampp looked suspiciously at Phillips' generalizations about the
kindness of masters and insisted that slaveholders ranged from
kind to cruel with any master being both to some degree and in
some circumstances. These observations make good sense so far
as they go, but they miss the main point. Phillips repeatedly shows
his awareness of cruelty and the harsher side of master-slave relationships, although he is open to severe criticism for under-
statement. The essential contribution he makes is to the notion of
Southern paternalism, which Stampp and many others too often
confuse with kindliness. Paternalism necessarily involves harshness and may even involve cruelty so long as it is within the context of a strong sense of duty and responsibility toward those in
dependent status. A father may be cruel to disobedient children
and yet be deeply concerned with their material and moral welfare. Phillips also argues that the slaves' standard of material
comfort rose steadily during the nineteenth century, and Stampp,
in *The Peculiar Institution,* comes to a similar conclusion. The
difference is that Stampp sees economic interest dominating the
master-slave relationship and therefore treats the improvement as
a matter of small importance, whereas Phillips describes a process
of deepening patriarchal commitment as the slave society matured.
Phillips does so in a somewhat contradictory or inconsistent way,
for he is loathe to dwell too much on the harsher side of eight-
eenth-century slavery and blunts the very point he is making for
the later period. His obsession with the problem of racial hege-
mony prevents him from developing his insights into the class
character of patriarchal ideology. Notwithstanding these objec-
tions, his viewpoint is decidedly more fruitful than that of his

critic and permits him, for example, to treat the improvement in
the slaves' conditions of life as an illustration of the advance of a
distinct world view.

Stampp repeatedly strikes blows at Phillips, some of which are
on the mark, but rarely transcends his performance. He takes
Phillips to task for insisting on the Negro's docility and argues
that the slave population had its share of active rebels, who in
any case constitute a minority in any society. Thus, Phillips'
pleasant judgment is replaced by an unpleasant one (or vice
versa), but the principal historical questions remain unanswered:
What accounts for the extent of docility? Under what conditions
does individual and collective rebellion occur? What are the
specific historical forms of accommodation, docility, and rebellion,
and what is the significance of these forms for Southern culture?
So long as we remain on the level on which Phillips placed the
discussion and Stampp chose to keep it, we cannot get much further
along, but if we must choose between two one-sided views, it is
difficult not to regard Phillips' as closer to the norm.

Similarly, whereas Phillips stresses the lighter side of slave life,
Stampp brushes the singing and dancing aside as unworthy of
close attention. One may and should criticize Phillips for not
analyzing these activities more closely to see the extent of group
consciousness as well as of ordinary diversions and for not seeing
how deeply they penetrated the life of the master in a thousand
subtle ways. Yet, Phillips gives us food for thought with his
descriptions, anecdotes, and sense of plantation community life;
Stampp pictures a prison camp peopled by jailers and inmates.
Whereas Phillips sees only the bare outlines of the road ahead,
Stampp would take us in the wrong direction.

The difference may be perceived most sharply in Stampp's
discussion of so narrow a question as investment in slaves: "And
what is to be made of the oft-repeated argument that the planters
got nowhere because 'they bought lands and slaves wherewith
to grow cotton, and with the proceeds ever bought more slaves
to make more cotton'? If this is the essence of economic futility,

then one must also pity the late Andrew Carnegie who built a
mill wherewith to make steel, and with the proceeds ever built
more mills to make more steel." [14] The economic consequences of
reliance on direct investments in labor and therefore on a labor-
intensive path to economic growth were grasped by Phillips but
elude his critic. Beyond economics, the social relations inherent
in the two cases cited by Stampp are diametrically opposed and
give rise to different ways of life and thought which themselves
have profound consequences for the economy; this Phillips understood and stressed.

How then does Phillips' racism return again and again to plague
him? And why have his successors, friendly and critical, not done
better? Phillips willingly displayed the many-sidedness of plantation life and presented it as a community of white men and black
struggling to find a way to live together. Yet, he stopped short
precisely where he ought to have begun. Because he did not take
the Negroes seriously as men and women he could not believe that
in meaningful and even decisive ways they shaped the lives of
their masters. After discussing the impact of the white man on the
black he adds: "The Caucasian was also changed by the contact
in a far from negligible degree; but the negro's conversion was
much the more thorough, partly because the process in his case
was coercive, partly because his genius was imitative." [15] How
easily he dismisses the subject! If he believes his own words, why
should he have to introduce a silly theory from Gabriel Tarde
to tell us that masters do not learn from slaves but that slaves do
learn from masters? Throughout this book Phillips demonstrates
how well he knows better. On page 296 he tells us that "the relation of planter and slave was largely shaped by a sense of
propriety, proportion and cooperation." All that without significant impact on their respective personalities! Or again on page
327: "The plantations were homes to which, as they were fond
of singing, their hearts turned ever; and the negroes, exasperating

[14]*Ibid.*, 623.
[15]*Infra.*, 291.

as they often were to visiting strangers, were an element in the home itself . . . . The separate integration of the slaves was no more than rudimentary. They were always within the social mind and conscience of the whites, as the whites were in turn within the mind and conscience of the blacks." And yet again a few lines further along, Phillips quotes a "sagacious" slaveholder as saying that the Negro understood the white man better than the white man understood the Negro. To which Phillips adds: "This knowledge gave a power all its own. The general régime was in fact shaped by mutual requirements, concessions and understandings, producing reciprocal codes of conventional morality." [16] Now, if such was the case—as indeed it was—how absurd to deny the profound impact of the Negro on every aspect of the white man's being. Phillips brings us to the brink of profound insight only to call a retreat made necessary by the poisonous demands of white supremacy. Yet, his critics have done no better. They have in fact not done so well, for his perceptive descriptions and flashes of insight are a beginning, whereas their sermons on the guilt complexes and sadism inherent in slaveownership tell us no more than the obvious.

To supplement Phillips' work the student must certainly read Stampp's passionate *The Peculiar Institution*, which is so rich in insights and which for all its faults brings to the surface much that Phillips obscures. He must read other works as well, particularly Gilberto Freyre's great essay on Brazilian slavery *The Masters and the Slaves*, which takes us into the kitchen and the bedroom, explores architecture and folklore, and slides from black to white and back again. He must read Frank Tannenbaum's *Slave & Citizen*, which in little more than one hundred pages brings the contrast between Hispanic and American slavery into unforgettable focus. And he must read Frantz Fanon's *The Wretched of the Earth,* [17] which provides all the answer one needs

[16] *Ibid.,* 327.

to Phillips' curious suggestion that a slave revolt ought to be discussed under the rubric of "crime." If our tender sensibilities choke on Fanon's notion that the colonial (read: slave) comes to manhood through the act of violence against his tormentors, so much the worse for our sensibilities. The point is not that this road to manhood is the best road, nor even a "good" one; the point is that it is better than none and that a society which provides no other has no right to complain.

Phillips' racism blinded him, corroded his enormous talent, and kept him short of the greatness he approached. Our revulsion at it ought not be blind us to the wisdom that constantly breaks through his work: "For him . . . who has known the considerate and cordial, courteous and charming men and women, white and black, which that picturesque life in its best phases produced, it is impossible to agree that its basis and its operation were wholly evil, the law and the prophets to the contrary notwithstanding" (p. 514). Those who see in these words merely the nostalgia of a latter-day proslavery writer may be left to contemplate their own moral virtue. The South, white and black, has given America some of its finest traditions and sensibilities and certainly its best manners. These were once firmly rooted in the plantation way of life and especially in the master-slave relationship. Their preservation does not require the preservation of the injustice and brutality with which they were originally and inseparably linked, but it does require a full understanding and appreciation of those origins. In this sense Phillips, despite his bias, still has much to say to us, however much more remains to be said by a new generation. *American Negro Slavery* is not the last word on its subject; merely the indispensable first.

[17]Frantz Fanon was a Negro psychiatrist from Martinique who served with the rebels during the Algerian War. He died of cancer in 1961 at the age of 36 after apparently refusing to leave his post to get the treatment he needed. Passionately committed to colonial independence and revolutionary socialism, he left behind several other books dealing with his life as a Negro colonial, the Algerian War, and his political thought.

PREFACE

For twenty years I have panned the sands of the stream of Southern life and garnered their golden treasure. Many of the nuggets rewarding the search have already been displayed in their natural form; [1] and this now is a coinage of the grains great and small. The metal is pure, the minting alone may be faulty. The die is the author's mind, which has been shaped as well by a varied Northern environment in manhood as by a Southern one in youth. In the making of coins and of histories, however, locality is of less moment than are native sagacity, technical training and a sense of truth and proportion. For these no warrant will hold. The product must stand or fall by its own quality.

The wide ramifications of negro slavery are sketched in these pages, but the central concern is with its rise, nature and influence in the regions of its concentration. In these the plantation régime prevailed. The characteristic American slave, indeed, was not only a negro, but a plantation workman; and for the present purpose a knowledge of the plans and requirements of plantation industry is no less vital than an understanding of human nature. While the latter is of course taken for granted, the former has been elaborated as a principal theme. Slaves were both persons and property, and as chattels they were investments. This phase has invited analysis at some length in the two chapters following those on the plantation régime.

Ante-bellum conditions were sharply different in some respects from those of colonial times, largely because of legislation enacted in the last quarter of the eighteenth century and the first decade of the nineteenth. For this reason the politics of that period of sharp transition are given attention herein. Otherwise the words and deeds of public men have been mostly left aside. Polemic writings also have been little used, for their fuel went so much to

[1] Ulrich B. Phillips, ed., *Plantation and Frontier Documents*, printed also as vols. I and II of the *Documentary History of American Industrial Society* (Cleveland, Ohio, 1909), and cited in the present work as *Plantation and Frontier*.

heat that their light upon the living conditions is faint. Reminiscences are likewise disregarded, for the reason that the lapse of decades has impaired inevitably the memories of men. The contemporary records of slaves, masters and witnesses may leave gaps and have their shortcomings, but the asseverations of politicians, pamphleteers, and aged survivors are generally unsafe even in supplement.

On the other hand, the tone of social elements in the Black Belt of the present is something of a gauge of the temper of generations past. My sojourn in a National Army Camp in the South while this book has been going through the press has reënforced my earlier conviction that Southern racial asperities are mainly superficial, and that the two great elements are fundamentally in accord. That the harmony is not a new thing is evinced by the very tone of the camp. The men of the two races are of course quartered separately; but it is a daily occurrence for white Georgian troops to go to the negro companies to seek out their accustomed friends and compare home news and experiences. The negroes themselves show the same easy-going, amiable, seriocomic obedience and the same personal attachments to white men, as well as the same sturdy light-heartedness and the same love of laughter and of rhythm, which distinguished their forbears. The non-commissioned officers among them show a punctilious pride of place which matches that of the plantation foremen of old; and the white officers who succeed best in the command of these companies reflect the planter's admixture of tact with firmness of control, the planter's patience of instruction, and his crisp though cordial reciprocation of sentiment. The negroes are not enslaved but drafted; they dwell not in cabins but in barracks; they shoulder the rifle, not the hoe; but the visitor to their company streets in evening hours enters nevertheless a plantation atmosphere. A hilarious party dashes in pursuit of a fugitive, and gives him lashes with a belt "moderately laid on." When questioned, the explanation is given that the victim is "a awnrooly nigger" whose ways must be mended. In the quiet which follows, a throng fills the quarter with an old-time unmartial refrain:

> I ain' go' study war no mo',
> I ain' go' study war no mo',
> Study war no mo'!

As the music pauses there comes through a nearby window the mention of two bits as a wager, and an earnest adjuration of "sebben or lebben." The drill which they do by day with splendid snap is wonderfully out of their minds by night. The grim realities of war, though a constant theme in the inculcation of discipline, is as remote in the thought of these men as is the planet Mars. Yet each of their lieutenants is justly confident that his platoon will follow whithersoever he may lead. It may be that the change of African nature by plantation slavery has been exaggerated. At any rate a generation of freedom has wrought less transformation in the bulk of the blacks than might casually be supposed.

Some of the many debts incurred in the prosecution of researches leading to this book have been acknowledged in my previous publications, and others are indicated in the footnotes herein. It remains to say that in stimulus and criticism, as well as in the revision of proofs while exigent camp duties have engrossed my main attention, my wife has given great and unflagging aid.

U. B. P.

Army Y.M.C.A.,
Camp Gordon, Ga.

CONTENTS

AMERICAN NEGRO SLAVERY

CHAPTER I

THE DISCOVERY AND EXPLOITATION OF GUINEA

THE Portuguese began exploring the west coast of Africa shortly before Christopher Columbus was born; and no sooner did they encounter negroes than they began to seize and carry them in captivity to Lisbon. The court chronicler Azurara set himself in 1452, at the command of Prince Henry, to record the valiant exploits of the negro-catchers. Reflecting the spirit of the time, he praised them as crusaders bringing savage heathen for conversion to civilization and christianity. He gently lamented the massacre and sufferings involved, but thought them infinitely outweighed by the salvation of souls. This cheerful spirit of solace was destined long to prevail among white peoples when contemplating the hardships of the colored races. But Azurara was more than a moralizing annalist. He acutely observed of the first cargo of captives brought from southward of the Sahara, less than a decade before his writing, that after coming to Portugal "they never more tried to fly, but rather in time forgot all about their own country," that "they were very loyal and obedient servants, without malice"; and that "after they began to use clothing they were for the most part very fond of display, so that they took great delight in robes of showy colors, and such was their love of finery that they picked up the rags that fell from the coats of other people of the country and sewed them on their own garments, taking great pleasure in these, as though it were matter of some greater perfection." [1] These few broad strokes would portray with

[1] Gomez Eannes de Azurara, *Chronicle of the Discovery and Conquest of Guinea*, translated by C. R. Beazley and E. P. Prestage, in the Hakluyt Society *Publications*, XCV, 85.

equally happy precision a myriad other black servants born centuries after the writer's death and dwelling in a continent of whose existence he never dreamed. Azurara wrote further that while some of the captives were not able to endure the change and died happily as Christians, the others, dispersed among Portuguese households, so ingratiated themselves that many were set free and some were married to men and women of the land and acquired comfortable estates. This may have been an earnest of future conditions in Brazil and the Spanish Indies; but in the British settlements it fell out far otherwise.

As the fifteenth century wore on and fleets explored more of the African coast with the double purpose of finding a passage to India and exploiting any incidental opportunities for gain, more and more human cargoes were brought from Guinea to Portugal and Spain. But as the novelty of the blacks wore off they were held in smaller esteem and treated with less liberality. Gangs of them were set to work in fields from which the Moorish occupants had recently been expelled. The labor demand was not great, however, and when early in the sixteenth century West Indian settlers wanted negroes for their sugar fields, Spain willingly parted with some of hers. Thus did Europe begin the coercion of African assistance in the conquest of the American wilderness.

Guinea comprises an expanse about a thousand miles wide lying behind three undulating stretches of coast, the first reaching from Cape Verde southeastward nine hundred miles to Cape Palmas in four degrees north latitude, the second running thence almost parallel to the equator a thousand miles to Old Calabar at the head of "the terrible bight of Biafra," the third turning abruptly south and extending some fourteen hundred miles to a short distance below Benguela where the southern desert begins. The country is commonly divided into Upper Guinea or the Sudan, lying north and west of the great angle of the coast, and Lower Guinea, the land of the Bantu, to the southward. Separate zones may also be distinguished as having different systems of economy: in the jungle belt along the equator bananas are the staple diet; in the belts bordering this on the north and south the growing of millet and manioc respectively, in small clearings, are the characteristic industries; while beyond the edges of the continental forest cattle contribute much of the food supply. The banana, millet and manioc zones, and especially their swampy coastal plains, were of course the chief sources of slaves for the transatlantic trade.

Of all regions of extensive habitation equatorial Africa is the worst. The climate is not only monotonously hot, but for the greater part of each year is excessively moist. Periodic rains bring deluge and periodic tornadoes play havoc. The dry seasons give partial relief, but they bring occasional blasts from the desert so dry and burning that all nature droops and is grateful at the return of the rains. The general dank heat stimulates vegetable growth in every scale from mildew to mahogany trees, and multiplies the members of the animal kingdom, be they mosquitoes, elephants or boa constrictors. There would be abundant food but for the superabundant creatures that struggle for it and prey upon one another. For mankind life is at once easy and hard. Food of a sort may often be had for the plucking, and raiment is needless; but aside from the menace of the elements human life is endangered by beasts and reptiles in the forest, crocodiles and hippopotami in the rivers, and sharks in the sea, and existence is made a burden to all but the happy-hearted by plagues of insects and parasites. In many districts tse-tse flies exterminate the cattle and spread the fatal sleeping-sickness among men; everywhere swarms of locusts occasionally destroy the crops; white ants eat timbers and any other useful thing, short of metal, which may come in their way; giant cockroaches and dwarf brown ants and other pests in great variety swarm in the dwellings continuously—except just after a village has been raided by the great black ants which are appropriately known as "drivers." These drivers march in solid columns miles on miles until, when they reach food resources to their fancy, they deploy for action and take things with a rush. To stay among them is to die; but no human being stays. A cry of "Drivers!" will depopulate a village instantly, and a missionary who at one moment has been combing brown ants from his hair will in the next find

himself standing safely in the creek or the water barrel, to stay
until the drivers have taken their leave.   Among less spectacular
things, mosquitoes fly in crowds and leave fevers in their wake,
gnats and flies are always on hand, chigoes bore and breed under
toe-nails, hook-worms hang themselves to the walls of the in-
testines, and other threadlike worms enter the eyeballs and the
flesh of the body.   Endurance through generations has given
the people large immunity from the effects of hook-worm and
malaria, but not from the indigenous diseases, kraw-kraw, yaws
and elephantiasis, nor of course from dysentery and smallpox
which the Europeans introduced.   Yet robust health is fairly common, and where health prevails there is generally happiness, for
the negroes have that within their nature.   They could not thrive
in Guinea without their temperament.

It is probable that no people ever became resident on or near
the west coast except under compulsion.   From the more favored
easterly regions successive hordes have been driven after defeat
in war.   The Fangs on the Ogowé are an example in the recent
past.   Thus the inhabitants of Guinea, and of the coast lands
especially, have survived by retreating and adapting themselves to
conditions in which no others wished to dwell.   The requirements
of adaptation were peculiar.   To live where nature supplies Turkish baths without the asking necessitates relaxation.   But since
undue physical indolence would unfit people for resistance to
parasites and hostile neighbors, the languid would perish.   Relaxation of mind, however, brought no penalties.   The climate
in fact not only discourages but prohibits mental effort of severe
or sustained character, and the negroes have submitted to that
prohibition as to many others, through countless generations, with
excellent grace.   So accustomed were they to interdicts of nature
that they added many of their own through conventional taboo,
some of them intended to prevent the eating of supposedly injurious food, others calculated to keep the commonalty from in-
fringing upon the preserves of the dignitaries.[2]

[2] A convenient sketch of the primitive African régime is J. A. Tilling-
hast's *The Negro in Africa and America*, part I.   A fuller survey is
Jerome Dowd's *The Negro Races*, which contains a bibliography of the
sources.   Among the writings of travelers and sojourners particularly

No people is without its philosophy and religion. To the Africans the forces of nature were often injurious and always impressive. To invest them with spirits disposed to do evil but capable of being placated was perhaps an obvious recourse; and this investiture grew into an elaborate system of superstition. Not only did the wind and the rain have their gods but each river and precipice, and each tribe and family and person, a tutelary spirit. These might be kept benevolent by appropriate fetish ceremonies; they might be used for evil by persons having specially great powers over them. The proper course for commonplace persons at ordinary times was to follow routine fetish observances; but when beset by witch-work the only escape lay in the services of witch-doctors or priests. Sacrifices were called for, and on the greatest occasions nothing short of human sacrifice was acceptable.

As to diet, vegetable food was generally abundant, but the negroes were not willingly complete vegetarians. In the jungle game animals were scarce, and everywhere the men were ill equipped for hunting. In lieu of better they were often fain to satisfy their craving for flesh by eating locusts and larvæ, as tribes in the interior still do. In such conditions cannibalism was fairly common. Especially prized was an enemy slain in war, for not only would his body feed the hungry but fetish taught that his bravery would pass to those who shared the feast.

In African economy nearly all routine work, including agriculture, was classed as domestic service and assigned to the women for performance. The wife, bought with a price at the time of marriage, was virtually a slave; her husband her master. Now one woman might keep her husband and children in but moderate comfort. Two or more could perform the family tasks much better. Thus a man who could pay the customary price would be inclined to add a second wife, whom the first

notable are Mary Kingsley's *Travels in West Africa* as a vivid picture of coast life, and her *West African Studies* for its elaborate and convincing discussion of fetish, and the works of Sir A. B. Ellis on the Tshi-, Ewe- and Yoruba-speaking peoples for their analyses of institutions along the Gold Coast.

would probably welcome as a lightener of her burdens. Polygamy prevailed almost everywhere.

Slavery, too, was generally prevalent except among the few tribes who gained their chief sustenance from hunting. Along with polygamy, it perhaps originated, if it ever had a distinct beginning, from the desire to lighten and improve the domestic service.[3] Persons became slaves through capture, debt or malfeasance, or through the inheritance of the status. While the ownership was absolute in the eyes of the law and captives were often treated with great cruelty, slaves born in the locality were generally regarded as members of their owner's family and were shown much consideration. In the millet zone where there was much work to be done the slaveholdings were in many cases very large and the control relatively stringent; but in the banana districts an easy-going schedule prevailed for all. One of the chief hardships of the slaves was the liability of being put to death at their master's funeral in order that their spirits might continue in his service. In such case it was customary on the Gold Coast to give the victim notice of his approaching death by suddenly thrusting a knife through each cheek with the blades crossing in his mouth so that he might not curse his master before he died. With his hands tied behind him he would then be led to the ceremonial slaughter. The Africans were in general eager traders in slaves as well as other goods, even before the time when the transatlantic trade, by giving excessive stimulus to raiding and trading, transformed the native economy and deranged the social order.

Apart from a few great towns such as Coomassee and Benin, life in Guinea was wholly on a village basis, each community dwelling in its own clearing and having very slight intercourse with its neighbors. Politically each village was governed by its chief and its elders, oftentimes in complete independence. In occasional instances, however, considerable states of loose organization were under the rule of central authorities. Such

---

[3] Slavery among the Africans and other primitive peoples has been elaborately discussed by H. J. Nieboer, *Slavery as an Industrial System: Ethnological Researches* (The Hague, 1900).

states were likely to be the creation of invaders from the eastward, the Dahomans and Ashantees for example; but the kingdom of Benin appears to have arisen indigenously. In many cases
the subordination of conquered villages merely resulted in their
paying annual tribute. As to language, Lower Guinea spoke
multitudinous dialects of the one Bantu tongue, but in Upper
Guinea there were many dialects of many separate languages.

Land was so abundant and so little used industrially that as
a rule it was not owned in severalty; and even the villages and
tribes had little occasion to mark the limits of their domains.
For travel by land there were nothing but narrow, rough and
tortuous foot-paths, with makeshift bridges across the smaller
streams. The rivers were highly advantageous both as avenues
and as sources of food, for the negroes were expert at canoeing
and fishing.

Intertribal wars were occasional, but a crude comity lessened
their frequency. Thus if a man of one village murdered one of
another, the aggrieved village if too weak to procure direct redress might save its face by killing someone in a third village,
whereupon the third must by intertribal convention make common cause with the second at once, or else coerce a fourth into
the punitive alliance by applying the same sort of persuasion that
it had just felt. These later killings in the series were not regarded as murders but as diplomatic overtures. The system
was hard upon those who were sacrificed in its operation, but
it kept a check upon outlawry.

A skin stretched over the section of a hollow tree, and usually
so constructed as to have two tones, made an instrument of extraordinary use in communication as well as in music. By a
system long anticipating the Morse code the Africans employed
this "telegraph drum" in sending messages from village to village
for long distances and with great speed. Differences of speech
were no bar, for the tom tom code was interlingual. The official
drummer could explain by the high and low alternations of his
taps that a deed of violence just done was not a crime but a
pourparler for the forming of a league. Every week for three
months in 1800 the tom toms doubtless carried the news through-

out Ashantee land that King Quamina's funeral had just been repeated and two hundred more slaves slain to do him honor. In 1806 they perhaps reported the ending of Mungo Park's travels by his death on the Niger at the hands of the Boussa people. Again and again drummers hired as trading auxiliaries would send word along the coast and into the country that white men's vessels lying at Lagos, Bonny, Loango or Benguela as the case might be were paying the best rates in calico, rum or Yankee notions for all slaves that might be brought.

In music the monotony of the tom tom's tone spurred the drummers to elaborate variations in rhythm. The stroke of the skilled performer could make it mourn a funeral dirge, voice the nuptial joy, throb the pageant's march, and roar the ambush alarm. Vocal music might be punctuated by tom toms and primitive wind or stringed instruments, or might swell in solo or chorus without accompaniment. Singing, however, appears not so characteristic of Africans at home as of the negroes in America. On the other hand garrulous conversation, interspersed with boisterous laughter, lasted well-nigh the livelong day. Daily life, indeed, was far from dull, for small things were esteemed great, and every episode was entertaining. It can hardly be maintained that savage life is idyllic. Yet the question remains, and may long remain, whether the manner in which the negroes were brought into touch with civilization resulted in the greater blessing or the greater curse. That manner was determined in part at least by the nature of the typical negroes themselves. Impulsive and inconstant, sociable and amorous, voluble, dilatory, and negligent, but robust, amiable, obedient and contented, they have been the world's premium slaves. Prehistoric Pharaohs, mediaeval Pashas and the grandees of Elizabethan England esteemed them as such; and so great a connoisseur in household service as the Czar Alexander added to his palace corps in 1810 two free negroes, one a steward on an American merchant ship and the other a body-servant whom John Quincy Adams, the American minister, had brought from Massachusetts to St. Petersburg.[4]

[4] *Writings of John Quincy Adams*, Ford ed., III, 471, 472 (New York, 1914).

The impulse for the enslavement of negroes by other peoples came from the Arabs who spread over northern Africa in the eighth century, conquering and converting as they went, and stimulating the trade across the Sahara until it attained large dimensions. The northbound caravans carried the peculiar variety of pepper called "grains of paradise" from the region later known as Liberia, gold from the Dahomey district, palm oil from the lower Niger, and ivory and slaves from far and wide. A small quantity of these various goods was distributed in southern Europe and the Levant. And in the same general period Arab dhows began to take slave cargoes from the east coast of Africa as far south as Mozambique, for distribution in Arabia, Persia and western India. On these northern and eastern flanks of Guinea where the Mohammedans operated and where the most vigorous of the African peoples dwelt, the natives lent ready assistance in catching and buying slaves in the interior and driving them in coffles to within reach of the Moorish and Arab traders. Their activities, reaching at length the very center of the continent, constituted without doubt the most cruel of all branches of the slave-trade. The routes across the burning Sahara sands in particular came to be strewn with negro skeletons.[5]

This overland trade was as costly as it was tedious. Dealers in Timbuctoo and other centers of supply must be paid their price; camels must be procured, many of which died on the journey; guards must be hired to prevent escapes in the early marches and to repel predatory Bedouins in the later ones; food supplies must be bought; and allowance must be made for heavy mortality among the slaves on their terrible trudge over the burning sands and the chilling mountains. But wherever Mohammedanism prevailed, which gave particular sanction to slavery as well as to polygamy, the virtues of the negroes as laborers and as eunuch harem guards were so highly esteemed that the trade was maintained on a heavy scale almost if not quite to the present day. The demand of the Turks in the Levant and the Moors in Spain was met by exportations from the various Barbary ports. Part

---

[5] Jerome Dowd, "The African Slave Trade," in the *Journal of Negro History*, II (1917), 1-20.

of this Mediterranean trade was conducted in Turkish and Moorish vessels, and part of it in the ships of the Italian cities and Marseilles and Barcelona. Venice for example had treaties with certain Saracen rulers at the beginning of the fourteenth century authorizing her merchants not only to frequent the African ports, but to go in caravans to interior points and stay at will. The principal commodities procured were ivory, gold, honey and negro slaves.[6]

The states of Christian Europe, though little acquainted with negroes, had still some trace of slavery as an inheritance from imperial Rome and barbaric Teutondom. The chattel form of bondage, however, had quite generally given place to serfdom; and even serfdom was disappearing in many districts by reason of the growth of towns and the increase of rural population to the point at which abundant labor could be had at wages little above the cost of sustaining life. On the other hand so long as petty wars persisted the enslavement of captives continued to be at least sporadic, particularly in the south and east of Europe, and a considerable traffic in white slaves was maintained from east to west on the Mediterranean. The Venetians for instance, in spite of ecclesiastical prohibitions, imported frequent cargoes of young girls from the countries about the Black Sea, most of whom were doomed to concubinage and prostitution, and the rest to menial service.[7] The occurrence of the Crusades led to the enslavement of Saracen captives in Christendom as well as of Christian captives in Islam.

The waning of the Crusades ended the supply of Saracen slaves, and the Turkish capture of Constantinople in 1453 destroyed the Italian trade on the Black Sea. No source of supply now remained, except a trickle from Africa, to sustain the moribund institution of slavery in any part of Christian Europe east of the Pyrenees. But in mountain-locked Roussillon and Asturias remnants of slavery persisted from Visigothic times to the seventeenth century; and in other parts of the peninsula

---

[6] The leading authority upon slavery and the slave-trade in the Mediterranean countries of Europe is J. A. Saco, *Historia de la Esclavitud desde los Tiempos mas remotas hasta nuestros Dias* (Barcelona, 1877), vol. III.
[7] W. C. Hazlitt, *The Venetian Republic* (London, 1900), pp. 81, 82.

the intermittent wars against the Moors of Granada supplied captives and to some extent reinvigorated slavery among the Christian states from Aragon to Portugal. Furthermore the conquest of the Canaries at the end of the fourteenth century and of Teneriffe and other islands in the fifteenth led to the bringing of many of their natives as slaves to Castille and the neighboring kingdoms.

Occasional documents of this period contain mention of negro slaves at various places in the Spanish peninsula, but the number was clearly small and it must have continued so, particularly as long as the supply was drawn through Moorish channels. The source whence the negroes came was known to be a region below the Sahara which from its yield of gold and ivory was called by the Moors the land of wealth, "Bilad Ghana," a name which on the tongues of European sailors was converted into "Guinea." To open a direct trade thither was a natural effort when the age of maritime exploration began. The French are said to have made voyages to the Gold Coast in the fourteenth century, though apparently without trading in slaves. But in the absence of records of their activities authentic history must confine itself to the achievements of the Portuguese.

In 1415 John II of Portugal, partly to give his five sons opportunity to win knighthood in battle, attacked and captured the Moorish stronghold of Ceuta, facing Gibraltar across the strait. For several years thereafter the town was left in charge of the youngest of these princes, Henry, who there acquired an enduring desire to gain for Portugal and Christianity the regions whence the northbound caravans were coming. Returning home, he fixed his residence at the promontory of Sagres, on Cape St. Vincent, and made his main interest for forty years the promotion of maritime exploration southward.[8] His perseverance won him fame as "Prince Henry the Navigator," though he was not himself an active sailor; and furthermore, after many disappointments, it resulted in exploration as far as the Gold Coast in his lifetime and the rounding of the Cape of Good Hope

[8] The chief source for the early Portuguese voyages is Azurara's *Chronicle of the Discovery and Conquest of Guinea*, already cited.

twenty-five years after his death. The first decade of his endeavor brought little result, for the Sahara shore was forbidding and the sailors timid. Then in 1434 Gil Eannes doubled Cape Bojador and found its dangers imaginary. Subsequent voyages added to the extent of coast skirted until the desert began to give place to inhabited country. The Prince was now eager for captives to be taken who might inform him of the country, and in 1441 Antam Gonsalvez brought several Moors from the southern edge of the desert, who, while useful as informants, advanced a new theme of interest by offering to ransom themselves by delivering on the coast a larger number of non-Mohammedan negroes, whom the Moors held as slaves. Partly for the sake of profit, though the chronicler says more largely to increase the number of souls to be saved, this exchange was effected in the following year in the case of two of the Moors, while a third took his liberty without delivering his ransom. After the arrival in Portugal of these exchanged negroes, ten in number, and several more small parcels of captives, a company organized at Lagos under the direction of Prince Henry sent forth a fleet of six caravels in 1444 which promptly returned with 225 captives, the disposal of whom has been recounted at the beginning of this chapter.

In the next year the Lagos Company sent a great expedition of twenty-six vessels which discovered the Senegal River and brought back many natives taken in raids thereabout; and by 1448 nearly a thousand captives had been carried to Portugal. Some of these were Moorish Berbers, some negroes, but most were probably Jolofs from the Senegal, a warlike people of mixed ancestry. Raiding in the Jolof country proved so hazardous that from about 1454 the Portuguese began to supplement their original methods by planting "factories" on the coast where slaves from the interior were bought from their native captors and owners who had brought them down in caravans and canoes. Thus not only was missionary zeal eclipsed but the desire of conquest likewise, and the spirit of exploration erelong partly subdued, by commercial greed. By the time of Prince Henry's death in 1460 Portugal was importing seven or eight hundred negro slaves each year. From this time, forward the traffic was conducted by a succession of companies and individual grantees, to whom the government gave the exclusive right for short terms of years in consideration of money payments and pledges of adding specified measures of exploration. As new coasts were reached additional facilities were established for trade in pepper, ivory and gold as well as in slaves. When the route round Africa to India was opened at the end of the century the Guinea trade fell to secondary importance, but it was by no means discontinued.

Of the negroes carried to Portugal in the fifteenth century a large proportion were set to work as slaves on great estates in the southern provinces recently vacated by the Moors, and others were employed as domestic servants in Lisbon and other towns. Some were sold into Spain where they were similarly employed, and where their numbers were recruited by a Guinea trade in Spanish vessels in spite of Portugal's claim of monopoly rights, even though Isabella had recognized these in a treaty of 1479. In short, at the time of the discovery of America Spain as well as Portugal had quite appreciable numbers of negroes in her population and both were maintaining a system of slavery for their control.

When Columbus returned from his first voyage in the spring of 1493 and announced his great landfall, Spain promptly entered upon her career of American conquest and colonization. So great was the expectation of adventure and achievement that the problem of the government was not how to enlist participants but how to restrain a great exodus. Under heavy penalties emigration was restricted by royal decrees to those who procured permission to go. In the autumn of the same year fifteen hundred men, soldiers, courtiers, priests and laborers, accompanied the discoverer on his second voyage, in radiant hopes. But instead of wealth and high adventure these Argonauts met hard labor and sickness. Instead of the rich cities of Japan and China sought for, there were found squalid villages of Caribs and Lucayans. Of gold there was little, of spices none.

Columbus, when planting his colony at Isabella, on the northern coast of Hispaniola (Hayti), promptly found need of draught animals and other equipment. He wrote to his sovereigns in January, 1494, asking for the supplies needed; and he offered, pending the discovery of more precious things, to defray expenses by shipping to Spain some of the island natives, "who are a wild people fit for any work, well proportioned and very intelligent, and who when they have got rid of their cruel habits to which they have been accustomed will be better than any other kind of slaves." [9] Though this project was discouraged by the crown, Columbus actually took a cargo of Indians for sale in Spain on his return from his third voyage; but Isabella stopped the sale and ordered the captives taken home and liberated. Columbus, like most of his generation, regarded the Indians as infidel foreigners to be exploited at will. But Isabella, and to some extent her successors, considered them Spanish subjects whose helplessness called for special protection. Between the benevolence of the distant monarchs and the rapacity of the present conquerors, however, the fate of the natives was in little doubt. The crown's officials in the Indies were the very conquerors themselves, who bent their soft instructions to fit their own hard wills. A native rebellion in Hispaniola in 1495 was crushed with such slaughter that within three years the population is said to have been reduced by two thirds. As terms of peace Columbus required annual tribute in gold so great that no amount of labor in washing the sands could furnish it. As a commutation of tribute and as a means of promoting the conversion of the Indians there was soon inaugurated the encomienda system which afterward spread throughout Spanish America. To each Spaniard selected as an encomendero was allotted a certain quota of Indians bound to cultivate land for his benefit and entitled to receive from him tutelage in civilization and christianity. The grantees, however, were not assigned specified Indians but merely specified numbers of them, with power to seize new ones to replace any who might die or run away. Thus the encomendero was given little

[9] R. H. Major, *Select Letters of Columbus*, 2d. ed., 1890, p. 88.

economic interest in preserving the lives and welfare of his workmen.

In the first phase of the system the Indians were secured in the right of dwelling in their own villages under their own chiefs. But the encomenderos complained that the aloofness of the natives hampered the work of conversion and asked that a fuller and more intimate control be authorized. This was promptly granted and as promptly abused. Such limitations as the law still imposed upon encomendero power were made of no effect by the lack of machinery for enforcement. The relationship in short, which the law declared to be one of guardian and ward, became harsher than if it had been that of master and slave. Most of the island natives were submissive in disposition and weak in physique, and they were terribly driven at their work in the fields, on the roads, and at the mines. With smallpox and other pestilences added to their hardships, they died so fast that before 1510 Hispaniola was confronted with the prospect of the complete disappearance of its laboring population.[10] Meanwhile the same régime was being carried to Porto Rico, Jamaica and Cuba with similar consequences in its train.

As long as mining remained the chief industry the islands failed to prosper; and the reports of adversity so strongly checked the Spanish impulse for adventure that special inducements by the government were required to sustain any flow of emigration. But in 1512-1515 the introduction of sugar-cane culture brought the beginning of a change in the industrial situation. The few surviving gangs of Indians began to be shifted from the mines to the fields, and a demand for a new labor supply arose which could be met only from across the sea.

Apparently no negroes were brought to the islands before 1501. In that year, however, a royal decree, while excluding Jews and Moors, authorized the transportation of negroes born in Christian lands; and some of these were doubtless carried to Hispaniola in the great fleet of Ovando, the new governor, in

---

[10] E. G. Bourne, *Spain in America* (New York, 1904); Wilhelm Roscher, *The Spanish Colonial System*, Bourne ed. (New York, 1904); Konrad Habler, "The Spanish Colonial Empire," in Helmolt, *History of the World*, vol I.

1502. Ovando's reports of this experiment were conflicting. In the year following his arrival he advised that no more negroes be sent, because of their propensity to run away and band with and corrupt the Indians. But after another year had elapsed he requested that more negroes be sent. In this interim the humane Isabella died and the more callous Ferdinand acceded to full control. In consequence a prohibition of the negro trade in 1504 was rescinded in 1505 and replaced by orders that the bureau in charge of colonial trade promote the sending of negroes from Spain in large parcels. For the next twelve years this policy was maintained—the sending of Christian negroes was encouraged, while the direct slave trade from Africa to America was prohibited. The number of negroes who reached the islands under this régime is not ascertainable. It was clearly almost negligible in comparison with the increasing demand.[11]

The policy of excluding negroes fresh from Africa—"bozal negroes" the Spaniards called them—was of course a product of the characteristic resolution to keep the colonies free from all influences hostile to Catholic orthodoxy. But whereas Jews, Mohammedans and Christian heretics were considered as champions of rival faiths, the pagan blacks came increasingly to be reckoned as having no religion and therefore as a mere passive element ready for christianization. As early as 1510, in fact, the Spanish crown relaxed its discrimination against pagans by ordering the purchase of above a hundred negro slaves in the Lisbon market for dispatch to Hispaniola. To quiet its religious scruples the government hit upon the device of requiring the baptism of all pagan slaves upon their disembarkation in the colonial ports.

The crown was clearly not prepared to withstand a campaign for supplies direct from Africa, especially after the accession of the youth Charles I in 1517. At that very time a clamor from the islands reached its climax. Not only did many civil offi-

---

[11] The chief authority upon the origin and growth of negro slavery in the Spanish colonies is J. A. Saco, *Historia de la Esclavitud de la Raza Africana en el Nuevo Mundo y en especial en los Paises Americo-Hispanos.* (Barcelona, 1879.) This book supplements the same author's *Historia de la Esclavitud desde los Tiempos remotos* previously cited.

cials, voicing public opinion in their island communities, urge that the supply of negro slaves be greatly increased as a means of preventing industrial collapse, but a delegation of Jeronimite friars and the famous Bartholomeo de las Casas, who .had formerly been a Cuban encomendero and was now a Dominican priest, appeared in Spain to press the same or kindred causes. The Jeronimites, themselves concerned in industrial enterprises, were mostly interested in the labor supply. But the well-born and highly talented Las Casas, earnest and full of the milk of human kindness, was moved entirely by humanitarian and religious considerations. He pleaded primarily for the abolition of the encomienda system and the establishment of a great Indian reservation under missionary control, and he favored the increased transfer of Christian negroes from Spain as a means of relieving the Indians from their terrible sufferings. The lay spokesmen and the Jeronimites asked that provision be made for the sending of thousands of negro slaves, preferably bozal negroes for the sake of cheapness and plenty; and the supporters of this policy were able to turn to their use the favorable impression which Las Casas was making, even though his programme and theirs were different.[12]   The outcome was that while the settling of the encomienda problem was indefinitely postponed, authorization was promptly given for a supply of bozal negroes.

The crown here had an opportunity to get large revenues, of which it was in much need, by letting the slave trade under contract or by levying taxes upon it. The young king, however, freshly arrived from the Netherlands with a crowd of Flemish favorites in his train, proceeded to issue gratuitously a license for the trade to one of the Flemings at court, Laurent de Gouvenot, known in Spain as Garrevod, the governor of Breza. This license empowered the grantee and his assigns to ship from Guinea to the Spanish islands four thousand slaves. All the historians until recently have placed this grant in the year 1517 and have called it a contract (asiento); but Georges Scelle has now discovered and printed the document itself which

[12] Las Casas, *Historia de las Indias* (Madrid, 1875, 1876); Arthur Helps, *Life of Las Casas* (London, 1873); Saco, *op. cit.*, pp. 62-104.

bears the date August 18, 1518, and is clearly a license of grace
bearing none of the distinctive asiento features.[13] Garrevod,
who wanted ready cash rather than a trading privilege, at once
divided his license into two and sold them for 25,000 ducats
to certain Genoese merchants domiciled at Seville, who in turn
split them up again and put them on the market where they
became an object of active speculation at rapidly rising prices.
The result was that when slaves finally reached the islands under Garrevod's grant the prices demanded for them were so
exorbitant that the purposes of the original petitioners were in
large measure defeated. Meanwhile the king, in spite of the
nominally exclusive character of the Garrevod grant, issued
various other licenses on a scale ranging from ten to four hundred slaves each. For a decade the importations were small,
however, and the island clamor increased.

In 1528 a new exclusive grant was issued to two German
courtiers at Seville, Eynger and Sayller, empowering them to
carry four thousand slaves from Guinea to the Indies within
the space of the following four years. This differed from Garrevod's in that it required a payment of 20,000 ducats to the
crown and restricted the price at which the slaves were to be
sold in the islands to forty ducats each. In so far it approached
the asientos of the full type which became the regular recourse of
the Spanish government in the following centuries; but it fell
short of the ultimate plan by failing to bind the grantees to the
performance of their undertaking and by failing to specify
the grades and the proportion of the sexes among the slaves
to be delivered. In short the crown's regard was still directed
more to the enrichment of courtiers than to the promotion of
prosperity in the islands.

After the expiration of the Eynger and Sayller grant the
king left the control of the slave trade to the regular imperial
administrative boards, which, rejecting all asiento overtures for
half a century, maintained a policy of granting licenses for com-

[13] Georges Scelle, *Histoire Politique de la Traité Négrière aux Indes de
Castille: Contrats et Traités d'Asiento* (Paris, 1906), I, 755. Book I,
chapter 2 of the same volume is an elaborate discussion of the Garrevod
grant.

petitive trade in return for payments of eight or ten ducats per head until 1560, and of thirty ducats or more thereafter. At length, after the Spanish annexation of Portugal in 1580, the government gradually reverted to monopoly grants, now however in the definite form of asientos, in which by intent at least the authorities made the public interest, with combined regard to the revenue and a guaranteed labor supply, the primary consideration.[14] The high prices charged for slaves, however, together with the burdensome restrictions constantly maintained upon trade in general, steadily hampered the growth of Spanish colonial industry. Furthermore the allurements of Mexico and Peru drained the older colonies of virtually all their more vigorous white inhabitants, in spite of severe penalties legally imposed upon emigration but never effectively enforced.

The agricultural régime in the islands was accordingly kept relatively stagnant as long as Spain preserved her full West Indian domination. The sugar industry, which by 1542 exported the staple to the amount of 110,000 arrobas of twenty-five pounds each, was standardized in plantations of two types—the *trapiche* whose cane was ground by ox power and whose labor force was generally thirty or forty negroes (each reckoned as capable of the labor of four Indians); and the *ingenio*, equipped with a water-power mill and employing about a hundred slaves.[15] Occasional slave revolts disturbed the Spanish islanders but never for long diminished their eagerness for slave recruits. The slave laws were relatively mild, the police administration extremely casual, and the plantation managements easy-going. In short, after introducing slavery into the new world the Spaniards maintained it in sluggish fashion, chiefly in the islands, as an institution which peoples more vigorous industrially might borrow and adapt to a more energetic plantation régime.

[14] Scelle, I, books 1-3.
[15] Saco, pp. 127, 128, 188; Oviedo, *Historia General de las Indias*, book 4, chap. 8.

CHAPTER II

THE MARITIME SLAVE TRADE

AT the request of a slaver's captain the government of
Georgia issued in 1772 a certificate to a certain Fenda
Lawrence reciting that she, "a free black woman and
heretofore a considerable trader in the river Gambia on the coast
of Africa, hath voluntarily come to be and remain for some time
in this province," and giving her permission to "pass and repass
unmolested within the said province on her lawfull and necessary
occations." [1] This instance is highly exceptional. The millions
of African expatriates went against their own wills, and their
transporters looked upon the business not as passenger traffic but
as trade in goods. Earnings came from selling in America the
cargoes bought in Africa; the transportation was but an item
in the trade.

The business bulked so large in the world's commerce in the
seventeenth and eighteenth centuries that every important maritime community on the Atlantic sought a share, generally with
the sanction and often with the active assistance of its respective
sovereign. The preliminaries to the commercial strife occurred
in the Elizabethan age. French traders in gold and ivory found
the Portuguese police on the Guinea Coast to be negligible; but
poaching in the slave trade was a harder problem, for Spain
held firm control of her colonies which were then virtually the
world's only slave market.

The test of this was made by Sir John Hawkins who at the
beginning of his career as a great English sea captain had
informed himself in the Canary Islands of the Afro-American
opportunity awaiting exploitation. Backed by certain English

[1] U. B. Phillips, *Plantation and Frontier Documents*, printed also as
vols. I and II of the *Documentary History of American Industrial Society*
(Cleveland, O., 1909), II, 141, 142. This publication will be cited here-
after as *Plantation and Frontier*.

financiers, he set forth in 1562 with a hundred men in three small ships, and after procuring in Sierra Leone, "partly by the sword and partly by other means," above three hundred negroes he sailed to Hispaniola where without hindrance from the authorities he exchanged them for colonial produce. "And so, with prosperous success, and much gain to himself and the aforesaid adventurers, he came home, and arrived in the month of September, 1563."[2] Next year with 170 men in four ships Hawkins again captured as many Sierra Leone natives as he could carry, and proceeded to peddle them in the Spanish islands. When the authorities interfered he coerced them by show of arms and seizure of hostages, and when the planters demurred at his prices he brought them to terms through a mixture of diplomacy and intimidation. After many adventures by the way he reached home, as the chronicler concludes, "God be thanked! in safety: with the loss of twenty persons in all the voyage; as with great profit to the venturers in the said voyage, so also to the whole realm, in bringing home both gold, silver, pearls, and other jewels in great store. His name therefore be praised for evermore! Amen." Before two years more had passed Hawkins put forth for a third voyage, this time with six ships, two of them among the largest then afloat. The cargo of slaves, procured by aiding a Guinea tribe in an attack upon its neighbor, had been duly sold in the Indies when dearth of supplies and stress of weather drove the fleet into the Mexican port of San Juan de Ulloa. There a Spanish fleet of thirteen ships attacked the intruders, capturing their treasure ship and three of her consorts. Only the *Minion* under Hawkins and the bark *Judith* under the young Francis Drake escaped to carry the harrowing tale to England. One result of the episode was that it filled Hawkins and Drake with desire for revenge on Spain, which was wreaked in due time but in European waters. Another consequence was a discouragement of English slave trading for nearly a century to follow.

[2] Hakluyt, *Voyages,* ed. 1589. This and the accounts of Hawkins' later exploits in the same line are reprinted with a valuable introduction in C. R. Beazley, ed., *Voyages and Travels* (New York, 1903), I, 29-126.

The defeat of the Armada in 1588 led the world to suspect the decline of Spain's maritime power, but only in the lapse of decades did the suspicion of her helplessness become a certainty. Meantime Portugal was for sixty years an appanage of the Spanish crown, while the Netherlands were at their heroic labor for independence. Thus when the Dutch came to prevail at sea in the early seventeenth century the Portuguese posts in Guinea fell their prey, and in 1621 the Dutch West India Company was chartered to take them over. Closely identified with the Dutch government, this company not only founded the colony of New Netherland and endeavored to foster the employment of negro slaves there, but in 1634 it seized the Spanish island of Curaçao near the Venezuelan coast and made it a basis for smuggling slaves into the Spanish dominions. And now the English, the French and the Danes began to give systematic attention to the African and West Indian opportunities, whether in the form of buccaneering, slave trading or colonization.

The revolt of Portugal in 1640 brought a turning point. For a quarter-century thereafter the Spanish government, regarding the Portuguese as rebels, suspended all trade relations with them, the asiento included. But the trade alternatives remaining were all distasteful to Spain. The English were heretics; the Dutch were both heretics and rebels; the French and the Danes were too weak at sea to handle the great slave trading contract with security; and Spain had no means of her own for large scale commerce. The upshot was that the carriage of slaves to the Spanish colonies was wholly interdicted during the two middle decades of the century. But this gave the smugglers their highest opportunity. The Spanish colonial police collapsed under the pressure of the public demand for slaves, and illicit trading became so general and open as to be pseudo legitimate. Such a boom came as was never felt before under Protestant flags in tropical waters. The French, in spite of great exertions, were not yet able to rival the Dutch and English. These in fact had such an ascendency that when in 1663 Spain revived the asiento by a contract with two Genoese, the contractors must needs procure their slaves by arrangement with Dutch and English who delivered them at Curaçao and Jamaica. Soon after this contract expired the asiento itself was converted from an item of Spanish internal policy into a shuttlecock of international politics. It became in fact the badge of maritime supremacy, possessed now by the Dutch, now by the French in the greatest years of Louis XIV, and finally by the English as a trophy in the treaty of Utrecht.

By this time, however, the Spanish dominions were losing their primacy as slave markets. Jamaica, Barbados and other Windward Islands under the English; Hayti, Martinique and Guadeloupe under the French, and Guiana under the Dutch were all more or less thriving as plantation colonies, while Brazil, Virginia, Maryland and the newly founded Carolina were beginning to demonstrate that slave labor had an effective calling without as well as within the Caribbean latitudes. The closing decades of the seventeenth century were introducing the heyday of the slave trade, and the English were preparing for their final ascendency therein.

In West African waters in that century no international law prevailed but that of might. Hence the impulse of any new country to enter the Guinea trade led to the project of a chartered monopoly company; for without the resources of share capital sufficient strength could not be had, and without the monopoly privilege the necessary shares could not be sold. The first English company of moment, chartered in 1618, confined its trade to gold and other produce. Richard Jobson while in its service on the Gambia was offered some slaves by a native trader. "I made answer," Jobson relates, "we were a people who did not deal in any such commodities; neither did we buy or sell one another, or any that had our own shapes; at which he seemed to marvel much, and told us it was the only merchandize they carried down, and that they were sold to white men, who earnestly desired them. We answered, they were another kind of people, different from us; but for our part, if they had no other commodities, we would return again." [3] This company speedily ending its life, was followed by another in 1631 with a similarly short career; and in 1651 the African privilege was granted for a time to the East India Company.

Under Charles II activities were resumed vigorously by a company chartered in 1662; but this promptly fell into such conflict with the Dutch that its capital of £122,000 vanished. In a drastic reorganization its affairs were taken over by a new corporation, the Royal African Company, chartered in 1672 with the Duke of York at its head and vested in its turn with monopoly rights under the English flag from Sallee on the Moroccan coast to the Cape of Good Hope. [4] For two decades this company prospered greatly, selling some two thousand slaves a year in Jamaica alone, and paying large cash dividends on its £100,000 capital and then a stock dividend of 300 per cent. But now came reverses through European war and through the competition of English and Yankee private traders who shipped slaves legitimately from Madagascar and illicitly from Guinea. Now came also a clamor from the colonies, where the company was never popular, and from England also where oppression and abuses were charged against it by would-be free traders. After a parliamentary investigation an act of 1697 restricted the monopoly by empowering separate traders to traffic in Guinea upon paying to the company for the maintenance of its forts ten per cent. on the value of the cargoes they carried thither and a percentage on certain minor exports carried thence.

The company soon fell upon still more evil times, and met them by evil practices. To increase its capital it offered new stock for sale at reduced prices and borrowed money for dividends in order to encourage subscriptions. The separate traders meanwhile were winning nearly all its trade. In 1709-1710, for

---

[3] Richard Jobson, *The Golden Trade* (London 1623,), pp. 29, 87, quoted in James Bandinel, *Some Account of the Trade in Slaves from Africa* (London, 1842), p. 43.

[4] The financial career of the company is described by W. R. Scott, "The Constitution and Finances of the Royal African Company of England till 1720," in the *American Historical Review*, VIII. 241-259.

example, forty-four of their vessels made voyages as compared with but three ships of the company, and Royal African stock sold as low as 2⅛ on the £100. A reorganization in 1712 however added largely to the company's funds, and the treaty of Utrecht brought it new prosperity. In 1730 at length Parliament relieved the separate traders of all dues, substituting a public grant of £10,000 a year toward the maintenance of the company's forts. For twenty years more the company, managed in the early thirties by James Oglethorpe, kept up the unequal contest until 1751 when it was dissolved.

The company régime under the several flags was particularly dominant on the coasts most esteemed in the seventeenth century; and in that century they reached a comity of their own on the basis of live and let live. The French were secured in the Senegal sphere of influence and the English on the Gambia, while on the Gold Coast the Dutch and English divided the trade between them. Here the two headquarters were in forts lying within sight of each other: El Mina of the Dutch, and Cape Coast Castle of the English. Each was commanded by a governor and garrisoned by a score or two of soldiers; and each with its outlying factories had a staff of perhaps a dozen factors, as many sub-factors, twice as many assistants, and a few bookkeepers and auditors, as well as a corps of white artisans and an abundance of native interpreters, boatmen, carriers and domestic servants. The Dutch and English stations alternated in a series east and west, often standing no further than a cannon-shot apart. Here and there one of them had acquired a slight domination which the other respected; but in the case of the Coromantees (or Fantyns) William Bosman, a Dutch company factor about 1700, wrote that both companies had "equal power, that is none at all. For when these people are inclined to it they shut up the passes so close that not one merchant can come from the inland country to trade with us; and sometimes, not content with this, they prevent the bringing of provisions to us till we have made peace with them." The tribe was in fact able to exact heavy tribute from both companies; and to stretch the

treaty engagements at will to its own advantage.[5] Further eastward, on the densely populated Slave Coast, the factories were
few and the trade virtually open to all comers. Here, as was
common throughout Upper Guinea, the traits and the trading
practices of adjacent tribes were likely to be in sharp contrast.
The Popo (or Paw Paw) people, for example, were so notorious
for cheating and thieving that few traders would go thither
unless prepared to carry things with a strong hand. The Portuguese alone bore their grievances without retaliation, Bosman
said, because their goods were too poor to find markets elsewhere.[6] But Fidah (Whydah), next door, was in Bosman's esteem the most agreeable of all places to trade in. The people
were honest and polite, and the red-tape requirements definite
and reasonable. A ship captain after paying for a license and
buying the king's private stock of slaves at somewhat above
the market price would have the news of his arrival spread
afar, and at a given time the trade would be opened with
prices fixed in advance and all the available slaves herded in
an open field. There the captain or factor, with the aid of a
surgeon, would select the young and healthy, who if the purchaser were the Dutch company were promptly branded to prevent their being confused in the crowd before being carried on
shipboard. The Whydahs were so industrious in the trade, with
such far reaching interior connections, that they could deliver a
thousand slaves each month.[7]

Of the operations on the Gambia an intimate view may be
had from the journal of Francis Moore, a factor of the Royal
African Company from 1730 to 1735.[8] Here the Jolofs on
the north and the Mandingoes on the south and west were divided
into tribes or kingdoms fronting from five to twenty-five leagues
on the river, while tributary villages of Arabic-speaking Foulahs
were scattered among them. In addition there was a small independent population of mixed breed, with very slight European

[5] Bosman's *Guinea* (London, 1705), reprinted in Pinkerton's *Voyages*,
XVI, 363.
[6] *Ibid.*, XVI, 474-476.
[7] *Ibid.*, XVI, 489-491.
[8] Francis Moore, *Travels in Africa* (London, 1738).

infusion but styling themselves Portuguese and using a "bastard language" known locally as Creole. Many of these last were busy in the slave trade. The Royal African headquarters, with a garrison of thirty men, were on an island in the river some thirty miles from its mouth, while its trading stations dotted the shores for many leagues upstream, for no native king was content without a factory near his "palace." The slaves bought were partly of local origin but were mostly brought from long distances inland. These came generally in strings or coffles of thirty or forty, tied with leather thongs about their necks and laden with burdens of ivory and corn on their heads. Mungo Park when exploring the hinterland of this coast in 1795-1797, traveling incidentally with a slave coffle on part of his journey, estimated that in the Niger Valley generally the slaves outnumbered the free by three to one.[9] But as Moore observed, the domestic slaves were rarely sold in the trade, mainly for fear it would cause their fellows to run away. When captured by their master's enemies however, they were likely to be sent to the coast, for they were seldom ransomed.

The diverse goods bartered for slaves were rated by units of value which varied in the several trade centers. On the Gold Coast it was a certain length of cowrie shells on a string; at Loango it was a "piece" which had the value of a common gun or of twenty pounds of iron; at Kakongo it was twelve- or fifteen-yard lengths of cotton cloth called "goods";[10] while on the Gambia it was a bar of iron, apparently about forty pounds in weight. But in the Gambia trade as Moore described it the unit or "bar" in rum, cloth and most other things became depreciated until in some commodities it was not above a shilling's value in English money. Iron itself, on the other hand, and crystal beads, brass pans and spreadeagle dollars appreciated in comparison. These accordingly became distinguished as the "heads of goods," and the inclusion of three or four units of them was required in the forty or fifty bars of miscellaneous

[9] Mungo Park, *Travels in the Interior Districts of Africa* (4th ed., London, 1800), pp. 287, 428.
[10] The Abbé Proyart, *History of Loango* (1776), in Pinkerton's *Voyages*, XVI, 584-587.

goods making up the price of a prime slave.[11] In previous years grown slaves alone had brought standard prices; but in Moore's time a specially strong demand for boys and girls in the markets of Cadiz and Lisbon had raised the prices of these almost to a parity. All defects were of course discounted. Moore, for example, in buying a slave with several teeth missing made the seller abate a bar for each tooth. The company at one time forbade the purchase of slaves from the self-styled Portuguese because they ran the prices up; but the factors protested that these dealers would promptly carry their wares to the separate traders, and the prohibition was at once withdrawn.

The company and the separate traders faced different problems. The latter were less easily able to adjust their merchandise to the market. A Rhode Island captain, for instance, wrote his owners from Anamabo in 1736, "heare is 7 sails of us rume men, that we are ready to devour one another, for our case is desprit"; while four years afterward another wrote after trading at the same port, "I have repented a hundred times ye lying in of them dry goods", which he had carried in place of the customary rum.[12] Again, a veteran Rhode Islander wrote from Anamabo in 1752, "on the whole I never had so much trouble in all my voiges", and particularized as follows: "I have Gott on bord 61 Slaves and upards of thirty ounces of Goold, and have Gott 13 or 14 hhds of Rum yet Left on bord, and God noes when I shall Gett Clear of it ye trade is so very Dull it is actuly a noof to make a man Creasey my Cheef mate after making foor or five Trips in the boat was taken Sick and Remains very bad yett then I sent Mr. Taylor, and he got not well, and three more of my men has [been] sick. . . . I should be Glad I coold Com Rite home with my slaves, for my vesiel will not Last to proceed farr we can see Day Lite al Roond her bow under Deck. . . . heare Lyes Captains hamlet, James, Jepson, Carpenter, Butler, Lindsay; Gardner is Due; Ferguson has Gone to Leward all these is Rum ships." [13]

[11] Francis Moore, *Travels in Africa*, p. 45.
[12] *American Historical Record*, I (1872), 314, 317.
[13] Massachusetts Historical Society *Collections*, LXIX, 59, 60.

The separate traders also had more frequent quarrels with the natives. In 1732 a Yankee captain was killed in a trade dispute and his crew' set adrift. Soon afterward certain Jolofs took another ship's officers captive and required the value of twenty slaves as ransom. And in 1733 the natives at Yamyamacunda, up the Gambia, sought revenge upon Captain Samuel Moore for having paid them in pewter dollars on his previous voyage, and were quieted through the good offices of a company factor.[14] The company suffered far less from native disorders, for a threat of removing its factory would bring any chief to terms. In 1731, however, the king of Barsally brought a troop of his kinsmen and subjects to the Joar factory where Moore was in charge, got drunk, seized the keys and rifled the stores.[15] But the company's chief trouble was with its own factors. The climate and conditions were so trying that illness was frequent and insanity and suicide occasional; and the isolation encouraged fraudulent practices. It was usually impossible to tell the false from the true in the reports of the loss of goods by fire and flood, theft and rapine, mildew and white ants, or the loss of slaves by death or mutiny. The expense of the salary list, ship hire, provisions and merchandise was heavy and continuous, while the returns were precarious to a degree. Not often did such great wars occur as the Dahomey invasion of the Whidah country in 1726[16] and the general fighting of the Gambia peoples in 1733-1734[17] to glut the outward bound ships with slave cargoes. As a rule the company's advantage of steady markets and friendly native relations appears to have been more than offset by the freedom of the separate traders from fixed charges and the necessity of dependence upon lazy and unfaithful employees.

Instead of jogging along the coast, as many had been accustomed to do, and casting anchor here and there upon sighting signal smokes raised by natives who had slaves to sell,[18] the separate traders began before the close of the colonial period to get

[14] Moore, pp. 112, 164, 182.
[15] Ibid., p. 82.
[16] William Snelgrave, A New Account of Some Parts of Guinea and the Slave Trade (London, 1734), pp. 8-32.
[17] Moore, p. 157.
[18] Snelgrave, introduction.

their slaves from white factors at the "castles," which were then a relic from the company régime. So advantageous was this that in 1772 a Newport brig owned by Colonel Wanton cleared £500 on her voyage, and next year the sloop *Adventure*, also of Newport, Christopher and George Champlin owners, made such speedy trade that after losing by death one slave out of the ninety-five in her cargo she landed the remainder in prime order at Barbados and sold them immediately in one lot at £35 per head.[19]

In Lower Guinea the Portuguese held an advantage, partly through the influence of the Catholic priests. The Capuchin missionary Merolla, for example, relates that while he was in service at the mouth of the Congo in 1685 word came that the college of cardinals had commanded the missionaries in Africa to combat the slave trade. Promptly deciding this to be a hopeless project, Merolla and his colleagues compromised with their instructions by attempting to restrict the trade to ships of Catholic nations and to the Dutch who were then supplying Spain under the asiento. No sooner had the chiefs in the district agreed to this than a Dutch trading captain set things awry by spreading Protestant doctrine among the natives, declaring baptism to be the only sacrament required for salvation, and confession to be superfluous. The priests then put all the Dutch under the ban, but the natives raised a tumult saying that the Portuguese, the only Catholic traders available, not only paid low prices in poor goods but also aspired to a political domination. The crisis was relieved by a timely plague of small-pox which the priests declared and the natives agreed was a divinely sent punishment for their contumacy,—and for the time at least, the exclusion of heretical traders was made effective.[20] The English appear never to have excelled the Portuguese on the Congo and southward except perhaps about the close of the eighteenth century.

The markets most frequented by the English and American separate traders lay on the great middle stretches of the coast

[19] Massachusetts Historical Society *Collections*, LXIX, 398, 429.
[20] Jerom Merolla da Sorrente, *Voyage to Congo* (translated from the Italian), in Pinkerton's *Voyages*, XVI, 253-260.

—Sierra Leone, the Grain Coast (Liberia), the Ivory, Gold and Slave Coasts, the Oil Rivers as the Niger Delta was then called, Cameroon, Gaboon and Loango. The swarm of their ships was particularly great in the Gulf of Guinea upon whose shores the vast fan-shaped hinterland poured its exiles along converging lines.

The coffles came from distances ranging to a thousand miles or more, on rivers and paths whose shore ends the European traders could see but did not find inviting. These paths, always of single-file narrowness, tortuously winding to avoid fallen trees and bad ground, never straightened even when obstructions had rotted and gone, branching and crossing in endless network, penetrating jungles and high-grass prairies, passing villages that were and villages that had been, skirting the lairs of savage beasts and the haunts of cannibal men, beset with drought and famine, storm and flood, were threaded only by negroes, bearing arms or bearing burdens. Many of the slaves fell exhausted on the paths and were cut out of the coffles to die. The survivors were sorted by the purchasers on the coast into the fit and the unfit, the latter to live in local slavery or to meet either violent or lingering deaths, the former to be taken shackled on board the strange vessels of the strange white men and carried to an unknown fate. The only consolations were that the future could hardly be worse than the recent past, that misery had plenty of company, and that things were interesting by the way. The combination of resignation and curiosity was most helpful.

It was reassuring to these victims to see an occasional American negro serving in the crew of a slaver and to know that a few specially favored tribesmen had returned home with vivid stories from across the sea. On the Gambia for example there was Job Ben Solomon who during a brief slavery in Maryland attracted James Oglethorpe's attention by a letter written in Arabic, was bought from his master, carried to England, presented at court, loaded with gifts and sent home as a freeman in 1734 in a Royal African ship with credentials requiring the governor and factors to show him every respect. Thereafter, a celebrity on the river, he spread among his fellow Foulahs and the neighboring Jolofs and Mandingoes his cordial praises of the English nation.[21] And on the Gold Coast there was Amissa to testify to British justice, for he had shipped as a hired sailor on a Liverpool slaver in 1774, had been kidnapped by his employer and sold as a slave in Jamaica, but had been redeemed by the king of Anamaboe and brought home with an award by Lord Mansfield's court in London of £500 damages collected from the slaving captain who had wronged him.[22]

The bursting of the South Sea bubble in 1720 shifted the bulk of the separate trading from London to the rival city of Bristol. But the removal of the duties in 1730 brought the previously unimportant port of Liverpool into the field with such vigor that ere long she had the larger half of all the English slave trade. Her merchants prospered by their necessary parsimony. The wages they paid were the lowest, and the commissions and extra allowances they gave in their early years were nil.[23] By 1753 her ships in the slave traffic numbered eighty-seven, totaling about eight thousand tons burthen and rated to carry some twenty-five thousand slaves. Eight of these vessels were trading on the Gambia, thirty-eight on the Gold and Slave Coasts, five at Benin, three at New Calabar, twelve at Bonny, eleven at Old Calabar, and ten in Angola.[24] For the year 1771 the number of slavers bound from Liverpool was reported at one hundred and seven with a capacity of 29,250 negroes, while fifty-eight went from London rated to carry 8,136, twenty-five from Bristol to carry 8,810, and five from Lancaster with room for 950. Of this total of 195 ships 43 traded in Senegambia, 29 on the Gold Coast, 56 on the Slave Coast, 63 in the bights of Benin and Biafra, and 4 in Angola. In addition there were sixty or seventy slavers from North America and the West Indies, and these were yearly increasing.[25] By 1801 the Liverpool ships had increased to 150, with capacity for 52,557 slaves according to the reduced rating

[21] Francis Moore, *Travels in Africa*, pp. 69, 202-203.
[22] Gomer Williams, *History of the Liverpool Privateers, with an Account of the Liverpool Slave Trade* (London, 1897), pp. 563, 564.
[23] *Ibid.*, p. 471, quoting *A General and Descriptive History of Liverpool* (1795).
[24] *Ibid.*, p. 472 and appendix 7.
[25] Edward Long, *History of Jamaica* (London, 1774), p. 492 note.

of five slaves to three tons of burthen as required by the parliamentary act of 1788. About half of these traded in the Gulf
of Guinea, and half in the ports of Angola.[26] The trade in American vessels, particularly those of New England, was also large.
The career of the town of Newport in fact was a small scale
replica of Liverpool's. But acceptable statistics of the American ships are lacking.

The ship captains in addition to their salaries generally received commissions of "4 in 104," on the gross sales, and also
had the privilege of buying, transporting and selling specified
numbers of slaves on their private account. When surgeons
were carried they also were allowed commissions and privileges
at a smaller rate, and "privileges" were often allowed the mates
likewise. The captains generally carried more or less definite instructions. Ambrose Lace, for example, master of the Liverpool
ship *Marquis of Granby* bound in 1762 for Old Calabar, was ordered to combine with any other ships on the river to keep down
rates, to buy 550 young and healthy slaves and such ivory as his
surplus cargo would purchase, and to guard against fire, fever
and attack. When laden he was to carry the slaves to agents
in the West Indies, and thence bring home according to opportunity sugar, cotton, coffee, pimento, mahogany and rum, and
the balance of the slave cargo proceeds in bills of exchange.[27] Simeon Potter, master of a Rhode Island slaver about
the same time, was instructed by his owners: "Make yr Cheaf
Trade with The Blacks and little or none with the white people if
possible to be avoided. Worter yr Rum as much as possible and
sell as much by the short mesuer as you can." And again: "Order
them in the Bots to worter thear Rum, as the proof will Rise by
the Rum Standing in ye Son."[28] As to the care of the slave
cargo a Massachusetts captain was instructed in 1785 as follows:
"No people require more kind and tender treatment to exhil-
arate their spirits than the Africans; and while on the one hand

[26] Gomer Williams, Appendix 13.
[27] *Ibid.*, pp. 486-489.
[28] W. B. Weeden, *Economic and Social History of New England* (Boston [1890]), II, 465.

you are attentive to this, remember that on the other hand too much circumspection cannot be observed by yourself and people to prevent their taking advantage of such treatment by insurrection, etc. When you consider that on the health of your slaves almost your whole voyage depends—for all other risques but mortality, seizures and bad debts the underwriters are accountable for—you will therefore particularly attend to smoking your vessel, washing her with vinegar, to the clarifying your water with lime or brimstone, and to cleanliness among your own people as well as among the slaves." [29]

Ships were frequently delayed for many months on the pestilent coast, for after buying their licenses in one kingdom and finding trade slack there they could ill afford to sail for another on the uncertain chance of a more speedy supply. Sometimes when weary of higgling the market, they tried persuasion by force of arms; but in some instances as at Bonny, in 1757,[30] this resulted in the victory of the natives and the destruction of the ships. In general the captains and their owners appreciated the necessity of patience, expensive and even deadly as that might prove to be.

The chiefs were eager to foster trade and cultivate good will, for it brought them pompous trappings as well as useful goods. "Grandy King George" of Old Calabar, for example, asked of his friend Captain Lace a mirror six feet square, an arm chair "for my salf to sat in," a gold mounted cane, a red and a blue coat with gold lace, a case of razors, pewter plates, brass flagons, knives and forks, bullet and cannon-ball molds, and sailcloth for his canoes, along with many other things for use in trade.[31]

The typical New England ship for the slave trade was a sloop, schooner or barkentine of about fifty tons burthen, which when engaged in ordinary freighting would have but a single deck. For a slaving voyage a second flooring was laid some three feet below the regular deck, the space between forming the slave

[29] G. H. Moore, *Notes on the History of Slavery in Massachusetts* (New York, 1866), pp. 66, 67, citing J. O. Felt, *Annals of Salem*, 2d ed., II, 289, 290.
[30] Gomer Williams, pp. 481, 482.
[31] *Ibid.*, pp. 545-547.

quarters. Such a vessel was handled by a captain, two mates, and from three to six men and boys. It is curious that a vessel of this type, with capacity in the hold for from 100 to 120 hogsheads of rum was reckoned by the Rhode Islanders to be "full bigg for dispatch," [32] while among the Liverpool slave traders such a ship when offered for sale could not find a purchaser.[33] The reason seems to have been that dry-goods and sundries required much more cargo space for the same value than did rum.

The English vessels were generally twice as great of burthen and with twice the height in their 'tween decks. But this did not mean that the slaves could stand erect in their quarters except along the center line; for when full cargoes were expected platforms of six or eight feet in width were laid on each side, halving the 'tween deck height and nearly doubling the floor space on which the slaves were to be stowed. Whatever the size of the ship, it loaded slaves if it could get them to the limit of its capacity. Bosman tersely said, "they lie as close together as it is possible to be crowded." [34] The women's room was divided from the men's by a bulkhead, and in time of need the captain's cabin might be converted into a hospital.

While the ship was taking on slaves and African provisions and water the negroes were generally kept in a temporary stockade on deck for the sake of fresh air. But on departure for the "middle passage," as the trip to America was called by reason of its being the second leg of the ship's triangular voyage in the trade, the slaves were kept below at night and in foul weather, and were allowed above only in daylight for food, air and exercise while the crew and some of the slaves cleaned the quarters and swabbed the floors with vinegar as a disinfectant. The negro men were usually kept shackled for the first part of the passage until the chances of mutiny and return to Africa dwindled and the captain's fears gave place to confidence. On various occa-

[32] Massachusetts Historical Society, *Collections*, LXIX, 524.
[33] *Ibid.*, 500.
[34] Bosman's *Guinea*, in Pinkerton's *Voyages*, XVI, 490.

sions when attacks of privateers were to be repelled weapons were issued and used by the slaves in loyal defense of the vessel.[35] Systematic villainy in the handling of the human cargo was perhaps not so characteristic in this trade as in the transport of poverty-stricken white emigrants. Henry Laurens, after withdrawing from African factorage at Charleston because of the barbarities inflicted by some of the participants in the trade, wrote in 1768: "Yet I never saw an instance of cruelty in ten or twelve years' experience in that branch equal to the cruelty exercised upon those poor Irish. . . . Self interest prompted the baptized heathen to take some care of their wretched slaves for a market, but no other care was taken of those poor Protestant Christians from Ireland but to deliver as many as possible alive on shoar upon the cheapest terms, no matter how they fared upon the voyage nor in what condition they were landed." [36]

William Snelgrave, long a ship captain in the trade, relates that he was accustomed when he had taken slaves on board to acquaint them through his interpreter that they were destined to till the ground in America and not to be eaten; that if any person on board abused them they were to complain to the interpreter and the captain would give them redress, but if they struck one of the crew or made any disturbance they must expect to be severely punished. Snelgrave nevertheless had experience of three mutinies in his career; and Coromantees figured so prominently in these that he never felt secure when men of that stock were in his vessel, for, he said, "I knew many of these Cormantine negroes despised punishment and even death itself." In one case when a Coromantee had brained a sentry he was notified by Snelgrave that he was to die in the sight of his fellows at the end of an hour's time. "He answered, 'He must confess it was a rash action in him to kill him; but he desired me to consider that if I put him to death I should lose all the money I had paid for him.'" When the captain professed himself un-

[35] E. g., Gomer Williams, pp. 560, 561.
[36] D. D. Wallace, *Life of Henry Laurens* (New York, 1915), pp. 67, 68. For the tragic sufferings of an English convict shipment in 1768 see *Plantation and Frontier*, I, 372-373.

moved by this argument the negro spent his last moments assuring his fellows that his life was safe.[37]

The discomfort in the densely packed quarters of the slave ships may be imagined by any who have sailed on tropic seas. With seasickness added it was wretched; when dysentery prevailed it became frightful; if water or food ran short the suffering was almost or quite beyond endurance; and in epidemics of scurvy, small-pox or ophthalmia the misery reached the limit of human experience. The average voyage however was rapid and smooth by virtue of the steadily blowing trade winds, the food if coarse was generally plenteous and wholesome, and the sanitation fairly adequate. In a word, under stern and often brutal discipline, and with the poorest accommodations, the slaves encountered the then customary dangers and hardships of the sea.[38]

Among the disastrous voyages an example was that of the Dutch West India Company's ship *St. John* in 1659. After buying slaves at Bonny in April and May she beat about the coast in search of provisions but found barely enough for daily consumption until at the middle of August on the island of Amebo she was able to buy hogs, beans, cocoanuts and oranges. Meanwhile bad food had brought dysentery, the surgeon, the cooper and a sailor had died, and the slave cargo was daily diminishing. Five weeks of sailing then carried the ship across the Atlantic, where she put into Tobago to refill her leaking water casks. Sailing thence she struck a reef near her destination at Curaçao and was abandoned by her officers and crew. Finally a sloop sent by the Curaçao governor to remove the surviving slaves was captured by a privateer with them on board. Of the 195 negroes comprising the cargo on June 30, from one to five died nearly

[37] Snelgrave, *Guinea and the Slave Trade* (London, 1734), pp. 162-185. Snelgrave's book also contains vivid accounts of tribal wars, human sacrifices, traders' negotiations and pirate captures on the Grain and Slave Coasts.
[38] Voluminous testimony in regard to conditions on the middle passage was published by Parliament and the Privy Council in 1789-1791. Summaries from it may be found in T. F. Buxton, *The African Slave Trade and the Remedy* (London, 1840), part I, chap. 2; and in W. O. Blake, *History of Slavery and the Slave Trade* (Columbus, Ohio, 1859), chaps. 9, 10.

every day, and one leaped overboard to his death. At the end of the record on October 29 the slave loss had reached 110, with the mortality rate nearly twice as high among the men as among the women.[39] About the same time, on the other hand, Captain John Newton of Liverpool, who afterwards turned preacher, made a voyage without losing a sailor or a slave.[40] The mortality on the average ship may be roughly conjectured from the available data at eight or ten per cent.

Details of characteristic outfit, cargo, and expectations in the New England branch of trade may be had from an estimate made in 1752 for a projected voyage.[41] A sloop of sixty tons, valued at £300 sterling, was to be overhauled and refitted, armed, furnished with handcuffs, medicines and miscellaneous chandlery at a cost of £65, and provisioned for £50 more. Its officers and crew, seven hands all told, were to draw aggregate wages of £10 per month for an estimated period of one year. Laden with eight thousand gallons of rum at 1s. 8d. per gallon and with forty-five barrels, tierces and hogsheads of bread, flour, beef, pork, tar, tobacco, tallow and sugar—all at an estimated cost of £775—it was to sail for the Gold Coast. There, after paying the local charges from the cargo, some 35 slave men were to be bought at 100 gallons per head, 15 women at 85 gallons, and 15 boys and girls at 65 gallons; and the residue of the rum and miscellaneous cargo was expected to bring some seventy ounces of gold in exchange as well as to procure food supplies for the westward voyage. Recrossing the Atlantic, with an estimated death loss of a man, a woman and two children, the surviving slaves were to be sold in Jamaica at about £21, £18, and £14 for the respective classes. Of these proceeds about one-third was to be spent for a cargo of 105 hogsheads of molasses at 8d. per gallon, and

[39] E. B. O'Callaghan ed., *Voyages of the Slavers St. John and Arms of Amsterdam* (Albany, N. Y., 1867), pp. 1-13.
[40] Gomer Williams, p. 515.
[41] "An estimate of a voyage from Rhode Island to the Coast of Guinea and from thence to Jamaica and so back to Rhode Island for a sloop of 60 Tons." The authorities of Yale University, which possesses the manuscript, have kindly permitted the publication of these data. The estimates in Rhode Island and Jamaica currencies, which were then depreciated, as stated in the document, to twelve for one and seven for five sterling respectively, are here changed into their approximate sterling equivalents.

the rest of the money remitted to London, whither the gold dust
was also to be sent. The molasses upon reaching Newport was
expected to bring twice as much as it had cost in the tropics. After deducting factor's commissions of from 2½ to 5 per cent. on
all sales and purchases, and of "4 in 104" on the slave sales as the
captain's allowance, after providing for insurance at four per
cent. on ship and cargo for each leg of the voyage, and for leak-
age of ten per cent. of the rum and five per cent. of the molasses,
and after charging off the whole cost of the ship's outfit and one-
third of her original value, there remained the sum of £357, 8s. 2d.
as the expected profits of the voyage.

As to the gross volume of the trade, there are few statistics.
As early as 1734 one of the captains engaged in it estimated that
a maximum of seventy thousand slaves a year had already been
attained.[42] For the next half century and more each passing
year probably saw between fifty thousand and a hundred thousand shipped. The total transportation from first to last may
well have numbered more than five million souls. Prior to the
nineteenth century far more negro than white colonists crossed
the seas, though less than one tenth of all the blacks brought to the
western world appear to have been landed on the North American
continent. Indeed, a statistician has reckoned, though not con-
vincingly, that in the whole period before 1810 these did not ex
ceed 385,500.[43]

In selling the slave cargoes in colonial ports the traders of
course wanted minimum delay and maximum prices. But as a
rule quickness and high returns were not mutually compatible.
The Royal African Company tended to lay chief stress upon
promptness of sale. Thus at the end of 1672 it announced that
if persons would contract to receive whole cargoes upon their arrival and to accept all slaves between twelve and forty years of
age who were able to go over the ship's side unaided they would
be supplied at the rate of £15 per head in Barbados, £16 in Nevis,

[42] Snelgrave, *Guinea and the Slave Trade*, p. 159.
[43] H. C. Carey, *The Slave Trade, Domestic and Foreign* (Philadelphia, 1853), chap. 3.

£17 in Jamaica, and £18 in Virginia.[44] The colonists were for a time disposed to accept this arrangement where they could. For example Charles Calvert, governor of Maryland, had already written Lord Baltimore in 1664: "I have endeavored to see if I could find as many responsible men that would engage to take 100 or 200 neigros every year from the Royall Company at that rate mentioned in your lordship's letter; but I find that we are nott men of estates good enough to undertake such a buisnesse, but could wish we were for we are naturally inclined to love neigros if our purses could endure it." [45] But soon complaints arose that the slaves delivered on contract were of the poorest quality, while the better grades were withheld for other means of sale at higher prices. Quarrels also developed between the company on the one hand and the colonists and their legislatures on the other over the rating of colonial moneys and the obstructions placed by law about the collection of debts; and the colonists proceeded to give all possible encouragement to the separate traders, legal or illegal as their traffic might be.[46]

Most of the sales, in the later period at least, were without previous contract. A practice often followed in the British West Indian ports was to advertise that the cargo of a vessel just arrived would be sold on board at an hour scheduled and at a uniform price announced in the notice. At the time set there would occur a great scramble of planters and dealers to grab the choicest slaves. A variant from this method was reported in 1670 from Guadeloupe, where a cargo brought in by the French African company was first sorted into grades of prime men, (*pièces d'Inde*), prime women, boys and girls rated at two-thirds of prime, and children rated at one-half. To each slave was attached a ticket bearing a number, while a corresponding ticket was deposited in one of four boxes according to the grade. At prices then announced for the several grades, the planters bought the privilege of drawing tickets from the appropriate boxes and

[44] E. D. Collins, "Studies in the Colonial Policy of England, 1672-1680," in the American Historical Association *Report* for 1901, I, 158.
[45] Maryland Historical Society *Fund Publications*, no. 28, p. 249.
[46] G. L. Beer, *The Old Colonial System* (New York, 1912), part I, vol. I, chap. 5.

acquiring thereby title to the slaves to which the numbers they drew were attached.[47] In the chief ports of the British continental colonies the maritime transporters usually engaged merchants on shore to sell the slaves as occasion permitted, whether by private sale or at auction. At Charleston these merchants charged a ten per cent. commission on slave sales, though their factorage rate was but five per cent. on other sorts of merchandise; and they had credits of one and two years for the remittance of the proceeds.[48] The following advertisement, published at Charleston in 1785 jointly by Ball, Jennings and Company, and Smiths, DeSaussure and Darrell is typical of the factors' announcements: "GOLD COAST NEGROES. On Thursday, the 17th. of March instant, will be exposed to public sale near the Exchange (if not before disposed of by private contract) the remainder of the cargo of negroes imported in the ship *Success,* Captain John Conner, consisting chiefly of likely young boys and girls in good health, and having been here through the winter may be considered in some degree seasoned to this climate. The conditions of the sale will be credit to the first of January, 1786, on giving bond with approved security where required—the negroes not to be delivered till the terms are complied with." [49] But in such colonies as Virginia where there was no concentration of trade in ports, the ships generally sailed from place to place peddling their slaves, with notice published in advance when practicable. The diseased or otherwise unfit negroes were sold for whatever price they would bring. In some of the ports it appears that certain physicians made a practise of buying these to sell the survivors at a profit upon their restoration to health.[50]

That by no means all the negroes took their enslavement grievously is suggested by a traveler's note at Columbia, South Carolina, in 1806: "We met . . . a number of new negroes, some of whom had been in the country long enough to talk intelligibly.

[47] Lucien Peytraud, *L'Esclavage aux Antilles, Françaises avant 1789* (Paris, 1897), pp. 122, 123.
[48] D. D. Wallace, *Life of Henry Laurens,* p. 75.
[49] *The Gazette of the State of South Carolina,* Mch. 10, 1785.
[50] C. C. Robin, *Voyages* (Paris, 1806), II, 170.

Their likely looks induced us to enter into a talk with them. One of them, a very bright, handsome youth of about sixteen, could talk well. He told us the circumstances of his being caught and enslaved, with as much composure as he would any common occurrence, not seeming to think of the injustice of the thing nor to speak of it with indignation. . . . He spoke of his master and his work as though all were right, and seemed not to know he had a right to be anything but a slave." [51]

In the principal importing colonies careful study was given to the comparative qualities of the several African stocks. The consensus of opinion in the premises may be gathered from several contemporary publications, the chief ones of which were written in Jamaica.[52]   The Senegalese, who had a strong Arabic strain in their ancestry, were considered the most intelligent of Africans and were especially esteemed for domestic service, the handicrafts and responsible positions. "They are good commanders over other negroes, having a high spirit and a tolerable share of fidelity; but they are unfit for hard work; their bodies are not robust nor their constitutions vigorous." The Mandingoes were reputed to be especially gentle in demeanor but peculiarly prone to theft. They easily sank under fatigue, but might be employed with advantage in the distillery and the boiling house or as watchmen against fire and the depredations of cattle. The Coromantees of the Gold Coast stand salient in all accounts as hardy and stalwart of mind and body. Long calls them haughty, ferocious and stubborn; Edwards relates examples of their Spartan fortitude; and it was generally agreed that they were frequently instigators of slave conspiracies and insurrections. Yet their spirit of loyalty made them the most highly prized of servants by those who could call it forth. Of them

[51] "Diary of Edward Hooker," in the American Historical Association *Report* for 1906, p. 882.
[52] Edward Long, *History of Jamaica* (London, 1774), II, 403, 404; Bryan Edwards, *History of the British Colonies in the West Indies,* various editions, book IV, chap. 3; and "A Professional Planter," *Practical Rules for the Management and Medical Treatment of Negro Slaves in the Sugar Colonies* (London, 1803), pp. 39-48. The pertinent portion of this last is reprinted in *Plantation and Frontier,* II, 127-133. For the similar views of the French planters in the West Indies see Peytraud, *L'Esclavage aux Antilles Françaises,* pp. 87-90.

Christopher Codrington, governor of the Leeward Islands, wrote in 1701 to the English Board of Trade: "The Corramantes are not only the best and most faithful of our slaves, but are really all born heroes. There is a differance between them and all other negroes beyond what 'tis possible for your Lordships to conceive. There never was a raskal or coward of that nation. Intrepid to the last degree, not a man of them but will stand to be cut to pieces without a sigh or groan, grateful and obedient to a kind master, but implacably revengeful when ill-treated. My father, who had studied the genius and temper of all kinds of negroes forty-five years with a very nice observation, would say, noe man deserved a Corramante that would not treat him like a friend rather than a slave." [53]

The Whydahs, Nagoes and Pawpaws of the Slave Coast were generally the most highly esteemed of all. They were lusty and industrious, cheerful and submissive. "That punishment which excites the Koromantyn to rebel, and drives the Ebo negro to suicide, is received by the Pawpaws as the chastisement of legal authority to which it is their duty to submit patiently." As to the Eboes or Mocoes, described as having a sickly yellow tinge in their complection, jaundiced eyes, and prognathous faces like baboons, the women were said to be diligent but the men lazy, despondent and prone to suicide. "They require therefore the gentlest and mildest treatment to reconcile them to their situation; but if their confidence be once obtained they manifest as great fidelity, affection and gratitude as can reasonably be expected from men in a state of slavery."

The "kingdom of Gaboon," which straddled the equator, was the worst reputed of all. "From thence a good negro was scarcely ever brought. They are purchased so cheaply on the coast as to tempt many captains to freight with them; but they generally die either on the passage or soon after their arrival in the islands. The debility of their constitutions is astonishing." From this it would appear that most of the so-called Gaboons must have been in reality Pygmies caught in the inland equa-

[53] *Calendar of State Papers, Colonial Series, America and West Indies,* 1701, pp. 720, 721.

torial forests, for Bosman, who traded among the Gaboons, merely inveighed against their garrulity, their indecision, their gullibility and their fondness for strong drink, while as to their physique he observed: "they are mostly large, robust well shaped men." [54] Of the Congoes and Angolas the Jamaican writers had little to say except that in their glossy black they were slender and sightly, mild in disposition, unusually honest, but exceptionally stupid.

In the South Carolina market Gambia negroes, mainly Mandingoes, were the favorites, and Angolas also found ready sale; but cargoes from Calabar, which were doubtless comprised mostly of Eboes, were shunned because of their suicidal proclivity. Henry Laurens, who was then a commission dealer at Charleston, wrote in 1755 that the sale of a shipload from Calabar then in port would be successful only if no other Guinea ships arrived before its quarantine was ended, for the people would not buy negroes of that stock if any others were to be had.[55]

It would appear that the Congoes, Angolas and Eboes were especially prone to run away, or perhaps particularly easy to capture when fugitive, for among the 1046 native Africans advertised as runaways held in the Jamaica workhouses in 1803 there were 284 Eboes and Mocoes, 185 Congoes and 259 Angolas as compared with 101 Mandingoes, 60 Chambas (from Sierra Leone), 70 Coromantees, 57 Nagoes and Pawpaws, and 30 scattering, along with a total of 488 American-born negroes and mulattoes, and 187 unclassified.[56]

This huge maritime slave traffic had great consequences for all the countries concerned. In Liverpool it made millionaires,[57] and elsewhere in England, Europe and New England it brought prosperity not only to ship owners but to the distillers of rum and manufacturers of other trade goods. In the American plantation districts it immensely stimulated the production of the

[54] Bosman in Pinkerton's *Voyages*, XVI, 509, 510.
[55] D. D. Wallace, *Life of Henry Laurens*, pp. 76, 77.
[56] These data were generously assembled for me by Professor Chauncey S. Boucher of Washington University, St. Louis, from a file of the *Royal Gazette* of Kingston, Jamaica, for the year 1803, which is preserved in the Charleston, S. C., Library.
[57] Gomer Williams, chap. 6.

staple crops. On the other hand it kept the planters constantly in debt for their dearly bought labor, and it left a permanent and increasingly complex problem of racial adjustments. In Africa, it largely transformed the primitive scheme of life, and for the worse. It created new and often unwholesome wants; it destroyed old industries and it corrupted tribal institutions. The rum, the guns, the utensils and the gewgaws were irresistible temptations. Every chief and every tribesman acquired a potential interest in slave getting and slave selling. Charges of witchcraft, adultery, theft and other crimes were trumped up that the number of convicts for sale might be swelled; debtors were pressed that they might be adjudged insolvent and their persons delivered to the creditors; the sufferings of famine were left unrelieved that parents might be forced to sell their children or themselves; kidnapping increased until no man or woman and especially no child was safe outside a village; and wars and raids were multiplied until towns by hundreds were swept from the earth and great zones lay void of their former teeming population.[58]

The slave trade has well been called the systematic plunder of a continent. But in the irony of fate those Africans who lent their hands to the looting got nothing but deceptive rewards, while the victims of the rapine were quite possibly better off on the American plantations than the captors who remained in the African jungle. The only participants who got unquestionable profit were the English, European and Yankee traders and manufacturers.

[58] C. B. Wadstrom, *Observations on the Slave Trade* (London, 1789); Lord Muncaster, *Historical Sketches of the Slave Trade and of its Effects in Africa* (London, 1792); Jerome Dowd, *The Negro Races*, vol. 3, chap. 2 (MS).

CHAPTER III

THE SUGAR ISLANDS

AS regards negro slavery the history of the West Indies is inseparable from that of North America. In them the plantation system originated and reached its greatest scale, and from them the institution of slavery was extended to the continent. The industrial system on the islands, and particularly on those occupied by the British, is accordingly instructive as an introduction and a parallel to the continental régime.

The early career of the island of Barbados gives a striking instance of a farming colony captured by the plantation system. Founded in 1624 by a group of unprosperous English emigrants, it pursued an even and commonplace tenor until the Civil War in England sent a crowd of royalist refugees thither, together with some thousands of Scottish and Irish prisoners converted into indentured servants. Negro slaves were also imported to work alongside the redemptioners in the tobacco, cotton, ginger, and indigo crops, and soon proved their superiority in that climate, especially when yellow fever, to which the Africans are largely immune, decimated the white population. In 1643, as compared with some five thousand negroes of all sorts, there were about eighteen thousand white men capable of bearing arms; and in the little island's area of 166 square miles there were nearly ten thousand separate landholdings. Then came the introduction of sugar culture, which brought the beginning of the end of the island's transformation. A fairly typical plantation in the transition period was described by a contemporary. Of its five hundred acres about two hundred were planted in sugar-cane, twenty in tobacco, five in cotton, five in ginger and seventy in provision crops; several acres were devoted to pineapples, bananas, oranges and the like; eighty acres were in pasturage, and one hundred and twenty in woodland. There were a sugar mill, a boiling house, a curing house, a distillery, tne master's residence, laborers' cabins, and barns and stables.   The live-stock numbered forty-five oxen, eight cows, twelve horses and sixteen asses; and the labor force comprised ninety-eight "Christians," ninety-six negroes and three Indian women with their children. In general, this writer said, "The slaves and their posterity, being subject to their masters forever, are kept and preserved with greater care than the (Christian) servants, who are theirs for but five years according to the laws of the island.[1] So that for the time being the servants have the worser lives, for they are put to very hard labor, ill lodging and their dyet very light."

As early as 1645 George Downing, then a young Puritan preacher recently graduated from Harvard College but later a distinguished English diplomat, wrote to his cousin John Winthrop, Jr., after a voyage in the West Indies: "If you go to Barbados, you shal see a flourishing Iland, many able men.   I beleive they have bought this year no lesse than a thousand Negroes, and the more they buie the better they are able to buye, for in a yeare and halfe they will earne (with God's blessing) as much as they cost." [2]   Ten years later, with bonanza prices prevailing in the sugar market, the Barbadian planters declared their colony to be "the most envyed of the world" and estimated the value of its annual crops at a million pounds sterling.[3] But in the early sixties a severe fall in sugar prices put an end to the boom period and brought the realization that while sugar was the rich man's opportunity it was the poor man's ruin.   By 1666 emigration to other colonies had halved the white population; but the slave trade had increased the negroes to forty thousand, most of whom were employed on the eight hundred sugar estates.[4] For the rest of the century Barbados held her place as the leading producer of British sugar and the most esteemed of the British colonies; but as the decades passed the fertility of her limited

---

[1] Richard Ligon, *History of Barbados* (London, 1657).
[2] Massachusetts Historical Society *Collections*, series 4, vol. 6, p. 536.
[3] G. L. Beer, *Origins of the British Colonial System* (New York, 1908), p. 413.
[4] G. L. Beer, *The Old Colonial System*, part I, vol. 2, pp. 9, 10.

fields became depleted, and her importance gradually fell secondary to that of the growing Jamaica.

The Barbadian estates were generally much smaller than those of Jamaica came to be. The planters nevertheless not only controlled their community wholly in their interest but long maintained a unique "planters' committee" at London to make representations to the English government on behalf of their class. They pleaded for the colony's freedom of trade, for example, with no more vigor than they insisted that England should not interfere with the Barbadian law to prohibit Quakers from admitting negroes to their meetings. An item significant of their attitude upon race relations is the following from the journal of the Crown's committee of trade and plantations, Oct. 8, 1680: "The gentlemen of Barbados attend, . . . who declare that the conversion of their slaves to Christianity would not only destroy their property but endanger the island, inasmuch as converted negroes grow more perverse and intractable than others, and hence of less value for labour or sale. The disproportion of blacks to white being great, the whites have no greater security than the diversity of the negroes' languages, which would be destroyed by conversion in that it would be necessary to teach them all English. The negroes are a sort of people so averse to learning that they will rather hang themselves or run away than submit to it." The Lords of Trade were enough impressed by this argument to resolve that the question be left to the Barbadian government.[5]

As illustrating the plantation régime in the island in the period of its full industrial development, elaborate instructions are extant which were issued about 1690 to Richard Harwood, manager or overseer of the Drax Hall and Hope plantations belonging to the Codrington family. These included directions for planting, fertilizing and cultivating the cane, for the operation of the wind-driven sugar mill, the boiling and curing houses and the distillery, and for the care of the live stock; but the main concern was with the slaves. The number in the gangs was not

[5] Calendar of State Papers, Colonial Series, America and West Indies, 1677-1680, p. 611.

stated, but the expectation was expressed that in ordinary years from ten to twenty new negroes would have to be bought to keep the ranks full, and it was advised that Coromantees be preferred, since they had been found best for the work on these estates. Plenty was urged in provision crops with emphasis upon plantains and cassava,—the latter because of the certainty of its harvest, the former because of the abundance of their yield in years of no hurricanes and because the negroes especially delighted in them and found them particularly wholesome as a dysentery diet. The services of a physician had been arranged for, but the manager was directed to take great care of the negroes' health and pay special attention to the sick. The clothing was not definitely stated as to periods. For food each was to receive weekly a pound of fish and two quarts of molasses, tobacco occasionally, salt as needed, palm oil once a year, and home-grown provisions in abundance. Offenses committed by the slaves were to be punished immediately, "many of them being of the houmer of avoiding punishment when threatened: to hang themselves." For drunkenness the stocks were recommended. As to theft, recognized as especially hard to repress, the manager was directed to let hunger give no occasion for it.[6]

Jamaica, which lies a thousand miles west of Barbados and has twenty-five times her area, was captured by the English in 1655 when its few hundreds of Spaniards had developed nothing but cacao and cattle raising. English settlement began after the Restoration, with Roundhead exiles supplemented by immigrants from the Lesser Antilles and by buccaneers turned farmers. Lands were granted on a lavish scale on the south side of the island where an abundance of savannahs facilitated tillage; but the development of sugar culture proved slow by reason of the paucity of slaves and the unfamiliarity of the settlers with the peculiarities of the soil and climate. With the increase of prosperity, and by the aid of managers brought from Barbados, sugar plantations gradually came to prevail all round the coast and in favorable mountain valleys, while smaller establishments here

Original MS. in the Bodleian Library, A. 248, 3. Copy used through the courtesy of Dr. F. W. Pitman of Yale University.

and there throve more moderately in the production of cotton, pimento, ginger, provisions and live stock. For many years the legislature, prodded by occasional slave revolts, tried to stimulate the increase of whites by requiring the planters to keep a fixed proportion of indentured servants; but in the early eighteenth century this policy proved futile, and thereafter the whites numbered barely one-tenth as many as the negroes. The slaves were reported at 86,546 in 1734; 112,428 in 1744; 166,914 in 1768; and 210,894 in 1787. In addition there were at the last date some 10,000 negroes legally free, and 1400 maroons or escaped slaves dwelling permanently in the mountain fastnesses. The number of sugar plantations was 651 in 1768, and 767 in 1791; and they contained about three-fifths of all the slaves on the island. Throughout this latter part of the century the average holding on the sugar estates was about 180 slaves of all ages.[7]

When the final enumeration of slaves in the British possessions was made in the eighteen-thirties there were no single Jamaica holdings reported as large as that of 1598 slaves held by James Blair in Guiana; but occasional items were of a scale ranging from five to eight hundred each, and hundreds numbered above one hundred each. In many of these instances the same persons are listed as possessing several holdings, with Sir Edward Hyde East particularly notable for the large number of his great squads. The degree of absenteeism is indicated by the frequency of English nobles, knights and gentlemen among the large proprietors. Thus the Earl of Balcarres had 474 slaves; the Earl of Harwood 232; the Earl and Countess of Airlie 59; Earl Talbot and Lord Shelborne jointly 79; Lord Seaford 70; Lord Hatherton jointly with Francis Downing, John Benbow and the Right Reverend H. Philpots, Lord Bishop of Exeter, two holdings of 304 and 236 slaves each; and the three Gladstones, Thomas, William and Robert 468 slaves jointly.[8]

Such an average scale and such a prevalence of absenteeism never prevailed in any other Anglo-American plantation com-

[7] Edward Long, *History of Jamaica*, I, 494, Bryan Edwards, *History of the British Colonies in the West Indies,* book II, appendix.
[8] "Accounts of Slave Compensation Claims," in the British official *Accounts and Papers, 1837-1838,* vol. XLVIII.

munity, largely because none of the other staples required so much manufacturing as sugar did in preparing the crops for market. As Bryan Edwards wrote in 1793: "the business of sugar planting is a sort of adventure in which the man that engages must engage deeply. . . . It requires a capital of no less than thirty thousand pounds sterling to embark in this employment with a fair prospect of success." Such an investment, he particularized, would procure and establish as a going concern a plantation of 300 acres in cane and 100 acres each in provision crops, forage and woodland, together with the appropriate buildings and apparatus, and a working force of 80 steers, 60 mules and 250 slaves, at the current price for these last of £50 sterling a head.[9] So distinctly were the plantations regarded as capitalistic ventures that they came to be among the chief speculations of their time for absentee investors.

When Lord Chesterfield tried in 1767 to buy his son a seat in Parliament he learned "that there was no such thing as a borough to be had now, for that the rich East and West Indians had secured them all at the rate of three thousand pounds at the least." [10] And an Englishman after traveling in the French and British Antilles in 1825 wrote: "The French colonists, whether Creoles or Europeans, consider the West Indies as their country; they cast no wistful looks toward France. . . . In our colonies it is quite different; . . . every one regards the colony as a temporary lodging place where they must sojourn in sugar and molasses till their mortgages will let them live elsewhere. They call England their home though many of them have never been there. . . . The French colonist deliberately expatriates himself; the Englishman never." [11] Absenteeism was throughout a serious detriment. Many and perhaps most of the Jamaica proprietors were living luxuriously in England instead of industriously on their estates. One of them, the talented author "Monk" Lewis, when he visited his own plantation in 1815-1817, near the end of his life, found as much novelty in the doings of his slaves

[9] Bryan Edwards, *History of the West Indies*, book 5, chap. 3.
[10] Lord Chesterfield, *Letters to his Son* (London, 1774), II, 525.
[11] H. N. Coleridge, *Six Months in the West Indies*, 4th ed. (London, 1832), pp. 131, 132.

as if he had been drawing his income from shares in the Bank of England; but even he, while noting their clamorous good nature was chiefly impressed by their indolence and perversity.[12] It was left for an invalid traveling for his health to remark most vividly the human equation: "The negroes cannot be silent; they talk in spite of themselves. Every passion acts upon them with strange intensity, their anger is sudden and furious, their mirth clamorous and excessive, their curiosity audacious, and their love the sheer demand for gratification of an ardent animal desire. Yet by their nature they are good-humored in the highest degree, and I know nothing more delightful than to be met by a group of negro girls and to be saluted with their kind 'How d'ye massa? how d'ye massa?' "[13]

On the generality of the plantations the tone of the management was too much like that in most modern factories. The laborers were considered more as work-units than as men, women and children. Kindliness and comfort, cruelty and hardship, were rated at balance-sheet value; births and deaths were reckoned in profit and loss, and the expense of rearing children was balanced against the cost of new Africans. These things were true in some degree in the North American slave-holding communities, but in the West Indies they excelled.

In buying new negroes a practical planter having a preference for those of some particular tribal stock might make sure of getting them only by taking with him to the slave ships or the "Guinea yards" in the island ports a slave of the stock wanted and having him interrogate those for sale in his native language to learn whether they were in fact what the dealers declared them to be. Shrewdness was even more necessary to circumvent other tricks of the trade, especially that of fattening up, shaving and oiling the skins of adult slaves to pass them off as youthful. The ages most desired in purchasing were between fifteen and twenty-five years. If these were not to be had well grown children were preferable to the middle-aged, since they were much less

[12] Matthew G. Lewis, *Journal of a West Indian Proprietor, kept during a Residence in the Island of Jamaica* (London, 1834).
[13] H. N. Coleridge, p. 76.

apt to die in the "seasoning," they would learn English readily, and their service would increase instead of decreasing after the lapse of the first few years. The conversion of new negroes into plantation laborers, a process called "breaking in," required always a mingling of delicacy and firmness. Some planters distributed their new purchases among the seasoned households, thus delegating the task largely to the veteran slaves. Others housed and tended them separately under the charge of a select staff of nurses and guardians and with frequent inspection from headquarters. The mortality rate was generally high under either plan, ranging usually from twenty to thirty per cent. in the seasoning period of three or four years. The deaths came from diseases brought from Africa, such as the yaws which was similar to syphilis; from debilities and maladies acquired on the voyage; from the change of climate and food; from exposure incurred in running away; from morbid habits such as dirt-eating; and from accident, manslaughter and suicide.[14]

The seasoned slaves were housed by families in separate huts grouped into "quarters," and were generally assigned small tracts on the outskirts of the plantation on which to raise their own provision crops. Allowances of clothing, dried fish, molasses, rum, salt, etc., were issued them from the commissary, together with any other provisions needed to supplement their own produce. The field force of men and women, boys and girls was generally divided according to strength into three gangs, with special details for the mill, the coppers and the still when needed; and permanent corps were assigned to the handicrafts, to domestic service and to various incidental functions. The larger the plantation, of course, the greater the opportunity of differentiating tasks and assigning individual slaves to employments fitted to their special aptitudes.

The planters put such emphasis upon the regularity and vigor of the routine that they generally neglected other equally vital

[14] Long, *Jamaica*, II, 435; Edwards, *West Indies*, book 4, chap. 5; A Professional Planter, *Rules*, chap. 2; Thomas Roughley, *Jamaica Planter's Guide* (London, 1823), pp. 118-120.

things. They ignored the value of labor-saving devices, most of them even shunning so obviously desirable an implement as the plough and using the hoe alone in breaking the land and cultivating the crops. But still more serious was the passive acquiescence in the depletion of their slaves by excess of deaths over births. This decrease amounted to a veritable decimation, requiring the frequent importation of recruits to keep the ranks full. Long estimated this loss at about two per cent. annually, while Edwards reckoned that in his day there were surviving in Jamaica little more than one-third as many negroes as had been imported in the preceding career of the colony.[15] The staggering mortality rate among the new negroes goes far toward accounting for this; but even the seasoned groups generally failed to keep up their numbers. The birth rate was notoriously small; but the chief secret of the situation appears to have lain in the poor care of the newborn children. A surgeon of long experience said that a third of the babies died in their first month, and that few of the imported women bore children; and another veteran resident said that commonly more than a quarter of the babies died within the first nine days, of "jaw-fall," and nearly another fourth before they passed their second year.[16] At least one public-spirited planter advocated in 1801 the heroic measure of closing the slave trade in order to raise the price of labor and coerce the planters into saving it both by improving their apparatus and by diminishing the death rate.[17] But his fellows would have none of his policy.

While in the other plantation staples the crop was planted and reaped in a single year, sugar cane had a cycle extending through several years. A typical field in southside Jamaica would be "holed" or laid off in furrows between March and June, planted in the height of the rainy season between July and September, cultivated for fifteen months, and harvested in the first half of the second year after its planting. Then when the rains returned new shoots, "rattoons," would sprout from the old roots to yield

[15] Long, III, 432; Edwards, book 4, chap. 2.
[16] *Abridgement of the evidence taken before a committee of the whole House: The Slave Trade*, no. 2 (London, 1790), pp. 48, 80.
[17] Clement Caines, *Letters on the Cultivation of the Otaheite Cane* (London, 1801), pp. 274-283.

a second though diminished harvest in the following spring, and so on for several years more until the rattoon or "stubble" yield became too small to be worth while. The period of profitable rattooning ran in some specially favorable districts as high as fourteen years, but in general a field was replanted after the fourth crop. In such case the cycles of the several fields were so arranged on any well managed estate that one-fifth of the area in cane was replanted each year and four-fifths harvested.

This coördination of cycles brought it about that oftentimes almost every sort of work on the plantation was going on simultaneously. Thus on the Lodge and Grange plantations which were apparently operated as a single unit, the extant journal of work during the harvest month of May, 1801,[18] shows a distribution of the total of 314 slaves as follows: ninety of the "big gang" and fourteen of the "big gang feeble" together with fifty of the "little gang" were stumping a new clearing, "holing" or laying off a stubble field for replanting, weeding and filling the gaps in the field of young first-year or "plant" cane, and heaping the manure in the ox-lot; ten slaves were cutting, ten tying and ten more hauling the cane from the fields in harvest; fifteen were in a "top heap" squad whose work was conjecturally the saving of the green cane tops for forage and fertilizer; nine were tending the cane mill, seven were in the boiling house, producing a hogshead and a half of sugar daily, and two were at the two stills making a puncheon of rum every four days; six watchmen and fence menders, twelve artisans, eight stockminders, two hunters, four domestics, and two sick nurses were at their appointed tasks; and eighteen invalids and pregnant women, four disabled with sores, forty infants and one runaway were doing no work. There were listed thirty horses, forty mules and a hundred oxen and other cattle; but no item indicates that a single plow was in use.

The cane-mill in the eighteenth century consisted merely of three iron-sheathed cylinders, two of them set against the third, turned by wind, water or cattle. The canes, tied into small bundles for greater compression, were given a double squeezing while

[18] Printed by Clement Caines in a table facing p. 246 of his *Letters.*

passing through the mill. The juice expressed found its way through a trough into the boiling house while the flattened stalks, called mill trash or megass in the British colonies and bagasse in Louisiana, were carried to sheds and left to dry for later use as fuel under the coppers and stills.

In the boiling house the cane-juice flowed first into a large receptacle, the clarifier, where by treatment with lime and moderate heat it was separated from its grosser impurities. It then passed into the first or great copper, where evaporation by boiling began and some further impurities, rising in scum, were taken off. After further evaporation in smaller coppers the thickened fluid was ladled into a final copper, the teache, for a last boiling and concentration; and when the product of the teache was ready for crystallization it was carried away for the curing. In Louisiana the successive caldrons were called the grande, the propre, the flambeau and the batterie, the last of these corresponding to the Jamaican teache.

The curing house was merely a timber framework with a roof above and a great shallow sloping vat below. The sugary syrup from the teache was generally potted directly into hogsheads resting on the timbers, and allowed to cool with occasional stirrings. Most of the sugar stayed in the hogsheads, while some of it trickled with the mother liquor, molasses, through perforations in the bottoms into the vat beneath. When the hogsheads were full of the crudely cured, moist, and impure "muscovado" sugar, they were headed up and sent to port. The molasses, the scum, and the juice of the canes tainted by damage from rats and hurricanes were carried to vats in the distillery where, with yeast and water added, the mixture fermented and when distilled yielded rum.

The harvest was a time of special activity, of good feeling, and even of a certain degree of pageantry. Lafcadio Hearn, many years after the slaves were freed, described the scene in Martinique as viewed from the slopes of Mont Pelée: "We look back over the upreaching yellow fan-spread of cane-fields, and winding of tortuous valleys, and the sea expanding beyond an opening to the west. . . . Far down we can distinguish a line of field-hands—

the whole *atelier*, as it is called, of a plantation—slowly descending a slope, hewing the canes as they go. There is a woman to every two men, a binder (amarreuse) : she gathers the canes as they are cut down, binds them with their own tough long leaves into a sort of sheaf, and carries them away on her head;—the men wield their cutlasses so beautifully that i' is a delight to watch them. One cannot often enjoy such a spectacle nowadays; tor the introduction of the piece-work system has destroyed the picturesqueness of plantation labor throughout the islands, with rare exceptions. Formerly the work of cane-cutting resembled the march of an army;—first advanced the cutlassers in line, naked to the waist; then the amarreuses, the women who tied and carried; and behind these the *ka*, the drum,—with a paid *crieur* or *crieuse* to lead the song;—and lastly the black Commandeur, for general." [19]

After this bit of rhapsody the steadying effect of statistics may be abundantly had from the records of the great Worthy Park plantation, elaborated expressly for posterity's information. This estate, lying in St. John's parish on the southern slope of the Jamaica mountain chain, comprised not only the plantation proper, which had some 560 acres in sugar cane and smaller fields in food and forage crops, but also Spring Garden, a nearby cattle ranch, and Mickleton which was presumably a relay station for the teams hauling the sugar and rum to Port Henderson. The records, which are available for the years from 1792 to 1796 inclusive, treat the three properties as one establishment. [20]

The slaves of the estate at the beginning of 1792 numbered 355, apparently all seasoned negroes, of whom 150 were in the main field gang. But this force was inadequate for the full routine, and in that year "jobbing gangs" from outside were employed at rates from 2*s*. 6*d*. to 3*s*. per head per day and at a total cost of £1832, reckoned probably in Jamaican currency which stood at thirty per cent. discount. In order to relieve the need of this outside labor the management began that year to buy new

[19] Lafcadio Hearn, *Two Years in the French West Indies* (New York, 1890), p. 275.
[20] These records have been analyzed in U. B. Phillips, "A Jamaica Slave Plantation," in the *American Historical Review*, XIX, 543-558.

Africans on a scale considered reckless by all the island authorities. In March five men and five women were bought; and in October 25 men, 27 women, 16 boys, 16 girls and 6 children, all new Congoes; and in the next year 51 males and 30 females, part Congoes and part Coromantees and nearly all of them eighteen to twenty years old. Thirty new huts were built; special cooks and nurses were detailed; and quantities of special foodstuffs were bought—yams, plantains, flour, fresh and salt fish, and fresh beef heads, tongues, hearts and bellies; but it is not surprising to find that the next outlay for equipment was for a large new hospital in 1794, costing £341 for building its brick walls alone. Yaws became serious, but that was a trifle as compared with dysentery; and pleurisy, pneumonia, fever and dropsy had also to be reckoned with. About fifty of the new negroes were quartered for several years in a sort of hospital camp at Spring Garden, where the routine even for the ablebodied was much lighter than on Worthy Park.

One of the new negroes died in 1792, and another in the next year. Then in the spring of 1794 the heavy mortality began. In that year at least 31 of the newcomers died, nearly all of them from the "bloody flux" (dysentery) except two who were thought to have committed suicide. By 1795, however, the epidemic had passed. Of the five deaths of the new negroes that year, two were attributed to dirt-eating,[21] one to yaws, and two to ulcers, probably caused by yaws. The three years of the seasoning period were now ended, with about three-fourths of the number imported still alive. The loss was perhaps less than usual where such large batches were bought; but it demonstrates the strength of the shock involved in the transplantation from Africa, even after the severities of the middle passage had been survived and after the weaklings among the survivors had been culled out at the ports. The outlay for jobbing gangs on Worthy Park rapidly diminished.

The list of slaves at the beginning of 1794 is the only one giving full data as to ages, colors and health as well as occupations.

[21] The "fatal habit of eating dirt" is described by Thomas Roughley in his *Planter's Guide* (London. 1823), pp. 118-120.

The ages were of course in many cases mere approximations. The "great house negroes" head the list, fourteen in number. They comprised four housekeepers, one of whom however was but eight years old, three waiting boys, a cook, two washerwomen, two gardeners and a grass carrier, and included nominally Quadroon Lizette who after having been hired out for several years to Peter Douglass, the owner of a jobbing gang, was this year manumitted.

The overseer's house had its proportionate staff of nine domestics with two seamstresses added, and it was also headquarters both for the nursing corps and a group engaged in minor industrial pursuits. The former, with a "black doctor" named Will Morris at its head, included a midwife, two nurses for the hospital, four (one of them blind) for the new negroes, two for the children in the day nursery, and one for the suckling babies of the women in the gangs. The latter comprised three cooks to the gangs, one of whom had lost a hand; a groom, three hog tenders, of whom one was ruptured, another "distempered" and the third a ten-year-old boy, and ten aged idlers including Quashy Prapra and Abba's Moll to mend pads, Yellow's Cuba and Peg's Nancy to tend the poultry house, and the rest to gather grass and hog feed.

Next were listed the watchmen, thirty-one in number, to guard against depredations of men, cattle and rats and against conflagrations which might sweep the ripening cane-fields and the buildings. All of these were black but the mulatto foreman, and only six were described as able-bodied. The disabilities noted were a bad sore leg, a broken back, lameness, partial blindness, distemper, weakness, and cocobees which was a malady of the blood.

A considerable number of the slaves already mentioned were in such condition that little work might be expected of them. Those completely laid off were nine superannuated ranging from seventy to eighty-five years old, three invalids, and three women relieved of work as by law required for having reared six children each.

Among the tradesmen, virtually all the blacks were stated to be fit for field work, but the five mulattoes and the one quadroon, though mostly youthful and healthy, were described as not fit for the field. There were eleven carpenters, eight coopers, four sawyers, three masons and twelve cattlemen, each squad with a foreman; and there were two ratcatchers whose work was highly important, for the rats swarmed in incredible numbers and spoiled the cane if left to work their will. A Jamaican author wrote, for example, that in five or six months on one plantation "not less than nine and thirty thousand were caught." [22]

In the "weeding gang," in which most of the children from five to eight years old were kept as much for control as for achievement, there were twenty pickaninnies, all black, under Mirtilla as "driveress," who had borne and lost seven children of her own. Thirty-nine other children were too young for the weeding gang, at least six of whom were quadroons. Two of these last, the children of Joanny, a washerwoman at the overseer's house, were manumitted in 1795.

Fifty-five, all new negroes except Darby the foreman, and including Blossom the infant daughter of one of the women, comprised the Spring Garden squad. Nearly all of these were twenty or twenty-one years old. The men included Washington, Franklin, Hamilton, Burke, Fox, Milton, Spencer, Hume and Sheridan; the women Spring, Summer, July, Bashfull, Virtue, Frolic, Gamesome, Lady, Madame, Dutchess, Mirtle and Cowslip. Seventeen of this distinguished company died within the year.

The "big gang" on Worthy Park numbered 137, comprising 64 men from nineteen to sixty years old and 73 women from nineteen to fifty years, though but four of the women and nine of the men, including Quashy the "head driver" or foreman, were past forty years. The gang included a "head home wainman," a "head road wainman," who appears to have been also the sole slave plowman on the place, a head muleman, three distillers, a boiler, two sugar potters, and two "sugar guards" for the wagons carrying the crop to port. All of the gang

─────

* William Beckford, *A Descriptive Account of Jamaica* (London, 1790), I, 55, 56.

were described as healthy, able-bodied and black. A considerable number in it were new negroes, but only seven of the whole
died in this year of heaviest mortality.

The "second gang," employed in a somewhat lighter routine
under Sharper as foreman, comprised 40 women and 27 men
ranging from fifteen to sixty years, all black. While most of
them were healthy, five were consumptive, four were ulcerated,
one was "inclined to be bloated," one was "very weak," and
Pheba was "healthy but worthless."

Finally in the third or "small gang," for yet lighter work
under Baddy as driveress with Old Robin as assistant, there
were 68 boys and girls, all black, mostly between twelve and
fifteen years old. The draught animals comprised about 80 mules
and 140 oxen.

Among the 528 slaves all told—284 males and 244 females—
74, equally divided between the sexes, were fifty years old and
upwards. If the new negroes, virtually all of whom were
doubtless in early life, be subtracted from the gross, it appears
that one-fifth of the seasoned stock had reached the half century,
and one-eighth were sixty years old and over. This is a good
showing of longevity.

About eighty of the seasoned women were within the age
limits of childbearing. The births recorded were on an average
of nine for each of the five years covered, which was hardly
half as many as might have been expected under favorable conditions. Special entry was made in 1795 of the number of children each woman had borne during her life, the number of these
living at the time this record was made, and the number of miscarriages each woman had had. The total of births thus recorded was 345; of children then living 159; of miscarriages
75. Old Quasheba and Betty Madge had each borne fifteen
children, and sixteen other women had borne from six to eleven
each. On the other hand, seventeen women of thirty years and
upwards had had no children and no miscarriages. The childbearing records of the women past middle age ran higher than
those of the younger ones to a surprising degree. Perhaps conditions on Worthy Park had been more favorable at an earlier

period, when the owner and his family may possibly have been resident there. The fact that more than half of the children whom these women had borne were dead at the time of the record comports with the reputation of the sugar colonies for heavy infant mortality. With births so infrequent and infant deaths so many it may well appear that the notorious failure of the island-bred stock to maintain its numbers was not due to the working of the slaves to death. The poor care of the young children may be attributed largely to the absence of a white mistress, an absence characteristic of Jamaica plantations. There appears to have been no white woman resident on Worthy Park during the time of this record. In 1795 and perhaps in other years the plantation had a contract for medical service at the rate of £140 a year.

"Robert Price of Penzance in the Kingdom of Great Britain Esquire" was the absentee owner of Worthy Park. His kinsman Rose Price Esquire who was in active charge was not salaried but may have received a manager's commission of six per cent. on gross crop sales as contemplated in the laws of the colony. In addition there were an overseer at £200, later £300, a year, four bookkeepers at £50 to £60, a white carpenter at £120, and a white plowman at £56. The overseer was changed three times during the five years of the record, and the bookkeepers were generally replaced annually. The bachelor staff was most probably responsible for the mulatto and quadroon offspring and was doubtless responsible also for the occasional manumission of a woman or child.

Rewards for zeal in service were given chiefly to the "drivers" or gang foremen. Each of these had for example every year a "doubled milled cloth colored great coat" costing 11s. 6d and a "fine bound hat with girdle and buckle" costing 10s. 6d. As a more direct and frequent stimulus a quart of rum was served weekly to each of three drivers, three carpenters, four boilers, two head cattlemen, two head mulemen, the "stoke-hole boatswain," and the black doctor, and to the foremen respectively of the sawyers, coopers, blacksmiths, watchmen, and road wainmen, and a pint weekly to the head home wainman, the potter, the midwife, and the young children's field nurse. These allowances totaled about three hundred gallons yearly. But a considerably greater quantity than this was distributed, mostly at Christmas perhaps, for in 1796 for example 922 gallons were recorded of "rum used for the negroes on the estate." Upon the birth of each child the mother was given a Scotch rug and a silver dollar.

No record of whippings appears to have been kept, nor of any offenses except absconding. Of the runaways, reports were made to the parish vestry of those lying out at the end of each quarter. At the beginning of the record there were no runaways and at the end there were only four; but during 1794 and 1795 there were eight or nine listed in each report, most of whom were out for but a few months each, but several for a year or two; and several furthermore absconded a second or third time after returning. The runaways were heterogeneous in age and occupation, with more old negroes among them than might have been expected. Most of them were men; but the women Ann, Strumpet and Christian Grace made two flights each, and the old pad-mender Abba's Moll stayed out for a year and a quarter. A few of those recovered were returned through the public agency of the workhouse. Some of the rest may have come back of their own accord.

In the summer of 1795, when absconding had for some time been too common, the recaptured runaways and a few other offenders were put for disgrace and better surveillance into a special "vagabond gang." This comprised Billy Scott, who was usually a mason and sugar guard, Oxford who as head cooper had enjoyed a weekly quart of rum, Cesar a sawyer, and Moll the old pad-mender, along with three men and two women from the main gangs, and three half-grown boys. The vagabond gang was so wretchedly assorted for industrial purposes that it was probably soon disbanded and its members distributed to their customary tasks. For use in marking slaves a branding iron was inventoried, but in the way of arms there were merely two muskets, a fowling piece and twenty-four old guns without locks. Evidently no turbulence was anticipated.

Worthy Park bought nearly all of its hardware, dry goods, drugs and sundries in London, and its herrings for the negroes and salt pork and beef for the white staff in Cork. Corn was cultivated between the rows in some of the cane fields on the plantation, and some guinea-corn was bought from neighbors. The negroes raised their own yams and other vegetables, and doubtless pigs and poultry as well; and plantains were likely to be plentiful.

Every October cloth was issued at the rate of seven yards of osnaburgs, three of checks, and three of baize for each adult and proportionately for children. The first was to be made into coats, trousers and frocks, the second into shirts and waists, the third into bedclothes. The cutting and sewing were done in the cabins. A hat and a cap were also issued to each negro old enough to go into the field, and a clasp-knife to each one above the age of the third gang. From the large purchases of Scotch rugs recorded it seems probable that these were issued on other occasions than those of childbirth. As to shoes, however, the record is silent.

The Irish provisions cost annually about £300, and the English supplies about £1000, not including such extra outlays as that of £1355 in 1793 for new stills, worms, and coppers. Local expenditures were probably reckoned in currency. Converted into sterling, the salary list amounted to about £500, and the local outlay for medical services, wharfage, and petty supplies came to a like amount. Taxes, manager's commissions, and the depreciation of apparatus must have amounted collectively to £800. The net death-loss of slaves, not including that from the breaking-in of new negroes, averaged about two and a quarter per cent.; that of the mules and oxen ten per cent. When reckoned upon the numbers on hand in 1796 when the plantation with 470 slaves was operating with very little outside help, these losses, which must be replaced by new purchases if the scale of output was to be maintained, amounted to about £900. Thus a total of £4000 sterling is reached as the average current expense in years when no mishaps occurred.

The crops during the years of the record averaged 311 hogsheads of sugar, sixteen hundredweight each, and 133 puncheons of rum, 110 gallons each.   This was about the common average on the island, of two-thirds as many hogsheads as there were slaves of all ages on a plantation.[23] If the prices had been those current in the middle of the eighteenth century these crops would have yielded the proprietor great profits.   But at £15 per hogshead and £10 per puncheon, the prices generally current in the island in the seventeen-nineties, the gross return was but about £6000 sterling, and the net earnings of the establishment accordingly not above £2000.   The investment in slaves, mules and oxen was about £28,000, and that in land, buildings and equipment according to the island authorities, would reach a like sum.[24]   The net earnings in good years were thus less than four per cent. on the investment; but the liability to hurricanes, earthquakes, fires, epidemics and mutinies would bring the safe expectations considerably lower.   A mere pestilence which carried off about sixty mules and two hundred oxen on Worthy Park in 1793-1794 wiped out more than a year's earnings.

In the twenty years prior to the beginning of the Worthy Park record more than one-third of all the sugar plantations in Jamaica had gone through bankruptcy.   It was generally agreed that, within the limits of efficient operation, the larger an estate was, the better its prospect for net earnings.   But though Worthy Park had more than twice the number of slaves that the average plantation employed, it was barely paying its way.

In the West Indies as a whole there was a remarkable repetition of developments and experiences in island after island, similar to that which occurred in the North American plantation regions, but even more pronounced.   The career of Barbados was followed rapidly by the other Lesser Antilles under the English and French flags; these were all exceeded by the greater scale of Jamaica; she in turn yielded the primacy in sugar to Hayti only to have that French possession, when overwhelmed by its great negro insurrection, give the paramount place to

[23] Long, Jamaica, II, 433, 439.
[24] Edwards, West Indies, book 5, chap. 3.

the Spanish Porto Rico and Cuba. In each case the opening of a fresh area under imperial encouragement would promote rapid immigration and vigorous industry on every scale; the land would be taken up first in relatively small holdings; the prosperity of the pioneers would prompt a more systematic husbandry and the consolidation of estates, involving the replacement of the free small proprietors by slave gangs; but diminishing fertility and intensifying competition would in the course of years more than offset the improvement of system. Meanwhile more pioneers, including perhaps some of those whom the planters had bought out in the original colonies, would found new settlements; and as these in turn developed, the older colonies would decline and decay in spite of desperate efforts by their plantation proprietors to hold their own through the increase of investments and the improvement of routine.[25]

[25] Herman Merivale, *Colonisation and Colonies* (London, 1841), pp. 92, 93.

CHAPTER IV

THE TOBACCO COLONIES

THE purposes of the Virginia Company of London and of the English public which gave it sanction were profit for the investors and aggrandizement for the nation, along with the reduction of pauperism at home and the conversion of the heathen abroad. For income the original promoters looked mainly toward a South Sea passage, gold mines, fisheries, Indian trade, and the production of silk, wine and naval stores. But from the first they were on the alert for unexpected opportunities to be exploited. The following of the line of least resistance led before long to the dominance of tobacco culture, then of the plantation system, and eventually of negro slavery. At the outset, however, these developments were utterly unforeseen. In short, Virginia was launched with varied hopes and vague expectations. The project was on the knees of the gods, which for a time proved a place of extreme discomfort and peril.

The first comers in the spring of 1607, numbering a bare hundred men and no women, were moved by the spirit of adventure. With a cumbrous and oppressive government over them, and with no private ownership of land nor other encouragement for steadygoing thrift, the only chance for personal gain was through a stroke of discovery. No wonder the loss of time and strength in futile excursions. No wonder the disheartening reaction in the malaria-stricken camp of Jamestown.

A second hundred men arriving early in 1608 found but forty of the first alive. The combined forces after lading the ships with "gilded dirt" and cedar logs, were left facing the battle with Indians and disease. The dirt when it reached London proved valueless, and the cedar, of course, worth little. The company that summer sent further recruits including two women and several Poles and Germans to make soap-ashes, glass and

pitch—"skilled workmen from foraine parts which may teach
and set ours in the way where we may set thousands a work in
these such like services." [1] At the same time it instructed the
captain of the ship to explore and find either a lump of gold, the
South Sea passage, or some of Raleigh's lost colonists, and it
sent the officials at Jamestown peremptory notice that unless the
£2000 spent on the present supply be met by the proceeds of
the ship's return cargo, the settlers need expect no further aid.
The shrewd and redoubtable Captain John Smith, now president
in the colony, opposed the vain explorings, and sent the council
in London a characteristic "rude letter." The ship, said he, kept
nearly all the victuals for its crew, while the settlers, "the one
halfe sicke, the other little better," had as their diet "a little
meale and water, and not sufficient of that." The foreign ex-
perts had been set at their assigned labors; but "it were better
to give five hundred pound a tun for those grosse commodities
in Denmarke than send for them hither till more necessary
things be provided. For in over-toyling our weake and unskil-
full bodies to satisfie this desire of present profit we can scarce
ever recover ourselves from one supply to another. . . . As yet
you must not looke for any profitable returnes." [2]

This unwelcome advice while daunting all mercenary promoters gave spur to strong-hearted patriots. The prospect of
profits was gone; the hope of an overseas empire survived.
The London Company, with a greatly improved charter, appealed
to the public through sermons, broadsides, pamphlets, and personal canvassing, with such success that subscriptions to its
stock poured in from "lords, knights, gentlemen and others,"
including the trade guilds and the town corporations. In lieu of
cash dividends the company promised that after a period of seven
years, during which the settlers were to work on the company's
account and any surplus earnings were to be spent on the colony
or funded, a dividend in land would be issued. In this the settlers were to be embraced as if instead of emigrating each of

[1] Alexander Brown, *The First Republic in America* (Boston, 1898), p. 68.
[2] Capt. John Smith, *Works*, Arber ed. (Birmingham, 1884), pp. 442-445. Smith's book. it should be said, is the sole source for this letter.

them had invested £12 10s. in a share of stock. Several hundred recruits were sent in 1609, and many more in the following years; but from the successive governors at Jamestown came continued reports of disease, famine and prostration, and pleas ever for more men and supplies. The company, bravely keeping up its race with the death rate, met all demands as best it could.

To establish a firmer control, Sir Thomas Dale was sent out in 1611 as high marshal along with Sir Thomas Gates as governor. Both of these were men of military training, and they carried with them a set of stringent regulations quite in keeping with their personal proclivities. These rulers properly regarded their functions as more industrial than political. They for the first time distributed the colonists into a series of settlements up and down the river for farming and live-stock tending; they spurred the willing workers by assigning them three-acre private gardens; and they mercilessly coerced the laggard. They transformed the colony from a distraught camp into a group of severely disciplined farms, owned by the London Company, administered by its officials, and operated partly by its servants, partly by its tenants who paid rent in the form of labor. That is to say, Virginia was put upon a schedule of plantation routine, producing its own food supply and wanting for the beginning of prosperity only a marketable crop. This was promptly supplied through John Rolfe's experiment in 1612 in raising tobacco. The English people were then buying annually some £200,000 worth of that commodity, mainly from the Spanish West Indies, at prices which might be halved or quartered and yet pay the freight and yield substantial earnings; and so rapid was the resort to the staple in Virginia that soon the very market place in Jamestown was planted in it. The government in fact had to safeguard the food supply by forbidding anyone to plant tobacco until he had put two acres in grain.

When the Gates-Dale administration ended, the seven year period from 1609 was on the point of expiry; but the temptation of earnings from tobacco persuaded the authorities to delay the land dividend. Samuel Argall, the new governor, while continuing the stringent discipline, robbed the company for his own profit; and the news of his misdeeds reaching London in 1618 discredited the faction in the company which had supported his régime. The capture of control by the liberal element among the stockholders, led by Edwin Sandys and the Earl of Southampton, was promptly signalized by measures for converting Virginia into a commonwealth. A land distribution was provided on a generous scale, and Sir George Yeardley was dispatched as governor with instructions to call a representative assembly of the people to share in the making of laws. The land warrants were issued at the rate of a hundred acres on each share of stock and a similar amount to each colonist of the time, to be followed in either case by the grant of a second hundred acres upon proof that the first had been improved; and fifty acres additional in reward for the future importation of every laborer.

While the company continued as before to send colonists on its own account, notably craftsmen, indigent London children, and young women to become wives for the bachelor settlers, it now offered special stimulus to its members to supplement its exertions. To this end it provided that groups of its stockholders upon organizing themselves into sub-companies or partnerships might consolidate their several grants into large units called particular plantations; and it ordered that "such captaines or leaders of perticulerr plantations that shall goe there to inhabite by vertue of their graunts and plant themselves, their tenants and servants in Virginia, shall have liberty till a forme of government be here settled for them, associatinge unto them divers of the gravest and discreetes of their companies, to make orders, ordinances and constitutions for the better orderinge and dyrectinge of their servants and buisines, provided they be not repugnant to the lawes of England." [3]

To embrace this opportunity some fifty grants for particular plantations were taken out during the remaining life of the London Company. Among them were Southampton Hundred

[3] *Records of the Virginia Company of London*, Kingsbury ed. (Washington, 1906), I, 303.

and Martin's Hundred, to each of which two or three hundred
settlers were sent prior to 1620,[4] and Berkeley Hundred whose
records alone are available. The grant for this last was issued
in February, 1619, to a missionary enthusiast, George Thorpe,
and his partners, whose collective holdings of London Company
stock amounted to thirty-five shares. To them was given and
promised land in proportion to stock and settlers, together with
a bonus of 1500 acres in view of their project for converting
the Indians. Their agent in residence was as usual vested with
public authority over the dwellers on the domain, limited only
by the control of the Virginia government in military matters
and in judicial cases on appeal.[5] After delays from bad weather,
the initial expedition set sail in September comprising John
Woodleaf as captain and thirty-four other men of diverse trades
bound to service for terms ranging from three to eight years at
varying rates of compensation. Several of these were designated
respectively as officers of the guard, keeper of the stores, care-
taker of arms and implements, usher of the hall, and clerk of the
kitchen. Supplies of provisions and equipment were carried, and
instructions in detail for the building of houses, the fencing of
land, the keeping of watch, and the observances of religion.
Next spring the settlement, which had been planted near the
mouth of the Appomattox River, was joined by Thorpe himself,
and in the following autumn by William Tracy who had entered
the partnership and now carried his own family together with a
preacher and some forty servants. Among these were nine women
and the two children of a man who had gone over the year before.
As giving light upon indented servitude in the period it may
be noted that many of those sent to Berkeley Hundred were
described as "gentlemen," and that five of them within the first
year besought their masters to send them each two indented
servants for their use and at their expense. Tracy's vessel however was too small to carry all whom it was desired to send.

[4] *Records of the Virginia Company of London,* Kingsbury ed. (Washington, 1906), I, 350.
[5] The records of this enterprise (the Smyth of Nibley papers) have
been printed in the New York Public Library *Bulletin,* III, 160-171, 208-
233, 248-258, 276-295.

It was in fact so crowded with plantation supplies that Tracy wrote on the eve of sailing: "I have throw out mani things of my own yet is ye midill and upper extre[m]li pestered so that ouer men will not lie like men and ye mareners hath not rome to stir   God is abel ih ye gretest weknes to helpe   we will trust to marsi for he must help be yond hope." Fair winds appear to have carried the vessel to port, whereupon Tracy and Thorpe jointly took charge of the plantation, displacing Woodleaf whose services had given dissatisfaction. Beyond this point the records are extremely scant; but it may be gathered that the plantation was wrecked and most of its inhabitants, including Thorpe, slain in the great Indian massacre of 1622. The restoration of the enterprise was contemplated in an after year, but eventually the land was sold to other persons.

The fate of Berkeley Hundred was at the same time the fate of most others of the same sort; and the extinction of the London Company in 1624 ended the granting of patents on that plan. The owners of the few surviving particular plantations, furthermore, found before long that ownership by groups of absentees was poorly suited to the needs of the case, and that the exercise of public jurisdiction was of more trouble than it was worth. The particular plantation system proved accordingly but an episode, yet it furnished a transition, which otherwise might not readily have been found, from Virginia the plantation of the London Company, to Virginia the colony of private plantations and farms. When settlement expanded afresh after the Indians were driven away many private estates gradually arose to follow the industrial routine of those which had been called particular.

The private plantations were hampered in their development by dearth of capital and labor and by the extremely low prices of tobacco which began at the end of the sixteen-twenties as a consequence of overproduction. But by dint of good management and the diversification of their industry the exceptional men led the way to prosperity and the dignity which it carried. Of Captain Samuel Matthews, for example, "an old Planter of above thirty years standing," whose establishment was at Blunt

Point on the lower James, it was written in 1648: "He hath
a fine house and all things answerable to it; he sowes yeerly
store of hempe and flax, and causes it to be spun; he keeps
weavers, and hath a tan-house, causes leather to be dressed, hath
eight shoemakers employed in this trade, hath forty negroe servants, brings them up to trades in his house: he yeerly sowes
abundance of wheat, barley, etc. The wheat he selleth at four
shillings the bushell; kills store of beeves, and sells them to
victuall the ships when they come thither; hath abundance of
kine, a brave dairy, swine great store, and poltery. He married the daughter of Sir Tho. Hinton, and in a word, keeps a
good house, lives bravely, and a true lover of Virginia. He is
worthy of much honour." [6] Many other planters were thriving
more modestly, most of them giving nearly all their attention to
the one crop. The tobacco output was of course increasing
prodigiously. The export from Virginia in 1619 had amounted
to twenty thousand pounds; that from Virginia and Maryland
in 1664 aggregated fifty thousand hogsheads of about five hundred pounds each.[7]

The labor problem was almost wholly that of getting and
managing bondsmen. Land in the colony was virtually to be
had for the taking; and in general no freemen arriving in the
colony would engage for such wages as employers could afford to
pay. Workers must be imported. Many in England were willing
to come, and more could be persuaded or coerced, if their
passage were paid and employment assured. To this end indentured servitude had already been inaugurated by the London Company as a modification of the long used system of ap-
prenticeship. And following that plan, ship captains brought
hundreds, then thousands of laborers a year and sold their indentures to the planters either directly or through dealers in
such merchandize. The courts took the occasion to lessen the
work of the hangman by sentencing convicts to deportation in
servitude; the government rid itself of political prisoners dur-

[6] *A Perfect Description of Virginia* (London, 1649), reprinted in Peter
Force *Tracts*, vol. II.
[7] Bruce, *Economic History of Virginia in the Seventeenth Century* (New
York, 1896), I, 391.

ing the civil war by the same method; and when servant prices
rose the supply was further swelled by the agency of professional kidnappers.

The bondage varied as to its terms, with two years apparently
the minimum. The compensation varied also from mere transportation and sustenance to a payment in advance and a stipula-
tion for outfit in clothing, foodstuffs and diverse equipment at
the end of service. The quality of redemptioners varied from
the very dregs of society to well-to-do apprentice planters; but
the general run was doubtless fairly representative of the English working classes. Even the convicts under the terrible laws
of that century were far from all being depraved. This labor in
all its grades, however, had serious drawbacks. Its first cost
was fairly heavy; it was liable to an acclimating fever with a high
death rate; its term generally expired not long after its adjustment and training were completed; and no sooner was its service
over than it set up for itself, often in tobacco production, to
compete with its former employers and depress the price of
produce. If the plantation system were to be perpetuated an entirely different labor supply must be had.

"About the last of August came in a Dutch man of warre that
sold us twenty negars." Thus wrote John Rolfe in a report of
happenings in 1619;[8] and thus, after much antiquarian dispute,
the matter seems to stand as to the first bringing of negroes to
Virginia. The man-of-war, or more accurately the privateer,
had taken them from a captured slaver, and it seems to have
sold them to the colonial government itself, which in turn sold
them to private settlers. At the beginning of 1625, when a
census of the colony was made,[9] the negroes, then increased to
twenty-three in a total population of 1232 of which about one-
half were white servants, were distributed in seven localities
along the James River. In 1630 a second captured cargo was
sold in the colony, and from 1635 onward small lots were imported nearly every year.[10] Part of these came from England,

[8] John Smith *Works*, Arber ed., p. 541.
[9] Tabulated in the *Virginia Magazine*, VII, 364-367.
[10] Bruce, *Economic History of Virginia*, II, 72-77.

part from New Netherland and most of the remainder doubtless from the West Indies. In 1649 Virginia was reckoned to have some three hundred negroes mingled with its fifteen thousand whites.[11] After two decades of a somewhat more rapid importation Governor Berkeley estimated the gross population in 1671 at forty thousand, including six thousand white servants and two thousand negro slaves.[12] Ere this there was also a small number of free negroes. But not until near the end of the century, when the English government had restricted kidnapping, when the Virginia assembly had forbidden the bringing in of convicts, and when the direct trade from Guinea had reached considerable dimensions, did the negroes begin to form the bulk of the Virginia plantation gangs.

Thus for two generations the negroes were few, they were employed alongside the white servants, and in many cases were members of their masters' households. They had by far the best opportunity which any of their race had been given in America to learn the white men's ways and to adjust the lines of their bondage into as pleasant places as might be. Their importation was, for the time, on but an experimental scale, and even their legal status was during the early decades indefinite.

The first comers were slaves in the hands of their maritime sellers; but they were not fully slaves in the hands of their Virginian buyers, for there was neither law nor custom then establishing the institution of slavery in the colony. The documents of the times point clearly to a vague tenure. In the county court records prior to 1661 the negroes are called negro servants or merely negroes—never, it appears, definitely slaves. A few were expressly described as servants for terms of years, and others were conceded property rights of a sort incompatible with the institution of slavery as elaborated in later times. Some of the blacks were in fact liberated by the courts as having served out the terms fixed either by their indentures or by the custom of the country. By the middle of the century several had become free landowners, and at least one of them owned a negro servant who

[11] *A New Description of Virginia* (London, 1649).
[12] W. W. Hening, *Statutes at Large of Virginia*, II, 515.

went to court for his freedom but was denied it because he could not produce the indenture which he claimed to have possessed. Nevertheless as early as the sixteen-forties the holders of negroes were falling into the custom of considering them, and on occasion selling them along with the issue of the females, as servants for life and perpetuity. The fact that negroes not bound for a term were coming to be appraised as high as £30, while the most valuable white redemptioners were worth not above £15 shows also the tendency toward the crystallization of slavery before any statutory enactments declared its existence.[13]

Until after the middle of the century the laws did not discriminate in any way between the races. The tax laws were an index of the situation. The act of 1649, for example, confined the poll tax to male inhabitants of all sorts above sixteen years old. But the act of 1658 added imported female negroes, along with Indian female servants; and this rating of negro women as men for tax purposes was continued thenceforward as a permanent practice. A special act of 1668, indeed, gave sharp assertion to the policy of using taxation as a token of race distinction: "Whereas some doubts have arisen whether negro women set free were still to be accompted tithable according to a former act, it is declared by this grand assembly that negro women, though permitted to enjoy their freedome yet ought not in all respects to be admitted to a full fruition of the exemptions and impunities of the English, and are still liable to the payment of taxes."[14]

As to slavery itself, the earliest laws giving it mention did not establish the institution but merely recognized it, first indirectly then directly, as in existence by force of custom. The initial act of this series, passed in 1656, promised the Indian tribes that when they sent hostages the Virginians would not "use them as slaves."[15] The next, an act of 1660, removing impediments to trade by the Dutch and other foreigners, contemplated specifically their bringing in of "negro slaves."[16] The third, in the fol-

[13] The substance of this paragraph is drawn mainly from the illuminating discussion of J. H. Russell, *The Free Negro in Virginia* (Johns Hopkins University *Studies*, XXXI, no. 3, Baltimore, 1913), pp. 24-35.
[14] W. W. Hening, *Statutes at Large of Virginia*, I, 361, 454; II, 267.
[15] *Ibid.*, I, 396.   [16] *Ibid.*, 540.

lowing year, enacted that if any white servants ran away in company with "any negroes who are incapable of making satisfaction by addition of time," the white fugitives must serve for the time of the negroes' absence in addition to suffering the usual penalties on their own score.[17] A negro whose time of service could not be extended must needs have been a servant for life—in other words a slave. Then in 1662 it was enacted that "whereas some doubts have arrisen whether children got by any Englishman upon a negro woman shall be slave or free, . . . all children born in this colony shall be bond or free only according to the condition of the mother." [18] Thus within six years from the first mention of slaves in the Virginia laws, slavery was definitely recognized and established as the hereditary legal status of such negroes and mulattoes as might be held therein. Eighteen years more elapsed before a distinctive police law for slaves was enacted; but from 1680 onward the laws for their control were as definite and for the time being virtually as stringent as those which in the same period were being enacted in Barbados and Jamaica.

In the first decade or two after the London Company's end the plantation and farm clearings broke the Virginian wilderness only in a narrow line on either bank of the James River from its mouth to near the present site of Richmond, and in a small district on the eastern shore of the Chesapeake. Virtually all the settlers were then raising tobacco, all dwelt at the edge of navigable water, and all were neighbors to the Indians. As further decades passed the similar shores of the parallel rivers to the northward, the York, then the Rappahannock and the Potomac, were occupied in a similar way, though with an increasing predominance of large landholdings. This broadened the colony and gave it a shape conducive to more easy frontier defence. It also led the way to an eventual segregation of industrial pursuits, for the tidewater peninsulas were gradually occupied more or less completely by the planters; while the farmers of less estate, weaned from tobacco by its fall in price, tended

[17] Hening, II, 26.
[18] *Ibid.*, 170.

to move west and south to new areas on the mainland, where they dwelt in self-sufficing democratic neighborhoods, and formed incidentally a buffer between the plantations on the seaboard and the Indians round about.

With the lapse of years the number of planters increased, partly through the division of estates, partly through the immigration of propertied Englishmen, and partly through the rise of exceptional yeomen to the planting estate. The farmers increased with still greater speed; for the planters in recruiting their gangs of indented laborers were serving constantly as immigration agents and as constantly the redemptioners upon completing their terms were becoming yeomen, marrying and multiplying. Meanwhile the expansion of Maryland was extending an identical régime of planters and farmers from the northern bank of the Potomac round the head of the Chesapeake all the way to the eastern shore settlements of Virginia.

In Maryland the personal proprietorship of Lord Baltimore and his desire to found a Catholic haven had no lasting effect upon the industrial and social development. The geographical conditions were so like those in Virginia and the adoption of her system so obviously the road to success that no other plans were long considered. Even the few variations attempted assimilated themselves more or less promptly to the régime of the older colony. The career of the manor system is typical. The introduction of that medieval régime was authorized by the charter for Maryland and was provided for in turn by the Lord Proprietor's instructions to the governor. Every grant of one thousand, later two thousand acres, was to be made a manor, with its appropriate court to settle differences between lord and tenant, to adjudge civil cases between tenants where the issues involved did not exceed the value of two pounds sterling, and to have cognizance of misdemeanors committed on the manor. The fines and other profits were to go to the manorial lord.

Many of these grants were made, and in a few instances the manorial courts duly held their sessions. For St. Clement's Manor, near the mouth of the Potomac, for example, court records between 1659 and 1672 are extant. John Ryves, steward of Thomas Gerard the proprietor, presided; Richard Foster assisted as the elected bailiff; and the classified freeholders, leaseholders, "essoines" and residents served as the "jury and homages." Characteristic findings were "that Samuell Harris broke the peace with a stick"; that John Mansell illegally entertained strangers; that land lines "are at this present unperfect and very obscure"; that a Cheptico Indian had stolen a shirt from Edward Turner's house, for which he is duly fined "if he can be knowne"; "that the lord of the mannor hath not provided a paire of stocks, pillory and ducking stoole—Ordered that these instruments of justice be provided by the next court by a generall contribution throughout the manor"; that certain freeholders had failed to appear, "to do their suit at the lord's court, wherefore they are amerced each man 50l. of tobacco to the lord"; that Joshua Lee had injured "Jno. Hoskins his hoggs by setting his doggs on them and tearing their eares and other hurts, for which he is fined 100l. of tobacco and caske"; "that upon the death of Mr. Robte Sly there is a reliefe due to the lord and that Mr. Gerard Sly is his next heire, who hath sworne fealty accordingly." [19]

St. Clement's was probably almost unique in its perseverance as a true manor; and it probably discarded its medieval machinery not long after the end of the existing record. In general, since public land was to be had virtually free in reward for immigration whether in freedom or service, most of the so-called manors doubtless procured neither leaseholders nor essoines nor any other sort of tenants, and those of them which survived as estates found their salvation in becoming private plantations with servant and slave gangs tilling their tobacco fields. In short, the Maryland manors began and ended much as the Virginia particular plantations had done before them. Maryland on the whole assumed the features of her elder sister. Her tobacco was of lower grade, partly because of her long delay in providing public inspection; her people in consequence were generally less prosperous, her plantations fewer in proportion to her farms, and her labor supply more largely of convicts and other white servants and correspondingly less of negroes. But aside from these variations in degree the developments and tendencies in the one were virtually those of the other. Before the end of the seventeenth century William Fitzhugh of Virginia wrote that his plantations were being worked by "fine crews" of negroes, the majority of whom were natives of the colony. Mrs. Elizabeth Digges owned 108 slaves, John Carter 106, Ralph Wormeley 91, Robert Beverly 42, Nathaniel Bacon, Sr., 40, and various other proprietors proportionate numbers.[20] The conquest of the wilderness was wellnigh complete on tidewater, and the plantation system had reached its full type for the Chesapeake latitudes. Broad forest stretches divided most of the plantations from one another and often separated the several fields on the same estate; but the cause of this was not so much the paucity of population as the character of the land and the prevalent industry. The sandy expanses, and the occasional belts of clay likewise, had but a surface fertility, and the cheapness of land prevented the conservation of the soil. Hence the fields when rapidly exhausted by successive cropping in tobacco were as a rule abandoned to broomsedge and scrub timber while new and still newer grounds were cleared and cropped. Each estate therefore, if its owner expected it to last a lifetime, must comprise an area in forestry much larger than that at any one time in tillage. The great reaches of the bay and the deep tidal rivers, furthermore, afforded such multitudinous places of landing for ocean-going ships that all efforts to modify the wholly rural condition of the tobacco colonies by concentrating settlement were thwarted. It is true that Norfolk and Baltimore grew into consequence during the eighteenth century; but the one throve mainly on the trade of landlocked North Carolina, and the other on that of Pennsylvania. Not until the plantation area had spread well into the piedmont hinterland did Richmond and her sister towns near the falls on the rivers begin to focus Virginia and Maryland trade; and even they had little influence upon life on the tidewater peninsulas.

[20] Bruce, *Economic History of Virginia*, II, 88.

The third tobacco-producing colony, North Carolina, was the product of secondary colonization. Virginia's expansion happened to send some of her people across the boundary, where upon finding themselves under the jurisdiction of the Lord Proprietors of Carolina they took pains to keep that authority upon a strictly nominal basis. The first comers, about 1660, and most of those who followed, were and continued to be small farmers; but in the course of decades a considerable number of plantations arose in the fertile districts about Albemarle Sound. Nearly everywhere in the lowlands, however, the land was too barren for any distinct prosperity. The settlements were quite isolated, the communications very poor, and the social tone mostly that of the backwoods frontier. An Anglican missionary when describing his own plight there in 1711 discussed the industrial régime about him: "Men are generally of all trades and women the like within their spheres, except some who are the posterity of old planters and have great numbers of slaves who understand most handicraft. Men are generally carpenters, joiners, wheelwrights, coopers, butchers, tanners, shoemakers, tallow-chandlers, watermen and what not; women, soap-makers, starch-makers, dyers, etc. He or she that cannot do all these things, or hath not slaves that can, over and above all the common occupations of both sexes, will have but a bad time of it; for help is not to be had at any rate, every one having business enough of his own. This makes tradesmen turn planters, and these become tradesmen. No society one with another, but all study to live by their own hands, of their own produce; and what they can spare goes for foreign goods. Nay, many live on a slender diet to buy rum, sugar and molasses, with other such like necessaries, which are sold at such a rate that the planter here is but a slave to raise a provision for other colonies, and dare not allow himself to partake of his own creatures, except it be the corn of the country in hominy bread."[21] Some of the farmers and probably all the planters raised tobacco according

[21] Letter of Rev. John Urmstone, July 7, 1711, to the secretary of the Society for Propagating the Gospel, printed in F. L. Hawks, *History of North Carolina* (Fayetteville, N. C., 1857, 1858), II, 215, 216.

to the methods prevalent in Virginia. Some also made tar for sale from the abounding pine timber; but with most of the families intercourse with markets must have been at an irreducible minimum.

Tobacco culture, while requiring severe exertion only at a few crises, involved a long painstaking routine because of the delicacy of the plant and the difficulty of producing leaf of good quality, whether of the original varieties, oronoko and sweet-scented, or of the many others later developed. The seed must be sown in late winter or early spring in a special bed of deep forest mold dressed with wood ashes; and the fields must be broken and laid off by shallow furrows into hills three or four feet apart by the time the seedlings were grown to a finger's length. Then came the first crisis. During or just after an April, May or June rain the young plants must be drawn carefully from their beds, distributed in the fields, and each plant set in its hill. Able-bodied, expert hands could set them at the rate of thousands a day; and every nerve must be strained for the task's completion before the ground became dry enough to endanger the seedlings' lives. Then began a steady repetition of hoeings and plowings, broken by the rush after a rain to replant the hills whose first plants had died or grown twisted. Then came also several operations of special tedium. Each plant at the time of forming its flower bud must be topped at a height to leave a specified number of leaves growing on the stalk, and each stalk must have the suckers growing at the base of the leaf-stems pulled off; and the under side of every leaf must be examined twice at least for the destruction of the horn-worms. These came each year in two successive armies or "gluts," the one when the plants were half grown, the other when they were nearly ready for harvest. When the crop began to turn yellow the stalks must be cut off close to the ground, and after wilting carried to a well ventilated tobacco house and there hung speedily for curing. Each stalk must hang at a proper distance from its neighbor, attached to laths laid in tiers on the joists. There the crop must stay for some months, with the windows open in dry weather and closed in wet. Finally came the striking, sorting and prizing in weather moist enough to make the leaves pliable. Part of the gang would lower the stalks to the floor, where the rest working in trios would strip them, the first stripper taking the culls, the second the bright leaves, the third the remaining ones of dull color. Each would bind his takings into "hands" of about a quarter of a pound each and throw them into assorted piles. In the packing or "prizing" a barefoot man inside the hogshead would lay the bundles in courses, tramping them cautiously but heavily. Then a second hogshead, without a bottom, would be set atop the first and likewise filled, and then perhaps a third, when the whole stack would be put under blocks and levers compressing the contents into the one hogshead at the bottom, which when headed up was ready for market. Oftentimes a crop was not cured enough for prizing until the next crop had been planted. Meanwhile the spare time of the gang was employed in clearing new fields, tending the subsidiary crops, mending fences, and performing many other incidental tasks. With some exaggeration an essayist wrote, "The whole circle of the year is one scene of bustle and toil, in which tobacco claims a constant and chief share." [22]

The general scale of slaveholdings in the tobacco districts cannot be determined prior to the close of the American Revolution; but the statistics then available may be taken as fairly representative for the eighteenth century at large. A state census taken in certain Virginia counties in 1782-1783 [23] permits the following analysis for eight of them selected for their large proportions of slaves. These counties, Amelia, Hanover, Lancaster, Middlesex, New Kent, Richmond, Surry and Warwick, are scattered through the Tidewater and the lower Piedmont. For each one of their citizens, fifteen altogether, who held upwards of one hundred slaves, there were approximately three who had from 50

[22] C. W. Gooch, "Prize Essay on Agriculture in Virginia," in the *Lynchburg Virginian*, July 14, 1833. More detailed is W. W. Bowie, "Prize Essay on the Cultivation and Management of Tobacco," in the U. S. Patent Office *Report*, 1849-1850, pp. 318-324. E. R. Billings, *Tobacco* (Hartford, 1875) is a good general treatise.

[23] Printed in lieu of the missing returns of the first U. S. census, in *Heads of Families at the First Census of the United States: Virginia* (Washington, 1908).

to 99; seven with from 30 to 49; thirteen with from 20 to 29; forty with from 10 to 19; forty with from 5 to 9; seventy with from 1 to 4; and sixty who had none. In the three chief plantation counties of Maryland, viz. Ann Arundel, Charles, and Prince George, the ratios among the slaveholdings of the several scales, according to the United States census of 1790, were almost identical with those just noted in the selected Virginia counties, but the non-slaveholders were nearly twice as numerous in proportion. In all these Virginia and Maryland counties the average holding ranged between 8.5 and 13 slaves. In the other districts in both commonwealths, where the plantation system was not so dominant, the average slaveholding was smaller, of course, and the non-slaveholders more abounding.

The largest slaveholding in Maryland returned in the census of 1790 was that of Charles Carroll of Carrollton, comprising 316 slaves. Among the largest reported in Virginia in 1782-1783 were those of John Tabb, Amelia County, 257; William Allen, Sussex County, 241; George Chewning, 224, and Thomas Nelson, 208, in Hanover County; Wilson N. Cary, Fluvanna County, 200; and George Washington, Fairfax County, 188. Since the great planters occasionally owned several scattered plantations it may be that the censuses reported some of the slaves under the names of the overseers rather than under those of the owners; but that such instances were probably few is indicated by the fact that the holdings of Chewning and Nelson above noted were each listed by the census takers in several parcels, with the names of owners and overseers both given.

The great properties were usually divided, even where the lands lay in single tracts, into several plantations for more convenient operation, each under a separate overseer or in some cases under a slave foreman. If the working squads of even the major proprietors were of but moderate scale, those in the multitude of minor holdings were of course lesser still. On the whole, indeed, slave industry was organized in smaller units by far than most writers, whether of romance or history, would have us believe.

CHAPTER V

THE RICE COAST

THE impulse for the formal colonization of Carolina came from Barbados, which by the time of the Restoration was both overcrowded and torn with dissension. Sir John Colleton, one of the leading planters in that little island, proposed to several of his powerful Cavalier friends in England that they join him in applying for a proprietary charter to the vacant region between Virginia and Florida, with a view of attracting Barbadians and any others who might come. In 1663 accordingly the "Merry Monarch" issued the desired charter to the eight applicants as Lords Proprietors. They were the Duke of Albemarle, the Earl of Clarendon, Earl Craven, Lord Ashley (afterward the Earl of Shaftesbury), Lord Berkeley, Sir George Carteret, Sir William Berkeley, and Sir John Colleton. Most of these had no acquaintance with America, and none of them had knowledge of Carolina or purpose of going thither. They expected that the mere throwing open of the region under their distinguished patronage would bring settlers in a rush; and to this end they published proposals in England and Barbados offering lands on liberal terms and providing for a large degree of popular self-government. A group of Barbadians promptly made a tentative settlement at the mouth of the Cape Fear River; but finding the soil exceedingly barren, they almost as promptly scattered to the four winds. Meanwhile in the more southerly region nothing was done beyond exploring the shore.

Finding their passive policy of no avail, the Lords Proprietors bestirred themselves in 1669 to the extent of contributing several hundred pounds each toward planting a colony on their southward coast. At the same time they adopted the "fundamental constitutions" which John Locke had framed for the province. These contemplated land grants in huge parcels to a provincial nobility, and a cumbrous oligarchical government with a minimum participation of popular representatives. The grandiloquent feudalism of the scheme appealed so strongly to the aristocratic Lords Proprietors that in spite of their usual acumen in politics they were blinded to its conflicts with their charter and to its utter top-heaviness. They rewarded Locke with the first patent of Carolina nobility, which carried with it a grant of forty-eight thousand acres. For forty years they clung to the fundamental constitutions, notwithstanding repeated rejections of them by the colonists.

The fund of 1669 was used in planting what proved a permanent settlement of English and Barbadians on the shores of Charleston Harbor. Thereafter the Lords Proprietors relapsed into passiveness, commissioning a new governor now and then and occasionally scolding the colonists for disobedience. The progress of settlement was allowed to take what course it might.

The fundamental constitutions recognized the institution of negro slavery, and some of the first Barbadians may have carried slaves with them to Carolina. But in the early decades Indian trading, lumbering and miscellaneous farming were the only means of livelihood, none of which gave distinct occasion for employing negroes. The inhabitants, furthermore, had no surplus income with which to buy slaves. The recruits who continued to come from the West Indies doubtless brought some blacks for their service; but the Huguenot exiles from France, who comprised the chief other streamlet of immigration, had no slaves and little money. Most of the people were earning their bread by the sweat of their brows. The Huguenots in particular, settling mainly in the interior on the Cooper and Santee Rivers, labored with extraordinary diligence and overcame the severest handicaps. That many of the settlers whether from France or the West Indies were of talented and sturdy stock is witnessed by the mention of the family names of Legaré, Laurens, Marion and Ravenel among the Huguenots, Drayton, Elliot, Gibbes and Middleton among the Barbadians, Lowndes and Rawlins from St. Christopher's, and Pinckney from Jamaica. Some of the people were sluggards, of course, but the rest, heterogeneous as they were, were living and laboring as best they might, trying such new projects as they could, building a free government in spite of the Lords Proprietors, and awaiting the discovery of some staple resource from which prosperity might be won.

Among the crops tried was rice, introduced from Madagascar by Landgrave Thomas Smith about 1694, which after some preliminary failures proved so great a success that from about the end of the seventeenth century its production became the absorbing concern. Now slaves began to be imported rapidly. An official account of the colony in 1708[1] reckoned the population at about 3500 whites, of whom 120 were indentured servants, 4100 negro slaves, and 1400 Indians captured in recent wars and held for the time being in a sort of slavery. Within the preceding five years, while the whites had been diminished by an epidemic, the negroes had increased by about 1,100. The negroes were governed under laws modeled quite closely upon the slave code of Barbados, with the striking exception that in this period of danger from Spanish invasion most of the slave men were required by law to be trained in the use of arms and listed as an auxiliary militia.

During the rest of the colonial period the production of rice advanced at an accelerating rate and the slave population increased in proportion, while the whites multiplied somewhat more slowly. Thus in 1724 the whites were estimated at 14,000, the slaves at 32,000, and the rice export was about 4000 tons; in 1749 the whites were said to be nearly 25,000, the slaves at least 39,000, and the rice export some 14,000 tons, valued at nearly £100,000 sterling;[2] and in 1765 the whites were about 40,000, the slaves about 90,000, and the rice export about 32,000 tons, worth some £225,000.[3] Meanwhile the rule of the Lords Proprietors had been replaced for the better by that of the crown, with South Carolina politically separated from her northern

[1] Text printed in Edward McCrady, *South Carolina under the Proprietary Government* (New York, 1897), pp. 477-481.
[2] Governor Glen, in B. R. Carroll, *Historical Collections of South Carolina* (New York, 1836), II, 218, 234, 266.
[3] McCrady, *South Carolina under the Royal Government* (New York, 1899), pp. 389, 390, 807.

sister; and indigo had been introduced as a supplementary staple. The Charleston district was for several decades perhaps the most prosperous area on the continent.

While rice culture did not positively require inundation, it was facilitated by the periodical flooding of the fields, a practice which was introduced into the colony about 1724. The best lands for this purpose were level bottoms with a readily controllable water supply adjacent. During most of the colonial period the main recourse was to the inland swamps, which could be flooded only from reservoirs of impounded rain or brooks. The frequent shortage of water in this régime made the flooding irregular and necessitated many hoeings of the crop. Furthermore, the dearth of watersheds within reach of the great cypress swamps on the river borders hampered the use of these which were the most fertile lands in the colony. Beginning about 1783 there was accordingly a general replacement of the reservoir system by the new one of tide-flowing.[4] For this method tracts were chosen on the flood-plains of streams whose water was fresh but whose height was controlled by the tide. The land lying between the levels of high and low tide was cleared, banked along the river front and on the sides, elaborately ditched for drainage, and equipped with "trunks" or sluices piercing the front embankment. On a frame above either end of each trunk a door was hung on a horizontal pivot and provided with a ratchet. When the outer door was raised above the mouth of the trunk and the inner door was lowered, the water in the stream at high tide would sluice through and flood the field, whereas at low tide the water pressure from the land side would shut the door and keep the flood in. But when the elevation of the doors was reversed the tide would be kept out and at low tide any water collected in the ditches from rain or seepage was automatically drained into the river. Occasional cross embankments divided the fields for greater convenience of control. The tide-flow system had its own limitations and handicaps. Many of the available tracts were so narrow that the cost of embankment was very high in proportion

[4] David Ramsay, *History of South Carolina* (Charleston, 1809), II, 201-206.

to the area secured; and hurricanes from oceanward sometimes raised the streams until they over-topped the banks and broke them. If these invading waters were briny the standing crop would be killed and the soil perhaps made useless for several years until fresh water had leached out the salt. At many places, in fact, the water for the routine flowing of the crop had to be inspected and the time awaited when the stream was not brackish.

Economy of operation required cultivation in fairly large units. Governor Glen wrote about 1760, "They reckon thirty slaves a proper number for a rice plantation, and to be tended by one overseer." [5] Upon the resort to tide-flowing the scale began to increase. For example, Sir James Wright, governor of Georgia, had in 1771 eleven plantations on the Savannah, Ogeechee and Canoochee Rivers, employing from 33 to 72 slaves each, the great majority of whom were working hands.[6] At the middle of the nineteenth century the single plantation of Governor Aiken on Jehossee Island, South Carolina, of which more will be said in another chapter, had some seven hundred slaves of all ages.

In spite of many variations in the details of cultivation, the tide-flow system led to a fairly general standard of routine. After perhaps a preliminary breaking of the soil in the preceding fall, operations began in the early spring with smoothing the fields and trenching them with narrow hoes into shallow drills about three inches wide at the bottom and twelve or fourteen inches apart. In these between March and May the seed rice was carefully strewn and the water at once let on for the "sprout flow" About a week later the land was drained and kept so until the plants appeared plentifully above ground. Then a week of "point flow" was followed by a fortnight of dry culture in which the spaces between the rows were lightly hoed and the weeds amidst the rice pulled up. Then came the "long flow" for two or three weeks, followed by more vigorous hoeing, and finally the "lay-by flow" extending for two or three months until the crop, then standing shoulder high and thick with bending heads, was ready for harvest. The flowings served a triple purpose

[5] Carroll, *Historical Collections of South Carolina,* II, 202.
[6] American Historical Association *Report* for 1903, p. 445.

in checking the weeds and grass, stimulating the rice, and saving the delicate stalks from breakage and matting by storms.

A curious item in the routine just before the grain was ripe was the guarding of the crop from destruction by rice birds. These bobolinks timed their southward migration so as to descend upon the fields in myriads when the grain was "in the milk." At that stage the birds, clinging to the stalks, could squeeze the substance from within each husk by pressure of the beak. Negroes armed with guns were stationed about the fields with instructions to fire whenever a drove of the birds alighted nearby. This fusillade checked but could not wholly prevent the bobolink ravages. To keep the gunners from shattering the crop itself they were generally given charges of powder only; but sufficient shot was issued to enable the guards to kill enough birds for the daily consumption of the plantation. When dressed and broiled they were such fat and toothsome morsels that in their season other sorts of meat were little used.

For the rice harvest, beginning early in September, as soon as a field was drained the negroes would be turned in with sickles, each laborer cutting a swath of three or four rows, leaving the stubble about a foot high to sustain the cut stalks carefully laid upon it in handfuls for a day's drying. Next day the crop would be bound in sheaves and stacked for a brief curing. When the reaping was done the threshing began, and then followed the tedious labor of separating the grain from its tightly adhering husk. In colonial times the work was mostly done by hand, first the flail for threshing, then the heavy fat-pine pestle and mortar for breaking off the husk. Finally the rice was winnowed of its chaff, screened of the "rice flour" and broken grain, and barreled for market.[7]

The ditches and pools in and about the fields of course bred swarms of mosquitoes which carried malaria to all people subject. Most of the whites were afflicted by that disease in the warmer

[7] The best descriptions of the rice industry are Edmund Ruffin, *Agricultural Survey of South Carolina* (Columbia, S. C., 1843); and R. F. W. Allston, *Essay on Sea Coast Crops* (Charleston, 1854), which latter is printed also in *DeBow's Review*, XVI, 589-615.

half of the year, but the Africans were generally immune. Negro labor was therefore at such a premium that whites were virtually never employed on the plantations except as overseers and occasionally as artisans. In colonial times the planters, except the few quite wealthy ones who had town houses in Charleston, lived on their places the year round; but at the close of the eighteenth century they began to resort in summer to "pine land" villages within an hour or two's riding distance from their plantations. In any case the intercourse between the whites and blacks was notably less than in the tobacco region, and the progress of the negroes in civilization correspondingly slighter. The plantations were less of homesteads and more of business establishments; the race relations, while often cordial, were seldom intimate.

The introduction of indigo culture was achieved by one of America's greatest women, Eliza Lucas, afterward the wife of Charles Pinckney (chief-justice of the province) and mother of the two patriot statesmen Thomas and Charles Cotesworth Pinckney. Her father, the governor of the British island of Antigua, had been prompted by his wife's ill health to settle his family in South Carolina, where the three plantations he acquired near Charleston were for several years under his daughter's management. This girl while attending her father's business found time to keep up her music and her social activities, to teach a class of young negroes to read, and to carry on various undertakings in economic botany. In 1741 her experiments with cotton, guinea-corn and ginger were defeated by frost, and alfalfa proved unsuited to her soil; but in spite of two preliminary failures that year she raised some indigo plants with success. Next year her father sent a West Indian expert named Cromwell to manage her indigo crop and prepare its commercial product. But Cromwell, in fear of injuring the prosperity of his own community, purposely mishandled the manufacturing. With the aid of a neighbor, nevertheless, Eliza not only detected Cromwell's treachery but in the next year worked out the true process. She and her father now distributed indigo seed to a number of planters;

and from 1744 the crop began to reach the rank of a staple.[8] The arrival of Carolina indigo at London was welcomed so warmly that in 1748 Parliament established a bounty of sixpence a pound on indigo produced in the British dominions. The Carolina output remained of mediocre quality until in 1756 Moses Lindo, after a career in the indigo trade in London, emigrated to Charleston and began to teach the planters to distinguish the grades and manufacture the best.[9] At excellent prices, ranging generally from four to six shillings a pound, the indigo crop during the rest of the colonial period, reaching a maximum output of somewhat more than a million pounds from some twenty thousand acres in the crop, yielded the community about half as much gross income as did its rice. The net earnings of the planters were increased in a still greater proportion than this, for the work-seasons in the two crops could be so dovetailed that a single gang might cultivate both staples.

Indigo grew best in the light, dry soil so common on the coastal plain. From seed sown in the early spring the plant would reach its full growth, from three to six feet high, and begin to bloom in June or early July. At that stage the plants were cut off near the ground and laid under water in a shallow vat for a fermentation which in the course of some twelve hours took the dye-stuff out of the leaves. The solution then drawn into another vat was vigorously beaten with paddles for several hours to renew and complete the foaming fermentation. Samples were taken at frequent intervals during the latter part of this process, and so soon as a blue tinge became apparent lime water, in carefully determined proportions, was gently stirred in to stop all further action and precipitate the "blueing." When this had settled, the water was drawn off, the paste on the floor was collected, drained in bags, kneaded, pressed, cut into cubes, dried in the shade and packed for market.[10] A second crop usually sprang from the roots of the first and was harvested in August or September.

[8] *Journal and Letters of Eliza Lucas* (Wormesloe, Ga., 1850) ; Mrs. St. Julien Ravenel, *Eliza Pinckney* (New York, 1896) ; *Plantation and Frontier*, I, 265, 266.
[9] B. A. Elzas, *The Jews of South Carolina* (Philadelphia, 1905), chap. 3.
[10] B. R. Carroll, *Historical Collections of South Carolina*, II, 532-535.

Indigo production was troublesome and uncertain of results. Not only did the furrows have to be carefully weeded and the caterpillars kept off the plants, but when the stalks were being cut and carried to the vats great pains were necessary to keep the bluish bloom on the leaves from being rubbed off and lost, and the fermentation required precise control for the sake of quality in the product.[11] The production of the blue staple virtually ended with the colonial period. The War of Independence not only cut off the market for the time being but ended permanently, of course, the receipt of the British bounty. When peace returned the culture was revived in a struggling way; but its vexations and vicissitudes made it promptly give place to sea-island cotton.[12]

The plantation of the rice-coast type had clearly shown its tendency to spread into all the suitable areas from Winyah Bay to St. John's River, when its southward progress was halted for a time by the erection of the peculiar province of Georgia. The launching of this colony was the beginning of modern philanthropy. Upon procuring a charter in 1732 constituting them trustees of Georgia, James Oglethorpe and his colleagues began to raise funds from private donations and parliamentary grants for use in colonizing English debtor-prisoners and other unfortunates. The beneficiaries, chosen because of their indigence, were transported at the expense of the trust and given fifty-acre homesteads with equipment and supplies. Instruction in agriculture was provided for them at Savannah, and various regulations were established for making them soberly industrious on a small-farming basis. The land could not be alienated, and neither slaves nor rum could be imported. Persons immigrating at their own expense might procure larger land grants, but no one could own more than five hundred acres; and all settlers must plant specified numbers of grape vines and mulberry trees with a view to establishing wine and silk as the staples of the colony.

[11] Johann David Schoepf, *Travels in the Confederation, 1783-1784*, A. J. Morrison tr. (Philadelphia, 1911), pp. 187-189.
[12] David Ramsay, *History of South Carolina*, II, 212; D. D. Wallace, *Life of Henry Laurens*, p. 132.

In the first few years, while Oglethorpe was in personal charge at Savannah and supplies from England were abundant, there was an appearance of success, which soon proved illusory. Not only were the conditions unfit for silk and wine, but the fertile tracts were malarial and the healthy districts barren, and every industry suited to the climate had to meet the competition of the South Carolinians with their slave labor and plantation system. The ne'er-do-weels from England proved ne'er-do-weels again. They complained of the soil, the climate, and the paternalistic regulations under which they lived. They protested against the requirements of silk and wine culture; they begged for the removal of all peculiar restrictions and for the institution of self-government. They bombarded the trustees with petitions saying "rum punch is very wholesome in this climate," asking fee-simple title to their lands, and demanding most vigorously the right of importing slaves. But the trustees were deaf to complaints. They maintained that the one thing lacking for prosperity from silk and wine was perseverance, that the restriction on land tenure was necessary on the one hand to keep an arms-bearing population in the colony and on the other hand to prevent the settlers from contracting debts by mortgage, that the prohibitions of rum and slaves were essential safeguards of sobriety and industry, and that discontent under the benevolent care of the trustees evidenced a perversity on the part of the complainants which would disqualify them for self-government. Affairs thus reached an impasse. Contributions stopped; Parliament gave merely enough money for routine expenses; the trustees lost their zeal but not their crotchets; the colony went from bad to worse. Out of perhaps five thousand souls in Georgia about 1737 so many departed to South Carolina and other free settlements that in 1741 there were barely more than five hundred left. This extreme depression at length forced even the staunchest of the trustees to relax. First the exclusion of rum was repealed, then the introduction of slaves on lease was winked at, then in 1749 and 1750 the overt importation of slaves was authorized and all restrictions on land tenure were canceled. Finally the stoppage of the parliamentary subvention in 1751 forced the trustees in the following year to resign their charter. Slaveholders had already crossed the Savannah River in appreciable numbers to erect plantations on favorable tracts. The lapse of a few more transition years brought Georgia to the status on the one hand of a self-governing royal province and on the other of a plantation community prospering, modestly for the time being, in the production of rice and indigo. Her peculiarities under the trustee régime were gone but not forgotten. The rigidity of paternalism, well meant though it had been, was a lesson against future submission to outward control in any form; and their failure as a peasantry in competition with planters across the river persuaded the Georgians and their neighbors that slave labor was essential for prosperity.

It is curious, by the way, that the tender-hearted, philanthropic Oglethorpe at the very time of his founding Georgia was the manager of the great slave-trading corporation, the Royal African Company. The conflict of the two functions cannot be relieved except by one of the greatest of all reconciling considerations, the spirit of the time. Whatever else the radicals of that period might wish to reform or abolish, the slave trade was held either as a matter of course or as a positive benefit to the people who constituted its merchandise.

The narrow limits of the rice and indigo régime in the two colonies made the plantation system the more dominant in its own area. Detailed statistics are lacking until the first federal census, when indigo was rapidly giving place to sea-island cotton; but the requirements of the new staple differed so little from those of the old that the plantations near the end of the century were without doubt on much the same scale as before the Revolution. In the four South Carolina parishes of St. Andrew's, St. John's Colleton, St. Paul's and St. Stephen's the census-takers of 1790 found 393 slaveholders with an average of 33.7 slaves each, as compared with a total of 28 non-slaveholding families. In these and seven more parishes, comprising together the rural portion of the area known politically as the Charleston District, there were among the 1643 heads of families 1318 slaveholders owning 42,949 slaves. William Blake had 695; Ralph Izard had

594 distributed on eight plantations in three parishes, and ten more at his Charleston house; Nathaniel Heyward had 420 on his plantations and 13 in Charleston; William Washington had 380 in the country and 13 in town; and three members of the Horry family had 340, 229 and 222 respectively in a single neighborhood. Altogether there were 79 separate parcels of a hundred slaves or more, 156 of between fifty and ninety-nine, 318 of between twenty and forty-nine, 251 of between ten and nineteen, 206 of from five to nine, and 209 of from two to four, 96 of one slave each, and 3 whose returns in the slave column are illegible.[18] The statistics of the Georgetown and Beaufort districts, which comprised the rest of the South Carolina coast, show a like analysis except for a somewhat larger proportion of non-slaveholders and very small slaveholders, who were, of course, located mostly in the towns and on the sandy stretches of pine-barren. The detailed returns for Georgia in that census have been lost. Were those for her coastal area available they would surely show a similar tendency toward slaveholding concentration.

Avenues of transportation abundantly penetrated the whole district in the form of rivers, inlets and meandering tidal creeks. Navigation on them was so easy that watermen to the manner born could float rafts or barges for scores of miles in any desired direction, without either sails or oars, by catching the strong ebb and flow of the tides at the proper points. But unlike the Chesapeake estuaries, the waterways of the rice coast were generally too shallow for ocean-going vessels. This caused a notable growth of seaports on the available harbors. Of those in South Carolina, Charleston stood alone in the first rank, flanked by Georgetown and Beaufort. In the lesser province of Georgia, Savannah found supplement in Darien and Sunbury. The two leading ports were also the seats of government in their respective colonies. Charleston was in fact so complete a focus of commerce, politics and society that South Carolina was in a sense a city-state.

[18] *Heads of Families at the First Census of the United States, 1790: State of South Carolina* (Washington, 1908) ; *A Century of Population Growth* (Washington, 1909), pp. 190, 191, 197, 198.

The towns were in sentiment and interest virtually a part of the plantation community. The merchants were plantation factors; the lawyers and doctors had country patrons; the wealthiest planters were town residents from time to time; and many prospering townsmen looked toward plantation retirement, carrying as it did in some degree the badge of gentility, as the crown of their careers. Furthermore the urban negroes, more numerous proportionately than anywhere else on the continent, kept the citizens as keenly alive as the planters to the intricacies of racial adjustments. For example Charleston, which in 1790 had 8089 whites, 7864 slaves and 586 free negroes, felt as great anxiety as did the rural parishes at rumors of slave conspiracies, and on the other hand she had a like interest in the improvement of negro efficiency, morality and good will.

The rice coast community was a small one. Even as measured in its number of slaves it bulked only one-fourth as large, say in 1790, as the group of tobacco commonwealths or the single sugar island of Jamaica. Nevertheless it was a community to be reckoned with. Its people were awake to their peculiar conditions and problems; it had plenty of talented citizens to formulate policies; and it had excellent machinery for uniting public opinion. In colonial times, plying its trade mainly with England and the West Indies, it was in little touch with its continental neighbors, and it developed a sense of separateness. As part of a loosely administered empire its people were content in prosperity and self-government. But in a consolidated nation of diverse and conflicting interests it would be likely on occasion to assert its own will and resist unitedly anything savoring of coercion. In a double sense it was of the *southern* South.

CHAPTER VI

THE NORTHERN COLONIES

HAD any American colony been kept wholly out of touch with both Indians and negroes, the history of slavery therein would quite surely have been a blank. But this was the case nowhere. A certain number of Indians were enslaved in nearly every settlement as a means of disposing of captives taken in war; and negro slaves were imported into every prosperous colony as a mere incident of its prosperity. Among the Quakers the extent of slaveholding was kept small partly, or perhaps mainly, by scruples of conscience; in virtually all other cases the scale was determined by industrial conditions. Here the plantation system flourished and slaves were many; there the climate prevented profits from crude gang labor in farming, and slaves were few.

The nature and causes of the contrast will appear from comparing the careers of two Puritan colonies launched at the same time but separated by some thirty degrees of north latitude. The one was planted on the island of Old Providence lying off the coast of Nicaragua, the other was on the shores of Massachusetts bay. The founders of Old Providence were a score of Puritan dignitaries, including the Earl of Warwick, Lord Saye and Sele, and John Pym, incorporated into the Westminster Company in 1630 with a combined purpose of erecting a Puritanic haven and gaining profits for the investors. The soil of the island was known to be fertile, the nearby Spanish Main would yield booty to privateers, and a Puritan government would maintain orthodoxy. These enticements were laid before John Winthrop and his companions; and when they proved steadfast in the choice of New England, several hundred others of their general sort embraced the tropical Providence alternative. Equipped as it was with all the apparatus of a "New England Canaan," the founders anticipated a far greater career than seemed likely of

achievement in Massachusetts. Prosperity came at once in the
form of good crops and rich prizes taken at sea. Some of the
latter contained cargoes of negro slaves, as was of course expected, who were distributed among the settlers to aid in raising
tobacco; and when a certain Samuel Rishworth undertook to
spread ideas of liberty among them he was officially admonished
that religion had no concern with negro slavery and that his in-
discretions must stop. Slaves were imported so rapidly that the
outnumbered whites became apprehensive of rebellion. In the
hope of promoting the importation of white labor, so greatly
preferable from the public point of view, heavy impositions were
laid upon the employment of negroes, but with no avail. The
apprehension of evils was promptly justified. A number of the
blacks escaped to the mountains where they dwelt as maroons;
and in 1638 a concerted uprising proved so formidable that the
suppression of it strained every resource of the government and
the white inhabitants. Three years afterward the weakened settlement was captured by a Spanish fleet; and this was the end
of the one Puritan colony in the tropics.[1]

Massachusetts was likewise inaugurated by a corporation of
Puritans, which at the outset endorsed the institution of unfree
labor, in a sense, by sending over from England 180 indentured
servants to labor on the company's account. A food shortage
soon made it clear that in the company's service they could not
earn their keep; and in 1630 the survivors of them were set
free.[2] Whether freedom brought them bread or whether they
died of famine, the records fail to tell. At any rate the loss of the
investment in their transportation, and the chagrin of the officials.
materially hastened the conversion of the colony from a company enterprise into an industrial democracy. The use of unfree labor nevertheless continued on a private basis and on a
relatively small scale. Until 1642 the tide of Puritan immigration continued, some of the newcomers of good estate bringing

[1] A. P. Newton, *The Colonizing Activities of the English Puritans* (New
Haven, 1914).
[2] Thomas Dudley, letter to the Countess of Lincoln, in Alex. Young,
Chronicles of the First Planters of Massachusetts Bay (Boston, 1846),
p. 312.

servants in their train. The authorities not only countenanced this but forbade the freeing of servants before the ends of their terms, and in at least one instance the court fined a citizen for such a manumission.³ Meanwhile the war against the Pequots in 1637 yielded a number of captives, whereupon the squaws and girls were distributed in the towns of Massachusetts and Connecticut, and a parcel of the boys was shipped off to the tropics in the Salem ship *Desire*. On its return voyage this thoroughly Puritan vessel brought from Old Providence a cargo of tobacco, cotton, and negroes.⁴ About this time the courts began to take notice of Indians as runaways; and in 1641 a "blackmore," Mincarry, procured the inscription of his name upon the public records by drawing upon himself an admonition from the magistrates.⁵ This negro, it may safely be conjectured, was not a freeman. That there were at least several other blacks in the colony, one of whom proved unamenable to her master's improper command, is told in the account of a contemporary traveler.⁶ In the same period, furthermore, the central court of the colony condemned certain white criminals to become slaves to masters whom the court appointed.⁷ In the light of these things the pro-slavery inclination of the much-disputed paragraph in the Body of Liberties, adopted in 1641, admits of no doubt. The passage reads: "There shall never be any bond slaverie, villinage or captivitie amongst us unles it be lawfull captives taken in just warres, and such strangers as willingly selle themselves or are sold to us. And these shall have all the liberties and Christian usages which the law of God established in Israell concerning such persons doeth morally require. This exempts none from servitude who shall be judged thereto by authoritie." ⁸

On the whole it seems that the views expressed a few years

³ *Records of the Court of Assistants of the Colony of Massachusetts Bay, 1630-1692* (Boston, 1904), pp. 135, 136.
⁴ Letter of John Winthrop to William Bradford, Massachusetts Historical Society *Collections*, XXXIII, 360; Winthrop, *Journal* (Original Narratives edition, New York, 1908), I, 260.
⁵ *Records of the Court of Assistants*, p. 118.
⁶ John Josslyn, "Two Voyages to New England," in Massachusetts Historical Society *Collections*, XXIII, 231.
⁷ *Records of the Court of Assistants*, pp. 78, 79, 86.
⁸ Massachusetts Historical Society *Collections*, XXVIII, 231.

later by Emanuel Downing in a letter to his brother-in-law John Winthrop were not seriously out of harmony with the prevailing sentiment. Downing was in hopes of a war with the Narragansetts for two reasons, first to stop their "worship of the devill," and "2lie, If upon a just warre the Lord should deliver them into our hands, we might easily have men, women and children enough to exchange for Moores,⁹ which wil be more gaynful pilladge for us than wee conceive, for I doe not see how wee can thrive untill wee get into a stock of slaves sufficient to doe all our buisines, for our children's children will hardly see this great continent filled with people, soe that our servants will still desire freedome to plant for themselves, and not stay but for verie great wages.¹⁰ And I suppose you know verie well how we shall mayntayne 20 Moores cheaper than one Englishe servant."

When the four colonies, Massachusetts, Plymouth, Connecticut and New Haven, created the New England Confederation in 1643 for joint and reciprocal action in matters of common concern, they provided not only for the intercolonial rendition of runaway servants, including slaves of course, but also for the division of the spoils of Indian wars, "whether it be in lands, goods or persons," among the participating colonies.¹¹ But perhaps the most striking action taken by the Confederation in these regards was a resolution adopted by its commissioners in 1646, in time of peace and professedly in the interests of peace, authorizing reprisals for depredations. This provided that if any citizen's property suffered injury at the hands of an Indian, the offender's village or any other which had harbored him might be raided and any inhabitants thereof seized in satisfaction "either to serve or to be shipped out and exchanged for negroes as the cause will justly beare." ¹² Many of these captives were in fact exported as merchandise, whether as private property or on the public account of the several colonies.¹³ The value of Indians for export was greater than for local employment by reason of

⁹ *I. e.* negroes.
¹⁰ Massachusetts Historical Society *Collections,* XXXVI, 65.
¹¹ *New Haven Colonial Records, 1653-1665,* pp. 562-566.
¹² *Plymouth Records,* IX, 71.
¹³ G. H. Moore, *Notes on the History of Slavery in Massachusetts* (New York, 1866), pp. 30-48.

their facility in escaping to their tribal kinsmen. Toward the end of the seventeenth century, however, there was some importation of "Spanish Indians" as slaves.[14]

An early realization that the price of negroes also was greater than the worth of their labor under ordinary circumstances in New England led the Yankee participants in the African trade to market their slave cargoes in the plantation colonies instead of bringing them home. Thus John Winthrop entered in his journal in 1645: "One of our ships which went to the Canaries with pipestaves in the beginning of November last returned now and brought wine and sugar and salt, and some tobacco, which she had at Barbadoes in exchange for Africoes which she carried from the Isle of Maio."[15] In their domestic industry the Massachusetts people found by experience that "many hands make light work, many hands make a full fraught, but many mouths eat up all";[16] and they were shrewd enough to apply the adage in keeping the scale of their industrial units within the frugal requirements of their lives.

That the laws of Massachusetts were enforced with special severity against the blacks is indicated by two cases before the central court in 1681, both of them prosecutions for arson. Maria, a negress belonging to Joshua Lamb of Roxbury, having confessed the burning of two dwellings, was sentenced by the Governor "yt she should goe from the barr to the prison whence she came and thence to the place of execution and there be burnt. —ye Lord be mercifull to thy soule, sd ye Govr." The other was Jack, a negro belonging to Samuel Wolcott of Weathersfield, who upon conviction of having set fire to a residence by waving a fire brand about in search of victuals, was condemned to be hanged until dead and then burned to ashes in the fire with the negress Maria.[17]

In this period it seems that Indian slaves had almost disappeared, and the number of negroes was not great enough to call

[14] Cotton Mather, "Diary," in Massachusetts Historical Society *Collections*, LXVII, 22, 203.
[15] Winthrop, *Journal*, II, 227.
[16] John Josslyn, "Two Voyages to New England," in Massachusetts Historical Society *Collections*, XXIII, 332.
[17] *Records of the Court of Assistants, 1630-1692* (Boston, 1901), p. 198.

for special police legislation. Governor Bradstreet, for example, estimated the "blacks or slaves" in the colony in 1680 at "about one hundred or one hundred and twenty." [18] But in 1708 Governor Dudley reckoned the number in Boston at four hundred, one-half of whom he said had been born there, and those in the rest of the colony at one hundred and fifty; and in the following decades their number steadily mounted, as a concomitant of the colony's increasing prosperity, until on the eve of the American Revolution they were reckoned at well above five thousand. Although they never exceeded two per cent. of the gross population, their presence prompted characteristic legislation, dating from about the beginning of the eighteenth century. This on the one hand taxed the importation of negroes unless they were promptly exported again on the other hand it forbade trading with slaves, restrained manumission, established a curfew, provided for the whipping of any negro or mulatto who should strike a "Christian," and prohibited the intermarriage of the races. On the other hand it gave the slaves the privilege of legal marriage with persons of their own race, though it did not attempt to prevent the breaking up of such a union by the sale and removal of the husband or wife.[19] Regarding the status of children there was no law enacted, and custom ruled. The children born of Indian slave mothers appear generally to have been liberated, for as willingly would a man nurse a viper in his bosom as keep an aggrieved and able-bodied redskin in his household. But as to negro children, although they were valued so slightly that occasionally it is said they were given to any one who would take them, there can be no reasonable doubt that by force of custom they were the property of the owners of their mothers.[20]

The New Englanders were "a plain people struggling for existence in a poor wilderness. . . . Their lives were to the last degree matter of fact, realistic, hard." [21] Shrewd in consequence

[18] Massachusetts Historical Society *Collections*, XXVIII, 337.
[19] Moore, *Slavery in Massachusetts*, pp. 52-55.
[20] *Ibid.*, pp. 20-27.
[21] C. F. Adams, *Massachusetts, its Historians and its History* (Boston, 1893), p. 106.

of their poverty, self-righteous in consequence of their religion, they took their slave-trading and their slaveholding as part of their day's work and as part of God's goodness to His elect. In practical effect the policy of colonial Massachusetts toward the backward races merits neither praise nor censure; it was merely commonplace.

What has been said in general of Massachusetts will apply with almost equal fidelity to Connecticut.[22] The number of negroes in that colony was hardly appreciable before 1720. In that year Governor Leete when replying to queries from the English committee on trade and plantations took occasion to emphasize the poverty of his people, and said as to bond labor: "There are but fewe servants amongst us, and less slaves; not above 30, as we judge, in the colony. For English, Scotts and Irish, there are so few come in that we cannot give a certain acco[un]t. Some yeares come none; sometimes a famaly or two in a year. And for Blacks, there comes sometimes 3 or 4 in a year from Barbadoes; and they are sold usually at the rate of 22*l* a piece, sometimes more and sometimes less, according as men can agree with the master of vessels or merchants that bring them hither." Few negroes had been born in the colony, "and but two blacks christened, as we know of." [23] A decade later the development of a black code was begun by an enactment declaring that any negro, mulatto, or Indian servant wandering outside his proper town without a pass would be accounted a runaway and might be seized by any person and carried before a magistrate for return to his master. A free negro so apprehended without a pass must pay the court costs. An act of 1702 discouraged manumission by ordering that if any freed negroes should come to want, their former owners were to be held responsible for their maintenance. Then came legislation forbidding the sale of liquors to slaves without special orders from their masters, prohibiting the purchase of

[22] The scanty materials available are summarized in B. C. Steiner, *History of Slavery in Connecticut* (Johns Hopkins University *Studies*, XI, nos. 9, 10, Baltimore, 1893), pp. 9-23, 84. See also W. C. Fowler, "The Historical Status of the Negro in Connecticut," in the *Historical Magazine and Notes and Queries*, III, 12-18, 81-85, 148-153, 260-266.
[23] *Public Records of the Colony of Connecticut*, III, 298.

goods from slaves without such orders, and providing a penalty
of not more than thirty lashes for any negro who should offer to
strike a white person; and finally a curfew law, in 1723, ordering
not above ten lashes for the negro, and a fine of ten shillings upon
the master, for every slave without a pass apprehended for being
out of doors after nine o'clock at night.[24] These acts, which remained in effect throughout the colonial period, constituted a code
of slave police which differed only in degree and fullness from
those enacted by the more southerly colonies in the same generation. A somewhat unusual note, however, was struck in an act
of 1730 which while penalizing with stripes the speaking by a
slave of such words as would be actionable if uttered by a free
person provided that in his defence the slave might make the
same pleas and offer the same evidence as a freeman. The number of negroes in the colony rose to some 6500 at the eve of the
American Revolution. Most of them were held in very small
parcels, but at least one citizen, Captain John Perkins of Nor-
wich, listed fifteen slaves in his will.

Rhode Island was distinguished from her neighbors by her diversity and liberalism in religion, by her great activity in the African slave trade, and by the possession of a tract of unusually
fertile soil. This last, commonly known as the Narragansett district and comprised in the two so-called towns of North and
South Kingstown, lay on the western shore of the bay, in the
southern corner of the colony. Prosperity from tillage, and especially from dairying and horse-breeding, caused the rise in that
neighborhood of landholdings and slaveholdings on a scale more
commensurate with those in Virginia than with those elsewhere
in New England. The Hazards, Champlins, Robinsons, and
some others accumulated estates ranging from five to ten thousand acres in extent, each with a corps of bondsmen somewhat in
proportion. In 1730, for example, South Kingstown had a population of 965 whites, 333 negroes and 233 Indians; and for a
number of years afterward those who may safely be assumed to
have been bondsmen, white, red and black, continued to be from

[24] *Public Records of the Colony of Connecticut*, IV, 40, 376; V, 52, 53;
VI, 390, 391.

a third to a half as many as the free inhabitants.[25] It may be noted that the prevalent husbandry was not such as generally attracted unfree labor in other districts, and that the climate was poorly suited to a negro population. The question then arises, Why was there so large a recourse to negro slave labor? The answer probably lies in the proximity of Newport, the main focus of African trading in American ships. James Browne wrote in 1737 from Providence, which was also busy in the trade, to his brother Obadiah who was then in Southern waters with an African cargo and who had reported poor markets: "If you cannot sell all your slaves to your mind, bring some of them home; I believe they will sell well." [26] This bringing of remainders home doubtless enabled the nearby townsmen and farmers to get slaves from time to time at bargain prices. The whole colony indeed came to have a relatively large proportion of blacks. In 1749 there were 33,773 whites and 3077 negroes; in 1756 there were 35,939 and 4697 respectively; and in 1774, 59,707 and 3668. Of this last number Newport contained 1246, South Kingstown 440, Providence 303, Portsmouth 122, and Bristol 114.[27]

The earliest piece of legislation in Rhode Island concerning negroes was of an anti-slavery character. This was an act adopted by the joint government of Providence and Warwick in 1652, when for the time being those towns were independent of the rest. It required, under a penalty of £40, that all negroes be freed after having rendered ten years of service.[28] This act may be attributed partly perhaps to the liberal influence of Roger Williams, and partly to the virtual absence of negroes in the towns near the head of the bay. It long stood unrepealed, but it was probably never enforced, for no sooner did negroes become numerous than a conservative reaction set in which deprived this peculiar law of any public sanction it may have had at the time of enactment. When in the early eighteenth century legislation was

[25] Edward Channing, *The Narragansett Planters* (Johns Hopkins University *Studies*, IV, no. 3, Baltimore, 1886).

[26] Gertrude S. Kimball, *Providence in Colonial Times* (Boston, 1912), p. 247.

[27] W. D. Johnston, "Slavery in Rhode Island, 1755-1776," in Rhode Island Historical Society *Publications,* new series, II, 126, 127.

[28] *Rhode Island Colonial Records,* I, 243.

resumed in regard to negroes, it took the form of a slave code much like that of Connecticut but with an added act, borrowed perhaps from a Southern colony, providing that slaves charged with theft be tried by impromptu courts consisting of two or more justices of the peace or town officers, and that appeal might be taken to a court of regular session only at the master's request and upon his giving bond for its prosecution. Some of the towns, furthermore, added by-laws of their own for more thorough police. South Kingstown for instance adopted an order that if any slave were found in the house of a free negro, both guest and host were to be whipped.[29]   The Rhode Island Quakers in annual meeting began as early as 1717 to question the propriety of importing slaves, and other persons from time to time echoed their sentiments; but it was not until just before the American Revolution that legislation began to interfere with the trade or the institution.

The colonies of Plymouth and New Haven in the period of their separate existence, and the colonies of Maine and New Hampshire throughout their careers, are negligible in a general account of negro slavery because their climate and their industrial requirements, along with their poverty, prevented them from importing any appreciable number of negroes.

New Netherland had the distinction of being founded and governed by a great slave-trading corporation—the Dutch West India Company—which endeavored to extend the market for its human merchandise whithersoever its influence reached.   This pro-slavery policy was not wholly selfish, for the directors appear to have believed that the surest way to promote a colony's welfare was to make slaves easy to buy.   In the infancy of New Netherland, when it consisted merely of two trading posts, the company delivered its first batch of negroes at New Amsterdam. But to its chagrin, the settlers would buy very few; and even the company's grant of great patroonship estates failed to promote a plantation régime.   Devoting their energies more to the Indian trade than to agriculture, the people had little use for farm hands, while in domestic service, if the opinion of the Reverend

  ²⁹ Channing, *The Narragansett Planters*, p. 11.

Jonas Michaelius be a true index, the negroes were found "thievish, lazy and useless trash." It might perhaps be surmised that the Dutch were too easy-going for success in slave management, were it not that those who settled in Guiana became reputed the severest of all plantation masters. The bulk of the slaves in New Netherland, left on the company's hands, were employed now in building fortifications, now in tillage. But the company, having no adequate means of supervising them in routine, changed the status of some of the older ones in 1644 from slavery to tribute-paying. That is to say, it gave eleven of them their freedom on condition that each pay the company every year some twenty-two bushels of grain and a hog of a certain value. At the same time it provided, curiously, that their children already born or yet to be born were to be the company's slaves. It was proposed at one time by some of the inhabitants, and again by Governor Stuyvesant, that negroes be armed with tomahawks and sent in punitive expeditions against the Indians, but nothing seems to have come of that.

The Dutch settlers were few, and the Dutch farmers fewer. But as years went on a slender stream of immigration entered the province from New England, settling mainly on Long Island and in Westchester; and these came to be among the company's best customers for slaves. The villagers of Gravesend, indeed, petitioned in 1651 that the slave supply might be increased. Soon afterward the company opened the trade to private ships, and then sent additional supplies on its own account to be sold at auction. It developed hopes, even, that New Amsterdam might be made a slave market for the neighboring English colonies. A parcel sold at public outcry in 1661 brought an average price of 440 florins,[80] which so encouraged the authorities that larger shipments were ordered. Of a parcel arriving in the spring of 1664 and described by Stuyvesant as on the average old and inferior, six men were reserved for the company's use in cutting timber, five women were set aside as unsalable, and the remaining twenty-nine, of both sexes, were sold at auction at prices ranging from 255 to 615 florins. But a great cargo of two or three hundred

[80] The florin has a value of forty cents.

slaves which followed in the same year reached port only in time for the vessel to be captured by the English fleet which took possession of New Netherland and converted it into the province of New York.[31]

The change of the flag was very slow in bringing any pronounced change in the colony's general régime. The Duke of York's government was autocratic and pro-slavery and the inhabitants, though for some decades they bought few slaves, were nothing averse to the institution. After the colony was converted into a royal province by the accession of James II to the English throne popular self-government was gradually introduced and a light import duty was laid upon slaves. But increasing prosperity caused the rise of slave importations to an average of about one hundred a year in the first quarter of the eighteenth century;[32] and in spite of the rapid increase of the whites during the rest of the colonial period the proportion of the negroes was steadily maintained at about one-seventh of the whole. They became fairly numerous in all districts except the extreme frontier, but in the counties fronting New York Harbor their ratio was somewhat above the average.[33] In 1755 a special census was taken of slaves older than fourteen years, and a large part of its detailed returns has been preserved. These reports from some two-score scattered localities enumerate 2456 slaves, about one-third of the total negro population of the specified age; and they yield unusually definite data as to the scale of slaveholdings. Lewis Morris of Morrisania had twenty-nine slaves above fourteen years old; Peter DeLancy of Westchester Borough had twelve; and the following had ten each: Thomas Dongan of Staten Island, Martinus Hoffman of Dutchess County, David Jones of Oyster Bay, Rutgert Van Brunt of New Utrecht, and Isaac Willett of Westchester Borough. Seventy-two others had

[31] This account is mainly drawn from A. J. Northrup, "Slavery in New York," in the New York State Library *Report* for 1900, pp. 246-254, and from E. B. O'Callaghan ed., *Voyages of the Slavers St. John and Arms of Amsterdam, with additional papers illustrative of the slave trade under the Dutch* (Albany, 1867), pp. 99-213.
[32] *Documentary History of New York* (Albany, 1850), I, 482.
[33] *Ibid.*, I, 467-474.

from five to nine each, and 1048 had still smaller holdings.[84] The average quota was two slaves of working age, and presumably the same number of slave children. That is to say, the typical slaveholding family had a single small family of slaves in its service. From available data it may be confidently surmised, furthermore, that at least one household in every ten among the eighty-three thousand white inhabitants of the colony held one or more slaves. These two features—the multiplicity of slaveholdings and the virtually uniform pettiness of their scale—constituted a régime never paralleled in equal volume elsewhere. The economic interest in slave property, nowhere great, was widely diffused. The petty masters, however, maintained so little system in the management of their slaves that the public problem of social control was relatively intense. It was a state of affairs conducing to severe legislation, and to hysterical action in emergencies.

The first important law, enacted in 1702, repeated an earlier prohibition against trading with slaves; authorized masters to chastise their slaves at discretion; forbade the meeting of more than three slaves at any time or place unless in their masters' service or by their consent; penalized with imprisonment and lashes the striking of a "Christian" by a slave; made the seductor or harborer of a runaway slave liable for heavy damages to the owner; and excluded slave testimony from the courts except as against other slaves charged with conspiracy. In order, however, that undue loss to masters might be averted, it provided that if by theft or other trespass a slave injured any person to the extent of not more than five pounds, the slave was not to be sentenced to death as in some cases a freeman might have been under the laws of England then current, but his master was to be liable for pecuniary satisfaction and the slave was merely to be whipped. Three years afterward a special act to check the fleeing to Canada provided a death penalty for any slave from the city and county of Albany found traveling more than forty miles north of that city, the master to be compensated from a special tax on slave property in the district. And in 1706 an act, passed

[84] *Documentary History of New York*, III, 505-521.

mainly to quiet any fears as to the legal consequences of Christianization, declared that baptism had no liberating effect, and that every negro or mulatto child should inherit the status of its mother.

The murder of a white family by a quartet of slaves in conspiracy not only led to their execution, by burning in one case, but prompted an enactment in 1708 that slaves charged with the murder of whites might be tried summarily by three justices of the peace and be put to death in such manner as the enormity of their crimes might be deemed to merit, and that slaves executed under this act should be paid for by the public. Thus stood the law when a negro uprising in the city of New York in 1712 and a reputed conspiracy there in 1741 brought atrociously numerous and severe punishments, as will be related in another chapter.[35] On the former of these occasions the royally appointed governor intervened in several cases to prevent judicial murder. The assembly on the other hand set to work at once on a more elaborate negro law which restricted manumissions, prohibited free negroes from holding real estate, and increased the rigor of slave control. Though some of the more drastic provisions were afterward relaxed in response to the more sober sense of the community, the negro code continued for the rest of the colonial period to be substantially as elaborated between 1702 and 1712.[36] The disturbance of 1741 prompted little new legislation and left little permanent impress upon the community. When the panic passed the petty masters resumed their customary indolence of control and the police officers, justly incredulous of public danger, let the rigors of the law relapse into desuetude.

As to New Jersey, the eastern half, settled largely from New England, was like in conditions and close in touch with New York, while the western half, peopled considerably by Quakers, had a much smaller proportion of negroes and was in sentiment akin to Pennsylvania. As was generally the case in such contrast of circumstances, that portion of the province which faced the greater problem of control determined the legislation for the whole. New Jersey, indeed, borrowed the New York slave code in all essentials. The administration of the law, furthermore, was about as it was in New York, in the eastern counties at least. An alleged conspiracy near Somerville in 1734 while it cost the reputed ringleader his life, cost his supposed colleagues their ears only. On the other hand sentences to burning at the stake were more frequent as punishment for ordinary crimes; and on such occasions the citizens of the neighborhood turned honest shillings by providing faggots for the fire. For the western counties the published annals concerning slavery are brief wellnigh to blankness.[37]

Pennsylvania's place in the colonial slaveholding sisterhood was a little unusual in that negroes formed a smaller proportion of the population than her location between New York and Maryland might well have warranted. This was due not to her laws nor to the type of her industry but to the disrelish of slaveholding felt by many of her Quaker and German inhabitants and to the greater abundance of white immigrant labor whether wage-earning or indentured. Negroes were present in the region before Penn's colony was founded. The new government recognized slavery as already instituted. Penn himself acquired a few slaves; and in the first quarter of the eighteenth century the assembly legislated much as New York was doing, though somewhat more mildly, for the fuller control of the negroes both slave and free. The number of blacks and mulattoes reached at the middle of the century about eleven thousand, the great majority of them slaves. They were most numerous, of course, in the older counties which lay in the southeastern corner of the province, and particularly in the city of Philadelphia. Occasional owners had as many as twenty or thirty slaves, employed either on country estates or in iron-works, but the typical holding was on a petty scale. There were no slave insurrections in the colony, no plots of any moment, and no panics of dread. The po-

[37] H. S. Cooley, *A Study of Slavery in New Jersey* (Johns Hopkins University *Studies,* XIV, nos. 9, 10, Baltimore, 1896).

lice was apparently a little more thorough than in New York, partly because of legislation, which the white mechanics procured, lessening negro competition by forbidding masters to hire out their slaves. From travelers' accounts it would appear that the relation of master and slave in Pennsylvania was in general more kindly than anywhere else on the continent; but from the abundance of newspaper advertisements for runaways it would seem to have been of about average character. The truth probably lies as usual in the middle ground, that Pennsylvania masters were somewhat unusually considerate. The assembly attempted at various times to check slave importations by levying prohibitive duties, which were invariably disallowed by the English crown. On the other hand, in spite of the endeavors of Sandiford, Lay, Woolman and Benezet, all of them Pennsylvanians, it took no steps toward relaxing racial control until the end of the colonial period.[38]

In the Northern colonies at large the slaves imported were more generally drawn from the West Indies than directly from Africa. The reasons were several. Small parcels, better suited to the retail demand, might be brought more profitably from the sugar islands whither New England, New York and Pennsylvania ships were frequently plying than from Guinea whence special voyages must be made. Familiarity with the English language and the rudiments of civilization at the outset were more essential to petty masters than to the owners of plantation gangs who had means for breaking in fresh Africans by deputy. But most important of all, a sojourn in the West Indies would lessen the shock of acclimatization, severe enough under the best of circumstances. The number of negroes who died from it was probably not small, and of those who survived some were incapacitated and bedridden with each recurrence of winter.

Slavery did not, and perhaps could not, become an important industrial institution in any Northern community; and the problem of racial adjustments was never as acute as it was generally thought to be. In not more than two or three counties do

[38] E. R. Turner, *The Negro in Pennsylvania* (Washington, 1911); R. R. Wright, Jr., *The Negro in Pennsylvania* (Philadelphia, 1912).

the negroes appear to have numbered more than one fifth of the population; and by reason of being distributed in detail they were more nearly assimilated to the civilization of the dominant race than in southerly latitudes where they were held in gross. They nevertheless continued to be regarded as strangers within the gates, by some welcomed because they were slaves, by others not welcomed even though they were in bondage. By many they were somewhat unreasonably feared; by few were they even reasonably loved. The spirit not of love but of justice and the public advantage was destined to bring the end of their bondage.

CHAPTER VII

REVOLUTION AND REACTION

AFTER the whole group of colonies had long been left in salutary neglect by the British authorities, George III and his ministers undertook the creation of an imperial control; and Parliament was too much at the king's command for opposing statesmen to stop the project. The Americans wakened resentfully to the new conditions. The revived navigation laws, the stamp act, the tea duty, and the dispatch of redcoats to coerce Massachusetts were a cumulation of grievances not to be borne by high-spirited people. For some years the colonial spokesmen tried to persuade the British government that it was violating historic and constitutional rights; but these efforts had little success. To the argument that the empire was composed of parts mutually independent in legislation, it was replied that Parliament had legislated imperially ever since the empire's beginning, and that the colonial assemblies possessed only such powers as Parliament might allow. The plea of no taxation without representation was answered by the doctrine that all elements in the empire were virtually represented in Parliament. The stress laid by the colonials upon their rights as Britons met the administration's emphasis upon the duty of all British subjects to obey British laws. This countering of pleas of exemption with pronouncements of authority drove the complainants at length from proposals of reform to projects of revolution. For this the solidarity of the continent was essential, and that was to be gained only by the most vigorous agitation with the aid of the most effective campaign cries. The claim of historic immunities was largely discarded in favor of the more glittering doctrines current in the philosophy of the time. The demands for local self-government or for national independence, one or both of which were the genuine issues at stake, were subordinated to the claim of the inherent and inalienable rights of man. Hence the culminating formulation in the Declaration of Independence: "We hold these truths to be self-evident, that all men are created equal, that they are endowed by their Creator with certain inalienable rights, that among these are life, liberty and the pursuit of happiness." The cause of the community was to be won under the guise of the cause of individuals.

In Jefferson's original draft of the great declaration there was a paragraph indicting the king for having kept open the African slave trade against colonial efforts to close it, and for having violated thereby the "most sacred rights of life and liberty of a distant people, who never offended him, captivating them into slavery in another hemisphere, or to incur miserable death in their transportation thither." This passage, according to Jefferson's account, "was struck out in complaisance to South Carolina and Georgia, who had never attempted to restrain the importation of slaves and who on the contrary still wished to continue it. Our Northern brethren also I believe," Jefferson continued, "felt a little tender under these censures, for though their people have very few slaves themselves, yet they have been pretty considerable carriers of them to others."[1] By reason of the general stress upon the inherent liberty of all men, however, the question of negro status, despite its omission from the Declaration, was an inevitable corollary to that of American independence.

Negroes had a barely appreciable share in precipitating the Revolution and in waging the war. The "Boston Massacre" was occasioned in part by an insult offered by a slave to a British soldier two days before; and in that celebrated affray itself, Crispus Attucks, a mulatto slave, was one of the five inhabitants of Boston slain. During the course of the war free negro and slave enlistments were encouraged by law in the states where racial control was not reckoned vital, and they were informally permitted in the rest. The British also utilized this resource in some degree. As early as November 7, 1775, Lord Dunmore, the ousted royal governor of Virginia, issued a proclamation offering free-

[1] Herbert Friedenwald, *The Declaration of Independence* (New York, 1904), pp. 130, 272.

dom to all slaves "appertaining to rebels" who would join him "for the more speedy reducing this colony to a proper sense of their duty to his Majesty's crown and dignity." [2] In reply the Virginia press warned the negroes against British perfidy; and the revolutionary government, while announcing the penalties for servile revolt, promised freedom to such as would promptly desert the British standard. Some hundreds of negroes appear to have joined Dunmore, but they did not save him from being driven away.[3]

When several years afterward military operations were transferred to the extreme South, where the whites were few and the blacks many, the problem of negro enlistments became at once more pressing and more delicate. Henry Laurens of South Carolina proposed to General Washington in March, 1779, the enrollment of three thousand blacks in the Southern department. Hamilton warmly endorsed the project, and Washington and Madison more guardedly. Congress recommended it to the states concerned, and pledged itself to reimburse the masters and to set the slaves free with a payment of fifty dollars to each of these at the end of the war. Eventually Colonel John Laurens, the son of Henry, went South as an enthusiastic emissary of the scheme, only to meet rebuff and failure.[4] Had the negroes in general possessed any means of concerted action, they might conceivably have played off the British and American belligerents to their own advantage. In actuality, however, they were a passive element whose fate was affected only so far as the master race determined.

Some of the politicians who championed the doctrine of liberty inherent and universal used it merely as a means to a specific and somewhat unrelated end. Others endorsed it literally and with resolve to apply it wherever consistency might require. How could they justly continue to hold men in bondage when in vindication of their own cause they were asserting the right of

[2] *American Archives,* Force ed., fourth series, III, 1385.
[3] *Ibid.,* III, 1387; IV, 84, 85; V, 160, 162.
[4] G. W. Williams, *History of the Negro Race in America* (New York. [1882]), I. 353-362.

all men to be free? Thomas Jefferson, Patrick Henry, Edmund
Randolph and many less prominent slaveholders were disquieted
by the question. Instances of private manumission became frequent, and memorials were fairly numerous advocating anti-
slavery legislation. Indeed Samuel Hopkins of Rhode Island in
a pamphlet of 1776 declared that slavery in Anglo-America was
"without the express sanction of civil government," and censured
the colonial authorities and citizens for having connived in the
maintenance of the wrongful institution.

As to public acts, the Vermont convention of 1777 when claiming statehood for its community framed a constitution with a bill
of rights asserting the inherent freedom of all men and attaching to it an express prohibition of slavery. The opposition of
New York delayed Vermont's recognition until 1791 when she
was admitted as a state with this provision unchanged. Similar
inherent-liberty clauses but without the expressed anti-slavery application were incorporated into the bills of rights adopted severally by Virginia in 1776, Massachusetts in 1780, and New
Hampshire in 1784. In the first of these the holding of slaves
persisted undisturbed by this action; and in New Hampshire the
custom died from the dearth of slaves rather than from the nat-
ural-rights clause. In Massachusetts likewise it is plain from
copious contemporary evidence that abolition was not intended
by the framers of the bill of rights nor thought by the people or
the officials to have been accomplished thereby.[5] One citizen,
indeed, who wanted to keep his woman slave but to be rid of her
child soon to be born, advertised in the *Independent Chronicle* of
Boston at the close of 1780: "A negro child, soon expected, of
a good breed, may be owned by any person inclining to take it,
and money with it."[6] The courts of the commonwealth, however, soon began to reflect anti-slavery sentiment, as Lord Mansfield had done in the preceding decade in England,[7] and to make
use of the bill of rights to destroy the masters' dominion. The

[5] G. H. Moore, *Notes on the History of Slavery in Massachusetts*, pp.
181-209.
[6] *Ibid.*, p. 208. So far as the present writer's knowledge extends, this
item is without parallel at any other time or place.
[7] The case of James Somerset on *habeas corpus*, in Howell's *State
Trials*, XX, § 548.

decisive case was the prosecution of Nathaniel Jennison of Worcester County for assault and imprisonment alleged to have been committed upon his absconded slave Quork Walker in the process of his recovery. On the trial in 1783 the jury responded to a strong anti-slavery charge from Chief Justice Cushing by returning a verdict against Jennison, and the court fined him £50 and costs.

This action prompted the negroes generally to leave their masters, though some were deterred "on account of their age and infirmities, or because they did not know how to provide for themselves, or for some pecuniary consideration." [8] The former slaveholders now felt a double grievance: they were deprived of their able-bodied negroes but were not relieved of the legal obligation to support such others as remained on their hands. Petitions for their relief were considered by the legislature but never acted upon. The legal situation continued vague, for although an act of 1788 forbade citizens to trade in slaves and another penalized the sojourn for more than two months in Massachusetts of negroes from other states,[9] no legislation defined the status of colored residents. In the federal census of 1790, however, this was the only state in which no slaves were listed.

Racial antipathy and class antagonism among the whites appear to have contributed to this result. John Adams wrote in 1795, with some exaggeration and incoherence: "Argument might have [had] some weight in the abolition of slavery in Massachusetts, but the real cause was the multiplication of labouring white people, who would no longer suffer the rich to employ these sable rivals so much to their injury. . . . If the gentlemen had been permitted by law to hold slaves, the common white people would have put the negroes to death, and their masters too, perhaps. . . . The common white people, or rather the labouring people, were the cause of rendering negroes unprofitable servants. Their scoffs and insults, their continual insinuations, filled the negroes with discontent, made them lazy, idle, proud, vicious,

[8] Massachusetts Historical Society *Collections*, XLIII, 386.
[9] Moore, pp. 227-229.

and at length wholly useless to their masters, to such a degree that the abolition of slavery became a measure of economy." [10]

Slavery in the rest of the Northern states was as a rule not abolished, but rather put in process of gradual extinction by legislation of a peculiar sort enacted in response to agitations characteristic of the times. Pennsylvania set the pattern in an act of 1780 providing that all children born thereafter of slave mothers in the state were to be the servants of their mothers' owners until reaching twenty-eight years of age, and then to become free. Connecticut followed in 1784 with an act of similar purport but with a specification of twenty-five years, afterward reduced to twenty-one, as the age for freedom; and in 1840 she abolished her remnant of slavery outright. In Rhode Island an act of the same year, 1784, enacted that the children thereafter born of slave mothers were to be free at the ages of twenty-one for males and eighteen for females, and that these children were meanwhile to be supported and instructed at public expense; but an amendment of the following year transferred to the mothers' owners the burden of supporting the children, and ignored the matter of their education. New York lagged until 1799, and then provided freedom for the after-born only at twenty-eight and twenty-five years for males and females respectively; but a further act of 1817 set the Fourth of July in 1827 as a time for the emancipation for all remaining slaves in the state. New Jersey fell into line last of all by an act of 1804 giving freedom to the after-born at the ages of twenty-five for males and twenty-one for females; and in 1846 she converted the surviving slaves nominally into apprentices but without materially changing their condition. Supplementary legislation here and there in these states bestowed freedom upon slaves in military service, restrained the import and export of slaves, and forbade the citizens to ply the slave trade by land or sea. [11]

[10] Massachusetts Historical Society *Collections*, XLIII, 402.
[11] E. R. Turner, *The Negro in Pennsylvania*, pp. 77-85; B. C. Steiner, *Slavery in Connecticut*, pp. 30-32; *Rhode Island Colonial Records*, X, 132, 133; A. J. Northrup, "Slavery in New York," in the New York State Library *Report* for 1900, pp. 286-298; H. S. Cooley, "Slavery in New Jersey" (Johns Hopkins University *Studies*, XIV, nos. 9, 10), pp. 47-50 F. B. Lee, *New Jersey as a Colony and as a State* (New York, 1912), IV, 25-48.

Thus from Pennsylvania eastward the riddance of slavery was procured or put in train, generally by the device of emancipating the *post nati;* and in consequence the slave population in that quarter dwindled before the middle of the nineteenth century to a negligible residue. To the southward the tobacco states, whose industry had reached a somewhat stationary condition, found it a simple matter to prohibit the further importation of slaves from Africa. Delaware did this in 1776, Virginia in 1778, Maryland in 1783 and North Carolina in 1794. But in these commonwealths as well as in their more southerly neighbors, the contemplation of the great social and economic problems involved in disestablishing slavery daunted the bulk of the citizens and impelled their representatives to conservatism. The advocacy of abolition, whether sudden or gradual, was little more than sporadic. The people were not to be stampeded in the cause of inherent rights or any other abstract philosophy. It was a condition and not a theory which confronted them.

In Delaware, however, the problem was hardly formidable, for at the time of the first federal census there were hardly nine thousand slaves and a third as many colored freemen in her gross population of some sixty thousand souls. Nevertheless a bill for gradual abolition considered by the legislature in 1786 appears not to have been brought to a vote,[12] and no action in the premises was taken thereafter. The retention of slavery seems to have been mainly due to mere public inertia and to the pressure of political sympathy with the more distinctively Southern states. Because of her border position and her dearth of plantation industry, the slaves in Delaware steadily decreased to less than eighteen hundred in 1860, while the free negroes grew to more than ten times as many.

In Maryland various projects for abolition, presented by the Quakers between 1785 and 1791 and supported by William Pinckney and Charles Carroll, were successively defeated in the legislature ; and efforts to remove the legal restraints on private manu-

---

[12] J. R. Brackett, "The Status of the Slave, 1775-1789," in J. F. Jameson ed., *Essays in the Constitutional History of the United States, 1775-1789* (Boston, 1889), pp. 300-302.

mission were likewise thwarted.[18]   These restrictions, which applied merely to the freeing of slaves above middle age, were in
fact very slight.   The manumissions indeed were so frequent
and the conditions of life in Maryland were so attractive to free
negroes, or at least so much less oppressive than in most other
states, that while the slave population decreased between 1790
and 1860 from 103,036 to 87,189 souls the colored freemen multiplied from 8046 to 83,942, a number greater by twenty-five thousand than that in any other commonwealth.

Thomas Jefferson wrote in 1785 that anti-slavery men were
as scarce to the southward of Chesapeake Bay as they were common to the north of it, while in Maryland, and still more in Virginia, the bulk of the people approved the doctrine and a respectable minority were ready to adopt it in practice, "a minority
which for weight and worth of character preponderates against
the greater number who have not the courage to divest their families of a property which, however, keeps their conscience unquiet." Virginia, he continued, "is the next state to which we
may turn our eyes for the interesting spectacle of justice in conflict
with avarice and oppression, a conflict in which the sacred side is
gaining daily recruits from the influx into office of young men
grown and growing up.   These have sucked in the principles of
liberty as it were with their mother's milk, and it is to them that
I look with anxiety to turn the fate of the question." [14]   Jefferson had already tried to raise the issue by having a committee for
revising the Virginia laws, appointed in 1776 with himself a
member, frame a special amendment for disestablishing slavery.
This contemplated a gradual emancipation of the after-born children, their tutelage by the state, their colonization at maturity,
and their replacement in Virginia by white immigrants.[15]   But a
knowledge that such a project would raise a storm caused even
its framers to lay it aside.   The abolition of primogeniture and
the severance of church from state absorbed reformers' energies
at the expense of the slavery question.

[13] J. R. Brackett, *The Negro in Maryland* (Baltimore, 1899), pp. 52-64,
148-155.
[14] Jefferson, *Writings*, P. L. Ford ed., IV, 82-83.
[15] Jefferson, *Notes on Virginia*, various editions, query 14.

When writing his *Notes on Virginia* in 1781 Jefferson de-
nounced the slaveholding system in phrases afterward classic
among abolitionists: "With what execration should the statesman be loaded who, permitting one-half of the citizens thus to
trample on the rights of the other, transforms those into despots
and these into enemies. . . . And can the liberties of a nation be
thought secure when we have removed their only firm basis, a
conviction in the minds of the people that these liberties are the
gift of God? That they are not to be violated but with his wrath?
Indeed I tremble for my country when I reflect that God is just;
that his justice cannot sleep forever." [16] In the course of the
same work, however, he deprecated abolition unless it were to be
accompanied with deportation: "Why not retain and incor-
porate the blacks into the state . . . ? Deep rooted prejudices
entertained by the whites, ten thousand recollections by the
blacks of the injuries they have sustained, new provocations, the
real distinctions which nature has made, and many other circumstances, will divide us into parties and produce convulsions which
will probably never end but in the extermination of the one or the
other race. . . . This unfortunate difference of colour, and perhaps of faculty, is a powerful obstacle to the emancipation of
these people. Many of their advocates while they wish to vindi-
cate the liberty of human nature are anxious also to preserve its
dignity and beauty. Some of these, embarrassed by the question 'What further is to be done with them?' join themselves in
opposition with those who are actuated by sordid avarice only.
Among the Romans, emancipation required but one effort. The
slave when made free might mix without staining the blood of
his master. But with us a second is necessary unknown to history. When freed, he is to be removed beyond the reach of mixture." [17]

George Washington wrote in 1786 that one of his chief wishes
was that some plan might be adopted "by which slavery may be
abolished by slow, sure and imperceptible degrees." But he

_____
[16] Jefferson, *Notes on Virginia*, query 18.
[17] *Ibid.*, query 14.

noted in the same year that some abolition petitions presented to the Virginia legislature had barely been given a reading.[18]

Seeking to revive the issue, Judge St. George Tucker, professor of law in William and Mary College, inquired of leading citizens of Massachusetts in 1795 for data and advice, and undaunted by discouraging reports received in reply or by the specific dissuasion of John Adams, he framed an intricate plan for extremely gradual emancipation and for expelling the freedmen without expense to the state by merely making their conditions of life unbearable. This was presented to the legislature in a pamphlet of 1796 at the height of the party strife between the Federalists and Democratic-Republicans; and it was impatiently dismissed from consideration.[19] Tucker, still nursing his project, reprinted his "dissertation" as an appendix to his edition of Blackstone in 1803, where the people and the politicians let it remain buried. In public opinion, the problem as to the freedmen remained unsolved and insoluble.

Meanwhile the Virginia black code had been considerably moderated during and after the Revolution; and in particular the previous almost iron-clad prohibition of private manumission had been wholly removed in effect by an act of 1782. In spite of restrictions afterward imposed upon manumission and upon the residence of new freedmen in the state, the free negroes increased on a scale comparable to that in Maryland. As compared with an estimate of less than two thousand in 1782, there were 12,866 in 1790, 20,124 in 1800, and 30,570 in 1810. Thereafter the number advanced more slowly until it reached 58,042, about one-eighth as many as the slaves numbered, in 1860.

In the more southerly states condemnation of slavery was rare. Among the people of Georgia, the depressing experience of the colony under a prohibition of it was too fresh in memory for them to contemplate with favor a fresh deprivation. In South Carolina Christopher Gadsden had written in 1766 likening slav-

[18] Washington, *Writings*, W. C. Ford ed., XI, 20, 62.
[19] St. George Tucker, *A Dissertation on Slavery, with a proposal for the gradual abolition of it in the State of Virginia* (Philadelphia, 1796, reprinted New York, 1860). Tucker's Massachusetts correspondence is printed in the Massachusetts Historical Society *Collections*, XLIII (Belknap papers), 379-431.

ery to a crime, and a decade afterward Henry Laurens wrote: "You know, my dear son, I abhor slavery. . . . The day, I hope is approaching when from principles of gratitude as well as justice every man will strive to be foremost in showing his readiness to comply with the golden rule. Not less than twenty thousand pounds sterling would all my negroes produce if sold at public auction tomorrow. . . . Nevertheless I am devising means for manumitting many of them, and for cutting off the entail of slavery. Great powers oppose me—the laws and customs of my country, my own and the avarice of my countrymen. What will my children say if I deprive them of so much estate? These are difficulties, but not insuperable. I will do as much as I can in my time, and leave the rest to a better hand. I am not one of those . . . who dare trust in Providence for defence and security of their own liberty while they enslave and wish to continue in slavery thousands who are as well entitled to freedom as themselves. I perceive the work before me is great. I shall appear to many as a promoter not only of strange but of dangerous doctrines; it will therefore be necessary to proceed with caution." [20] Had either Gadsden or Laurens entertained thoughts of launching an anti-slavery campaign, however, the palpable hopelessness of such a project in their community must have dissuaded them. The negroes of the rice coast were so outnumbering and so crude that an agitation applying the doctrine of inherent liberty and equality to them could only have had the effect of discrediting the doctrine itself. Furthermore, the industrial prospect, the swamps and forests calling for conversion into prosperous plantations, suggested an increase rather than a diminution of the slave labor supply. Georgia and South Carolina, in fact, were more inclined to keep open the African slave trade than to relinquish control of the negro population. Revolutionary liberalism had but the slightest of echoes there.

[20] Frank Moore ed., *Correspondence of Henry Laurens* (New York, 1861), pp. 20, 21. The version of this letter given by Professor Wallace in his *Life of Henry Laurens*, p. 446, which varies from the present one, was derived from a paraphrase by John Laurens to whom the original was written. Cf. *South Carolina Historical and Genealogical Magazine*, X. 49. For related items in the Laurens correspondence *see* D. D. Wallace, *Life of Henry Laurens*, pp. 445, 447-455.

In North Carolina the prevailing lack of enterprise in public affairs had no exception in regard to slavery. The Quakers alone condemned it. When in 1797 Nathaniel Macon, a pronounced individualist and the chief spokesman of his state in Congress, discussed the general subject he said "there was not a gentleman in North Carolina who did not wish there were no blacks in the country. It was a misfortune—he considered it a curse; but there was no way of getting rid of them." Macon put his emphasis upon the negro problem rather than upon the question of slavery, and in so doing he doubtless reflected the thought of his community.[21] The legislation of North Carolina regarding racial control, like that of the period in South Carolina, Georgia, Tennessee and Kentucky, was more conservative than liberal.

The central government of the United States during the Revolution and the Confederation was little concerned with slavery problems except in its diplomatic affairs, where the question was merely the adjustment of property in slaves, and except in regard to the western territories. Proposals for the prohibition of slavery in these wilderness regions were included in the first projects for establishing governments in them. Timothy Pickering and certain military colleagues framed a plan in 1780 for a state beyond the Ohio River with slavery excluded; but it was allowed to drop out of consideration. In the next year an ordinance drafted by Jefferson was introduced into Congress for erecting territorial governments over the whole area ceded or to be ceded by the states, from the Alleghanies to the Mississippi and from Canada to West Florida; and one of its features was a prohibition of slavery after the year 1800 throughout the region concerned. Under the Articles of Confederation, the Congress could enact legislation only by the affirmative votes of seven state delegations. When the ballot was taken on the anti-slavery

[21] *Annals of Congress*, VII, 661. American historians, through preoccupation or inadvertence, have often confused anti-negro with anti-slavery expressions. In reciting the speech of Macon here quoted McMaster has replaced "blacks" with "slaves"; and incidentally he has made the whole discussion apply to Georgia instead of North Carolina. Rhodes in turn has implicitly followed McMaster in both errors. J. B. McMaster, *History of the People of the United States*, II, 359; J. F. Rhodes, *History of the United States*, I, 19.

clause the six states from Pennsylvania eastward voted aye: Maryland, Virginia and South Carolina voted no; and the other states were absent. Jefferson was not alone in feeling chagrin at the defeat and in resolving to persevere. Pickering expressed his own views in a letter to Rufus King: "To suffer the continuance of slaves till they can be gradually emancipated, in states already overrun with them, may be pardonable because unavoidable without hazarding greater evils; but to introduce them into countries where none already exist . . . can never be forgiven." King in his turn introduced a resolution virtually restoring the stricken clause, but was unable to bring it to a vote. After being variously amended, the ordinance without this clause was adopted. It was, however, temporary in its provision and ineffectual in character; and soon the drafting of one adequate for permanent purposes was begun. The adoption of this was hastened in July, 1787, by the offer of a New England company to buy from Congress a huge tract of Ohio land. When the bill was put to the final vote it was supported by every member with the sole exception of the New Yorker, Abraham Yates. Delegations from all of the Southern states but Maryland were present, and all of them voted aye. Its enactment gave to the country a basic law for the territories in phrasing and in substance comparable to the Declaration of Independence and the Federal Constitution. Applying only to the region north of the Ohio River, the ordinance provided for the erection of territories later to be admitted as states, guaranteed in republican government, secured in the freedom of religion, jury trial and all concomitant rights, endowed with public land for the support of schools and universities, and while obligated to render fugitive slaves on claim of their masters in the original states, shut out from the régime of slaveholding itself. [22] "There shall be neither slavery nor involuntary servitude in the said territory," it prescribed, "otherwise than in punishment of crimes whereof the party shall

[22] A. C. McLaughlin, *The Confederation and the Constitution* (New York [1905], chap. 7; B. A. Hinsdale, *The Old Northwest* (New York, 1888), chap. 15.

have been duly convicted." The first Congress under the new constitution reënacted the ordinance, which was the first and last antislavery achievement by the central government in the period.

By this time radicalism in general had spent much of its force. The excessive stress which the Revolution had laid upon the liberty of individuals had threatened for a time to break the community's grasp upon the essentials of order and self-restraint. Social conventions of many sorts were flouted; local factions resorted to terrorism against their opponents; legislatures abused their power by confiscating loyalist property and enacting laws for the dishonest promotion of debtor-class interests, and the central government, made pitiably weak by the prevailing jealousy of control, was kept wholly incompetent through the shirking of burdens by states pledged to its financial support. But populism and particularism brought their own cure. The paralysis of government now enabled sober statesmen to point the prospect of ruin through chaos and get a hearing in their advocacy of sound system. Exalted theorising on the principles of liberty had merely destroyed the old régime: matter-of-fact reckoning on principles of law and responsibility must build the new. The plan of organization, furthermore, must be enough in keeping with the popular will to procure a general ratification.

Negro slavery in the colonial period had been of continental extent but under local control. At the close of the Revolution, as we have seen, its area began to be sectionally confined while the jurisdiction over it continued to lie in the several state governments. The great convention at Philadelphia in 1787 might conceivably have undertaken the transfer of authority over the whole matter to the central government; but on the one hand the beginnings of sectional jealousy made the subject a delicate one, and on the other hand the members were glad enough to lay aside all problems not regarded as essential in their main task. Conscious ignorance by even the best informed delegates from one section as to affairs in another was a dissuasion from the centralizing of doubtful issues; and the secrecy of the convention's proceedings exempted it from any pressure of anti-slavery sentiment from outside.

On the whole the permanence of any critical problem in the premises was discredited. Roger Sherman of Connecticut "observed that the abolition of slavery seemed to be going on in the United States, and that the good sense of the people of the several states would by degrees compleat it." His colleague Oliver Ellsworth said, "The morality or wisdom of slavery are considerations belonging to the states themselves"; and again, "Let us not intermeddle. As population increases poor laborers will be so plenty as to render slaves useless. Slavery in time will not be a speck in our country." And Elbridge Gerry of Massachusetts "thought we had nothing to do with the conduct of states as to slaves, but ought to be careful not to give any sanction to it." The agreement was general that the convention keep its hands off so far as might be; but positive action was required upon incidental phases which involved some degree of sanction for the institution itself. These issues concerned the apportionment of representation, the regulation of the African trade, and the rendition of fugitives. This last was readily adjusted by the unanimous adoption of a clause introduced by Pierce Butler of South Carolina and afterward changed in its phrasing to read: "No person held to service or labour in one state under the laws thereof escaping into another shall in consequence of any law or regulation therein be discharged from such service or labour, but shall be delivered up on claim of the party to whom such service or labour may be due." After some jockeying, the other two questions were settled by compromise. Representation in the lower house of Congress was apportioned among the states "according to their several members, which shall be determined by adding to the whole number of free persons . . . three fifths of all other persons." As to the foreign slave trade, Congress was forbidden to prohibit it prior to the year 1808, and was merely permitted meanwhile to levy an import duty upon slaves at a rate of not more than ten dollars each.[23]

[23] Max Farrand ed., *The Records of the Federal Convention* (New Haven, 1911), *passim*.

In the state conventions to which the Constitution was referred for ratification the debates bore out a remark of Madison's at Philadelphia that the real difference of interests lay not between the large and small states but between those within and without the slaveholding influence. The opponents of the Constitution at the North censured it as a pro-slavery instrument, while its advocates apologized for its pertinent clauses on the ground that nothing more hostile to the institution could have been carried and that if the Constitution were rejected there would be no prospect of a federal stoppage of importations at any time. But at the South the opposition, except in Maryland and Virginia where the continuance of the African trade was deprecated, declared the slavery concessions inadequate, while the champions of the Constitution maintained that the utmost practicable advantages for their sectional interest had been achieved. Among the many amendments to the Constitution proposed by the ratifying conventions the only one dealing with any phase of slavery was offered, strange to say, by Rhode Island, whose inhabitants had been and still were so active in the African trade. It reads: "As a traffic tending to establish and continue the slavery of the human species is disgraceful to the cause of liberty and humanity, Congress shall as soon as may be promote and establish such laws as may effectually prevent the importation of slaves of every description." [24] The proposal seems to have received no further attention at the time.

In the early sessions of Congress under the new Constitution most of the few debates on slavery topics arose incidentally and ended without positive action. The taxation of slave imports was proposed in 1789, but was never enacted: sundry petitions of anti-slavery tenor, presented mostly by Quakers, were given brief consideration in 1790 and again at the close of the century but with no favorable results; and when, in 1797, a more concrete issue was raised by memorials asking intervention on behalf of some negroes whom Quakers had manumitted in North Carolina in disregard of legal restraints and who had again been reduced

[24] This was dated May 29, 1790. H. V. Ames, "Proposed Amendment to the Constitution of the United States," in the American Historical Association *Report* for 1896, p. 208

to slavery, a committee reported that the matter fell within the scope of judicial cognizance alone, and the House dismissed the subject. For more than a decade, indeed, the only legislation enacted by Congress concerned at all with slavery was the act of 1793 empowering the master of an interstate fugitive to seize him wherever found, carry him before any federal or state magistrate in the vicinage, and procure a certificate warranting his removal to the state from which he had fled. Proposals to supplement this rendition act on the one hand by safeguarding free negroes from being kidnapped under fraudulent claims and on the other hand by requiring employers of strange negroes to publish descriptions of them and thus facilitate the recovery of runaways, were each defeated in the House.

On the whole the glamor of revolutionary doctrines was passing, and self interest was regaining its wonted supremacy. While the rising cotton industry was giving the blacks in the South new value as slaves, Northern spokesmen were frankly stating an antipathy of their people toward negroes in any capacity whatever. [25] The succession of disasters in San Domingo, meanwhile, gave warning against the upsetting of racial adjustments in the black belts, and the Gabriel revolt of 1800 in Virginia drove the lesson home. On slavery questions for a period of several decades the policy of each of the two sections was merely to prevent itself from being overreached. The conservative trend, however, could not wholly remove the Revolution's impress of philosophical liberalism from the minds of men. Slavery was always a thing of appreciable disrelish in many quarters; and the slave trade especially, whether foreign or domestic, bore a permanent stigma.

[25] *E. g., Annals of Congress*, 1799-1801, pp. 230-246.

CHAPTER VIII

THE CLOSING OF THE AFRICAN SLAVE TRADE

THE many attempts of the several colonies to restrict or prohibit the importation of slaves were uniformly thwarted, as we have seen, by the British government. The desire for prohibition, however, had been far from constant or universal.[1] The first Continental Congress when declaring the Association, on October 18, 1774, resolved: "We will neither import, nor purchase any slave imported, after the first day of December next; after which time we will wholly discontinue the slave trade, and will neither be concerned in it ourselves nor will we hire our vessels nor sell our commodities or manufactures to those who are concerned in it."[2] But even this was mainly a political stroke against the British government; and the general effect of the restraint lasted not more than two or three years.[3] The ensuing war, of course, hampered the trade, and the legislatures of several Northern states, along with Delaware and Virginia, took occasion to prohibit slave importations. The return of peace, although followed by industrial depression, revived the demand for slave labor. Nevertheless, Maryland prohibited the import by an act of 1783; North Carolina laid a prohibitive duty in 1787; and South Carolina in the spring of that year enacted the first of a series of temporary laws which maintained a continuous prohibition for sixteen years. Thus at the time when the framers of the Federal Constitution were stopping congressional action for twenty years, the trade was legitimate only in a few of the Northern states, all of which soon

[1] The slave trade enactments by the colonies, the states and the federal government are listed and summarized in W. E. B. DuBois, *The Suppression of the African Slave Trade to the United States, 1638-1870* (New York, 1904), appendices.
[2] W. C. Ford, ed., *Journals of the Continental Congress* (Washington, 1904), I, 75, 77.
[3] DuBois, pp. 44-48.

enacted prohibitions, and in Georgia alone at the South. The San Domingan cataclysm prompted the Georgia legislature in an act of December 19, 1793, to forbid the importation of slaves from the West Indies, the Bahamas and Florida, as well as to require free negroes to procure magisterial certificates of industriousness and probity.[4] The African trade was left open by that state until 1798, when it was closed both by legislative enactment and by constitutional provision.

The scale of the importation in the period when Georgia alone permitted them appears to have been small. For the year 1796, for example, the imports at Savannah were officially reported at 2084, including some who had been brought coastwise from the northward for sale.[5] A foreign traveler who visited Savannah in the period noted that the demand was light because of the dearth of money and credit, that the prices were about three hundred dollars per head, that the carriers were mainly from New England, and that one third of each year's imports were generally smuggled into South Carolina.[6]

In the impulse toward the prohibitory acts the humanitarian motive was obvious but not isolated. At the North it was supplemented, often in the same breasts, by the inhumane feeling of personal repugnance toward negroes. The anti-slave-trade agitation in England also had a contributing influence; and there were no economic interests opposing the exclusion. At the South racial repugnance was fainter, and humanitarianism though of positive weight was but one of several factors. The distinctively Southern considerations against the trade were that its continuance would lower the prices of slaves already on hand, or at least prevent those prices from rising; that it would so increase the staple exports as to spoil the world's market for them; that it would drain out money and keep the community in debt; that it would retard the civilization of the negroes already on hand; and that by raising the proportion of blacks in the population it would

---

[4] The text of the act, which appears never to have been printed, is in the Georgia archives. For a transcript I am indebted to the Hon. Philip Cook, Secretary of State of Georgia.

[5] American Historical Association *Report* for 1903, pp. 459, 460.

[6] LaRochefoucauld-Liancourt, *Travels in the United States* (London, 1799), p. 605.

intensify the danger of slave insurrections. The several arguments had varying degrees of influence in the several areas. In the older settlements where the planters had relaxed into easy-going comfort, the fear of revolt was keenest; in the newer districts the settlers were more confident in their own alertness. Again, where prosperity was declining the planters were fairly sure to favor anything calculated to raise the prices of slaves which they might wish in future to sell, while on the other hand the people in districts of rising industry were tempted by programmes tending to cheapen the labor they needed.

The arguments used in South Carolina for and against exclusion may be gathered from scattering reports in the newspapers. In September, 1785, the lower house of the legislature upon receiving a message from the governor on the distressing condition of commerce and credit, appointed a committee of fifteen on the state of the republic. In this committee there was a vigorous debate on a motion by Ralph Izard to report a bill prohibiting slave importations for three years. John Rutledge opposed it. Since the peace with Great Britain, said he, not more than seven thousand slaves had been imported, which at £50 each would be trifling as a cause of the existing stringency; and the closing of the ports would therefore fail to relieve the distress [7] Thomas Pinckney supported Rutledge with an argument that the exclusion of the trade from Charleston would at once drive commerce in general to the ports of Georgia and North Carolina, and that the advantage of low prices, which he said had fallen from a level of £90 in 1783, would be lost to the planters. Judge Pendleton, on the other hand, stressed the need of retrenchment. Planters, he said, no longer enjoyed the long loans which in colonial times had protected them from distress; and the short credits now alone available put borrowers in peril of bankruptcy from a single season of short crops and low prices. [8] The committee reported Izard's bill; but it was defeated in the House by a vote of 47 to 51, and an act was passed instead for an emission of bills of credit by the state. The advocacy of the trade by Thomas Pinck-

[7] Charleston *Evening Gazette*, Sept. 26 and 28, 1785.
[8] *Ibid.*, Oct. 1, 1785.

ney indicates that at this time there was no unanimity of conservatives against it.

When two years later the stringency persisted, the radicals in
the legislature demanded a law to stay the execution of debts,
while the now unified conservatives proposed again the stoppage
of the slave trade.   In the course of the debate David Ramsay
"made a jocose remark that every man who went to church
last Sunday and said his prayers was bound by a spiritual obligation to refuse the importation of slaves.   They had devoutly
prayed not to be led into temptation, and negroes were a temptation too great to be resisted." [9]   The issue was at length adjusted by combining the two projects of a stay-law and a prohibition of slave importations for three years in a single bill.
This was approved on March 28, 1787; and a further act of the
same day added a penalty of fine to that of forfeiture for the
illegal introduction of slaves.   The exclusion applied to slaves
from every source, except those whose masters should bring them
when entering the state as residents.[10]

Early in the next year an attempt was made to repeal the
prohibition.   Its leading advocate was Alexander Gillon, a popu-
listic Charleston merchant who had been made a commodore by
the State of South Carolina but had never sailed a ship.   The
opposition was voiced so vigorously by Edward Rutledge, Charles
Pinckney, Chancellor Matthews, Dr. Ramsay, Mr. Lowndes, and
others that the project was crushed by 93 votes to 40.   The
strongest weapon in the hands of its opponents appears to have
been a threat of repealing the stay-law in retaliation.[11]   At the
end of the year the prohibitory act had its life prolonged until the
beginning of 1793; and continuation acts adopted every two or
three years thereafter extended the régime until the end of 1803.
The constitutionality of the prohibition was tested before the
judiciary of the state in January, 1802, when the five assembled
judges unanimously pronounced it valid.[12]

[9] Charleston *Morning Post,* March 23, 1787.
[10] *Ibid.,* March 29, 1787; Cooper and McCord, *Statutes at Large of
South Carolina,* VII, 430.
[11] *Georgia State Gazette* (Savannah), Feb. 17, 1788.
[12] Augusta, Ga., *Chronicle,* Jan. 30, 1802.

But at last the advocates of the open trade had their innings. The governor in a message of November 24, 1803, recited that his best exertions to enforce the law had been of no avail. Inhabitants of the coast and the frontier, said he, were smuggling in slaves abundantly, while the people of the central districts were suffering an unfair competition in having to pay high prices for their labor. He mentioned a recently enacted law of Congress reinforcing the prohibitory acts of the several states only to pronounce it already nullified by the absence of public sanction; and he dismissed any thought of providing the emancipation of smuggled slaves as "a remedy more mischievous than their introduction in servitude." [13] Having thus described the problem as insoluble by prohibitions, he left the solution to the legislature.

In spite of the governor's assertion, supported soon afterward by a statement of William Lowndes in Congress,[14] there is reason to believe that violations of the law had not been committed on a great scale. Slave prices could not have become nearly doubled, as they did during the period of legal prohibition, if African imports had been at all freely made. The governor may quite possibly have exaggerated the facts with a view to bringing the system of exclusion to an end.

However this may have been, a bill was promptly introduced in the Senate to repeal all acts against importations. Mr. Barnwell opposed this on the ground that the immense influx of slaves which might be expected in consequence would cut in half the value of slave property, and that the increase in the cotton output would lower the already falling prices of cotton to disastrous levels. The resumption of the great war in Europe, said he, had already diminished the supply of manufactured goods and raised their prices. "Was it under these circumstances that we ought to lay out the savings of our industry, the funds accumulated in many years of prosperity and peace, to increase that produce whose value had already fallen so much? He thought not. The permission given by the bill would lead to ruinous speculations. Everyone would purchase negroes. It was well known that those

[13] Charleston *Courier*, Dec. 5, 1803.
[14] *Annals of Congress*, 1803-1804, p. 992.

who dealt in this property would sell it at a very long credit. Our citizens would purchase at all hazards and trust to fortunate crops and favorable markets for making their payments; and it would be found that South Carolina would in a few years, if this trade continued open, be in the same situation of debt, and subject to all misfortunes which that situation had produced, as at the close of the Revolutionary war." The newspaper closed its report of the speech by a concealment of its further burden: "The Hon. member adduced in support of his opinion various other arguments, still more cogent and impressive, which from reasons very obvious we decline making public."[15] It may be surmised that the suppressed remarks dealt with the danger of slave revolts. In the further course of the debate, "Mr. Smith said he would agree to put a stop to the importation of slaves, but he believed it impossible. For this reason he would vote for the bill." The measure soon passed the Senate.

Meanwhile the lower house had resolved on December 8, in committee of the whole, "that the laws prohibiting the importation of negroes and other persons of colour in this state can be so amended as to prevent their introduction amongst us," and had recommended that a select committee be appointed to draft a bill accordingly.[16] Within the following week, however, the sentiment of the House was swung to the policy of repeal, and the Senate bill was passed. On the test vote the ayes were 55 and the noes 46.[17] The act continued the exclusion of West Indian negroes, and provided that slaves brought in from sister states of the Union must have official certificates of good character; but as to the African trade it removed all restrictions. In 1805 a bill to prohibit imports again was introduced into the legislature, but after debate it was defeated.[18]

The local effect of the repeal is indicated in the experience of E. S. Thomas, a Charleston bookseller of the time who in high prosperity had just opened a new importation of fifty thousand

[15] Charleston *Courier*, Dec. 26, 1803.
[16] *Ibid.*, Dec. 20, 1803.
[17] Charleston *City Gazette*, Dec. 22, 1803.
[18] "Diary of Edward Hooker" in the American Historical Association *Report* for 1896, p. 878.

volumes. As he wrote in after years, the news that the legislature had reopened the slave trade "had not been five hours in the city, before two large British Guineamen, that had been lying on and off the port for several days expecting it, came up to town; and from that day my business began to decline. . . . A great change at once took place in everything. Vessels were fitted out in numbers for the coast of Africa, and as fast as they returned their cargoes were bought up with avidity, not only consuming the large funds that had been accumulating, but all that could be procured, and finally exhausting credit and mortgaging the slaves for payment. . . . For myself, I was upwards of five years disposing of my large stock, at a sacrifice of more than a half, in all the principal towns from Augusta in Georgia to Boston." [19]

As reported at the end of the period, the importations amounted to 5386 slaves in 1804; 6790 in 1805; 11,458 in 1806; and 15,676 in 1807.[20] Senator William Smith of South Carolina upon examining the records at a later time placed the total at 39,310, and analysed the statistics as follows: slaves brought by British vessels, 19,449; by French vessels, 1078; by American vessels, operated mostly for the account of Rhode Islanders and foreigners, 18,048.[21] If an influx no greater than this could produce the effect which Thomas described, notwithstanding that many of the slaves were immediately reshipped to New Orleans and many more were almost as promptly sold into the distant interior, the scale of the preceding illicit trade must have been far less than the official statements and the apologies in Congress would indicate.

South Carolina's opening of the trade promptly spread dismay in other states. The North Carolina legislature, by a vote afterwards described as virtually unanimous in both houses, adopted resolutions in December, 1804, instructing the Senators from North Carolina and requesting her Congressmen to use their utmost exertions at the earliest possible time to procure an

[19] E. S. Thomas, *Reminiscences*, II, 35, 36.
[20] *Virginia Argus*, Jan. 19, 1808.
[21] *Annals of Congress*, 1821-1822, pp. 73-77.

amendment to the Federal Constitution empowering Congress at once to prohibit the further importation of slaves and other persons of color from Africa and the West Indies. Copies were ordered sent not only to the state's delegation in Congress but to the governors of the other states for transmission to the legislatures with a view to their concurrence.[22] In the next year similar resolutions were adopted by the legislatures of New Hampshire, Vermont, Maryland and Tennessee;[23] but the approach of the time when Congress would acquire the authority without a change of the Constitution caused a shifting of popular concern from the scheme of amendment to the expected legislation of Congress. Meanwhile, a bill for the temporary government of the Louisiana purchase raised the question of African importations there which occasioned a debate in the Senate at the beginning of 1804 [24] nearly as vigorous as those to come on the general question three years afterward.

In the winter of 1804-1805 bills were introduced in both Senate and House to prohibit slave importations at large; but the one was postponed for a year and the other was rejected,[25] doubtless because the time was not near enough when they could take effect. At last the matter was formally presented by President Jefferson. "I congratulate you, fellow-citizens," he said in his annual message of December 2, 1806, "on the approach of the period at which you may interpose your authority constitutionally to withdraw the citizens of the United States from all further participation in those violations of human rights which have been so long continued on the unoffending inhabitants of Africa, and which the morality, the reputation, and the best interests of our country have long been eager to proscribe. Although no law you can pass can take effect until the day of the year one thousand eight hundred and eight, yet the inter-

[22] Broadside copy of the resolution, accompanied by a letter of Governor James Turner of North Carolina to the governor of Connecticut, in the possession of the Pennsylvania Historical Society.
[23] H. V. Ames, *Proposed Amendments to the Constitution*, in the American Historical Association *Report* for 1896, pp. 208, 209.
[24] Printed from Senator Plumer's notes, in the *American Historical Review*, XXII, 340-364.
[25] W. E. B. DuBois, *Suppression of the African Slave Trade*, p. 105.

vening period is not too long to prevent, by timely notice, expeditions which cannot be completed before that day." [26] Next day Senator Bradley of Vermont gave notice of a bill which was shortly afterward introduced and which, after an unreported discussion, was passed by the Senate on January 27. Its conspicuous provisions were that after the close of the year 1807 the importation of slaves was to be a felony punishable with death, and that the interstate coasting trade in slaves should be illegal.

The report of proceedings in the House was now full, now scant. The paragraph of the President's message was referred on December 3 to a committee of seven with Peter Early of Georgia as chairman and three other Southerners in the membership. The committee's bill reported on December 15, proposed to prohibit slave importations, to penalize the fitting out of vessels for the trade by fine and forfeiture, to lay fines and forfeitures likewise upon the owners and masters found within the jurisdictional waters of the United States with slaves from abroad on board, and empowered the President to use armed vessels in enforcement. It further provided that if slaves illegally introduced should be found within the United States they should be forfeited, and any person wittingly concerned in buying or selling them should be fined; it laid the burden of proof upon defendants when charged on reasonable grounds of presumption with having violated the act; and it prescribed that the slaves forfeited should, like other goods in the same status, be sold at public outcry by the proper federal functionaries. [27]

Mr. Sloan of New Jersey instantly moved to amend by providing that the forfeited slaves be entitled to freedom. Mr. Early replied that this would rob the bill of all effect by depriving it of public sanction in the districts whither slaves were likely to be brought. Those communities, he said, would never tolerate the enforcement of a law which would set fresh Africans at large in their midst. Mr. Smilie, voicing the sentiment and indicating the dilemma of most of his fellow Pennsylvanians, declared his unconquerable aversion to any measure which would

[26] *Annals of Congress*, 1806-1807, p. 14.
[27] *Ibid.*, pp. 167, 168.

make the federal government a dealer in slaves, but confessed
that he had no programme of his own. Nathaniel Macon, the
Speaker, saying that he thought the desire to enact an effective
law was universal, agreed with Early that Sloan's amendment
would defeat the purpose. Early himself waxed vehement,
prophesying the prompt extermination of any smuggled slaves
emancipated in the Southern states. The amendment was defeated by a heavy majority.

Next day, however, Mr. Bidwell of Massachusetts renewed
Sloan's attack by moving to strike out the provision for the
forfeiture of the slaves; but his colleague Josiah Quincy, supported by the equally sagacious Timothy Pitkin of Connecticut,
insisted upon the necessity of forfeiture; and Early contended
that this was particularly essential to prevent the smuggling of
slaves across the Florida border where the ships which had
brought them would keep beyond the reach of congressional laws.
The House finding itself in an impasse referred the bill back
to the same committee, which soon reported it in a new form
declaring the illegal importation of slaves a felony punishable
with death. Upon Early's motion this provision was promptly
stricken out in committee of the whole by a vote of 60 to 41;
whereupon Bidwell renewed his proposal to strike out the forfeiture of slaves. He was numerously supported in speeches
whose main burden was that the United States government must
not become the receiver of stolen goods. The speeches in reply
stressed afresh the pivotal quality of forfeiture in an effective
law; and Bidwell when pressed for an alternative plan could
only say that he might if necessary be willing to leave them to
the disposal of the several states, but was at any rate "opposed
to disgracing our statute book with a recognition of the principle
of slavery." Quincy replied that he wished Bidwell and his
fellows "would descend from their high abstract ground to the
level of things in their own state—such as have, do and will
exist after your laws, and in spite of them." The Southern
members, said he, were anxious for nothing so much as a total
prohibition, and for that reason were insistent upon forfeiture.
For the sake of enforcing the law, and for the sake of controlling

the future condition of the smuggled slaves, forfeiture was imperative. Such a provision would not necessarily admit that the importers had had a title in the slaves before capture, but it and it alone would effectively divest them of any color of title to which they might pretend. The amendment was defeated by a vote of 36 to 63.

When the bill with amendments was reported to the House by the committee of the whole, on December 31, there was vigorous debate upon the question of substituting imprisonment of from five to ten years in place of the death penalty. Mr. Talmadge of Connecticut supported the provision of death with a biblical citation; and Mr. Smilie said he considered it the very marrow of the bill. Mr. Lloyd of Maryland thought the death penalty would be out of proportion to the crime, and considered the extract from Exodus inapplicable since few of the negroes imported had been stolen in Africa. But Mr. Olin of Vermont announced that the man-stealing argument had persuaded him in favor of the extreme penalty. Early now became furious, and in his fury, frank. In a preceding speech he had pronounced slavery "an evil regretted by every man in the country." [28] He now said: "A large majority of the people in the Southern states do not . . . believe it immoral to hold human flesh in bondage. Many deprecate slavery as an evil; as a political evil; but not as a crime. Reflecting men apprehend, at some future day, evils, incalculable evils, from it; but it is a fact that few, very few, consider it as a crime. It is best to be candid on this subject. . . . I will tell the truth. A large majority of people in the Southern states do not consider slavery as an evil. Let the gentleman go and travel in that quarter of the Union; let him go from neighborhood to neighborhood, and he will find that this is the fact. Some gentlemen appear to legislate for the sake of appearances. . . . I should like to know what honor you will derive from a law that will be broken every day of your lives." [29] Mr. Stanton said with an air of deprecation on behalf of his state of Rhode Island: "I wish the law made so strong

[28] *Annals of Congress*, 1806-1807, p. 174.
[29] *Ibid.*, pp. 238, 239.

THE CLOSING OF THE AFRICAN TRADE 143

as to prevent this trade in future; but I cannot believe that a man ought to be hung for only stealing a negro. Those who buy them are as bad as those who import them, and deserve hanging quite as much." The yeas and nays recorded at the end of the exhausting day showed 63 in favor and 53 against the substitution of imprisonment. The North was divided, 29 to 37, with the nays coming mostly from Pennsylvania, Massachusetts and Connecticut; the South, although South Carolina as well as Kentucky was evenly divided, cast 34 yeas to 16 nays. Virginia and Maryland, which might have been expected to be doubtful, virtually settled the question by casting 17 yeas against 6 nays.

When the consideration of the bill was resumed on January 7, Mr. Bidwell renewed his original attack by moving to strike out the confiscation of slaves; and when this was defeated by 39 to 77, he attempted to reach the same end by a proviso "That no person shall be sold as a slave by virtue of this act." This was defeated only by the casting vote of the Speaker. Those voting aye were all from Northern states, except Archer of Maryland, Broom of Delaware, Bedinger of Kentucky and Williams of North Carolina. The noes were all from the South except one from New Hampshire, ten from New York, and one from Pennsylvania. The outcome was evidently unsatisfactory to the bulk of the members, for on the next day a motion to recommit the bill to a new committee of seventeen prevailed by a vote of 76 to 46. Among the members who shifted their position over night were six of the ten from New York, four from Maryland, three from Virginia, and two from North Carolina. In the new committee Bedinger of Kentucky, who was regularly on the Northern side, was chairman, and Early was not included.

This committee reported in February a bill providing, as a compromise, that forfeited negroes should be carried to some place in the United States where slavery was either not permitted or was in course of gradual extinction, and there be indentured or otherwise employed as the President might deem best for them and the country. Early moved that for this there be substituted a provision that the slaves be delivered to the several states in which the captures were made, to be disposed of at discretion; and he said that the Southern people would resist the indenture provision with their lives. This reckless assertion suggests that Early was either set against the framing of an effective law, or that he spoke in mere blind rage.

Before further progress was made the House laid aside its bill in favor of the one which the Senate had now passed. An amendment to this, striking out the death penalty, was adopted on February 12 by a vote of 67 to 48. The North gave 31 ayes and 36 noes, quite evenly distributed among the states. The South cast 37 ayes to 11 noes, five of the latter coming from Virginia, two from North Carolina, and one each from Delaware, Maryland, Kentucky and South Carolina. A considerable shifting of votes appeared since the ballot on the same question six weeks before. Knight of Rhode Island, Sailly and Williams of New York, Helms of New Jersey and Wynns of North Carolina changed in favor of the extreme penalty; but they were more than offset by the opposite change of Bidwell of Massachusetts, Van Cortlandt of New York, Lambert of New Jersey, Clay and Gray of Virginia and McFarland of North Carolina. Numerous members from all quarters who voted on one of these roll-calls were silent at the other, and this variation also had a net result against the infliction of death. The House then filled the blank it had made in the bill by defining the offense as a high misdemeanor and providing a penalty of imprisonment of not less than five nor more than ten years. John Randolph opposed even this as excessive, but found himself unsupported. The House then struck out the prohibition of the coasting trade in slaves, and returned the bill as amended to the Senate. The latter concurred in all the changes except that as to the coastwise trade, and sent the bill back to the House.

John Randolph now led in the insistence that the House stand firm. If the bill should pass without the amendment, said he, the Southern people would set the law at defiance, and he himself would begin the violation of so unconstitutional an infringement of the rights of property. The House voted to insist upon its amendment, and sent the bill to conference where in compromise the prohibition as to the coastwise carriage of slaves for sale was made to apply only to vessels of less than forty tons burthen. The Senate agreed to this. In the House Mr. Early opposed it as improper in law and so easy of evasion that it would be perfectly futile for the prevention of smuggling from Florida. John Randolph said: "The provision of the bill touched the right of private property. He feared lest at a future period it might be made the pretext of universal emancipation. He had rather lose the bill, he had rather lose all the bills of the session, he had rather lose every bill passed since the establishment of the government, than agree to the provision contained in this slave bill. It went to blow up the Constitution in ruins."[30] Concurrence was carried, nevertheless, by a vote of 63 to 49, in which the North cast 51 ayes to 12 noes, and the South 12 ayes to 37 noes. The Southern ayes were four from Maryland, four from North Carolina, two from Tennessee, and one each from Virginia and Kentucky. The Northern noes were five from New York, two each from New Hampshire and Vermont, and one each from Massachusetts, Connecticut and Pennsylvania.

The bill then passed the House. Its variance from the original House bill was considerable, for it made the importation of slaves from abroad a high misdemeanor punishable with imprisonment; it prohibited the coastwise trade by sea in vessels of less than forty tons, and required the masters of larger vessels transporting negroes coastwise to deliver to the port officials classified manifests of the negroes and certificates that to the best of their knowledge and belief the slaves had not been imported since the beginning of 1808; and instead of forfeiture to the United States it provided that all smuggled slaves seized under the act should be subject to such disposal as the laws of the state or territory in which the seizure might be made should prescribe.[31] Randolph, still unreconciled, offered an explanatory act, February 27, that nothing in the preceding act should be construed to affect in any manner the absolute property right of masters in their slaves not imported contrary to the law, and that such masters should not be liable to any penalty for the coastwise transporta-

[30] *Annals of Congress*, 1806-1807, p. 626.
[31] *Ibid.*, pp. 1266-1270.

tion of slaves in vessels of less than forty tons. In attempting to force this measure through, he said that if it did not pass the House at once he hoped the Virginia delegation would wait on the President and remonstrate against his approving the act which had passed.[32] By a vote of 60 to 49 this bill was made the order for the next day; but its further consideration was crowded out by the rush of business at the session's close. The President signed the prohibitory bill on March 2, without having received the threatened Virginia visitation.

Among the votes in the House on which the yeas and nays were recorded in the course of these complex proceedings, six may be taken as tests. They were on striking out the death penalty, December 31; on striking out the forfeiture of slaves, January 7; on the proviso that no person should be sold by virtue of the act, January 7; on referring the bill to a new committee, January 8; on striking out the death penalty from the Senate bill, February 12; and on the prohibition of the coasting trade in slaves in vessels of under forty tons, February 26. In each case a majority of the Northern members voted on one side of the question, and a yet larger majority of Southerners voted on the other. Twenty-two members voted in every case on the side which the North tended to adopt. These comprised seven from Massachusetts, six from Pennsylvania, three from Connecticut, and one or two from each of the other Northern states except Rhode Island and Ohio. They comprised also Broom of Delaware, Bedinger of Kentucky, and Morrow of Virginia; while Williams of North Carolina was almost equally constant in opposing the policies advocated by the bulk of his fellow Southerners. On the other hand the regulars on the Southern side comprised not only ten Virginians, all of the six South Carolinians, except three of their number on the punishment questions, all of the four Georgians, three North Carolinians, two Marylanders and one Kentuckian, but in addition Tenney of New Hampshire, Schuneman, Van Rensselaer and Verplanck of New York on all but the punishment questions.

On the whole, sectional divergence was fairly pronounced, but

[32] *Annals of Congress*, 1806-1807, p. 637.

only on matters of detail. The expressions from all quarters of a common desire to make the prohibition of importations·effective were probably sincere without material exception. As regards the Virginia group of states, their economic interest in high prices for slaves vouches for the genuine purpose of their representatives, while that of the Georgians and South Carolinians may at the most be doubted and not disproved. The South in general wished to prevent any action which might by implication stigmatize the slaveholding régime, and was on guard also against precedents tending to infringe state rights. The North, on the other hand, was largely divided between a resolve to stop the sanction of slavery and a desire to enact an effective law in the premises directly at issue. The outcome was a law which might be evaded with relative ease wherever public sanction was weak, but which nevertheless proved fairly effective in operation.

When slave prices rose to high levels after the war of 1812 systematic smuggling began to prevail from Amelia Island on the Florida border, and on a smaller scale on the bayous of the Barataria district below New Orleans; but these operations were checked upon the passage of a congressional act in 1818 increasing the rewards to informers. Another act in the following year directed the President to employ armed vessels for police in both African and American waters, and incidentally made provisions contemplating the return of captured slaves to Africa. Finally Congress by an act of 1820 declared the maritime slave trade to be piracy.[33] Smuggling thereafter diminished though it never completely ceased.

As to the dimensions of the illicit importations between 1808 and 1860, conjectures have placed the gross as high as two hundred and seventy thousand.[34] Most of the documents in the premises, however, bear palpable marks of unreliability. It may suffice to say that these importations were never great enough to affect the labor supply in appreciable degree. So far as the

[33] DuBois, *Suppression of the Slave Trade*, pp. 118-123.
[34] W. H. Collins, *The Domestic Slave Trade of the Southern States* (New York [1904], pp. 12-20). *See also* W. E. B. DuBois, "Enforcement of the Slave Trade Laws," in the American Historical Association *Report* for 1891, p. 173.

general economic regime was concerned, the foreign slave trade was effectually closed in 1808.

At that time, however, there were already in the United States about one million slaves to serve as a stock from which other millions were to be born to replenish the plantations in the east and to aid in the peopling of the west. These were ample to maintain a chronic racial problem, and had no man invented a cotton gin their natural increase might well have glutted the market for plantation labor. Had the African source been kept freely open, the bringing of great numbers to meet the demand in prosperous times would quite possibly have so burdened the country with surplus slaves in subsequent periods of severe depression that slave prices would have fallen virtually to zero, and the slaveholding community would have been driven to emancipate them wholesale as a means of relieving the masters from the burden of the slaves' support. The foes of slavery had long reckoned that the abolition of 'he foreign trade would be a fatal blow to slavery itself. The event exposed their fallacy. Thomas Clarkson expressed the disappointment of the English abolitionists in a letter of 1830: "We certainly have been deceived in our first expectations relative to the fruit of our exertions. We supposed that when by the abolition of the slave trade the planters could get no more slaves, they would not only treat better those whom they then had in their power, but that they would gradually find it to their advantage to emancipate them. A part of our expectations have been realized; . . . but, alas! where the heart has been desperately wicked, we have found no change. We did not sufficiently take into account the effect of unlimited power on the human mind. No man likes to part with power, and the more unbounded it is, the less he likes to part with it. Neither did we sufficiently take into account the ignominy attached to a black skin as the badge of slavery, and how difficult it would be to make men look with a favourable eye upon what they had looked [upon] formerly as a disgrace. Neither did we take sufficiently into account the belief which every planter has, that such an unnatural state as that of slavery can be kept up only by a system of rigour, and how difficult therefore it would be to procure a relaxation from the ordinary discipline of a slave estate."[35]

If such was the failure in the British West Indies, the change in conditions in the United States was even greater; for the rise of the cotton industry concurred with the prohibition of the African trade to enhance immensely the preciousness of slaves and to increase in similar degree the financial obstacle to a sweeping abolition.

[35] MS. in private possession.

CHAPTER IX

THE INTRODUCTION OF COTTON AND SUGAR

THE decade following the peace of 1783 brought depression in all the plantation districts. The tobacco industry, upon which half of the Southern people depended in greater or less degree, was entering upon a half century of such wellnigh constant low prices that the opening of each new tract for its culture was offset by the abandonment of an old one, and the export remained stationary at a little less than half a million hogsheads. Indigo production was decadent; and rice culture was in painful transition to the new tide-flow system. Slave prices everywhere, like those of most other investments, were declining in so disquieting a manner that as late as the end of 1794 George Washington advised a friend to convert his slaves into other forms of property, and said on his own account: "Were it not that I am principled against selling negroes, as you would cattle in a market, I would not in twelve months hence be possessed of a single one as a slave. I shall be happily mistaken if they are not found to be a very troublesome species of property ere many years have passed over our heads."[1] But at that very time the addition of cotton and sugar to the American staples was on the point of transforming the slaveholders' prospects.

For centuries cotton had been among the world's materials for cloth, though the dearth of supply kept it in smaller use than wool or flax. This continued to be the case even when the original sources in the Orient were considerably supplemented from the island of Bourbon and from the colonies of Demarara, Berbice and Surinam which dotted the tropical South American coast now known as Guiana. Then, in the latter half of the eighteenth century, the great English inventions of spinning and

[1] New York Public Library *Bulletin*, 1898, pp. 14, 15.

weaving machinery so cheapened the manufacturing process that the world's demand for textiles was immensely stimulated. Europe was eagerly inquiring for new fiber supplies at the very time when the plantation states of America were under the strongest pressure for a new source of income.

The green-seed, short-staple variety of cotton had long been cultivated for domestic use in the colonies from New Jersey to Georgia, but on such a petty scale that spinners occasionally procured supplies from abroad. Thus George Washington, who amid his many activities conducted a considerable cloth-making establishment, wrote to his factor in 1773 that a bale of cotton received from England had been damaged in transit.[2] The cutting off of the foreign trade during the war for independence forced the Americans to increase their cotton production to supply their necessities for apparel. A little of it was even exported at the end of the war, eight bags of which are said to have been seized by the customs officers at Liverpool in 1784 on the ground that since America could not produce so great a quantity the invoice must be fraudulent. But cotton was as yet kept far from staple rank by one great obstacle, the lack of a gin. The fibers of the only variety at hand clung to the seed as fast as the wool to the sheep's back. It had to be cut or torn away; and because the seed-tufts were so small, this operation when performed by hand was exceedingly slow and correspondingly expensive. The preparation of a pound or two of lint a day was all that a laborer could accomplish.

The problem of the time had two possible solutions; the invention of a machine for cleaning the lint from the seed of the sort already at hand, or the introduction of some different variety whose lint was more lightly attached. Both solutions were applied, and the latter first in point of time though not in point of importance.

About 1786 seed of several strains was imported from as many quarters by planters on the Georgia-Carolina coast. Experiments with the Bourbon variety, which yielded the finest lint then in the market, showed that the growing season was too short for

[2] MS. in the Library of Congress, Washington letter-books, XVII, 90.

the ripening of its pods; but seed procured from the Bahama Islands, of the sort which has ever since been known as sea-island, not only made crops but yielded a finer fiber than they had in their previous home. This introduction was accomplished by the simultaneous experiments of several planters on the Georgia coast. Of these, Thomas Spaulding and Alexander Bissett planted the seed in 1786 but saw their plants fail to ripen any pods that year. But the ensuing winter happened to be so mild that, although the cotton is not commonly a perennial outside the tropics, new shoots grew from the old roots in the following spring and yielded their crop in the fall.[3] Among those who promptly adopted the staple was Richard Leake, who wrote from Savannah at the end of 1788 to Tench Coxe: "I have been this year an adventurer, and the first that has attempted on a large scale, in the article of cotton. Several here as well as in Carolina have followed me and tried the experiment. I shall raise about 5000 pounds in the seed from about eight acres of land, and the next year I expect to plant from fifty to one hundred acres." [4]

The first success in South Carolina appears to have been attained by William Elliott, on Hilton Head near Beaufort, in 1790. He bought five and a half bushels of seed in Charleston at 14s per bushel, and sold his crop at 10½d per pound. In the next year John Screven of St. Luke's parish planted thirty or forty acres, and sold his yield at from 1s. 2d. to 1s. 6d. sterling per pound. Many other planters on the islands and the adjacent mainland now joined the movement. Some of them encountered failure, among them General Moultrie of Revolutionary fame who planted one hundred and fifty acres in St. John's Berkeley in 1793 and reaped virtually nothing.[5]

The English market came promptly to esteem the long, strong, silky sea-island fiber as the finest of all cottons; and the prices

[3] Letter of Thomas Spaulding, Sapelo Island, Georgia, Jan. 20, 1844, to W. B. Seabrook, in J. A. Turner, ed., *The Cotton Planter's Manual* (New York, 1857), pp. 280-286.
[4] E. J. Donnell, *Chronological and Statistical History of Cotton* (New York, 1872), p. 45.
[5] Whitemarsh B. Seabrook, *Memoir on the Origin, Cultivation and Uses of Cotton* (Charleston, 1844), pp. 19, 20.

at Liverpool rose before the end of the century to as high as five shillings a pound. This brought fortunes in South Carolina. Captain James Sinkler from a crop of three hundred acres on his plantation, "Belvedere," in 1794 gathered 216 pounds to the acre, which at prices ranging from fifty to seventy-five cents a pound brought him a gross return of $509 per laborer employed.[6] Peter Gaillard of St. John's Berkeley received for his crop of the same year an average of $340 per hand; and William Brisbane of St. Paul's earned so much in the three years from 1796 to 1798 that he found himself rich enough to retire from work and spend several years in travel at the North and abroad. He sold his plantation to William Seabrook at a price which the neighbors thought ruinously high, but Seabrook recouped the whole of it from the proceeds of two years' crops.[7]

The methods of tillage were quickly systematized. Instead of being planted, as at first, in separate holes, the seed came to be drilled and plants grown at intervals of one or two feet on ridges five or six feet apart; and the number of hoeings was increased. But the thinner fruiting of this variety prevented the planters from attaining generally more than about half the output per acre which their upland colleagues came to reap from their crops of the shorter staple. A hundred and fifty pounds to the acre and three or four acres to the hand was esteemed a reasonable crop on the seaboard.[8] The exports of the sea-island staple rose by 1805 to nearly nine million pounds, but no further expansion occurred until 1819 when an increase carried the exports for a decade to about eleven million pounds a year. In the course of the 'twenties Kinsey Burden and Hugh Wilson, both of St. John's Colleton, began breeding superfine fiber through seed selection, with such success that the latter sold two of his bales in 1828 at the unequaled price of two dollars a pound. The practice of raising fancy grades became fairly common after 1830, with the result,

[6] Samuel DuBose, *Address delivered before the Black Oak Agricultural Society, April 28, 1858*, in T. G. Thomas, *The Huguenots of South Carolina* (New York, 1887).
[7] W. B. Seabrook, *Memoir on Cotton*, p. 20.
[8] John Drayton, *View of South Carolina* (Charleston, 1802), p. 132; J. A. Turner, ed., *Cotton Planter's Manual*, pp. 129, 131.

however, that for the following decade the exports fell again to about eight million pounds a year.[9]

Sea-island cotton, with its fibers often measuring more than two inches in length, had the advantages of easy detachment from its glossy black seed by squeezing it between a pair of simple rollers, and of a price for even its common grades ranging usually more than twice that of the upland staple. The disadvantages were the slowness of the harvesting, caused by the failure of the bolls to open wide; the smallness of the yield; and the necessity of careful handling at all stages in preparing the lint for market. Climatic requirements, furthermore, confined its culture within a strip thirty or forty miles wide along the coast of South Carolina and Georgia. In the first flush of the movement some of the rice fields were converted to cotton;[10] but experience taught the community ere long that the labor expense in the new industry absorbed too much of the gross return for it to displace rice from its primacy in the district.

In the Carolina-Georgia uplands the industrial and social developments of the eighteenth century had been in marked contrast with those on the seaboard. These uplands, locally known as the Piedmont, were separated from the tide-water tract by a flat and sandy region, the "pine barrens," a hundred miles or more in breadth, where the soil was generally too light for prosperous agriculture before the time when commercial fertilizers came into use. The Piedmont itself is a rolling country, extending without a break from Virginia to Alabama and from the mountains of the Blue Ridge to the line of the lowest falls on the rivers. The soil of mingled clay and sand was originally covered with rich forest mold. The climate was moderately suited to a great variety of crops; but nothing was found for which it had a marked superiority until short-staple cotton was made available.

In the second half of the eighteenth century this region had come to be occupied in scattered homesteads by migrants moving overland from Pennsylvania, Maryland and Virginia, extending their régime of frontier farms until the stubborn Creek and

[9] Seabrook, pp. 35-37, 53.
[10] F. A. Michaux, *Travels,* in R. G. Thwaites, ed., *Early Western Travels,* III, 303.

Cherokee Indian tribes barred further progress. Later comers from the same northeastward sources, some of them bringing a few slaves, had gradually thickened the settlement without changing materially its primitive system of life. Not many recruits had entered from the rice coast in colonial times, for the régime there was not such as to produce pioneers for the interior. The planters, unlike those of Maryland and Virginia, had never imported appreciable numbers of indentured servants to become in after years yeomen and fathers of yeomen; the slaves begat slaves alone to continue at their masters' bidding; and the planters themselves had for the time being little inducement to forsake the lowlands. The coast and the Piedmont were unassociated except by a trickle of trade by wagon and primitive river-boat across the barrens. The capture of Savannah and Charleston by the British during the War for Independence, however, doubtless caused a number of the nearby inhabitants to move into the Piedmont as refugees, carrying their slaves with them.

The commercial demands of the early settlers embraced hardly anything beyond salt, ammunition and a little hardware. The forest and their half-cleared fields furnished meat and bread; workers in the households provided rude furniture and homespun; and luxuries, except home-made liquors, were unknown. But the time soon came when zealous industry yielded more grain and cattle than each family needed for its own supply. The surplus required a market, which the seaboard was glad to furnish. The road and river traffic increased, and the procurement of miscellaneous goods from the ports removed the need of extreme diversity in each family's work. This treeing of energy led in turn to a search for more profitable market crops. Flax and hemp were tried, and tobacco with some success. Several new villages were founded, indeed, on the upper courses of the rivers to serve as stations for the inspection and shipment of tobacco; but their budding hopes of prosperity from that staple were promptly blighted. The product was of inferior grade, the price was low, and the cost of freightage high. The export from Charleston rose from 2680 hogsheads in 1784 to 9646 in 1799, but rapidly declined thereafter. Tobacco, never more than a makeshift staple, was gladly abandoned for cotton at the first opportunity.[11]

At the time of the federal census of 1790 there were in the main group of upland counties of South Carolina, comprised then in the two "districts" of Camden and Ninety-six, a total of 91,704 white inhabitants, divided into 15,652 families. Of these 3787 held slaves to the number of 19,934—an average of 5¼ slaves in each holding. No more than five of these parcels comprised as many as one hundred slaves each, and only 156 masters, about four per cent. of the whole, had as many as twenty each. These larger holdings, along with the 335 other parcels ranging from ten to nineteen slaves each, were of course grouped mainly in the river counties in the lower part of the Piedmont, while the smallest holdings were scattered far and wide. That is to say, there was already discoverable a tendency toward a plantation régime in the localities most accessible to market, while among the farmers about one in four had one or more slaves to aid in the family's work. The Georgia Piedmont, for which the returns of the early censuses have been lost, probably had a somewhat smaller proportion of slaves by reason of its closer proximity to the Indian frontier.

A sprinkling of slaves was enough to whet the community's appetite for opportunities to employ them with effect and to buy more slaves with the proceeds. It is said that in 1792 some two or three million pounds of short-staple cotton was gathered in the Piedmont,[12] perhaps in anticipation of a practicable gin, and that the state of Georgia had appointed a commission to promote the desired invention.[13] It is certain that many of the citizens were discussing the problem when in the spring of 1793 young Eli Whitney, after graduating at Yale College, left his home in Massachusetts intending to teach school in the South. While making a visit at the home of General Greene's widow, near Savannah, he listened to a conversation on the subject by visitors

[11] U. B. Phillips, *History of Transportation in the Eastern Cotton Belt to 1860* (New York, 1908), pp. 46-55.
[12] Letter of Phineas Miller to the Comptroller of South Carolina, in the *American Historical Review*, III, 115.
[13] M. B. Hammond, *The Cotton Industry* (New York, 1897), p. 23.

from upland Georgia, and he was urged by Phineas Miller, the manager of the Greene estate, to apply his Yankee ingenuity to the solution. When Miller offered to bear the expenses of the project, Whitney set to work, and within ten days made a model which met the essential requirements. This comprised a box with a slatted side against which a wooden cylinder studded with wire points was made to play. When seed cotton was fed into the box and the cylinder was revolved, the sharp wires passing between the slats would engage the lint and pull it through as they passed out in the further revolution of the cylinder. The seed, which were too large to pass through the grating, would stay within the hopper until virtually all the wool was torn off, whereupon they would fall through a crevice on the further side. The minor problem which now remained of freeing the cylinder's teeth from their congestion of lint found a solution in Mrs. Greene's stroke with a hearth-broom. Whitney, seizing the principle, equipped his machine with a second cylinder studded with brushes, set parallel to the first but revolving in an opposite direction and at a greater speed. This would sweep the teeth clean as fast as they emerged lint-laden from the hopper. Thus was the famous cotton-gin devised.[14]

Miller, who now married Mrs. Greene, promptly entered into partnership with Whitney not only to manufacture gins but also to monopolize the business of operating them, charging one-third of the cotton as toll. They even ventured into the buying and selling of the staple on a large scale. Miller wrote Whitney in 1797, for example, that he was trying to raise money for the purchase of thirty or forty thousand pounds of seed cotton at the prevailing price of three cents, and was projecting a trade in the lint to far-off Tennessee.[15] By this time the partners had as many as thirty gins in operation at various points in Georgia; but misfortune had already begun to pursue them. Their shop on the Greene plantation had been forced by a mob even before their patent was procured in 1793, and Jesse Bull, Charles M.

[14] Denison Olmstead, *Memoir of Eli Whitney, Esq.* (New Haven, 1846), reprinted in J. A. Turner, ed., *Cotton Planter's Manual*, pp. 297-320. **M. B.** Hammond, *The Cotton Industry*, pp. 25, 26.
[15] *American Historical Review*. III, 104.

Lin and Edward Lyons, collaborating near Wrightsboro, soon
put forth an improved gin in which saw-toothed iron discs replaced the wire points of the Whitney model.[16]   Whitney had
now returned to New Haven to establish a gin factory, and Miller wrote him in 1794 urging prompt shipments and saying:
"The people of the country are running mad for them, and much
can be said to justify their importunity.   When the present crop
is harvested there will be a real property of at least fifty thousand
dollars lying useless unless we can enable the holders to bring it
to market."   But an epidemic prostrated Whitney's workmen
that year, and a fire destroyed his factory in 1795.   Meanwhile
rival machines were appearing in the market, and Whitney and
Miller were beginning their long involvement in lawsuits.   Their
overreaching policy of monopolizing the operation of their gins
turned public sentiment against them and inclined the juries,
particularly in Georgia, to decide in favor of their opponents.
Not until 1807, when their patent was on the point of expiring
did they procure a vindication in the Georgia courts.   Meanwhile a grant of $50,000 from the legislature of South Carolina
to extinguish the patent right in that state, and smaller grants
from North Carolina and Tennessee did little more than counterbalance expenses.[17]   A petition which Whitney presented to Congress in 1812 for a renewal of his expired patent was denied,
and Whitney turned his talents to the manufacture of muskets.

In Georgia the contest of lawyers in the courts was paralleled
by a battle of advertisers in the newspapers.   Thomas Spaulding
offered to supply Joseph Eve's gins from the Bahama Islands at
fifty guineas each;[18] and Eve himself shortly immigrated to Augusta to contend for his patent rights on roller-gins, for some of
his workmen had changed his model in such a way as to increase
the speed, and had put their rival gins upon the market.[19]   Among
these may have been John Currie, who offered exclusive county
rights at $100 each for the making, using and vending of his

[16] J. A. Turner, ed., *Cotton Planter's Manual*, pp. 289, 290, 293-295.
[17] M. B. Hammond, "Correspondence of Eli Whitney relating to the Invention of the Cotton Gin," in the *American Historical Review*, III, 99-127.
[18] *Columbian Museum* (Savannah, Ga.), April 26, 1796.
[19] J. A. Turner, ed., *Cotton Planter's Manual*, p. 281.

type of gins,[20] also William Longstreet of Augusta who offered
to sell gins of his own devising at $150 each,[21] and Robert Wat-
kins of the short-lived town of Petersburg, Georgia, who de-
nounced Longstreet as an infringer of his patent and advertised
local non-exclusive rights for making and using his own style of
gins at the bargain rate of sixty dollars.[22] All of these were described as roller gins; but all were warranted to gin upland as
well as sea-island cotton.[23] By the year 1800 Miller and Whitney
had also adopted the practice of selling licenses in Georgia, as is
indicated by an advertisement from their agent at Augusta.
Meanwhile ginners were calling for negro boys and girls ten or
twelve years old on hire to help at the machines;[24] and were offering to gin for a toll of one-fifth of the cotton.[25] As years
passed the rates were still further lowered. At Augusta in 1809,
for example, cotton was ginned and packed in square bales of
350 pounds at a cost of $1.50 per hundredweight.[26]

The upland people of Georgia and the two Carolinas made
prompt response to the new opportunity. By 1800 even Tennessee had joined the movement, and a gin of such excellence was
erected near Nashville that the proprietors exacted fees from visitors wishing to view it;[27] and by 1802 not only were consign-
ments being shipped to New Orleans for the European market,
but part of the crop was beginning to be peddled in wagons to
Kentucky and in pole-boats on the Ohio as far as Pittsburg, for
the domestic making of homespun.[28] In 1805 John Baird advertised at Nashville that, having received a commission from
correspondents at Baltimore, he was ready to buy as much as
one hundred thousand pounds of lint at fifteen cents a
pound.[29] In the settlements about Vicksburg in the Mississippi
Territory, cotton was not only the staple product by 1809, but was

[20] Augusta, Ga., *Chronicle*, Dec. 10, 1796.
[21] *Southern Sentinel* (Augusta, Ga.), July 14, 1796.
[22] *Ibid.*, Feb. 7, 1797; Augusta *Chronicle*, June 10, 1797.
[23] Augusta *Chronicle*, Dec. 13, 1800.
[24] *Southern Sentinel*, April 23, 1795.
[25] Augusta *Chronicle*, Jan. 16, 1796.
[26] *Ibid.*, Sept. 9, 1809.
[27] *Tennessee Gazette* (Nashville, Tenn.), April 9, 1800.
[28] F. A. Michaux in Thwaites, ed., *Early Western Travels*, III, 252.
[29] *Tennessee Gazette*, March 27, 1805.

also for the time being the medium of exchange, while in Arkansas the squatters were debarred from the new venture only by the poverty which precluded them from getting gins.[30]   In Virginia also, in such of the southerly counties as had summers long enough for the crop to ripen in moderate security, cotton growing became popular.   But for the time being these were merely an out-lying fringe of cotton's principality.   The great rush to cotton growing prior to the war of 1812 occurred in the Carolina-Georgia Piedmont, with its trend of intensity soon pointing south-westward.

A shrewd contemporary observer found special reason to rejoice that the new staple required no large capital and involved no exposure to disease.   Rice and indigo, said he, had offered the poorer whites, except the few employed as overseers, no livelihood "without the degradation of working with slaves"; but cotton, stimulating and elevating these people into the rank of substantial farmers, tended "to fill the country with an independent industrious yeomanry." [31]   True as this was, it did not mean that producers on a plantation scale were at a disadvantage. Settlers of every type, in fact, adopted the crop as rapidly as they could get seed and ginning facilities, and newcomers poured in apace to share the prosperity.

The exports mounted swiftly, but the world's market readily absorbed them at rising prices until 1801 when the short-staple output was about forty million pounds and the price at the ports about forty-four cents a pound.   A trade in slaves promptly arose to meet the eager demand for labor; and migrants coming from the northward and the rice coast brought additional slaves in their train.   General Wade Hampton was the first conspicuous one of these.   With the masterful resolution which always characterized him, he carried his great gang from the seaboard to the neighborhood of Columbia and there in 1799 raised six hundred of the relatively light weight bales of that day on as

---

[30] F. Cuming, *Tour to the Western Country* (Pittsburg, 1810), in Thwaites, ed., *Early Western Travels*, IV, 272, 280, 298.
[31] David Ramsay, *History of South Carolina* (Charleston, 1808), II, 448-9.

many acres.[32]   His crop was reckoned to have a value of some ninety thousand dollars.[33]

The general run of the upland cultivators, however, continued as always to operate on a minor scale; and the high cost of transportation caused them generally to continue producing miscellaneous goods to meet their domestic needs. The diversified régime is pictured in Michaux's description of a North Carolina plantation in 1802: "In eight hundred acres of which it is composed, a hundred and fifty are cultivated in cotton, Indian corn, wheat and oats, and dunged annually, which is a great degree of perfection in the present state of agriculture in this part of the country. Independent of this [the proprietor] has built in his yard several machines that the same current of water puts in motion; they consist of a corn mill, a saw mill, another to separate the cotton seeds, a tan-house, a tan-mill, a distillery to make peach brandy, and a small forge where the inhabitants of the country go to have their horses shod. Seven or eight negro slaves are employed in the different departments, some of which are only occupied at certain periods of the year. Their wives are employed under the direction of the mistress in manufacturing cotton and linen for the use of the family." [34]

The speed of the change to a general slaveholding régime in the uplands may easily be exaggerated. In those counties of South Carolina which lay wholly within the Piedmont the fifteen thousand slaves on hand in 1790 formed slightly less than one-fifth of the gross population there. By 1800 the number of slaves increased by seventy per cent., and formed nearly one-fourth of the gross; in the following decade they increased by ninety per cent., until they comprised one-third of the whole; from 1810 to 1820 their number grew at the smaller rate of fifty per cent. and reached two-fifths of the whole; and by 1830, with a further increase of forty per cent., the number of slaves almost overtook that of the whites. The slaves were then counted at 101,982, the whites at 115,318, and the free negroes at 2,115.

[32] Seabrook, pp. 16, 17.
[33] Note made by L. C. Draper from the Louisville, Ga., *Gazette*, Draper MSS., series VV, vol. XVI, p. 84, Wisconsin Historical Society.
[34] F. A. Michaux in Thwaites, ed., *Early Western Travels*, III, 292.

In Georgia the slave proportion grew more rapidly than this because it was much smaller at the outset; in North Carolina, on the other hand, the rise was less marked because cotton never throve there so greatly.

In its industrial requirements cotton was much closer to tobacco than to rice or sugar. There was no vital need for large units of production. On soils of the same quality the farmer with a single plow, if his family did the hoeing and picking, was on a similar footing with the greatest planter as to the output per hand, and in similar case as to cost of production per bale. The scale of cotton-belt slaveholdings rose not because free labor was unsuited to the industry but because slaveholders from the outside moved in to share the opportunity and because every prospering non-slaveholder and small slaveholder was eager to enlarge his personal scale of operations. Those who could save generally bought slaves with their savings; those who could not, generally continued to raise cotton nevertheless.

The gross cotton output, in which the upland crop greatly and increasingly outweighed that of the sea-island staple, rapidly advanced from about forty-eight million pounds in 1801 to about eighty million in 1806; then it was kept stationary by the embargo and the war of 1812, until the return of peace and open trade sent it up by leaps and bounds again. The price dropped abruptly from an average of forty-four cents in the New York market in 1801 to nineteen cents in 1802, but there was no further decline until the beginning of the war with Great Britain.[35]

Cotton's absorption of the people's energies already tended to become excessive. In 1790 South Carolina had sent abroad a surplus of corn from the back country measuring well over a hundred thousand bushels. But by 1804 corn brought in brigs was being advertised in Savannah to meet the local deficit;[36] and in the spring of 1807 there seems to have been a dearth of grain in the Piedmont itself. At that time an editorial in the *Augusta Chronicle* ran as follows: "A correspondent would recommend

[35] M. B. Hammond, *The Cotton Industry*, table following p. 357.
[36] Savannah *Museum*, April 11, 1804.

to the planters of Georgia, now the season is opening, to raise more corn and less cotton. . . . The dear bought experience of the present season should teach us to be more provident for the future." [37] Under the conditions of the time this excess at the expense of grain was likely to correct itself at once, for men and their draught animals must eat to work, and in the prevailing lack of transportation facilities food could not be brought from a distance at a price within reach. The systematic basis of industry was the production, whether by planters or farmers, of such food as was locally needed and such supplies of cloth together with such other outfit as it was economical to make at home, and the devotion of all further efforts to the making of cotton.

Coincident with the rise of cotton culture in the Atlantic states was that of sugar in the delta lands of southeastern Louisiana. In this triangular district, whose apex is the junction of the Red and Mississippi rivers, the country is even more amphibious than the rice coast. Everywhere in fact the soil is too waterlogged for tillage except close along the Father of Waters himself and his present or aforetime outlets. Settlement must, therefore, take the form of strings of plantations and farms on these elevated riparian strips, with the homesteads fronting the streams and the fields stretching a few hundred or at most a few thousand yards to the rear; and every new establishment required its own levee against the flood. So long as there were great areas of unrestricted flood-plain above Vicksburg to impound the freshets and lower their crests, the levees below required no great height or strength; but the tasks of reclamation were at best arduous enough to make rapid expansion depend upon the spur of great expectations.

The original colony of the French, whose descendants called themselves Creoles, was clustered about the town of New Orleans. A short distance up stream the river banks in the parishes of St. Charles and St. John the Baptist were settled at an early period by German immigrants; thence the settlements were extended after the middle of the eighteenth century, first by

[37] Reprinted in the *Farmer's Gazette* (Sparta, Ga.), April 11, 1807.

French exiles from Acadia, next by Creole planters, and finally by Anglo-Americans who took their locations mostly above Baton Rouge. As to the westerly bayous, the initial settlers were in general Acadian small farmers. Negro slaves were gradually introduced into all these districts, though the Creoles, who were the most vigorous of the Latin elements, were the chief importers of them. Their numbers at the close of the colonial period equalled those of the whites, and more than a tenth of them had been emancipated.

The people in the later eighteenth century were drawing their livelihoods variously from hunting, fishing, cattle raising and Indian trading, from the growing of grain and vegetables for sale to the boatmen and townsmen, and from the production of indigo on a somewhat narrow margin of profit as the principal export crop. Attempts at sugar production had been made in 1725 and again in 1762, but the occurrence of winter frosts before the cane was fully ripe discouraged the enterprise; and in most years no more cane was raised than would meet the local demand for sirup and rum. In the closing decades of the century, however, worm pests devoured the indigo leaves with such thoroughness as to make harvesting futile; and thereby the planters were driven to seek an alternative staple. Projects of cotton were baffled by the lack of a gin, and recourse was once more had to sugar. A Spaniard named Solis had built a small mill below New Orleans in 1791 and was making sugar with indifferent success when, in 1794-1795, Etienne de Boré, a prominent Creole whose estate lay just above the town, bought a supply of seed cane from Solis, planted a large field with it, engaged a professional sugar maker, and installed grinding and boiling apparatus against the time of harvest. The day set for the test brought a throng of onlookers whose joy broke forth at the sight of crystals in the cooling fluid—for the good fortune of Boré, who received some $12,000 for his crop of 1796, was an earnest of general prosperity.

Other men of enterprise followed the resort to sugar when opportunity permitted them to get seed cane, mills and cauldrons. In spite of a dearth of both capital and labor and in spite of wartime restrictions on maritime commerce, the sugar estates within nine years reached the number of eighty-one, a good many of which were doubtless the property of San Domingan refugees who were now pouring into the province with whatever slaves and other movables they had been able to snatch from the black revolution. Some of these had fled first to Cuba and after a sojourn there, during which they found the Spanish government oppressive, removed afresh to Louisiana. As late as 1809 the year's immigration from the two islands was reported by the mayor of New Orleans to the governor of Louisiana at 2,731 whites and 3,102 free persons of color, together with 3,226 slaves warranted as the property of the free immigrants.[88] The volume of the San Domingan influx from first to last was great enough to double the French-speaking population. The newcomers settled mainly in the New Orleans neighborhood, the whites among them promptly merging themselves with the original Creole population. By reason of their previous familiarity with sugar culture they gave additional stimulus to that industry.

Meanwhile the purchase of Louisiana by the United States in 1803 had transformed the political destinies of the community and considerably changed its economic prospects. After prohibiting in 1804 the importation into the territory of any slaves who had been brought from Africa since 1798, Congress passed a new act in 1805 which, though probably intended to continue the prohibition, was interpreted by the attorney-general to permit the inhabitants to bring in any slaves whatever from any place within the United States.[39] This news was published with delight by the New Orleans newspapers at the end of February, 1806;[40] and from that time until the end of the following year their columns bristled with advertisements of slaves from African cargoes "just arrived from Charleston." Of these the following, issued by the firm of Kenner and Henderson, June 24, 1806, is an example: "The subscribers offer for sale 74 prime slaves of the Fantee nation on board the schooner *Reliance*, I. Potter

---

[88] *Moniteur de la Louisiane* (New Orleans), Jan. 27 and Mch. 24, 1810.
[39] W. E. B. DuBois, *Suppression of the African Slave Trade*, pp. 87-90. The acts of 1804 and 1805 are printed in B. P. Poore, *Charters and Constitutions* (Washington, 1877), I, 691-697.
[40] *Louisiana Gazette*, Feb. 28, 1806.

master, from Charleston, now lying opposite this city. The sales will commence on the 25th. inst. at 9 o'clock A.M., and will continue from day to day until the whole is sold.[41] Good endorsed notes will be taken in payment, payable the 1st. of January, 1807. Also [for sale] the above mentioned schooner *Reliance,* burthen about 60 tons, completely fitted for an African voyage."

Upon the prohibition of the African trade at large in 1808, the slave demand of the sugar parishes was diverted to the Atlantic plantation states where it served to advertise the Louisiana boom. Wade Hampton of South Carolina responded in 1811 by carrying a large force of his slaves to establish a sugar estate of his own at the head of Bayou Lafourche, and a few others followed his example. The radical difference of the industrial methods in sugar from those in the other staples, however, together with the predominance of the French language, the Catholic religion and a Creole social régime in the district most favorable for sugar, made Anglo-Americans chary of the enterprise; and the revival of cotton prices after 1815 strengthened the tendency of migrating planters to stay within the cotton latitudes. Many of those who settled about Baton Rouge and on the Red River with cotton as their initial concern shifted to sugar at the end of the 'twenties, however, in response to the tariff of 1828 which heightened sugar prices at a time when the cotton market was depressed. This was in response, also, to the introduction of ribbon cane which matured earlier than the previously used Malabar and Otaheite varieties and could accordingly be grown in a somewhat higher latitude.

The territorial spread was mainly responsible for the sudden advance of the number of sugar estates from 308 operating in 1827, estimated as employing 21,000 able-bodied slaves and having a gross value of $34,000,000, to 691 plantations in 1830,[42] with some 36,000 working slaves and a gross value of $50,000,000. At this time the output was at the rate of about 75,000 hogsheads containing 1,000 pounds of sugar each, together with some forty or fifty gallons of molasses per hogshead as a by-product. Lou-

[41] *Louisiana Gazette,* July 4, 1806.
[42] *DeBow's Review,* I, 55.

isiana.was at this time supplying about half of the whole country's consumption of sugar and bade fair to meet the whole demand ere long.[43] The reduction of protective tariff rates, coming simultaneously with a rise of cotton prices, then checked the spread of the sugar industry, and the substitution of steam engines for horse power in grinding the cane caused some consolidation of estates. In 1842 accordingly, when the slaves numbered 50,740 and the sugar crop filled 140,000 hogsheads, the plantations were but 668.[44] The raising of the tariff anew in that year increased the plantations to 762 in 1845 and they reached their maximum number of 1,536 in 1849, when more than half of their mills were driven by steam[45] and their slaves numbered probably somewhat more than a hundred thousand of all ages.[46] Thereafter the recovery of the cotton market from the severe depression of the early 'forties caused a strong advance in slave prices which again checked the sugar spread, while the introduction of vacuum pans and other improvements in apparatus[47] promoted further consolidations. The number of estates accordingly diminished to 1,298 in 1859, on 987 of which the mills were steam driven, and on 52 of which the extraction and evaporation of the sugar was done by one sort or another of the newly invented devices. The gross number of slaves in the sugar parishes was nearly doubled between 1830 and 1850, but in the final ante-bellum decade it advanced only at about the rate of natural increase.[48] The sugar output advanced to 200,000 hogsheads in 1844 and to 450,000 in 1853. Bad seasons then reduced it to 74,000 in 1856; and the previous maximum was not equaled in the remaining ante-bellum years.[49] The liability of

[43] V. Debouchel, *Histoire de la Louisiane* (New Orleans, 1851), pp. 151 ff.
[44] E. J. Forstall, *Agricultural Productions of Louisiana* (New Orleans, 1845).
[45] P. A. Champonier, *Statement of the Sugar Crop Made in Louisiana* (New Orleans, annual, 1848-1859).
[46] DeBow, in the *Compendium of the Seventh Census*, p. 94, estimated the sugar plantation slaves at 150,000; but this is clearly an overestimate.
[47] Some of these are described by Judah P. Benjamin in *DeBow's Review*, II, 322-345.
[48] *I. e.* from 150,000 to 180,000.
[49] The crop of 1853, indeed, was not exceeded until near the close of the nineteenth century.

the crop to damage from drought and early frost, and to destruction from the outpouring of the Mississippi through crevasses in the levees, explains the fluctuations in the yield. Outside of Louisiana the industry took no grip except on the Brazos River in Texas, where in 1858 thirty-seven plantations produced about six thousand hogsheads.[50]

In Louisiana in the banner year 1853, with perfect weather and no crevasses, each of some 50,000 able-bodied field hands cultivated, besides the incidental food crops, about five acres of cane on the average and produced about nine hogsheads of sugar and three hundred gallons of molasses per head. On certain specially favored estates, indeed, the product reached as much as fifteen hogsheads per hand.[51] In the total of 1407 fully equipped plantations 103 made less than one hundred hogsheads each, while forty produced a thousand hogsheads or more. That year's output, however, was nearly twice the size of the average crop in the period. A dozen or more proprietors owned two or more estates each, some of which were on the largest scale, while at the other extreme several dozen farmers who had no mills of their own sent cane from their few acres to be worked up in the spare time of some obliging neighbor's mill. In general the bulk of the crop was made on plantations with cane fields ranging from rather more than a hundred to somewhat less than a thousand acres, and with each acre producing in an ordinary year somewhat more than a hogshead of sugar.

Until about 1850 the sugar district as well as the cotton belt was calling for labor from whatever source it might be had; but whereas the uplands had work for people of both races and all conditions, the demand of the delta lands, to which the sugar crop was confined, was almost wholly for negro slaves. The only notable increase in the rural white population of the district came through the fecundity of the small-farming Acadians who had little to do with sugar culture.

[50] P. A. Champonier, *Statement of the Sugar Crop . . . in 1858-1859,* p. 40.
[51] *DeBow's Review,* XIV, 199, 200.

CHAPTER X

THE WESTWARD MOVEMENT

THE flow of population into the distant interior followed the lines of least resistance and greatest opportunity. In the earlier decades these lay chiefly in the Virginia latitudes. The Indians there were yielding, the mountains afforded passes thither, and the climate permitted the familiar tobacco industry. The Shenandoah Valley had been occupied mainly by Scotch-Irish and German small farmers from Pennsylvania; but the glowing reports, which the long hunters brought and the land speculators spread from beyond the further mountains, made Virginians to the manner born resolve to compete with the men of the backwoods for a share of the Kentucky lands. During and after the war for independence they threaded the gorges, some with slaves but most without. Here and there one found a mountain glade so fertile that he made it his permanent home, while his fellows pushed on to the greater promised land. Some of these emerging upon a country of low and uniform hills, closely packed and rounded like the backs of well-fed pigs crowding to the trough, staked out their claims, set up their cabins, deadened their trees, and planted wheat. Others went on to the gently rolling country about Lexington, let the luxuriant native bluegrass wean them from thoughts of tobacco, and became breeders of horses for evermore. A few, settling on the southerly edge of the bluegrass, mainly in and about Garrard County, raised hemp on a plantation scale. The rest, resisting all these allurements, pressed on still further to the pennyroyal country where tobacco would have no rival. While thousands made the whole journey overland, still more made use of the Ohio River for the later stages. The adjutant at Fort Harmar counted in seven months of 1786-1787, 177 boats descending the Ohio, carrying 2,689 persons, 1,333 horses, 766 cattle, 102 wagons and one phaëton, while still others passed by night uncounted.[1] The family establishments in Kentucky were always on a smaller scale, on an average, than those in Virginia. Yet the people migrating to the more fertile districts tended to maintain and even to heighten the spirit of gentility and the pride of type which they carried as part of their heritage. The laws erected by the community were favorable to the slaveholding régime; but after the first decades of the migration period, the superior attractions of the more southerly latitudes for plantation industry checked Kentucky's receipt of slaves.

The wilderness between the Ohio and the Great Lakes, meanwhile, was attracting Virginia and Carolina emigrants as well as those from the northerly states. The soil there was excellent, and some districts were suited to tobacco culture. The Ordinance of 1787, however, though it was not strictly enforced, made slaveholdings north of the Ohio negligible from any but an antiquarian point of view.

The settlement of Tennessee was parallel, though subsequent, to that of the Shenandoah and Kentucky. The eastern intramontane valley, broad and fertile but unsuited to the staple crops, gave homes to thousands of small farmers, while the Nashville basin drew planters of both tobacco and cotton, and the counties along the western and southern borders of the state made cotton their one staple. The scale of slaveholdings in middle and western Tennessee, while superior to that in Kentucky, was never so great as those which prevailed in Virginia and the lower South.

Missouri, whose adaptation to the southern staples was much poorer, came to be colonized in due time partly by planters from Kentucky but mostly by farmers from many quarters, including after the first decades a large number of Germans, some of whom entered through the eastern ports and others through New Orleans.

This great central region as a whole acquired an agricultural régime blending the features of the two national extremes. The staples were prominent but never quite paramount. Corn and

[1] *Massachusetts Centinel* (Boston), July 21, 1787.

wheat, cattle and hogs were produced regularly nearly everywhere, not on a mere home consumption basis, but for sale in the
cotton belt and abroad. This diversification caused the region
to wane in the esteem of the migrating planters as soon as the
Alabama-Mississippi country was opened for settlement.

Preliminaries of the movement into the Gulf region had begun
as early as 1768, when a resident of Pensacola noted that a group
of Virginians had been prospecting thereabouts with such favorable results that five of them had applied for a large grant of
lands, pledging themselves to bring in a hundred slaves and a
large number of cattle.[2] In 1777 William Bartram met a group
of migrants journeying from Georgia to settle on the lower
course of the Alabama River;[3] and in 1785 a citizen of Augusta
wrote that "a vast number" of the upland settlers were removing
toward the Mississippi in consequence of the relinquishment of
Natchez by the Spaniards.[4] But these were merely forerunners.
Alabama in particular, which comprises for the most part the
basin draining into Mobile Bay, could have no safe market for
its produce until Spain was dispossessed of the outlet. The taking of Mobile by the United States as an episode of the war of
1812, and the simultaneous breaking of the Indian strength, removed the obstacles. The influx then rose to immense proportions. The roads and rivers became thronged, and the federal
agents began to sell homesteads on a scale which made the "land
office business" proverbial.[5]

The Alabama-Mississippi population rose from 40,000 in round
numbers in 1810 to 200,000 in 1820, 445,000 in 1830, 965,000 in
1840, 1,377,000 in 1850, and 1,660,000 in 1860, while the proportion of slaves advanced from forty to forty-seven per cent. In
the same period the tide flowed on into the cotton lands of Arkansas and Louisiana and eventually into Texas. Florida alone
of the newer southern areas was left in relative neglect by reason of the barrenness of her soil. The states and territories

[2] Boston, Mass, *Chronicle*, Aug. 1-7, 1768.
[3] William Bartram, *Travels* (London, 1792), p. 441.
[4] *South Carolina Gazette*, May 26, 1785.
[5] C. F. Emerick, "The Credit System and the Public Domain," in the
Vanderbilt University *Southern History Publications*. no. 3 (Nashville,
Tenn., 1899).

from Alabama and Tennessee westward increased their proportion of the whole country's cotton output from one-sixteenth in 1811 to one-third in 1820, one-half before 1830, nearly two-thirds in 1840, and quite three-fourths in 1860; and all this was in spite of continued and substantial enlargements of the eastern output.

In the western cotton belt the lands most highly esteemed in the ante-bellum period lay in two main areas, both of which had soils far more fertile and lasting than any in the interior of the Atlantic states. One of these formed a crescent across south-central Alabama, with its western horn reaching up the Tombigbee River into northeastern Mississippi. Its soil of loose black loam was partly forested, partly open, and densely matted with grass and weeds except where limestone cropped out on the hill crests and where prodigious cane brakes choked the valleys. The area was locally known as the prairies or the black belt.[6] The process of opening it for settlement was begun by Andrew Jackson's defeat of the Creeks in 1814 but was not completed until some twenty years afterward. The other and greater tract extended along both sides of the Mississippi River from northern Tennessee and Arkansas to the mouth of the Red River. It comprised the broad alluvial bottoms, together with occasional hill districts of rich loam, especially notable among the latter of which were those lying about Natchez and Vicksburg. The southern end of this area was made available first, and the hills preceded the delta in popularity for cotton culture. It was not until the middle thirties that the broadest expanse of the bottoms, the Yazoo-Mississippi Delta, began to receive its great influx. The rest of the western cotton belt had soils varying through much the same range as those of Georgia and the Carolinas. Except in the bottoms, where the planters themselves did most of the pioneering, the choicer lands of the whole district were entered by a pell-mell throng of great planters, lesser planters and small farmers, with the farmers usually a little in the lead and the planters ready to buy them out of specially rich lands. Farmers refusing to sell

<hr/>

[6] This use of the term "black belt" is not to be confused with the other and more general application of it to such areas in the South at large as have a majority of negroes in their population.

might by their own thrift shortly rise into the planter class; or if they sold their homesteads at high prices they might buy slaves with the proceeds and remove to become planters in still newer districts.

The process was that which had already been exemplified abundantly in the eastern cotton belt. A family arriving perhaps in the early spring with a few implements and a small supply of food and seed, would build in a few days a cabin of rough logs with an earthen floor and a roof of bark or of riven clapboards. To clear a field they would girdle the larger trees and clear away the underbrush. Corn planted in April would furnish roasting ears in three months and ripe grain in six weeks more. Game was plenty; lightwood was a substitute for candles; and housewifely skill furnished homespun garments. Shelter, food and clothing and possibly a small cotton crop or other surplus were thus had the first year. Some rested with this; but the more thrifty would soon replace their cabins with hewn log or frame houses, plant kitchen gardens and watermelon patches, set out orchards and increase the cotton acreage. The further earnings of a year or two would supply window glass, table ware, coffee, tea and sugar, a stock of poultry, a few hogs and even perhaps a slave or two. The pioneer hardships decreased and the homely comforts grew with every passing year of thrift. But the orchard yield of stuff for the still, and the cotton field's furnishing the wherewithal to buy more slaves, brought temptations. Distilleries and slaves, a contemporary said, were blessings or curses according as they were used or abused; for drunkenness and idleness were the gates of the road to retrogression.[7]

The pathetic hardships which some of the poorer migrants underwent in their labors to reach the western opportunity are exemplified in a local item from an Augusta newspaper in 1819: "Passed through this place from Greenville District [South Carolina] bound for Chatahouchie, a man and his wife, his son and his wife, with a cart but no horse. The man had a belt over his shoulders and he drew in the shafts; the son worked by traces

[7] David Ramsay *History of South Carolina*, II, pp. 246 ff.

tied to the end of the shafts and assisted his father to draw the cart; the son's wife rode in the cart, and the old woman was walking, carrying a rifle, and driving a cow." [8] This example, while extreme, was not unique. [9]

The call of the west was carried in promoters' publications, [10] in private letters, in newspaper reports, and by word of mouth. A typical communication was sent home in 1817 by a Marylander who had moved to Louisiana: "In your states a planter with ten negroes with difficulty supports a family genteelly; here well managed they would be a fortune to him. With you the seasons are so irregular your crops often fail; here the crops are certain, and want of the necessaries of life never for a moment causes the heart to ache—abundance spreads the table of the poor man, and contentment smiles on every countenance." [11] Other accounts told glowingly of quick fortunes made and to be made by getting lands cheaply in the early stages of settlement and selling them at greatly enhanced prices when the tide of migration arrived in force. [12] Such ebullient expressions were taken at face value by thousands of the unwary; and other thousands of the more cautious followed in the trek when personal inquiries had reinforced the tug of the west. The larger planters generally removed only after somewhat thorough investigation and after procuring more or less acquiescence from their slaves; the smaller planters and farmers, with lighter stake in their homes and better opportunity to sell them, with lighter impedimenta for the journey, with less to lose by misadventure, and with poorer facilities for inquiry, responded more readily to the enticements.

The fever of migration produced in some of the people an unconquerable restlessness. An extraordinary illustration of this is given in the career of Gideon Lincecum as written by himself. In 1802, when Gideon was ten years old, his father, after farming successfully for some years in the Georgia uplands was lured by letters from relatives in Tennessee to sell out and remove

---

[8] Augusta, Ga., *Chronicle*, Sept. 24, 1819, reprinted in *Plantation and Frontier*, II, 196.
[9] *Niles' Register*, XX, 320.
[10] *E. g.*, the Washington, Ky., *Mirror*, Sept. 30, 1797.
[11] *Niles' Register*, XIII, 38.
[12] *E. g.*, *Federal Union* (Milledgeville, Ga.), March 11, 1836.

thither. Taking the roundabout road through the Carolinas to avoid the Cherokee country, he set forth with a wagon and four horses to carry a bed, four chests, four white and four negro children, and his mother who was eighty-eight years old. When but a few days on the road an illness of the old woman caused a halt, whereupon Lincecum rented a nearby farm and spent a year on a cotton crop. The journey was then resumed, but barely had the Savannah River been crossed when another farm was rented and another crop begun. Next year they returned to Georgia and worked a farm near Athens. Then they set out again for Tennessee; but on the road in South Carolina the wreck of the wagon and its ancient occupant gave abundant excuse for the purchase of a farm there. After another crop, successful as usual, the family moved back to Georgia and cropped still another farm. Young Gideon now attended school until his father moved again, this time southward, for a crop near Eatonton. Gideon then left his father after a quarrel and spent several years as a clerk in stores here and there, as a county tax collector and as a farmer, and began to read medicine in odd moments. He now married, about the beginning of the year 1815, and rejoined his father who was about to cross the Indian country to settle in Alabama. But they had barely begun this journey when the father, while tipsy, bought a farm on the Georgia frontier, where the two families settled and Gideon interspersed deer hunting with his medical reading. Next spring the cavalcade crossed the five hundred miles of wilderness in six weeks, and reached the log cabin village of Tuscaloosa, where Gideon built a house. But provisions were excessively dear, and his hospitality to other land seekers from Georgia soon consumed his savings. He began whipsawing lumber, but after disablement from a gunpowder explosion he found lighter employment in keeping a billiard room. He then set out westward again, breaking a road for his wagon as he went. Upon reaching the Tombigbee River he built a clapboard house in five days, cleared land from its canebrake, planted corn with a sharpened stick, and in spite of ravages from bears and raccoons gathered a hundred and fifty bushels from six acres. When the town of Columbus, Mississippi, was founded nearby in 1819 he sawed boards to build a house on speculation. From this he was diverted to the Indian trade, bartering whiskey, cloth and miscellaneous goods for peltries. He then became a justice of the peace and school commissioner at Columbus, surveyed and sold town lots on public account, and built two school houses with the proceeds. He then moved up the river to engage anew in the Indian trade with a partner who soon proved a drunkard. He and his wife there took a fever which after baffling the physicians was cured by his own prescription. He then moved to Cotton Gin Port to take charge of a store, but was invalided for three years by a sunstroke. Gradually recovering, he lived in the woods on light diet until the thought occurred to him of carrying a company of Choctaw ball players on a tour of the United States. The tour was made, but the receipts barely covered expenses. Then in 1830, Lincecum set himself up as a physician at Columbus. No sooner had he built up a practice, however, than he became dissatisfied with allopathy and went to study herb remedies among the Indians; and thereafter he practiced botanic medicine. In 1834 he went as surgeon with an exploring party to Texas and found that country so attractive that after some years further at Columbus he spent the rest of his long life in Texas as a planter, physician and student of natural history. He died there in 1873 at the age of eighty years.[13]

The descriptions and advice which prospectors in the west sent home are exemplified in a letter of F. X. Martin, written in New Orleans in 1911, to a friend in eastern North Carolina. The lands, he said, were the most remunerative in the whole country; a planter near Natchez was earning $270 per hand each year. The Opelousas and Attakapas districts for sugar, and the Red River bottoms for cotton, he thought, offered the best opportunities because of the cheapness of their lands. As to the journey from North Carolina, he advised that the start be made about the first of September and the course be laid through Knoxville to Nashville. Traveling thence through the Indian country,

[13] F. L. Riley, ed., "The Autobiography of Gideon Lincecum," in the Mississippi Historical Society *Publications*, VIII, 443-519.

safety would be assured by a junction with other migrants. Speed would be greater on horseback, but the route was feasible for vehicles, and a traveler would find a tent and a keg of water conducive to his comfort. The Indians, who were generally short of provisions in spring and summer, would have supplies to spare in autumn; and the prevailing dryness of that season would make the streams and swamps in the path less formidable. An alternative route lay through Georgia; but its saving of distance was offset by the greater expanse of Indian territory to be crossed, the roughness of the road and the frequency of rivers. The viewing of the delta country, he thought, would require three or four months of inspection before a choice of location could safely be made.[14]

The procedure of planters embarking upon long distance migration may be gathered from the letters which General Leonard Covington of Calvert County, Maryland, wrote to his brother and friends who had preceded him to the Natchez district. In August, 1808, finding a prospect of selling his Maryland lands, he formed a project of carrying his sixty slaves to Mississippi and hiring out some of them there until a new plantation should be ready for routine operation. He further contemplated taking with him ten or fifteen families of non-slaveholding whites who were eager to migrate under his guidance and wished employment by him for a season while they cast about for farms of their own. Covington accordingly sent inquiries as to the prevailing rates of hire and the customary feeding and treatment of slaves. He asked whether they were commonly worked only from "sun to sun," and explained his thought by saying, "It is possible that so much labor may be required of hirelings and so little regard may be had for their constitutions as to render them in a few years not only unprofitable but expensive." He asked further whether the slaves there were contented, whether they as universally took wives and husbands and as easily reared children as in Maryland, whether cotton was of more certain yield and sale than tobacco, what was the cost of clearing land

and erecting rough buildings, what the abundance and quality of fruit, and what the nature of the climate.

The replies he received were quite satisfactory, but a failure to sell part of his Maryland lands caused him to leave twenty-six of his slaves in the east. The rest he sent forward with a neighbor's gang. Three white men were in charge, but one of the negroes escaped at Pittsburg and was apparently not recaptured. Covington after detention by the delicacy of his wife's health and by duties in the military service of the United States, set out at the beginning of October, 1809, with his wife and five children, a neighbor named Waters and his family, several other white persons, and eleven slaves. He described his outfit as "the damnedest cavalcade that ever man was burdened with; not less than seven horses compose my troop; they convey a close carriage (Jersey stage), a gig and horse cart, so that my family are transported with comfort and convenience, though at considerable expense. All these odd matters and contrivances I design to take with me to Mississippi if possible. Mr. Waters will also take down his waggon and team." Upon learning that the Ohio was in low water he contemplated journeying by land as far as Louisville; but he embarked at Wheeling instead, and after tedious dragging "through shoals, sandbars and ripples" he reached Cincinnati late in November. When the last letter on the journey was written he was on the point of embarking afresh on a boat so crowded, that in spite of his desire to carry a large stock of provisions he could find room for but a few hundredweight of pork and a few barrels of flour. He apparently reached his destination at the end of the year and established a plantation with part of his negroes, leaving the rest on hire. The approach of the war of 1812 brought distress; cotton was low, bacon was high, and the sale of a slave or two was required in making ends meet. Covington himself was now ordered by the Department of War to take the field in command of dragoons, and in 1813 was killed in a battle beyond the Canadian border. The fate of his family and plantation does not appear in the records.[15]

[15] *Plantation and Frontier*, II, 201-208.

A more successful migration was that of Col. Thomas S. Dabney in 1835. After spending the years of his early manhood on his ancestral tide-water estate, Elmington, in Gloucester County, Virginia, he was prompted to remove by the prospective needs of his rapidly growing family. The justice of his anticipations appears from the fact that his second wife bore him eventually sixteen children, ten of whom survived her. After a land-looking tour through Alabama and Louisiana, Dabney chose a tract in Hinds County, Mississippi, some forty miles east of Vicksburg, where he bought the property of several farmers as the beginning of a plantation which finally engrossed some four thousand acres. Returning to Virginia, he was given a great farewell dinner at Richmond, at which Governor Tyler presided and many speakers congratulated Mississippi upon her gain of such a citizen at Virginia's expense.[16] Several relatives and neighbors resolved to accompany him in the migration. His brother-in-law, Charles Hill, took charge of the carriages and the white families, while Dabney himself had the care of the wagons and the many scores of negroes. The journey was accomplished without mishap in two months of perfect autumn weather. Upon arriving at the new location most of the log houses were found in ruins from a recent hurricane; but new shelters were quickly provided, and in a few months the great plantation, with its force of two hundred slaves, was in routine operation. In the following years Dabney made it a practice to clear about a hundred acres of new ground annually. The land, rich and rolling, was so varied in its qualities and requirements that a general failure of crops was never experienced—the bottoms would thrive in dry seasons, the hill crops in wet, and moderation in rainfall would prosper them all. The small farmers who continued to dwell nearby included Dabney at first in their rustic social functions; but when he carried twenty of his slaves to a house-raising and kept his own hands gloved while directing their work, the beneficiary and his fellows were less grateful for the service than offended at the undemocratic manner of its rendering. When

---

[16] *Richmond Enquirer*, Sept. 22, 1835, reprinted in Susan D. Smedes, *Memorials of a Southern Planter* (2d. ed., Baltimore, 1888), pp. 43-47.

Dabney, furthermore, made no return calls for assistance, the restraint was increased. The rich might patronize the poor in the stratified society of old Virginia; in young Mississippi such patronage was an unpleasant suggestion that stratification was beginning.[17] With the passage of years and the continued influx of planters ready to buy their lands at good prices, such farmers as did not thrive tended to vacate the richer soils. The Natchez-Vicksburg district became largely consolidated into great plantations,[18] and the tract extending thence to Tuscaloosa, as likewise the district about Mongtomery, Alabama, became occupied mostly by smaller plantations on a scale of a dozen or two slaves each,[19] while the non-slaveholders drifted to the southward pine-barrens or the western or northwestern frontiers.

The caravans of migrating planters were occasionally described by travelers in the period. Basil Hall wrote of one which he overtook in South Carolina in 1828: "It . . . did not consist of above thirty persons in all, of whom five-and-twenty at least were slaves. The women and children were stowed away in wagons, moving slowly up a steep, sandy hill; but the curtains being let down we could see nothing of them except an occasional glance of an eye, or a row of teeth as white as snow. In the rear of all came a light covered vehicle, with the master and mistress of the party. Along the roadside, scattered at intervals, we observed the male slaves trudging in front. At the top of all, against the sky line, two men walked together, apparently hand in hand pacing along very sociably. There was something, however, in their attitude, which seemed unusual and constrained. When we came nearer, accordingly, we discovered that this couple were bolted together by a short chain or bar riveted to broad iron clasps secured in like manner round the wrists. 'What have you been doing, my boys,' said our coachman in passing, 'to entitle you to these ruffles?' 'Oh, sir,' cried one of them quite gaily, 'they are the best things in the world to travel with.' The other man said nothing.

[a] Smedes, *Memorials of a Southern Planter*, pp. 42-68.
[18] F. L. Olmsted, *A Journey in the Back Country* (New York, 1860), pp. 20, 28.
[19] *Ibid.*, pp. 160, 161; Robert Russell, *North America* (Edinburgh, 1857), p. 297.

I stopped the carriage and asked one of the slave drivers why these men were chained, and how they came to take the matter so differently. The answer explained the mystery. One of them, it appeared, was married, but his wife belonged to a neighboring planter, not to his master. When the general move was made the proprieter of the female not choosing to part with her, she was necessarily left behind. The wretched husband was therefore shackled to a young unmarried man who having no such tie to draw him back might be more safely trusted on the journey." [20]

Timothy Flint wrote after observing many of these caravans: "The slaves generally seem fond of their masters, and as much delighted and interested in their migration as their masters. It is to me a very pleasing and patriarchal sight." [21] But Edwin L. Godkin, who in his transit of a Mississippi swamp in 1856 saw a company in distress, used the episode as a peg on which to hang an anti-slavery sentiment: "I fell in with an emigrant party on their way to Texas. Their mules had sunk in the mud, . . . the wagons were already embedded as far as the axles. The women of the party, lightly clad in cotton, had walked for miles, knee-deep in water, through the brake, exposed to the pitiless pelting of the storm, and were now crouching forlorn and woe-begone under the shelter of a tree. . . . The men were making feeble attempts to light a fire. . . . 'Colonel,' said one of them as I rode past, 'this is the gate of hell, ain't it?' . . . The hardships the negroes go through who are attached to one of these emigrant parties baffle description. . . . They trudge on foot all day through mud and thicket without rest or respite. . . . Thousands of miles are traversed by these weary wayfarers without their knowing or caring why, urged on by the whip and in the full assurance that no change of place can bring any change to them. . . . Hard work, coarse food, merciless floggings, are all that await them, and all that they can look to. I have never passed them, staggering along in the rear of the wagons at the

[20] Basil Hall, *Travels in North America* (Edinburgh, 1829), III, 128, 129. *See also* for similar scenes, Adam Hodgson, *Letters from North America* (London, 1854), I, 113.
[21] Timothy Flint, *History and Geography of the Western States* (Cincinnati, 1828), p. 11.

close of a long day's march, the weakest furthest in the rear, the strongest already utterly spent, without wondering how Christendom, which eight centuries ago rose in arms for a sentiment, can look so calmly on at so foul and monstrous a wrong as this American slavery." [22] If instead of crossing the Mississippi bottoms and ascribing to slavery the hardships he observed, Godkin had been crossing the Nevada desert that year and had come upon, as many others did, a train of emigrants with its oxen dead, its women and children perishing of thirst, and its men with despairing eyes turned still toward the goldfields of California, would he have inveighed against freedom as the cause? Between Flint's impression of pleasure and Godkin's of gloom no choice need be made, for either description was often exemplified. In general the slaves took the fatigues and the diversions of the route merely as the day's work and the day's play.

Many planters whose points of departure and of destination were accessible to deep water made their transit by sea. Thus on the brig *Calypso* sailing from Norfolk to New Orleans in April, 1819, Benjamin Ballard and Samuel T. Barnes, both of Halifax County, North Carolina, carrying 30 and 196 slaves respectively, wrote on the margins of their manifests, the one "The owner of these slaves is moving to the parish of St. Landry near Opelousas where he has purchased land and intends settling, and is not a dealer in human flesh," the other, "The owner of these slaves is moving to Louisiana to settle, and is not a dealer in human flesh." On the same voyage Augustin Pugh of the adjoining Bertie County carried seventy slaves whose manifest, though it bears no such asseveration, gives evidence that they likewise were not a trader's lot; for some of the negroes were sixty years old, and there were as many children as adults in the parcel. Lots of such sizes as these were of course exceptional. In the packages of manifests now preserved in the Library of Congress the lists of from one to a dozen slaves outnumbered those of fifty or more by perhaps a hundred fold.

[22] Letter of E. L. Godkin to the *London News*, reprinted in the *North American Review*, CLXXXV (1907), 46, 47.

The western cotton belt not only had a greater expanse and richer lands than the eastern, but its cotton tended to have a longer fiber, ranging, particularly in the district of the "bends" of the Mississippi north of Vicksburg, as much as an inch and a quarter in length and commanding a premium in the market. Its far reaching waterways, furthermore, made freighting easy and permitted the planters to devote themselves the more fully to their staple. The people in the main made their own food supplies; yet the market demand of the western cotton belt and the sugar bowl for grain and meat contributed much toward the calling of the northwestern settlements into prosperous existence.[23]

This thriving of the West, however, was largely at the expense of the older plantation states.[24] In 1813 John Randolph wrote: "The whole country watered by the rivers which fall into the Chesapeake is in a state of paralysis. . . . The distress is general and heavy, and I do not see how the people can pay their taxes." And again: "In a few years more, those of us who are alive will move off to Kaintuck or the Mississippi, where corn can be had for sixpence a bushel and pork for a penny a pound. I do not wonder at the rage for emigration. What do the bulk of the people get here that they cannot have there for one fifth the labor in the western country?" Next year, after a visit to his birthplace, he exclaimed: "What a spectacle does our lower country present! Deserted and dismantled country-houses once the seats of cheerfulness and plenty, and the temples of the Most High ruinous and desolate, 'frowning in portentous silence upon the land.'" And in 1819 he wrote from Richmond: "You have no conception of the gloom and distress that pervade this place. There has been nothing like it since 1785 when from the same causes (paper money and a general peace) there was a general depression of everything."[25]

The extreme depression passed, but the conditions prompting emigration were persistent and widespread. News items from

[23] G. S. Callender in the *Quarterly Journal of Economics*, XVII, 111-162.
[24] Edmund Quincy, *Life of Josiah Quincy* (Boston, 1869), p. 336.
[25] H. A. Garland, *Life of John Randolph* (Philadelphia, 1851), II, 15; I, 2; II, 105.

here and there continued for decades to tell of movement in large volume from Tide-water and Piedmont, from the tobacco states and the eastern cotton-belt, and even from Alabama in its turn, for destinations as distant and divergent as Michigan, Missouri and Texas. The communities which suffered cast about for both solace and remedy. An editor in the South Carolina uplands remarked at the beginning of 1833 that if emigration should continue at the rate of the past year the state would become a wilderness; but he noted with grim satisfaction that it was chiefly the "fire-eaters" that were moving out.[26] In 1836 another South Carolinian wrote: "The spirit of emigration is still rife in our community. From this cause we have lost many, and we are destined, we fear, to lose more, of our worthiest citizens." Though efforts to check it were commonly thought futile, he addressed himself to suasion. The movement, said he, is a mistaken one; South Carolina planters should let well enough alone. The West is without doubt the place for wealth, but prosperity is a trial to character. In the West money is everything. Its pursuit, accompanied as it is by baneful speculation, lawlessness, gambling, sabbath-breaking, brawls and violence, prevents moral attainment and mental cultivation. Substantial people should stay in South Carolina to preserve their pristine purity, hospitality, freedom of thought, fearlessness and nobility.[27]

An Alabama spokesman rejoiced in the manual industry of the white people in his state, and said if the negroes were only thinned off it would become a great and prosperous commonwealth.[28] But another Alabamian, A. B. Meek, found reason to eulogize both emigration and slavery. He said the roughness of manners prevalent in the haphazard western aggregation of New Englanders, Virginians, Carolinians and Georgians would prove but a temporary phase. Slavery would be of benefit through its tendency to stratify society, ennoble the upper classes, and give even the poorer whites a stimulating pride of race. "In a few

[26] Sumterville, S. C., *Whig*, Jan. 5, 1833.
[27] "The Spirit of Emigration," signed "A South Carolinian," in the *Southern Literary Journal*, II, 259-262 (June, 1836).
[28] Portland, Ala., *Evening Advertiser*, April 12, 1833.

years," said he, "owing to the operation of this institution upon
our unparalleled natural advantages, we shall be the richest people beneath the bend of the rainbow; and then the arts and the
sciences, which always follow in the train of wealth, will flourish to an extent hitherto unknown on this side of the Atlantic." [29]

As a practical measure to relieve the stress of the older districts a beginning was made in seed selection, manuring and crop
rotation to enhance the harvests; horses were largely replaced by
mules, whose earlier maturity, greater hardihood and longer lives
made their use more economical for plow and wagon work; [30] the
straight furrows of earlier times gave place in the Piedmont
to curving ones which followed the hill contours and when supplemented with occasional grass balks and ditches checked the
scouring of the rains and conserved in some degree the thin
soils of the region; a few textile factories were built to better the
local market for cotton and lower the cost of cloth as well as to
yield profits to their proprietors; the home production of grain
and meat supplies was in some measure increased; and river
and highway improvements and railroad construction were undertaken to lessen the expenses of distant marketing. [31] Some
of these recourses were promptly adopted in the newer settlements also; and others proved of little avail for the time being.
The net effect of the betterments, however, was an appreciable
offsetting of the western advantage; and this, when added to
the love of home, the disrelish of primitive travel and pioneer
life, and the dread of the costs and risks involved in removal,
dissuaded multitudes from the project of migration. The actual
depopulation of the Atlantic states was less than the plaints of
the time would suggest. The volume of emigration was undoubtedly great, and few newcomers came in to fill the gaps.
But the birth rate alone in those generations of ample families
more than replaced the losses year by year in most localities.

[29] *Southern Ladies' Book* (Macon, Ga.), April, 1840.
[30] H. T. Cook, *The Life and Legacy of David R. Williams* (New York, 1916), pp. 166-168.
[31] U. B. Phillips, *History of Transportation in the Eastern Cotton Belt to 1860.*

The sense of loss was in general the product not of actual depletion but of disappointment in the expectation of increase.

The non-slaveholding backwoodsmen formed the vanguard of settlement on each frontier in turn; the small slaveholders followed on their heels and crowded each fertile district until the men who lived by hunting as well as by farming had to push further westward; finally the larger planters with their crowded carriages, their lumbering wagons and their trudging slaves arrived to consolidate the fields of such earlier settlers as would sell. It often seemed to the wayfarer that all the world was on the move. But in the districts of durable soil thousands of men, clinging to their homes, repelled every attack of the western fever.

CHAPTER XI

THE DOMESTIC SLAVE TRADE

IN the New England town of Plymouth in November, 1729, a certain Thompson Phillips who was about to sail for Jamaica exchanged a half interest in his one-legged negro man for a similar share in Isaac Lathrop's negro boy who was to sail with Phillips and be sold on the voyage. Lathrop was meanwhile to teach the man the trade of cordwaining, and was to resell his share to Phillips at the end of a year at a price of £40 sterling.[1] This transaction, which was duly concluded in the following year, suggests the existence of a trade in slaves on a small scale from north to south in colonial times. Another item in the same connection is an advertisement in the Boston *Gazette* of August 17, 1761, offering for sale young slaves just from Africa and proposing to take in exchange "any negro men, strong and hearty though not of the best moral character, which are proper subjects of transportation";[2] and a third instance appears in a letter of James Habersham of Georgia in 1764 telling of his purchase of a parcel of negroes at New York for work on his rice plantation.[3] That the disestablishment of slavery in the North during and after the American Revolution enhanced the exportation of negroes was recited in a Vermont statute of 1787,[4] and is shown by occasional items in Southern archives. One of these is the registry at Savannah of a bill of sale made at New London in 1787 for a mulatto boy "as a servant for the term of ten years only, at the expiration of which time he is to be free."[5] Another is a report from an official at Norfolk to the

[1] Massachusetts Historical Society *Proceedings*, XXIV, 335, 336.
[2] Reprinted in Joshua Coffin, *An Account of Some of the Principal Slave Insurrections* (New York, 1860), p. 15.
[3] "The Letters of James Habersham," in the Georgia Historical Society *Collections*, VI, 22, 23.
[4] *New England Register*, XXIX, 248, citing Vermont *Statutes*, 1787, p. 105.
[5] U. B. Phillips, "Racial Problems, Adjustments and Disturbances in the Ante-bellum South," in *The South in the Building of the Nation*, IV, 218.

Governor of Virginia, in 1795, relating that the captain of a sloop from Boston with three negroes on board pleaded ignorance of the Virginia law against the bringing in of slaves.[6]

The federal census returns show that from 1790 onward the decline in the number of slaves in the Northern states was more than counterbalanced by the increase of their free negroes. This means either that the selling of slaves to the southward was very slight, or that the statistical effect of it was canceled by the northward flight of fugitive slaves and the migration of negroes legally free. There seems to be no evidence that the traffic across Mason and Dixon's line was ever of large dimensions, the following curious item from a New Orleans newspaper in 1818 to the contrary notwithstanding: "Jersey negroes appear to be peculiarly adapted to this market—especially those that bear the mark of Judge Van Winkle, as it is understood that they offer the best opportunity for speculation. We have the right to calculate on large importations in future, from the success which hitherto attended the sale."[7]

The internal trade at the South began to be noticeable about the end of the eighteenth century. A man at Knoxville, Tennessee, in December, 1795, sent notice to a correspondent in Kentucky that he was about to set out with slaves for delivery as agreed upon, and would carry additional ones on speculation; and he concluded by saying "I intend carrying on the business extensively."[8] In 1797 La Rochefoucauld-Liancourt met a "drove of negroes" about one hundred in number,[9] whose owner had abandoned the planting business in the South Carolina uplands and was apparently carrying them to Charleston for sale. In 1799 there was discovered in the Georgia treasury a shortage of some ten thousand dollars which a contemporary news item explained as follows: Mr. Sims, a member of the legislature, having borrowed the money from the treasurer, entrusted it to a certain Speers for the purchase of slaves in Virginia.

[6] *Calendar of Virginia State Papers*, VIII, 255.
[7] Augusta, Ga., *Chronicle*, Aug. 22, 1818, quoting the New Orleans *Chronicle*, July 14, 1818.
[8] Unsigned MS. draft in the Wisconsin Historical Society, Draper collection, printed in *Plantation and Frontier*, II, 55, 56.
[9] La Rochefoucauld-Liancourt, *Travels in the United States*, p. 592.

"Speers accordingly went and purchased a considerable number of negroes; and on his way returning to this state the negroes rose and cut the throats of Speers and another man who accompanied him. The slaves fled, and about ten of them, I think, were killed. In consequence of this misfortune Mr. Sims was rendered unable to raise the money at the time the legislature met." [10]   Another transaction achieved record because of a literary effusion which it prompted. Charles Mott Lide of South Carolina, having inherited a fortune, went to Virginia early in 1802 to buy slaves, and began to establish a sea-island cotton plantation in Georgia. But misfortune in other investments forced him next year to sell his land, slaves and crops to two immigrants from the Bahama Islands. Thereupon, wrote he, "I composed the following valedictory, which breathes something of the tenderness of Ossian." [11] Callous history is not concerned in the farewell to his "sweet asylum," but only in the fact that he bought slaves in Virginia and carried them to Georgia. A grand jury at Alexandria presented as a grievance in 1802, "the practice of persons coming from distant parts of the United States into this district for the purpose of purchasing slaves." [12] Such fugitive items as these make up the whole record of the trade in its early years, and indeed constitute the main body of data upon its career from first to last.

As soon as the African trade was closed, the interstate traffic began to assume the aspect of a regular business though for some years it not only continued to be of small scale but was oftentimes merely incidental in character. That is to say, migrating planters and farmers would in some cases carry extra slaves bought with a view to reselling them at western prices and applying the proceeds toward the expense of their new homesteads. The following advertisement by William Rochel at Natchez in 1810 gives an example of this: "I have upwards of twenty likely Virginia born slaves now in a flat bottomed boat lying in the river at Natchez, for sale cheaper than has been sold here

[10] Charleston, S. C., *City Gazette*, Dec. 21, 1799.
[11] Alexander Gregg, *History of the Old Cheraws* (New York, 1877), pp. 480-482.
[12] Quoted in a speech in Congress in 1829, *Register of Debates*, V, 177.

in years.[13] Part of said negroes I wish to barter for a small farm. My boat may be known by a large cane standing on deck.

The heyday of the trade fell in the piping times of peace and migration from 1815 to 1860. Its greatest activity was just prior to the panic of 1837, for thereafter the flow was held somewhat in check, first by the hard times in the cotton belt and then by an agricultural renaissance in Virginia. A Richmond newspaper reported in the fall of 1836 that estimates by intelligent men placed Virginia's export in the preceding year at 120,000 slaves, of whom at least two thirds had been carried by emigrating owners, and the rest by dealers.[14] This was probably an exaggeration for even the greatest year of the exodus. What the common volume of the commercial transport was can hardly be ascertained from the available data.

The slave trade was partly systematic, partly casual. For local sales every public auctioneer handled slaves along with other property, and in each city there were brokers buying them to sell again or handling them on commission. One of these at New Orleans in 1854 was Thomas Foster who advertised that he would pay the highest prices for sound negroes as well as sell those whom merchants or private citizens might consign him. Expecting to receive negroes throughout the season, he said, he would have a constant stock of mechanics, domestics and field hands; and in addition he would house as many as three hundred slaves at a time, for such as were importing them from other states.[15] Similarly Clark and Grubb, of Whitehall Street in Atlanta, when advertising their business as wholesale grocers, commission merchants and negro brokers, announced that they kept slaves of all classes constantly on hand and were paying the highest market prices for all that might be offered.[16] At Nashville, William L. Boyd, Jr., and R. W. Porter advertised as rival slave dealers in 1854;[17] and in the directory of that city for 1860 E. S. Hawkins, G. H. Hitchings, and Webb, Merrill and Company were also listed in this traffic. At St. Louis in 1859 Corbin

[13] Natchez, Miss., *Weekly Chronicle,* April 2, 1810.
[14] *Niles' Register,* LI, 83 (Oct. 8, 1836), quoting the *Virginia Times.*
[15] *Southern Business Directory* (Charleston, 1854), I, 163.
[16] Atlanta *Intelligencer,* Mch. 7, 1860.
[17] *Southern Business Directory,* II, 131.

Thompson and Bernard M. Lynch were the principal slave dealers. The rates of the latter, according to his placard, were 37½ cents per day for board and 2½ per cent. commission on sales; and all slaves entrusted to his care were to be held at their owners' risk.[18]

On the other hand a rural owner disposed to sell a slave locally would commonly pass the word round among his neighbors or publish a notice in the county newspaper. To this would sometimes be appended a statement that the slave was not to be sent out of the state, or that no dealers need apply. The following is one of many such Maryland items: "Will be sold for cash or good paper, a negro woman, 22 years old, and her two female children. She is sold for want of employment, and will not be sent out of the state. Apply to the editor." [19] In some cases, whether rural or urban, the slave was sent about to find his or her purchaser. In the city of Washington in 1854, for example, a woman, whose husband had been sold South, was furnished with the following document: "The bearer, Mary Jane, and her two daughters, are for sale. They are sold for no earthly fault whatever. She is one of the most ladylike and trustworthy servants I ever knew. She is a first rate parlour servant; can arrange and set out a dinner or party supper with as much taste as the most of white ladies. She is a pretty good mantua maker; can cut out and make vests and pantaloons and roundabouts and joseys for little boys in a first rate manner. Her daughters' ages are eleven and thirteen years, brought up exclusively as house servants. The eldest can sew neatly, both can knit stockings; and all are accustomed to all kinds of house work. They would not be sold to speculators or traders for any price whatever." The price for the three was fixed at $1800, but a memorandum stated that a purchaser taking the daughters at $1000 might have the mother on a month's trial. The girls were duly bought by Dr. Edward Maynard, who we may hope took the mother also at the end of the stipulated month.[20] In the cities a few

[18] H. A. Trexler, *Slavery in Missouri, 1804-1865* (Baltimore, 1914), p. 49.
[19] Charleston, Md., *Telegraph*, Nov. 7, 1828.
[20] MSS. in the New York Public Library, MSS. division, filed under "slavery."

slaves were sold by lottery. One Boulmay, for example, advertised at New Orleans in 1819 that he would sell fifty tickets at twenty dollars each, the lucky drawer to receive his girl Amelia, thirteen years old.[21]

The long distance trade, though open to any who would engage in it, appears to have been conducted mainly by firms plying it steadily. Each of these would have an assembling headquarters with field agents collecting slaves for it, one or more vessels perhaps for the coastwise traffic, and a selling agency at one of the centers of slave demand. The methods followed by some of the purchasing agents, and the local esteem in which they were held, may be gathered by an item written in 1818 at Winchester in the Shenandoah Valley: "Several wretches, whose hearts must be as black as the skins of the unfortunate beings who constitute their inhuman traffic, have for several days been impudently prowling about the streets of this place with labels on their hats exhibiting in conspicuous characters the words 'Cash for negroes.' "[22] That this repugnance was genuine enough to cause local sellers to make large concessions in price in order to keep faithful servants out of the hands of the long-distance traders is evidenced by the following report in 1824 from Hillsborough on the eastern shore of Maryland: "Slaves in this county, and I believe generally on this shore, have always had two prices, viz. a neighbourhood or domestic and a foreign or Southern price. The domestic price has generally been about a third less than the foreign, and sometimes the difference amounts to one half."[23]

The slaves of whom their masters were most eager to be rid were the indolent, the unruly, and those under suspicion. A Creole settler at Mobile wrote in 1748, for example, to a friend living on the Mississippi: "I am sending you l'Eveille and his wife, whom I beg you to sell for me at the best price to be had. If however they will not bring 1,500 francs each, please keep them on your land and make them work. What makes me sell them is that l'Eveille is accused of being the head of a plot of

[21] *Louisiana Courier* (New Orleans), Aug. 17, 1819.
[22] *Virginia Northwestern Gazette*, Aug. 15, 1818.
[23] *American Historical Review*, XIX, 818.

some thirty Mobile slaves to run away. He stoutly denies this; but since there is rarely smoke without fire I think it well to take the precaution." [24] The converse of this is a laconic advertisement at Charleston in 1800: "Wanted to purchase one or two negro men whose characters will not be required." [25] It is probable that offers were not lacking in response.

Some of the slaves dealt in were actually convicted felons sold by the states in which their crimes had been committed. The purchasers of these were generally required to give bond to transport them beyond the limits of the United States; but some of the traders broke their pledges on the chance that their breaches would not be discovered. One of these, a certain W. H. Williams, when found offering his outlawed merchandize of twenty-four convict slaves at New Orleans in 1841, was prosecuted and convicted. His penalty included the forfeiture of the twenty-four slaves, a fine of $500 to the state of Louisiana for each of the felons introduced, and the forfeiture to the state of Virginia of his bond in the amount of $1,000 per slave. The total was reckoned at $48,000.[26]

The slaves whom the dealers preferred to buy for distant sale were "likely negroes from ten to thirty years old." [27] Faithfulness and skill in husbandry were of minor importance, for the trader could give little proof of them to his patrons. Demonstrable talents in artisanry would of course enhance a man's value; and unusual good looks on the part of a young woman might stimulate the bidding of men interested in concubinage. Episodes of the latter sort were occasionally reported; but in at least one instance inquiry on the spot showed that sex was not involved. This was the case of the girl Sarah, who was sold to the highest bidder on the auction block in the rotunda of the St. Louis Hotel at New Orleans in 1841 at a price of eight thousand dollars. The onlookers were set agog, but a newspaper man

---

[24] MS. in private possession, here translated from the French.
[25] Charleston *City Gazette*, Jan. 8, 1800.
[26] *Niles' Register*, LX, 189, quoting the New Orleans *Picayune*, May 2, 1841.
[27] Advertisement in the *Western Carolinian* (Salisbury, N. C.), July 12, 1834.

promptly found that the sale had been made as a mere form in the course of litigation and that the bidding bore no relation to the money which was to change hands.[28] Among the thousands of bills of sale which the present writer has scanned, in every quarter of the South, many have borne record of exceptional prices for men, mostly artisans and "drivers"; but the few women who brought unusually high prices were described in virtually every case as fine seamstresses, parlor maids, laundresses, hotel cooks, and the like. Another indication against the multiplicity of purchases for concubinage is that the great majority of the women listed in these records were bought in family groups. Concubinage itself was fairly frequent, particularly in southern Louisiana; but no frequency of purchases for it as a predominant purpose can be demonstrated from authentic records.

Some of the dealers used public jails, taverns and warehouses for the assembling of their slaves, while others had stockades of their own. That of Franklin and Armfield at Alexandria, managed by the junior member of the firm, was described by a visitor in July, 1835. In addition to a brick residence and office, it comprised two courts, for the men and women respectively, each with whitewashed walls, padlocked gates, cleanly barracks and eating sheds, and a hospital which at this time had no occupants. In the men's yards "the slaves, fifty or sixty in number, were standing or moving about in groups, some amusing themselves with rude sports, and others engaged in conversation which was often interrupted by loud laughter in all the varied tones peculiar to negroes." They were mostly young men, but comprised a few boys of from ten to fifteen years old. In the women's yard the ages ranged similarly, and but one woman had a young child. The slaves were neatly dressed in clothes from a tailor shop within the walls, and additional clothing was already stored ready to be sent with the coffle and issued to its members at the end of the southward journey. In a yard behind the stockade there were wagons and tents made ready for the departure. Shipments were commonly made by the firm once every two

[28] New Orleans *Bee*, Oct. 16, 1841.

months in a vessel for New Orleans, but the present lot was to march overland. Whether by land or sea, the destination was Natchez, where the senior partner managed the selling end of the business. Armfield himself was "a man of fine personal appearance, and of engaging and graceful manners"; and his firm was said to have gained the confidence of all the countryside by its honorable dealings and by its resolute efforts to discourage kidnapping. It was said to be highly esteemed even among the negroes.[29]

Soon afterward this traveler made a short voyage on the Potomac with a trader of a much more vulgar type who was carrying about fifty slaves, mostly women with their children, to Fredericksburg and thence across the Carolinas. Overland, the trader said, he was accustomed to cover some twenty-five miles a day, with the able-bodied slaves on foot and the children in wagons. The former he had found could cover these marches, after the first few days, without much fatigue. His firm, he continued, had formerly sent most of its slaves by sea, but one of the vessels carrying them had been driven to Bermuda, where all the negroes had escaped to land and obtained their freedom under the British flag.[30]

The scale of the coasting transit of slaves may be ascertained from the ship manifests made under the requirements of the congressional act of 1808 and now preserved in large numbers in the manuscripts division of the Library of Congress. Its volume appears to have ranged commonly, between 1815 and 1860, at from two to five thousand slaves a year. Several score of these, or perhaps a few hundred, annually were carried as body servants by their owners when making visits whether to southern cities or to New York or Philadelphia. Of the rest about half were sent or carried without intent of sale. Thus in 1831 James L. Pettigru and Langdon Cheves sent from Charleston to Savannah 85 and 64 slaves respectively of ages ranging from ninety and seventy years to infancy, with obvious purpose to develop newly acquired plantations in Georgia. Most

[29] E. A. Andrews, *Slavery and the Domestic Slave Trade in the United States* (Boston, 1836), pp. 135, 143, 150.
[30] *Ibid.*, pp. 145-149.

of the non-commercial shipments, however, were in lots of from one to a dozen slaves each. The traders' lots, on the other hand, which were commonly of considerable dimensions, may be somewhat safely distinguished by the range of the negroes' ages, with heavy preponderance of those between ten and thirty years, and by the recurrence of shippers' and consignees' names. The Chesapeake ports were the chief points of departure, and New Orleans the great port of entry. Thus in 1819 Abner Robinson at Baltimore shipped a cargo of 99 slaves to William Kenner and Co. at New Orleans, whereas by 1832 Robinson had himself removed to the latter place and was receiving shipments from Henry King at Norfolk. In the latter year Franklin and Armfield sent from Alexandria *via* New Orleans to Isaac Franklin at Natchez three cargoes of 109, 117 and 134 slaves, mainly of course within the traders' ages; R. C. Ballard and Co. sent batches from Norfolk to Franklin at Natchez and to John Hogan and Co. at New Orleans; and William T. Foster, associated with William Rollins who was master of the brig *Ajax,* consigned numerous parcels to various New Orleans correspondents. About 1850 the chief shippers were Joseph Donovan of Baltimore, B. M. and M. L. Campbell of the same place, David Currie of Richmond and G. W. Apperson of Norfolk, each of whom sent each year several shipments of several score slaves to New Orleans. The principal recipients there were Thomas Boudar, John Hogan, W. F. Talbott, Buchanan, Carroll and Co., Masi and Bourk, and Sherman Johnson. The outward manifests from New Orleans show in turn a large maritime distribution from that port, mainly to Galveston and Matagorda Bay. The chief bulk of this was obviously migrant, not commercial; but a considerable dependence of all the smaller Gulf ports and even of Montgomery upon the New Orleans labor market is indicated by occasional manifests bulking heavily in the traders' ages. In 1850 and thereabouts, it is curious to note, there were manifests for perhaps a hundred slaves a year bound for Chagres *en route* for San Francisco. They were for the most part young men carried singly, and were obviously intended to share their masters' adventures in the California gold fields.

Many slaves carried by sea were covered by marine insurance.
Among a number of policies issued by the Louisiana Insurance
Company to William Kenner and Company was one dated
February 18, 1822, on slaves in transit in the brig *Fame*. It
was made out on a printed form of the standard type for the
marine insurance of goods, with the words "on goods" stricken
out and "on slaves" inserted. The risks, specified as assumed
in the printed form were those "of the sea, men of war, fire,
enemies, pirates, rovers, thieves, jettison, letters of mart and
counter-mart, surprisals, taking at sea, arrests, restraints and
detainments of all kings, princes or people of what nation, condition or quality soever, barratry of the master and mariners, and
all other perils, losses and misfortunes that have or shall come
to the hurt, detriment or damage of the said goods or merchandize, or any part thereof." In manuscript was added: "This
insurance is declared to be made on one hundred slaves, valued
at $40,000 and warranted by the insured to be free from insur-
rection, elopement, suicide and natural death." The premium
was one and a quarter per cent. of the forty thousand dollars.[31] That the insurers were not always free from serious
risk is indicated by a New Orleans news item in 1818 relating
that two local insurance companies had recently lost more than
forty thousand dollars in consequence of the robbery of seventy-
two slaves out of a vessel from the Chesapeake by a piratical
boat off the Berry Islands.[32]

Overland coffles were occasionally encountered and described
by travelers. Featherstonhaugh overtook one at daybreak one
morning in southwestern Virginia bound through the Tennessee
Valley and wrote of it as follows: "It was a camp of negro
slave drivers, just packing up to start. They had about three
hundred slaves with them, who had bivouacked the preceding
night in chains in the woods. These they were conducting to
Natchez on the Mississippi River to work upon the sugar plantations in Louisiana. It resembled one of the coffles spoken of
by Mungo Park, except that they had a caravan of nine wagons

[31] Original in private possession.
[32] Augusta, Ga., *Chronicle*, Sept. 23, 1818, quoting the *Orleans Gazette*.

and single-horse carriages for the purpose of conducting the white people and any of the blacks that should fall lame. . . . The female slaves, some of them sitting on logs of wood, while others were standing, and a great many little black children, were warming themselves at the fire of the bivouac. In front of them all, and prepared for the march, stood in double files about two hundred men slaves, manacled and chained to each other." The writer went on to ejaculate upon the horror of "white men with liberty and equality in their mouths," driving black men "to perish in the sugar mills of Louisiana, where the duration of life for a sugar mill hand does not exceed seven years." [33] Sir Charles Lyell, who was less disposed to moralize or to repeat slanders of the Louisiana régime, wrote upon reaching the outskirts of Columbus, Georgia, in January, 1846: "The first sight we saw there was a long line of negroes, men, women and boys, well dressed and very merry, talking and laughing, who stopped to look at our coach. On inquiry we were told that it was a gang of slaves, probably from Virginia, going to the market to be sold." [34] Whether this laughing company wore shackles the writer failed to say.

Some of the slaves in the coffles were peddled to planters and townsmen along the route; the rest were carried to the main distributing centers and there either kept in stock for sale at fixed prices to such customers as might apply, or sold at auction. Oftentimes a family group divided for sale was reunited by purchase. Johann Schoepf observed a prompt consummation of the sort when a cooper being auctioned continually called to the bidders that whoever should buy him must buy his son also, an injunction to which his purchaser duly conformed. [35] Both hardness of heart and shortness of sight would have been involved in the neglect of so ready a means of promoting the workman's equanimity; and the good nature of the competing bidders doubtless made the second purchase easy. More commonly the sellers

[33] G. W. Featherstonhaugh, *Excursion through the Slave States* (London, 1844), I, 120.
[34] Sir Charles Lyell, *A Second Visit to the United States* (New York, 1849), II, 35.
[35] Johann David Schoepf, *Travels in the Confederation, 1783-1784*, A. J. Morrison tr. (Philadelphia, 1911), I, 148.

offered the slaves in family groups outright. By whatever method the sales were made, the slaves of both sexes were subjected to such examination of teeth and limbs as might be desired.[36] Those on the block oftentimes praised their own strength and talents, for it was a matter of pride to fetch high prices. On the other hand if a slave should bear a grudge against his seller, or should hope to be bought only by someone who would expect but light service, he might pretend a disability though he had it not. The purchasers were commonly too shrewd to be deceived in either way; yet they necessarily took risks in every purchase they made. If horse trading is notoriously fertile in deception, slave trading gave opportunity for it in as much greater degree as human nature is more complex and uncertain than equine and harder to fathom from surface indications.

There was also some risk of loss from defects of title. The negroes offered might prove to be kidnapped freemen, or stolen slaves, or to have been illegally sold by their former owners in defraud of mortgagees. The last of these considerations was particularly disquieting in times of financial stress, for suspicion of wholesale frauds then became rife. At the beginning of 1840, for example, the offerings of slaves from Mississippi in large numbers and at bargain prices in the New Orleans market prompted a local editor to warn the citizens against buying cheap slaves who might shortly be seized by the federal marshal at the suit of citizens in other states. A few days afterward the same journal printed in its local news the following: "Many slaves were put up this day at the St. Louis exchange. Few if any were sold. It is very difficult now to find persons willing to buy slaves from Mississippi or Alabama on account of the fears entertained that such property may be already mortgaged to the banks of the above named states. Our moneyed men and specu-

[36] The proceedings at typical slave auctions are narrated by Basil Hall, *Travels in North America* (Edinburgh, 1829), III, 143-145; and by William Chambers, *Things as they are in America* (2d edition, London, 1857), pp. 273-284.

lators are now wide awake. It will take a pretty cunning child to cheat them." [37]

The disesteem in which the slavetraders were held was so great and general in the Southern community as to produce a social ostracism. The prevailing sentiment was expressed, with perhaps a little exaggeration, by D. R. Hundley of Alabama in his analysis of Southern social types: "Preëminent in villainy and a greedy love of filthy lucre stands the hard-hearted negro trader. . . . Some of them, we do not doubt, are conscientious men, but the number is few. Although honest and honorable when they first go into the business, the natural result of their calling seems to corrupt them; for they usually have to deal with the most refractory and brutal of the slave population, since good and honest slaves are rarely permitted to fall into the unscrupulous clutches of the speculator. . . . [He] is outwardly a coarse, ill-bred person, provincial in speech and manners, with a cross-looking phiz, a whiskey-tinctured nose, cold hard-looking eyes, a dirty tobacco-stained mouth, and shabby dress. . . . He is not troubled evidently with a conscience, for although he habitually separates parent from child, brother from sister, and husband from wife, he is yet one of the jolliest dogs alive, and never evinces the least sign of remorse. . . . Almost every sentence he utters is accompanied by an oath. . . . Nearly nine tenths of the slaves he buys and sells are vicious ones sold for crimes and misdemeanors, or otherwise diseased ones sold because of their worthlessness as property. These he purchases for about one half what healthy and honest slaves would cost him; but he sells them as both honest and healthy, mark you! So soon as he has completed his 'gang' he dresses them up in good clothes, makes them comb their kinky heads into some appearance of neatness, rubs oil on their dusky faces to give them a sleek healthy color, gives them a dram occasionally to make them sprightly, and teaches each one the part he or she has to play; and then he sets out for the extreme South. . . . At every village of importance he sojourns for a day or two, each day ranging his 'gang' in a line on the most busy street, and whenever a customer

Louisiana Courier, Feb. 12 and 15, 1840.

makes his appearance the oily speculator button-holes him immediately and begins to descant in the most highfalutin fashion
upon the virtuous lot of darkeys he has for sale. Mrs. Stowe's
Uncle Tom was not a circumstance to any one of the dozens he
points out. So honest! so truthful! so dear to the hearts of their
former masters and mistresses! Ah! Messrs. stock-brokers of
Wall Street—you who are wont to cry up your rotten railroad,
mining, steamboat and other worthless stocks [38]—for ingenious
lying you should take lessons from the Southern negro trader!"
Some of the itinerant traders were said, however, and probably
with truth, to have had silent partners among the most substantial capitalists in the Southern cities.[39]

The social stigma upon slave dealing doubtless enhanced the
profits of the traders by diminishing the competition. The difference in the scales of prices prevailing at any time in the cheapest and the dearest local markets was hardly ever less than
thirty per cent. From such a margin, however, there had to be
deducted not only the cost of feeding, clothing, sheltering, guarding and transporting the slaves for the several months commonly
elapsing between purchase and sale in the trade, but also allowances for such loss as might occur in transit by death, illness,
accident or escape. At some periods, furthermore, slave prices
fell so rapidly that the prospect of profit for the speculator
vanished. At Columbus, Georgia, in December, 1844, for example, it was reported that a coffle from North Carolina had been
marched back for want of buyers.[40] But losses of this sort were
more than offset in the long run by the upward trend of prices
which was in effect throughout the most of the ante-bellum
period. The Southern planters sometimes cut into the business
of the traders by going to the border states to buy and bring home
in person the slaves they needed.[41] The building of railways
speeded the journeys and correspondingly reduced the costs. The
Central of Georgia Railroad improved its service in 1858 by insti-

[38] D. R. Hundley, *Social Relations in our Southern States* (New York,
1860), pp. 139-142.
[39] *Ibid.*, p. 145.
[40] *Federal Union* (Milledgeville, Ga.), Dec. 31, 1844.
[41] Andrews, *Slavery and the Domestic Slave Trade*, p. 171.

tuting a negro sleeping car [42]—an accommodation which apparently no railroad has furnished in the post-bellum decades.

While the traders were held in common contempt, the incidents and effects of their traffic were viewed with mixed emotions. Its employment of shackles was excused only on the ground of necessary precaution. Its breaking up of families was generally deplored, although it was apologized for by thick-and-thin champions of everything Southern with arguments that negro domestic ties were weak at best and that the separations were no more frequent than those suffered by free laborers at the North under the stress of economic necessity. Its drain of money from the districts importing the slaves was regretted as a financial disadvantage. On the other hand, the citizens of the exporting states were disposed to rejoice doubly at being saved from loss by the depreciation of property on their hands [43] and at seeing the negro element in their population begin to dwindle; [44] but even these considerations were in some degree offset, in Virginia at least, by thoughts that the shrinkage of the blacks was not enough to lessen materially the problem of racial adjustments, that it was prime young workmen and women rather than culls who were being sold South, that white immigration was not filling their gaps, and that accordingly land prices were falling as slave prices rose. [45]

Delaware alone among the states below Mason and Dixon's line appears to have made serious effort to restrict the outgoing trade in slaves; but all the states from Maryland and Kentucky to Louisiana legislated from time to time for the prohibition of the inward trade. [46] The enforcement of these laws was called for by citizen after citizen in the public press, as demanded by "every principle of justice. humanity, policy and interest," and particularly on the ground that if the border states were drained

[42] Central of Georgia Railroad Company *Report* for 1859.
[43] *National Intelligencer* (Washington, D. C.), Jan. 19, 1833.
[44] R. R. Howison, *History of Virginia* (Richmond, Va., 1846-1848), II. 519, 520.
[45] Edmund Ruffin, "The Effects of High Prices of Slaves," in *DeBow's Review*, XXVI, 647-657 (June, 1859).
[46] These acts are summarized in W. H. Collins, *Domestic Slave Trade*, chap. 7.

of slaves they would be transferred from the pro-slavery to the anti-slavery group in politics.[47] The state laws could not constitutionally debar traders from the right of transit, and as a rule they did not prohibit citizens from bringing in slaves for their own use. These two apertures, together with the passiveness of the public, made the legislative obstacles of no effect whatever. As to the neighborhood trade within each community, no prohibition was attempted anywhere in the South.

On the whole, instead of hampering migration, as serfdom would have done, the institution of slavery made the negro population much more responsive to new industrial opportunity than if it had been free. The long distance slave trade found its principal function in augmenting the westward movement. No persuasion of the ignorant and inert was required; the fiat of one master set them on the road, and the fiat of another set them to new tasks. The local branch of the trade had its main use in transferring labor from impoverished employers to those with better means, from passive owners to active, and from persons with whom relations might be strained to others whom the negroes might find more congenial. That this last was not negligible is suggested by a series of letters in 1860 from William Capers, overseer on a Savannah River rice plantation, to Charles Manigault his employer, concerning a slave foreman or "driver" named John. In the first of these letters, August 5, Capers expressed pleasure at learning that John, who had in previous years been his lieutenant on another estate, was for sale. He wrote: "Buy him by all means. There is but few negroes more competent than he is, and he was not a drunkard when under my management. . . . In speaking with John he does not answer like a smart negro, but he is quite so. You had better say to him who is to manage him on Savannah." A week later Capers wrote: "John arrived safe and handed me yours of the 9th inst. I congratulate you on the purchase of said negro.

[47] *Louisiana Gazette,* Feb. 25, 1818 and Jan. 29, 1823; *Louisiana Courier,* Jan. 13, 1831; *Georgia Journal* (Milledgeville, Ga.), Dec. 4, 1821, reprinted in *Plantation and Frontier,* II, 67-70; *Federal Union* (Milledgeville, Ga.), Feb. 6, 1847.

He says he is quite satisfied to be here and will do as he has always done 'during the time I have managed him.' No drink will be offered him. All on my part will be done to bring John all right." Finally, on October 15, Capers reported: "I have found John as good a driver as when I left him on Santee. Bad management was the cause of his being sold, and [I] am glad you have been the fortunate man to get him."[48]

Leaving aside for the present, as topics falling more fitly under the economics of slavery, the questions of the market breeding of slaves in the border states and the working of them to death in the lower South, as well as the subject of inflations and depressions in slave prices, it remains to mention the chief defect of the slave trade as an agency for the distribution of labor. This lay in the fact that it dealt only in lifetime service. Employers, it is true, might buy slaves for temporary employment and sell them when the need for their labor was ended; but the fluctuations of slave prices and of the local opportunity to sell those on hand would involve such persons in slave trading risks on a scale eclipsing that of their industrial earnings. The fact that slave hiring prevailed extensively in all the Southern towns demonstrates the eagerness of short term employers to avoid the toils of speculation.

[48] *Plantation and Frontier*, I, 337, 338.

CHAPTER XII

THE COTTON RÉGIME

IT would be hard to overestimate the predominance of the special crops in the industry and interest of the Southern community. For good or ill they have shaped its development from the seventeenth to the twentieth century. Each characteristic area had its own staple, and those districts which had none were scorned by all typical Southern men. The several areas expanded and contracted in response to fluctuations in the relative prices of their products. Thus when cotton was exceptionally high in the early 'twenties many Virginians discarded tobacco in its favor for a few years,[1] and on the Louisiana lands from Baton Rouge to Alexandria, the planters from time to time changed from sugar to cotton and back again.[2] There were local variations also in scale and intensity; but in general the system in each area tended to be steady and fairly uniform. The methods in the several staples, furthermore, while necessarily differing in their details, were so similar in their emphasis upon routine that each reinforced the influence of the others in shaping the industrial organization of the South as a whole.

At the height of the plantation system's career, from 1815 to 1860, indigo production was a thing of the past; hemp was of negligible importance; tobacco was losing in the east what it gained in the west; rice and sea-island cotton were stationary; but sugar was growing in local intensity, and upland cotton was "king" of a rapidly expanding realm. The culture of sugar, tobacco and rice has been described in preceding chapters; that of the fleecy staple requires our present attention.

The outstanding features of the landscape on a short-staple

[1] *Richmond Compiler,* Nov. 25, 1825, and *Alexandria Gazette,* Feb. 11, 1826, quoted in the *Charleston City Gazette,* Dec. 1, 1825 and Feb. 20, 1826; *The American Farmer* (Baltimore, Dec. 29, 1825), VII, 299.
[2] *Hunt's Merchant's Magazine,* IX, 149.

cotton plantation were the gin house and its attendant baling press. The former was commonly a weatherboarded structure some forty feet square, raised about eight feet from the ground by wooden pillars. In the middle of the space on the ground level, a great upright hub bore an iron-cogged pinion and was pierced by a long horizontal beam some three feet from the ground. Draught animals hitched to the ends of this and driven in a circular path would revolve the hub and furnish power for transmission by cogs and belts to the gin on the floor above. At the front of the house were a stair and a platform for unloading seed cotton from the wagons; inside there were bins for storage, as well as a space for operating the gin; and in the rear a lean-to room extending to the ground level received the flying lint and let it settle on the floor. The press, a skeleton structure nearby, had in the center a stout wooden box whose interior length and width determined the height and thickness of the bales but whose depth was more than twice as great as the intended bale's width. The floor, the ends and the upper halves of the sides of the box were built rigidly, but the lower sides were hinged at the bottom, and the lid was a block sliding up and down according as a great screw from above was turned to left or right. The screw, sometimes of cast iron but preferably of wood as being less liable to break under strain without warning, worked through a block mortised into a timber frame above the box, and at its upper end it supported two gaunt beams which sloped downward and outward to a horse path encircling the whole. A cupola roof was generally built on the revolving apex to give a slight shelter to the apparatus; and in some cases a second roof, with the screw penetrating its peak, was built near enough the ground to escape the whirl of the arms. When the contents of the lint room were sufficient for a bale, a strip of bagging was laid upon the floor of the press and another was attached to the face of the raised lid; the sides of the press were then made fast, and the box was filled with cotton. The draught animals at the beam ends were then driven round the path until the descent of the lid packed the lint firmly; whereupon the sides were lowered, the edges of the bagging drawn into place, ropes were passed through transverse slots in the lid and floor and tied round the bale in its bagging, the pressure was released, and the bale was ready for market. Between 1820 and 1860 improvements in the apparatus promoted an increase in the average weight of the bales from 250 to 400 pounds; while in still more recent times the replacement of horse power by steam and the substitution of iron ties for rope have caused the average bale to be yet another hundredweight heavier. The only other distinctive equipment for cotton harvesting comprised cloth bags with shoulder straps, and baskets of three or four bushels capacity woven of white-oak splits to contain the contents of the pickers' bags until carried to the gin house to be weighed at the day's end.

Whether on a one-horse farm or a hundred-hand plantation, the essentials in cotton growing were the same. In an average year a given force of laborers could plant and cultivate about twice as much cotton as it could pick. The acreage to be seeded in the staple was accordingly fixed by a calculation of the harvesting capacity, and enough more land was put into other crops to fill out the spare time of the hands in spring and summer. To this effect it was customary to plant in corn, which required less than half as much work, an acreage at least equal to that in cotton, and to devote the remaining energy to sweet potatoes, peanuts, cow peas and small grain. In 1820 the usual crop in middle Georgia for each full hand was reported at six acres of cotton and eight of corn;[3] but in the following decades during which mules were advantageously substituted for horses and oxen, and the implements of tillage were improved and the harvesters grew more expert, the annual stint was increased to ten acres in cotton and ten in corn.

At the Christmas holiday when the old year's harvest was nearly or quite completed, well managed plantations had their preliminaries for the new crop already in progress. The winter months were devoted to burning canebrakes, clearing underbrush and rolling logs in the new grounds, splitting rails and

[3] *The American Farmer* (Baltimore), II, 359.

ₘending fences, cleaning ditches, spreading manure, knocking down the old cotton and corn stalks, and breaking the soil of the fields to be planted. Some planters broke the fields completely each year and then laid off new rows. Others merely "listed" the fields by first running a furrow with a shovel plow where each cotton or corn row was to be and filling it with a single furrow of a turn plow from either side; then when planting time approached they would break out the remaining balks with plows, turning the soil to the lists and broadening them into rounded plant beds. This latter plan was advocated as giving a firm seed bed while making the field clean of all grass at the planting. The spacing of the cotton rows varied from three to five feet according to the richness of the soil. The policy was to put them at such distance that the plants when full grown would lightly interlace their branches across the middles.

In March the corn fields were commonly planted, not so much because this forehandedness was better for the crop as for the sake of freeing the choicer month of April for the more important planting of cotton. In this operation a narrow plow lightly opened the crests of the beds; cotton seed were drilled somewhat thickly therein; and a shallow covering of earth was given by means of a concave board on a plow stock, or by a harrow, a roller or a small shallow plow.

Within two or three weeks, as soon as the young plants had put forth three or four leaves, thinning and cultivation was begun. Hoe hands, under orders to chop carefully, stirred the crust along the rows and reduced the seedlings to a "double stand," leaving only two plants to grow at each interval of twelve or eighteen inches. The plows then followed, stirring the soil somewhat deeply near the rows. In another fortnight the hoes gave another chopping, cutting down the weaker of each pair of plants, thus reducing the crop to a "single stand"; and where plants were missing they planted fresh seed to fill the gaps. The plows followed again, with broad wings to their shares, to break the crust and kill the grass throughout the middles. Similar alternations of chipping and plowing then ensued until near the end of July, each cultivation shallower than the last in order that the roots of the cotton should not be cut.[4]

When the blossoms were giving place to bolls in midsummer, "lay-by time" was at hand. Cultivation was ended, and the labor was diverted to other tasks until in late August or early September the harvest began. The corn, which had been worked at spare times previously, now had its blades stripped and bundled for fodder; the roads were mended, the gin house and press put in order, the premises in general cleaned up, and perhaps a few spare days given to recreation.

The cotton bolls ripened and opened in series, those near the center of the plant first, then the outer ones on the lower branches, and finally the top crop. If subjected unduly to wind and rain the cotton, drooping in the bolls, would be blown to the ground or tangled with dead leaves or stained with mildew. It was expedient accordingly to send the pickers through the fields as early and as often as there was crop enough open to reward the labor.

Four or five compartments held the contents of each boll; from sixty to eighty bolls were required to yield a pound in the seed; and three or four pounds of seed cotton furnished one pound of lint. When a boll was wide open a deft picker could empty all of its compartments by one snatch of the fingers; and a specially skilled one could keep both hands flying independently, and still exercise the small degree of care necessary to keep the lint fairly free from the trash of the brittle dead calyxes. As to the day's work, a Georgia planter wrote in 1830: "A hand will pick or gather sixty to a hundred pounds of cotton in the seed, with ease, per day. I have heard of some hands gathering a hundred and twenty pounds in a day. The hands on a plantation ought to average sixty-five pounds."[5] But actual records in the following decades made these early pickers appear very inept. On Levin Covington's plantation near Natchez in 1844, in a typical

[4] Cotton Culture is described by M. W. Philips in the *American Agriculturist*, II (New York, 1843), 51, 81, 117, 149; by various writers in J. A. Turner, ed., *The Cotton Planter's Manual* (New York, 1856), chap. I; Harry Hammond, *The Cotton Plant* (U. S. Department of Agriculture, Experiment Station, *Bulletin* 33, 1896); and in the U. S. Census, 1880, vols. V and VI.
[5] *American Farmer*, II, 359.

week of October, Bill averaged 220 pounds a day, Dred 205 pounds, Aggy 215, and Delia 185; and on Saturday of that week all the twenty-eight men and boys together picked an average of 160 pounds, and all the eighteen women and girls an average of 125.[6] But these were dwarfed in turn by the pickings on J. W. Fowler's Prairie plantation, Coahoma County, Mississippi, at the close of the ante-bellum period. In the week of September 12 to 17, 1859, Sandy, Carver and Gilmore each averaged about three hundred pounds a day, and twelve other men and five women ranged above two hundred, while the whole gang of fifty-one men and women, boys and girls average 157 pounds each.[7]

The picking required more perseverance than strength. Dexterity was at a premium, but the labors of the slow, the youthful and the aged were all called into requisition. When the fields were white with their fleece and each day might bring a storm to stop the harvesting, every boll picked might well be a boll saved from destruction. Even the blacksmith was called from his forge and the farmer's children from school to bend their backs in the cotton rows. The women and children picked steadily unless rains drove them in; the men picked as constantly except when the crop was fairly under control and some other task, such as breaking in the corn, called the whole gang for a day to another field or when the gin house crew had to clear the bins by working up their contents to make room for more seed cotton.

In the Piedmont where the yield was lighter the harvest was generally ended by December; but in the western belt, particularly when rains interrupted the work, it often extended far into the new year. Lucien Minor, for example, wrote when traveling through the plantations of northern Alabama, near Huntsville, in December, 1823: "These fields are still white with cotton, which frequently remains unpicked until March or April, when the ground is wanted to plant the next crop."[8] Planters

<hr/>

[6] MS. in the Mississippi Department of History and Archives, Jackson, Miss.
[7] MS. in the possession of W. H. Stovall, Stovall, Miss.
[8] *Atlantic Monthly*, XXVI, 175.

occasionally noted in their journals that for want of pickers the top crop was lost.

As to the yield, an adage was current, that cotton would promise more and do less and promise less and do more than any other green thing that grew. The plants in the earlier stages were very delicate. Rough stirring of the clods would kill them; excess of rain or drought would be likewise fatal; and a choking growth of grass would altogether devastate the field. Improvement of conditions would bring quick recuperation to the surviving stalks, which upon attaining their full growth became quite hardy; but undue moisture would then cause a shedding of the bolls, and the first frost of autumn would stop the further fruiting. The plants, furthermore, were liable to many diseases and insect ravages. In infancy cut-worms might sever the stalks at the base, and lice might sap the vitality; in the full flush of blooming luxuriance, wilt and rust, the latter particularly on older lands, might blight the leaves, or caterpillars in huge armies reduce them to skeletons and blast the prospect; and even when the fruit was formed, boll-worms might consume the substance within, or dry-rot prevent the top crop from ripening. The ante-bellum planters, however, were exempt from the Mexican boll-weevil, the great pest of the cotton belt in the twentieth century.

While every planter had his fat years and lean, and the yield of the belt as a whole alternated between bumper crops and short ones, the industry was in general of such profit as to maintain a continued expansion of its area and a never ending though sometimes hesitating increase of its product. The crop rose from eighty-five million pounds in 1810 to twice as much in 1820; it doubled again by 1830 and more than doubled once more by 1840. Extremely low prices for the staple in the early 'forties and again in 1849 prompted a campaign for crop reduction; and in that decade the increase was only from 830,000,000 to 1,000,-000,000 pounds. But the return of good prices in the 'fifties caused a fresh and huge enlargement to 2,300,000,000 pounds in the final census year of the ante-bellum period. While this was little more than one fourth as great as the crops of sixteen million bales in 1912 and 1915, it was justly reckoned in its time, at home and abroad, a prodigious output. All the rest of the world then produced barely one third as much. The cotton sent abroad made up nearly two thirds of the value of the gross export trade of the United States, while the tobacco export had hardly a tenth of the cotton's worth. In competition with all the other staples, cotton engaged the services of some three fourths of all the country's plantation labor, in addition to the labor of many thousands of white farmers and their families.

The production and sale of the staple engrossed no less of the people's thought than of their work. A traveler who made a zig-zag journey from Charleston to St. Louis in the early months of 1827, found cotton "a plague." At Charleston, said he, the wharves were stacked and the stores and ships packed with the bales, and the four daily papers and all the patrons of the hotel were "teeming with cotton." At Augusta the thoroughfares were thronged with groaning wagons, the warehouses were glutted, the open places were stacked, and the steamboats and barges hidden by their loads. On the road beyond, migrating planters and slaves bound for the west, " 'where the cotton land is not worn out,' " met cotton-laden wagons townward bound, whereupon the price of the staple was the chief theme of roadside conversation. Occasionally a wag would have his jest. The traveler reported a tilt between two wagoners: " 'What's cotton in Augusta?' says the one with a load. . . . 'It's cotton,' says the other. 'I know that,' says the first, 'but what is it?' 'Why,' says the other, 'I tell you it's cotton. Cotton is cotton in Augusta and everywhere else that I ever heard of.' 'I know that as well as you,' says the first, 'but what does cotton bring in Augusta?' 'Why, it brings nothing there, but everybody brings cotton.' " Whereupon the baffled inquirer appropriately relieved his feelings and drove on. At his crossing of the Oconee River the traveler saw pole-boats laden with bales twelve tiers high; at Milledgeville and Macon cotton was the absorbing theme; in the newly opened lands beyond he "found cotton land speculators thicker than locusts in Egypt"; in the neighborhood of Montgomery cotton fields adjoined one another in a solid stretch **for**

fourteen miles along the road; Montgomery was congested beyond the capacity of the boats; and journeying thence to Mobile
he "met and overtook nearly one hundred cotton waggons travelling over a road so bad that a state prisoner could hardly walk
through it to make his escape." As to Mobile, it was "a receptacle monstrous for the article. Look which way you will you
see it, and see it moving; keel boats, steamboats, ships, brigs,
schooners, wharves, stores, and press-houses, all appeared to be
full; and I believe that in the three days I was there, boarding
with about one hundred cotton factors, cotton merchants and
cotton planters, I must have heard the word cotton pronounced
more than three thousand times." New Orleans had a similar
glut.

On the journey up the Mississippi the plaint heard by this traveler from fellow passengers who lived at Natchitoches, was that
they could not get enough boats to bring the cotton down the
Red. The descending steamers and barges on the great river
itself were half of them heavy laden with cotton and at the head
of navigation on the Tennessee, in northwestern Alabama, bales
enough were waiting to fill a dozen boats. "The Tennesseeans,"
said he, "think that no state is of any account but their own;
Kentucky, they say, would be if it could grow cotton, but as it
is, it is good for nothing. They count on forty or fifty thousand
bales going from Nashville this season; that is, if they can get
boats to carry it all." The fleet on the Cumberland River was
doing its utmost, to the discomfort of the passengers; and it was
not until the traveler boarded a steamer for St. Louis at the middle of March, that he escaped the plague which had surrounded
him for seventy days and seventy nights. This boat, at last,
"had not a bale of cotton on board, nor did I hear it named more
than twice in thirty-six hours. . . . I had a pretty tolerable
night's sleep, though I dreamed of cotton."[9]

This obsession was not without its undertone of disquiet.
Foresighted men were apprehensive lest the one-crop system
bring distress to the cotton belt as it had to Virginia. As early

[9] *Georgia Courier* (Augusta, Ga.), Oct. 11, 1827, reprinted in *Plantation
and Frontier*, I, 283-289.

as 1818 a few newspaper editors [10] began to decry the régime; and one of them in 1821 rejoiced in a widespread prevalence of rot in the crop of the preceding year as a blessing, in that it staved off the rapidly nearing time when the staple's price would fall below the cost of production.[11] A marked rise of the price to above twenty cents a pound at the middle of the decade, however, silenced these prophets until a severe decline in the later twenties prompted the sons of Jeremiah to raise their voices again, and the political crisis procured them a partial hearing. Politicians were advocating the home production of cloth and foodstuffs as a demonstration against the protective tariff, while the economists pleaded for diversification for the sake of permanent prosperity, regardless of tariff rates. One of them wrote in 1827: "That we have cultivated cotton, cotton, cotton and bought everything else, has long been our opprobrium. It is time that we should be aroused by some means or other to see that such a course of conduct will inevitably terminate in our ultimate poverty and ruin. Let us manufacture, because it is our best policy. Let us go more on provision crops and less on cotton, because we have had everything about us poor and impoverished long enough. . . . We have good land, unlimited water powers, capital in plenty, and a patriotism which is running over in some places. If the tariff drives us to this, we say, let the name be sacred in all future generations." [12] Next year William Ellison of the South Carolina uplands welcomed even the low price of cotton as a lever [13] which might pry the planters out of the cotton rut and shift them into industries less exhausting to the soil.

But in the breast of the lowlander, William Elliott, the depression of the cotton market produced merely a querulous complaint that the Virginians, by rushing into the industry several years before when the prices were high, had spoiled the market. Each region, said he, ought to devote itself to the staples best suited to its climate and soil; this was the basis of profitable commerce. The proper policy for Virginia and most of North Carolina was

---

[10] Augusta *Chronicle*, Dec. 23, 1818.
[11] *Georgia Journal* (Milledgeville), June 5, 1821.
[12] *Georgia Courier* (Augusta), June 21, 1827.
[13] *Southern Agriculturist*, II, 13.

to give all their labor spared from tobacco to the growing of corn which South Carolina would gladly buy of them if undisturbed in her peaceful concentration upon cotton.[14] The advance of cotton prices throughout most of the thirties suspended the discussion, and the régime went on virtually unchanged. As an evidence of the specialization of the Piedmont in cotton, it was reported in 1836 that in the town of Columbia alone the purchases of bacon during the preceding year had amounted to three and a half million pounds.[15]

The world-wide panic of 1837 began to send prices down, and the specially intense cotton crisis of 1839 broke the market so thoroughly that for five years afterward the producers had to take from five to seven cents a pound for their crops. Planters by thousands were bankrupted, most numerously in the inflated southwest; and thoughtful men everywhere set themselves afresh to study the means of salvation. Edmund Ruffin, the Virginian enthusiast for fertilizers, was employed by the authority of the South Carolina legislature to make an agricultural survey of that state with a view to recommending improvements. Private citizens made experiments on their estates; and the newspapers and the multiplying agricultural journals published their reports and advice. Most prominent among the cotton belt planters who labored in the cause of reform were ex-Governor James H. Hammond of South Carolina, Jethro V. Jones of Georgia, Dr. N. B. Cloud of Alabama, and Dr. Martin W. Philips of Mississippi. Of these, Hammond was chiefly concerned in swamp drainage, hillside terracing, forage increase, and livestock improvement; Jones was a promoter of the breeding of improved strains of cotton; Cloud was a specialist in fertilizing; and Philips was an all-round experimenter and propagandist. Hammond and Philips, who were both spurred to experiments by financial stress, have left voluminous records in print and manuscript. Their careers illustrate the handicaps under which innovators labored.

[14] *Southern Agriculturist*, I, 61.
[15] *Niles' Register*, LI, 46.

Hammond's estate [16] lay on the Carolina side of the Savannah River, some sixteen miles below Augusta. Impressed by the depletion of his upland soils, he made a journey in 1838 through southwestern Georgia and the adjacent portion of Florida in search of a new location; but finding land prices inflated, he returned without making a purchase,[17] and for the time being sought relief at home through the improvement of his methods. He wrote in 1841: "I have tried almost all systems, and unlike most planters do not like what is old. I hardly know anything old in corn or cotton planting but what is wrong." His particular enthusiasm now was for plow cultivation as against the hoe. The best planter within his acquaintance, he said, was Major Twiggs, on the opposite bank of the Savannah, who ran thirty-four plows with but fourteen hoes. Hammond's own plowmen were now nearly as numerous as his full hoe hands, and his crops were on a scale of twenty acres of cotton, ten of corn and two of oats to the plow. He was fertilizing each year a third of his corn acreage with cotton seed, and a twentieth of his cotton with barnyard manure; and he was making a surplus of thirty or forty bushels of corn per hand for sale.[18] This would perhaps have contented him in normal times, but the severe depression of cotton prices drove him to new prognostications and plans. His confidence in the staple was destroyed, he said, and he expected the next crop to break the market forever and force virtually everyone east of the Chattahoochee to abandon the culture. "Here and there," he continued, "a plantation may be found; but to plant an acre that will not yield three hundred pounds net will be folly. I cannot make more than sixty dollars clear to the hand on my whole plantation at seven cents. . . . The western plantations have got fairly under way; Texas is coming in, and the game is up with us." He intended to change his own activities in the main to the raising of cattle and hogs; and he thought also of sending part of his slaves to Louisiana or Texas, with a view to remov-

[16] Described in 1846 in the *American Agriculturist*, VI, 113, 114.
[17] MS. diary, April 13 to May 14, 1838, in Hammond papers, Library of Congress.
[18] Letters of Hammond to William Gilmore Simms, Jan. 27 and Mch. 9, 1841. Hammond's MS. drafts are in the Library of Congress.

ing thither himself after a few years if the project should prove successful.[19] In an address of the same year before the Agricultural Society of South Carolina, he advised those to emigrate who intended to continue producing cotton, and recommended for those who would stay in the Piedmont a diversified husbandry including tobacco but with main emphasis upon cereals and livestock.[20] Again at the end of 1849, he voiced similar views at the first annual fair of the South Carolina Institute. The first phase of the cotton industry, said he, had now passed; and the price henceforward would be fixed by the cost of production, and would yield no great profits even in the most fertile areas. The rich expanses of the Southwest, he thought, could meet the whole world's demand at a cost of less than five cents a pound, for the planters there could produce two thousand pounds of lint per hand while those in the Piedmont could not exceed an average of twelve hundred pounds. This margin of difference would deprive the slaves of their value in South Carolina and cause their owners to send them West, unless the local system of industry should be successfully revolutionized. The remedies he proposed were the fertilization of the soil, the diversification of crops, the promotion of commerce, and the large development of cotton manufacturing.[21]

Hammond found that not only the public but his own sons also, with the exception of Harry, were cool toward his advice and example; and he himself yielded to the temptation of the higher cotton prices in the 'fifties, and while not losing interest in cattle and small grain made cotton and corn his chief reliance. He appears to have salved his conscience in this relapse by devoting part of his income to the reclamation of a great marsh on his estate. He operated two plantations, the one at his home, "Silver Bluff," the other, "Cathwood," near by. The field force on the former comprised in 1850 sixteen plow hands, thirty-four full hoe hands, six three-quarter hands, two

[19] Letter to Isaac W. Hayne, Jan. 21, 1841.
[20] MS. oration in the Library of Congress.
[21] James H. Hammond, *An Address delivered before the South Carolina Institute, at the first annual Fair, on the 20th November, 1849* (Charleston, 1849).

half hands and a water boy, the whole rated at fifty-five **full** hands. At Cathwood the force, similarly grouped, was rated at seventy-one hands; but at either place the force was commonly subject to a deduction of some ten per cent. of its rated strength, on the score of the loss of time by the "breeders and suckers" among the women. In addition to their field strength and the children, of whom no reckoning was made in the schedule of employments, the two plantations together had five stable men, two carpenters, a miller and job worker, a keeper of the boat landing, three nurses and two overseers' cooks; and also thirty-five ditchers in the reclamation work.

At Silver Bluff, the 385 acres in cotton were expected to yield 330 bales of 400 pounds each; the 400 acres in corn had an expectation of 9850 bushels; and 10 acres of rice, 200 bushels. At Cathwood the plantings and expectations were 370 acres in cotton to yield 280 bales, 280 in corn to yield 5000 bushels, 15 in wheat to yield 100 bushels, 11 in rye to yield 50, and 2 in rice to yield 50. In financial results, after earning in 1848 only $4334.91, which met barely half of his plantation and family expenses for the year, his crop sales from 1849 to 1853 ranged from seven to twenty thousand dollars annually in cotton and from one and a half to two and a half thousand dollars in corn. His gross earnings in these five years averaged $16,217.76, while his plantation expenses averaged $5393.87, and his family outlay $6392.67, leaving an average "clear gain per annum," as he called it, of $4431.10. The accounting, however, included no reckoning of interest on the investment or of anything else but money income and outgo. In 1859 Hammond put upon the market his 5500 acres of uplands with their buildings, livestock, implements and feed supplies, together with 140 slaves including 70 full hands. His purpose, it may be surmised, was to confine his further operations to his river bottoms.[22]

Philips, whom a dearth of patients drove early from the practice of medicine, established in the 'thirties a plantation which he named Log Hall, in Hinds County, Mississippi. After nar-

* Hammond MSS., Library of Congress.

rowly escaping the loss of his lands and slaves in 1840 through
his endorsement of other men's notes, he launched into experimental farming and agricultural publication. He procured various fancy breeds of cattle and hogs, only to have most of them
die on his hands. He introduced new sorts of grasses and
unfamiliar vegetables and field crops, rarely with success.
Meanwhile, however, he gained wide reputation through his
many writings in the periodicals, and in the 'fifties he turned this
to some advantage in raising fancy strains of cotton and selling
their seed. His frequent attendance at fairs and conventions
and his devotion to his experiments and to his pen caused him to
rely too heavily upon overseers in the routine conduct of his
plantation. In consequence one or more slaves occasionally
took to the woods; the whole force was frequently in bad health;
and his women, though remarkably fecund, lost most of their
children in infancy. In some degree Philips justified the prevalent scorn of planters for "book farming." [23]

The newspapers and farm journals everywhere printed arguments in the 'forties in behalf of crop diversification, and *De-
Bow's Review*, founded in 1846, joined in the campaign; but the
force of habit, the dearth of marketable substitutes and the
charms of speculation conspired to make all efforts of but temporary avail. The belt was as much absorbed in cotton in the
'fifties as it had ever been before.

Meanwhile considerable improvement had been achieved in
cotton methods. Mules, mainly bred in Tennessee, Kentucky
and Missouri, largely replaced the less effective horses and oxen;
the introduction of horizontal plowing with occasional balks
and hillside ditches, checked the washing of the Piedmont soils;
the use of fertilizers became fairly common; and cotton seed
was better selected. These last items of manures and seed were
the subject of special campaigns. The former was begun as
early as 1808 by the Virginian John Taylor of Caroline in his
"Arator" essays, and was furthered by the publications of Ed-

[23] M. W. Phillips, "Diary," F. L. Riley, ed., in the Mississippi Historical
Society *Publications*, X, 305-481; letters of Philips in the *American Agriculturist, DeBow's Review*, etc., and in J. A. Turner, ed., *The Cotton Planter's Manual*, pp. 98-123.

mund Ruffin and many others. But an adequate available source of fertilizers long remained a problem without solution. Taylor stressed the virtues of dung and rotation; but the dearth of forage hampered the keeping of large stocks of cattle, and soiling crops were thought commonly to yield too little benefit for the expense in labor. Ruffin had great enthusiasm for the marl or phosphate rock of the Carolina coast; but until the introduction in much later decades of a treatment by sulphuric acid this was too little soluble to be really worth while as a plant food. Lime was also praised; but there were no local sources of it in the districts where it was most needed.

Cotton seed, in fact, proved to be the only new fertilizer generally available in moderate abundance prior to the building of the railroads. In early years the seed lay about the gins as refuse until it became a public nuisance. To abate it the village authorities of Sparta, Georgia, for example, adopted in 1807 an ordinance "that the owner of each and every cotton machine within the limits of said town shall remove before the first day of May in each year all seed and damaged cotton that may be about such machines, or dispose of such seed or cotton so as to prevent its unhealthy putrefaction." [24] Soon after this a planter in St. Stephen's Parish, South Carolina, wrote: "We find from experience our cotton seed one of the strongest manures we make use of for our Indian corn; a pint of fresh seed put around or in the corn hole makes the corn produce wonderfully", [25] but it was not until the lapse of another decade or two that such practice became widespread. In the thirties Harriet Martineau and J. S. Buckingham noted that in Alabama the seed was being strewn as manure on a large scale.[26] As an improvement of method the seed was now being given in many cases a preliminary rotting in compost heaps, with a consequent speeding of its availability as plant food;[27] and cotton seed rose to

[24] *Farmer's Gazette* (Sparta, Ga.), Jan. 31, 1807.
[25] Letter of John Palmer. Dec. 3, 1808, to David Ramsay. MS. in the Charleston Library.
[26] Harriet Martineau, *Retrospect of Western Travel* (London, 1838), I, 218; I. S. Buckingham, *The Slave States of America* (London, 1842), I, 257.
[27] D. R. Williams of South Carolina described his own practice to this effect in an essay of 1825 contributed to the *American Farmer* and re-

such esteem as a fertilizer for general purposes that many planters rated it to be worth from sixteen to twenty-five cents a bushel of twenty-five pounds.[28]   As early as 1830, furthermore a beginning was made in extracting cottonseed oil for use both in painting and illumination, and also in utilizing the by-product of cottonseed meal as a cattle feed.[29]   By the 'fifties the oil was coming to be an unheralded substitute for olive oil in table use; but the improvements which later decades were to introduce in its extraction and refining were necessary for the raising of the manufacture to the scale of a substantial industry.

The importation of fertilizers began with guano. This material, the dried droppings of countless birds, was discovered in the early 'forties on islands off the coast of Peru;[30] and it promptly rose to such high esteem in England that, according to an American news item, Lloyd's listed for 1845 not less than a thousand British vessels as having sailed in search of guano cargoes. The use of it in the United States began about that year; and nowhere was its reception more eager than in the upland cotton belt.   Its price was about fifty dollars a ton in the seaports.   To stimulate the use of fertilizers, the Central of Georgia Railroad Company announced in 1858 that it would carry all manures for any distance on its line in carload lots at a flat rate of two dollars per ton; and the connecting roads concurred in this policy. In consequence the Central of Georgia carried nearly two thousand tons of guano in 1859, and more than nine thousand tons in 1860, besides lesser quantities of lime, salt and bone dust. The superintendent reported that while the rate failed to cover the cost of transportation, the effect in increasing the amount of cotton to be freighted, and in checking emigration, fully compensated the road.[31]   A contributor to the *North American Review* in January, 1861, wrote: "The use of guano is increasing.   The

printed in H. T. Cook, *The Life and Legacy of David R. Williams* (New York, 1916), pp. 226, 227.
[28] J. A. Turner, ed., *Cotton Planter's Manual*, p. 99; Robert Russell, *North America*, p. 269.
[29] *Southern Agriculturist*, II, 563; *American Farmer*, II, 98; H. T. Cook, *Life and Legacy of David R. Williams*, pp. 197-209.
[30] *American Agriculturist*, III, 283.
[31] Central of Georgia Railroad Company *Reports*, 1858-1860.

average return for each pound used in the cotton field is estimated to be a pound and a half of cotton; and the planter who could raise but three bales to the hand on twelve acres of exhausted soil has in some instances by this appliance realized ten bales from the same force and area. In North Carolina guano is reported to accelerate the growth of the plant, and this encourages the culture on the northern border of the cotton-field, where early frosts have proved injurious."

Widespread interest in agricultural improvement was reported by *DeBow's Review* in the 'fifties, taking the form partly of local and general fairs, partly of efforts at invention. A citizen of Alabama, for example, announced success in devising a cotton picking machine; but as in many subsequent cases in the same premises, the proclamation was premature.

As to improved breeds of cotton, public interest appears to have begun about 1820 in consequence of surprisingly good results from seed newly procured from Mexico. These were in a few years widely distributed under the name of Petit Gulf cotton. Colonel Vick of Mississippi then began to breed strains from selected seed; and others here and there followed his example, most of them apparently using the Mexican type. The more dignified of the planters who prided themselves on selling nothing but cotton, would distribute among their friends parcels of seed from any specially fine plants they might encounter in their fields, and make little ado about it. Men of a more flamboyant sort, such as M. W. Philips, contemning such "ruffle-shirt cant," would christen their strains with attractive names, publish their virtues as best they might, and offer their fancy seed for sale at fancy prices. Thus in 1837 the Twin-seed or Okra cotton was in vogue, selling at many places for five dollars a quart. In 1839 this was eclipsed by the Alvarado strain, which its sponsors computed from an instance of one heavily fruited stalk nine feet high and others not so prodigious, might yield three thousand pounds per acre.[32] Single Alvarado seeds were sold at fifty cents each, or a bushel might be had at $160. In the succeeding years Vick's Hundred Seed, Brown's, Pitt's,

[32] *Southern Banner* (Athens, Ga.), Sept. 20, 1839.

Prolific, Sugar Loaf, Guatemala, Cluster, Hogan's, Banana, Pomegranate, Dean, Multibolus, Mammoth, Mastodon and many others competed for attention and sale. Some proved worth while either in increasing the yield, or in producing larger bolls and thereby speeding the harvest, or in reducing the proportionate weight of the seed and increasing that of the lint; but the test of planting proved most of them to be merely commonplace and not worth the cost of carriage. Extreme prices for seed of any strain were of course obtainable only for the first year or two; and the temptation to make fraudulent announcement of a wonder-working new type was not always resisted. Honest breeders improved the yield considerably; but the succession of hoaxes roused abundant skepticism. In 1853 a certain Miller of Mississippi confided to the public the fact that he had discovered by chance a strain which would yield three hundred pounds more of seed cotton per acre than any other sort within his knowledge, and he alluringly named it Accidental Poor Land Cotton. John Farrar of the new railroad town Atlanta was thereby moved to irony. "This kind of cotton," he wrote in a public letter, "would run a three million bale crop up to more than four millions; and this would reduce the price probably to four or five cents. Don't you see, Mr. Miller, that we had better let you keep and plant your seed? You say that you had rather plant your crop with them than take a dollar a pint. . . . Let us alone, friend, we are doing pretty well— we might do worse." [33]

In the sea-island branch of the cotton industry the methods differed considerably from those in producing the shorter staple. Seed selection was much more commonly practiced, and extraordinary care was taken in ginning and packing the harvest. The earliest and favorite lands for this crop were those of exceedingly light soil on the islands fringing the coast of Georgia and South Carolina. At first the tangle of live-oak and palmetto roots discouraged the use of the plow; and afterward the need of heavy fertilization with swamp mud and seaweed kept the acreage so small in proportion to the laborers that hoes contin-

* J. A. Turner, ed., *Cotton Planter's Manual*, p. 98-128.

ued to be the prevalent means of tillage. Operations were commonly on the basis of six or seven acres to the hand, half in cotton and the rest in corn and sweet potatoes. In the swamps on the mainland into which this crop was afterwards extended, the use of the plow permitted the doubling of the area per hand; but the product of the swamp lands was apparently never of the first grade.

The fields were furrowed at five-foot intervals during the winter, bedded in early spring, planted in late April or early May, cultivated until the end of July, and harvested from September to December. The bolls opened but narrowly and the fields had to be reaped frequently to save the precious lint from damage by the weather. Accordingly the pickers are said to have averaged no more than twenty-five pounds a day. The preparation for market required the greatest painstaking of all. First the seed cotton was dried on a scaffold; next it was whipped for the removal of trash and sand; then it was carefully sorted into grades by color and fineness; then it went to the roller gins, whence the lint was spread upon tables where women picked out every stained or matted bit of the fiber; and finally when gently packed into sewn bags it was ready for market. A few gin houses were equipped in the later decades with steam power; but most planters retained the system of a treadle for each pair of rollers as the surest safeguard of the delicate filaments. A plantation gin house was accordingly a simple barn with perhaps a dozen or two foot-power gins, a separate room for the whipping, a number of tables for the sorting and moting, and a round hole in the floor to hold open the mouth of the long bag suspended for the packing.[34] In preparing a standard bale of three hundred pounds, it was reckoned that the work required of the laborers at the gin house was as follows: the dryer, one day; the whipper, two days; the sorters, at fifty pounds of seed cotton per day for

[34] The culture and apparatus are described by W. B. Seabrook, *Memoir on Cotton*, pp. 23-25; Thomas Spaulding in the *American Agriculturist*, III, 244-246; R. F. W. Allston, *Essay on Sea Coast Crops* (Charleston, 1854), reprinted in *DeBow's Review*, XVI, 589-615; J. A. Turner, ed., *Cotton Planter's Manual*, pp. 131-136. The routine of operations is illustrated in the diary of Thomas P. Ravenel, of Woodboo plantation, 1847-1850, printed in *Plantation and Frontier*, I, 195-208.

each, thirty days; the ginners, each taking 125 pounds in the seed per day and delivering therefrom 25 pounds of lint, twelve days; the moters, at 43 pounds, seven days; the inspector and packer, two days; total fifty-four days.

The roller gin was described in a most untechnical manner by Basil Hall: "It consists of two little wooden rollers, each about as thick as a man's thumb, placed horizontally and touching each other. On these being put into rapid motion, handfulls of the cotton are cast upon them, which of course are immediately sucked in. . . . A sort of comb fitted with iron teeth . . . is made to wag up and down with considerable velocity in front of the rollers. This rugged comb, which is equal in length to the rollers, lies parallel to them, with the sharp ends of its teeth almost in contact with them. By the quick wagging motion given to this comb by the machinery, the buds of cotton cast upon the rollers are torn open just as they are beginning to be sucked in. The seeds, now released . . . fly off like sparks to the right and left, while the cotton itself passes between the rollers." [35]

As to yields and proceeds, a planter on the Georgia seaboard analyzed his experience from 1830 to 1847 as follows: the harvest average per acre ranged from 68 pounds of lint in 1846 to 223 pounds in 1842, with a general average for the whole period of 137 pounds; the crop's average price per pound ranged from 14 cents in 1847 to 41 cents in 1838, with a general average of 23½ cents; and the net proceeds per hand were highest at $137 in 1835, lowest at $41 in 1836, and averaged $83 for the eighteen years.[36]

In the cotton belt as a whole the census takers of 1850 enumerated 74,031 farms and plantations each producing five bales or more,[37] and they reckoned the crop at 2,445,793 bales of four hundred pounds each. Assuming that five bales were commonly the product of one full hand, and leaving aside a tenth of the gross output as grown perhaps on farms where the cotton was not the main product, it appears that the cotton farms and plan-

[35] Basil Hall, *Travels in North America* (Edinburgh, 1829), III, 221, 222.
[36] J. A. Turner, ed., *Cotton Planter's Manual*, pp. 128, 129.
[37] *Compendium of the Seventh Census*, p. 178

tations averaged some thirty bales each, and employed on the average about six full hands. That is to say, there were very many more small farms than large plantations devoted to cotton; and among the plantations, furthermore, it appears that very few were upon a scale entitling them to be called great, for the nature of the industry did not encourage the engrossment of more than sixty laborers under a single manager.[38] It is true that some proprietors operated on a much larger scale than this. It was reported in 1859, for example, that Joseph Bond of Georgia had marketed 2199 bales of his produce, that numerous Louisiana planters, particularly about Concordia Parish, commonly exceeded that output; that Dr. Duncan of Mississippi had a crop of 3000 bales; and that L. R. Marshall, who lived at Natchez and had plantations in Louisiana, Mississippi and Arkansas, was accustomed to make more than four thousand bales.[39] The explanation lies of course in the possession by such men of several more or less independent plantations of manageable size. Bond's estate, for example, comprised not less than six plantations in and about Lee County in southwestern Georgia, while his home was in the town of Macon. The areas of these, whether cleared or in forest, ranged from 1305 to 4756 acres.[40] But however large may have been the outputs of exceptionally great planters, the fact remains on the other hand that virtually half of the total cotton crop each year was made by farmers whose slaves were on the average hardly more numerous than the white members of their own families. The plantation system nevertheless dominated the régime.

The British and French spinners, solicitous for their supply of material, attempted at various times and places during the ante-bellum period to enlarge the production of cotton where it was already established and to introduce it into new regions. The result was a complete failure to lessen the predominance of the United States as a source. India, Egypt and Brazil might enlarge their outputs considerably if the rates in the market were

[38] *DeBow's Review*, VIII, 16.
[39] *Ibid.*, XXVI, 581.
[40] Advertisement of Bond's executors offering the plantations for sale in the *Federal Union* (Milledgeville, Ga.), Nov. 8, 1859.

raised to twice or thrice their wonted levels; but so long as the price held a moderate range the leadership of the American cotton belt could not be impaired, for its facilities were unequaled. Its long growing season, hot in summer by day and night, was perfectly congenial to the plant, its dry autumns permitted the reaping of full harvests, and its frosty winters decimated the insect pests. Its soil was abundant, its skilled managers were in full supply, its culture was well systematized, and its labor adequate for the demand. To these facilities there was added in the Southern thought of the time, as no less essential for the permanence of the cotton belt's primacy, the plantation system and the institution of slavery.

CHAPTER XIII

TYPES OF LARGE PLANTATIONS

THE tone and method of a plantation were determined partly by the crop and the lie of the land, partly by the characters of the master and his men, partly by the local tradition. Some communities operated on the basis of time-work, or the gang system; others on piece-work or the task system. The former was earlier begun and far more widely spread, for Sir Thomas Dale used it in drilling the Jamestown settlers at their work, it was adopted in turn on the "particular" and private plantations thereabout, and it was spread by the migration of the sons and grandsons of Virginia throughout the middle and western South as far as Missouri and Texas. The task system, on the other hand, was almost wholly confined to the rice coast.

The gang method was adaptable to operations on any scale. If a proprietor were of the great majority who had but one or two families of slaves, he and his sons commonly labored alongside the blacks, giving not less than step for step at the plow and stroke for stroke with the hoe. If there were a dozen or two working hands, the master, and perhaps the son, instead of laboring manually would superintend the work of the plow and hoe gangs. If the slaves numbered several score the master and his family might live in leisure comparative or complete, while delegating the field supervision to an overseer, aided perhaps by one or more slave foremen. When an estate was inherited by minor children or scattered heirs, or where a single proprietor had several plantations, an overseer would be put into full charge of an establishment so far as the routine work was concerned; and when the plantations in one ownership were quite numerous or of a great scale a steward might be employed to supervise the several overseers. Thus in the latter part of the eighteenth century, Robert Carter of Nomoni Hall on the Potomac had a steward to assist in the administration of his many scattered properties, and Washington after dividing the Mount Vernon lands into several units had an overseer upon each and a steward for the whole during his own absence in the public service. The neighboring estate of Gunston Hall, belonging to George Mason, was likewise divided into several units for the sake of more detailed supervision. Even the 103 slaves of James Mercer, another neighbor, were distributed on four plantations under the management in 1771 of Thomas Oliver. Of these there were 54 slaves on Marlborough, 19 on Acquia, 12 on Belviderra and 9 on Accokeek, besides 9 hired for work elsewhere. Of the 94 not hired out, 64 were field workers. Nearly all the rest, comprising the house servants, the young children, the invalids and the superannuated, were lodged on Marlborough, which was of course the owner's "home place." Each of the four units had its implements of husbandry, and three of them had tobacco houses; but the barn and stables were concentrated on Marlborough. This indicates that the four plantations were parts of a single tract so poor in soil that only pockets here and there would repay cultivation.[1] This presumption is reinforced by an advertisement which Mercer published in 1767: "Wanted soon, . . . a farmer who will undertake the management of about 80 slaves, all settled within six miles of each other, to be employed in making of grain." [2]   In such a case the superintendent would combine the functions of a regular overseer on the home place with those of a "riding boss" inspecting the work of the three small outlying squads from time to time. Grain crops would facilitate this by giving more frequent intermissions than tobacco in the routine. The Mercer estate might indeed be

[1] Robert Carter's plantation affairs are noted in Philip V. Fithian, *Journal and Letters* (Princeton, N. J., 1900) ; the Gunston Hall estate is described in Kate M. Rowland, *Life of George Mason* (New York, 1892), I, 98-102; many documents concerning Mt. Vernon are among the George Washington MSS. in the Library of Congress, and Washington's letters, 1793-179 , to his steward are printed in the Long Island Historical Society *Memoirs* v. 4; of James Mercer's establishments an inventory taken in 1771 is reproduced in *Plantation and Frontier*, I, 249.

[2] *Virginia Gazette* (Williamsburg, Va.), Oct. 22, 1767, reprinted in *Plantation and Frontier*, I, 133.

more correctly described as a plantation and three subsidiary farms than as a group of four plantations. The occurrence of tobacco houses in the inventory and of grain crops alone in the advertisement shows a recent abandonment of the tobacco staple; and the fact of Mercer's financial embarrassment [3] suggests, what was common knowledge, that the plantation system was ill suited to grain production as a central industry.

The organization and routine of the large plantations on the James River in the period of an agricultural renaissance are illustrated in the inventory and work journal of Belmead, in Powhatan County, owned by Philip St. George Cocke and superintended by S. P. Collier.[4] At the beginning of 1854 the 125 slaves were scheduled as follows: the domestic staff comprised a butler, two waiters, four housemaids, a nurse, a laundress, a seamstress, a dairy maid and a gardener; the field corps had eight plowmen, ten male and twelve female hoe hands, two wagoners and four ox drivers, with two cooks attached to its service; the stable and pasture staff embraced a carriage driver, a hostler, a stable boy, a shepherd, a cowherd and a hog herd; in outdoor crafts there were two carpenters and five stone masons; in indoor industries a miller, two blacksmiths, two shoemakers, five women spinners and a woman weaver; and in addition there were forty-five children, one invalid, a nurse for the sick, and an old man and two old women hired off the place, and finally Nancy for whom no age, value or classification is given. The classified workers comprised none younger than sixteen years except the stable boy of eleven, a waiter of twelve, and perhaps some of the housemaids and spinners whose ages are not recorded. At the other extreme there were apparently no slaves on the plantation above sixty years old except Randal, a stone mason, who in spite of his sixty-six years was valued at $300, and the following who had no appraisable value: Old Jim the shepherd, Old Maria the dairy maid, and perhaps two of the spinners. The highest appraisal, $800, was given to Pay-

[3] S. M. Hamilton ed., *Letters to Washington*, IV, 286.
[4] These records are in the possession of Wm. Bridges of Richmond, Va. For copies of them, as well as for many other valuable items, I am indebted to Alfred H. Stone of Dunleith, Miss.

ton, an ox driver, twenty-eight years old. The $700 class comprised six plowmen, five field hands, the three remaining ox drivers, both wagoners, both blacksmiths, the carriage driver, four stone masons, a carpenter, and Ned the twenty-eight year old invalid whose illness cannot have been chronic. The other working men ranged between $250 and $500 except the two shoemakers whose rating was only $200 each. None of the women were appraised above $400, which was the rating also of the twelve and thirteen year old boys. The youngest children were valued at $100 each. These ratings were all quite conservative for that period. The fact that an ox driver overtopped all others in appraisal suggests that the artisans were of little skill. The masons, the carpenters and various other specialists were doubtless impressed as field hands on occasion.

The livestock comprised twelve mules, nine work horses, a stallion, a brood mare, four colts, six pleasure horses and "William's team" of five head; sixteen work oxen, a beef ox, two bulls, twenty-three cows, and twenty-six calves; 150 sheep and 115 swine. The implements included two reaping machines, three horse rakes, two wheat drills, two straw cutters, three wheat fans, and a corn sheller; one two-horse and four four-horse wagons, two horse carts and four ox carts; nine one-horse and twelve two-horse plows, six colters, six cultivators, eight harrows, two earth scoops, and many scythes, cradles, hoes, pole-axes and miscellaneous farm implements as well as a loom and six spinning wheels.

The bottom lands of Belmead appear to have been cultivated in a rotation of tobacco and corn the first year, wheat the second and clover the third, while the uplands had longer rotations with more frequent crops of clover and occasional interspersions of oats. The work journal of 1854 shows how the gang dove-tailed the planting, cultivation, and harvesting of the several crops and the general upkeep of the plantation.

On specially moist days from January to the middle of April all hands were called to the tobacco houses to strip and prize the cured crop; when the ground was frozen they split and hauled firewood and rails, built fences, hauled stone to line the ditches or build walls and culverts, hauled wheat to the mill, tobacco and flour to the boat landing, and guano, land plaster, barnyard manure and straw to the fields intended for the coming tobacco crop; and in milder dry weather they spread and plowed in these fertilizers, prepared the tobacco seed bed by heaping and burning brush thereon and spading it mellow, and also sowed clover and oats in their appointed fields. In April also the potato patch and the corn fields were prepared, and the corn planted; and the tobacco bed was seeded at the middle of the month. In early May the corn began to be plowed, and the soil of the tobacco fields drawn by hoes into hills with additional manure in their centers. From the end of May until as late as need be in July the occurrence of every rain sent all hands to setting the tobacco seedlings in their hills at top speed as long as the ground stayed wet enough to give prospect of success in the process. In the interims the corn cultivation was continued, hay was harvested in the clover fields and the meadows, and the tobacco fields first planted began to be scraped with hoe and plow. The latter half of June was devoted mainly to the harvesting of small grain with the two reaping machines and the twelve cradles; and for the following two months the main labor force was divided between threshing the wheat and plowing, hoeing, worming and suckering the tobacco, while the expert Daniel was day after day steadily topping the plants. In late August the plows began breaking the fallow fields for wheat. Early in September the cutting and housing of tobacco began, and continued at intervals in good weather until the middle of October. Then the corn was harvested and the sowing of wheat was the chief concern until the end of November when winter plowing was begun for the next year's tobacco. Two days in December were devoted to the housing of ice; and Christmas week, as well as Easter Monday and a day or two in summer and fall, brought leisure. Throughout the year the overseer inspected the negroes' houses and yards every Sunday morning and regularly reported them in good order.

The greatest of the tobacco planters in this period was Samuel Hairston, whose many plantations lying in the upper Piedmont on both sides of the Virginia-North Carolina boundary were reported in 1854 to have slave populations aggregating some 1600 souls, and whose gardens at his homestead in Henry County, Virginia, were likened to paradise. Of his methods of management nothing more is known than that his overseers were systematically superintended and that his negroes were commonly both fed and clothed with the products of the plantations themselves.[5]

In the eastern cotton belt a notable establishment of earlier decades was that of Governor David R. Williams, who began operations with about a hundred slaves in Chesterfield County, South Carolina, near the beginning of the nineteenth century and increased their number fivefold before his death in 1830. While each of his four plantations gave adequate yields of the staple as well as furnishing their own full supplies of corn and pork, the central feature and the chief source of prosperity was a great bottom tract safeguarded from the floods of the Pee Dee by a levee along the river front. The building of this embankment was but one of many enterprises which Williams undertook in the time spared from his varied political and military services. Others were the improvement of manuring methods, the breeding of mules, the building of public bridges, the erection and management of a textile factory, the launching of a cottonseed oil mill, of which his talents might have made a success even in that early time had not his untimely death intervened. The prosperity of Williams' main business in the face of his multifarious diversions proves that his plantation affairs were administered in thorough fashion. His capable wife must have supplemented the husband and his overseers constantly and powerfully in the conduct of the routine. The neighboring plantation of a kinsman, Benjamin F. Williams, was likewise notable in after years for its highly improved upland fields as well as for the excellent specialized work of its slave craftsmen.[6]

[5] William Chambers, *American Slavery and Colour* (London, 1857), pp. 194, 195, quoting a Richmond newspaper of 1854.
[6] Harvey T. Cooke, *The Life and Legacy of David Rogerson Williams* (New York, 1916), chaps. XIV, XVI, XIX, XX, XXV. This book, though bearing a New York imprint, is actually published, as I have been at pains to learn, by Mr. J. W. Norwood of Greenville, South Carolina.

In the fertile bottoms on the Congaree River not far above Columbia, lay the well famed estate of Colonel Wade Hampton, which in 1846 had some sixteen hundred acres of cotton and half as much of corn. The traveler, when reaching it after long faring past the slackly kept fields and premises common in the region, felt equal enthusiasm for the drainage and the fencing, the avenues, the mansion and the mill, the stud of blooded horses, the herd of Durham cattle, the flock of long-wooled sheep, and the pens of Berkshire pigs.[7] Senator McDuffie's plantation in the further uplands of the Abbeville district was likewise prosperous though on a somewhat smaller scale. Accretions had enlarged it from three hundred acres in 1821 to five thousand in 1847, when it had 147 slaves of all ages. Many of these were devoted to indoor employments, and seventy were field workers using twenty-four mules. The 750 acres in cotton commonly yielded crops of a thousand pounds in the seed; the 325 acres in corn gave twenty-five or thirty bushels; the 300 in oats, fifteen bushels; and ten acres in peas, potatoes and squashes yielded their proportionate contribution.[8]

The conduct and earnings of a cotton plantation fairly typical among those of large scale, may be gathered from the overseer's letters and factor's accounts relating to Retreat, which lay in Jefferson County, Georgia. This was one of several establishments founded by Alexander Telfair of Savannah and inherited by his two daughters, one of whom became the wife of W. B. Hodgson. For many years Elisha Cain was its overseer. The first glimpse which the correspondence affords is in the fall of 1829, some years after Cain had taken charge. He then wrote to Telfair that many of the negroes young and old had recently been ill with fever, but most of them had recovered without a physician's aid. He reported further that a slave named John had run away "for no other cause than that he did not feel disposed to be governed by the same rules and regulations that the

[7] Described by R. L. Allen in the *American Agriculturist*, VI, 20, 21.
[8] *DeBow's Review*, VI, 149.

other negroes on the land are governed by." Shortly afterward John returned and showed willingness to do his duty. But now Cain encountered a new sort of trouble. He wrote Telfair in January, 1830: "Your negroes have a disease now among them that I am fully at a loss to know what I had best to do. Two of them are down with the venereal disease, Die and Sary. Doctor Jenkins has been attending Die four weeks, and very little alteration as I can learn. It is very hard to get the truth; but from what I can learn, Sary got it from Friday." A note appended to this letter, presumably by Telfair, reads: "Friday is the house servant sent to Retreat every summer. I have all the servants examined before they leave Savannah."

In a letter of February, 1831, Cain described his winter work and his summer plans. The teams had hauled away nearly all the cotton crop of 205 bales; the hog killing had yielded thirteen thousand pounds of pork, from which some of the bacon and lard was to be sent to Telfair's town house; the cotton seed were abundant and easily handled, but they were thought good for fertilizing corn only; the stable and cowpen manure was embarrassingly plentiful in view of the pressure of work for the mules and oxen; and the encumbrance of logs and brush on the fields intended for cotton was straining all the labor available to clear them. The sheep, he continued, had not had many lambs; and many of the pigs had died in spite of care and feeding; but "the negroes have been healthy, only colds, and they have for some time now done their work in as much peace and have been as obedient as I could wish."

One of the women, however, Darkey by name, shortly became a pestilent source of trouble. Cain wrote in 1833 that her termagant outbreaks among her fellows had led him to apply a "moderate correction," whereupon she had further terrorized her housemates by threats of poison. Cain could then only unbosom himself to Telfair: "I will give you a full history of my belief of Darkey, to wit: I believe her disposition as to temper is as bad as any in the whole world. I believe she is as unfaithful as any I have ever been acquainted with. In every respect I believe she has been more injury to you in the place where she is than two such negroes would sell for. . . . I have tryed and done all I could to get on with her, hopeing that she would mend; but I have been disappointed in every instant. I can not hope for the better any longer."

The factor's record becomes available from 1834, with the death of Telfair. The seventy-six pair of shoes entered that year tells roughly the number of working hands, and the ninety-six pair in 1842 suggests the rate of increase. Meanwhile the cotton output rose from 166 bales of about three hundred pounds in 1834 to 407 bales of four hundred pounds in the fine weather of 1841. In 1836 an autumn report from Cain is available, dated November 20. Sickness among the negroes for six weeks past had kept eight or ten of them in their beds; the resort to Petit Gulf seed had substantially increased the cotton yield; and the fields were now white with a crop in danger of ruin from storms. "My hands." he said, "have picked well when they were able, and some of them appear to have a kind of pride in making a good crop." A gin of sixty saws newly installed had proved too heavy for the old driving apparatus, but it was now in operation with shifts of four mules instead of two as formerly. This pressure, in addition to the hauling of cotton to market had postponed the gathering of the corn crop. The corn would prove adequate for the plantation's need, and the fodder was plentiful, but the oats had been ruined by the blast. The winter cloth supply had been spun and woven, as usual, on the place; but Cain now advised that the cotton warp for the jeans in future be bought. "The spinning business on this plantation," said he, "is very ungaining. In the present arrangement there is eight hands regular imployed in spinning and weaving, four of which spin warpe, and it could be bought at the factory at 120 dollars annually. Besides, it takes 400 pounds of cotton each year, leaveing 60 dollars only to the four hands who spin warp. . . . These hands are not old negroes, not all of them. Two of Nanny's daughters, or three I may say, are all able hands . . . and these make neither corn nor meat. Take out $20 to pay their borde, and it leaves them in debt. I give them their task to spin, and they say they cannot do more. That is, they have what is jenerly given as a task."

In 1840 Cain raised one of the slaves to the rank of driver, whereupon several of the men ran away in protest, and Cain was impelled to defend his policy in a letter to Mary Telfair, explaining that the new functionary had not been appointed "to lay off tasks and use the whip." The increase of the laborers and the spread of the fields, he said, often required the working of three squads, the plowmen, the grown hoe hands, and the younger hoe hands. "These separate classes are frequently separate a considerable distance from each other, and so soon as I am absent from either they are subject to quarrel and fight, or to idle time, or beat and abuse the mules; and when called to account each negro present when the misconduct took place will deny all about the same. I therefore thought, and yet believe, that for the good order of the plantation and faithful performance of their duty, it was proper to have some faithful and trusty hand whose duty it should be to report to me those in fault, and that is the only dread they have of John, for they know he is not authorized to beat them. You mention in your letter that you do not wish your negroes treated with severity. I have ever thought my fault on the side of lenity; if they were treated severe as many are, I should not be their overseer on any consideration." In the same letter Cain mentioned that the pork made on the place the preceding year had yielded eleven monthly allowances to the negroes at the rate of 1050 pounds per month, and that the deficit for the twelfth month had been filled as usual by a shipment from Savannah.

From 407 bales in 1841 the cotton output fell rapidly, perhaps because of restriction prompted by the low prices, to 198 bales in 1844. Then it rose to the maximum of 438 bales in 1848. Soon afterwards Cain's long service ended, and after two years during which I. Livingston was in charge, I. N. Bethea was engaged and retained for the rest of the ante-bellum period. The cotton crops in the 'fifties did not commonly exceed three hundred bales of a weight increasing to 450 pounds, but they were supplemented to some extent by the production of wheat and rve for market. The overseer's wages were sometimes as low as $600, but were generally $1000 a year. In the expense accounts ·the annual charges for shoes, blankets and oznaburgs were no more regular than the items of "cotton money for the people." These sums, averaging about a hundred dollars a year, were distributed among the slaves in payment for the little crops of nankeen cotton which they cultivated in spare time on plots assigned to the several families. Other expense items mentioned salt, sugar, bacon, molasses, tobacco, wool and cotton cards, loom sleighs, mules and machinery. Still others dealt with drugs and doctor's bills. In 1837, for example, Dr. Jenkins was paid $90 for attendance on Priscilla. In some years the physician's payment was a round hundred dollars, indicating services on contract. In May, 1851, there are debits of $16.16 for a constable's reward, a jail fee and a railroad fare, and of $1.30 for the purchase of a pair of handcuffs, two padlocks and a trace chain. These constitute the financial record of a runaway's recapture.

From 1834 to 1841 the gross earnings on Retreat ranged between eight and fifteen thousand dollars, of which from seven to twelve thousand each year was available for division between the owners. The gross then fell rapidly to $4000 in 1844, of which more than half was consumed in expenses. It then rose as rapidly to its maximum of $21,300 in 1847, when more than half of it again was devoted to current expenses and betterments. Thereafter the range of the gross was between $8000 and $17,-000 except for a single year of crop failure, 1856, when the 109 bales brought $5750. During the 'fifties the current expenses ranged usually between six and ten thousand dollars, as compared with about one third as much in the 'thirties. This is explained partly by the resolution of the owners to improve the fields, now grown old, and to increase the equipment. For the crop of 1856, for example, purchases were made of forty tons of Peruvian guano at $56 per ton, and nineteen tons of Mexican guano at $25 a ton. In the following years lime, salt and dried blood were included in the fertilizer purchases. At length Hodgson himself gave over his travels and his ethnological studies to take personal charge on Retreat. He wrote in June, 1859, to his friend Senator Hammond, of whom we have seen something in the preceding chapter, that he had seriously engaged in "high farming," and was spreading huge quantities of fertilizers. He continued: "My portable steam engine is the *delicia domini* and of overseer too. It follows the reapers beautifully in a field of wheat, 130 acres, and then in the rye fields. In August it will be backed up to the gin house and emancipate from slavery eighteen mules and four little nigger drivers." [9]

The factor's books for this plantation continue their records into the war time. From the crop of 1861 nothing appears to have been sold but a single bale of cotton, and the year's deficit was $6,721. The proceeds from the harvests of 1862 were $500 from nineteen bales of cotton, and some $10,000 from fodder, hay, peanuts and corn. The still more diversified market produce of 1863 comprised also wheat, which was impressed by the Confederate government, syrup, cowpeas, lard, hams and vinegar. The proceeds were $17,000 and the expenses about $9000, including the overseer's wages at $1300 and the purchase of 350 bushels of peanuts from the slaves at $1.50 per bushel. The reckonings in the war period were made of course in the rapidly depreciating Confederate currency. The stoppage of the record in 1864 was doubtless a consequence of Sherman's march through Georgia.[10]

In the western cotton belt the plantations were much like those of the eastern, except that the more uniform fertility often permitted the fields to lie in solid expanses instead of being sprawled and broken by waste lands as in the Piedmont. The scale of operations tended accordingly to be larger. One of the greatest proprietors in that region, unless his display were far out of proportion to his wealth, was Joseph A. S. Acklen whose group of plantations was clustered near the junction of the Red and Mississippi Rivers. In 1859 he began to build a country house on the style of a Gothic castle, with a great central hall and fifty

[9] MS. among the Hammond papers in the Library of Congress.
[10] The Retreat records are in the possession of the Georgia Historical Society, trustee for the Telfair Academy of Art, Savannah, Ga. The overseer's letters here used are printed in *Plantation and Frontier*, I, 314, 330-336, II, 39, 85.

rooms exclusive of baths and closets.[11] The building was expected to cost $150,000, and the furnishings $125,000 more. Acklen's rules for the conduct of his plantations will be discussed in another connection;[12] but no description of his estate or his actual operations is available.

Olmsted described in detail a plantation in the neighborhood of Natchez. Its thirteen or fourteen hundred acres of cotton, corn and incidental crops were tilled by a plow gang of thirty and a hoe gang of thirty-seven, furnished by a total of 135 slaves on the place. A driver cracked a whip among the hoe hands, occasionally playing it lightly upon the shoulders of one or another whom he thought would be stimulated by the suggestion. "There was a nursery for sucklings at the quarters, and twenty women at this time left their work four times a day, for half an hour, to nurse the young ones, and whom the overseer counted as half hands—that is, expected to do half an ordinary day's work." At half past nine every night the hoe and plow foremen, serving alternately, sounded curfew on a horn, and half an hour afterward visited each cabin to see that the households were at rest and the fires safely banked. The food allowance was a peck of corn and four pounds of pork weekly. Each family, furthermore, had its garden, fowl house and pigsty; every Christmas the master distributed among them coffee, molasses, tobacco, calico and "Sunday tricks" to the value of from a thousand to fifteen hundred dollars; and every man might rive boards in the swamp on Sundays to buy more supplies, or hunt and fish in leisure times to vary his family's fare. Saturday afternoon was also free from the routine. Occasionally a slave would run away, but he was retaken sooner or later, sometimes by the aid of dogs. A persistent runaway was disposed of by sale.[13]

Another estate in the same district, which Olmsted observed more cursorily, comprised four adjoining plantations, each with its own stables and quarter, each employing more than a hundred slaves under a separate overseer, and all directed by a steward

[11] *Federal Union* (Milledgeville, Ga.), Aug. 2, 1859.
[12] Below, pp. 262 ff.
[13] F. L. Olmsted, *A Journey in the Back Country* (New York, 1860), pp. 46-54.

whom the traveler described as cultured, poetic and delightful. An observation that women were at some of the plows prompted Olmsted to remark that throughout the Southwest the slaves were worked harder as a rule than in the easterly and northerly slaveholding states. On the other hand he noted: "In the main the negroes appeared to be well cared for and abundantly supplied with the necessaries of vigorous physical existence. A large part of them lived in commodious and well built cottages, with broad galleries in front, so that each family of five had two rooms on the lower floor and a large loft. The remainder lived in log huts, small and mean in appearance; [14] but those of their overseers were little better, and preparations were being made to replace all of these by neat boarded cottages."

In the sugar district Estwick Evans when on his "pedestrious tour" in 1817 found the shores of the Mississippi from a hundred miles above New Orleans to twenty miles below the city in a high state of cultivation. "The plantations within these limits," he said, "are superb beyond description. . . . The dwelling houses of the planters are not inferior to any in the United States, either with respect to size, architecture, or the manner in which they are furnished. The gardens and yards contiguous to them are formed and decorated with much taste. The cotton, sugar and ware houses are very large, and the buildings for the slaves are well finished. The latter buildings are in some cases forty or fifty in number, and each of them will accommodate ten or twelve persons. . . . The planters here derive immense profits from the cultivation of their estates.[15] The yearly income from them is from twenty thousand to thirty thousand dollars."

Gross proceeds running into the tens of thousands of dollars were indeed fairly common then and afterward among Louisiana sugar planters, for the conditions of their industry conduced strongly to a largeness of plantation scale. Had railroad facilities been abundant a multitude of small cultivators might have shipped their cane to central mills for manufacture, but as things

---

[14] Olmsted, *Back Country*, pp. 72-92.
[15] Estwick Evans, *A Pedestrious Tour . . . through the Western States and Territories* (Concord, N. H., 1817), p. 219, reprinted in R. G. Thwaites ed., *Early Western Travels*, VIII, 325, 326.

were the weight and the perishableness of the cane made milling within the reach of easy cartage imperative. It was inexpedient even for two or more adjacent estates to establish a joint mill, for the imminence of frost in the harvest season would make wrangles over the questions of precedence in the grinding almost inevitable. As a rule, therefore, every unit in cane culture was also a unit in sugar manufacture. Exceptions were confined to the scattering instances where some small farm lay alongside a plantation which had a mill of excess capacity available for custom grinding on slack days.

The type of plantation organization in the sugar bowl was much like that which has been previously described for Jamaica. Mules were used as draught animals instead of oxen, however, on account of their greater strength and speed, and all the seeding and most of the cultivation was done with deep-running plows. Steam was used increasingly as years passed for driving the mills, railways were laid on some of the greater estates for hauling the cane, more suitable varieties of cane were introduced, guano was imported soon after its discovery to make the rich fields yet more fertile, and each new invention of improved mill apparatus was readily adopted for the sake of reducing expenses. In consequence the acreage cultivated per hand came to be several times greater than that which had prevailed in Jamaica's heyday. But the brevity of the growing season kept the saccharine content of the canes below that in the tropics, and together with the mounting price of labor made prosperity depend in some degree upon protective tariffs. The dearth of land available kept the sugar output well below the domestic demand, though the molasses market was sometimes glutted.

A typical prosperous estate of which a description and a diary are extant [16] was that owned by Valcour Aime, lying on the right bank of the Mississippi about sixty miles above New Orleans. Of the 15,000 acres which it comprised in 1852, 800 were in cane, 300 in corn, 150 in crops belonging to the slaves, and most of the rest in swampy forest from which two or three thousand cords

[16] *Harper's Magazine*, VII, 758, 759 (November, 1853) ; Valcour Aime, *Plantation Diary* (New Orleans, 1878), partly reprinted in *Plantation and Frontier*, I, 214, 230.

of wood were cut each year as fuel for the sugar mill and the boiling house. The slaves that year numbered 215 of all ages, half of them field hands,[17] and the mules 64. The negroes were well housed, clothed and fed; the hospital and the nursery were capacious, and the stables likewise. The mill was driven by an eighty-horse-power steam engine, and the vacuum pans and the centrifugals were of the latest types. The fields were elaborately ditched, well manured, and excellently tended. The land was valued at $360,000, the buildings at $100,000, the machinery at $60,-ooo, the slaves at $170,000, and the livestock at $11,000; total, $701,000. The crop of 1852, comprising 1,300,000 pounds of white centrifugal sugar at 6 cents and 60,000 gallons of syrup at 36 cents, yielded a gross return of almost $100,000. The expenses included 4,629 barrels of coal from up the river, in addition to the outlay for wages and miscellaneous supplies.

In the routine of work, each January was devoted mainly to planting fresh canes in the fields from which the stubble canes or second rattoons had recently been harvested. February and March gave an interval for cutting cordwood, cleaning ditches, and such other incidentals as the building and repair of the plantation's railroad. Warm weather then brought the corn planting and cane and corn cultivation. In August the laying by of the crops gave time for incidentals again. Corn and hay were now harvested, the roads and premises put in order, the cordwood hauled from the swamp, the coal unladen from the barges, and all things made ready for the rush of the grinding season which began in late October. In the first phase of harvesting the main gang cut and stripped the canes, the carters and the railroad crew hauled them to the mill, and double shifts there kept up the grinding and boiling by day and by night. As long as the weather continued temperate the mill set the pace for the cutters. But when frost grew imminent every hand who could wield a knife was sent to the fields to cut the still standing stalks and se-

[17] According to the MS. returns of the U. S. census of 1850 Aime's slaves at that time numbered 231, of whom 58 were below fifteen years old, 164 were between 15 and 65, and 9 (one of them blind, another insane) were from 66 to 80 years old. Evidently there was a considerable number of slaves of working age not classed by him as field hands.

cure them against freezing. For the first few days of this phase, the stalks as fast as cut were laid, in their leaves, in great mats with the tops turned south to prevent the entrance of north winds, with the leaves of each layer covering the butts of that below, and with a blanket of earth over the last butts in the mat. Here these canes usually stayed until January when they were stripped and strewn in the furrows of the newly plowed "stubble" field as the seed of a new crop. After enough seed cane were "matlayed," the rest of the cut was merely laid lengthwise in the adjacent furrows to await cartage to the mill.[18] In the last phase of the harvest, which followed this work of the greatest emergency, these "windrowed" canes were stripped and hauled, with the mill setting the pace again, until the grinding was ended, generally in December.

Another typical sugar estate was that of Dr. John P. R. Stone, comprising the two neighboring though not adjacent plantations called Evergreen and Residence, on the right bank of the Mississippi in Iberville Parish. The proprietor's diary is much like Aime's as regards the major crop routine but is fuller in its mention of minor operations. These included the mending and heightening of the levee in spring, the cutting of staves, the shaving of hoops and the making of hogsheads in summer, and, in their fitting interims, the making of bricks, the sawing of lumber, enlarging old buildings, erecting new ones, whitewashing, ditching, pulling fodder, cutting hay, and planting and harvesting corn, sweet potatoes, pumpkins, peas and turnips. There is occasional remark upon the health of the slaves, usually in the way of rejoicing at its excellence. Apparently no outside help was employed except for an Irish carpenter during the construction of a sugar house on Evergreen in 1850.[19] The slaves on Evergreen in 1850 numbered 44 between the ages of 15 and 60 years and 26 children; on Residence, 25 between 15 and 65 years and

[18] These processes of matlaying and windrowing are described in L. Bouchereau, *Statement of the Sugar and Rice Crops made in Louisiana in 1870-71* (New Orleans, 1871), p. xii.

[19] Diary of Dr. J. P. R. Stone. MS. in the possession of Mr. John Stone Ware, White Castle, La. For the privilege of using the diary I am indebted to Mr. V. Alton Moody of the University of Michigan, now Lieutenant in the American Expeditionary Force in France.

6 children.[20]   The joint crop in 1850, ground in the Residence mill, amounted to 312 hogsheads of brown sugar and sold for 4¾ to 5 cents a pound; that of the phenomenal year 1853, when the Evergreen mill was also in commission, reached 520 hogsheads on that plantation and 179 on Residence, but brought only 3 cents a pound.   These prices were much lower than those of white sugar at the time; but as Valcour Aime found occasion to remark, the refining reduced the weight of the product nearly as much as it heightened the price, so that the chief advantage of the centrifugals lay in the speed of their process.

All of the characteristic work in the sugar plantation routine called mainly for able-bodied laborers.   Children were less used than in tobacco and cotton production, and the men and women, like the mules, tended to be of sturdier physique.   This was the result partly of selection, partly of the vigorous exertion required.

Among the fourteen hundred and odd sugar plantations of this period, the average one had almost a hundred slaves of all ages, and produced average crops of nearly three hundred hogsheads or a hundred and fifty tons.   Most of the Anglo-Americans among the planters lived about Baton Rouge and on the Red River, where they or their fathers had settled with an initial purpose of growing cotton.   Their fellows who acquired estates in the Creole parishes were perhaps as often as otherwise men who had been merchants and not planters in earlier life.   One of these had removed from New York in the eighteenth century and had thriven in miscellaneous trade at Pensacola and on the Mississippi.   In 1821 he bought for $140,000 a plantation and its complement of slaves on Bayou Lafourche, and he afterward acquired a second one in Plaquemines Parish.   In the conduct of his plantation business he shrewdly bought blankets by the bale in Philadelphia, and he enlarged his gang by commissioning agents to buy negroes in Virginia and Maryland.   The nature of the instructions he gave may be gathered from the results, for there duly arrived in several parcels between 1828 and 1832, fully cov-

[20] MS. returns in the U. S. Census Bureau, data procured through the courtesy of the Carnegie Institution of Washington and Mr. (now Lieutenant) V. Alton Moody.

ered by marine insurance for the coastwise voyage, fifty slaves, male and female, virtually all of whom ranged between the ages of ten and twenty-five years.[21]   This planter prospered, and his children after him; and while he may have had a rugged nature, his descendants to-day are among the gentlest of Louisianians. Another was Duncan F. Kenner, who was long a slave trader with headquarters at New Orleans before he became a planter in Ascension Parish on a rapidly increasing scale.   His crop advanced from 580 hogsheads in 1849 to 1,370 hogsheads in 1853 and 2,002 hogsheads in 1858 when he was operating two mills, one equipped with vacuum pans and the other with Rillieux apparatus.[22]   A third example was John Burnside, who emigrated from the North of Ireland in his youth rose rapidly from grocery clerk in upland Virginia to millionaire merchant in New Orleans, and then in the fifties turned his talents to sugar growing.   He bought the three contiguous plantations of Col. J. S. Preston lying opposite Donaldsonville, and soon added a fourth one to the group.   In 1858 his aggregate crop was 3,701 hogsheads; and in 1861 his fields were described by William H. Russell as exhibiting six thousand acres of cane in an unbroken tract.   By employing squads of immigrant Irishmen for ditching and other severe work he kept his literally precious negroes, well housed and fed, in fit condition for effective routine under his well selected staff of overseers.[23]   Even after the war Burnside kept on acquiring plantations, and with free negro labor kept on making large sugar crops.   At the end of his long life, spent frugally as a bachelor and somewhat of a recluse, he was doubtless by far the richest man in all the South.   The number of planters who had been merchants and the frequency of partnerships and corporations operating sugar estates, as well as the magnitude of scale characteristic of the industry, suggest that methods of a strictly business kind were more common in sugar production

[21] MSS. in private possession, data from which were made available through the kindness of Mr. V. A. Moody.

[22] The yearly product of each sugar plantation in Louisiana between 1849 and 1858 is reported in P. A. Champonier's *Annual Statement* of the crop. (New Orleans, 1850-1859).

[23] William H. Russell, *My Diary North and South* (Boston, 1863), pp. 268-279

than in that of cotton or tobacco. Domesticity and paternalism were nevertheless by no means alien to the sugar régime.

Virtually all of the tobacco, short staple cotton and sugar plantations were conducted on the gang system. The task system, on the other hand, was instituted on the rice coast, where the drainage ditches checkering the fields into half or quarter acre plots offered convenient units of performance in the successive processes. The chief advantage of the task system lay in the ease with which it permitted a planter or an overseer to delegate much of his routine function to a driver. This official each morning would assign to each field hand his or her individual plot, and spend the rest of the day in seeing to the performance of the work. At evening or next day the master could inspect the results and thereby keep a check upon both the driver and the squad. Each slave when his day's task was completed had at his own disposal such time as might remain. The driver commonly gave every full hand an equal area to be worked in the same way, and discriminated among them only in so far as varying conditions from plot to plot would permit the assignment of the stronger and swifter workmen to tracts where the work required was greater, and the others to plots where the labor was less. Fractional hands were given fractional tasks, or were combined into full hands for full tasks. Thus a woman rated at three quarters might be helped by her own one quarter child, or two half-hand youths might work a full plot jointly. The system gave some stimulus to speed of work, at least from time to time, by its promise of afternoon leisure in reward. But for this prospect to be effective the tasks had to be so limited that every laborer might have the hope of an hour or two's release as the fruit of diligence. The performance of every hand tended accordingly to be standardized at the customary accomplishment of the weakest and slowest members of the group. This tendency, however, was almost equally strong in the gang system also.

The task acre was commonly not a square of 210 feet, but a rectangle 300 feet long and 150 feet broad, divided into square halves and rectangular quarters, and further divisible into "compasses" five feet wide and 150 feet long, making one sixtieth of an acre. The standard tasks for full hands in rice culture were scheduled in 1843 as follows: plowing with two oxen, with the animals changed at noon, one acre; breaking stiff land with the hoe and turning the stubble under, ten compasses; breaking such land with the stubble burnt off, or breaking lighter land, a quarter acre or slightly more; mashing the clods to level the field, from a quarter to half an acre; trenching the drills, if on well prepared land, three quarters of an acre; sowing rice, from three to four half-acres; covering the drills, three quarters; the first hoeing, half an acre, or slightly less if the ground were lumpy and the drills hard to clear; second hoeing, half an acre, or slightly less or more according to the density of the grass; third hoeing with hand picking of the grass from the drills, twenty compasses; fourth hoeing, half an acre; reaping with the sickle, three quarters, or much less if the ground were new and cumbered or if the stalks were tangled; and threshing with the flail, six hundred sheaves for the men, five hundred for the women.[24] Much of the incidental work was also done by tasks, such as ditching, cutting cordwood, squaring timber, splitting rails, drawing staves and hoop poles, and making barrels. The scale of the crop was commonly five acres of rice to each full hand, together with about half as much in provision crops for home consumption.

Under the task system, Olmsted wrote: "most of the slaves work rapidly and well. . . . Custom has settled the extent of the task, and it is difficult to increase it. The driver who marks it out has to remain on the ground until it is finished, and has no interest in over-measuring it; and if it should be systematically increased very much there is the danger of a general stampede to the 'swamp'—a danger a slave can always hold before his master's cupidity. . . . It is the driver's duty to make the tasked hands do their work well.[25] If in their haste to finish it they neglect to do it properly he 'sets them back,' so that carelessness will hinder more than it hastens the completion of their tasks." But Olmsted's view was for once rose colored. A planter who lived in the régime wrote: "The whole task system . . . is one

[24] Edmund Ruffin, *Agricultural Survey of South Carolina* (Columbia, 1843), p. 118.
[25] Olmsted, *Seaboard Slave States*, pp. 435, 436.

that I most unreservedly disapprove of, because it promotes idleness, and that is the parent of mischief." [26]   Again the truth lies in the middle ground.   The virtue or vice of the system, as with the gang alternative, depended upon its use by a diligent master or its abuse by an excessive delegation of responsibility.

That the tide when taken at the flood on the rice coast as elsewhere would lead to fortune is shown by the career of the greatest of all rice planters, Nathaniel Heyward.   At the time of his birth, in 1766, his father was a planter on an inland swamp near Port Royal.   Nathaniel himself after establishing a small plantation in his early manhood married Harriett Manigault, an heiress with some fifty thousand dollars.   With this, when both lands and slaves were cheap, Heyward bought a tide-land tract and erected four plantations thereon, and soon had enough accrued earnings to buy the several inland plantations of the Gibbes brothers, who had fallen into debt from luxurious living.   With the proceeds of his large crops at high prices during the great wars in Europe, he bought more slaves year after year, preferably fresh Africans as long as that cheap supply remained available, and he bought more land when occasion offered.   Joseph Manigault wrote of him in 1806: "Mr. Heyward has lately made another purchase of land, consisting of 300 acres of tide swamp, joining one of his Combahee plantations and belonging to the estate of Mrs. Bell.   I believe he has made a good bargain.   It is uncleared and will cost him not quite £20 per acre. I have very little doubt that he will be in a few years, if he lives, the richest, as he is the best planter in the state.   The Cooper River lands give him many a long ride."   Heyward was venturesome in large things, conservative in small.   He long continued to have his crops threshed by hand, saying that if it were done by machines his darkies would have no winter work; but when eventually he instituted mechanical threshers, no one could discern an increase of leisure.   In the matter of pounding mills likewise, he clung for many years to those driven by the tides and operating slowly and crudely; but at length he built two new ones driven by steam and so novel and complete in their ap-

[26] J. A. Turner. ed., *Cotton Planter's Manual*, p. 34.

paratus as to be the marvels of the countryside. He necessarily depended much upon overseers; but his own frequent visits of inspection and the assistance rendered by his sons kept the scattered establishments in an efficient routine. The natural increase of his slaves was reckoned by him to have ranged generally between one and five per cent annually, though in one year it rose to seven per cent. At his death in 1851 he owned fourteen rice plantations with fields ranging from seventy to six hundred acres in each, and comprising in all 4,390 acres in cultivation. He had also a cotton plantation, much pine land and a sawmill, nine residences in Charleston, appraised with their furniture at $180,-000; securities and cash to the amount of $200,000; $20,000 worth of horses, mules and cattle; $15,000 worth of plate; and $3000 worth of old wine. His slaves, numbering 2,087 and appraised at an average of $550, made up the greater part of his two million dollar estate. His heirs continued his policy. In 1855, for example, they bought a Savannah River plantation called Fife, containing 500 acres of prime rice land at $150 per acre, together with its equipment and 120 slaves, at a gross price of $135,600.[27]

The history of the estate of James Heyward, Nathaniel's brother, was in striking contrast with this. When on a tour in Ireland he met and married an actress, who at his death in 1796 inherited his plantation and 214 slaves. Two suitors for the widow's hand promptly appeared in Alexander Baring, afterwards Lord Ashburton, and Charles Baring, his cousin. Mrs. Heyward married the latter, who increased the estate to seven or eight hundred acres in rice, yielding crops worth from twelve to thirty thousand dollars. But instead of superintending its work in person Baring bought a large tract in the North Carolina mountains, built a house there, and carried thither some fifty slaves for his service. After squandering the income for nearly fifty years, he sold off part of the slaves and mortgaged the land; and when the plantation was finally surrendered in set-

[27] MSS. in the possession of Mrs. Hawkins K. Jenkins, Pinopolis, S. C., including a "Memoir of Nathaniel Heyward," written in 1895 by Gabriel E. Manigault.

tlement of Baring's debts, it fell into Nathaniel Heyward's possession.[28]

Another case of absentee neglect, made notorious through Fanny Kemble's *Journal,* was the group of rice and sea-island cotton plantations founded by Senator Pierce Butler on and about Butler's Island near the mouth of the Altamaha River. When his two grandsons inherited the estate, they used it as a source of revenue but not as a home. One of these was Pierce Butler the younger, who lived in Philadelphia. When Fanny Kemble, with fame preceding her, came to America in 1832, he became infatuated, followed her troupe from city to city, and married her in 1834. The marriage was a mistake. The slaveholder's wife left the stage for the time being, but retained a militant English abolitionism. When in December, 1838, she and her husband were about to go South for a winter on the plantations, she registered her horror of slavery in advance, and resolved to keep a journal of her experiences and observations. The resulting record is gloomy enough. The swarms of negroes were stupid and slovenly, the cabins and hospitals filthy, the women overdriven, the overseer callous, the master indifferent, and the new mistress herself, repudiating the title, was more irritable and meddlesome than helpful.[29] The short sojourn was long enough. A few years afterward the ill-mated pair were divorced and Fanny Kemble resumed her own name and career. Butler did not mend his ways. In 1859 his half of the slaves, 429 in number, were sold at auction in Savannah to pay his debts.

A pleasanter picture is afforded by the largest single unit in rice culture of which an account is available. This was the plantation of William Aiken, at one time governor of South Carolina, occupying Jehossee Island near the mouth of the Edisto River. It was described in 1850 by Solon Robinson, an Iowa farmer then on tour as correspondent for the *American Agriculturist.* The two or three hundred acres of firm land above tide comprised the homestead, the negro quarter, the stables, the stock yard, the threshing mill and part of the provision fields. Of the land which could be flooded with the tide, about fifteen hundred acres were diked and drained. About two-thirds of this appears to have been cropped in rice each year, and the rest in corn, oats and sweet potatoes. The steam-driven threshing apparatus was described as highly efficient. The sheaves were brought on the heads of the negroes from the great smooth stack yard, and opened in a shed where the scattered grain might be saved. A mechanical carrier led thence to the threshing machines on the second floor, whence the grain descended through a winnowing fan. The pounding mill, driven by the tide, was a half mile distant at the wharf, whence a schooner belonging to the plantation carried the hulled and polished rice in thirty-ton cargoes to Charleston. The average product per acre was about forty-five bushels in the husk, each bushel yielding some thirty pounds of cleaned rice, worth about three cents a pound. The provision fields commonly fed the force of slaves and mules; and the slave families had their own gardens and poultry to supplement their fare. The rice crops generally yielded some twenty-five thousand dollars in gross proceeds, while the expenses, including the two-thousand-dollar salary of the overseer, commonly amounted to some ten thousand dollars. During the summer absence of the master, the overseer was the only white man on the place. The engineers, smiths, carpenters and sailors were all black. "The number of negroes upon the place," wrote Robinson, "is just about 700, occupying 84 double frame houses, each containing two tenements of three rooms to a family besides the cockloft. . . . There are two common hospitals and a 'lying-in hospital,' and a very neat, commodious church, which is well filled every Sabbath. . . . Now the owner of all this property lives in a very humble cottage, embowered in dense shrubbery and making no show. . . . He and his family are as plain and unostentatious in their manners as the house they live in. . . . Nearly all the land has been reclaimed and the buildings, except the house, erected new within the twenty years that Governor Aiken has owned the island. I fully believe that he is more concerned to make his people comfortable and happy than he is to make money." [80]   When the present writer visited Jehossee in the harvest season sixty years after Robinson, the fields were dotted with reapers, wage earners now instead of slaves, but still using sickles on half-acre tasks; and the stack yard was aswarm with sable men and women carrying sheaves on their heads and chattering as of old in a dialect which a stranger can hardly understand.   The ante-bellum hospital and many of the cabins in their far-thrown quadruple row were still standing.   The site of the residence, however, was marked only by desolate chimneys, a live-oak grove and a detached billiard room, once elegant but now ruinous, the one indulgence which this planter permitted himself.

The ubiquitous Olmsted chose for description two rice plantations operated as one, which he inspected in company with the owner, whom he calls "Mr. X."   Frame cabins at intervals of three hundred feet constituted the quarters; the exteriors were whitewashed, the interiors lathed and plastered, and each family had three rooms and a loft, as well as a chicken yard and pigsty not far away.   "Inside, the cabins appeared dirty and disordered, which was rather a pleasant indication that their home life was not much interfered with, though I found certain police regulations enforced."   Olmsted was in a mellow mood that day. At the nursery "a number of girls eight or ten years old were occupied in holding and tending the youngest infants.   Those a little older—the crawlers—were in the pen, and those big enough to toddle were playing on the steps or before the house.   Some of these, with two or three bigger ones, were singing and dancing about a fire they had made on the ground. . . . The nurse was a kind-looking old negro woman. . . . I watched for half an hour, and in all that time not a baby of them began to cry; nor have I ever heard one, at two or three other plantation nurseries which I have visited."   The chief slave functionary was a "gentlemanly-mannered mulatto who . . . carried by a strap at his waist a very large bunch of keys and had charge of all the stores of provisions, tools and materials on the plantations, as

---

[80] *American Agriculturist*, IX, 187, 188, reprinted in *DeBow's Review,* IX, 201-203.

well as of their produce before it was shipped to market. He
weighed and measured out all the rations of the slaves and the
cattle. . . . In all these departments his authority was superior
to that of the overseer; . . . and Mr. X. said he would trust him
with much more than he would any overseer he had ever known."
The master explained that this man and the butler, his brother,
having been reared with the white children, had received special
training to promote their sense of dignity and responsibility.
The brothers, Olmsted further observed, rode their own horses
the following Sunday to attend the same church as their master,
and one of them slipped a coin into the hand of the boy who had
been holding his mount. The field hands worked by tasks under
their drivers. "I saw one or two leaving the field soon after one
o'clock, several about two; and between three and four I met a
dozen men and women coming home to their cabins, having finished their day's work." As to punishment, Olmsted asked how
often it was necessary. The master replied: " 'Sometimes perhaps not once for two or three weeks; then it will seem as if the
devil had gotten into them all and there is a good deal of it.' "
As to matings: "While watching the negroes in the field, Mr.
X. addressed a girl who was vigorously plying a hoe near us:
'Is that Lucy?—Ah, Lucy, what's this I hear about you?' The
girl simpered, but did not answer or discontinue her work.
'What is this I hear about you and Sam, eh?' The girl grinned
and still hoeing away with all her might whispered 'Yes, sir.'
'Sam came to see me this morning.' 'If master pleases.' 'Very
well; you may come up to the house Saturday night, and your
mistress will have something for you.' " [31] We may hope that
the pair whose prospective marriage was thus endorsed with the
promise of a bridal gift lived happily ever after.

The most detailed record of rice operations available is that
made by Charles Manigault from the time of his purchase in
1833 of "Gowrie," on the Savannah River, twelve miles above the
city of Savannah.[32] The plantation then had 220 acres in rice

[31] Olmsted, *Seaboard Slave States*, 418-448.
[32] The Manigault MSS. are in the possession of Mrs. H. K. Jenkins,
Pinopolis, S. C. Selections from them are printed in *Plantation and Frontier*, I, 134-139 *et passim*.

fields, 80 acres unreclaimed, a good pounding mill, and 50 slaves. The price of $40,000 was analyzed by Manigault as comprising $7500 for the mill, $70 per acre for the cleared, and $37 for the uncleared, and an average of $300 for the slaves. His maintenance expense per hand he itemized at a weekly peck of corn, $13 a year; summer and winter clothes, $7; shoes, $1; meat at times, salt, molasses and medical attention, not estimated. In reward for good service, however, Manigault usually issued broken rice worth $2.50 per bushel, instead of corn worth $1. Including the overseer's wages the current expense for the plantation for the first six years averaged about $2000 annually. Meanwhile the output increased from 200 barrels of rice in 1833 to 578 in 1838. The crop in the latter year was particularly notable, both in its yield of three barrels per acre, or 16½ barrels per working hand, and its price of four cents per pound or $24 per barrel. The net proceeds of the one crop covered the purchase in 1839 of two families of slaves, comprising sixteen persons, mostly in or approaching their prime, at a price of $640 each.

Manigault and his family were generally absent every summer and sometimes in winter, at Charleston or in Europe, and once as far away as China. His methods of administration may be gathered from his letters, contracts and memoranda. In January, 1848, he wrote from Naples to I. F. Cooper whom his factor had employed at $250 a year as a new overseer on Gowrie: "My negroes have the reputation of being orderly and well disposed; but like all negroes they are up to anything if not watched and attended to. I expect the kindest treatment of them from you, for this has always been a principal thing with me. I never suffer them to work off the place, or exchange work with any plantation. . . . It has always been my plan to give out allowance to my negroes on Sunday in preference to any other day, because this has much influence in keeping them at home that day, whereas if they received allowance on Saturday for instance some of them would be off with it that same evening to the shops to trade, and perhaps would not get back until Monday morning. I allow no strange negro to take a wife on my place, and none of mine to keep a boat." [33]

A few years after this, Manigault bought an adjoining plantation, "East Hermitage," and consolidated it with Gowrie, thereby increasing his rice fields to 500 acres and his slaves to about 90 of all ages. His draught animals appear to have comprised merely five or six mules. A new overseer, employed in 1853 at wages of $500 together with corn and rice for his table and the services of a cook and a waiting boy, was bound by a contract stipulating the duties described in the letter to Cooper above quoted, along with a few additional items. He was, for example, to procure a book of medical instructions and a supply of the few requisite "plantation medicines" to be issued to the nurses with directions as needed. In case of serious injury to a slave, however, the sufferer was to be laid upon a door and sent by the plantation boat to Dr. Bullock's hospital in Savannah. Except when the work was very pressing the slaves were to be sent home for the rest of the day upon the occurrence of heavy rains in the afternoon, for Manigault had found by experience "that always after a complete wetting, particularly in cold rainy weather in winter or spring, one or more of them are made sick and lie up, and at times serious illness ensues." [34]

In 1852 and again in 1854 storms and freshets heavily injured Manigault's crops, and cholera decimated his slaves. In 1855 the fields were in bad condition because of volunteer rice, and the overseer was dying of consumption. The slaves, however, were in excellent health, and the crop, while small, brought high prices because of the Crimean war. In 1856 a new overseer named Venters handled the flooding inexpertly and made but half a crop, yielding $12,660 in gross proceeds. For the next year Venters was retained, on the maxim "never change an overseer if you can help it," and nineteen slaves were bought for $11,850 to fill the gaps made by the cholera. Furthermore a tract of pine forest was bought to afford summer quarters for the negro children, who did not thrive on the malarial plantation, and to pro-

[33] MS. copy in Manigault letter book.
[34] *Plantation and Frontier*, I, 122-126.

vide a place of isolation for cholera cases. In 1857 Venters made a somewhat better crop, but as Manigault learned and wrote at the end of the year, "elated by a strong and very false religious feeling, he began to injure the plantation a vast deal, placing himself on a par with the negroes by even joining in with them at their prayer meetings, breaking down long established discipline which in every case is so difficult to preserve, favoring and siding in any difficulty with the people against the drivers, besides causing numerous grievances." The successor of the eccentric Venters in his turn proved grossly neglectful; and it was not until the spring of 1859 that a reliable overseer was found in William Capers, at a salary of $1000. Even then the year's experience was such that at its end Manigault recorded the sage conclusion: "The truth is, on a plantation, to attend to things properly it requires both master and overseer."

The affairs of another estate in the Savannah neighborhood, "Sabine Fields," belonging to the Alexander Telfair estate, may be gleaned from its income and expense accounts. The purchases of shoes indicate a working force of about thirty hands. The purchases of woolen clothing and waterproof hats tell of adequate provision against inclement weather; but the scale of the doctor's bills suggest either epidemics or serious occasional illnesses. The crops from 1845 to 1854 ranged between seventeen and eighty barrels of rice; and for the three remaining years of the record they included both rice and sea-island cotton. The gross receipts were highest at $1,695 in 1847 and lowest at $362 in 1851; the net varied from a surplus of $995 in 1848 to a deficit of $2,035 in the two years 1853 and 1854 for which the accounting was consolidated. Under E. S. Mell, who was overseer until 1854 at a salary of $350 or less, there were profits until 1849, losses thereafter. The following items of expense in this latter period, along with high doctor's bills, may explain the reverse: for taking a negro from the guardhouse, $5; for court costs in the case of a boy prosecuted for larceny, $9.26; jail fees of Cesar, $2.69; for the apprehension of a runaway, $5; paid Jones for trying to capture a negro, $5. In February, 1854, Mell was paid off, and a voucher made record of a newspaper advertisement for another overseer. What happened to the new incumbent is told by the expense entries of March 9, 1855: "Paid . . . amount Jones' bill for capturing negroes, $25. Expenses of Overseer Page's burial as follows, Ferguson's bill, $25; Coroner's, $14; Dr. Kollock's, $5; total $69." A further item in 1856 of twenty-five dollars paid for the arrest of Bing and Tony may mean that two of the slaves who shared in the killing of the overseer succeeded for a year in eluding capture, or it may mean that disorders continued under Page's successor.[35]

Other lowland plantations on a scale similar to that of Sabine Fields showed much better earnings. One of these, in Liberty County, Georgia, belonged to the heirs of Dr. Adam Alexander of Savannah. It was devoted to sea-island cotton in the 'thirties, but rice was added in the next decade. While the output fluctuated, of course, the earnings always exceeded the expenses and sometimes yielded as much as a hundred dollars per hand for distribution among the owners.[36]

The system of rice production was such that plantations with less than a hundred acres available for the staple could hardly survive in the competition. If one of these adjoined another estate it was likely to be merged therewith; but if it lay in isolation the course of years would probably bring its abandonment. The absence of the proprietors every summer in avoidance of malaria, and the consequent expense of overseer's wages, hampered operations on a small scale, as did also the maintenance of special functionaries among the slaves, such as drivers, boatswains, trunk minders, bird minders, millers and coopers. In 1860 Louis Manigault listed the forty-one rice plantations on the Savannah River and scheduled their acreage in the crop. Only one of them had as little as one hundred acres in rice, and it seems to have been an appendage of a larger one across the river. On the other hand, two of them had crops of eleven hundred, and two more of twelve hundred acres each. The average was about 425

---

[35] Account book of Sabine Fields plantation, among the Telfair MSS. in the custody of the Georgia Historical Society, Savannah, Ga.
[36] The accounts for selected years are printed in *Plantation and Frontier*, I, 150-165.

acres per plantation, expected to yield about 1200 pounds of rice per acre each year.[37] A census tabulation in 1850, ignoring any smaller units, numbered the plantations which produced annually upwards of 20,000 pounds of rice at 446 in South Carolina, 80 in Georgia, and 25 in North Carolina.[38]

Indigo and sea-island cotton fields had no ditches dividing them permanently into task units; but the fact that each of these in its day was often combined with rice on the same plantations, and that the separate estates devoted to them respectively lay in the region dominated by the rice régime, led to the prevalence of the task system in their culture also. The soils used for these crops were so sandy and light, however, that the tasks, staked off each day by the drivers, ranged larger than those in rice. In the cotton fields they were about half an acre per hand, whether for listing, bedding or cultivation. In the collecting and spreading of swamp mud and other manures for the cotton the work was probably done mostly by gangs rather than by task, since the units were hard to measure. In cotton picking, likewise, the conditions of the crop were so variable and the need of haste so great that time work, perhaps with special rewards for unusually heavy pickings, was the common resort. Thus the lowland cotton régime alternated the task and gang systems according to the work at hand; and even the rice planters of course abandoned all thoughts of stinted performance when emergency pressed, as in the mending of breaks in the dikes, or when joint exertion was required, as in log rolling, or when threshing and pounding with machinery to set the pace.

That the task system was extended sporadically into the South Carolina Piedmont, is indicated by a letter of a certain Thomas Parker of the Abbeville district, in 1831,[39] which not only described his methods but embodied an essential plantation precept. He customarily tasked his hoe hands, he said, at rates determined by careful observation as just both to himself and the workers. These varied according to conditions, but ranged usually about

[37] MS. in the possession of Mrs. H. K. Jenkins, Pinopolis, S. C.
[38] *Compendium of the Seventh U. S. Census*, p. 178.
[39] *Southern Agriculturist*, March. 1831, reprinted in the *American Farmer*, XIII, 105, 106.

three quarters of an acre. He continued: "I plant six acres of cotton to the hand, which is about the usual quantity planted in my neighborhood. I do not make as large crops as some of my neighbors. I am content with three to three and a half bales of cotton to the hand, with my provisions and pork; but some few make four bales, and last year two of my neighbors made five bales to the hand. In such cases I have vanity enough, however, to attribute this to better lands. I have no overseer, nor indeed is there one in the neighborhood. We personally attend to our planting, believing that as good a manure as any, if not the best we can apply to our fields, is the print of the master's footstep."

CHAPTER XIV

PLANTATION MANAGEMENT

TYPICAL planters though facile in conversation seldom resorted to their pens. Few of them put their standards into writing except in the form of instructions to their stewards and overseers. These counsels of perfection, drafted in widely separated periods and localities, and varying much in detail, concurred strikingly in their main provisions. Their initial topic was usually the care of the slaves. Richard Corbin of Virginia wrote in 1759 for the guidance of his steward: "The care of negroes is the first thing to be recommended, that you give me timely notice of their wants that they may be provided with all necessarys. The breeding wenches more particularly you must instruct the overseers to be kind and indulgent to, and not force them when with child upon any service or hardship that will be injurious to them, . . . and the children to be well looked after, . . . and that none of them suffer in time of sickness for want of proper care." P. C. Weston of South Carolina wrote in 1856: "The proprietor, in the first place, wishes the overseer most distinctly to understand that his first object is to be, under all circumstances, the care and well being of the negroes. The proprietor is always ready to excuse such errors as may proceed from want of judgment; but he never can or will excuse any cruelty, severity or want of care towards the negroes. For the well being, however, of the negroes it is absolutely necessary to maintain obedience, order and discipline, to see that the tasks are punctually and carefully performed, and to conduct the business steadily and firmly, without weakness on the one hand or harshness on the other." Charles Manigault likewise required of his overseer in Georgia a pledge to treat his negroes "all with kindness and consideration in sickness and health." On J. W.

Fowler's plantation in the Yazoo-Mississippi delta from which
we have seen in a preceding chapter such excellent records of
cotton picking, the preamble to the rules framed in 1857 ran as
follows: "The health, happiness, good discipline and obedience,
good, sufficient and comfortable clothing, a sufficiency of good,
wholesome and nutritious food for both man and beast being in-
dispensably necessary to successful planting, as well as for reasonable dividends for the amount of capital invested, without
saying anything about the Master's duty to his dependents, to
himself, and his God, I do hereby establish the following rules
and regulations for the management of my Prairie plantation,
and require an observance of the same by any and all overseers
I may at any time have in charge thereof." [1]

Joseph A. S. Acklen had his own rules printed in 1861 for the
information of applicants and the guidance of those who were
employed as his overseers.[2] His estate was one of the greatest
in Louisiana, his residence one of the most pretentious,[3] and his
rules the most sharply phrased. They read in part: "Order
and system must be the aim of everyone on this estate, and the
maxim strictly pursued of a time for everything and everything
done in its time, a place for everything and everything kept in
its place, a rule for everything and everything done according to
rule. In this way labor becomes easy and pleasant. No man
can enforce a system of discipline unless he himself conforms
strictly to rules. . . . No man should attempt to manage negroes
who is not perfectly firm and fearless and [in] entire control of
his temper."

James H. Hammond's "plantation manual" which is the fullest of such documents available, began with the subject of the
crop, only to subordinate it at once to the care of the slaves and
outfit: "A good crop means one that is good taking into consideration everything, negroes, land, mules, stock, fences, ditches,
farming utensils, etc., etc., all of which must be kept up and

---

[1] The Corbin, Weston, Manigault and Fowler instructions are printed
in *Plantation and Frontier*, I, 109-129.
[2] They were also printed in *DeBow's Review*, XXII, 617-620, XXIII,
376-381 (Dec., 1856, and April, 1857).
[3] *See above*, p. 239.

improved in value. The effort must therefore not be merely to make so many cotton bales or such an amount of other produce, but as much as can be made without interrupting the steady increase in value of the rest of the property. . . . There should be an increase in number and improvement in condition of negroes." [4]

For the care of the sick, of course, all these planters were solicitous. Acklen, Manigault and Weston provided that mild cases be prescribed for by the overseer in the master's absence, but that for any serious illness a doctor be summoned. One of Telfair's women was a semi-professional midwife and general practitioner, permitted by her master to serve blacks and whites in the neighborhood. For home needs Telfair wrote of her: "Elsey is the doctoress of the plantation. In case of extraordinary illness, when she thinks she can do no more for the sick, you will employ a physician." Hammond, however, was such a devotee of homeopathy that in the lack of an available physician of that school he was his own practitioner. He wrote in his manual: "No negro will be allowed to remain at his own house when sick, but must be confined to the hospital. Every reasonable complaint must be promptly attended to; and with any marked or general symptom of sickness, however trivial, a negro may lie up a day or so at least. . . . Each case has to be examined carefully by the master or overseer to ascertain the disease. The remedies next are to be chosen with the utmost discrimination; . . . the directions for treatment, diet, etc., most implicitly followed; the effects and changes cautiously observed. . . . In cases where there is the slightest uncertainty, the books must be taken to the bedside and a careful and thorough examination of the case and comparison of remedies made before administering them. The overseer must record in the prescription book every dose of medicine administered." Weston said he would never grudge a doctor's bill, however large; but he was anxious to prevent idleness under pretence of illness. "Nothing," said he, "is so subversive of discipline, or so unjust, as to

[4] MS. bound volume, "Plantation Manual," among the Hammond papers in the Library of Congress.

allow people to sham, for this causes the well-disposed to do the work of the lazy."

Pregnancy, childbirth and the care of children were matters of special concern. Weston wrote: "The pregnant women are always to do some work up to the time of their confinement, if it is only walking into the field and staying there. If they are sick, they are to go to the hospital and stay there until it is pretty certain their time is near." "Lying-in women are to be attended by the midwife as long as is necessary, and by a woman put to nurse them for a fortnight. They will remain at the negro houses for four weeks, and then will work two weeks on the highland. In some cases, however, it is necessary to allow them to lie up longer. The health of many women has been ruined by want of care in this particular." Hammond's rules were as follows: "Sucklers are not required to leave their homes until sunrise, when they leave their children at the children's house before going to field. The period of suckling is twelve months. Their work lies always within half a mile of the quarter. They are required to be cool before commencing to suckle—to wait fifteen minutes at least in summer, after reaching the children's house before nursing. It is the duty of the nurse to see that none are heated when nursing, as well as of the overseer and his wife occasionally to do so. They are allowed forty-five minutes at each nursing to be with their children. They return three times a day until their children are eight months old—in the middle of the forenoon, at noon, and in the middle of the afternoon; till the twelfth month but twice a day, missing at noon; during the twelfth month at noon only. . . . The amount of work done by a suckler is about three fifths of that done by a full hand, a little increased toward the last. . . . Pregnant women at five months are put in the sucklers' gang. No plowing or lifting must be required of them. Sucklers, old, infirm and pregnant receive the same allowances as full-work hands. The regular plantation midwife shall attend all women in confinement. Some other woman learning the art is usually with her during delivery. The confined woman lies up one month, and the midwife remains in constant attendance for seven days.

Each woman on confinement has a bundle given her containing articles of clothing for the infant, pieces of cloth and rag, and some nourishment, as sugar, coffee, rice and flour for the mother."

The instructions with one accord required that the rations issued to the negroes be never skimped. Corbin wrote, "They ought to have their belly full, but care must be taken with this plenty that no waste is committed." Acklen, closely followed by Fowler, ordered his overseer to "see that their necessities be supplied, that their food and clothing be good and sufficient, their houses comfortable; and be kind and attentive to them in sickness and old age." And further: "There will be stated hours for the negroes to breakfast and dine [in the field], and those hours must be regularly observed. The manager will frequently inspect the meals as they are brought by the cook—see that they have been properly prepared, and that vegetables be at all times served with the meat and bread." At the same time he forbade his slaves to use ardent spirits or to have such about their houses. Weston wrote: "Great care should be taken that the negroes should never have less than their regular allowance. In all cases of doubt, it should be given in favor of the largest quantity. The measure should not be struck, but rather heaped up over. None but provisions of the best quality should be used." Telfair specified as follows: "The allowance for every grown negro, however old and good for nothing, and every young one that works in the field, is a peck of corn each week and a pint of salt, and a piece of meat, not exceeding fourteen pounds, per month. . . . The suckling children, and all other small ones who do not work in the field, draw a half allowance of corn and salt. . . . . Feed everything plentifully, but waste nothing." He added that beeves were to be killed for the negroes in July, August and September. Hammond's allowance to each working hand was a heaping peck of meal and three pounds of bacon or pickled pork every week. In the winter, sweet potatoes were issued when preferred, at the rate of a bushel of them in lieu of the peck of meal; and fresh beef, mutton or pork, at increased weights, were to be substituted for the salt pork from time to time. The ditchers and drivers were to have extra allowances in meat and molasses. Furthermore, "Each ditcher receives every night, when ditching, a dram (jigger) consisting of two-thirds whiskey and one-third water, with as much asafoetida as it will absorb, and several strings of red peppers added in the barrel. The dram is a large wine-glass full. In cotton picking time when sickness begins to be prevalent, every field hand gets a dram in the morning before leaving for the field. After a soaking rain all exposed to it get a dram before changing their clothes; also those exposed to the dust from the sheller and fan in corn shelling, on reaching the quarter at night; or anyone at any time required to keep watch in the night. Drams are not given as rewards, but only as medicinal. From the second hoeing, or early in May, every work hand who uses it gets an occasional allowance of tobacco, about one sixth of a pound, usually after some general operation, as a hoeing, plow-ing, etc. This is continued until their crops are gathered, when they can provide for themselves." The families, furthermore, shared in the distribution of the plantation's peanut crop every fall. Each child was allowed one third as much meal and meat as was given to each field hand, and an abundance of vegetables to be cooked with their meat. The cooking and feeding was to be done at the day nursery. For breakfast they were to have hominy and milk and cold corn bread; for dinner, vege-table soup and dumplings or bread; and cold bread or potatoes were to be kept on hand for demands between meals. They were also to have molasses once or twice a week. Each child was provided with a pan and spoon in charge of the nurse.

Hammond's clothing allowance was for each man in the fall two cotton shirts, a pair of woolen pants and a woolen jacket, and in the spring two cotton shirts and two pairs of cotton pants, with privilege of substitution when desired; for each woman six yards of woolen cloth and six yards of cotton cloth in the fall, six yards of light and six of heavy cotton cloth in the spring, with needles, thread and buttons on each occasion. Each worker was to have a pair of stout shoes in the fall, and a heavy blanket every third year. Children's cloth allowances were proportionate and their mothers were required to dress them in clean clothes twice a week.

In the matter of sanitation, Acklen directed the overseer to see that the negroes kept clean in person, to inspect their houses at least once a week and especially during the summer, to examine their bedding and see to its being well aired, to require that their clothes be mended, "and everything attended to which conduces to their comfort and happiness." In these regards, as in various others, Fowler incorporated Acklen's rules in his own, almost verbatim. Hammond scheduled an elaborate cleaning of the houses every spring and fall. The houses were to be completely emptied and their contents sunned, the walls and floors were to be scrubbed, the mattresses to be emptied and stuffed with fresh hay or shucks, the yards swept and the ground under the houses sprinkled with lime. Furthermore, every house was to be whitewashed inside and out once a year; and the negroes must appear once a week in clean clothes, "and every negro habitually uncleanly in person must be washed and scrubbed by order of the overseer—the driver and two other negroes officiating."

As to schedules of work, the Carolina and Georgia lowlanders dealt in tasks; all the rest in hours. Telfair wrote briefly: "The negroes to be tasked when the work allows it. I require a reasonable day's work, well done—the task to be regulated by the state of the ground and the strength of the negro." Weston wrote with more elaboration: "A task is as much work as the meanest full hand can do in nine hours, working industriously. . . . This task is never to be increased, and no work is to be done over task except under the most urgent necessity; which over-work is to be reported to the proprietor, who will pay for it. No negro is to be put into a task which [he] cannot finish with tolerable ease. It is a bad plan to punish for not finishing tasks; it is subversive of discipline to leave tasks unfinished, and contrary to justice to punish for what cannot be done. In nothing does a good manager so much excel a bad as in being able to discern what a hand is capable of doing, and in never attempting to make him do more." In Hammond's schedule the first horn was blown an hour before daylight as a summons for work-hands to rise and do their cooking and other preparations for the day. Then at the summons of the plow driver, at first break of day, the plowmen went to the stables whose doors the overseer opened. At the second horn, "just at good daylight," the hoe gang set out for the field. At half past eleven the plowmen carried their mules to a shelter house in the fields, and at noon the hoe hands laid off for dinner, to resume work at one o'clock, except that in hot weather the intermission was extended to a maximum of three and a half hours. The plowmen led the way home by a quarter of an hour in the evening, and the hoe hands followed at sunset. "No work," said Hammond, "must ever be required after dark." Acklen contented himself with specifying that "the negroes must all rise at the ringing of the first bell in the morning, and retire when the last bell rings at night, and not leave their houses after that hour unless on business or called." Fowler's rule was of the same tenor: "All hands should be required to retire to rest and sleep at a suitable hour and permitted to remain there until such time as it will be necessary to get out in time to reach their work by the time they can see well how to work."

Telfair, Fowler and Hammond authorized the assignment of gardens and patches to such slaves as wanted to cultivate them at leisure times. To prevent these from becoming a cloak for thefts from the planter's crops, Telfair and Fowler forbade the growing of cotton in the slaves' private patches, and Hammond forbade both cotton and corn. Fowler specifically gave his negroes the privilege of marketing their produce and poultry "at suitable leisure times." Hammond had a rule permitting each work hand to go to Augusta on some Sunday after harvest; but for some reason he noted in pencil below it: "This is objectionable and must be altered." Telfair and Weston directed that their slaves be given passes on application, authorizing them to go at proper times to places in the neighborhood. The negroes, however, were to be at home by the time of the curfew horn about nine o'clock each night. Mating with slaves on other plantations was discouraged as giving occasion for too much journeying.

"Marriage is to be encouraged," wrote Hammond, "as it adds to the comfort, happiness and health of those who enter upon it, besides insuring a greater increase. Permission must always be obtained from the master before marriage, but no marriage will be allowed with negroes not belonging to the master. When sufficient cause can be shewn on either side, a marriage may be annulled; but the offending party must be severely punished. Where both are in wrong, both must be punished, and if they insist on separating must have a hundred lashes apiece. After such a separation, neither can marry again for three years. For first marriage a bounty of $5.00, to be invested in household articles, or an equivalent of articles, shall be given. If either has been married before, the bounty shall be $2.50. A third marriage shall be not allowed but in extreme cases, and in such cases, or where both have been married before, no bounty will be given."

"Christianity, humanity and order elevate all, injure none," wrote Fowler, "whilst infidelity, selfishness and disorder curse some, delude others and degrade all. I therefore want all of my people encouraged to cultivate religious feeling and morality, and punished for inhumanity to their children or stock, for profanity, lying and stealing." And again: "I would that every human being have the gospel preached to them in its original purity and simplicity. It therefore devolves upon me to have these dependants properly instructed in all that pertains to the salvation of their souls. To this end whenever the services of a suitable person can be secured, have them instructed in these things. In view of the fanaticism of the age, it behooves the master or overseer to be present on all such occasions. They should be instructed on Sundays in the day time if practicable; if not, then on Sunday night." Acklen wrote in his usual peremptory tone: "No negro preachers but my own will be permitted to preach or remain on any of my places. The regularly appointed minister for my places must preach on Sundays during daylight, or quit. The negroes must not be suffered to continue their night meetings beyond ten o'clock." Telfair in his rules merely permitted religious meetings on Saturday nights and Sunday mornings. Hammond encouraged his negroes to go to church on Sundays, but permitted no exercises on the plantation beyond singing and praying. He, and many others, encouraged his negroes to bring him their complaints against drivers and overseers, and even against their own ecclesiastical authorities in the matter of interference with recreations.

Fighting among the negroes was a common bane of planters. Telfair prescribed: "If there is any fighting on the plantation, whip all engaged in it, for no matter what the cause may have been, all are in the wrong." Weston wrote: "Fighting, particularly amongst women, and obscene or abusive language, is to be always rigorously punished."

"Punishment must never be cruel or abusive," wrote Acklen, closely followed by Fowler, "for it is absolutely mean and unmanly to whip a negro from mere passion and malice, and any man who can do so is utterly unfit to have control of negroes; and if ever any of my negroes are cruelly or inhumanly treated, bruised, maimed or otherwise injured, the overseer will be promptly discharged and his salary withheld." Weston recommended the lapse of a day between the discovery of an offense and the punishment, and he restricted the overseer's power in general to fifteen lashes. He continued: "Confinement (not in the stocks) is to be preferred to whipping; but the stoppage of Saturday's allowance, and doing whole task on Saturday, will suffice to prevent ordinary offenses. Special care must be taken to prevent any indecency in punishing women. No driver or other negro is to be allowed to punish any person in any way except by order of the overseer and in his presence." And again: "Every person should be made perfectly to understand what they are punished for, and should be made to perceive that they are not punished in anger or through caprice. All abusive language or violence of demeanor should be avoided; they reduce the man who uses them to a level with the negro, and are hardly ever forgotten by those to whom they are addressed." Ham-

mond directed that the overseer "must never threaten a negro,
but punish offences immediately on knowing them; otherwise he
will soon have runaways." As a schedule he wrote: "The following is the order in which offences must be estimated and
punished: 1st, running away; 2d, getting drunk or having
spirits; 3d, stealing hogs; 4th, stealing; 5th, leaving plantation
without permission; 6th, absence from house after horn-blow at
night; 7th, unclean house or person; 8th, neglect of tools; 9th,
neglect of work. The highest punishment must not exceed a
hundred lashes in one day, and to that extent only in extreme
cases. The whip lash must be one inch in width, or a strap of
one thickness of leather 1½ inches in width, and never severely
administered. In general fifteen to twenty lashes will be a sufficient flogging. The hands in every case must be secured by a
cord. Punishment must always be given calmly, and never when
angry or excited." Telfair was as usual terse: "No negro
to have more than fifty lashes for any offense, no matter how
great the crime." Manigault said nothing of punishments in
his general instructions, but sent special directions when a case
of incorrigibility was reported: "You had best think carefully
respecting him, and always keep in mind the important old
plantation maxim, viz: 'never to threaten a negro,' or he will
do as you and I would when at school—he will run. But with
such a one, . . . if you wish to make an example of
him, take him down to the Savannah jail and give him prison
discipline, and by all means solitary confinement, for three
weeks, when he will be glad to get home again. . . . Mind
then and tell him that you and he are quits, that you will never
dwell on old quarrels with him, that he has now a clear track
before him and all depends on himself, for he now sees how
easy it is to fix 'a bad disposed nigger.' Then give my com-
pliments to him and tell him that you wrote me of his conduct,
and say if he don't change for the better I'll sell him to a slave
trader who will send him to New Orleans, where I have already
sent several of the gang for misconduct, or their running away
for no cause." In one case Manigault lost a slave by suicide

in the river when a driver brought him up for punishment but allowed him to run before it was administered.[5]

As to rewards, Hammond was the only one of these writers to prescribe them definitely. His head driver was to receive five dollars, the plow driver three dollars, and the ditch driver and stock minder one dollar each every Christmas day, and the nurse a dollar and the midwife two dollars for every actual increase of two on the place. Further, "for every infant thirteen months old and in sound health, that has been properly attended to, the mother shall receive a muslin or calico frock."

"The head driver," Hammond wrote, "is the most important negro on the plantation, and is not required to work like other hands. He is to be treated with more respect than any other negro by both master and overseer. . . . He is to be required to maintain proper discipline at all times; to see that no negro idles or does bad work in the field, and to punish it with discretion on the spot. . . . He is a confidential servant, and may be a guard against any excesses or omissions of the overseer." Weston, forbidding his drivers to inflict punishments except at the overseer's order and in his presence, described their functions as the maintenance of quiet in the quarter and of discipline at large, the starting of the slaves to the fields each morning, the assignment and supervision of tasks, and the inspection of "such things as the overseer only generally superintends." Telfair informed his overseer: "I have no driver. You are to task the negroes yourself, and each negro is responsible to you for his own work, and nobody's else."

Of the master's own functions Hammond wrote in another place: "A planter should have all his work laid out, days, weeks, months, seasons and years ahead, according to the nature of it. He must go from job to job without losing a moment in turning round, and he must have all the parts of his work so arranged that due proportion of attention may be bestowed upon each at the proper time. More is lost by doing work out of season, and doing it better or worse than is requisite, than can readily be supposed. Negroes are harassed by it, too, instead of being

[5] *Plantation and Frontier*, II, 32, 94.

indulged; so are mules, and everything else. A halting, vacil-
lating, undecided course, now idle, now overstrained, is more
fatal on a plantation than in any other kind of business—
ruinous as it is in any."[6]

In the overseer all the virtues of a master were desired,
with a deputy's obedience added. Corbin enjoined upon his staff
that they "attend their business with diligence, keep the negroes
in good order, and enforce obedience by the example of their
own industry, which is a more effectual method in every respect
than hurry and severity. The ways of industry," he continued,
"are constant and regular, not to be in a hurry at one time
and do nothing at another, but to be always usefully and steadily
employed. A man who carries on business in this manner will
be prepared for every incident that happens. He will see what
work may be proper at the distance of some time and be
gradually and leisurely preparing for it. By this foresight he
will never be in confusion himself, and his business, instead
of a labor, will be a pleasure to him." Weston wrote: "The
proprietor wishes particularly to impress upon the overseer the
criterions by which he will judge of his usefullness and capacity.
First, by the general well-being of all the negroes; their cleanly
appearance, respectful manners, active and vigorous obedience;
their completion of their tasks well and early; the small amount
of punishment; the excess of births over deaths; the small number of persons in hospital; and the health of the children. Sec-
ondly, the condition and fatness of the cattle and mules; the
good repair of all the fences and buildings, harness, boats,
flats and ploughs; more particularly the good order of the banks
and trunks, and the freedom of the fields from grass and volunteer
[rice]. Thirdly, the amount and quality of the rice and provision
crops. . . . The overseer is expressly forbidden from three
things, viz.: bleeding, giving spirits to any negro without a doctor's order, and letting any negro on the place have or keep any
gun, powder or shot." One of Acklen's prohibitions upon his
overseers was: "Having connection with any of my female

---

[6] Letter of Hammond to William Gilmore Simms, Jan. 21, 1841, from
Hammond's MS. copy in the Library of Congress.

servants will most certainly be visited with a dismissal from my employment, and no excuse can or will be taken."

Hammond described the functions as follows: "The overseer will never be expected to work in the field, but he must always be with the hands when not otherwise engaged in the employer's business. . . . The overseer must never be absent a single night, nor an entire day, without permission previously obtained. Whenever absent at church or elsewhere he must be on the plantation by sundown without fail. He must attend every night and morning at the stables and see that the mules are watered, cleaned and fed, and the doors locked. He must keep the stable keys at night, and all the keys, in a safe place, and never allow anyone to unlock a barn, smoke-house or other depository of plantation stores but himself. He must endeavor, also, to be with the plough hands always at noon." He must also see that the negroes are out promptly in the morning, and in their houses after curfew, and must show no favoritism among the negroes. He must carry on all experiments as directed by the employer, and use all new implements and methods which the employer may determine upon; and he must keep a full plantation diary and make monthly inventories. Finally, "The negroes must be made to obey and to work, which may be done, by an overseer who attends regularly to his business, with very little whipping. Much whipping indicates a bad tempered or inattentive manager, and will not be allowed." His overseer might quit employment on a month's notice, and might be discharged without notice. Acklen's dicta were to the same general effect.

As to the relative importance of the several functions of an overseer, all these planters were in substantial agreement. As Fowler put it: "After taking proper care of the negroes, stock, etc., the next most important duty of the overseer is to make, if practicable, a sufficient quantity of corn, hay, fodder, meat, potatoes and other vegetables for the consumption of the plantation, and then as much cotton as can be made by requiring good and reasonable labor of operatives and teams." Likewise Henry Laurens, himself a prosperous planter of the earlier time as well as a statesman, wrote to an overseer of whose heavy tasking he had learned: "Submit to make less rice and keep my negroes at home in some degree of happiness in preference to large crops acquired by rigour and barbarity to those poor creatures." And to a new incumbent: "I have now to recommend to you the care of my negroes in general, but particularly the sick ones. Desire Mrs. White not to be sparing of red wine for those who have the flux or bad loosenesses; let them be well attended night and day, and if one wench is not sufficient add another to nurse them. With the well ones use gentle means mixed with easy authority first—if that does not succeed, make choice of the most stubborn one or two and chastise them severely but properly and with mercy, that they may be convinced that the end of correction is to be amendment." Again, alluding to one of his slaves who had been gathering the pennies of his fellows: "Amos has a great inclination to turn rum merchant. If his confederate comes to that plantation, I charge you to discipline him with thirty-nine sound lashes and turn him out of the gate and see that he goes quite off."[7]

The published advice of planters to their fellows was quite in keeping with these instructions to overseers. About 1809, for example, John Taylor, of Caroline, the leading Virginian advocate of soil improvement in his day, wrote of the care and control of slaves as follows: "The addition of comfort to mere necessaries is a price paid by the master for the advantages he will derive from binding his slave to his service by a ligament stronger than chains, far beneath their value in a pecuniary point of view; and he will moreover gain a stream of agreeable reflections throughout life, which will cost him nothing." He recommended fireproof brick houses, warm clothing, and abundant, varied food. Customary plenty in meat and vegetables, he said, would not only remove occasions for pilfering, but would give the master effective power to discourage it; for upon discovering the loss of any goods by theft he might put his whole force of slaves upon a limited diet for a time and thus suggest to the thief that on any future occasion his fellows would be under pressure to inform on him as a means of relieving their own privations. "A daily

[7] D. D. Wallace, *Life of Henry Laurens*, pp. 133, 192.

allowance of cyder," Taylor continued, "will extend the success of this system for the management of slaves, and particularly its effect of diminishing corporal punishments. But the reader is warned that a stern authority, strict discipline and complete subordination must be combined with it to gain any success at all."[8]

Another Virginian's essay, of 1834, ran as follows: Virginia negroes are generally better tempered than any other people; they are kindly, grateful, attached to persons and places, enduring and patient in fatigue and hardship, contented and cheerful. Their control should be uniform and consistent, not an alternation of rigor and laxity. Punishment for real faults should be invariable but moderate. "The best evidence of the good management of slaves is the keeping up of good discipline with little or no punishment." The treatment should be impartial except for good conduct which should bring rewards. Praise is often a better cure for laziness than stripes. The manager should know the temper of each slave. The proud and high spirited are easily handled: "Your slow and sulky negro, although he may have an even temper, is the devil to manage. The negro women are all harder to manage than the men. The only way to get along with them is by kind words and flattery. If you want to cure a sloven, give her something nice occasionally to wear, and praise her up to the skies whenever she has on anything tolerably decent." Eschew suspicion, for it breeds dishonesty. Promote harmony and sound methods among your neighbors. "A good disciplinarian in the midst of bad managers of slaves cannot do much; and without discipline there cannot be profit to the master or comfort to the slaves." Feed and clothe your slaves well. The best preventive of theft is plenty of pork. Let them have poultry and gardens and fruit trees to attach them to their houses and promote amenability. "The greatest bar to good discipline in Virginia is the number of grog shops in every farmer's neighborhood." There is no severity in the state,

[8] John Taylor, of Caroline County, Virginia, *Arator, Being a Series of Agricultural Essays* (2d ed., Georgetown, D. C., 1814), pp. 122-125.

and there will be no occasion for it again if the fanatics will only let us alone.[9]

An essay written after long experience by Robert Collins, of Macon, Georgia, which was widely circulated in the 'fifties, was in the same tone: "The best interests of all parties are promoted by a kind and liberal treatment on the part of the owner, and the requirement of proper discipline and strict obedience on the part of the slave. . . . Every attempt to force the slave beyond the limits of reasonable service by cruelty or hard treatment, so far from extorting more work, only tends to make him unprofitable, unmanageable, a vexation and a curse." The quarters should be well shaded, the houses free of the ground, well ventilated, and large enough for comfort; the bedding and blankets fully adequate. "In former years the writer tried many ways and expedients to economize in the provision of slaves by using more of the vegetable and cheap articles of diet, and less of the costly and substantial. But time and experience have fully proven the error of a stinted policy. . . . The allowance now given per week to each hand . . . is five pounds of good clean bacon and one quart of molasses, with as much good bread as they require; and in the fall, or sickly season of the year, or on sickly places, the addition of one pint of strong coffee, sweetened with sugar, every morning before going to work." The slaves may well have gardens, but the assignment of patches for market produce too greatly "encourages a traffic on their own account, and presents a temptation and opportunity, during the process of gathering, for an unscrupulous fellow to mix a little of his master's produce with his own. It is much better to give each hand whose conduct has been such as to merit it an equivalent in money at the end of the year; it is much less trouble, and more advantageous to both parties." Collins further advocated plenty of clothing, moderate hours, work by tasks in cotton picking and elsewhere when feasible, and firm though kindly discipline. "Slaves," he said, "have no respect or affection for a master who indulges them over much.

[9] "On the Management of Negroes. Addressed to the Farmers and Overseers of Virginia," signed "H. C.," in the *Farmer's Register*, I, 564, 565 (February, 1834).

. . . Negroes are by nature tyrannical in their dispositions, and if allowed, the stronger will abuse the weaker, husbands will often abuse their wives and mothers their children, so that it becomes a prominent duty of owners and overseers to keep peace and prevent quarrelling and disputes among them; and summary punishment should follow any violation of this rule. Slaves are also a people that enjoy religious privileges. Many of them place much value upon it; and to every reasonable extent that advantage should be allowed them. They are never injured by preaching, but thousands become wiser and better people and more trustworthy servants by their attendance at church. Religious services should be provided and encouraged on every plantation. A zealous and vehement style, both in doctrine and manner, is best adapted to their temperament. They are good believers in mysteries and miracles, ready converts, and adhere with much pertinacity to their opinions when formed." [10] It is clear that Collins had observed plantation negroes long and well.

Advice very similar to the foregoing examples was also printed in the form of manuals at the front of blank books for the keeping of plantation records; [11] and various planters described their own methods in operation as based on the same principles. One of these living at Chunnennuggee, Alabama, signing himself "N. B. P.," wrote in 1852 an account of the problems he had met and the solutions he had applied. Owning some 150 slaves, he had lived away from his plantation until about a decade prior to this writing; but in spite of careful selection he could never get an overseer combining the qualities necessary in a good manager. "They were generally on extremes; those celebrated for making large crops were often too severe, and did everything by

[10] Robert Collins, "Essay on the Management of Slaves," reprinted in *DeBow's Review*, XVII, 421-426, and partly reprinted in F. L. Olmsted, *Seaboard Slave States*, pp. 692-697.
[11] Pleasant Suit, *Farmer's Accountant and Instructions for Overseers* (Richmond, Va., 1828); *Affleck's Cotton Plantation Record and Account Book*, reprinted in *DeBow's Review*, XVIII, 339-345, and in Thomas W. Knox, *Campfire and Cotton Field* (New York, 1865), pp. 358-364. *See also* for varied and interesting data as to rules, experience and advice; Thomas S. Clay (of Bryan County, Georgia), *Detail of a Plan for the Moral Improvement of Negroes on Plantations* (1833); and *DeBow's Review*, XII, 291, 292; XIX, 358-363; XXI, 147-149, 277-279; XXIV, 321-326; XXV, 463; XXVI, 579, 580; XXIX, 112-115, 357-368.

coercion. Hence turmoil and strife ensued. The negroes were ill treated and ran away. On the other hand, when he employed a good-natured man there was a want of proper discipline; the negroes became unmanageable and, as a natural result, the farm was brought into debt." The owner then entered residence himself and applied methods which resulted in contentment, health and prolific increase among the slaves, and in consistently good crops. The men were supplied with wives at home so far as was practicable; each family had a dry and airy house to itself, with a poultry house and a vegetable garden behind; the rations issued weekly were three and a half pounds of bacon to each hand over ten years old, together with a peck of meal, or more if required; the children in the day nursery were fed from the master's kitchen with soup, milk, bacon, vegetables and bread; the hands had three suits of working clothes a year; the women were given time off for washing, and did their mending in bad weather; all hands had to dress up and go to church on Sunday when preaching was near; and a clean outfit of working clothes was required every Monday. The chief distinction of this plantation, however, lay in its device for profit sharing. To each slave was assigned a half-acre plot with the promise that if he worked with diligence in the master's crop the whole gang would in turn be set to work his crop. This was useful in preventing night and Sunday work by the negroes. The proceeds of their crops, ranging from ten to fifty dollars, were expended by the master at their direction for Sunday clothing and other supplies.[12] On a sugar plantation visited by Olmsted a sum of as many dollars as there were hogsheads in the year's crop was distributed among the slaves every Christmas.[13]

Of overseers in general, the great variety in their functions, their scales of operation and their personal qualities make sweeping assertions hazardous. Some were at just one remove from the authority of a great planter, as is suggested by the following advertisement: "Wanted, a manager to superintend several rice plantations on the Santee River. As the business is extensive,

[12] Southern Quarterly Review, XXI, 215, 216.
[13] Olmsted, Seaboard Slave States, p. 660.

a proportionate salary will be made, and one or two young men of his own selection employed under him.[14]   A healthful summer residence on the seashore is provided for himself and family. Others were hardly more removed from the status of common field hands.   Lawrence Tompkins, for example, signed with his mark in 1779 a contract to oversee the four slaves of William Allason, near Alexandria, and to work steadily with them.   He was to receive three barrels of corn and three hundred pounds of pork as his food allowance, and a fifth share of the tobacco, hemp and flax crops and a sixth of the corn; but if he neglected his work he might be dismissed without pay of any sort.[15]   Some overseers were former planters who had lost their property, some were planters' sons working for a start in life, some were English and German farmers who had brought their talents to what they hoped might prove the world's best market, but most of them were of the native yeomanry which abounded in virtually all parts of the South.   Some owned a few slaves whom they put on hire into their employers' gangs, thereby hastening their own attainment of the means to become planters on their own score.[16]

If the master lived on the plantation, as was most commonly the case, the overseer's responsibilities were usually confined to the daily execution of orders in supervising the slaves in the fields and the quarters.   But when the master was an absentee the opportunity for abuses and misunderstandings increased. Jurisdiction over slaves and the manner of its exercise were the grounds of most frequent complaint.   On the score of authority, for example, a Virginia overseer in the employ of Robert Carter wrote him in 1787 in despair at the conduct of a woman named Suckey: "I sent for hir to Come in the morning to help Secoure the foder, but She Sent me word that She would not come to worke that Day, and that you had ordered her to wash hir Cloaiths and goo to Any meeting She pleased any time in the weke without my leafe, and on monday when I Come to Reken with hir about it She Said it was your orders and She would

[14] *Southern Patriot* (Charleston, S. C.), Jan. 9, 1821.
[15] MS. Letter book, 1770-1787, among the Allason papers in the New York Public Library.
[16] D. D. Wallace, *Life of Henry Laurens*, pp. 21, 135.

do it in Defiance of me. . . . I hope if Suckey is aloud that privilige more than the Rest, that she will bee moved to some other place, and one Come in her Room."[17] On the score of abuses, Stancil Barwick, an overseer in southwestern Georgia, wrote in 1855 to John B. Lamar: "I received your letter on yesterday ev'ng. Was vary sorry to hear that you had heard that I was treating your negroes so cruely. Now, sir, I do say to you in truth that the report is false. Thear is no truth in it. No man nor set of men has ever seen me mistreat one of the negroes on the place." After declaring that miscarriages by two of the women had been due to no require-ment of work, he continued: "The reports that have been sent must have been carried from this place by negroes. The fact is I have made the negro men work, an made them go strait. That is what is the matter, an is the reason why my place is talk of the settlement. I have found among the negro men two or three hard cases an I have had to deal rite ruff, but not cruly at all. Among them Abram has been as triflin as any man on the place. Now, sir, what I have wrote you is truth, and it cant be disputed by no man on earth."[18]

To diminish the inducement for overdriving, the method of paying the overseers by crop shares, which commonly prevailed in the colonial period, was generally replaced in the nineteenth century by that of fixed salaries. As a surer preventive of embezzlement, a trusty slave was in some cases given the store-house keys in preference to the overseer; and sometimes even when the master was an absentee an overseer was wholly dis-pensed with and a slave foreman was given full charge. This practice would have been still more common had not the laws discouraged it.[19] Some planters refused to leave their slaves in the full charge of deputies of any kind, even for short periods. For example, Francis Corbin in 1819 explained to James Madison that he must postpone an intended visit because of the absence of his son. "Until he arrives," Corbin wrote, "I dare not, in common prudence, leave my affairs to the sole management of

[17] *Plantation and Frontier,* I, 325.
[18] *Ibid.,* I, 312, 313.
[19] Olmsted, *Seaboard States,* p. 206.

overseers, who in these days are little respected by our intelligent negroes, many of whom are far superior in mind, morals and manners to those who are placed in authority over them."[20]

Various phases of the problem of management are illustrated in a letter of A. H. Pemberton of the South Carolina midlands to James H. Hammond at the end of 1846. The writer described himself as unwilling to sacrifice his agricultural reading in order to superintend his slaves in person, but as having too small a force to afford the employment of an overseer pure and simple. For the preceding year he had had one charged with the double function of working in person and supervising the slaves' work also; but this man's excess of manual zeal had impaired his managerial usefulness. What he himself did was well done, said Pemberton, "and he would do *all* and leave the negroes to do virtually nothing; and as they would of course take advantage of this, what he did was more than counterbalanced by what they did not." Furthermore, this employee, "who worked harder than any man I ever saw," used little judgment or foresight. "Withal, he has always been accustomed to the careless Southern practice generally of doing things temporarily and in a hurry, just to last for the present, and allowing the negroes to leave plows and tools of all kinds just where they use them, no matter where, so that they have to be hunted all over the place when wanted. And as to stock, he had no idea of any more attention to them than is common in the ordinarily cruel and neglectful habits of the South." Pemberton then turned to lamentation at having let slip a recent opportunity to buy at auction "a remarkably fine looking negro as to size and strength, very black, about thirty-five or forty, and so intelligent and trustworthy that he had charge of a separate plantation and eight or ten hands some ten or twelve miles from home." The procuring of such a foreman would precisely have solved Pemberton's problem; the failure to do so left him in his far from hopeful search for a paragon manager and workman combined.[21]

On the whole, the planters were disposed to berate the overseers as a class for dishonesty, inattention and self indulgence. The demand for new and better ones was constant. For example, the editor of the *American Agriculturist,* whose office was at New York, announced in 1846: "We are almost daily beset with applications for properly educated managers for farms and plantations—we mean for such persons as are up to the improvements of the age, and have the capacity to carry them into effect."[22] Youths occasionally offered themselves as apprentices. One of them, in Louisiana, published the following notice in 1822: "A young man wishing to acquire knowledge of cotton planting would engage for twelve months as overseer and keep the accounts of a plantation. . . . Unquestionable reference as to character will be given."[23] And a South Carolinian in 1829 proposed that the practice be systematized by the appointment of local committees to bring intelligent lads into touch with planters willing to take them as indentured apprentices.[24] The lack of system persisted, however, both in agricultural education and in the procuring of managers. In the opinion of Basil Hall and various others the overseers were commonly better than the reputation of their class,[25] but this is not to say that they were conspicuous either for expertness or assiduity. On the whole they had about as much human nature, with its merits and failings, as the planters or the slaves or anybody else.

It is notable that George Washington was one of the least tolerant employers and masters who put themselves upon record.[26] This was doubtless due to his own punctiliousness and thorough devotion to system as well as to his often baffled wish to diversify his crops and upbuild his fields. When in 1793 he engaged William Pearce as a new steward for the group of plantations comprising the Mount Vernon estate, he enjoined strict super-

[22] *American Agriculturist,* V, 24.
[23] *Louisiana Herald* (Alexandria, La.), Jan. 12, 1822, advertisement.
[24] *Southern Agriculturist,* II, 271.
[25] Basil Hall, *Travels in North America,* III, 193.
[26] Voluminous plantation data are preserved in the Washington MSS. in the Library of Congress. Those here used are drawn from the letters of Washington published in the Long Island Historical Society *Memoirs,* vol. IV; entitled *George Washington and Mount Vernon.* A map of the Mount Vernon estate is printed in Washington's *Writings* (W. C. Ford ed.), XII, 358.

vision of his overseers "to keep them from running about and to oblige them to remain constantly with their people, and moreover to see at what time they turn out in the morning—for," said he, "I have strong suspicions that this with some of them is at a late hour, the consequences of which to the negroes is not difficult to foretell." "To treat them civilly," Washington continued, "is no more than what all men are entitled to; but my advice to you is, keep them at a proper distance, for they will grow upon familiarity in proportion as you will sink in authority if you do not. Pass by no faults or neglects, particularly at first, for overlooking one only serves to generate another, and it is more than probable that some of them, one in particular, will try at first what lengths he may go." Particularizing as to the members of his staff, Washington described their several characteristics: Stuart was intelligent and apparently honest and attentive, but vain and talkative, and usually backward in his schedule; Crow would be efficient if kept strictly at his duty, but seemed prone to visiting and receiving visits. "This of course leaves his people too much to themselves, which produces idleness or slight work on the one side and flogging on the other, the last of which, besides the dissatisfaction which it creates, has in one or two instances been productive of serious consequences." McKay was a "sickly, slothful and stupid sort of fellow," too much disposed to brutality in the treatment of the slaves in his charge; Butler seemed to have "no more authority over the negroes . . . than an old woman would have"; and Green, the overseer of the carpenters, was too much on a level with the slaves for the exertion of control. Davy, the negro foreman at Muddy Hole, was rated in his master's esteem higher than some of his white colleagues, though Washington had suspicions concerning the fate of certain lambs which had vanished while in his care. Indeed the overseers all and several were suspected from time to time of drunkenness, waste, theft and miscellaneous rascality. In the last of these categories Washington seems to have included their efforts to secure higher wages.

The slaves in their turn were suspected of ruining horses by

riding them at night, and of embezzling grain issued for planting, as well as of lying and malingering in general. The carpenters, Washington said, were notorious piddlers; and not a
slave about the mansion house was worthy of trust. Pretences
of illness as excuses for idleness were especially annoying. "Is
there anything particular in the cases of Ruth, Hannah and
Pegg," he enquired, "that they have been returned as sick
for several weeks together? . . . If they are not made to
do what their age and strength will enable them, it will be a
very bad example to others, none of whom would work if by
pretexts they can avoid it." And again: "By the reports I
perceive that for every day Betty Davis works she is laid up
two. If she is indulged in this idleness she will grow worse and
worse, for she has a disposition to be one of the most idle
creatures on earth, and is besides one of the most deceitful."
Pearce seems to have replied that he was at a loss to tell the false
from the true. Washington rejoined: "I never found so much
difficulty as you seem to apprehend in distinguishing between real
and feigned sickness, or when a person is much afflicted with
pain. Nobody can be very sick without having a fever, or any
other disorder continue long upon anyone without reducing them.
. . . But my people, many of them, will lay up a month, at
the end of which no visible change in their countenance nor the
loss of an ounce of flesh is discoverable; and their allowance of
provision is going on as if nothing ailed them." Runaways were
occasional. Of one of them Washington directed: "Let Abram
get his deserts when taken, by way of example; but do not trust
Crow to give it to him, for I have reason to believe he is swayed
more by passion than by judgment in all his corrections." Of
another, whom he had previously described as an idler beyond
hope of correction: "Nor is it worth while, except for the sake
of example, . . . to be at much trouble, or any expence over
a trifle, to hunt him up." Of a third, who was thought to have
escaped in company with a neighbor's slave: "If Mr. Dulany
is disposed to pursue any measure for the purpose of recovering
his man, I will join him in the expence so far as it may respect
Paul; but I would not have my name appear in any adver-

tisement, or other measure, leading to it." Again, when asking
that a woman of his who had fled to New Hampshire be seized
and sent back if it could be done without exciting a mob: "However well disposed I might be to gradual abolition, or even to an
entire emancipation of that description of people (if the latter
was in itself practicable), at this moment it would neither be
politic nor just to reward unfaithfulness with a premature preference, and thereby discontent beforehand the minds of all her
fellow serv'ts who, by their steady attachment, are far more
deserving than herself of favor."[27] Finally: "The running off
of my cook has been a most inconvenient thing to this family,
and what rendered it more disagreeable is that I had resolved
never to become the master of another slave by purchase. But
this resolution I fear I must break. I have endeavored to hire,
black or white, but am not yet supplied." As to provisions, the
slaves were given fish from Washington's Potomac fishery while
the supply lasted, "meat, fat and other things . . . now and
then," and of meal "as much as they can eat without waste, and
no more." The housing and clothing appear to have been adequate. The "father of his country" displayed little tenderness
for his slaves. He was doubtless just, so far as a business-like
absentee master could be; but his only generosity to them seems
to have been the provision in his will for their manumission after
the death of his wife.

Lesser men felt the same stresses in plantation management.
An owner of ninety-six slaves told Olmsted that such was the
trouble and annoyance his negroes caused him, in spite of his
having an overseer, and such the loneliness of his isolated life,
that he was torn between a desire to sell out at once and a
temptation to hold on for a while in the expectation of higher
prices. At the home of another Virginian, Olmsted wrote: "During three hours or more in which I was in company with the
proprietor I do not think there were ten consecutive minutes
uninterrupted by some of the slaves requiring his personal direction or assistance. He was even obliged three times to leave
the dinner table. 'You see,' said he smiling, as he came in the

[*] Marion G. McDougall, *Fugitive Slaves* (Boston, 1891), p. 36.

last time, 'a farmer's life in this country is no sinecure.' " A third Virginian, endorsing Olmsted's observations, wrote that a planter's cares and troubles were endless; the slaves, men, women and children, infirm and aged, had wants innumerable; some were indolent, some obstinate, some fractious, and each class required different treatment. With the daily wants of food, clothing and the like, "the poor man's time and thoughts, indeed every faculty of mind, must be exercised on behalf of those who have no minds of their own."[28]

Harriet Martineau wrote on her tour of the South: "Nothing struck me more than the patience of slave-owners . . . with their slaves. . . . When I considered how they love to be called 'fiery Southerners,' I could not but marvel at their mild forbearance under the hourly provocations to which they are liable in their homes. Persons from New England, France or England, becoming slave-holders, are found to be the most severe masters and mistresses, however good their tempers may always have appeared previously. They cannot, like the native proprietor, sit waiting half an hour for the second course, or see everything done in the worst possible manner, their rooms dirty, their property wasted, their plans frustrated, their infants slighted,—themselves deluded by artifices—they cannot, like the native proprietor, endure all this unruffled." [29] It is clear from every sort of evidence, if evidence were needed, that life among negro slaves and the successful management of them promoted, and wellnigh necessitated, a blending of foresight and firmness with kindliness and patience. The lack of the former qualities was likely to bring financial ruin; the lack of the latter would make life not worth living; the possession of all meant a toleration of slackness in every concern not vital to routine. A plantation was a bed of roses only if the thorns were turned aside. Charles Eliot Norton, who like Olmsted, Hall, Miss Martineau and most other travelers, was hostile to slavery, wrote after a journey to Charleston in 1855: "The change to a Northerner in coming South is always a great one when

[28] F. L. Olmsted, *Seaboard Slave States*, pp. 44, 58, 718.
[29] Harriet Martineau, *Society in America* (London, 1837), II, 315, 316.

he steps over the boundary of the free states; and the farther you go towards the South the more absolutely do shiftlessness and careless indifference take the place of energy and active precaution and skilful management. . . . The outside first aspect of slavery has nothing horrible and repulsive about it. The slaves do not go about looking unhappy, and are with difficulty, I fancy, persuaded to feel so. Whips and chains, oaths and brutality, are as common, for all that one sees, in the free as the slave states. We have come thus far, and might have gone ten times as far, I dare say, without seeing the first sign of negro misery or white tyranny."[30] If, indeed, the neatness of aspect be the test of success, most plantations were failures; if the test of failure be the lack of harmony and good will, it appears from the available evidence that most plantations were successful.

The concerns and the character of a high-grade planter may be gathered from the correspondence of John B. Lamar, who with headquarters in the town of Macon administered half a dozen plantations belonging to himself and his kinsmen scattered through central and southwestern Georgia and northern Florida.[31] The scale of his operations at the middle of the nineteenth century may be seen from one of his orders for summer cloth, presumably at the rate of about five yards per slave. This was to be shipped from Savannah to the several plantations as follows: to Hurricane, the property of Howell Cobb, Lamar's brother-in-law, 760 yards; to Letohatchee, a trust estate in Florida belonging to the Lamar family, 500 yards; and to Lamar's own plantations the following: Swift Creek, 486; Harris Place, 360; Domine, 340; and Spring Branch, 229. Of his course of life Lamar wrote: "I am one half the year rattling over rough roads with Dr. Physic and Henry, stopping at farm houses in the country, scolding overseers in half a dozen counties and two states, Florida and Georgia, and the other half in the largest cities of the Union, or those of Europe, living on dainties

[30] Charles Eliot Norton, *Letters* (Boston, 1913), I, 121.
[31] Lamar's MSS. are in the possession of Mrs. A. S. Erwin, Athens, Ga. Selections from them are printed in *Plantation and Frontier*, I, 167-183, 309-312, II, 38, 41.

and riding on rail-cars and steamboats. When I first emerge
from Swift Creek into the hotels and shops on Broadway of a
summer, I am the most economical body that you can imagine.
The fine clothes and expensive habits of the people strike me
forcibly. . . . In a week I become used to everything, and
in a month I forget my humble concern on Swift Creek and
feel as much a nabob as any of them. . . . At home where
everything is plain and comfortable we look on anything beyond
that point as extravagant. When abroad where things are on
a greater scale, our ideas keep pace with them. I always find
such to be my case; and if I live to a hundred I reckon it will
always be so."

Lamar could command strong words, as when a physician
demanded five hundred dollars for services at Hurricane in
1844, or when overseers were detected in drunkenness or cruelty;
but his most characteristic complaints were of his own shortcomings as a manager and of the crotchets of his relatives. His
letters were always cheery, and his repeated disappointments in
overseers never damped his optimism concerning each new incumbent. His old lands contented him until he found new and
more fertile ones to buy, whereupon his jubilation was great.
When cotton was low he called himself a toad under the harrow; but rising markets would set him to counting bales before
the seed had more than sprouted and to building new plantations in the air. In actual practice his log-cabin slave quarters
gave place to frame houses; his mules were kept in full force;
his production of corn and bacon was nearly always ample for
the needs of each place; his slaves were permitted to raise
nankeen cotton on their private accounts; and his own frequent
journeys of inspection and stimulus, as he said, kept up an
esprit du corps. When an overseer reported that his slaves
were down with fever by the dozen and his cotton wasting in
the fields, Lamar would hasten thither with a physician and a
squad of slaves impressed from another plantation, to care for
the sick and the crop respectively. He redistributed slaves
among his plantations with a view to a better balancing of
land and labor, but was deterred from carrving this policy as

far as he thought might be profitable by his unwillingness to separate the families. His absence gave occasion sometimes for discontent among his slaves; yet when the owners of others who were for sale authorized them to find their own purchasers his well known justice, liberality and good nature made "Mas John" a favorite recourse.

As to crops and management, Lamar indicated his methods in criticizing those of a relative: "Uncle Jesse still builds air castles and blinds himself to his affairs. Last year he tinkered away on tobacco and sugar cane, things he knew nothing about. . . . He interferes with the arrangements of his overseers, and has no judgment of his own. . . . If he would employ a competent overseer and move off the plantation with his family he could make good crops, as he has a good force of hands and good lands. . . . I have found that it is unprofitable to undertake anything on a plantation out of the regular routine. If I had a little place off to itself, and my business would admit of it, I should delight in agricultural experiments." In his reliance upon staple routine, as in every other characteristic, Lamar rings true to the planter type.

CHAPTER XV

PLANTATION LABOR

WHILE produced only in America, the plantation slave was a product of old-world forces. His nature was an African's profoundly modified but hardly transformed by the requirements of European civilization. The wrench from Africa and the subjection to the new discipline while uprooting his ancient language and customs had little more effect upon his temperament than upon his complexion. Ceasing to be Foulah, Coromantee, Ebo or Angola, he became instead the American negro. The Caucasian was also changed by the contact in a far from negligible degree; but the negro's conversion was much the more thorough, partly because the process in his case was coercive, partly because his genius was imitative.

The planters had a saying, always of course with an implicit reservation as to limits, that a negro was what a white man made him. The molding, however, was accomplished more by groups than by individuals. The purposes and policies of the masters were fairly uniform, and in consequence the negroes, though with many variants, became largely standardized into the predominant plantation type. The traits which prevailed were an eagerness for society, music and merriment, a fondness for display whether of person, dress, vocabulary or emotion, a not flagrant sensuality, a receptiveness toward any religion whose exercises were exhilarating, a proneness to superstition, a courteous acceptance of subordination, an avidity for praise, a readiness for loyalty of a feudal sort, and last but not least, a healthy human repugnance toward overwork. "It don't do no good to hurry," was a negro saying, "'caze you're liable to run by mo'n you overtake." Likewise painstaking was reckoned painful; and tomorrow was always waiting for today's work, while

today was ready for tomorrow's share of play. On the other
hand it was a satisfaction to work sturdily for a hard boss, and
so be able to say in an interchange of amenities: "Go long,
half-priced nigger! You wouldn't fotch fifty dollars, an' I'm
wuth a thousand!"[1]

Contrasts were abundant. John B. Lamar, on the one hand,
wrote: "My man Ned the carpenter is idle or nearly so at
the plantation. He is fixing gates and, like the idle groom in
Pickwick, trying to fool himself into the belief that he is
doing something. . . . He is an eye servant. If I was
with him I could have the work done soon and cheap; but I
am afraid to trust him off where there is no one he fears."[2] On
the other hand, M. W. Philips inscribed a page of his plantation
diary as follows:[3]

<blockquote>
Sunday
July 10, 1853
Peyton is no more
Aged 42
Though he was a bad man in many respects
yet he was a most excellent field
hand, always at his
post.
On this place for 21 years.
Except the measles and its sequence, the
injury rec'd by the mule last Nov'r and its sequence,
he has not lost 15 days' work, I verily believe, in the
remaining 19 years. I wish we could hope for his
eternal state.
</blockquote>

Should anyone in the twentieth century wish to see the old-
fashioned prime negro at his best, let him take a Mississippi
steamboat and watch the roustabouts at work—those chaffing and
chattering, singing and swinging, lusty and willing freight han-
dlers, whom a river captain plying out of New Orleans has
called the noblest black men that God ever made.[4] Ready at

[1] *Daily Tropic* (New Orleans), May 18, 1846.
[2] *Plantation and Frontier*, II, 38.
[3] Mississippi Historical Society *Publications*, X, 444.
[4] Captain L. V. Cooley, *Address Before the Tulane Society of Economics, New Orleans, April 11th, 1911, on River Transportation and Its Relation to New Orleans, Past, Present and Future*. [New Orleans, 1911.]

every touching of the shore day and night, resting and sleeping only between landings, they carry their loads almost at running speed, and when returning for fresh burdens they "coonjine" by flinging their feet in semi-circles at every step, or cutting other capers in rhythm to show their fellows and the gallery that the strain of the cotton bales, the grain sacks, the oil barrels and the timbers merely loosen their muscles and lighten their spirits.

Such an exhibit would have been the despair of the average ante-bellum planter, for instead of choosing among hundreds of applicants and rejecting or discharging those who fell short of a high standard, he had to make shift with such laborers as the slave traders chanced to bring or as his women chanced to rear. His common problem was to get such income and comfort as he might from a parcel of the general run; and the creation of roustabout energy among them would require such vigor and such iron resolution on his own part as was forthcoming in extremely few cases.

Theoretically the master might be expected perhaps to expend the minimum possible to keep his slaves in strength, to discard the weaklings and the aged, to drive his gang early and late, to scourge the laggards hourly, to secure the whole with fetters by day and with bolts by night, and to keep them in perpetual terror of his wrath. But Olmsted, who seems to have gone South with the thought of finding some such theory in application, wrote: "I saw much more of what I had not anticipated and less of what I had in the slave states than. with a somewhat extended travelling experience, in any other country I ever visited"; [5] and Nehemiah Adams, who went from Boston to Georgia prepared to weep with the slaves who wept, found himself laughing with the laughing ones instead.[6]

The theory of rigid coercion and complete exploitation was as strange to the bulk of the planters as the doctrine and practice of moderation was to those who viewed the régime from afar and with the mind's eye. A planter in explaining his

[5] Olmsted, *Seaboard Slave States*, p. 179.
[6] Nehemiah Adams, *A Southside View of Slavery, or Three Months in the South in 1854* (Boston, 1854), chap. 2.

mildness might well have said it was due to his being neither a knave nor a fool. He refrained from the use of fetters not so much because they would have hampered the slaves in their work as because the general use of them never crossed his mind. And since chains and bolts were out of the question, the whole system of control must be moderate; slaves must be impelled as little as possible by fear, and as much as might be by loyalty, pride and the prospect of reward.

Here and there a planter applied this policy in an exceptional degree. A certain Z. Kingsley followed it with marked success even when his whole force was of fresh Africans. In a pamphlet of the late eighteen-twenties he told of his method as follows: "About twenty-five years ago I settled a plantation on St. John's River in Florida with about fifty new negroes, many of whom I brought from the Coast myself. They were mostly fine young men and women, and nearly in equal numbers. I never interfered in their connubial concerns nor domestic affairs, but let them regulate these after their own manner. I taught them nothing but what was useful, and what I thought would add to their physical and moral happiness. I encouraged as much as possible dancing, merriment and dress, for which Saturday afternoon and night and Sunday morning were dedicated. [Part of their leisure] was usually employed in hoeing their corn and getting a supply of fish for the week. Both men and women were very industrious. Many of them made twenty bushels of corn to sell, and they vied with each other in dress and dancing. . . . They were perfectly honest and obedient, and appeared perfectly happy, having no fear but that of offending me; and I hardly ever had to apply other correction than shaming them. If I exceeded this, the punishment was quite light, for they hardly ever failed in doing their work well. My object was to excite their ambition and attachment by kindness, not to depress their spirits by fear and punishment. . . . Perfect confidence, friendship and good understanding reigned between us." During the War of 1812 most of these negroes were killed or carried off in a Seminole raid. When peace returned and Kingsley attempted to restore

his Eden with a mixture of African and American negroes, a
serpent entered in the guise of a negro preacher who taught
the sinfulness of dancing, fishing on Sunday and eating the
catfish which had no scales. In consequence the slaves "became
poor, ragged, hungry and disconsolate. To steal from me was
only to do justice—to take what belonged to them, because I
kept them in unjust bondage." They came to believe "that all
pastime or pleasure in this iniquitous world was sinful; that this
was only a place of sorrow and repentance, and the sooner they
were out of it the better; that they would then go to a good
country where they would experience no want of anything, and
have no work nor cruel taskmaster, for that God was merciful
and would pardon any sin they committed; only it was necessary to pray and ask forgiveness, and have prayer meetings and
contribute what they could to the church, etc. . . . Finally
myself and the overseer became completely divested of all authority over the negroes. . . . Severity had no effect; it
only made it worse."[7]

This experience left Kingsley undaunted in his belief that
liberalism and profit-sharing were the soundest basis for the
plantation régime. To support this contention further he cited
an experiment by a South Carolinian who established four or
five plantations in a group on Broad River, with a slave foreman on each and a single overseer with very limited functions
over the whole. The cotton crop was the master's, while the
hogs, corn and other produce belonged to the slaves for their
sustenance and the sale of any surplus. The output proved
large, "and the owner had no further trouble nor expense than
furnishing the ordinary clothing and paying the overseer's wages,
so that he could fairly be called free, seeing that he could realize
his annual income wherever he chose to reside, without paying
the customary homage to servitude of personal attendance on
the operation of his slaves." In Kingsley's opinion the system
"answered extremely well, and offers to us a strong case in

[7] [Z. Kingsley] *A Treatise on the Patriarchal System of Society as It
exists . . . under the Name of Slavery.* By an inhabitant of Florida.
Fourth edition (1834), pp. 21, 22. (Copy in the Library of Congress.)

favor of exciting ambition by cultivating utility, local attachment and moral improvement among the slaves."[8]

The most thoroughgoing application on record of self-government by slaves is probably that of the brothers Joseph and
Jefferson Davis on their plantations, Hurricane and Brierfield, in
Warren County, Mississippi. There the slaves were not only
encouraged to earn money for themselves in every way they
might, but the discipline of the plantations was vested in courts
composed wholly of slaves, proceeding formally and imposing
penalties to be inflicted by slave constables except when the
master intervened with his power of pardon. The régime was
maintained for a number of years in full effect until in 1862
when the district was invaded by Federal troops.[9]

These several instances were of course exceptional, and they
merely tend to counterbalance the examples of systematic severity at the other extreme. In general, though compulsion was
always available in last resort, the relation of planter and slave
was largely shaped by a sense of propriety, proportion and cooperation.

As to food, clothing and shelter, a few concrete items will
reinforce the indications in the preceding chapters that crude
comfort was the rule. Bartram the naturalist observed in 1776
that a Georgia slaveholder with whom he stopped sold no dairy
products from his forty cows in milk. The proprietor explained this by saying: "I have a considerable family of black
people who though they are slaves must be fed and cared for
Those I have were either chosen for their good qualities or
born in the family; and I find from long experience and observation that the better they are fed, clothed and treated, the more
service and profit we may expect to derive from their labour.
In short, I find my stock produces no more milk, or any article
of food or nourishment, than what is expended to the best
advantage amongst my family and slaves." At another place
Bartram noted the arrival at a plantation of horse loads of

[Z. Kingsley] *Treatise*, p. 22.
[9] W. L. Fleming, "Jefferson Davis, the Negroes and the Negro Problem,"
in the *Sewanee Review* (October, 1908).

wild pigeons taken by torchlight from their roosts in a neighboring swamp.[10]

On Charles Cotesworth Pinckney's two plantations on the South Carolina coast, as appears from his diary of 1818, a detail of four slaves was shifted from the field work each week for a useful holiday in angling for the huge drumfish which abounded in those waters; and their catches augmented the fare of the white and black families alike.[11] Game and fish, however, were extras. The staple meat was bacon, which combined the virtues of easy production, ready curing and constant savoriness. On Fowler's "Prairie" plantation, where the field hands numbered a little less than half a hundred, the pork harvest throughout the eighteen-fifties, except for a single year of hog cholera, yielded from eleven to twenty-three hundred pounds; and when the yield was less than the normal, northwestern bacon or barreled pork made up the deficit.[12]

In the matter of clothing, James Habersham sent an order to London in 1764 on behalf of himself and two neighbors for 120 men's jackets and breeches and 80 women's gowns to be made in assorted sizes from strong and heavy cloth. The purpose was to clothe their slaves "a little better than common" and to save the trouble of making the garments at home.[13] In January, 1835, the overseer of one of the Telfair plantations reported that the woolen weaving had nearly supplied the full needs of the place at the rate of six or six and a half yards for each adult and proportionately for the children.[14] In 1847, in preparation for winter, Charles Manigault wrote from Paris to his overseer: "I wish you to count noses among the negroes and see how many jackets and trousers you want for the men at Gowrie, . . . and then write to Messrs. Matthiessen and Co. of Charleston to send them to you, together with the same quantity of twilled red flannel shirts, and a large woolen Scotch cap for each man and youth on the place. . . . Send back

[10] William Bartram, *Travels* (London, 1792), pp. 307-310, 467, 468.
[11] *Plantation and Frontier*, I, 203-208.
[12] MS. records in the possession of W. H. Stovall, Stovall, Miss.
[13] *Plantation and Frontier*, I, 293, 294.
[14] *Ibid.*, 192, 193.

anything which is not first rate. You will get from Messrs. Habersham and Son the twilled wool and cotton, called by some 'Hazzard's cloth,' for all the women and children, and get two or three dozen handkerchiefs so as to give each woman and girl one. . . . The shoes you will procure as usual from Mr. Habersham by sending down the measures in time."[15] Finally, the register of A. L. Alexander's plantation in the Georgia Piedmont contains record of the distributions from 1851 to 1864 on a steady schedule. Every spring each man drew two cotton shirts and two pair of homespun woolen trousers, each woman a frock and chemises, and each child clothing or cloth in proportion; and every fall the men drew shirts, trousers and coats, the women shifts, petticoats, frocks and sacks, the children again on a similar scale, and the several families blankets as needed.[16]

As for housing, the vestiges of the old slave quarters, some of which have stood abandoned for half a century, denote in many cases a sounder construction and greater comfort than most of the negroes in freedom have since been able to command.

With physical comforts provided, the birth-rate would take care of itself. The pickaninnies were winsome, and their parents, free of expense and anxiety for their sustenance, could hardly have more of them than they wanted. A Virginian told Olmsted, "he never heard of babies coming so fast as they did on his plantation; it was perfectly surprising";[17] and in Georgia, Howell Cobb's negroes increased "like rabbits."[18] In Mississippi M. W. Philips' woman Amy had borne eleven children when at the age of thirty she was married by her master to a new husband, and had eight more thereafter, including a set of triplets.[19] But the culminating instance is the following as reported by a newspaper at Lynchburg, Virginia: "VERY REMARKABLE. There is now living in the vicinity of Campbell a negro woman belonging to a gentleman by the name of Todd; this

[15] MS. copy in Manigault's letter book.
[16] MS. in the possession of Mrs. J. F. Minis, Savannah, Ga.
[17] Olmsted, *Seaboard Slave States*, p. 57.
[18] *Plantation and Frontier*, I, 179.
[19] Mississippi Historical Society *Publications*, X, 439, 443, 447, 480.

woman is in her forty-second year and has had forty-one children and at this time is pregnant with her forty-second child, and possibly with her forty-third, as she has frequently had doublets."[20] Had childbearing been regulated in the interest of the masters, Todd's woman would have had less than forty-one and Amy less than her nineteen, for such excesses impaired the vitality of the children. Most of Amy's, for example, died a few hours or days after birth.

A normal record is that of Fowler's plantation, the "Prairie." Virtually all of the adult slaves were paired as husbands and wives except Caroline who in twenty years bore ten children. Her husband was presumably the slave of some other master. Tom and Milly had nine children in eighteen years; Harry and Jainy had seven in twenty-two years; Fanny had five in seventeen years with Ben as the father of all but the first born; Louisa likewise had five in nineteen years with Bob as the father of all but the first; and Hector and Mary had five in seven years. On the other hand, two old couples and one in their thirties had had no children, while eight young pairs had from one to four each.[21] A lighter schedule was recorded on a Louisiana plantation called Bayou Cotonier, belonging to E. Tanneret, a Creole. The slaves listed in 1859 as being fifteen years old and upwards comprised thirty-six males and thirty-seven females. The "livre des naissances" showed fifty-six births between 1833 and 1859, distributed among twenty-three women, two of whom were still in their teens when the record ended. Rhodé bore six children between her seventeenth and thirty-fourth years; Henriette bore six between twenty-one and forty; Esther six between twenty-one and thirty-six; Fanny, four between twenty-five and thirty-two; Annette, four between thirty-three and forty; and the rest bore from one to three children each, including Celestine who had her first baby when fifteen and her second two years after. None of the matings or paternities appear in the record, though the christenings and the slave godparents are registered.[22]

[20] *Louisiana Gazette* (New Orleans), June 11, 1822, quoting the Lynchburg *Press.*
[21] MS. in the possession of W. H. Stovall, Stovall, Miss.
[22] MS. in the Howard Memorial Library, New Orleans.

The death rate was a subject of more active solicitude. This may be illustrated from the journal for 1859-1860 of the Magnolia plantation, forty miles below New Orleans. Along with its record of rations to 138 hands, and of the occasional births, deaths, runaways and recaptures, and of the purchase of a man slave for $2300, it contains the following summary under date of October 4, 1860: "We have had during the past eighteen months over 150 cases of measles and numerous cases of whooping cough, and then the diphtheria, all of which we have gone through with but little loss save in the whooping cough when we lost some twelve children." This entry was in the spirit of rejoicing at escape from disasters. But on December 18 there were two items of another tone. One of these was entered by an overseer named Kellett: "[I] shot the negro boy Frank for attempting to cut at me and three boys with his cane knife with intent to kill." The other, in a different handwriting, recorded tersely: "J. A. Randall commenst buisnass this mornung. J. Kellett discharged this morning." The owner could not afford to keep an overseer who killed negroes even though it might be in self defence.[23]

Of epidemics, yellow fever was of minor concern as regards the slaves, for negroes were largely immune to it; but cholera sometimes threatened to exterminate the slaves and bankrupt their masters. After a visitation of this in and about New Orleans in 1832, John McDonogh wrote to a friend: "All that you have seen of yellow fever was nothing in comparison. It is supposed that five or six thousand souls, black and white, were carried off in fourteen days."[24] The pecuniary loss in Louisiana from slave deaths in that epidemic was estimated at four million dollars.[25] Two years afterward it raged in the Savannah neighborhood. On Mr. Wightman's plantation, ten miles above the city, there were in the first week of September fifty-three cases and eighteen deaths. The overseer then

---

[23] MS. preserved on the plantation, owned by ex-Governor H. C. Warmoth.
[24] William Allen, *Life of John McDonogh* (Baltimore, 1886), p. 54.
[25] *Niles' Register*, XLV, 84.

checked the spread by isolating the afflicted ones in the church, the barn and the mill. The neighboring planters awaited only the first appearance of the disease on their places to abandon their crops and hurry their slaves to lodges in the wilderness.[26] Plagues of smallpox were sometimes of similar dimensions. Even without pestilence, deaths might bring a planter's ruin. A series of them drove M. W. Philips to exclaim in his plantation journal: "Oh! my losses almost make me crazy. God alone can help." In short, planters must guard their slaves' health and life as among the most vital of their own interests; for while crops were merely income, slaves were capital. The tendency appears to have been common, indeed, to employ free immigrant labor when available for such work as would involve strain and exposure. The documents bearing on this theme are scattering but convincing. Thus E. J. Forstall when writing in 1845 of the extension of the sugar fields, said thousands of Irishmen were seen in every direction digging plantation ditches;[27] T. B. Thorpe when describing plantation life on the Mississippi in 1853 said the Irish proved the best ditchers;[28] and a Georgia planter when describing his drainage of a swamp in 1855 said that Irish were hired for the work in order that the slaves might continue at their usual routine.[29] Olmsted noted on the Virginia seaboard that "Mr. W. . . . had an Irish gang draining for him by contract." Olmsted asked, "why he should employ Irishmen in preference to doing the work with his own hands. 'It's dangerous work,' the planter replied, 'and a negro's life is too valuable to be risked at it. If a negro dies, it is a considerable loss you know.' "[30] On a Louisiana plantation W. H. Russell wrote in 1860: "The labor of ditching, trenching, cleaning the waste lands and hewing down the forests is generally done by Irish laborers who travel about the country under contractors or are engaged by resident gangsmen for the task. Mr. Seal lamented the high prices of this work; but then, as he said, 'It was much

[26] *Federal Union* (Milledgeville, Ga.), Sept. 14 and 17 and Oct. 22, 1834.
[27] Edward J. Forstall, *The Agricultural Productions of Louisiana* (New Orleans, 1845).
[28] *Harper's Magazine*, VII, 755.
[29] *DeBow's Review*, XI, 401.
[30] Olmsted, *Seaboard Slave States*, pp. 90, 91.

better to have Irish do it, who cost nothing to the planter if they died, than to use up good field-hands in such severe employment.' " Russell added on his own score: "There is a wonderful mine of truth in this observation. Heaven knows how many poor Hibernians have been consumed and buried in these Louisianian swamps, leaving their earnings to the dramshop keeper and the contractor, and the results of their toil to the planter." On another plantation the same traveller was shown the débris left by the last Irish gang and was regaled by an account of the methods by which their contractor made them work.[31] Robert Russell made a similar observation on a plantation near New Orleans, and was told that even at high wages Irish laborers were advisable for the work because they would do twice as much ditching as would an equal number of negroes in the same time.[32] Furthermore, A. de Puy Van Buren, noted as a common sight in the Yazoo district, "especially in the ditching season, wandering 'exiles of Erin,' straggling along the road"; and remarked also that the Irish were the chief element among the straining roustabouts, on the steamboats of that day.[33] Likewise Olmsted noted on the Alabama River that in lading his boat with cotton from a towering bluff, a slave squad was appointed for the work at the top of the chute, while Irish deck hands were kept below to capture the wildly bounding bales and stow them. As to the reason for this division of labor and concentration of risk, the traveller had his own surmise confirmed when the captain answered his question by saying, "The niggers are worth too much to be risked here; if the Paddies are knocked overboard, or get their backs broke, nobody loses anything!"[34] To these chance observations it may be added that many newspaper items and canal and railroad company reports from the 'thirties to the 'fifties record that the construction gangs were largely of Irish and Germans. The pay attracted those

[31] W. H. Russell, *My Diary North and South* (Boston, 1863), pp 272, 273, 278.
[32] Robert Russell, *North America, Its Agriculture and Climate* (Edinburgh, 1857), p. 272.
[33] A. de Puy Van Buren, *Jottings of a Year's Sojourn in the South* (Battle Creek, Mich., 1859), pp. 84, 318.
[34] Olmsted, *Seaboard Slave States*, pp. 550, 551.

whose labor was their life; the risk repelled those whose labor was their capital. There can be no doubt that the planters cherished the lives of their slaves.

Truancy was a problem in somewhat the same class with disease, disability and death, since for industrial purposes a slave absent was no better than a slave sick, and a permanent escape was the equivalent of a death on the plantation. The character of the absconding was various. Some slaves merely took vacations without leave, some fled in postponement of threatened punishments, and most of the rest made resolute efforts to escape from bondage altogether.

Occasionally, however, a squad would strike in a body as a protest against severities. An episode of this sort was recounted in a letter of a Georgia overseer to his absent employer: "Sir: I write you a few lines in order to let you know that six of your hands has left the plantation—every man but Jack. They displeased me with their worke and I give some of them a few lashes, Tom with the rest. On Wednesday morning they were missing. I think they are lying out until they can see you or your uncle Jack, as he is expected daily. They may be gone off, or they may be lying round in this neighbourhood, but I don't know. I blame Tom for the whole. I don't think the rest would of left the plantation if Tom had not of persuaded them of for some design. I give Tom but a few licks, but if I ever get him in my power I will have satisfaction. There was a part of them had no cause for leaving, only they thought if they would all go it would injure me moore. They are as independent a set for running of as I have ever seen, and I think the cause is they have been treated too well. They want more whipping and no protecter; but if our country is so that negroes can quit their homes and run of when they please without being taken they will have the advantage of us. If they should come in I will write to you immediately and let you know." [35]

Such a case is analogous to that of wage-earning laborers

[35] Letter of I. E. H. Harvey, Jefferson County, Georgia, April 16, 1837, to H. C. Flournoy, Athens, Ga. MS. in private possession. Punctuation and capitals, which are conspicuously absent in the original, have here been supplied for the sake of clarity.

on strike for better conditions of work. The slaves could not
negotiate directly at such a time, but while they lay in the woods
they might make overtures to the overseer through slaves on a
neighboring plantation as to terms upon which they would
return to work, or they might await their master's posthaste
arrival and appeal to him for a redress of grievances. Humble
as their demeanor might be, their power of renewing the pressure by repeating their flight could not be ignored. A happy
ending for all concerned might be reached by mutual concessions and pledges. That the conclusion might be tragic is illustrated in a Louisiana instance where the plantation was in charge
of a negro foreman. Eight slaves after lying out for some
weeks because of his cruelty and finding their hardships in the
swamp intolerable returned home together and proposed to go
to work again if granted amnesty. When the foreman promised a multitude of lashes instead, they killed him with their
clubs. The eight then proceeded to the parish jail at Vidalia,
told what they had done, and surrendered themselves. The
coroner went to the plantation and found the foreman dead
according to specifications.[36] The further history of the eight
is unknown.

Most of the runaways went singly, but some of them went
often. Such chronic offenders were likely to be given exemplary
punishment when recaptured. In the earlier decades branding
and shackling were fairly frequent. Some of the punishments
were unquestionably barbarous, the more so when inflicted upon
talented and sensitive mulattoes and quadroons who might be
quite as fit for freedom as their masters. In the later period
the more common resorts were to whipping, and particularly to
sale. The menace of this last was shrewdly used by making a
bogey man of the trader and a reputed hell on earth of any
district whither he was supposed to carry his merchandise. "They
are taking her to Georgia for to wear her life away" was a slave
refrain welcome to the ears of masters outside that state; and
the slanderous imputation gave no offence even to Georgians,
for they recognized that the intention was benevolent, and they

[36] *Daily Delta* (New Orleans), April 17, 1849.

were in turn blackening the reputations of the more westerly states in the amiable purpose of keeping their own slaves content.

Virtually all the plantations whose records are available suffered more or less from truancy, and the abundance of newspaper advertisements for fugitives reinforces the impression that the need of deterrence was vital. Whippings, instead of proving a cure, might bring revenge in the form of sabotage, arson or murder. Adequacy in food, clothing and shelter might prove of no avail, for contentment must be mental as well as physical. The preventives mainly relied upon were holidays, gifts and festivities to create lightness of heart; overtime and overtask payments to promote zeal and satisfaction; kindliness and care to call forth loyalty in return; and the special device of crop patches to give every hand a stake in the plantation. This last raised a minor problem of its own, for if slaves were allowed to raise and sell the plantation staples, pilfering might be stimulated more than industry and punishments become more necessary than before. In the cotton belt a solution was found at last in nankeen cotton.[37] This variety had been widely grown for domestic use as early as the beginning of the nineteenth century, but it was left largely in neglect until when in the thirties it was hit upon for negro crops. While the prices it brought were about the same as those of the standard upland staple, its distinctive brown color prevented the admixture of the planter's own white variety without certain detection when it reached the gin. The scale which the slave crops attained on some plantations is indicated by the proceeds of $1,969.65 in 1859 from the nankeen of the negroes on the estate of Allen McWalker in Taylor County, Georgia.[38] Such returns might be distributed in cash; but planters generally preferred for the sake of sobriety that money should not be freely handled by the slaves. Earnings as well as gifts were therefore likely to be issued in the form of tickets for merchandise. David Ross, for example, addressed

[37] John Drayton, *View of South Carolina* (Charleston, 1802), p. 128.
[38] Macon, Ga., *Telegraph*, Feb. 3, 1859, quoted in *DeBow's Review*, XXIX, 362, note.

the following to the firm of Allen and Ellis at Fredericksburg
in the Christmas season of 1802: "Gentlemen: Please to let
the bearer George have ten dollars value in anything he chooses";
and the merchants entered a memorandum that George chose
two handkerchiefs, two hats, three and a half yards of linen, a
pair of hose, and six shillings in cash.[89]

In general the most obvious way of preventing trouble was to
avoid the occasion for it. If tasks were complained of as too
heavy, the simplest recourse was to reduce the schedule. If
jobs were slackly done, acquiescence was easier than correction.
The easy-going and plausible disposition of the blacks conspired
with the heat of the climate to soften the resolution of the whites
and make them patient. Severe and unyielding requirements
would keep everyone on edge; concession when accompanied
with geniality and not indulged so far as to cause demoralization
would make plantation life not only tolerable but charming.

In the actual régime severity was clearly the exception, and
kindliness the rule. The Englishman Welby, for example, wrote
in 1820: "After travelling through three slave states I am
obliged to go back to theory to raise any abhorrence of it. Not
once during the journey did I witness an instance of cruel treatment, nor could I discover anything to excite commiseration in
the faces or gait of the people of colour. They walk, talk and
appear at least as independent as their masters; in animal spirits
they have greatly the advantage."[40] Basil Hall wrote in 1828:
"I have no wish, God knows! to defend slavery in the abstract;
. . . but . . . nothing during my recent journey gave me
more satisfaction than the conclusion to which I was gradually
brought that the planters of the Southern states of America,
generally speaking, have a sincere desire to manage their estates
with the least possible severity. I do not say that undue severity
is nowhere exercised; but the discipline, taken upon the average, as far as I could learn, is not more strict than is necessary
for the maintenance of a proper degree of authority, without
which the whole framework of society in that quarter would be

[89] MS. among the Allen and Ellis papers in the Library of Congress.
[40] Adlard Welby, *Visit to North America* (London, 1821), reprinted in
Thwaites ed., *Early Western Travels*, XII, 289.

blown to atoms."[41] And Olmsted wrote: "The only whipping of slaves that I have seen in Virginia has been of these wild, lazy children as they are being broke in to work."[42]

As to the rate and character of the work, Hall said that in contrast with the hustle prevailing on the Northern farms, "in Carolina all mankind appeared comparatively idle."[43] Olmsted, when citing a Virginian's remark that his negroes never worked enough to tire themselves, said on his own account: "This is just what I have thought when I have seen slaves at work—they seem to go through the motions of labor without putting strength into them. They keep their powers in reserve for their own use at night, perhaps."[44] And Solon Robinson reported tersely from a rice plantation that the negroes plied their hoes "at so slow a rate, the motion would have given a quick-working Yankee convulsions."[45]

There was clearly no general prevalence of severity and strain in the régime. There was, furthermore, little of that curse of impersonality and indifference which too commonly prevails in the factories of the present-day world where power-driven machinery sets the pace, where the employers have no relations with the employed outside of work hours, where the proprietors indeed are scattered to the four winds, where the directors confine their attention to finance, and where the one duty of the superintendent is to procure a maximum output at a minimum cost. No, the planters were commonly in residence, their slaves were their chief property to be conserved, and the slaves themselves would not permit indifference even if the masters were so disposed. The generality of the negroes insisted upon possessing and being possessed in a cordial but respectful intimacy. While by no means every plantation was an Arcadia there were many on which the industrial and racial relations deserved almost as glowing accounts as that which the Englishman William Faux wrote in 1819 of the "goodly plantation" of the venerable Mr.

[41] Basil Hall, *Travels in the United States*, III, 227, 228.
[42] Olmsted, *Seaboard Slave States*, p. 146.
[43] Basil Hall, III, 117.
[44] *Seaboard Slave States*, p. 91.
[45] *American Agriculturist*, IX, 93.

Mickle in the uplands of South Carolina.[46] "This gentleman,"
said he, "appears to me to be a rare example of pure and
undefiled religion, kind and gentle in manners. . . . Seeing
a swarm, or rather herd, of young negroes creeping and dancing
about the door and yard of his mansion, all appearing healthy,
happy and frolicsome and withal fat and decently clothed, both
young and old, I felt induced to praise the economy under which
they lived. 'Aye,' said he, 'I have many black people, but I
have never bought nor sold any in my life. All that you see
came to me with my estate by virtue of my father's will. They
are all, old and young, true and faithful to my interests. They
need no taskmaster, no overseer. They will do all and more
than I expect them to do, and I can trust them with untold gold.
All the adults are well instructed, and all are members of Christian churches in the neighbourhood; and their conduct is becoming their professions. I respect them as my children, and they
look on me as their friend and father. Were they to be taken
from me it would be the most unhappy event of their lives.'
This conversation induced me to view more attentively the faces
of the adult slaves; and I was astonished at the free, easy, sober,
intelligent and thoughtful impression which such an economy as
Mr. Mickle's had indelibly made on their countenances."

[46] William Faux, *Memorable Days in America* (London, 1823), p. 68, re
printed in Thwaites, ed., *Early Western Travels*, XI, 87.

CHAPTER XVI

PLANTATION LIFE

W HEN Hakluyt wrote in 1584 his *Discourse of Western Planting,* his theme was the project of American colonization; and when a settlement was planted at Jamestown, at Boston or at Providence as the case might be, it was called, regardless of the type, a plantation. This usage of the word in the sense of a colony ended only upon the rise of a new institution to which the original name was applied. The colonies at large came then to be known as provinces or dominions, while the sub-colonies, the privately owned village estates which prevailed in the South, were alone called plantations. In the Creole colonies, however, these were known as *habitations*—dwelling places. This etymology of the name suggests the nature of the thing—an isolated place where people in somewhat peculiar groups settled and worked and had their being. The standard community comprised a white household in the midst of several or many negro families. The one was master, the many were slaves; the one was head, the many were members; the one was teacher, the many were pupils.

The scheme of the buildings reflected the character of the group. The "big house," as the darkies loved to call it, might be of any type from a double log cabin to a colonnaded mansion of many handsome rooms, and its setting might range from a bit of primeval forest to an elaborate formal garden. Most commonly the house was commodious in a rambling way, with no pretense to distinction without nor to luxury within. The two fairly constant features were the hall running the full depth of the house, and the verandah spanning the front. The former by day and the latter at evening served in all temperate seasons as the receiving place for guests and the gathering place for the household at all its leisure times. The house was likely to have a quiet dignity of its own; but most of such beauty as the homestead possessed was contributed by the canopy of live-oaks if on the rice or sugar coasts, or of oaks, hickories or cedars, if in the uplands. Flanking the main house in many cases were an office and a lodge, containing between them the administrative headquarters, the schoolroom, and the apartments for any bachelor overflow whether tutor, sons or guests. Behind the house and at a distance of a rod or two for the sake of isolating its noise and odors, was the kitchen. Near this, unless a spring were available, stood the well with its two buckets dangling from the pulley; and near this in turn the dairy and the group of pots and tubs which constituted the open air laundry. Bounding the back yard there were the smoke-house where bacon and hams were cured, the sweet potato pit, the ice pit except in the southernmost latitudes where no ice of local origin was to be had, the carriage house, the poultry house, the pigeon cote, and the lodgings of the domestic servants. On plantations of small or medium scale the cabins of the field hands generally stood at the border of the master's own premises; but on great estates, particularly in the lowlands, they were likely to be somewhat removed, with the overseer's house, the smithy, and the stables, corn cribs and wagon sheds nearby. At other convenient spots were the buildings for working up the crops—the tobacco house, the threshing and pounding mills, the gin and press, or the sugar house as the respective staples required. The climate conduced so strongly to out of door life that as a rule each roof covered but a single unit of residence, industry or storage.

The fields as well as the buildings commonly radiated from the planter's house. Close at hand were the garden, the orchards and the horse lot; and behind them the sweet potato field, the watermelon patch and the forage plots of millet, sorghum and the like. Thence there stretched the fields of the main crops in a more or less solid expanse according to the local conditions. Where ditches or embankments were necessary, as for sugar and rice fields, the high cost of reclamation promoted compactness; elsewhere the prevailing cheapness of land promoted dispersion.

Throughout the uplands, accordingly, the area in crops was likely to be broken by wood lots and long-term fallows. The scale of tillage might range from a few score acres to a thousand or two; the expanse of unused land need have no limit but those of the proprietor's purse and his speculative proclivity.

The scale of the orchards was in some degree a measure of the domesticity prevailing. On the rice coast the unfavorable character of the soil and the absenteeism of the planter's families in summer conspired to keep the fruit trees few. In the sugar district oranges and figs were fairly plentiful. But as to both quantity and variety in fruits the Piedmont was unequaled. Figs, plums, apples, pears and quinces were abundant, but the peaches excelled all the rest. The many varieties of these were in two main groups, those of clear stones and soft, luscious flesh for eating raw, and those of clinging stones and firm flesh for drying, preserving, and making pies. From June to September every creature, hogs included, commonly had as many peaches as he cared to eat; and in addition great quantities might be carried to the stills. The abandoned fields, furthermore, contributed dewberries, blackberries, wild strawberries and wild plums in summer, and persimmons in autumn, when the forest also yielded its muscadines, fox grapes, hickory nuts, walnuts, chestnuts and chinquapins, and along the Gulf coast pecans.

The resources for edible game were likewise abundant, with squirrels, opossums and wild turkeys, and even deer and bears in the woods, rabbits, doves and quail in the fields, woodcock and snipe in the swamps and marshes, and ducks and geese on the streams. Still further, the creeks and rivers yielded fish to be taken with hook, net or trap, as well as terrapin and turtles, and the coastal waters added shrimp, crabs and oysters. In most localities it required little time for a household, slave or free, to lay forest, field or stream under tribute.

The planter's own dietary, while mostly home grown, was elaborate. Beef and mutton were infrequent because the pastures were poor; Irish potatoes were used only when new, for they did not keep well in the Southern climate; and wheaten loaves were seldom seen because hot breads were universally preferred. The standard meats were chicken in its many guises, ham and bacon. Wheat flour furnished relays of biscuit and waffles, while corn yielded lye hominy, grits, muffins, batter cakes, spoon bread, hoe cake and pone. The gardens provided in season lettuce, cucumbers, radishes and beets, mustard greens and turnip greens, string beans, snap beans and butter beans, asparagus and artichokes, Irish potatoes, squashes, onions, carrots, turnips, okra, cabbages and collards. The fields added green corn for boiling, roasting, stewing and frying, cowpeas and black-eyed peas, pumpkins and sweet potatoes, which last were roasted, fried or candied for variation. The people of the rice coast, furthermore, had a special fondness for their own pearly staple; and in the sugar district *sirop de batterie* was deservedly popular. The pickles, preserves and jellies were in variety and quantity limited only by the almost boundless resources and industry of the housewife and her kitchen corps. Several meats and breads and relishes would crowd the table simultaneously, and, unless unexpected guests swelled the company, less would be eaten during the meal than would be taken away at the end, never to return. If ever tables had a habit of groaning it was those of the planters. Frugality, indeed, was reckoned a vice to be shunned, and somewhat justly so since the vegetables and eggs were perishable, the bread and meat of little cost, and the surplus from the table found sure disposal in the kitchen or the quarters. Lucky was the man whose wife was the "big house" cook, for the cook carried a basket, and the basket was full when she was homeward bound.

The fare of the field hands was, of course, far more simple. Hoecake and bacon were its basis and often its whole content. But in summer fruit and vegetables were frequent; there was occasional game and fish at all seasons; and the first heavy frost of winter brought the festival of hog-killing time. While the shoulders, sides, hams and lard were saved, all other parts of the porkers were distributed for prompt consumption. Spare ribs and backbone, jowl and feet, souse and sausage, liver and chitterlings greased every mouth on the plantation; and the cracklingbread, made of corn meal mixed with the crisp tidbits left from the trying of the lard, carried fullness to repletion. Christmas and the summer lay-by brought recreation, but the hog-killing brought fat satisfaction.[1]

The warmth of the climate produced some distinctive customs. One was the high seasoning of food to stimulate the appetite; another was the afternoon siesta of summer; a third the well-nigh constant leaving of doors ajar even in winter when the roaring logs in the chimney merely took the chill from the draughts. Indeed a door was not often closed on the plantation except those of the negro cabins, whose inmates were hostile to night air, and those of the storerooms. As a rule, it was only in the locks of the latter that keys were ever turned by day or night.

The lives of the whites and the blacks were partly segregate, partly intertwined. If any special link were needed, the children supplied it. The whites ones, hardly knowing their mothers from their mammies or their uncles by blood from their "uncles" by courtesy, had the freedom of the kitchen and the cabins, and the black ones were their playmates in the shaded sandy yard the livelong day. Together they were regaled with folklore in the quarters, with Bible and fairy stories in the "big house," with pastry in the kitchen, with grapes at the scuppernong arbor, with melons at the spring house and with peaches in the orchard. The half-grown boys were likewise almost as undiscriminating among themselves as the dogs with which they chased rabbits by day and 'possums by night. Indeed, when the fork in the road of life was reached, the white youths found something to envy in the freedom of their fellows' feet from the cramping weight of shoes and the freedom of their minds from the restraints of school. With the approach of maturity came routine and responsibility for the whites, routine alone for the generality of the blacks. Some of the males of each race grew into ruffians, others into gentlemen in the literal sense, some of

<hr/>

[1] This account of plantation homesteads and dietary is drawn mainly from the writer's own observations in post-bellum times in which, despite the shifting of industrial arrangements and the decrease of wealth, these phases have remained apparent. Confirmation may be had in Philip Fithian *Journal* (Princeton, 1900); A. de Puy Van Buren, *Jottings of a Year's Sojourn in the South* (Battle Creek, Mich., 1859); Susan D. Smedes, *Memorials of a Southern Planter* (Baltimore, 1887); Mary B. Chestnutt, *A Diary from Dixie* (New York, 1905); and many other memoirs and traveller's accounts.

the females into viragoes, others into gentlewomen; but most of both races and sexes merely became plain, wholesome folk of a somewhat distinctive plantation type.

In amusements and in re'' ion the activities of the whites and blacks were both mingled and separate. Fox hunts when occurring by day were as a rule diversions only for the planters and their sons and guests, but when they occurred by moonlight the chase was joined by the negroes on foot with halloos which rivalled the music of the hounds. By night also the blacks, with the whites occasionally joining in, sought the canny 'possum and the embattled 'coon; in spare times by day they hied their curs after the fleeing Brer Rabbit, or built and baited seductive traps for turkeys and quail; and fishing was available both by day and by night. At the horse races of the whites the jockeys and many of the spectators were negroes; while from the cock fights and even the "crap" games of the blacks, white men and boys were not always absent.

Festivities were somewhat more separate than sports, though by no means wholly so. In the gayeties of Christmas the members of each race were spectators of the dances and diversions of the other. Likewise marriage merriment in the great house would have its echo in the quarters; and sometimes marriages among the slaves were grouped so as to give occasion for a general frolic. Thus Daniel R. Tucker in 1858 sent a general invitation over the countryside in central Georgia to a sextuple wedding among his slaves, with dinner and dancing to follow.[2] On the whole, the fiddle, the banjo and the bones were not seldom in requisition.

It was a matter of discomfort that in the evangelical churches dancing and religion were held to be incompatible. At one time on Thomas Dabney's plantation in Mississippi, for instance, the whole negro force fell captive in a Baptist "revival" and forswore the double shuffle. "I done buss' my fiddle an' my banjo, and done fling 'em away," the most music-loving fellow on the place said to the preacher when asked for his religious experi-

---

[2] *Federal Union* (Milledgeville, Ga.), April 20, 1858.

ences.[3] Such a condition might be tolerable so long as it was
voluntary; but the planters were likely to take precautions
against its becoming coercive. James H. Hammond, for instance,
penciled a memorandum in his plantation manual: "Church
members are privileged to dance on all holyday occasions; and
the class-leader or deacon who may report them shall be repri-
manded or punished at the discretion of the master."[4] The
logic with which sin and sanctity were often reconciled is illustrated in Irwin Russell's remarkably faithful "Christmas in the
Quarters." "Brudder Brown" has advanced upon the crowded
floor to "beg a blessin' on dis dance:"

O Mashr! let dis gath'rin' fin' a blessin' in yo' sight!
Don't jedge us hard fur what we does—you knows it's Chrismus
    night;
An' all de balunce ob de yeah we does as right's we kin.
Ef dancin's wrong, O Mashr! let de time excuse de sin!

We labors in de vineya'd, wukin' hard and wukin' true;
Now, shorely you won't notus, ef we eats a grape or two,
An' takes a leetle holiday,—a leetle restin' spell,—
Bekase, nex' week we'll start in fresh, an' labor twicet as well.

Remember, Mashr,—min' dis, now,—de sinfulness ob sin
Is 'pendin' 'pon de sperrit what we goes an' does it in;
An' in a righchis frame ob min' we's gwine to dance an' sing,
A-feelin' like King David, when he cut de pigeon-wing.

It seems to me—indeed it do—I mebbe mout be wrong—
That people raly *ought* to dance, when Chrismus comes along;
Des dance bekase dey's happy—like de birds hops in de trees,
De pine-top fiddle soundin' to de blowin' ob de breeze.

We has no ark to dance afore, like Isrul's prophet king;
We has no harp to soun' de chords, to holp us out to sing;
But 'cordin' to de gif's we has we does de bes' we knows,
An' folks don't 'spise de vi'let-flower bekase it ain't de rose.

You bless us, please, sah, eben ef we's doin' wrong tonight:
Kase den we'll need de blessin' more'n ef we's doin' right;
An' let de blessin' stay wid us, untel we comes to die,
An' goes to keep our Chrismus wid dem sheriffs in de sky!

[3] S. D. Smedes, *Memorials of a Southern Planter*, pp. 161, 162.
[4] MS. among the Hammond papers in the Library of Congress.

Yes, tell dem preshis anjuls we's a-gwine to jine 'em soon:
Our voices we's a-trainin' fur to sing de glory tune;
We's ready when you wants us, an' it ain't no matter when—
O Mashr! call yo' chillen soon, an' take 'em home! Amen.[5]

The churches which had the greatest influence upon the negroes
were those which relied least upon ritual and most upon exhilara-
tion. The Baptist and Methodist were foremost, and the latter
had the special advantage of the chain of camp meetings which
extended throughout the inland regions. At each chosen spot
the planters and farmers of the countryside would jointly erect
a great shed or "stand" in the midst of a grove, and would severally build wooden shelters or "tents" in a great square surrounding it. When the crops were laid by in August, the households would remove thither, their wagons piled high with bedding, chairs and utensils to keep "open house" with heavy-laden
tables for all who might come to the meeting. With less elaborate equipment the negroes also would camp in the neighborhood and attend the same service as the whites, sitting generally
in a section of the stand set apart for them. The camp meeting, in short, was the chief social and religious event of the year
for all the Methodist whites and blacks within reach of the
ground and for such non-Methodists as cared to attend. For
some of the whites this occasion was highly festive, for others,
intensely religious; but for any negro it might easily be both at
once. Preachers in relays delivered sermons at brief intervals
from sunrise until after nightfall; and most of the sermons were
followed by exhortations for sinners to advance to the mourners'
benches to receive the more intimate and individual suasion of
the clergy and their corps of assisting brethren and sisters. The
condition was highly hypnotic, and the professions of conversion
were often quite as ecstatic as the most fervid ministrant could
wish. The negroes were particularly welcome to the preachers,
for they were likely to give the promptest response to the pulpit's challenge and set the frenzy going. A Georgia preacher,
for instance, in reporting from one of these camps in 1807, wrote:
"The first day of the meeting, we had a gentle and comfortable

[5] Irwin Russell, *Poems* (New York [1888]), pp. 5-7.

moving of the spirit of the Lord among us; and at night it was much more powerful than before, and the meeting was kept up all night without intermission. However, before day the white people retired, and the meeting was continued by the black people." It is easy to see who led the way to the mourners' bench. "Next day," the preacher continued, "at ten o'clock the meeting was remarkably lively, and many souls were deeply wrought upon; and at the close of the sermon there was a general cry for mercy, and before night there were a good many persons who professed to get converted. That night the meeting continued all night, both by the white and black people, and many souls were converted before day." The next day the stir was still more general. Finally, "Friday was the greatest day of all. We had the Lord's Supper at night, . . . and such a solemn time I have seldom seen on the like occasion. Three of the preachers fell helpless within the altar, and one lay a considerable time before he came to himself. From that the work of convictions and conversions spread, and a large number were converted during the night, and there was no intermission until the break of day. At that time many stout hearted sinners were conquered. On Saturday we had preaching at the rising of the sun; and then with many tears we took leave of each other." [6]

The tone of the Baptist "protracted meetings" was much like that of the Methodist camps. In either case the rampant emotionalism, effective enough among the whites, was with the negroes a perfect contagion. With some of these the conversion brought lasting change; with others it provided a garment of piety to be donned with "Sunday-go-to-meeting clothes" and doffed as irksome on week days. With yet more it merely added to the joys of life. The thrill of exaltation would be followed by pleasurable "sin," to give place to fresh conversion when the furor season recurred. The rivalry of the Baptist and Methodist churches, each striving by similar methods to excel the other, tempted many to become oscillating proselytes, yielding to the allurements first of the one and then of the other, and on each

[6] *Farmer's Gazette* (Sparta, Ga.), Aug. 8, 1807, reprinted in *Plantation and Frontier*, II, 285, 286.

occasion holding the center of the stage as a brand snatched from the burning, a lost sheep restored to the fold, a cause and participant of rapture.

In these manifestations the negroes merely followed and enlarged upon the example of some of the whites. The similarity of practices, however, did not promote a permanent mingling of the two races in the same congregations, for either would feel some restraint upon its rhapsody imposed by the presence of the other. To relieve this there developed in greater or less degree a separation of the races for purposes of worship, white ministers preaching to the blacks from time to time in plantation missions, and home talent among the negroes filling the intervals. While some of the black exhorters were viewed with suspicion by the whites, others were highly esteemed and unusually privileged. One of these at Lexington, Kentucky, for example, was given the following pass duly signed by his master: "Tom is my slave, and has permission to go to Louisville for two or three weeks and return here after he has made his visit. Tom is a preacher of the reformed Baptist church, and has always been a faithful servant." [7] As a rule the greater the proportion of negroes in a district or a church connection, the greater the segregation in worship. If the whites were many and the negroes few, the latter would be given the gallery or some other group of pews; but if the whites were few and the negroes many, the two elements would probably worship in separate buildings. Even in such case, however, it was very common for a parcel of black domestics to flock with their masters rather than with their fellows.

The general régime in the fairly typical state of South Carolina was described in 1845 in a set of reports procured preliminary to a convention on the state of religion among the negroes and the means of its betterment. Some of these accounts were from the clergy of several denominations, others from the laity; some treated of general conditions in the several districts, others

[7] Dated Aug. 6, 1856, and signed E. McCallister. MS. in the New York Public Library.

in detail of systems on the writers' own plantations. In the latter group, N. W. Middleton, an Episcopalian of St. Andrew's parish, wrote that he and his wife and sons were the only religious teachers of his slaves, aside from the rector of the parish. He read the service and taught the catechism to all every Sunday afternoon, and taught such as came voluntarily to be instructed after family prayers on Wednesday nights. His wife and sons taught the children "constantly during the week," chiefly in the catechism. On the other hand R. F. W. Allston, a fellow Episcopalian of Prince George, Winyaw, had on his plantation a place of worship open to all denominations. A Methodist missionary preached there on alternate Sundays, and the Baptists were less regularly cared for. Both of these sects, furthermore, had prayer meetings, according to the rules of the plantation, on two nights of each week. Thus while Middleton endeavored to school his slaves in his own faith, Allston encouraged them to seek salvation by such creed as they might choose.

An Episcopal clergyman in the same parish with Allston wrote that he held fortnightly services among the negroes on ten plantations, and enlisted some of the literate slaves as lay readers. His restriction of these to the text of the prayer book, however, seems to have shorn them of power. The bulk of the slaves flocked to the more spontaneous exercises elsewhere; and the clergyman could find ground for satisfaction only in saying that frequently as many as two hundred slaves attended services at one of the parish churches in the district.

The Episcopal failure was the "evangelical" opportunity. Of the thirteen thousand slaves in Allston's parish some 3200 were Methodists and 1500 Baptists, as compared with 300 Episcopalians. In St. Peter's parish a Methodist reported that in a total of 6600 slaves, 1335 adhered to his faith, about half of whom were in mixed congregations of whites and blacks under the care of two circuit-riders, and the rest were in charge of two missionaries who ministered to negroes alone. Every large plantation, furthermore, had one or more "so-called negro preachers, but more properly exhorters." In St. Helena parish the Baptists led with 2132 communicants; the Methodists followed with

314 to whom a missionary holding services on twenty plantations devoted the whole of his time; and the Episcopalians as usual brought up the rear with fifty-two negro members of the church at Beaufort and a solitary additional one in the chapel on St. Helena island.

Of the progress and effects of religion in the lowlands Allston and Middleton thought well. The latter said, "In every respect I feel encouraged to go on." The former wrote: "Of my own negroes and those in my immediate neighborhood I may speak with confidence. They are attentive to religious instruction and greatly improved in intelligence and morals, in domestic relations, etc. Those who have grown up under religious training are more intelligent and generally, though not always, more improved than those who have received religious instruction as adults. Indeed the degree of intelligence which as a class they are acquiring is worthy of deep consideration." Thomas Fuller, the reporter from the Beaufort neighborhood, however, was as much apprehensive as hopeful. While the negroes had greatly improved in manners and appearance as a result of coming to worship in town every Sunday, said he, the freedom which they were allowed for the purpose was often misused in ways which led to demoralization. He strongly advised the planters to keep the slaves at home and provide instruction there.

From the upland cotton belt a Presbyterian minister in the Chester district wrote: "You are all aware, gentlemen, that the relation and intercourse between the whites and the blacks in the up-country are very different from what they are in the low-country. With us they are neither so numerous nor kept so entirely separate, but constitute a part of our households, and are daily either with their masters or some member of the white family. From this circumstance they feel themselves more identified with their owners than they can with you. I minister steadily to two different congregations. More than one hundred blacks attend. . . . The gallery, or a quarter of the house, is appropriated to them in all our churches, and they enjoy the preached gospel in common with the whites." Finally, from the Greenville district, on the upper edge of the Piedmont, where the

Methodists and Baptists were completely dominant among whites and blacks alike, it was reported: "About one fourth of the members in the churches are negroes. In the years 1832, '3 and '4 great numbers of negroes joined the churches during a period of revival. Many, I am sorry to say, have since been excommunicated. As the general zeal in religion declined, they backslid." There were a few licensed negro preachers, this writer continued, who were thought to do some good; but the general improvement in negro character, he thought, was mainly due to the religious and moral training given by their masters, and still more largely by their mistresses. From all quarters the expression was common that the promotion of religion among the slaves was not only the duty of masters but was to their interest as well in that it elevated the morals of the workmen and improved the quality of the service they rendered.[8]

In general, the less the cleavage of creed between master and man, the better for both, since every factor conducing to solidarity of sentiment was of advantage in promoting harmony and progress. When the planter went to sit under his rector while the slave stayed at home to hear an exhorter, just so much was lost in the sense of fellowship. It was particularly unfortunate that on the rice coast the bulk of the blacks had no co-religionists except among the non-slaveholding whites with whom they had more conflict than community of economic and sentimental interest. On the whole, however, in spite of the contrary suggestion of irresponsible religious preachments and manifestations, the generality of the negroes everywhere realized, like the whites, that virtue was to be acquired by consistent self-control

---

[8] *Proceedings of the Meeting in Charleston, S. C., May 13-15, 1845, on the Religious Instruction of the Negroes, together with the Report of the Committee and the Address to the Public* (Charleston, 1845). The reports of the Association for the Religious Instruction of Negroes in Liberty County, Georgia, printed annually for a dozen years or more in the 'thirties and 'forties, relate the career of a particularly interesting missionary work in that county on the rice coast, under the charge of the Reverend C. C. Jones. The tenth report in the series (1845) summarizes the work of the first decade, and the twelfth (1847) surveys the conditions then prevalent. In C. F. Deems ed., *Annals of Southern Methodism for 1856* (Nashville, [1857]) the ninth chapter is made up of reports on the mission activities of that church among the negroes in various quarters of the South.

in the performance of duty rather than by the alternation of spasmodic reforms and relapses.

Occasionally some hard-headed negro would resist the hypnotic suggestion of his preacher, and even repudiate glorification on his death-bed. A Louisiana physician recounts the final episode in the career of "Old Uncle Caleb," who had long been a-dying. "Before his departure, Jeff, the negro preacher of the place, gathered his sable flock of saints and sinners around the bed. He read a chapter and prayed, after which they sang a hymn. . . . Uncle Caleb lay motionless with closed eyes, and gave no sign. Jeff approached and took his hand. 'Uncle Caleb,' said he earnestly, 'de doctor says you are dying; and all de bredderin has come in for to see you de last time. And now, Uncle Caleb, dey wants to hear from your own mouf de precious words, dat you feels prepared to meet your God, and is ready and willin' to go.' Old Caleb opened his eyes suddenly, and in a very peevish, irritable tone, rebuffed the pious functionary in the following unexpected manner: 'Jeff, don't talk your nonsense to me! You jest knows dat I an't ready to go, nor willin' neder; and dat I an't prepared to meet nobody.' Jeff expatiated largely not only on the mercy of God, but on the glories of the heavenly kingdom, as a land flowing with milk and honey, etc. 'Dis ole cabin suits me mon'sus well!' was the only reply he could elicit from the old reprobate. And so he died." [9]

The slaves not only had their own functionaries in mystic matters, including a remnant of witchcraft, but in various temporal concerns also. Foremen, chosen by masters with the necessary sanction of the slaves, had industrial and police authority; nurses were minor despots in sick rooms and plantation hospitals; many an Uncle Remus was an oracle in folklore; and many an Aunt Dinah was arbitress of style in turbans and of elegancies in general. Even in the practice of medicine a negro here and there gained a sage's reputation. The governor of Virginia reported in 1729 that he had "met with a negro, a very old man, who has performed many wonderful cures of diseases. For the sake of

---

[9] William H. Holcombe, "Sketches of Plantation Life," in the *Knickerbocker Magazine*, LVII, 631 (June, 1861).

his freedom he has revealed the medicine, a concoction of roots and barks. . . . There is no room to doubt of its being a certain remedy here, and of singular use among the negroes—it is well worth the price (£60) of the negro's freedom, since it is now known how to cure slaves without mercury." [10] And in colonial South Carolina a slave named Caesar was particularly famed for his cure for poison, which was a decoction of plantain, hoarhound and golden rod roots compounded with rum and lye, together with an application of tobacco leaves soaked in rum in case of rattlesnake bite. In 1750 the legislature ordered his prescription published for the benefit of the public, and the Charleston journal which printed it found its copies exhausted by the demand.[11] An example of more common episodes appears in a letter from William Dawson, a Potomac planter, to Robert Carter of Nomoni Hall, asking that "Brother Tom," Carter's coachman, be sent to see a sick child in his quarter. Dawson continued: "The black people at this place hath more faith in him as a doctor than any white doctor; and as I wrote you in a former letter I cannot expect you to lose your man's time, etc., for nothing, but am quite willing to pay for same." [12]

Each plantation had a double head in the master and the mistress. The latter, mother of a romping brood of her own and over-mother of the pickaninny throng, was the chatelaine of the whole establishment. Working with a never flagging constancy, she carried the indoor keys, directed the household routine and the various domestic industries, served as head nurse for the sick, and taught morals and religion by precept and example. Her hours were long, her diversions few, her voice quiet, her influence firm.[13] Her presence made the plantation a home; her absence would have made it a factory. The master's concern was mainly with the able-bodied in the routine of the crops. He laid the plans, guessed the weather, ordered the work, and saw to its performance. He was out early and in late, directing, teaching,

[10] J. H. Russell, *The Free Negro in Virginia* (Baltimore, 1913), p. 53, note.
[11] *South Carolina Gazette*, Feb. 25, 1751.
[12] MS. in the Carter papers, Virginia Historical Society.
[13] Emily J. Putnam, *The Lady* (New York, 1910), pp. 282-323.

encouraging, and on occasion punishing. Yet he found time for going to town and for visits here and there, time for politics, and time for sports. If his duty as he saw it was sometimes grim, and his disappointments keen, hearty diversions were at hand to restore his equanimity. His horn hung near and his hounds made quick response on Reynard's trail, and his neighbors were ready to accept his invitations and give theirs lavishly in return, whether to their houses or to their fields. When their absences from home were long, as they might well be in the public service, they were not unlikely upon return to meet such a reception as Henry Laurens described: "I found nobody there but three of our old domestics—Stepney, Exeter and big Hagar. These drew tears from me by their humble and affectionate salutes. My knees were clasped, my hands kissed, my very feet embraced, and nothing less than a very—I can't say fair, but full —buss of my lips would satisfy the old man weeping and sobbing in my face. . . . They . . . held my hands, hung upon me; I could scarce get from them. 'Ah,' said the old man, 'I never thought to see you again; now I am happy; Ah, I never thought to see you again.' " [14]

Among the clearest views of plantation life extant are those of two Northern tutors who wrote of their Southern sojourns. One was Philip Fithian who went from Princeton in 1773 to teach the children of Colonel Robert Carter of Nomoni Hall in the "Northern Neck" of Virginia, probably the most aristocratic community of the whole South: the other was A. de Puy Van Buren who left Battle Creek in the eighteen-fifties to seek health and employment in Mississippi and found them both, and happiness too, amid the freshly settled folk on the banks of the Yazoo River. Each of these made jottings now and then of the work and play of the negroes, but both of them were mainly impressed by the social régime in which they found themselves among the whites. Fithian marveled at the evidences of wealth and the stratification of society, but he reckoned that a well recommended Princeton graduate, with no questions asked as to his family, fortune or business, would be rated socially as on an

[14] D. D. Wallace, *Life of Henry Laurens*, p. 436.

equal footing with the owner of a £10,000 estate, though this might be discounted one-half if he were unfashionably ignorant of dancing, boxing, fencing, fiddling and cards.[15] He was attracted by the buoyancy, the good breeding and the cordiality of those whom he met, and particularly by the sound qualities of Colonel and Mrs. Carter with whom he dwelt; but as a budding Presbyterian preacher he was a little shocked at first by the easygoing conduct of the Episcopalian planters on Sundays. The time at church, he wrote, falls into three divisions: first, that before service, which is filled by the giving and receiving of business letters, the reading of advertisements and the discussion of crop prices and the lineage and qualities of favorite horses; second, "in the church at service, prayrs read over in haste, a sermon seldom under and never over twenty minutes, but always made up of sound morality or deep, studied metaphysicks;"[16] third, "after service is over, three quarters of an hour spent in strolling round the church among the crowd, in which time you will be invited by several different gentlemen home with them to dinner."

Van Buren found the towns in the Yazoo Valley so small as barely to be entitled to places on the map; he found the planters' houses to be commonly mere log structures, as the farmers' houses about his own home in Michigan had been twenty years before; and he found the roads so bad that the mule teams could hardly draw their wagons nor the spans of horses their chariots except in dry weather. But when on his horseback errands in search of a position he learned to halloo from the roadway and was regularly met at each gate with an extended hand and a friendly "How do you do, sir? Won't you alight, come in, take a seat and sit awhile?"; when he was invariably made a member of any circle gathered on the porch and refreshed with cool water from the cocoanut dipper or with any other beverages in circulation; when he was asked as a matter of course to share any meal in prospect and to spend the night or day, he discovered charms even in the crudities of the pegs for hanging saddles on the porch and the crevices between the logs of the wall for the

[15] Philip V. Fithian, *Journal and Letters* (Princeton, 1900), p. 287.
[16] Fithian *Journal and Letters*, p. 296.

keeping of pipes and tobacco, books and newspapers. Finally, when the planter whose house he had made headquarters for two months declined to accept a penny in payment, Van Buren's heart overflowed. The boys whom he then began to teach he found particularly apt in historical studies, and their parents with whom he dwelt were thorough gentlefolk.

Toward the end of his narrative, Van Buren expressed the thought that Mississippi, the newly settled home of people from all the older Southern states, exemplified the manners of all. He was therefore prompted to generalize and interpret: "A Southern gentleman is composed of the same material that a Northern gentleman is, only it is tempered by a Southern clime and mode of life. And if in this temperament there is a little more urbanity and chivalry, a little more politeness and devotion to the ladies, a little more *suaviter in modo,* why it is theirs—be fair and acknowledge it, and let them have it. He is from the mode of life he lives, especially at home, more or less a cavalier; he invariably goes a-horseback. His boot is always spurred, and his hand ensigned with the riding-whip. Aside from this he is known by his bearing—his frankness and firmness." Furthermore he is a man of eminent leisureliness, which Van Buren accounts for as follows: "Nature is unloosed of her stays there; she is not crowded for time; the word haste is not in her vocabulary. In none of the seasons is she stinted to so short a space to perform her work as at the North. She has leisure enough to bud and blossom—to produce and mature fruit, and do all her work. While on the other hand in the North right the reverse is true. Portions are taken off the fall and spring to lengthen out the winter, making his reign nearly half the year. This crowds the work of the whole year, you might say, into about half of it. This . . . makes the essential difference between a Northerner and a Southerner. They are children of their respective climes; and this is why Southrons are so indifferent about time; they have three months more of it in a year than we have." [17]

A key to Van Buren's enthusiasm is given by a passage in the

[17] A. de Puy Van Buren, *Jottings of a Year's Sojourn in the South,* pp. 232-236.

diary of the great English reporter, William H. Russell: "The
more one sees of a planter's life the greater is the conviction that
its charms come from a particular turn of mind, which is separated by a wide interval from modern ideas in Europe. The
planter is a denomadized Arab;—he has fixed himself with horses
and slaves in a fertile spot, where he guards his women with Ori-
ental care, exercises patriarchal sway, and is at once fierce, tender and hospitable. The inner life of his household is exceedingly charming, because one is astonished to find the graces and
accomplishments of womanhood displayed in a scene which has
a certain sort of savage rudeness about it after all, and where
all kinds of incongruous accidents are visible in the service of the
table, in the furniture of the house, in its decorations, menials,
and surrounding scenery." [18]   The Southerners themselves took
its incongruities much as a matter of course. The régime was
to their minds so clearly the best attainable under the circumstances that its roughnesses chafed little. The plantations were
homes to which, as they were fond of singing, their hearts turned
ever; and the negroes, exasperating as they often were to visiting
strangers, were an element in the home itself. The problem of
accommodation, which was the central problem of the life, was
on the whole happily solved.

The separate integration of the slaves was no more than rudimentary. They were always within the social mind and conscience of the whites, as the whites in turn were within the mind
and conscience of the blacks. The adjustments and readjustments were mutually made, for although the masters had by far
the major power of control, the slaves themselves were by no
means devoid of influence. A sagacious employer has well said,
after long experience, "a negro understands a white man better
than the white man understands the negro." [19]   This knowledge
gave a power all its own. The general régime was in fact shaped
by mutual requirements, concessions and understandings, producing reciprocal codes of conventional morality. Masters of

[18] William H. Russell, *My Diary North and South* (Boston, 1863), p. 285.
[19] Captain L. V. Cooley, *Address Before the Tulane Society of Economics* [New Orleans, 1911], p. 8.

the standard type promoted Christianity and the customs of marriage and parental care, and they instructed as much by example
as by precept; they gave occasional holidays, rewards and indulgences, and permitted as large a degree of liberty as they thought
the slaves could be trusted not to abuse; they refrained from
selling slaves except under the stress of circumstances; they
avoided cruel, vindictive and captious punishments, and endeavored to inspire effort through affection rather than through
fear; and they were content with achieving quite moderate industrial results.   In short their despotism, so far as it might
properly be so called, was benevolent in intent and on the whole
beneficial in effect.

Some planters there were who inflicted severe punishments for
disobedience and particularly for the offense of running away;
and the community condoned and even sanctioned a certain degree of this.   Otherwise no planter would have printed such descriptions of scars and brands as were fairly common in the
newspaper advertisements offering rewards for the recapture of
absconders.[20]   When severity went to an excess that was reckoned as positive cruelty, however, the law might be invoked if
white witnesses could be had; or the white neighbors or the
slaves themselves might apply extra-legal retribution.   The former were fain to be content with inflicting social ostracism or
with expelling the offender from the district;[21] the latter sometimes went so far as to set fire to the oppressor's house or to accomplish his death by poison, cudgel, knife or bullet.[22]

In the typical group there was occasion for terrorism on neither
side.   The master was ruled by a sense of dignity, duty and
moderation, and the slaves by a moral code of their own.   This
embraced a somewhat obsequious obedience, the avoidance of
open indolence and vice, the attainment of moderate skill in industry, and the cultivation of the master's good will and affection.   It winked at petty theft, loitering and other little laxities,

[20] Examples are reprinted in *Plantation and Frontier*, II, 79-91.
[21] An instance is given in H. M. Henry, *Police Control of the Slave in South Carolina* (Emory, Va., [1914]), p. 75.
[22] For instances *see Plantation and Frontier*, II, 117-121.

while it stressed good manners and a fine faithfulness in major concerns. While the majority were notoriously easy-going, very many made their master's interests thoroughly their own; and many of the masters had perfect confidence in the loyalty of the bulk of their servitors. When on the eve of secession Edmund Ruffin foretold [23] the fidelity which the slaves actually showed when the war ensued, he merely voiced the faith of the planter class.

In general the relations on both sides were felt to be based on pleasurable responsibility. The masters occasionally expressed this in their letters. William Allason, for example, who after a long career as a merchant at Falmouth, Virginia, had retired to plantation life, declined his niece's proposal in 1787 that he return to Scotland to spend his declining years. In enumerating his reasons he concluded: "And there is another thing which in your country you can have no trial of: that is, of selling faithful slaves, which perhaps we have raised from their earliest breath. Even this, however, some can do, as with horses, etc., but I must own that it is not in my disposition." [24]

Others were yet more expressive when they came to write their wills. Thus [25] Howell Cobb of Houston County, Georgia, when framing his testament in 1817 which made his body-servant "to be what he is really deserving, a free man," and gave an annuity along with virtual freedom to another slave, of an advanced age, said that the liberation of the rest of his slaves was prevented by a belief that the care of generous and humane masters would be much better for them than a state of freedom. Accordingly he bequeathed these to his wife who he knew from her goodness of temper would treat them with unflagging kindness. But should the widow remarry, thereby putting her property under the control of a stranger, the slaves and the plantation were at once to revert to the testator's brother who was recommended to bequeath them in turn to his son Howell if he

[23] *Debow's Review*, XXX, 118-120 (January, 1861).
[24] Letter dated Jan. 22, 1787, in the Allason MS. mercantile books, Virginia State Library.
[25] MS. copy in the possession of Mrs. A. S. Erwin, Athens, Ga. The nephew mentioned in the will was Howell Cobb of Confederate prominence.

were deemed worthy of the trust. "It is my most ardent desire that in whatsoever hands fortune may place said negroes," the will enjoined, "that all the justice and indulgence may be shown them that is consistent with a state of slavery. I flatter myself with the hope that none of my relations or connections will be so ungrateful to my memory as to treat or use them otherwise." Surely upon the death of such a master the slaves might, with even more than usual unction, raise their melodious refrain:

> Down in de cawn fiel'
> Hear dat mo'nful soun';
> All de darkies am aweepin',
> Massa's in de col', col' ground.

CHAPTER XVII

PLANTATION TENDENCIES

EVERY typical settlement in English America was in its first phase a bit of the frontier. Commerce was rudimentary, capital scant, and industry primitive. Each family had to suffice itself in the main with its own direct produce. No one could afford to specialize his calling, for the versatility of the individual was wellnigh a necessity of life. This phase lasted only until some staple of export was found which permitted the rise of external trade. Then the fruit of such energy as could be spared from the works of bodily sustenance was exchanged for the goods of the outer world; and finally in districts of special favor for staples, the bulk of the community became absorbed in the special industry and procured most of its consumption goods from without.

In the hidden coves of the Southern Alleghanies the primitive régime has proved permanent. In New England where it was but gradually replaced through the influence first of the fisheries and then of manufacturing, it survived long enough to leave an enduring spirit of versatile enterprise, evidenced in the plenitude of "Yankee notions." In the Southern lowlands and Piedmont, however, the pristine advantages of self-sufficing industry were so soon eclipsed by the profits to be had from tobacco, rice, indigo, sugar or cotton, that in large degree the whole community adopted a stereotyped economy with staple production as its cardinal feature. The earnings obtained by the more efficient producers brought an early accumulation of capital, and at the same time the peculiar adaptability of all the Southern staples to production on a large scale by unfree labor prompted the devotion of most of the capital to the purchase of servants and slaves. Thus in every district suited to any of these staples, the growth of an industrial and social system like that of Europe and the Northern States was cut short and the distinctive Southern scheme of things developed instead.

This régime was conditioned by its habitat, its products and the racial quality of its labor supply, as well as by the institution of slavery and the traditional predilections of the masters. The climate of the South was generally favorable to one or another of the staples except in the elevated tracts in and about the mountain ranges. The soil also was favorable except in the pine barrens which skirted the seaboard. Everywhere but in the alluvial districts, however, the land had only a surface fertility, and all the staples, as well as their great auxiliary Indian corn, required the fields to be kept clean and exposed to the weather; and the heavy rainfall of the region was prone to wash off the soil from the hillsides and to leach the fertile ingredients through the sands of the plains. But so spacious was the Southern area that the people never lacked fresh fields when their old ones were outworn. Hence, while public economy for the long run might well have suggested a conservation of soil at the expense of immediate crops, private economy for the time being dictated the opposite policy; and its dictation prevailed, as it has done in virtually all countries and all ages. Slaves working in squads might spread manure and sow soiling crops if so directed, as well as freemen working individually; and their failure to do so was fully paralleled by similar neglect at the North in the same period. New England, indeed, was only less noted than the South for exhausted fields and abandoned farms. The newness of the country, the sparseness of population and the cheapness of land conspired with crops, climate and geological conditions to promote exploitive methods. The planters were by no means alone in shaping their program to fit these circumstances.[1] The heightened speed of the consequences was in a sense merely an unwelcome proof of their system's efficiency. Their laborers, by reason of being slaves, must at word of command set forth on a trek of a hundred or a thousand miles. No

[1] Edmund Ruffin, *Address on the opposite results of exhausting and fertilizing systems of agriculture. Read before the South Carolina Institute, November 18, 1852* (Charleston, 1853), pp. 12, 13.

racial inertia could hinder nor local attachments hold them.   In
the knowledge of this the masters were even more alert than other
men of the time for advantageous new locations; and they were
accordingly fain to be content with rude houses and flimsy fences
in any place of sojourn, and to let their hills remain studded with
stumps as well as to take the exhaustion of the soil as a matter
of course.[2]

Migration produced a more or less thorough segregation of
types, for planters and farmers respectively tended to enter and
remain in the districts most favorable to them.[3]   The monopoliza-
tion of the rice and sugar industries by the planters, has been described in previous chapters.   At the other extreme the farming
régime was without a rival throughout the mountain regions, in
the Shenandoah and East Tennessee Valleys and in large parts
of Kentucky and Missouri where the Southern staples would not
flourish, and in great tracts of the pine barrens where the quality of the soil repelled all but the unambitious.   The tobacco and
cotton belts remained as the debatable ground in which the two
systems might compete on more nearly even terms, though in
some cotton districts the planters had always an overwhelming
advantage.   In the Mississippi bottoms, for example, the solid
spread of the fields facilitated the supervision of large gangs at
work, and the requirement of building and maintaining great
levees on the river front virtually debarred operations by small
proprietors.   The extreme effects of this are illustrated in Issa-
quena County, Mississippi, and Concordia Parish, Louisiana,
where in 1860 the slaveholdings averaged thirty and fifty slaves
each, and where except for plantation overseers and their families there were virtually no non-slaveholders present.   The Alabama prairies, furthermore, showed a plantation predominance
almost as complete.   In the six counties of Dallas, Greene,
Lowndes, Macon, Perry, Sumter and Wilcox, for example, the

[2] W. L. Trenholm, "The Southern States, their social and industrial
history, conditions and needs," in the *Journal of Social Science*, no. IX
(January, 1878).
[3] F. V. Emerson, "Geographical Influences in American Slavery," in the
American Geographical Society *Bulletin*, XLIII (1911), 13-26, 106-118, 170-
181.

average slaveholdings ranged from seventeen to twenty-one each, and the slaveholding families were from twice to six times as numerous as the non-slaveholding ones. Even in the more rugged parts of the cotton belt and in the tobacco zone as well, the same tendency toward the engrossment of estates prevailed, though in milder degree and with lesser effects.

This widespread phenomenon did not escape the notice of contemporaries. Two members of the South Carolina legislature described it as early as 1805 in substance as follows: "As one man grows wealthy and thereby increases his stock of negroes, he wants more land to employ them on; and being fully able, he bids a large price for his less opulent neighbor's plantation, who by selling advantageously here can raise money enough to go into the back country, where he can be more on a level with the most forehanded, can get lands cheaper, and speculate or grow rich by industry as he pleases." [4] Some three decades afterward another South Carolinian spoke sadly "on the incompatibleness of large plantations with neighboring farms, and their uniform tendency to destroy the yeoman." [5] Similarly Dr. Basil Manly,[6] president of the University of Alabama, spoke in 1841 of the inveterate habit of Southern farmers to buy more land and slaves and plod on captive to the customs of their ancestors; and C. C. Clay, Senator from Alabama, said in 1855 of his native county of Madison, which lay on the Tennessee border: "I can show you . . . the sad memorials of the artless and exhausting culture of cotton. Our small planters, after taking the cream off their lands, unable to restore them by rest, manures or otherwise, are going further west and south in search of other virgin lands which they may and will despoil and impoverish in like manner. Our wealthier planters, with greater means and no more skill, are buying out their poorer neighbors, extending their plantations and adding to their slave force. The wealthy few, who are able to live on smaller profits and to give their blasted

[4] "Diary of Edward Hooker," in the American Historical Association *Report* for 1896, p. 878.
[5] Quoted in Francis Lieber, *Slavery, Plantations and the Yeomanry* (Loyal Publication Society, no. 29, New York, 1863), p. 5.
[6] *Tuscaloosa Monitor*, April 13, 1842.

fields some rest, are thus pushing off the many who are merely independent. . . . In traversing that county one will discover numerous farm houses, once the abode of industrious and intelligent freemen, now occupied by slaves, or tenantless, deserted and dilapidated; he will observe fields, once fertile, now unfenced, abandoned, and covered with those evil harbingers fox-tail and broomsedge; he will see the moss growing on the mouldering walls of once thrifty villages; and will find 'one only master grasps the whole domain' that once furnished happy homes for a dozen white families. Indeed, a country in its infancy, where fifty years ago scarce a forest tree had been felled by the axe of the pioneer, is already exhibiting the painful signs of senility and decay apparent in Virginia and the Carolinas; the freshness of its agricultural glory is gone, the vigor of its youth is extinct, and the spirit of desolation seems brooding over it." [7]

The census returns for Madison County show that in 1830 when the gross population was at its maximum the whites and slaves were equally numerous, and that by 1860 while the whites had diminished by a fourth the slaves had increased only by a twentieth. This suggests that the farmers were drawn, not driven, away.

The same trend may be better studied in the uplands of eastern Georgia where earlier settlements gave a longer experience and where fuller statistics permit a more adequate analysis. In the county of Oglethorpe, typical of that area, the whites in the year 1800 were more than twice as many as the slaves, the non-slaveholding families were to the slaveholders in the ratio of 8 to 5, and slaveholders on the average had but 5 slaves each. In 1820 the county attained its maximum population for the antebellum period, and competition between the industrial types was already exerting its full effect. The whites were of the same number as twenty years before, but the slaves now exceeded them; the slaveholding families also slightly exceeded those who had none, and the scale of the average slaveholding had risen to 8.5. Then in the following forty years while the whites diminished and the number of slaves remained virtually constant, the

[7] DeBow's Review, XIX, 727.

scale of the average slaveholding rose to 12.2; the number of
slaveholders shrank by a third and the non-slaveholders by two
thirds.[8] The smaller slaveholders, those we will say with less
than ten slaves each, ought of course to be classed among the
farmers. When this is done the farmers of Oglethorpe appear
to have been twice as many as the planters even in 1860. But
this is properly offset by rating the average plantation there at
four or five times the industrial scale of the average farm, which
makes it clear that the plantation régime had grown dominant.

In such a district virtually everyone was growing cotton to the
top of his ability. When the price of the staple was high, both
planters and farmers prospered in proportion to their scales.
Those whose earnings were greatest would be eager to enlarge
their fields, and would make offers for adjoining lands too tempting for some farmers to withstand. These would sell out and
move west to resume cotton culture to better advantage than before. When cotton prices were low, however, the farmers, feeling the stress most keenly, would be inclined to forsake staple
production. But in such case there was no occasion for them
to continue cultivating lands best fit for cotton. The obvious
policy would be to sell their homesteads to neighboring planters
and move to cheaper fields beyond the range of planters' competition. Thus the farmers were constantly pioneering in districts
of all sorts, while the plantation régime, whether by the prosperity and enlargement of the farms or by the immigration of
planters, or both, was constantly replacing the farming scale in
most of the staple areas.

In the oldest districts of all, however, the lowlands about the
Chesapeake, the process went on to a final stage in which the bulk
of the planters, after exhausting the soil for staple purposes, departed westward and were succeeded in their turn by farmers,
partly native whites and free negroes and partly Northerners
trickling in, who raised melons, peanuts, potatoes, and garden
truck for the Northern city markets.

Throughout the Southern staple areas the plantations waxed

U. B. Phillips, "The Origin and Growth of the Southern Black Belts,"
in the *American Historical Review*, XI, 810-813 (July, 1906).

and waned in a territorial progression.   The régime was a broad billow moving irresistibly westward and leaving a trough behind.   At the middle of the nineteenth century it was entering Texas, its last available province, whose cotton area it would have duly filled had its career escaped its catastrophic interruption. What would have occurred after that completion, without the war, it is interesting to surmise.   Probably the crest of the billow would have subsided through the effect of an undertow setting eastward again.   Belated immigrants, finding the good lands all engrossed, would have returned to their earlier homes, to hold their partially exhausted soils in higher esteem than before and to remedy the depletion by reformed cultivation.   That the billow did not earlier give place to a level flood was partly due to the shortage of slaves; for the African trade was closed too soon for the stock to fill the country in these decades.   To the same shortage was owing such opportunity as the white yeomanry had in staple production.   The world offered a market, though not at high prices, for a greater volume of the crops than the plantation slaves could furnish; the farmers supplied the deficit.

Free workingmen in general, whether farmers, artisans or unskilled wage earners, merely filled the interstices in and about the slave plantations.   One year in the eighteen-forties a planter near New Orleans, attempting to dispense with slave labor, assembled a force of about a hundred Irish and German immigrants for his crop routine.   Things went smoothly until the midst of the grinding season, when with one accord the gang struck for double pay.   Rejecting the demand the planter was unable to proceed with his harvest and lost some ten thousand dollars worth of his crop.[9]   The generality of the planters realized, without such a demonstration, that each year must bring its crop crisis during which an overindulgence by the laborers in the privileges of liberty might bring ruin to the employers.   To secure immunity from this they were the more fully reconciled to the limitations of their peculiar labor supply.   Freemen white or black might be convenient as auxiliaries, and were indeed employed in many in-

---

[9] Sir Charles Lyell, *Second Visit to the United States*, 2d ed. (London, 1850), II, 162, 163.

stances whether on annual contract as blacksmiths and the like or temporarily as emergency helpers in the fields; but negro slaves were the standard composition of the gangs. This brought it about that whithersoever the planters went they carried with them crowds of negro slaves and all the problems and influences to which the presence of negroes and the prevalence of slavery gave rise.

One of the consequences was to keep foreign immigration small. In the colonial period the trade in indentured servants recruited the white population, and most of those who came in that status remained as permanent citizens of the South; but such Europeans as came during the nineteenth century were free to follow their own reactions without submitting to a compulsory adjustment. Many of them found the wage-earning opportunity scant, for the slaves were given preference by their masters when steady occupations were to be filled, and odd jobs were often the only recourse for outsiders. This was an effect of the slavery system. Still more important, however, was the repugnance which the newcomers felt at working and living alongside the blacks; and this was a consequence not of the negroes being slaves so much as of the slaves being negroes. It was a racial antipathy which when added to the experience of industrial disadvantage pressed the bulk of the newcomers northwestward beyond the confines of the Southern staple belts, and pressed even many of the native whites in the same direction.

This intrenched the slave plantations yet more strongly in their local domination, and by that very fact it hampered industrial development. Great landed proprietors, it is true, have oftentimes been essential for making beneficial innovations. Thus the remodeling of English agriculture which Jethro Tull and Lord Townsend instituted in the eighteenth century could not have been set in progress by any who did not possess their combination of talent and capital[10] In the ante-bellum South, likewise, it was the planters, and necessarily so, who introduced the new staples of sea-island cotton and sugar, the new devices of horizontal

[10] R. E. Prothero, *English Farming, past and present* (London, 1912), chap. 7.

plowing and hillside terracing, the new practice of seed selection, and the new resource of commercial fertilizers. Yet their constant bondage to the staples debarred the whole community in large degree from agricultural diversification, and their dependence upon gangs of negro slaves kept the average of skill and assiduity at a low level.

The negroes furnished inertly obeying minds and muscles; slavery provided a police; and the plantation system contributed the machinery of direction. The assignment of special functions to slaves of special aptitudes would enhance the general efficiency; the coördination of tasks would prevent waste of effort; and the conduct of a steady routine would lessen the mischiefs of irresponsibility. But in the work of a plantation squad no delicate implements could be employed, for they would be broken; and no discriminating care in the handling of crops could be had except at a cost of supervision which was generally prohibitive. The whole establishment would work with success only when the management fully recognized and allowed for the crudity of the labor.

The planters faced this fact with mingled resolution and resignation. The sluggishness of the bulk of their slaves they took as a racial trait to be conquered by discipline, even though their ineptitude was not to be eradicated; the talents and vigor of their exceptional negroes and mulattoes, on the other hand, they sought to foster by special training and rewards. But the prevalence of slavery which aided them in the one policy hampered them in the other, for it made the rewards arbitrary instead of automatic and it restricted the scope of the laborers' employments and of their ambitions as well. The device of hiring slaves to themselves, which had an invigorating effect here and there in the towns, could find little application in the country; and the paternalism of the planters could provide no fully effective substitute. Hence the achievements of the exceptional workmen were limited by the status of slavery as surely as the progress of the generality was restricted by the fact of their being negroes.

A further influence of the plantation system was to hamper the growth of towns. This worked in several ways. As for manufactures, the chronic demand of the planters for means with which to enlarge their scales of operations absorbed most of the capital which might otherwise have been available for factory promotion. A few cotton mills were built in the Piedmont where water power was abundant, and a few small ironworks and other industries; but the supremacy of agriculture was nowhere challenged. As for commerce, the planters plied the bulk of their trade with distant wholesale dealers, patronizing the local shopkeepers only for petty articles or in emergencies when transport could not be awaited; and the slaves for their part, while willing enough to buy of any merchant within reach, rarely had either money or credit.

Towns grew, of course, at points on the seaboard where harbors were good, and where rivers or railways brought commerce from the interior. Others rose where the fall line marked the heads of river navigation, and on the occasional bluffs of the Mississippi, and finally a few more at railroad junctions. All of these together numbered barely three score, some of which counted their population by hundreds rather than by thousands; and in the wide intervals between there was nothing but farms, plantations and thinly scattered villages. In the Piedmont, country towns of fairly respectable dimensions rose here and there, though many a Southern county-seat could boast little more than a court house and a hitching rack. Even as regards the seaports, the currents of trade were too thin and divergent to permit of large urban concentration, for the Appalachian watershed shut off the Atlantic ports from the commerce of the central basin; and even the ambitious construction of railroads to the northwest, fostered by the seaboard cities, merely enabled the Piedmont planters to get their provisions overland, and barely affected the volume of the seaboard trade. New Orleans alone had a location promising commercial greatness; but her prospects were heavily diminished by the building of the far away Erie Canal and the Northern trunk line railroads which diverted the bulk of Northwestern trade from the Gulf outlet.

As conditions were, the slaveholding South could have realized a metropolitan life only through absentee proprietorships.

In the Roman *latifundia,* which overspread central and southern Italy after the Hannibalic war, absenteeism was a chronic feature and a curse. The overseers there were commonly not helpers in the proprietors' daily routine, but sole managers charged with a paramount duty of procuring the greatest possible revenues and transmitting them to meet the urban expenditures of their patrician employers. The owners, having no more personal touch with their great gangs of slaves than modern stockholders have with the operatives in their mills, exploited them accordingly. Where humanity and profits were incompatible, business considerations were likely to prevail. Illustrations of the policy may be drawn from Cato the Elder's treatise on agriculture. Heavy work by day, he reasoned, would not only increase the crops but would cause deep slumber by night, valuable as a safeguard against conspiracy; discord was to be sown instead of harmony among the slaves, for the same purpose of hindering plots; capital sentences when imposed by law were to be administered in the presence of the whole corps for the sake of their terrorizing effect; while rations for the able-bodied were not to exceed a fixed rate, those for the sick were to be still more frugally stinted; and the old and sick slaves were to be sold along with other superfluities.[11] Now, Cato was a moralist of wide repute, a stoic it is true, but even so a man who had a strong sense of duty. If such were his maxims, the oppressions inflicted by his fellow proprietors and their slave drivers must have been stringent indeed.

The heartlessness of the Roman *latifundiarii* was the product partly of their absenteeism, partly of the cheapness of their slaves which were poured into the markets by conquests and raids in all quarters of the Mediterranean world, and partly of the lack of difference between masters and slaves in racial traits. In the ante-bellum South all these conditions were reversed: the planters were commonly resident; the slaves were costly; and the slaves were negroes, who for the most part were by racial qual-

[11] A. H. J. Greenidge, *History of Rome during the later Republic and the early Principate* (New York, 1905), I, 64-85; M. Porcius Cato, *De Agri Cultura,* Keil ed. (Leipsig, 1882).

ity submissive rather than defiant, light-hearted instead of gloomy, amiable and ingratiating instead of sullen, and whose very defects invited paternalism rather than repression. Many a city slave in Rome was the boon companion of his master, sharing his intellectual pleasures and his revels, while most of those on the *latifundia* were driven cattle. It was hard to maintain a middle adjustment for them. In the South, on the other hand, the medium course was the obvious thing. The bulk of the slaves, because they were negroes, because they were costly, and because they were in personal touch, were pupils and working wards, while the planters were teachers and guardians as well as masters and owners. There was plenty of coercion in the South; but in comparison with the harshness of the Roman system the American régime was essentially mild.

Every plantation of the standard Southern type was, in fact, a school constantly training and controlling pupils who were in a backward state of civilization. Slave youths of special promise, or when special purposes were in view, might be bound as apprentices to craftsmen at a distance. Thus James H. Hammond in 1859 apprenticed a fourteen-year-old mulatto boy, named Henderson, for four years to Charles Axt, of Crawfordville, Georgia, that he might be taught vine culture. Axt agreed in the indenture to feed and clothe the boy, pay for any necessary medical attention, teach him his trade, and treat him with proper kindness. Before six months were ended Alexander H. Stephens, who was a neighbor of Axt and a friend of Hammond, wrote the latter that Henderson had run away and that Axt was unfit to have the care of slaves, especially when on hire, and advised Hammond to take the boy home. Soon afterward Stephens reported that Henderson had returned and had been whipped, though not cruelly, by Axt.[12] The further history of this episode is not ascertainable. Enough of it is on record, however, to suggest reasons why for the generality of slaves home training was thought best.

This, rudimentary as it necessarily was, was in fact just what the bulk of the negroes most needed. They were in an alien

[12] MSS. among the Hammond papers in the Library of Congress.

land, in an essentially slow process of transition from barbarism to civilization. New industrial methods of a simple sort they might learn from precepts and occasional demonstrations; the habits and standards of civilized life they could only acquire in the main through examples reinforced with discipline. These the plantation régime supplied. Each white family served very much the function of a modern social settlement, setting patterns of orderly, well bred conduct which the negroes were encouraged to emulate; and the planters furthermore were vested with a coercive power, salutary in the premises, of which settlement workers are deprived. The very aristocratic nature of the system permitted a vigor of discipline which democracy cannot possess. On the whole the plantations were the best schools yet invented for the mass training of that sort of inert and backward people which the bulk of the American negroes represented. The lack of any regular provision for the discharge of pupils upon the completion of their training was, of course, a cardinal shortcoming which the laws of slavery imposed; but even in view of this, the slave plantation régime, after having wrought the initial and irreparable misfortune of causing the negroes to be imported, did at least as much as any system possible in the period could have done toward adapting the bulk of them to life in a civilized community.

CHAPTER XVIII

ECONOMIC VIEWS OF SLAVERY: A SURVEY OF THE LITERATURE

IN barbaric society slavery is a normal means of conquering the isolation of workers and assembling them in more productive coördination. Where population is scant and money little used it is almost a necessity in the conduct of large undertakings, and therefore more or less essential for the advancement of civilization. It is a means of domesticating savage or barbarous men, analogous in kind and in consequence to the domestication of the beasts of the field.[1] It was even of advantage to some of the people enslaved, in that it saved them from extermination when defeated in war, and in that it gave them touch with more advanced communities than their own. But this was counterbalanced by the stimulus which the profits of slave catching gave to wars and raids with all their attendant injuries. Any benefit to the slave, indeed, was purely incidental. The reason for the institution's existence was the advantage which accrued to the masters. So positive and pronounced was this reckoned to be, that such highly enlightened people as the Greeks and Romans maintained it in the palmiest days of their supremacies.

Western Europe in primitive times was no exception. Slavery in a more or less fully typical form was widespread. When the migrations ended in the middle ages, however, the rise of feudalism gave the people a thorough territorial regimentation. The dearth of commerce whether in goods or in men led gradually to the conversion of the unfree laborers from slaves into serfs or villeins attached for generations to the lands on which they wrought. Finally, the people multiplied so greatly and the land-

[1] This thought was expressed, perhaps for the first time, in T. R. Dew's essay on slavery (1832); it is elaborated in Gabriel Tarde, *The Laws of Imitation* (Parsons tr., New York, 1903), pp. 278, 279.

less were so pressed for livelihood that at the beginning of modern times European society found the removal of bonds conducive to the common advantage. Serfs freed from their inherited obligations could now seek employment wherever they would, and landowners, now no longer lords, might employ whom they pleased. Bondmen gave place to hirelings and peasant proprietors, status gave place to contract, industrial society was enabled to make redistributions and readjustments at will, as it had never been before. In view of the prevailing traits and the density of the population a general return whether to slavery or serfdom was economically unthinkable. An intelligent Scotch philanthropist, Fletcher of Saltoun, it is true, proposed at the end of the seventeenth century that the indigent and their children be bound as slaves to selected masters as a means of relieving the terrible distresses of unemployment in his times; [2] but his project appears to have received no public sanction whatever. The fact that he published such a plan is more a curious antiquarian item than one of significance in the history of slavery. Not even the thin edge of a wedge could possibly be inserted which might open a way to restore what everyone was on virtually all counts glad to be free of.

When the American mining and plantation colonies were established, however, some phases of the most ancient labor problems recurred. Natural resources invited industry in large units. but wage labor was not to be had. The Spaniards found a temporary solution in impressing the tropical American aborigines, and the English in a recourse to indented white immigrants. But both soon resorted predominantly for plantation purposes to the importation of Africans, for whom the ancient institution of slavery was revived. Thus from purely economic considerations the sophisticated European colonists of the sixteenth and seventeenth centuries involved themselves and their descendants, with the connivance of their home governments, in the toils of a system which on the one hand had served their remote forbears with good effect, but which on the other hand civilized peoples

[2] W. E. H. Lecky, *History of England in the Eighteenth Century* (New York, 1879), II, 43, 44.

had long and almost universally discarded as an incubus. In these colonial beginnings the negroes were to be had so cheaply and slavery seemed such a simple and advantageous device when applied to them, that no qualms as to the future were felt. At least no expressions of them appear in the records of thought extant for the first century and more of English colonial experience. And when apprehensions did arise they were concerned with the dangers of servile revolt, not with any deleterious effects to arise from the economic nature of slavery in time of peace.

Now, slavery and indented servitude are analogous to serfdom in that they may yield to the employers all the proceeds of industry beyond what is required for the sustenance of the laborers; but they have this difference, immense for American purposes, that they permit labor to be territorially shifted, while serfdom keeps it locally fixed. By choosing these facilitating forms of bondage instead of the one which would have attached the laborers to the soil, the founders of the colonial régime in industry doubtless thought they had avoided all economic handicaps in the premises. Their device, however, was calculated to meet the needs of a situation where the choice was between bond labor and no labor. As generations passed and workingmen multiplied in America, the system of indentures for white immigrants was automatically dissolved; but slavery for the bulk of the negroes persisted as an integral feature of economic life Whether this was conducive or injurious to the prosperity of employers and to the community's welfare became at length a question to which students far and wide applied their faculties Some of the participants in the discussion considered the problem as one in pure theory; others examined not only the abstract ratio of slave and free labor efficiency but included in their view the factor of negro racial traits and the prospects and probable consequences of abolition under existing circumstances. On the one point that an average slave might be expected to accomplish less in an hour's work than an average free laborer, agreement was unanimous; on virtually every other point the views published were so divergent as to leave the public more or less distracted.

Adam Smith, whose work largely shaped the course of economic thought for a century following its publication in 1776, said of slave labor merely that its cost was excessive by reason of its lack of zest, frugality and inventiveness. The tropical climate of the sugar colonies, he conceded, might require the labor of negro slaves, but even there its productiveness would be enhanced by liberal policies promoting intelligence among the slaves and assimilating their condition to that of freemen.[3] To some of these points J. B. Say, the next economist to consider the matter, took exception. Common sense must tell us, said he, that a slave's maintenance must be less than that of a free workman, since the master will impose a more drastic frugality than a freeman will adopt unless a dearth of earnings requires it. The slave's work, furthermore, is more constant, for the master will not permit so much leisure and relaxation as the freeman customarily enjoys. Say agreed, however, that slavery, causing violence and brutality to usurp the place of intelligence, both hampered the progress of invention and enervated such free laborers as were in touch with the régime.[4]

The translation of Say's book into English evoked a reply to his views on slavery by Adam Hodgson, an Englishman with anti-slavery bent who had made an American tour; but his essay, though fortified with long quotations, was too rambling and ill digested to influence those who were not already desirous of being convinced.[5] More substantial was an essay of 1827 by a Marylander, James Raymond, who cited the experiences of his own commonwealth to support his contentions that slavery hampered economy by preventing seasonal shiftings of labor, by requiring employers to support their operatives in lean years as well as fat, and by hindering the accumulation of wealth by the laborers. The system, said he, could yield profits to the masters

---

[3] Adam Smith, *The Wealth of Nations*, various editions, book I, chap. 8; book III, chap. 2; book IV, chaps. 7 and 9.
[4] J. B. Say, *Traité d'Economie Politique* (Paris, 1803), book I, chap. 28; in various later editions, book I, chap. 19.
[5] Adam Hodgson, *A Letter to M. Jean-Baptiste Say, on the comparative expense of free and slave labour* (Liverpool, 1823; New York, 1823).

only in specially fertile districts; and even there it kept down the growth of population and of land values.[6]

About the same time Dr. Thomas Cooper, president of South Carolina College, wrote: "Slave labour is undoubtedly the dearest kind of labour; it is all forced, and forced too from a class of human beings who have the least propensity to voluntary labour even when it is to benefit themselves alone." The cost of rearing a slave to the age of self support, he reckoned, including insurance, at forty dollars a year for fifteen years. The usual work of a slave field hand, he thought, was barely two-thirds of what a white laborer at usual wages would perform, and from his earnings about forty dollars a year must be deducted for his maintenance. When interest on the investment and a proportion of an overseer's wages were deducted in addition, he thought the prevalent rate, six to eight dollars a month and board valued at forty or fifty dollars a year, for free white farm hands in the Northern states gave a decisive advantage to those who hired laborers over those who owned them. "Nothing will justify slave labour in point of economy," he concluded, "but the nature of the soil and climate which incapacitates a white man from labouring in the summer time, as on the rich lands in Carolina and Georgia extending one hundred miles from the seaboard."[7]

The economic vices of slavery as exemplified in Virginia were elaborated in an essay printed in 1832 attributed to Jesse Burton Harrison of that state. Slavery, said this essay, drives away free workmen by stigmatizing labor, for "nothing but the most abject necessity would lead a white man to hire himself to work in the fields under the overseer"; it causes exhaustion of the soil by reason of the negligence it promotes in the workmen and the stress which overseers are fain to put upon immediate returns; it discourages all forms of industry but plantation tillage, furthermore, for although it has not and perhaps cannot be proved that slaves may not be successfully employed in manufactures,

---

[6] James Raymond, *Prize Essay on the Comparative Economy of Free and Slave Labor in Agriculture* (Frederick [Md.], 1827), reprinted in the *African Repository*, III, 97-110 (June, 1827).

[7] Thomas Cooper, *Lectures on the Elements of Political Economy* (Columbia [S. C.], 1826), pp. 94, 95.

the community has gone and tends still to go, on that assumption; it discourages mechanic skill, for the slaves never acquire more than the rudiments of artisanry, and the planters discourage white craftsmen by giving preference uniformly to their own laborers. Slave labor is dearer than free, because of its lack of incentive; the régime costs the community the services of the immigrants who would otherwise enter; and finally it promotes waste instead of frugality on the part of both masters and slaves. The only means by which Virginia could procure profit from slaves, it concluded, was that of raising them for sale to the lower South; but such profit could only be gained systematically at a complete sacrifice of honor.[8]

Daniel R. Goodloe of North Carolina wrote in 1846 in a similar tone but with original arguments. Beginning with an exposition of the South's comparative backwardness in economic development, he showed a twofold working of the institution of slavery as the cause. For one thing it lessened the vigor of industry by degrading labor in the estimation of the poor and engendering pride in the rich; but far more important, it required employers to sink large amounts of capital in the purchase of laborers instead of permitting them to pay for work, as the wage system does, out of current proceeds. It thereby particularly hampered the growth of manufactures, for in such lines, as well as in commerce, "the fact that slavery absorbs the bulk of Southern capital must always present an obstacle to extensive operations." The holding of laborers as property, he continued, can contribute nothing to production, for the destruction of the property by the liberation of the slaves would not impair their laboring efficiency. Hence all the individual wealth which has assumed that shape has added nothing to the resources of the community. "Slavery merely serves to appropriate the wages of labor—it distributes wealth, but cannot create it." It involves expenditure in acquiring early population, then operates to prevent land improvements and

[8] [Jesse Burton Harrison], *Review of the Slave Question, extracted from the American Quarterly Review, Dec. 1832.* By a Virginian (Richmond, 1833).

the diversification of industry, restricting, indeed, even the range of agriculture. The monopoly which the South has enjoyed in the production of the staples has palliated the evils of slavery, but at the same time has expanded the system to the point of great injury to the public. Goodloe accordingly advocated the riddance of the institution, contending that both landowners and laborers would thereby benefit. The continued maintenance of the institution, on the other hand, would bring severe loss to the slaveholders, for within the coming decade the demand of the Southwest for slaves would be sated, he thought, and nothing but a great advancement of cotton prices and an unlimited supply of fertile land for its production could sustain slave prices. "It is evident that the Southern country approaches a period of great and sudden depreciation in the value of slave property."[9]

The statistical theme of the South's backwardness was used by many other essayists in the period for indicting the slaveholding régime. With most of these, however, exemplified saliently by H. R. Helper, logic was to such extent replaced with vehemence as to transfer their writings from the proper purview of economics to that of sectional controversy.

On the other hand, Thomas R. Dew, whose cogent essay of 1832 marks the turn of the prevailing Southern sentiment toward a firm support of slavery, attributed the lack of prosperity in the South to the tariff policy of the United States, while he largely ignored the question of labor efficiency. His central theme was the imperative necessity of maintaining the enslavement of the negroes on hand until a sound plan was devised and made applicable for their peaceful and prosperous disposal elsewhere. Among Dew's disciples, William Harper of South Carolina admitted that slave labor was dear and unskillful, though he thought it essential for productive industry in the tropics and sub-tropics,

---

[9] [D. R. Goodloe], *Inquiry into the Causes which have retarded the Accumulation of Wealth and Increase of Population in the Southern States, in which the question of slavery is considered in a politico-economic point of view. By a Carolinian.* (Washington, 1846.) *See also* a similar essay by the same author in the U. S. Commissioner of Agriculture's *Report* for 1865, pp. 102-135.

and he considered coercion necessary for the negroes elsewhere in civilized society. James H. Hammond, likewise, agreed that "as a general rule . . . free labor is cheaper than slave labor," but in addition to the factor of race he stressed the sparsity of population in the South as a contributing element in economically necessitating the maintenance of slavery.[10]

Most of the foregoing Southern writers were men of substantial position and systematic reasoning. N. A. Ware, on the other hand who in 1844 issued in the capacity of a Southern planter a slender volume of *Notes on Political Economy* was both obscure and irresponsible. Contending as his main theme that protective tariffs were of no injury to the plantation interests, he asserted that slave labor was incomparably cheaper than free, and attempted to prove it by ignoring the cost of capital and by reckoning the price of bacon at four cents a pound and corn at fifteen cents a bushel. Then, curiously, he delivered himself of the following: "When slavery shall have run itself out or yielded to the changes and ameliorations of the times, the owners and all dependent upon it will stand appalled and prostrate, as the sot whose liquor has been withheld, and nothing but the bad and worthless habit left to remind the country of its ruinous effects. The political economist, as well as all wise statesmen in this country, cannot think of any measure going to discharge slavery that would not be a worse state than its existence." His own remedy for the depression prevailing at the time when he wrote, was to divert a large proportion of the slaves from the glutted business of staple agriculture into manufacturing, for which he thought them well qualified.[11] Equally fantastic were the ideas of H. C. Carey of Pennsylvania who dealt here and there with slavery in the course of his three stout volumes on political economy. His lucubrations are negligible for the present survey.

All these American writers except Goodloe accomplished little

[10] Dew's "Essay" (1832), Harper's "Memoir" (1838), and Hammond's "Letters to Clarkson" (1845) are collected in the *Pro-Slavery Argument* (Philadelphia, 1852).
[11] [N. A. Ware] *Notes on Political Economy as applicable to the United States.* By a Southern Planter (New York, 1844), pp. 200-204.

of substantial quality in the field of economic thought beyond adding details to the doctrines of Adam Smith and Say. John Stuart Mill in turn did little more than combine the philosophies of his predecessors. "It is a truism to assert," said he, "that labour extorted by fear of punishment is insufficient and unproductive"; yet some people can be driven by the lash to accomplish what no feasible payment would have induced them to undertake. In sparsely settled regions, furthermore, slavery may afford the otherwise unobtainable advantages of labour combination, and it has undoubtedly hastened industrial development in some American areas. Yet, since all processes carried on by slave labour are conducted in the rudest manner, virtually any employer may pay a considerably greater value in wages to free labour than the maintenance of his slaves has cost him and be a gainer by the change.[12]

Partly concurring and partly at variance with Mill's views were those which Edmund Ruffin of Virginia published in a well reasoned essay of 1857, *The Political Economy of Slavery*. "Slave labor in each individual case and for each small measure of time," he said, "is more slow and inefficient than the labor of a free man." On the other hand it is more continuous, for hirelings are disposed to work fewer hours per day and fewer days per year, except when wages are so low as to require constant exertion in the gaining of a bare livelihood. Furthermore, the consolidation of domestic establishments, which slavery promotes, permits not only an economy in the purchase of supplies but also a great saving by the specialization of labor in cooking, washing, nursing, and the care of children, thereby releasing a large proportion of the women from household routine and rendering them available for work in the field. An increasing density of population, however, would depress the returns of industry to the point where slaves would merely earn their keep, and free laborers would of necessity lengthen their hours. Finally a still greater glut of labor might come, and indeed had occurred in various countries of Europe, carrying wages so low

[12] John Stuart Mill, *Principles of Political Economy* (London, 1848, and later editions), book II, chap. 5.

that only the sturdiest free laborers could support themselves and all the weaker ones must enter a partial pauperism. At such a stage the employment of slaves could only be continued at a steady deficit, to relieve themselves from which the masters must resort to a general emancipation. In the South, however, there were special public reasons, lying in the racial traits of the slave population, which would make that recourse particularly deplorable; for the industrial collapse ensuing upon emancipation in the British West Indies on the one hand, and on the other the pillage and massacre which occurred in San Domingo and the disorder still prevailing there, were alternative examples of what might be apprehended from orderly or revolutionary abolition as the case might be. The Southern people, in short, might well congratulate themselves that no ending of their existing régime was within visible prospect.[13]

About the same time a writer in *DeBow's Review* elaborated the theme that the comparative advantages of slavery and freedom depended wholly upon the attainments of the laboring population concerned. "Both are necessarily recurring types of social organization, and each suited to its peculiar phase of society." "When a nation or society is in a condition unfit for self-government, . . . often the circumstance of contact with or subjection by more enlightened nations has been the means of transition to a higher development." "All that is now needed for the defence of United States negro slavery and its entire exoneration from reproach is a thorough investigation of fact; . . . and political economy . . . must . . . pronounce our system . . . no disease, but the normal and healthy condition of a society formed of such mixed material as ours." "The strong race and the weak, the civilized and the savage," the one by nature master, the other slave, "are here not only cast together, but have been born together, grown together, lived togther, worked together, each in his separate sphere striving for the good of each. . . . These two races of men are mutually assistant to each other and are contributing in the larg-

---

[13] Edmund Ruffin, *The Political Economy of Slavery* ([Richmond, 1857]).

est possible degree consistent with their mutual powers to the
good of each other and mankind." A general emancipation
therefore could bring nothing but a detriment.[14]

What proved to be the last work in the premises before the
overthrow of slavery in the United States was *The Slave Power,
its Character, Career and Probable Designs,* by J. E.
Cairnes, professor of political economy in the University of
Dublin and in Queen's College, Galway. It was published in
1862 and reissued with appendices in the following year. Cairnes
at the outset scouted the factors of climate and negro racial
traits. The sole economic advantage of slavery, said he, consists
in its facilitation of control in large units; its defects lay in its
causing reluctance, unskilfulness and lack of versatility. The
reason for its prevalence in the South he found in the high
fertility and the immense abundance of soil on the one hand,
and on the other the intensiveness of staple cultivation. A
single operative, said he, citing as authority Robert Russell's
erroneous assertion, "might cultivate twenty acres in wheat or
Indian corn, but could not manage more than two in tobacco or
three in cotton; therefore the supervision of a considerable squad
is economically feasible in these though it would not be so in
the cereals." These conditions might once have made slave labor
profitable, he conceded; but such possibility was now doubtless
a thing of the distant past. The persistence of the system did
not argue to the contrary, for it would by force of inertia
persist as long as it continued to be self-supporting.

Turning to a different theme, Cairnes announced that slave
labor, since it had never been and never could be employed with
success in manufacturing or commercial pursuits, must find its
whole use in agriculture; and even there it required large capital,
at the same time that the unthrifty habits inculcated in the
masters kept them from accumulating funds. The consequence
was that slaveholding society must necessarily be and remain
heavily in debt. The imperative confinement of slave labor to
the most fertile soils, furthermore, prevented the community

---

[14] *DeBow's Review,* XXI, 331-349, 443-467 (October and November,
1856).

from utilizing any areas of inferior quality; for slaveholding society is so exclusive that it either expels free labor from its vicinity or deprives it of all industrial vigor. It is true that some five millions of whites in the South have no slaves; but these "are now said to exist in this manner in a condition little removed from savage life, eking out a wretched subsistence by hunting, by fishing, by hiring themselves for occasidnal jobs, by plunder." These "mean whites . . . are the natural growth of the slave system; . . . regular industry is only known to them as the vocation of slaves, and it is the one fate which above all others they desire to avoid."[15]

"The constitution of a slave society," he says again, "resolves itself into three classes, broadly distinguished from each other and connected by no common interest—the slaves on whom devolves all the regular industry, the slaveholders who reap all its fruits, and an idle and lawless rabble who live dispessed over vast plains in a condition little removed from absolute barbarism."[16] Nowhere can any factors be found which will promote any progress of civilization so long as slavery persists. The non-slaveholders will continue in "a life alternating between listless vagrancy and the excitement of marauding expeditions." "If civilization is to spring up among the negro race, it will scarcely be contended that this will happen while they are still slaves; and if the present ruling class are ever to rise above the existing type, it must be in some other capacity than as slaveholders."[17] Even as a "probationary discipline" to prepare a backward people for a higher form of civilized existence, slavery as it exists in America cannot be justified; for that effect is vitiated by reason of the domestic slave trade. "Considerations of economy, . . . which under a natural system afford some security for humane treatment by identifying the master's interest with the slave's preservation, when once trading in slaves is practised become reasons for racking to the utmost the toil of the slave; for when his place can at once be supplied from foreign preserves the duration of his life becomes a matter of less moment than its productiveness while it lasts. It is accordingly a maxim of slave management in slave-importing countries, that the most effective economy is that which takes out of the human chattel in the shortest space of time the utmost amount of exertion it is capable of putting forth."[18]

The force of circumstances gave this book a prodigious and lasting vogue. Its confident and cogent style made skepticism difficult; the dearth of contrary data prevented impeachment on the one side of the Atlantic, and on the other side the whole Northern people would hardly criticise such a vindication of their cause in war by a writer from whose remoteness might be presumed fairness, and whose professional position might be taken as giving a stamp of thoroughness and accuracy. Yet the very conditions and method of the writer made his interpretations hazardous. An economist, using great caution, might possibly have drawn the whole bulk of his data from travelers' accounts, as Cairnes did, and still have reached fairly sound conclusions; but Cairnes gave preference not to the concrete observations of the travelers but to their generalizations, often biased or amateurish, and on them erected his own. Furthermore, he ignored such material as would conflict with his preconceptions. His conclusions, accordingly, are now true, now false, and while always vivid are seldom substantially illuminating. His picture of the Southern non-slaveholders, which, be it observed, he applied in his first edition to five millions or ten-elevenths of that whole white population, and which he restricted, under stress of contemporary criticism, only to four million souls in the second edition,[19] is merely the most extreme of his grotesqueries. The book was, in short, less an exposition than an exposure.

These criticisms of Cairnes will apply in varying lesser degrees to all of his predecessors in the field. Those who sought the truth merely were in general short of data; those who could get the facts in any fullness were too filled with partisan purpose.

[18] First American edition (New York, 1862), p. 73.
[19] *Ibid.*, second edition (London, 1863), appendix D.

What was begun as a study was continued as a dispute, necessarily endless so long as the political issue remained active. Many data which would have been illuminating, such as plantation records and slave price quotations, were never systematically assembled; and the experience resulting from negro emancipation was then too slight for use in substantial generalizations. The economist M'Culloch, for example, concluded from the experience of San Domingo and Jamaica that cane sugar production could not be sustained without slavery;[20] but the industrial careers of Cuba, Porto Rico and Louisiana since his time have refuted him. He, like virtually all his contemporaries in economic thought, confused the several factors of slavery, race traits and the plantation system; the consequent liability to error was inevitable.

Economists of later times have nearly all been too much absorbed in current problems to give attention to a discarded institution. Most of them have ignored the subject of slavery altogether, and the concern of the rest with it has been merely incidental. Nicholson, for example, alludes to it as [21] "one of the earliest and one of the most enduring forms of poverty," and again as "the original and universal form of bankruptcy." Smart deals with it only as concerns the care of workingmen's children: "The one good thing in slavery was the interest of the master in the future of his workers. The children of the slaves were the master's property. They were always at least a valuable asset. . . . But there is no such continuity in the relation between the employer [of free labor] and his human cattle. The best-intentioned employer cannot be expected to be much concerned about the efficient upkeep of the workman's child when the child is free to go where he likes. . . . The child's future is bound up with the father's wage. The wage may be enough, even when low, to support the father's efficiency, but it is not necessarily enough to keep up the efficiency

[20] J. R. M'Culloch, *Principles of Political Economy* (fourth edition, Edinburgh, 1849), p. 439.
[21] J. S. Nicholson, *Principles of Political Economy* (New York, 1898), I, 221, 391.

of the young laborer on which the future depends."[22]   Loria
deals more extensively with slavery as affected by the valuation
of labor,[23] and Gibson [24] examines elaborately the nature of hypo-
thetically absolute slavery in analyzing the earnings of labor.
The contributions of both Loria and Gibson will be used below.
The economic bearings of the institution in history still await
satisfactory analysis.

[22] William Smart, *The Distribution of Income* (London, 1899), pp. 296,
297.
[23] Achille Loria, *La Costitutione Economica Odierna* (Turin, 1899), chap.
6, part 2.
[24] Arthur H. Gibson, *Human Economics* (London, 1909).

CHAPTER XIX

BUSINESS ASPECTS OF SLAVERY

AN expert accountant has well defined the property of a master in his slave as an annuity extending throughout the slave's working life and amounting to the annual surplus which the labor of the slave produced over and above the cost of his maintenance.[1] Before any profit accrued to the master in any year, however, various deductions had to be subtracted from this surplus. These included interest on the slave's cost, regardless of whether he had been reared by his owner or had been bought for a price; amortization of the capital investment; insurance against the slave's premature death or disability and against his escape from service; insurance also for his support when incapacitated whether by illness, accident or old age; taxes; and wages of superintendence. None of these charges would any sound method of accounting permit the master to escape.

The maintenance of the slave at the full rate required for the preservation of lusty physique was essential. The master could not reduce it below that standard without impairing his property as well as lessening its immediate return; and as a rule he could shift none of the charge to other shoulders, for the public would grant his workmen no dole from its charity funds. On the other hand, he was often induced to raise the scale above the minimum standard in order to increase the zeal and efficiency of his corps. In any case, medical attendance and the like was necessarily included in the cost of maintenance.

The capital investment in a slave reared by his master would include charges for the insurance of the child's mother at the time of his birth and for her deficit of routine work before and

---

[1] Arthur H. Gibson, *Human Economics* (London, 1909), p. 202. The substance of the present paragraph and the three following ones is mostly in close accord with Gibson's analysis.

afterward; the food, clothing, nurse's care and incidentals furnished in childhood; the surplus of supplies over earnings in the period of youth while the slave was not fully earning his own keep and his overhead charges; compound interest on all of these until the slave reached adolescence or early manhood; and a proportion of similar charges on behalf of other children in his original group who had died in youth. In his teens the slave's earnings would gradually increase until they covered all his current charges, including the cost of supervision; and shortly before the age of twenty he would perhaps begin to yield a net return to the owner.

A slave's highest rate of earning would be reached of course when his physical maturity and his training became complete, and would normally continue until his bodily powers began to flag. This period would extend in the case of male field hands from perhaps twenty-five to possibly fifty years of age, and in the case of artizans from say thirty to fifty-five years. The maximum valuation of the slave as property, however, would come earlier, at the point when the investment in his production was first complete and when his maximum earnings were about to begin; and his value would thereafter decline, first slowly and then more swiftly with every passing year, in anticipation of the decline and final cessation of his earning power. Thus the ratio between the capital value of a slave and his annual net earnings, far from remaining constant, would steadily recede from the beginning to the end of his working life. At the age of twenty it might well be as ten to one; at the age of fifty it would probably not exceed four to one; at sixty-five it might be less than a parity.

In the buying and selling of nearly all non-human commodities the cost of production, or of reproduction, bears a definite relation to the market price, in that it fixes a limit below which owners will not continue to produce and sell. In the case of slaves, however, the cost of rearing had no practical bearing upon the market price, for the reason that the owners could not, or at least did not, increase or diminish the production at will.[2] It has been said by various anti-slavery spokesmen that many slaveowners systematically bred slaves for the market. They have adduced no shred of supporting evidence however; and although the present writer has long been alert for such data he has found but a single concrete item in the premises. This one came, curiously enough, from colonial Massachusetts, where John Josslyn recorded in 1636: "Mr. Maverick's negro woman came to my chamber window and in her own country language and tune sang very loud and shril. Going out to her, she used a great deal of respect towards me, and willingly would have expressed her grief in English. But I apprehended it by her countenance and deportment, whereupon I repaired to my host to learn of him the cause, for that I understood before that she had been a queen in her own countrey, and observed a very humble and dutiful garb used towards her by another negro who was her maid. Mr. Maverick was desirous to have a breed of negroes, and therefore seeing she would not yield to perswasions to company with a negro young man he had in his house, he commanded him, will'd she nill'd she to go to bed to her—which was no sooner done than she kickt him out again. This she took in high disdain beyond her slavery, and this was the cause of her grief." [3]

As for the ante-bellum South, the available plantation instructions, journals and correspondence contain no hint of such a practice. Jesse Burton Harrison, a Virginian in touch with planters' conversation and himself hostile to slavery,[4] went so far as to write, "It may be that there is a small section of Virginia (perhaps we could indicate it) where the theory of population is studied with reference to the yearly income from the sale of slaves," but he went no further; and this, be it noted, is not clearly to hint anything further than that the owners of multiplying slaves reckoned their own gains from the unstimulated increase. If pressure were commonly applied James H. Hammond would not merely have inserted the characteristic provision in his schedule

[2] This is at variance with Gibson's thesis which, professedly dealing always in pure hypothesis, assumes a state of "perfect" slavery in which breeding is controlled on precisely the same basis as in the case of cattle.
[3] John Josslyn, "Account of two Voyages to New England," in the Massachusetts Historical Society *Collections, XXIII*, 231.
[4] *Review of the Slave Question* (Richmond, 1833), p. 17.

of rewards: "For every infant thirteen months old and in sound health that has been properly attended to, the mother shall receive a muslin or calico frock."[5] A planter here and there may have exerted a control of matings in the interest of industrial and commercial eugenics, but it is extremely doubtful that any appreciable number of masters attempted any direct hastening of slave increase. The whole tone of the community was hostile to such a practice. Masters were in fact glad enough to leave the slaves to their own inclinations in all regards so long as the day's work was not obstructed and good order was undisturbed. They had of course everywhere and at all times an interest in the multiplication of their slaves as well as the increase of their industrial aptitudes. Thus William Lee wrote in 1778 concerning his plantation in Virginia: "I wish particular attention may be paid to rearing young negroes, and taking care of those grown up, that the number may be increased as much as possible; also putting several of the most promising and ingenious lads apprentices to different trades, such as carpenters, coopers, wheelwrights, sawyers, shipwrights, bricklayers, plasterers, shoemakers and blacksmiths; some women should also be taught to weave."[6]

But even if masters had stimulated breeding on occasion, that would have created but a partial and one-sided relationship between cost of production and market price. To make the connection complete it would have been requisite for them to check slave breeding when prices were low; and even the abolitionists, it seems, made no assertion to that effect. No, the market might decline indefinitely without putting an appreciable check upon the birth rate; and the master had virtually no choice but to rear every child in his possession. The cost of production, therefore, could not serve as a nether limit for slave prices at any time.

An upper limit to the price range was normally fixed by the reckoning of a slave's prospective earnings above the cost of

[5] See above, p. 272.
[6] W. C. Ford, ed., *Letters of William Lee* (Brooklyn, 1891), II, 363, 364.

his maintenance. The slave may here be likened to a mine operated by a corporation leasing the property. The slave's claim to his maintenance represents the prior claim of the landowner to his rent; the master's claim to the annual surplus represents the equity of the stockholders in the corporation. But the ore will some day be exhausted and the dividends cease. Purchasers of the stock should accordingly consider amortization and pay only such price as will be covered by the discounted value of the prospective dividends during the life of the mine. The price of the output fluctuates, however, and the rate of any year's earnings can only be conjectured. Precise reckoning is therefore impracticable, and the stock will rise and fall in the market in response to the play of conjectures as to the present value of the total future earnings applicable to dividends. So also a planter entering the slave market might have reckoned in advance the prospect of working life which a slave of given age would have, and the average earnings above maintenance which might be expected from his labor. By discounting each of those annual returns at the prevailing rate of interest to determine their present values, and adding up the resulting sums, he would ascertain the price which his business prospects would justify him in paying. Having bought a slave at such a price, an equally thoroughgoing caution would have led him to take out a life, health and accident insurance policy on the slave; but even then he must personally have borne the risk of the slave's running away. In practice the lives of a few slaves engaged in steamboat operation and other hazardous pursuits were insured,[7] but the total number of policies taken on their

<hr/>

[7] Dr. J. C. Nott, in J. B. D. DeBow, ed., *Industrial Resources of the Southern and Western States* (New Orleans, 1852), II, 299; F. L. Hoffman, in *The South in the Building of the Nation* (Richmond, Va. [1909]), 638-655. *DeBow's Review*, X, 241, contains an advertisement of a company offering life and accident insurance on slaves.

A typical policy is preserved in the MSS. division of the Library of Congress. It was issued Dec. 31, 1851, by the Louisville agent of the Mutual Benefit Fire and Life Insurance Company of Louisiana, to T. P. Linthicum of Bairdstown, Ky., insuring for $650 each the lives of Jack, 26 years old and Alexander, 31 years old, for one year, at the rates of 2 and 2½ per cent. respectively, plus one per cent., for permission to employ the slaves on steamboats during the first half of the period. They were employed as waiters. Jack died Nov. 20, and the insurance was duly paid.

lives, except as regards marine insurance in the coasting slave trade, was very small. The planters as a rule carried their own risks, and they generally dispensed with actuarial reckonings in determining their bids for slaves. About 1850 a rule of thumb was current that a prime hand was worth a hundred dollars for every cent in the current price of a pound of cotton. In general, however, the prospective purchaser merely "reckoned" in the Southern sense of conjecturing, at what price he could employ an added slave with probable advantage, and made his bid accordingly.

A slave's market price was affected by sex, age, physique, mental quality, industrial training, temper, defects and vices, so far as each of these could be ascertained. The laws of most of the states presumed a seller's warrant of health at the time of sale, unless expressly withheld, and in Louisiana this warrant extended to mental and moral soundness. The period in which the buyer might apply for redress, however, was limited to a few months, and the verdicts of juries were uncertain. On the whole, therefore, if the buyer were unacquainted with the slave's previous career and with his attitude toward the transfer of possession, he necessarily incurred considerable risk in making each purchase. But in general the taking of reasonable precautions would cause the loss through unsuspected vices in one case to be offset by gains through unexpected virtues in another.

The scale and the trend of slave prices are essential features of the régime which most economists have ignored and for which the rest have had too little data. For colonial times the quotations are scant. An historian of the French West Indies, however, has ascertained from the archives that whereas the prices ranged perhaps as low as 200 francs for imported Africans there at the middle of the seventeenth century, they rose to 450 francs by the year 1700 and continued in a strong and steady advance thereafter, except in war times, until the very eve of the French Revolution. Typical prices for prime field hands in San Domingo were 650 francs in 1716, 800 in 1728, 1,160 in

1750, 1,400 in 1755, 1,180 in 1764, 1,600 in 1769, 1,860 in 1772, 1,740 in 1777, and 2,200 francs in 1785.[8]

In the British West Indies it is apparent from occasional documents that the trend was similar. A memorial from Barbados in 1689, for example, recited that in earlier years the planters had been supplied with Africans at £7 sterling per head, of which forty shillings covered the Guinea cost and £5 paid the freightage; but now since the establishment of the Royal African company, "we buy negroes at the price of an engrossed commodity, the common rate of a good negro on shipboard being twenty pound. And we are forced to scramble for them in so shameful a manner that one of the great burdens of our lives is the going to buy negroes. But we must have them; we cannot be without them." [9] The overthrow of the monopoly, however, brought no relief. In 1766 the price of new negroes in the West Indies ranged at about £26; [10] and in 1788-1790 from £41 to £49. At this time the value of a prime field hand, reared in the islands, was reported to be twice as great as that of an imported African.[11]

In Virginia the rise was proportionate. In 1671 a planter wrote of his purchase of a negro for £26. 10s and said he supposed the price was the highest ever paid in those parts; but a few years afterward a lot of four men brought £30 a head, two women the same rate, and two more women £25 apiece; and before the end of the seventeenth century men were being appraised at £40.[12] An official report from the colony in 1708 noted a great increase of the slave supply in recent years, but observed that the prices had nevertheless risen.[13] In 1754 George

[8] Lucien Peytraud, *L'Esclavage aux Antilles Françaises avant 1789* (Paris, 1897), pp. 122-127.
[9] *Groans of the Plantations* (1679), p. 5, quoted in W. Cunningham, *Growth of English Industry and Commerce* (Cambridge, 1892), II, 278, note.
[10] *Abridgement of the Evidence taken before a Committee of the whole House: The Slave Trade*, no. 2 (London, 1790), p. 37.
[11] "An Old Member of Parliament," *Doubts on the Abolition of the Slave Trade* (London, 1790), p. 72, quoting Dr. Adair's evidence in the *Privy Council Report*, part 3, Antigua appendix no. 11.
[12] P. A. Bruce, *Economic History of Virginia in the Seventeenth Century*, II, 88-92.
[13] *North Carolina Colonial Records*, I, 693.

Washington paid £52 for a man and nearly as much for a woman; in 1764 he bought a lot at £57 a head; in 1768 he bought two mulattoes at £50 and £61.15s respectively, a negro for £66.10s, another at public vendue for £72, and a girl for £49.10s. Finally in 1772 he bought five males, one of whom cost £50, another £65, a third £75, and the remaining two £90 each;[14] and in the same year he was offered £80 for a slave named Will Shagg whom his overseer described as an incorrigible runaway.[15]

Scattered items which might be cited from still other colonies make the evidence conclusive that there was a general and substantially continuous rise throughout colonial times. The advances which occurred in the principal British West India islands and in Virginia, indeed, were a consequence of advances elsewhere, for by the middle of the eighteenth century all of these colonies were already passing the zenith of their prosperity, whereas South Carolina, Georgia, San Domingo and Brazil, as well as minor new British tropical settlements, were in course of rapid plantation expansion. Prices in the several communities tended of course to be equalized partly by a slender intercolonial slave trade but mainly by the Guineamen's practice of carrying their wares to the highest of the many competing markets.

The war for American independence, bringing hard times, depressed all property values, those of slaves included. But the return of peace brought prompt inflation in response to exaggerated anticipations of prosperity to follow. Wade Hampton, for example, wrote to his brother from Jacksonborough in the South Carolina lowlands, January 30, 1782: "All attempts to purchase negroes have been fruitless, owing to the flattering state of our affairs in this quarter."[16] The sequel was sharply disappointing. The indigo industry was virtually dead, and rice prices, like those of tobacco, did not maintain their expected levels. The financial experience was described in 1786 by Henry

---

[14] W. C. Ford, *George Washington* (Paris and New York, 1900), I, 125-127; *Washington as an Employer and Importer of Labor* (Brooklyn, 1889).
[15] S. M. Hamilton, ed., *Letters to Washington*, IV, 127.
[16] MS. among the Gibbes papers in the capitol at Columbia, S. C.

Pendleton, a judge on the South Carolina bench, in words which doubtless would have been similarly justified in various other states: "No sooner had we recovered and restored the country to peace and order than a rage for running into debt became epidemical. . . . A happy speculation was almost every man's object and pursuit. . . . What a load of debt was in a short time contracted in the purchase of British superfluities, and of lands and slaves for which no price was too high if credit for the purchase was to be obtained! . . . How small a pittance of the produce of the years 1783, '4, '5, altho' amounting to upwards of 400,000*l* sterling a year on an average, hath been applied toward lessening old burdens! . . . What then was the consequence? The merchants were driven to the exportation of gold and silver, which so rapidly followed; . . . a diminution of the value of the capital as well as the annual produce of estates in consequence of the fallen price; . . . the recovery of new debts as well as old in effect suspended, while the numerous bankruptcies which have happened in Europe amongst the merchants trading to America, the reproach of which is cast upon us, have proclaimed to all the trading nations to guard against our laws and policy, and even against our moral principles."[17]

The depression continued with increasing severity into the following decade, when it appears that many of the planters in the Charleston district were saved from ruin only by the wages happily drawn from the Santee Canal Company in payment for the work of their slaves in the canal construction gangs.[18] The conditions and prospects in Virginia at the same time are suggested by a remark of George Washington in 1794 on slave investments: "I shall be happily mistaken if they are not found to be a very troublesome species of property ere many years have passed over our heads."[19]

[17] *Charleston Morning Post,* Dec. 13, 1786, quoted in the *American Historical Review,* XIV, 537, 538.
[18] Samuel DuBose, "Reminiscences of St. Stephen's Parish," in T. G. Thomas, ed., *History of the Huguenots in South Carolina* (New York, 1887), pp. 66-68.
[19] New York Public Library *Bulletin,* II, 15. This letter has been quoted at greater length at the beginning of chapter VIII above.

Prices in this period were so commonly stated in currency
of uncertain depreciation that a definite schedule by years may
not safely be made. It is clear, however, that the range in 1783
was little lower than it had been on the eve of the war, while
in 1795 it was hardly more than half as high. For the first
time in American history, in a period of peace, there was a
heavy and disquieting fall in slave prices. This was an earnest
of conditions in the nineteenth century when advances and
declines alternated. From about 1795 onward the stability of
the currency and the increasing abundance of authentic data
permit the fluctuations of prices to be measured and their causes
and effects to be studied with some assurance.

The materials extant comprise occasional travellers' notes,
fairly numerous newspaper items, and quite voluminous manuscript collections of appraisals and bills of sale, all of which
require cautious discrimination in their analysis.[20] The appraisals
fall mainly into two groups: the valuation of estates in probate,
and those for the purpose of public compensation to the
owners of slaves legally condemned for capital crimes. The
former were oftentimes purely perfunctory, and they are generally serviceable only as aids in ascertaining the ratios of value
between slaves of the diverse ages and sexes. The appraisals
of criminals, however, since they prescribed actual payments on
the basis of the market value each slave would have had if his
crime had not been committed, may be assumed under such
laws as Virginia maintained in the premises to be fairly accurate.
A file of more than a thousand such appraisals, with vouchers
of payment attached, which is preserved among the Virginia
archives in the State Library at Richmond, is particularly copious in regard to prices as well as in regard to crimes and punishments.

The bills of sale recording actual market transactions remain

[20] The difficulties to be encountered in ascertaining the values at any
time and place are exemplified in the documents pertaining to slave prices
in the various states in the year 1815, printed in the *American Historical
Review*, XIX, 813-838. In the gleaning of slave prices I have been actively
assisted by Professor R. P. Brooks of the University of Georgia and Miss
Lillie Richardson of New Orleans.

as the chief and central source of information upon prices. Some thousands of these, originating in the city of Charleston, are preserved in a single file among the state archives of South Carolina at Columbia; other thousands are scattered through the myriad miscellaneous notarial records in the court house at New Orleans; many smaller accumulations are to be found in county court houses far and wide, particularly in the cotton belt; and considerable numbers are in private possession, along with plantation journals and letters which sometimes contain similar data.

Now these documents more often than otherwise record the sale of slaves in groups. One of the considerations involved was that a gang already organized would save its purchaser time and trouble in establishing a new plantation as a going concern, and therefore would probably bring a higher gross price than if its members were sold singly. Another motive was that of keeping slave families together, which served doubly in comporting with scruples of conscience and inducing to the greater contentment of slaves in their new employ. The documents of the time demonstrate repeatedly the appreciation of equanimity as affecting value. But group sales give slight information upon individual prices; and even the bills of individual sale yield much less than a statistician could wish. The sex is always presumable from the slave's name, the color is usually stated or implied, and occasionally deleterious proclivities are specified, as of a confirmed drunkard or a persistent runaway; but specifications of age, strength and talents are very often, one and all, omitted. The problem is how may these bare quotations of price be utilized. To strike an average of all prices in any year at any place would be fruitless, since an even distribution of slave grades cannot be assumed when quotations are not in great volume: the prices of young children are rarely ascertainable from the bills, since they were hardly ever sold separately; the prices of women likewise are too seldom segregated from those of their children to permit anything to be established beyond a ratio to some ascertained standard; and the prices of artizans varied too greatly with their skill to permit definite schedules of them. The only market grade, in fact, for which basic price tabulations can be made with any confidence is that of young male prime field hands, for these alone may usually be discriminated even when ages and qualities are not specified. The method here is to select in the group of bills for any time and place such maximum quotations for males as occur with any notable degree of frequency. Artizans, foremen and the like are thereby generally excluded by the infrequency of their sales, while the middle-aged, the old and the defective are eliminated by leaving aside the quotations of lower range. The more scattering bills in which ages and crafts are given will then serve, when supplemented from probate appraisals, to establish valuation ratios between these able-bodied unskilled young men and the several other classes of slaves. Thus, artizans often brought twice as much as field hands of similar ages, prime women generally brought three-fourths or four-fifths as much as prime men; boys and girls entering their teens, and men and women entering their fifties, brought about half of prime prices for their sexes; and infants were generally appraised at about a tenth or an eighth of prime. The average price for slaves of all ages and both sexes, furthermore, was generally about one-half of the price for male prime field hands. The fluctuation of prime prices, therefore, measures the rise and fall of slave values in general.

The accompanying chart will show the fluctuations of the average prices of prime field hands (unskilled young men) in Virginia, at Charleston, in middle Georgia, and at New Orleans, as well as the contemporary range of average prices for cotton of middling grade in the chief American market, that of New York. The range for prime slaves, it will be seen, rose from about $300 and $400 a head in the upper and lower South respectively in 1795 to a range of from $400 to $600 in 1803, in consequence of the initial impulse of cotton and sugar production and of the contemporary prohibition of the African slave trade by the several states. At those levels prices remained virtually fixed, in most markets, for nearly a decade as an effect of South Carolina's reopening of her ports and of the ham-

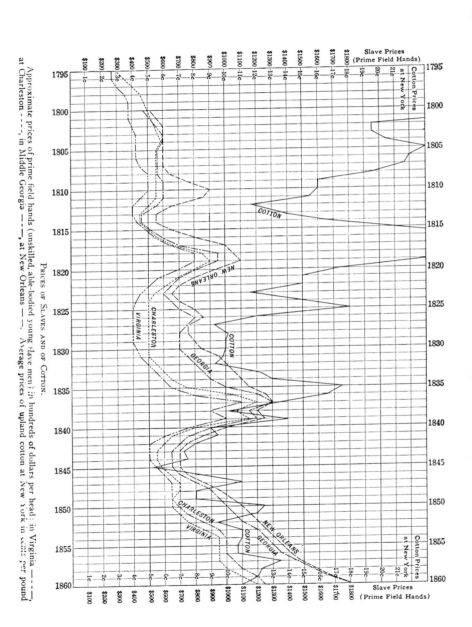

PRICES OF SLAVES AND OF COTTON.

Approximate prices of prime field hands (unskilled, able-bodied young slave men): in Virginia — - — - —, at Charleston - - - -, in Middle Georgia — - —, at New Orleans — —. Average prices of upland cotton at New York in cents per pound.

pering of export commerce by the Napoleonic war. The latter factor prevented even the congressional stoppage of the foreign slave trade in 1808 from exerting any strong effect upon slave prices for the time being except in the sugar district. The next general movement was in fact a downward one of about $100 a head caused by the War of 1812. At the return of peace the prices leaped with parallel perpendicularity in all the markets from $400-$500 in 1814 to twice that range in 1818, only to be upset by the world-wide panic of the following year and to descend to levels of $400 to $600 in 1823. Then came a new rise in the cotton and sugar districts responding to a heightened price of their staples, but for once not evoking a sympathetic movement in the other markets. A small decline then ensuing gave place to a soaring movement at New Orleans, in response to the great stimulus which the protective tariff of 1828 gave to sugar production. The other markets began in the early thirties to make up for the tardiness of their rise; and as a feature of the general inflation of property values then prevalent everywhere, slave prices rose to an apex in 1837 of $1,300 in the purchasing markets and $1,100 in Virginia. The general panic of 1837 began promptly to send them down; and though they advanced in 1839 as a consequence of a speculative bolstering of the cotton market that year, they fell all the faster upon the collapse of that project, finding new levels of rest only at a range of $500-$700. A final advance then set in at the middle of the forties which continued until the highest levels on record were attained on the eve of secession and war.

There are thus in the slave price diagram for the nineteenth century a plateau, with a local peak rising from its level in the sugar district, and three solid peaks—all of them separated by intervening valleys, and all corresponding more or less to the elevations and depressions in the cotton range. The plateau, 1803-1812, was prevented from producing a peak in the eastern markets by the South Carolina repeal of the slave trade prohibition and by the European imbroglio. The first common peak, 1818, and its ensuing trough came promptly upon the establishment of the characteristic régime of the ante-bellum period,

in which the African reservoir could no longer be drawn upon
to mitigate labor shortages and restrain the speculative enhancement of slave prices. The trough of the 'twenties was deeper
and broader in the upper and eastern South than elsewhere
partly because the panic of 1819 had brought a specially severe
financial collapse there from the wrecking of mushroom canal
projects and the like.[21] It is remarkable that so wide a spread
of rates in the several districts prevailed for so long a period as
here appears. The statistics may of course be somewhat at fault,
but there is reason for confidence that their margin of error is not
great enough to vitiate them.

The next peak, 1837-1839, was in most respects like the preceding one, and the drop was quite as sudden and even more
severe. The distresses of the time in the district where they
were the most intense were described in a diary of 1840 by a
North Carolinian, who had journeyed southwestward in the hope
of collecting payment for certain debts, but whose personal chagrin was promptly eclipsed by the spectacle of general disaster.
"Speculation," said he, "has been making poor men rich and
rich men princes." But now "a revulsion has taken place. Mississippi is ruined. Her rich men are poor, and her poor men
beggars. . . . We have seen hard times in North Carolina,
hard times in the east, hard times everywhere; but Mississippi
exceeds them all. . . . Lands . . . that once commanded from thirty to fifty dollars per acre may now be bought
for three or five dollars, and that with considerable improvements, while many have been sold at sheriff's sales at fifty cents
that were considered worth ten to twenty dollars. The people,
too, are running their negroes to Texas and to Alabama, and
leaving their real estate and perishable property to be sold, or
rather sacrificed. . . . So great is the panic and so dreadful
the distress that there are a great many farms prepared to receive
crops, and some of them actually planted, and yet deserted, not
a human being to be found upon them. I had prepared myself

---

[21] *E. g., The Papers of Archibald D. Murphey* (North Carolina Historical Commission *Publications*, Raleigh, 1914), I, 93 ff.

to see hard times here, but unlike most cases, the actual condition of affairs is much worse than the report."[22]

The fall of Mississippi slaves continued, accompanying that of cotton and even anticipating it in the later phase of the movement, until extreme depths were reached in the middle forties, though at New Orleans and in the Georgia uplands the decline was arrested in 1842 at a level of about $700. The sugar planters began prospering from the better prices established for their staple by the tariff of that year, and were able to pay more than panic prices for slaves; but as has been noted in an earlier chapter, suspicion of fraud in the cases of slaves offered from Mississippi militated against their purchase. A sugar planter would be willing to pay considerably more for a neighbor's negro than for one who had come down the river and who might shortly be seized on a creditor's attachment.

At the middle of the forties, with a rising cotton market, there began a strong and sustained advance, persisting throughout the fifties and carrying slave prices to unexampled heights. By 1856 the phenomenon was receiving comment in the newspapers far and wide. In the early months of that year the *Republican* of St. Louis reported field hand sales in Pike County, Missouri, at from $1,215 to $1,642; the *Herald* of Lake Providence, Louisiana, recorded the auction of General L. C. Polk's slaves at which "negro men ranged from $1,500 to $1,635, women and girls from $1,250 to $1,550, children in proportion—all cash" and concluded: "Such a sale, we venture to say, has never been equaled in the state of Louisiana." In Virginia, likewise, the Richmond *Despatch* in January told of the sale of an estate in Halifax County at which "among other enormous prices, one man brought $1,410 and another $1,425, and both were sold again privately the same day at advances of $50. They were ordinary field hands, not considered no. I. in any respect." In April the Lynchburg *Virginian* reported the sale of men in the auction of a large estate at from $1,120 to $2,110, with most of the prices ranging midway between; and in August the Richmond *Despatch* noted

[22] W. H. Wills, "Diary," in the Southern History Association *Publications. VIII* (Washington, 1904), 35.

that instead of the customary summer dullness in the demand for slaves, it was unprecedentedly vigorous, with men's prices ranging from $1,200 to $1,500.[23]

The *Southern Banner* of Athens, Georgia, said as early as January, 1855: "Everybody except the owners of slaves must feel and know that the price of slave labor and slave property at the South is at present too high when compared with the prices of everything else. There must ere long be a change; and . . . we advise parties interested to 'stand from under!' "[24] But the market belied the apprehensions. A neighboring journal noted at the beginning of 1858, that in the face of the current panic, slave prices as indicated in newspapers from all quarters of the South held up astonishingly. "This argues a confidence on the part of the planters that there is a good time coming. Well," the editor concluded with a hint of his own persistent doubts, "we trust they may not be deceived in their calculations."[25]

The market continued deaf to the Cassandra school. When in March, 1859, Pierce Butler's half of the slaves from the plantations which his quondam wife made notorious were auctioned to defray his debts, bidders who gathered from near and far offered prices which yielded an average rate of $708 per head for the 429 slaves of all ages.[26] And in January and February the still greater auction at Albany, Georgia, of the estate of Joseph Bond, lately deceased, yielded $2,850 for one of the men, about $1,900 as an average for such prime field hands as were sold separately, and a price of $958.64 as a general average for the 497 slaves of all ages and conditions.[27] Sales at similar prices

[23] These items were reprinted in George M. Weston, *Who are and who may be Slaves in the U. S.* [1856].
[24] *Southern Banner*, Jan. 11, 1855, endorsing an editorial of similar tone in the New York *Express*.
[25] *Southern Watchman* (Athens, Ga.), Jan. 21, 1858.
[26] *What Became of the Slaves on a Georgia Plantation Auction Sale of Slaves at Savannah, March 2d and 3d, 1859. A Sequel to Mrs. Kemble's Journal* [1863]. This appears to have been a reprint of an article in the New York *Tribune*. The slaves were sold in family parcels comprising from two to seven persons each.
[27] MS. record in the Ordinary's office at Macon, Ga. Probate Returns, vol. 9, pp. 2-7.

were at about the same time reported from various other quarters.[28]

Editorial warnings were now more vociferous than before. The *Federal Union* of Milledgeville said for example: "There is a perfect fever raging in Georgia now on the subject of buying negroes. . . . Men are borrowing money at exorbitant rates of interest to buy negroes at exorbitant prices. The speculation will not sustain the speculators, and in a short time we shall see many negroes and much land offered under the sheriff's hammer, with few buyers for cash; and then this kind of property will descend to its real value. The old rule of pricing a negro by the price of cotton by the pound—that is to say, if cotton is worth twelve cents a negro man is worth $1,200.00, if at fifteen cents then $1,500.00—does not seem to be regarded. Negroes are 25 per cent. higher now with cotton at ten and one half cents than they were two or three years ago when it was worth fifteen and sixteen cents. Men are demented upon the subject. A reverse will surely come."[29]

The fever was likewise raging in the western South,[30] and it persisted until the end of 1860. Indeed the peak of this price movement was evidently cut off by the intervention of war. How great an altitude it might have reached, and what shape its downward slope would have taken had peace continued, it is idle to conjecture. But that a crash must have come is beyond a reasonable doubt.

The Charleston *Mercury*[31] attributed the advance of slave prices in the fifties mainly to the demand of the railroads for labor. This was borne out in some degree by the transactions of the railroad companies whose headquarters were in that city. The president of the Charleston and Savannah Railroad Company, endorsing the arguments which had been advanced by a writer in

[28] Edward Ingle, *Southern Sidelights* (New York [1896]), p. 294, note.
[29] *Federal Union* (Milledgeville, Ga.), Jan. 17, 1860, reprinted with endorsement in the *Southern Banner* (Athens, Ga.), Jan. 26, 1860, and reprinted in *Plantation and Frontier*, II, 73, 74.
[30] Prices at Lebanon, Tenn., and Franklin, Ky., are given in *Hunt's Merchants' Magazine*, XI, 774 (Dec., 1859).
[31] Reprinted in William Chambers, *American Slavery and Colour* (London, 1857), p. 207.

DeBow's Review,[32] recommended in his first annual report, 1855, an extensive purchase of slaves for the company's construction gangs, reckoning that at the price of $1,000, with interest at 7 per cent. and life insurance at 2½ per cent. the annual charge would be little more than half the current cost in wages at $180. The yearly cost of maintenance and superintendence, reckoned at $20 for clothing, $15 for corn, molasses and tobacco, $1 for physician's fees, $10 for overseer's wages and $15 for tools and repairs, he said, would be the same whether the slaves were hired or bought.[33] How largely the company adopted its president's plan is not known. For the older and stronger South Carolina Railroad Company, however, whose lines extended from Charleston to Augusta, Columbia and Camden, detailed records in the premises are available. This company was created in 1843 by the merging of two earlier corporations, one of which already possessed eleven slaves. In February, 1845, the new company bought three more slaves, two of which cost $400 apiece and the third $686. At the end of the next year the superintendent reported: "After hands for many years in the company's service have acquired the knowledge and skill necessary to make them valuable, the company are either compelled to submit to higher rates of wages imposed or to pass others at a lower rate of compensation through the same apprenticeship, with all the hazard of a strike, in their turn, by the owners."[34] The directors, after studying the problem thus presented, launched upon a somewhat extensive slave-purchasing programme, buying one in 1848 and seven in 1849 at uniform prices of $900; one in 1851 at $800 thirty-seven in 1852, all but two of which were procured in a single purchase from J. C. Sproull and Company, at prices from $512.50 to $1,004.50, but mostly ranging near $900; and twenty-eight more at various times between 1853 and 1859, at prices rising to $1,500. Finally, when two or three years of war had put all property, of however precarious a nature, at a premium over Confederate currency, the company bought

[*] *DeBow's Review*, XVII, 76-82.
[*] *Ibid.*, XVIII, 404-406.
[*] U. B. Phillips, *Transportation in the Eastern Cotton Belt* (New York, 1908), p. 205.

another slave in August, 1863, for $2,050, and thirty-two more in 1864 at prices ranging from $2,450 to $6,005.[35] All of these slaves were males. No ages or trades are specified in the available records, and no statement of the advantages actually experienced in owning rather than hiring slaves.

The Brandon Bank, at Brandon, Mississippi, which was virtually identical with the Mississippi and Alabama Railroad Company, bought prior to 1839, $159,000 worth of slaves for railroad employment, but it presumably lost them shortly after that year when the bank and the railroad together went bankrupt.[36] The state of Georgia had bought about 190 slaves in and before 1830 for employment in river and road improvements, but it sold them in 1834,[37] and when in the late 'forties and the 'fifties it built and operated the Western and Atlantic Railroad it made no repetition of the earlier experiment. In the 'fifties, indeed, the South Carolina Railroad Company was almost unique in its policy of buying slaves for railroad purposes.

The most cogent reason against such a policy was not that the owned slaves increased the current charges, but that their purchase involved the diversion of capital in a way which none but abnormal circumstances could justify. In the year 1846 when the superintendent of the South Carolina company made his recommendation, slave prices were abnormally low and cotton prices were leaping in such wise as to make probable a strong advance in the labor market. By 1855, however, the price of slaves had nearly doubled, and by 1860 it was clearly inordinate. The special occasion for a company to divert its funds or increase its capital obligations had accordingly vanished, and sound policy would have suggested the sale of slaves on hand rather than the purchase of more. The state of Louisiana, indeed, sold in 1860[38] the force of nearly a hundred slave men which it had

[35] South Carolina Railroad Company *Reports* for 1860 and 1865.
[36] *Niles' Register*, LVI, 130 (April 27, 1839).
[37] U. B. Phillips, *Transportation in the Eastern Cotton Belt*, pp. 114, 115; W. C. Dawson, *Compilation of Georgia Laws*, p. 399; O. H. Prince, *Digest of the Laws of Georgia*, p. 742.
[38] Board of Public Works *Report* for 1860 (Baton Rouge, 1861), p. 7.

used on river improvements long enough for many of its members to have grown old in the service.[39]

Manufacturing companies here and there bought slaves to man their works, but in so doing added seriously to the risks of their business. A news item of 1849 reported that an outbreak of cholera at the Hillman Iron Works near Clarksville, Tenn., had brought the death of four or five slaves and the removal of the remainder from the vicinity until the epidemic should have passed.[40] A more normal episode of mere financial failure was that which wrecked the Nesbitt Manufacturing Company whose plant was located on Broad River in South Carolina. To complete its works and begin operations this company procured a loan of some $92,000 in 1837 from the Bank of the State of South Carolina on the security of the land and buildings and a hundred slaves owned by the company. After several years of operation during which the purchase of additional slaves raised the number to 194, twenty-seven of whom were mechanics, the company admitted its insolvency. When the mortgage was foreclosed in 1845 the bank bought in virtually the whole property to save its investment, and operated the works for several years until a new company, with a manager imported from Sweden, was floated to take the concern off its hands.[41]

Most of the cotton mills depended wholly upon white labor, though a few made experiments with slave staffs. One of these was in operation in Maury County, Tennessee, in 1827,[42] and another near Pensacola, Florida, twenty years afterward. Except for their foremen, each of these was run by slave operatives exclusively; and in the latter case, at least, all the slaves were owned by the company. These comprised in 1847 some forty boys and girls, who were all fed, and apparently well fed, at the

[39] State Engineer's *Report* for 1856 (New Orleans, 1857), p. 7.
[40] New Orleans *Delta*, Mch. 10, 1849.
[41] *Report of the Special Joint Committee appointed to examine the Bank of the State of South Carolina* (Charleston, 1849); *Report of the President and Directors of the Bank of the State of South Carolina, November, 1850* (Columbia, 1850).
[42] *Georgia Courier* (Augusta, Ga.), Apr. 24, 1828, reprinted in *Plantation and Frontier*, II, 258.

company's table.[43] The career of these enterprises is not ascertainable. A better known case is that of the Saluda Factory, near Columbia, South Carolina. When J. Graves came from New England in 1848 to assume the management of this mill he found several negroes among the operatives, all of whom were on hire. His first impulse was to replace all the negroes with whites; but before this was accomplished the newcomer was quite converted by their "activity and promptness," and he recommended that the number of black operatives be increased instead of diminished. "They are easily trained to habits of industry and patient endurance," he said, "and by the concentration of all their faculties . . . their imitative faculties become cultivated to a very high degree, their muscles become trained and obedient to the will, so that whatever they see done they are quick in learning to do." [44] The company was impelled by Graves' enthusiasm to resort to slave labor exclusively, partly on hire from their owners and partly by purchase. At the height of this regime, in 1851, the slave operatives numbered 158.[45] But whether from the incapacity of the negroes as mill hands or from the accumulation of debt through the purchase of slaves, the company was forced into liquidation at the close of the following year.[46]

Corporations had reason at all times, in fact, to prefer free laborers over slaves even on hire, for in so doing they escaped liabilities for injuries by fellow servants. When a firm of contractors, for example, advertised in 1833 for five hundred laborers at $15 per month to work on the Muscle Shoals canal in northern Alabama, it deemed it necessary to say that in cases of accidents to slaves it would assume financial responsibility "for any injury or damage that may hereafter happen in the process of blasting rock or of the caving of banks."[47] Free

[43] *DeBow's Review*, IV, 256.
[44] Letter of J. Graves, May 15, 1849, in the Augusta, Ga., *Chronicle*, June 1, 1849. Cf. also J. B. D Debow, *Industrial Resources of the Southern and Western States* (New Orleans, 1852), II, 339.
[45] *DeBow's Review*, XI, 319, 320.
[46] *Augusta Chronicle*, Jan. 5, 1853.
[47] Reprinted in E S. Abdy, *Journal of a Residence in the United States* (London, 1835), II, 109.

laborers, on the other hand, carried their own risks. Except when some planter would take a contract for grading in his locality, to be done under his own supervision in the spare time of his gang, slaves were generally called for in canal and railroad work only when the supply of free labor was inadequate.

Slaveowners, on the other hand, were equally reluctant to hire their slaves to such corporations or contractors except in times of special depression, for construction camps from their lack of sanitation, discipline, domesticity and stability were at the opposite pole from plantations as places of slave residence. High wages were no adequate compensation for the liability to contagious and other diseases, demoralization, and the checking of the birth rate by the separation of husbands and wives. The higher the valuation of slave property, the greater would be the strength of these considerations.

Slaves were a somewhat precarious property under all circumstances. Losses were incurred not only through disease[48] and flight but also through sudden death in manifold ways, and through theft. A few items will furnish illustration. An early Charleston newspaper printed the following: "On the ninth instant Mr. Edward North at Pon Pon sent a sensible negro fellow to Moon's Ferry for a jug of rum, which is about two miles from his house; and he drank to that excess in the path that he died within six or seven hours."[49] From the Eutaws in the same state a correspondent wrote in 1798 of a gin-house disaster: "I yesterday went over to Mr. Henry Middleton's plantation to view the dreadful effects of a flash of lightning which the day before fell on his machine house in which were about twenty negro men, fourteen of which were killed immediately."[50] In 1828 the following appeared in a newspaper at New Orleans: "Yesterday towards one o'clock P. M., as one of the ferry boats was crossing the river with sixteen slaves on board belonging to General Wade Hampton, with their baggage, a few rods distant from the

[48] For the effect of epidemics see above, pp. 300, 301.
[49] South Carolina Gazette, Feb. 12 to 19, 1741.
[50] Carolina Gazette (Charleston), Feb. 4, 1798, supplement.

shore these negroes, being frightened by the motion of the boat, all threw themselves on the same side, which caused the boat to fill; and notwithstanding the prompt assistance afforded, four or five of these unfortunates perished."[51] In 1839 William Lowndes Yancey, who was then a planter in South Carolina, lost his whole gang through the poisoning of a spring on his place, and was thereby bankrupted.[52] About 1858 certain bandits in western Louisiana abducted two slaves from the home of the Widow Bernard on Bayou Vermilion. After the lapse of several months they were discovered in the possession of one Apcher, who was tried for the theft but acquitted. The slaves when restored to their mistress were put in the kitchen, bound together by their hands. But while the family was at dinner the two ran from the house and drowned themselves in the bayou. The narrator of the episode attributed the impulse for suicide to the taste for vagabondage and the hatred for work which the negroes had acquired from the bandit.[53]

The governor of South Carolina reported the convictions of five white men for the crime of slave stealing in the one year 1809;[54] and in the penitentiary lists of the several states the designation of slave stealers was fairly frequent, in spite of the fact that the death penalty was generally prescribed for the crime. One method of their operation was described in a Georgia newspaper item of 1828 which related that two wagoners upon meeting a slave upon the road persuaded him to lend a hand in shifting their load. When the negro entered the wagon they overpowered him and drove on. When they camped for the night they bound him to the wheel; but while they slept he cut his thongs and returned to his master.[55] The greatest activities in this line, however, were doubtless those of the Murrell gang of desperadoes operating throughout the southwest in the early

[51] *Louisiana Courier*, Mch. 3, 1828.
[52] J. W. DuBose, *Life of W. L. Yancey* (Birmingham, Ala., 1892), p. 39.
[53] Alexandre Barbe, *Histoire des Comités de Vigilance aux Attakapas* (Louisiana, 1861), pp. 182-185.
[54] H. M. Henry, *The Police Control of the Slave in South Carolina* [1914], pp. 110-112.
[55] *The Athenian* (Athens, Ga.), Aug. 19, 1828.

thirties with a shrewd scheme for victimizing both whites and blacks. They would conspire with a slave, promising him his freedom or some other reward if he would run off with them and suffer himself to be sold to some unwary purchaser and then escape to join them again.[56] Sometimes they repeated this process over and over again with the same slave until a threat of exposure from him led to his being silenced by murder. In the same period a smaller gang with John Washburn as its leading spirit and with Natchez as informal headquarters, was busy at burglary, highway and flatboat robbery, pocket picking and slave stealing.[57] In 1846 a prisoner under arrest at Cheraw, South Carolina, professed to reveal a new conspiracy for slave stealing with ramifications from Virginia to Texas; but the details appear not to have been published.[58]

Certain hostile critics of slavery asserted that in one district or another masters made reckonings favorable to such driving of slaves at their work as would bring premature death. Thus Fanny Kemble wrote in 1838, when on the Georgia coast: "In Louisiana . . . the humane calculation was not only made but openly and unhesitatingly avowed that the planters found it upon the whole their most profitable plan to work off (kill with labour) their whole number of slaves about once in seven years, and renew the whole stock." [59] The English traveler Featherstonhaugh likewise wrote of Louisiana in 1844, when he had come as close to it as East Tennessee, that "the duration of

[56] H. R. Howard, compiler, *The History of Virgil A. Stewart and his Adventure in capturing and exposing the great "Western Land Pirate" and his Gang* (New York, 1836), pp. 63-68, 104, *et passim*. The truth of these accounts of slave stealings is vouched for in a letter to the editor of the New Orleans *Bulletin*, reprinted in the *Federal Union* (Milledgeville, Ga.), Nov. 5, 1835.
[57] The manifold felonies of the gang were described by Washburn in a dying confession after his conviction for a murder at Cincinnati. Natchez *Courier*, reprinted in the *Louisiana Courier* (New Orleans), Feb. 28, 1837. Other reports of the theft of slaves appear in the Charleston *Morning Post and Daily Advertiser*, Nov. 2, 1786; *Southern Banner* (Athens, Ga.), July 19, 1834, advertisement; *Federal Union* (Milledgeville, Ga.), July 18, 1835; and the following New Orleans journals: *Louisiana Gazette*, Apr. 1 and Sept. 10, 1819; *Mercantile Advertiser*, Sept. 29, 1831; *Bee*, Dec. 14, 1841; Mch. 10, 1845, and Aug. 1 and Nov. 11, 1848; *Louisiana Courier*, Mch. 29 and Sept. 18, 1840; *Picayune*, Aug. 21, 1845.
[58] New Orleans *Commercial Times*, Aug. 26, 1846.
[59] Frances A. Kemble, *Journal* (New York, 1863), p. 28.

life for a sugar mill hand does not exceed seven years."[60] William Goodell supported a similar assertion of his own in 1853 by a series of citations. The first of these was to Theodore Weld as authority, that "Professor Wright" had been told at New York by Dr. Deming of Ashland, Ohio, a story that Mr. Dickinson of Pittsburg had been told by Southern planters and slave dealers on an Ohio River steamboat. The tale thus vouched for contained the assertion that sugar planters found that by the excessive driving of slaves day and night in the grinding season they could so increase their output that "they could afford to sacrifice one set of hands in seven years," and "that this horrible system was now practised to a considerable extent." The second citation was likewise to Weld for a statement by Mr. Samuel Blackwell of Jersey City, whose testimonial lay in the fact of his membership in the Presbyterian church, that while on a tour in Louisiana "the planters generally declared to him that they were obliged so to overwork their slaves during the sugar-making season (from eight to ten weeks) as to use them up in seven or eight years." The third was to the Rev. Mr. Reed of London who after a tour in Maryland, Virginia and Kentucky in 1834 published the following: "I was told, confidentially, from excellent authority, that recently at a meeting of planters in South Carolina the question was seriously discussed whether the slave is more profitable to the owner if well fed, well clothed and worked lightly, or if made the most of at once and exhausted in some eight years. The decision was in favor of the last alternative "[61] An anonymous writer in 1857 repeated this last item without indication of its date or authority but with a shortening of the period of exhaustion to "some four or five years."[62]

These assertions, which have been accepted by some historians as valid, prompt a series of reflections. In the first place, anyone

[60] G. W. Featherstonhaugh, *Excursion Through the Slave States* (London, 1844), I, 120. Though Featherstonhaugh afterward visited New Orleans his book does not recur to this topic.
[61] William Goodell, *The American Slave Code in Theory and Practise* (New York, 1853), pp. 79-81, citing Theodore Weld, *Slavery as it is*, p 39, and Mattheson, *Visit to the American Churches*, II, 173.
[62] *The Suppressed Book about Slavery! Prepared for publication in 1857, never published until the present time* (New York, 1864), p. 211.

who has had experience with negro labor may reasonably be
skeptical when told that healthy, well fed negroes, whether slave
or free, can by any routine insistence of the employer be driven
beyond the point at which fatigue begins to be injurious.   In
the second place, plantation work as a rule had the limitation
of daylight hours; in plowing, mules which could not be hur-
ried set the pace; in hoeing, haste would imperil the plants by
enhancing the proportion of misdirected strokes; and in the
harvest of tobacco, rice and cotton much perseverance but little
strain was involved. The sugar harvest alone called for heavy
exertion and for night work in the mill. But common report in
that regard emphasized the sturdy sleekness as well as the jovi-
ality of the negroes in the grinding season;[63] and even if exhaustion had been characteristic instead, the brevity of the period
would have prevented any serious debilitating effect before the
coming of the more leisurely schedule after harvest. In fact
many neighboring Creole and Acadian farmers, fishermen and
the like were customarily enlisted on wages as plantation recruits
in the months of stress.[64] The sugar district furthermore was
the one plantation area within easy reach of a considerable city
whence a seasonal supply of extra hands might be had to save
the regular forces from injury. The fact that a planter, as reported by Sir Charles Lyell, failed to get a hundred recruits one
year in the midst of the grinding season [65] does not weaken this
consideration. It may well have been that his neighbors had
forestalled him in the wage-labor market, or that the remaining
Germans and Irish in the city refused to take the places of their
fellows who were on strike. It is well established that sugar
planters had systematic recourse to immigrant labor for ditching
and other severe work.[66] It is incredible that they ignored the
same recourse if at any time the requirements of their crop threatened injury to their property in slaves. The recommendation of
the old Roman, Varro, that freemen be employed in harvesting to

[63] E. g., Olmsted, *Seaboard Slave States*, p. 668.
[64] *DeBow's Review*, XI, 606.
[65] *See* above, p. 337.
[66] See above, pp. 301, 302.

save the slaves[67] would apply with no more effect, in case of need, to the pressing of oil and wine than to the grinding of sugar-cane.   Two months' wages to a Creole, a "'Cajun" or an Irishman would be cheap as the price of a slave's continued vigor, even when slave prices were low.   On the whole, however, the stress of the grinding was not usually as great as has been fancied. Some of the regular hands in fact were occasionally spared from the harvest at its height and set to plow and plant for the next year's crop.[68]

The further question arises: how could a master who set himself to work a slave to death in seven years make sure on the one hand that the demise would not be precipitated within a few months instead, and on the other that the consequence would not be merely the slave's incapacitation instead of his death?   In the one case a serious loss would be incurred at once; in the other the stoppage of the slave's maintenance, which would be the only conceivable source of gain in the premises, would not have been effected, but the planter would merely have an invalid on his hands instead of a worker.   Still further, the slaves had recourses of their own, even aside from appeals for legal redress. They might shoot or stab the oppressor, burn his house, or run away, or resort to any of a dozen other forms of sabotage.   These possibilities the masters knew as well as the slaves.   Mere passive resistance, however, in cases where even that was needed, would generally prove effective enough.

Finally, if all the foregoing arguments be dismissed as fallacious, there still remains the factor of slave prices as a deterrent in certain periods.   If when slaves were cheap and their produce dear it might be feasible and profitable to exhaust the one to increase the other, the opportunity would surely vanish when the price relations were reversed.   The trend of the markets was very strong in that direction.   Thus at the beginning of the nineteenth century a prime field hand in the upland cotton belt had

[67] Varro, *De Re Rustica*, I, XVII, 2.
[68] *E. g.*, items for November, 1849, in the plantation diary of Dr. John P. R. Stone, of Iberville Parish, Louisiana. For the use of this document, the MS. of which is in the possession of Mr. John Stone Ware, White-Castle, La., I am indebted to Mr. V. Alton Moody of the University of Michigan, now Lieutenant in the American Expeditionary Force in France.

the value of about 1,500 pounds of middling cotton; by 1810 this value had risen to 4,500 pounds; by 1820 to 5,500; by 1830 to 6,000; by 1840 to 8,300; from 1843 to 1853 it was currently about 10,000; and in 1860 it reached about 16,000 pounds. Comparison of slave values as measured in the several other staples would show quite similar trends, though these great appreciations were accompanied by no remotely proportionate increase of the slaves' industrial capacities. The figures tell their own tale of the mounting preposterousness of any calculated exhaustion of the human chattels.

The tradition in anti-slavery circles was however too strong to die. Various travelers touring the South, keen for corroborative evidence but finding none, still nursed the belief that a further search would bring reward. It was like the rainbow's end, always beyond the horizon. Thus the two Englishmen, Marshall Hall and William H. Russell, after scrutinizing many Southern localities and finding no slave exhaustion, asserted that it prevailed either in a district or in a type of establishment which they had not examined. Hall, who traveled far in the Southern states and then merely touched at Havana on his way home, wrote: "In the United States the life of the slave has been cherished and his offspring promoted. In Cuba the lives of the slaves have been 'used up' by excessive labour, and increase in number disregarded. It is said, indeed, that the slave-life did not extend beyond eight or ten years."[69] Russell recorded his surprise at finding that the Louisiana planters made no reckoning whatever of the cost of their slaves' labor, that Irish gangs nevertheless did the ditching, and that the slave children of from nine to eleven years were at play, "exempted from that cruel fate which befalls poor children of their age in the mining and manufacturing districts of England"; and then upon glimpsing the homesteads of some Creole small proprietors, he wrote: "It is among these men that, at times, slavery assumes its harshest aspect, and that slaves are exposed to the severest labor."[70] Johann Schoepf on the

[69] Marshall Hall, *The Two-fold Slavery of the United States* (London, 1854), p. 154.
[70] W. H. Russell, *My Diary North and South* (Boston, 1863), pp. 274, 278.

other hand while travelling many years before on the Atlantic seaboard had written: "They who have the largest droves [of slaves] keep them the worst, let them run naked mostly or in rags, and accustom them as much as possible to hunger, but exact of them steady work." [71] That no concrete observations were adduced in any of these premises is evidence enough, under the circumstances, that the charges were empty.

The capital value of the slaves was an increasingly powerful insurance of their lives and their health. In four days of June, 1836, Thomas Glover of Lowndes County, Alabama, incurred a debt of $35 which he duly paid, for three visits with mileage and prescriptions by Dr. Salley to his "wench Rina"; [72] and in the winter of 1858 Nathan Truitt of Troup County, Georgia, had medical attendance rendered to a slave child of his to the amount of $130.50.[73] These are mere chance items in the multitude which constantly recur in probate records. Business prudence required expenditure with almost a lavish hand when endangered property was to be saved. The same consideration applied when famines occurred, as in Alabama in 1828 [74] and 1855.[75] Poverty-stricken freemen might perish, but slaveowners could use the slaves themselves as security for credits to buy food at famine prices to feed them.[76] As Olmsted said, comparing famine effects in the South and in Ireland, "the slaves suffered no physical want—the peasant starved." [77] The higher the price of slaves, the more stringent the pressure upon the masters to safeguard them from disease, injury and risk of every sort.

Although this phase of the advancing valuation gave no occasion for regret, other phases brought a spread of dismay and apprehension. In an essay of 1859 Edmund Ruffin analyzed the effects in Virginia. In the last fifteen years, he said, the value

[71] Johann David Schoepf, *Travels in the Confederation*, A. J. Morrisson, tr. (Philadelphia, 1911), II, 147. But *see ibid.*, pp. 94, 116, for observations of a general air of indolence among whites and blacks alike.
[72] MS. receipt in private possession.
[73] MS. probate records at LaGrange, Ga.
[74] Charleston *City Gazette*, May 28, 1828.
[75] Olmsted, *Seaboard Slave States*, pp. 707, 708, quoting contemporary newspapers.
[76] Cf. D. D. Wallace, *Life of Henry Laurens*, p. 429.
[77] Olmsted, *Seaboard Slave States*, p. 244.

of slaves had been doubled, solely because of the demand from the lower South. The Virginians affected fell into three classes. The first were those who had slaves to be sold, whether through pressure of debt or in the legal division of estates or in the rare event of liquidating a surplus of labor. These would receive advantage from high prices. The second were those who wishing neither to buy nor sell slaves desired merely to keep their estates intact. These were, of course, unaffected by the fluctuations. The third were the great number of enterprising planters and farmers who desired to increase the scale of their industrial operations and who would buy slaves if conditions were propitious but were debarred therefrom by the immoderate prices. When these men stood aside in the bidding the manual force and the earning power of the commonwealth were depleted. The smaller volume of labor then remaining must be more thinly applied; land values must needs decline; and the shrewdest employers must join the southward movement. The draining of the slaves, he continued, would bring compensation in an inflow of white settlers only when the removal of slave labor had become virtually complete and had brought in consequence the most extreme prostration of land prices and of the incomes of the still remaining remnant of the original population. The exporting of labor, at whatever price it might be sold, he likened to a farmer's conversion of his plow teams into cash instead of using them in his work. According to these views, he concluded. "the highest prices yet obtained from the foreign purchasers of our slaves have never left a profit to the state or produced pecuniary benefit to general interests. And even if prices should continue to increase, as there is good reason to expect and to dread, until they reach $2000 or more for the best laborers, or $1200 for the general average of ages and sexes, these prices, though necessarily operating to remove every slave from Virginia, will still cause loss to agricultural and general interests in every particular sale, and finally render the state a desert and a ruin." [78]

[78] Edmund Ruffin, "The Effects of High Prices of Slaves," in *DeBow's Review*, XXVI, 647-657 (June, 1859).

At Charleston a similar plaint was voiced by L. W. Spratt. In early years when the African trade was open and slaves were cheap, said he, in the Carolina lowlands "enterprise found a profitable field, and necessarily therefore the fortunes of the country bloomed and brightened. But when the fertilizing stream of labor was cut off, when the opening West had no further supply to meet its requisitions, it made demands upon the accumulations of the seaboard. The limited amount became a prize to be contended for. Land in the interior offered itself at less than one dollar an acre. Land on the seaboard had been raised to fifty dollars per acre, and labor, forced to elect between them, took the cheaper. The heirs who came to an estate, or the men of capital who retired from business, sought a location in the West. Lands on the seaboard were forced to seek for purchasers; purchasers came to the seaboard to seek for slaves. Their prices were elevated to their value not upon the seaboard where lands were capital but in the interior where the interest upon the cost of labor was the only charge upon production. Labor therefore ceased to be profitable in the one place as it became profitable in the other. Estates which were wealth to their original proprietors became a charge to the descendants who endeavored to maintain them. Neglect soon came to the relief of unprofitable care; decay followed neglect. Mansions became tenantless and roofless. Trees spring in their deserted halls and wave their branches through dismantled windows. Drains filled up; the swamps returned. Parish churches in imposing styles of architecture and once attended by a goodly company in costly equipages, are now abandoned. Lands which had ready sale at fifty dollars per acre now sell for less than five dollars; and over all these structures of wealth, with their offices of art, and over these scenes of festivity and devotion, there now hangs the pall of an unalterable gloom." [79]   In a later essay the same writer dealt with developments in the 'fifties in more sober phrases which are corroborated by the census returns. Within the decade, he said, as many as ten thousand slaves had been

[79] L. W. Spratt, *The Foreign Slave Trade, the source of political power, of material progress, of social integrity and of social emancipation to the South* (Charleston, 1858), pp. 7, 8.

drawn from Charleston by the attractive prices of the west, and the towns of the interior had suffered losses in the same way. The slaves had been taken in large numbers from all manufacturing employments, and were now being sold by thousands each year from the rice fields. "They are as yet retained by cotton and the culture incident to cotton; but as almost every negro offered in our markets is bid for by the West, the drain is likely to continue." In the towns alone was the loss offset in any degree by an inflow of immigration.[80]

A similar trend as to slaves but with a sharply contrasting effect upon prosperity was described by Gratz Brown as prevailing in Missouri. The slave population, said he, is in process of rapid decline except in a dozen central counties along the Missouri River. "Hemp is the only staple here left that will pay for investment in negroes," and that can hardly hold them against the call of the cotton belt. Already the planters of the upland counties are beginning to send their slaves to southerly markets in response to the prices there offered. In most parts of Missouri, he continued, slavery could not be said to exist as a system. It accordingly served, not as an appreciable industrial agency, but only as a deterrent hampering the progress of immigration. Brown therefore advocated the complete extirpation of the institution as a means of giving great impetus to the state's prosperity.[81]

These accounts are colored by the pro-slavery views of Ruffin and Spratt and the opposite predilections of Brown. It is clear nevertheless that the net industrial effects of the exportation of slaves were strikingly diverse in the several regions. In Missouri, and in Delaware also, where plantations had never been dominant and where negroes were few, the loss of slaves was more than counterbalanced by the gain of freemen; in some portions of Maryland, Virginia and Kentucky the replacement of the one by the other was at so evenly compensating a rate that the volume of industry was not affected; but in other parts of

[80] L. W. Spratt, "Letter to John Perkins of Louisiana," in the Charleston *Mercury*, Feb. 13, 1861.
[81] B. Gratz Brown, *Speech in the Missouri Legislature, February 12, 1857 on gradual emancipation in Missouri* (St. Louis, 1857).

those states and in the rural districts of the rice coast the depletion of slaves was not in any appreciable measure offset by immigration. This applies also to the older portions of the eastern cotton belt.

Throughout the northern and eastern South doubts had often been expressed that slave labor was worth its price. Thus Philip Fithian recorded in his Virginia diary in 1774 a conversation with Mrs. Robert Carter in which she expressed an opinion, endorsed by Fithian, "that if in Mr. Carter's or in any gentleman's estate all the negroes should be sold and the money put to interest in safe hands, and let the land which the ne_ oes now work lie wholly uncultivated, the bare interest of the pric of the negroes would be a much greater yearly income than what is now received from their working the lands, making no allowance at all for the trouble and risk of the masters as to crops and negroes." [82] In 1824 John Randolph said: "It is notorious that the profits of slave labor have been for a long time on the decrease, and that on a fair average it scarcely reimburses the expense of the slave," and concluded by prophesying that a continuance of the tendency would bring it about "in case the slave shall not elope from his master, that his master will run away from him." [83] In 1818 William Elliott of Beaufort, South Carolina, had written that in the sea-island cotton industry for a decade past the high valuations of lands and slaves had been wholly unjustified. On the one hand, said he, the return on investments was extremely small; on the other, it was almost impossible to relieve an embarrassed estate by the sale of a part, for the reduction of the scale of operations would cause a more than proportionate reduction of income. [84]

The remorseless advance of slave prices as measured in their produce tended to spread the adverse conditions noted by Elliott into all parts of the South; and by the close of the 'fifties it is fairly certain that no slaveholders but those few whose plantations lay in the most advantageous parts of the cotton and sugar

[82] Philip V. Fithian, *Journal and Letters* (Princeton, 1900), p. 145.
[83] H. A. Garland, *Life of John Randolph* (New York, 1851), II, 215.
[84] *Southern Agriculturist*, I, 151-163.

districts and whose managerial ability was exceptionally great were earning anything beyond what would cover their maintenance and carrying charges.

Achille Loria has repeatedly expressed the generalization that slaves have been systematically overvalued wherever the institution has prevailed, and he has attempted to explain the phenomenon by reference to an economic law of his own formulation that capitalists always and everywhere exploit labor by devices peculiarly adapted to each régime in turn. His latest argument in the premises is as follows: Man, who is by nature dispersively individualistic, is brought into industrial coördination only by coercion. Isolated labor if on exceptionally fertile soil or if equipped with specially efficient apparatus or if supernormal in energy may produce a surplus income, but ordinarily it can earn no more than a bare subsistence. Associative labor yields so much greater returns that masters of one sort or another emerge in every progressive society to replace dispersion with concentration and to engross most of the accruing enhancement of produce to themselves as captains of industry. This "persistent and continuous coercion, compelling them to labour in conformity to a unitary plan or in accordance with a concentrating design" is commonly in its earlier form slavery, and slaveholders are thus the first possessors of capital. As capitalists they become perpetually concerned with excluding the laborers from the proprietorship of land and the other means of production. So long as land is relatively abundant this can be accomplished only by keeping labor enslaved, and enslavement cannot be maintained unless the slaves are prevented from buying their freedom. This prevention is procured by the heightening of slave prices at such a rate as to keep the cost of freedom always greater than the generality of the slaves can pay with their own accumulated savings or *peculia.* Slave prices in fact, whether in ancient Rome or in modern America, advanced disproportionately to the advantage which the owners could derive from the ownership. "This shows that an element of speculation enters into the valuation of the slave, or that there is a hypervaluation of the slave. *This is the central phenomenon of slavery;* and it is to this far more than to the indolence of slave labour that is due the low productivity of slave states, the permanently unstable equilibrium of the slaveholding enterprise, and its inevitable ruin." The decline of earnings and of slave prices promotes a more drastic oppression, as in Roman Sicily, to reduce the slave's *peculium* and continue the prevention of his self-purchase. When this device is about to fail of its purpose the masters may foil the intention of the slaves by changing them into serfs, attaching the lands to the laborers as an additional thing to be purchased as a condition of freedom. The value of the man may now be permitted to fall to its natural level. Finally, when the growth of population has made land so dear that common laborers in freedom cannot save enough to buy farms, the occasion for slavery and serfdom lapses. Laborers may now be freed to become a wage-earning proletariat, to take their own risks. An automatic coercion replaces the systematic; the labor stimulus is intensified, but the stress of the employer is diminished. The laborer does not escape from coercion, but merely exchanges one of its forms for another.[85]

Now Loria falls into various fallacies in other parts of his book, as when he says that southern lands are generally more fertile than northern and holds that alone, to the exclusion of climate and racial qualities, responsible for the greater prevalence of slavery ancient and modern in southerly latitudes; or when he follows Cairnes in asserting that upon the American slave plantations "the only form of culture practised was spade culture, merely agglomerating upon a single area of land a number of isolated laborers"; or when he contends that either slavery or serfdom since based on force and fraud "destroys the possibility of fiduciary credit by cancelling the conditions [of trust and confidence] which alone can foster it." [86] Such errors disturb one's faith. In the presentation of his main argument, furthermore, he not only exaggerates the cleavage between capitalists and laborers, the class consciousness of the two groups and the rationality of capitalistic purpose, but he falls into calami-

[85] Achille Loria, *The Economic Synthesis*, M. Eden Paul tr. (London, 1914), pp. 23-26, 91-99.
[86] *Ibid.*, pp. 26, 190, 260.

tous ambiguity and confusion. The central phenomenon of slavery, says he, is speculation or the overvaluation of the slave. He thereupon assumes that speculation always means overvaluation, ignoring its downward possibility, and he accounts for the asserted universal and continuously increasing overvaluation by reference to the desire of masters to prevent slaves from buying their freedom. Here he ignores essential historic facts. In American law a slave's *peculium* had no recognition; and the proportion of slaves, furthermore, who showed any firm disposition to accumulate savings for the purpose of buying their freedom was very small. Where such efforts were made, however, they were likely to be aided by the masters through facilities for cash earnings, price concessions and honest accounting of instalments, notwithstanding the lack of legal requirements in the premises. Loria's explanation of the "central phenomenon" is therefore hardly tenable.

A far sounder basic doctrine is that of the accountant Gibson, recited at the beginning of this chapter, that the valuation of a slave is theoretically determined by the reckoning of his prospective earnings above the cost of his maintenance. In the actual Southern régime, however, this was interfered with by several influences. For one thing, the successful proprietors of small plantations could afford to buy additional slaves at somewhat more than the price reckoned on *per capita* earnings, because the advance of their establishments towards the scale of maximum efficiency would reduce the proportionate cost of administration. Again, the scale of slaveholdings was in some degree a measure of social rank, and men were accordingly tempted by uneconomic motives to increase their trains of retainers. Both of these considerations stimulated the bidding. On the other hand conventional morality deterred many proprietors from selling slaves except under special stress, and thereby diminished the offers in the market. If the combination of these factors is not adequate as an explanation, there remain the spirit of inflation characteristic of a new country and the common desire for tangible investments of a popularly sanctioned sort. All staple producers were engaged in a venturesome business. Crops were highly uncertain, and staple prices even more so. The variability of earnings inured men to the taking of risks and spurred them to borrow money and buy more of both lands and slaves even at inflated prices in the hope of striking it rich with a few years' crops. On the other hand when profits actually accrued, there was nothing available as a rule more tempting than slaves as investments. Corporation securities were few and unseasoned; lands were liable to wear out and were painfully slow in liquidation; but slaves were a self-perpetuating stock whose ownership was a badge of dignity, whose management was generally esteemed a pleasurable responsibility, whose labor would yield an income, and whose value could be realized in cash with fair promptitude in time of need. No calculated overvaluation by proprietors for the sake of keeping the slaves enslaved need be invented. Loria's thesis is a work of supererogation.

But whatever may be the true explanation it is clear that slave prices did rise to immoderate heights, that speculation was kept rife, and that in virtually every phase, after the industrial occupation of each area had been accomplished, the maintenance of the institution was a clog upon material progress. The economic virtues of slavery lay wholly in its making labor mobile, regular and secure. These qualities accorded remarkably, so far as they went, with the requirements of the plantation system on the one hand and the needs of the generality of the negroes on the other. Its vices were more numerous, and in part more subtle.

The North was annually acquiring thousands of immigrants who came at their own expense, who worked zealously for wages payable from current earnings, and who possessed all the inventive and progressive potentialities of European peoples. But aspiring captains of industry at the South could as a rule procure labor only by remitting round sums in money or credit which depleted their working capital and for which were obtained slaves fit only for plantation routine, negroes of whom little initiative could be expected and little contribution to the community's welfare beyond their mere muscular exertions. The negroes were procured in the first instance mainly because white laborers were not to be had; afterward when whites might otherwise have been available the established conditions repelled them. The continued avoidance of the South by the great mass of incoming Europeans in post-bellum decades has now made it clear that it was the negro character of the slaves rather than the slave status of the negroes which was chiefly responsible. The racial antipathy felt by the alien whites, along with their cultural repugnance and economic apprehensions, intrenched the negroes permanently in the situation. The most fertile Southern areas when once converted into black belts tended, and still tend as strongly as ever, to be tilled only by inert negroes, the majority of whom are as yet perhaps less efficient in freedom than their forbears were as slaves.

The drain of funds involved in the purchase of slaves was impressive to contemporaries. Thus Governor Spotswood wrote from Virginia to the British authorities in 1711 explaining his assent to a £5 tax upon the importation of slaves. The members of the legislature, said he, "urged what is really true, that the country is already ruined by the great number of negros imported of late years, that it will be impossible for them in many years to discharge the debts already contracted for the purchase of those negroes if fresh supplys be still poured upon them while their tobacco continues so little valuable, but that the people will run more and more in debt." [87] And in 1769 a Charleston correspondent wrote to a Boston journal: "A calculation having been made of the amount of purchase money of slaves effected here the present year, it is computed at £270,000 sterling, which sum will by that means be drained off from this province." [88]

An unfortunate fixation of capital was likewise remarked. Thus Sir Charles Lyell noted at Columbus, Georgia, in 1846 that Northern settlers were "struck with the difficulty experienced in raising money here by small shares for the building of mills. 'Why,' say they, 'should all our cotton make so long a journey to the North, to be manufactured there, and come back to us at so high a price? It is because all spare cash is sunk here in purchasing negroes.'" And again at another stage of his tour:

[87] Virginia Historical Society *Collections*, I, 52.
[88] Boston *Chronicle*, Mch. 27, 1769.

"That slave labour is more expensive than free is an opinion which is certainly gaining ground in the higher parts of Alabama, and is now professed openly by some Northerners who have settled there.   One of them said to me, 'Half the population of the South is employed in seeing that the other half do their work, and they who do work accomplish half what they might do under a better system.'   'We cannot,' said another,[89] 'raise capital enough for new cotton factories because all our savings go to buy negroes, or as has lately happened, to feed them when the crop is deficient.''

The planters, who were the principal Southern capitalists, trod in a vicious circle. They bought lands and slaves wherewith to grow cotton, and with the proceeds ever bought more slaves to make more cotton; and oftentimes they borrowed heavily on their lands and slaves as collateral in order to enlarge their scale of production the more speedily. When slave prices rose the possessors of those in the cotton belt seldom took profit from the advance, for it was a rare planter who would voluntarily sell his operating force. When crops failed or prices fell, however, the loans might be called, the mortgages foreclosed, and the property sold out at panic levels. Thus while the slaves had a guarantee of their sustenance, their proprietors, themselves the guarantors, had a guarantee of nothing. By virtue, or more properly by vice, of the heavy capitalization of the control of labor which was a cardinal feature of the ante-bellum régime, they were involved in excessive financial risks.

The slavery system has often been said to have put so great a stigma on manual labor as to have paralyzed the physical energies of the Southern white population. This is a great exaggeration; and yet it is true that the system militated in quite positive degree against the productivity of the several white classes. Among the well-to-do it promoted leisure by giving rise to an abnormally large number of men and women who whether actually or nominally performing managerial functions, did little to bring sweat to their brows. The proportion of white collars to overalls and of muslin frocks to kitchen aprons was

---

* Sir Charles Lyell, *Second Visit to the United States* (London, 1850), II, 35, 84, 85.

greater than in any other Anglo-Saxon community of equal income. The contrast so often drawn between Southern gentility and Northern thrift had a concrete basis in fact. At the other extreme the enervation of the poor whites, while mainly due to malaria and hookworm, had as a contributing cause the limitation upon their wage-earning opportunity which the slavery system imposed. Upon the middle class and the yeomanry, which were far more numerous and substantial[90] than has been commonly realized, the slavery system exerted an economic influence by limiting the availability of capital and by offering the temptation of an unsound application of earnings. When a prospering farmer, for example, wanted help for himself in his fields or for his wife indoors, the habit of the community prompted him to buy or hire slaves at a greater cost than free labor would normally have required.[91] The high price of slaves, furthermore, prevented many a capable manager from exercising his talents by debarring him from the acquisition of labor and the other means of large-scale production.

Finally, the force of custom, together with the routine efficiency of slave labor itself, caused the South to spoil the market for its distinctive crops by producing greater quantities than the world would buy at remunerative prices. To this the solicitude of the masters for the health of their slaves contributed. The harvesting of wheat, for example, as a Virginian planter observed in a letter to his neighbor James Madison, in the days when harvesting machinery was unknown, required exertion much more severe than the tobacco routine, and was accordingly, as he put it, "by no means so conducive to the health of our negroes, upon whose increase (*miserabile dictu!*) our principal profit depends."[92] The same letter also said: "Where there is negro slavery there will be laziness, carelessness and wastefulness. Nor is it possible to prevent them. Severity increases the evil, and humanity does not lessen it."

[90] D. R. Hundley, *Social Relations in our Southern States* (New York, 1860), pp. 91-100, 193-303; John M. Aughey, *The Iron Furnace, or Slavery and Secession* (Philadelphia, 1863), p. 231.
[91] F. L. Olmsted, *Journey through Texas*, p. 513.
[92] Francis Corbin to James Madison, Oct. 10, 1819, in the Massachusetts Historical Society *Proceedings*, XLIII, 263.

On the whole, the question whether negro labor in slavery was more or less productive than free negro labor would have been is not the crux of the matter. The influence of the slaveholding régime upon the whites themselves made it inevitable that the South should accumulate real wealth more slowly than the contemporary North. The planters and their neighbors were in the grip of circumstance. The higher the price of slaves the greater was the absorption of capital in their purchase, the blacker grew the black belts, the more intense was the concentration of wealth and talent in plantation industry, the more complete was the crystallization of industrial society. Were there any remedies available? Certain politicians masquerading as economists advocated the territorial expansion of the régime as a means of relief. Their argument, however, would not stand analysis. On one hand virtually all the territory on the continent climatically available for the staples was by the middle of the nineteenth century already incorporated into slaveholding states; on the other hand, had new areas been available the chief effects of their exploitation would have been to heighten the prices of slaves and lower the prices of crops. Actual expansion had in fact been too rapid for the best interests of society, for it had kept the population too sparse to permit a proper development of schools and the agencies of communications.

With a view to increase the power of the South to expand, and for other purposes mainly political, a group of agitators in the 'fifties raised a vehement contention in favor of reopening the African slave trade in full volume. This, if accomplished, would have lowered the cost of labor, but its increase of the crops would have depressed staple prices in still greater degree; its unsettling of the slave market would have hurt vested interests; and its infusion of a horde of savage Africans would have set back the progress of the negroes already on hand and have magnified permanently the problems of racial adjustment.

The prohibition of the interstate slave trade was another project for modifying the situation. It was mooted in the main by politicians alien to the régime. If accomplished it would have wrought a sharp differentiation in the conditions within the several groups of Southern states. An analogy may be seen in the British possessions in tropical America, where, following the stoppage of the intercolonial slave trade in 1807, a royal commission found that the average slave prices as gathered from sale records between 1822 and 1830 varied from a range in the old and stagnant colonies of £27 4s. 11¾d. in Bermuda, £29 18s. 9¾d. in the Bahamas, £47 1s. in Barbados and £44 15s. 2¼d. in Jamaica, to £105 4s., £114 11s. and £120 4s. 7½d. respectively in the new and buoyant settlements of Trinidad, Guiana and British Honduras.[93] If the interstate transfer had been stopped, the Virginia, Maryland and Carolina slave markets would have been glutted while the markets of every southwestern state were swept bare. Slave prices in the former would have fallen to such levels that masters would have eventually resorted to manumission in self-defence, while in the latter all existing checks to the inflation of prices would have been removed and all the evils consequent upon the capitalization of labor intensified.

Another conceivable plan would have been to replace slavery at large by serfdom. This would have attached the negroes to whatever lands they chanced to occupy at the time of the legislation. By force of necessity it would have checked the depletion of soils; but by preventing territorial transfer it would have robbed the negroes and their masters of all advantages afforded by the virginity of unoccupied lands. Serfdom could hardly be seriously considered by the citizens of a new and sparsely settled country such as the South then was.

Finally the conversion of slaves into freemen by a sweeping emancipation was a project which met little endorsement except among those who ignored the racial and cultural complications. Financially it would work drastic change in private fortunes, though the transfer of ownership from the masters to the laborers themselves need not necessarily have great effect for the time being upon the actual wealth of the community as a whole. Emancipation would most probably, however, break down the plantation system by making the labor supply unstable, and fill the

[93] *Accounts and Papers* [of the British Government], 1837-1838, vol. 48, [p. 329].

country partly with peasant farmers and partly with an unattached and floating negro population. Exceptional negroes and mulattoes would be sure to thrive upon their new opportunities, but the generality of the blacks could be counted upon to relax into a greater slackness than they had previously been permitted to indulge in. The apprehension of industrial paralysis, however, appears to have been a smaller factor than the fear of social chaos as a deterrent in the minds of the Southern whites from thoughts of abolition.

The slaveholding régime kept money scarce, population sparse and land values accordingly low; it restricted the opportunities of many men of both races, and it kept many of the natural resources of the Southern country neglected. But it kept the main body of labor controlled, provisioned and mobile. Above all it maintained order and a notable degree of harmony in a community where confusion worse confounded would not have been far to seek. Plantation slavery had in strictly business aspects at least as many drawbacks as it had attractions. But in the large it was less a business than a life; it made fewer fortunes than it made men.

CHAPTER XX

TOWN SLAVES

SOUTHERN households in town as well as in country were commonly large, and the dwellings and grounds of the well-to-do were spacious. The dearth of gas and plumbing and the lack of electric light and central heating made for heavy chores in the drawing of water, the replenishment of fuel and the care of lamps. The gathering of vegetables from the kitchen garden, the dressing of poultry and the baking of relays of hot breads at meal times likewise amplified the culinary routine. Maids of all work were therefore seldom employed. Comfortable circumstances required at least a cook and a housemaid, to which might be added as means permitted a laundress, a children's nurse, a seamstress, a milkmaid, a butler, a gardener and a coachman. While few but the rich had such ample staffs as this, none but the poor were devoid of domestics, and the ratio of servitors to the gross population was large. The repugnance of white laborers toward menial employment, furthermore, conspired with the traditional predilection of householders for negroes in a lasting tenure for their intimate services and gave the slaves a virtual monopoly of this calling. A census of Charleston in 1848,[1] for example, enumerated 5272 slave domestics as compared with 113 white and 27 free colored servants. The slaves were more numerous than the free also in the semi-domestic employments of coachmen and porters, and among the draymen and the coopers and the unskilled laborers in addition.

On the other hand, although Charleston excelled every other city in the proportion of slaves in its population, free laborers

[1] J. L. Dawson and H. W. DeSaussure, *Census of Charleston for 1848* (Charleston, 1849), pp. 31-36. The city's population then comprised some 20,000 whites, a like number of slaves, and about 3,500 free persons of color. The statistics of occupations are summarized in the accompanying table.

MANUAL OCCUPATIONS IN CHARLESTON, 1848

	Slaves		Free Negroes		Whites	
	Men	Women	Men	Women	Men	Women
Domestic servants	1,888	3,384	9	28	13	100
Cooks and confectioners	7	12	18	18	....	5
Nurses and midwives	....	2	....	10	....	5
Laundresses	....	33	....	45	....	....
Seamstresses and mantua makers	....	24	....	196	....	125
Milliners	....	....	....	7	....	44
Fruiterers, hucksters and pedlers	....	18	6	5	46	18
Gardeners	3	....	....	....	5	1
Coachmen	15	....	4	....	2	....
Draymen	67	....	11	....	13	....
Porters	35	....	5	....	8	....
Wharfingers and stevedores	2	....	1	....	21	....
Pilots and sailors	50	....	1	....	176	....
Fishermen	11	....	14	....	10	....
Carpenters	120	....	27	....	119	....
Masons and bricklayers	68	....	10	....	60	....
Painters and plasterers	16	....	4	....	18	....
Tinners	3	....	1	....	10	....
Ship carpenters and joiners	51	....	6	....	52	....
Coopers	61	....	2	....	20	....
Coach makers and wheelwrights	3	....	1	....	26	....
Cabinet makers	8	....	....	....	26	....
Upholsterers	1	....	1	....	10	....
Gun, copper and locksmiths	2	....	1	....	16	....
Blacksmiths and horseshoers	40	....	4	....	51	....
Millwrights	....	....	5	....	4	....
Boot and shoemakers	6	....	17	....	30	....
Saddle and harness makers	2	....	1	....	29	....
Tailors and cap makers	36	....	42	6	68	6
Butchers	5	....	1	....	10	....
Millers	....	....	1	....	14	....
Bakers	39	....	1	....	35	1
Barbers and hairdressers	4	....	14	....	....	6
Cigarmakers	5	....	1	....	10	....
Bookbinders	3	....	....	....	10	....
Printers	5	....	....	....	65	....
Other mechanics*	45	....	2	....	182	....
Apprentices	43	8	14	7	55	5
Unclassified, unskilled laborers	838	378	19	2	192	....
Superannuated	38	54	1	5	....	....

* The slaves and free negroes in this group were designated merely as mechanics. The whites were classified as follows: 3 joiners, 1 plumber, 8 gas fitters, 7 bell hangers, 1 paper hanger, 6 carvers and gilders, 9 sail makers, 5 riggers, 1 bottler, 8 sugar makers, 43 engineers, 10 machinists, 6 boilermakers, 7 stone cutters, 4 piano and organ builders, 23 silversmiths, 15 watchmakers, 3 hair braiders, 1 engraver, 1 cutler, 3 molders, 3 pump and block makers, 2 turners, 2 wigmakers, 1 basketmaker, 1 bleacher, 4 dyers, and 4 journeymen. In addition there were enumerated of whites in non-mechanical employments in which the negroes did not participate, 7 omnibus drivers and 16 barkeepers.

predominated in all the other industrial groups, though but
slightly in the cases of the masons and carpenters. The whites,
furthermore, heavily outnumbered the free negroes in virtually
all the trades but that of barbering which they shunned. Among
women workers the free colored ranked first as seamstresses,
washerwomen, nurses and cooks, with white women competing
strongly in the sewing trades alone. A census of Savannah in
the same year shows a similar predominance of whites in all the
male trades but that of the barbers, in which there were counted
five free negroes, one slave and no whites.[2] From such statistics two conclusions are clear: first, that the repulsion of the
whites was not against manual work but against menial service;
second, that the presence of the slaves in the town trades was
mainly due to the presence of their fellows as domestics.

Most of the slave mechanics and out-of-door laborers were the
husbands and sons of the cooks and chambermaids, dwelling
with them on their masters' premises, where the back yard with
its crooning women and romping vari-colored children was as
characteristic a feature as on the plantations. Town slavery, indeed, had a strong tone of domesticity, and the masters were
often paternalistically inclined. It was a townsman, for example, who wrote the following to a neighbor: "As my boy Reu-
ben has formed an attachment to one of your girls and wants her
for a wife, this is to let you know that I am perfectly willing
that he should, with your consent, marry her. His character is
good; he is honest, faithful and industrious." The patriarchal
relations of the country, however, which depended much upon
the isolation of the groups, could hardly prevail in similar degree where the slaves of many masters intermingled. Even for
the care of the sick there was doubtless fairly frequent recourse
to such establishments as the "Surgical Infirmary for Negroes"
at Augusta which advertised its facilities in 1854,[3] though the
more common practice, of course, was for slave patients in town

[2] Joseph Bancroft, *Census of the City of Savannah* (Savannah, 1848).
[3] *Southern Business Directory* (Charleston, 1854), I, 289, advertisement.
The building was described as having accommodations for fifty or sixty
patients. The charge for board, lodging and nursing was $10 per month,
and for surgical operations and medical attendance "the usual rates of city
practice."

as well as country to be nursed at home. A characteristic note in this connection was written by a young Georgia townswoman: "No one is going to church today but myself, as we have a little negro very sick and Mama deems it necessary to remain at home to attend to him." [4]

The town régime was not so conducive to lifelong adjustments of masters and slaves except as regards domestic service; for whereas a planter could always expand his operations in response to an increase of his field hands and could usually provide employment at home for any artizan he might produce, a lawyer, a banker or a merchant had little choice but to hire out or sell any slave who proved a superfluity or a misfit in his domestic establishment. On the other hand a building contractor with an expanding business could not await the raising of children but must buy or hire masons and carpenters where he could find them.

Some of the master craftsmen owned their staffs. Thus William Elfe, a Charleston cabinet maker at the close of the colonial period, had title to four sawyers, five joiners and a painter, and he managed to keep some of their wives and children in his possession also by having a farm on the further side of the harbor for their residence and employment.[5] William Rouse, a Charleston leather worker who closed his business in 1825 when the supply of tan bark ran short, had for sale four tanners, a currier and seven shoemakers, with, however, no women or children;[6] and the seven slaves of William Brockelbank, a plastering contractor of the same city, sold after his death in 1850, comprised but one woman and no children.[7] Likewise when the rope walk of Smith, Dorsey and Co. at New Orleans was offered for sale in 1820, fourteen slave operatives were included without mention of their families.[8]

[4] Mary E. Harden to Mrs. Howell Cobb, Athens, Ga., Nov. 13, 1853. MS. in possession of Mrs. A. S. Erwin, Athens, Ga.
[5] MS. account book of William Elfe, in the Charleston Library.
[6] Charleston *City Gazette*, Jan. 5, 1826, advertisement.
[7] Charleston *Mercury*, quoted in the Augusta *Chronicle*, Dec. 5, 1850. This news item owed its publication to the "handsome prices" realized. A plasterer 28 years old brought $2,135; another, 30, $1,805; a third, 24, $1,775; a fourth, 24, $1,100; and a fifth, 20, $730.
[8] *Louisiana Advertiser* (New Orleans), May 13, 1820, advertisement.

Far more frequently such laborers were taken on hire. The following are typical of a multitude of newspaper advertisements: Michael Grantland at Richmond offered "good wages" for the year 1799 by piece or month for six or eight negro coopers.[9] At the same time Edward Rumsey was calling for strong negro men of good character at $100 per year at his iron works in Botetourt County, Virginia, and inviting free laboring men also to take employment with him.[10] In 1808 Daniel Weisinger and Company wanted three or four negro men to work in their factory at Frankfort, Kentucky, saying "they will be taught weaving, and liberal wages will be paid for their services."[11] George W. Evans at Augusta in 1818 "Wanted to hire, eight or ten white or black men for the purpose of cutting wood."[12] A citizen of Charleston in 1821 called for eight good black carpenters on weekly or monthly wages, and in 1825 a blacksmith and wheelwright of the same city offered to take black apprentices.[13] In many cases whites and blacks worked together in the same employ, as in a boat-building yard on the Flint River in 1836,[14] and in a cotton mill at Athens, Georgia, in 1839.[15]

In some cases the lessor of slaves procured an obligation of complete insurance from the lessee. An instance of this was a contract between James Murray of Wilmington in 1743, when he was departing for a sojourn in Scotland, and his neighbor James Hazel. The latter was to take the three negroes Glasgow, Kelso and Berwick for three years at an annual hire of £21 sterling for the lot. If death or flight among them should prevent Hazel from returning any of the slaves at the end of the term he was to reimburse Murray at full value scheduled in the lease, receiving in turn a bill of sale for any runaway. Furthermore if any of the slaves were permanently injured by willful abuse at the

[9] *Virginia Gazette* (Richmond), Nov. 20, 1798.
[10] Winchester, Va., *Gazette*, Jan. 30, 1799.
[11] The *Palladium* (Frankfort, Ky.), Dec. 1, 1808.
[12] Augusta, Ga., *Chronicle*, Aug. 1, 1818.
[13] Charleston *City Gazette*, Feb. 22, 1825.
[14] *Federal Union* (Milledgeville, Ga.), Mch. 18, 1836, reprinted in *Plantation and Frontier*, II, 356.
[15] J. S. Buckingham, *The Slave States of America* (London, [1842]), II, 112.

hands of Hazel's overseer, Murray was to be paid for the damage.[16] Leases of this type, however, were exceptional. As a rule the owners appear to have carried all risks except in regard to willful injury, and the courts generally so adjudged it where the contracts of hire had no stipulations in the premises.[17] When the Georgia supreme court awarded the owner a full year's hire of a slave who had died in the midst of his term the decision was complained of as an innovation "signally oppressive to the poorer classes of our citizens—the large majority—who are compelled to hire servants." [18]

The main supply of slaves for hire was probably comprised of the husbands and sons, and sometimes the daughters, of the cooks and housemaids of the merchants, lawyers and the like whose need of servants was limited but who in many cases made a point of owning their slaves in families. On the other hand, many townsmen whose capital was scant or whose need was temporary used hired slaves even for their kitchen work; and sometimes the filling of the demand involved the transfer of a slave from one town to another. Thus an innkeeper of Clarkesville, a summer resort in the Georgia mountains, published in the distant newspapers of Athens and Augusta in 1838 his offer of liberal wages for a first rate cook.[19] This hiring of domestics brought periodic embarrassments to those who depended upon them. A Virginia clergyman who found his wife and himself doing their own chores "in the interval between the hegira of the old hirelings and the coming of the new" [20] was not alone in his plight. At the same season, a Richmond editor wrote: "The negro hiring days have come, the most woeful of the year! So housekeepers think who do not own their own servants; and even this class is but a little better off than the rest, for all darkeydom must have holiday this week, and while their masters and mistresses are making fires and cooking victuals or attend-

[16] Nina M. Tiffany ed., *Letters of James Murray, Loyalist* (Boston, 1901), pp. 67-69.
[17] J. D. Wheeler, *The Law of Slavery* (New York, 1837), pp. 152-155.
[18] Editorial in the *Federal Union* (Milledgeville, Ga.), Dec. 12, 1854.
[19] *Southern Banner* (Athens, Ga.), June 21, 1838, advertisement ordering its own republication in the Augusta *Constitutionalist*.
[20] T. C. Johnson, *Life of Robert L. Dabney* (Richmond, 1905), p. 120.

ing to otner menial duties the negroes are promenading the
streets decked in their finest clothes." [21] Even the tobacco factories, which were constantly among the largest employers of
hired slaves, were closed fc. iack of laborers from Christmas day
until well into January.[22]

That the bargain of hire sometimes involved the consent of
more than two parties is suggested by a New Year's colloquy
overheard by Robert Russell on a Richmond street: "I was
rather amused at the efforts of a market gardener to hire a young
woman as a domestic servant. The price her owner put upon
her services was not objected to by him, but they could not agree
about other terms. The grand obstacle was that she would not
consent to work in the garden, even when she had nothing else to
do. After taking an hour's walk in another part of town I again
met the two at the old bargain. Stepping towards them, I now
learned that she was pleading for other privileges—her friends
and favourites must be allowed to visit her.[23] At length she agreed
to go and visit her proposed home and see how things looked."
That the scruples of proprietors occasionally prevented the placing of slaves is indicated by a letter of a Georgia woman anent
her girl Betty and a free negro woman, Matilda: "I cannot
agree for Betty to be hired to Matilda—her character is too bad.
I know her of old; she is a drunkard, and is said to be bad in
every respect. I would object her being hired to any colored
person no matter what their character was; and if she cannot get
into a respectable family I had rather she came home, and if she
can't work out put her to spinning and weaving. Her relations
here beg she may not be permitted to go to Matilda. She would
not be worth a cent at the end of the year."[24]

The coördination of demand and supply was facilitated in
some towns by brokers. Thus J. de Bellièvre of Baton Rouge
maintained throughout 1826 a notice in the local *Weekly Messenger* of "Servants to hire by the day or month," including both

[21] Richmond *Whig*, quoted in the *Atlanta Intelligencer*, Jan. 5, 1859.
[22] Robert Russell, *North America* (Edinburgh, 1857), p. 151.
[23] *Ibid.*
[24] Letter of Mrs. S. R. Cobb, Cowpens, Ga., Jan. 9, 1843, to her daugh-
ter-in-law at Athens. MS. in the possession of Mrs. A. S. Erwin, Athens,
Ga.

artizans and domestics; and in the Nashville city directory of
1860 Van B. Holman advertised his business as an agent for the
hiring of negroes as well as for the sale and rental of real estate.

Slave wages, generally quoted for the year and most frequently
for unskilled able-bodied hands, ranged materially higher, of
course, in the cotton belt than in the upper South. Women
usually brought about half the wages of men, though they were
sometimes let merely for the keep of themselves and their children. In middle Georgia the wages of prime men ranged about
$100 in the first decade of the nineteenth century, dropped to $60
or $75 during the war of 1812, and then rose to near $150 by
1818. The panic of the next year sent them down again; and
in the 'twenties they commonly ranged between $100 and $125.
Flush times then raised them in such wise that the contractors
digging a canal on the Georgia coast found themselves obliged in
1838 to offer $18 per month together with the customary weekly
rations of three and a half pounds of bacon and ten quarts of
corn and also the services of a staff physician as a sort of substitute for life and health insurance.[25] The beginning of the
distressful 'forties eased the market so that the town of Milledgeville could get its street gang on a scale of $125;[26] at the middle
of the decade slaveowners were willing to take almost any wages
offered; and in its final year the Georgia Railroad paid only $70
to $75 for section hands. In 1850, however, this rate leaped to
$100 and $110, and caused a partial substitution of white laborers for the hired slaves;[27] but the brevity of any relief procured
by this recourse is suggested by a news item from Chattanooga
in 1852 reporting that the commonest labor commanded a dollar
a day, that mechanics were all engaged far in advance, that much
building was perforce being postponed, and that all persons who
might be seeking employment were urged to answer the city's
call.[28] By 1854 the continuing advance began to discommode
rural employers likewise. A Norfolk newspaper of the time

[25] Advertisement in the Savannah newspapers, reprinted in J. S. Buckingham, *Slave States* (London, 1842), I, 137.
[26] MS. minutes of the board of aldermen, in the town hall at Milledgeville, Ga. Item dated Feb. 23, 1841.
[27] Georgia Railroad Company *Report* for 1850, p. 13.
[28] Chattanooga *Advertiser*, quoted in the Augusta *Chronicle*, June 6, 1852.

reported that the current wages of $150 for ordinary hands and $225 for the best laborers, together with life insurance for the full value of the slaves, were so high that prudent farmers were curtailing their operations.[29] At the beginning of 1856 the wages in the Virginia tobacco factories advanced some fifteen per cent. over the rates of the preceding year;[30] and shortly afterward several of these establishments took refuge in the employment of white women for their lighter processes.[31] In 1860 there was a culmination of this rise of slave wages throughout the South, contemporaneous with that of their purchase prices. First-rate hands were engaged by the Petersburg tobacco factories at $225;[32] and in northwestern Louisiana the prime field hands in a parcel of slaves hired for the year brought from $300 to $360 each, and a blacksmith $430.[33] The general average then prevalent for prime unskilled slaves, however, was probably not much above two hundred dollars. While the purchase price of slaves was wellnigh quadrupled in the three score years of the nineteenth century, slave wages were little more than doubled, for these were of course controlled not by the fluctuating hopes and fears of what the distant future might bring but by the sober prospect of the work at hand.

The proprietors of slaves for hire appear to have been generally as much concerned with questions of their moral and physical welfare as with the wages to be received, for no wage would compensate for the debilitation of the slave or his conversion into an inveterate runaway The hirers in their turn had the problem, growing more intense with the advance of costs, of procuring full work without resorting to such rigor of discipline as would disquiet the owners of their employees. The tobacco factories found solution in piece work with bonus for excess over the required stint. At Richmond in the middle 'fifties this was commonly yielding the slaves from two to five dollars a month for their own uses; and these establishments, along with all other

[29] Norfolk *Argus,* quoted in *Southern Banner* (Athens, Ga.), Jan. 12, 1854.
[30] Richmond *Dispatch,* Jan., 1856, quoted in G. M. Weston, *Who are and who may be Slaves in the U. S.* (caption).
[31] *Hunt's Merchants' Magazine*, XL, 522.
[32] Petersburg *Democrat,* quoted by the Atlanta *Intelligencer*, Jan., 1860.
[33] *DeBow's Review*, XXIX, 374.

slave employers, suspended work for more than a week at the Christmas season.[34]

The hiring of slaves from one citizen to another did not meet all the needs of the town industry, for there were many occupations in which the regular supervision of labor was impracticable. Hucksters must trudge the streets alone; and market women sit solitary in their stalls. If slaves were to follow such callings at all, and if other slaves were to utilize their talents in keeping cobbler and blacksmith shops and the like for public patronage,[35] they must be vested with fairly full control of their own activities. To enable them to compete with whites and free negroes in the trades requiring isolated and occasional work their masters early and increasingly fell into the habit of hiring many slaves to the slaves themselves, granting to each a large degree of industrial freedom in return for a stipulated weekly wage. The rates of hire varied, of course, with the slave's capabilities and the conditions of business in their trades. The practice brought friction sometimes between slaves and owners when wages were in default. An instance of this was published in a Charleston advertisement of 1800 announcing the auction of a young carpenter and saying as the reason of the sale that he had absconded because of a deficit in his wages.[36] Whether the sale was merely by way of punishment or was because the proprietor could not give personal supervision to the carpenter's work the record fails to say. The practice also injured the interests of white competitors in the same trades, who sometimes bitterly complained; [37] it occasionally put pressure upon the slaves to fill out their wages by theft; and it gave rise in some degree to a public apprehension that the liberty of movement might be perverted to purposes of conspiracy. The law came to frown upon it everywhere; but the device was too great a public and private convenience to be suppressed.

[34] Robert Russell, *North America*, p. 152.
[35] *E. g.*, "For sale: a strong, healthy Mulatto Man, about 24 years of age, by trade a blacksmith, and has had the management of a blacksmith shop for upwards of two years." Advertisement in the Alexandria, Va., *Times and Advertiser*, Sept. 26, 1797.
[36] Charleston *City Gazette*, May 12, 1800.
[37] *E. g.*, *Plantation and Frontier*, II, 367.

To procure the enforcement of such laws a vigilance committee was proposed at Natchez in 1824;[38] but if it was created it had no lasting effect. With the same purpose newspaper campaigns were waged from time to time. Thus in the spring of 1859 the *Bulletin* of Columbia, South Carolina, said editorially: "Despite the laws of the land forbidding under penalty the hiring of their time by slaves, it is much to be regretted that the pernicious practice still exists," and it censured the citizens who were consciously and constantly violating a law enacted in the public interest. The nearby Darlington *Flag* endorsed this and proposed in remedy that the town police and the rural patrols consider void all tickets issued by masters authorizing their slaves to pass and repass at large, that all slaves found hiring their time be arrested and punished, and that their owners be indicted as by law provided. The editor then ranged further. "There is another evil of no less magnitude," said he, "and perhaps the foundation of the one complained of. It is that of transferring slave labor from its legitimate field, the cultivation of the soil, into that of the mechanic arts. . . . Negro mechanics are an ebony aristocracy into which slaves seek to enter by teasing their masters for permission to learn a trade. Masters are too often seduced by the prospect of gain to yield their assent, and when their slaves have acquired a trade are forced to the violation of the law to realize their promised gain. We should therefore have a law to prevent slave mechanics going off their masters' premises to work. Let such a law be passed, and . . . there will no longer be need of a law to prohibit slaves hiring their own time." The *Southern Watchman* of Athens, Georgia, reprinted all of this in turn, along with a subscriber's communication entitled "free slaves." There were more negroes enjoying virtual freedom in the town of Athens, this writer said, than there were *bona fide* free negroes in any ten counties of the district. "Everyone who is at all acquainted with the character of the slave race knows that they have great ideas of liberty, and in order to get the enjoyment of it they make large offers for their time. And everyone who knows anything of the negro knows that he won't work unless he is obliged to. . . . The negro thus set free, in nine cases out of ten, idles away half of his time or gambles away what he does make, and then relies on his ingenuity in stealing to meet the demands pay day inevitably brings forth; and this is the way our towns are converted into dens of rogues and thieves." [39]

These arguments had been answered long before by a citizen of Charleston. The clamor, said he, was intended not so much to guard the community against theft and insurrection as to diminish the competition of slaves with white mechanics. The strict enforcement of the law would almost wholly deprive the public of the services of jobbing slaves, which were indispensable under existing circumstances. Let the statute therefore be left in the obscurity of the lawyers' bookshelves, he concluded, to be brought forth only in case of an emergency. [40] And so such laws were left to sleep, despite the plaints of self-styled reformers.

That self-hire may often have led to self-purchase is suggested by an illuminating letter of Billy Procter, a slave at Americus, Georgia, in 1854 to Colonel John B. Lamar of whom something has been seen in a foregoing chapter. The letter, presumably in the slave's own hand, runs as follows: "As my owner, Mr Chapman, has determined to dispose of all his Painters, I would prefer to have you buy me to any other man. And I am anxious to get you to do so if you will. You know me very well yourself, but as I wish you to be fully satisfied I beg to refer you to Mr. Nathan C. Monroe, Dr. Strohecker and Mr. Bogg. I am in distress at this time, and will be until I hear from you what you will do. I can be bought for $1000—and I think that you might get me for 50 Dolls less if you try, though that is Mr. Chapman's price. Now Mas John, I want to be plain and honest with you. If you will buy me I will pay you $600 per year untill this money is paid, or at any rate will pay for myself in two years. . . . I am fearfull that if you do not buy me, there

<hr/>

[39] *Southern Watchman* (Athens, Ga.), Apr. 20, 1859.
[40] Letter to the editor in the Charleston *City Gazette*, Nov. 1, 1825. To similar effect was an editorial in the Augusta *Chronicle*, Oct. 16, 1851.

is no telling where I may have to go, and Mr. C. wants me to go where I would be satisfied,—I promise to serve you faithfully, and I know that I am as sound and healthy as anyone you could find. You will confer a great favour, sir, by Granting my request, and I would be very glad to hear from you in regard to the matter at your earliest convenience." [41]

The hiring of slaves by one citizen to another prevailed to some extent in country as well as town, and the hiring of them to themselves was particularly notable in the forest labors of gathering turpentine and splitting shingles; [42] but slave hire in both its forms was predominantly an urban resort. On the whole, whereas the plantation system cherished slavery as a well-nigh fundamental condition, town industry could tolerate it only by modifying its features to make labor more flexibly responsive to the sharply distinctive urban needs.

As to routine control, urban proprietors were less complete masters even of slaves in their own employ than were those in the country. For example, Morgan Brown of Clarksville, Tennessee, had occasion to publish the following notice: "Whereas my negroes have been much in the habit of working at night for such persons as will employ them, to the great injury of their health and morals, I therefore forbid all persons employing them without my special permission in writing. I also forbid trading with them, buying from or selling to them, without my written permit stating the article they may buy or sell. The law will be strictly enforced against transgressors, without respect to persons." [43]

When broils occurred in which slaves were involved, the masters were likely to find themselves champions rather than judges. This may be illustrated by two cases tried before the town commissioners of Milledgeville, Georgia, in 1831. In the first of these Edward Cary was ordered to bring before the board his

[41] MS. in the possession of Mrs. A. S. Erwin, Athens, Ga., printed in *Plantation and Frontier*, II, 41. The writer must have been well advanced in years or else highly optimistic. Otherwise he could not have expected to earn his purchase price within two years.
[42] Olmsted, *Seaboard Slave States*, pp. 153-155.
[43] *Town Gazette and Farmers' Register* (Clarksville, Tenn.), Aug. 9, 1819, reprinted in *Plantation and Frontier*, II, 45, 46.

slave Nathan to answer a charge of assault upon Richard Mayhorn, a member of the town patrol, and show why punishment
should not be inflicted. On the day set Cary appeared without
the negro and made a counter charge supported by testimony
that Mayhorn had exceeded his authority under the patrol ordinance. The prosecution of the slave was thereupon dropped,
and the patrolman was dismissed from the town's employ. The
second case was upon a patrol charge against a negro named
Hubbard, whose master or whose master's attorney was one
Wiggins, reciting an assault upon Billy Woodliff, a slave apparently of Seaborn Jones. Billy being sworn related that Hubbard had come to the door of his blacksmith shop and "abused
and bruised him with a rock." Other evidence revealed that
Hubbard's grievance lay in Billy's having taken his wife from
him. "The testimony having been concluded, Mr. Wiggins addressed the board in a speech containing some lengthy, strengthy
and depthy argument: whereupon the board ordered that the
negro man Hubbard receive from the marshall ten lashes, moderately laid on, and be discharged." [44] Even in the maintenance of
household discipline masters were fain to apply chastisement
vicariously by having the town marshal whip their offending
servants for a small fee.

The variety in complexion, status and attainment among town
slaves led to a somewhat elaborate gradation of colored society.
One stratum comprised the fairly numerous quadroons and mulattoes along with certain exceptional blacks. The men among
these had a pride of place as butlers and coachmen, painters and
carpenters; the women fitted themselves trimly with the cast-off
silks and muslins of their mistresses, walked with mincing tread,
and spoke in quiet tones with impressive nicety of grammar.
This element was a conscious aristocracy of its kind, but its
members were more or less irked by the knowledge that no matter how great their merits they could not cross the boundary into
white society. The bulk of the real negroes on the other hand, with
an occasional mulatto among them, went their own way, the

[44] MS. archives in the town hall at Milledgeville, Ga., selected items from
which are printed in the American Historical Association *Report* for 1903,
I, 468, 469.

women frankly indulging a native predilection for gaudy colors, carrying their burdens on their heads, arms akimbo, and laying as great store in their kerchief turbans as their paler cousins did in their beflowered bonnets. The men of this class wore their shreds and patches with an easy swing, doffed their wool hats to white men as they passed, called themselves niggers or darkies as a matter of course, took the joys and sorrows of the day as they came, improvised words to the music of their work, and customarily murdered the Queen's English, all with a true if humble nonchalance and a freedom from carking care.

The differentiation of slave types was nevertheless little more than rudimentary; for most of those who were lowliest on work days assumed a grandiloquence of manner when they donned their holiday clothes. The gayeties of the colored population were most impressive to visitors from afar. Thus Adam Hodgson wrote of a spring Sunday at Charleston in 1820: "I was pleased to see the slaves apparently enjoying themselves on this day in their best attire, and was amused with their manners towards each other. They generally use Sir and Madam in addressing each other, and make the most formal and particular inquiries after each other's families." [45] J. S. Buckingham wrote at Richmond fifteen years afterward: "On Sundays, when the slaves and servants are all at liberty after dinner, they move about in every thoroughfare, and are generally more gaily dressed than the whites. The females wear white muslin and light silk gowns, with caps, bonnets, ribbons and feathers; some carry reticules on the arm and many are seen with parasols, while nearly all of them carry a white pocket-handkerchief before them in the most fashionable style. The young men among the slaves wear white trousers, black stocks, broad-brimmed hats, and carry walking-sticks; and from the bowings, curtseying and greetings in the highway one might almost imagine one's self to be at Hayti and think that the coloured people had got possession of the town and held sway, while the whites were living among them by sufferance." [46] Olmsted in his turn found

[45] Adam Hodgson, *Letters from North America*, I, 97.
[46] J. S. Buckingham, *Slave States*, II, 427.

the holiday dress of the slaves in many cases better than the whites,[47] and said their Christmas festivities were Saturnalia. The town ordinances, while commonly strict in regard to the police of slaves for the rest of the year, frequently gave special countenance to negro dances and other festive assemblies at Christmas tide.

Even in work-a-day seasons the laxity of control gave rise to occasional complaint. Thus the acting mayor of New Orleans recited in 1813, among matters needing correction, that loitering slaves were thronging the grog shops every evening and that negro dances were lasting far into the night, in spite of the prohibitions of the law.[48] A citizen of Charleston protested in 1835 against another and more characteristic form of dissipation. "There are," said he, "sometimes every evening in the week, funerals of negroes accompanied by three or four hundred negroes . . . who disturb all the inhabitants in the neighborhood of burying grounds in Pitt street near Boundary street. It appears to be a jubilee for every slave in the city. They are seen eagerly pressing to the place from all quarters, and such is frequently the crowd and noise made by them that carriages cannot safely be driven that way." [49]

The operations of urban constables and police courts are exemplified in some official statistics of Charleston. In the year ending September 1, 1837, the slave arrests, numbering 768 in all, were followed in 138 cases by prompt magisterial discharge, by fines in 309 cases, and by punishment in the workhouse or by remandment for trial on criminal charges in 264 of the remainder. The mayor said in summary: "Of the 573 slaves fined or committed to the workhouse nearly the whole were arrested for being out at night without tickets or being found in the dram shops or other unlawful places. The fines imposed did not in general exceed $1, and where corporal punishment was inflicted it was always moderate. It is worthy to remark that of the 460

[47] *Seaboard Slave States*, pp. 101, 103. Cf. also *DeBow's Review*, XII, 692, and XXVIII, 194-199.
[48] *Plantation and Frontier*, II, 153.
[49] Letter of a citizen in the *Southern Patriot*, quoted in H. M. Henry, *Police Control of the Slave in South Carolina* (Emory, Va., 1914), p. 144.

cases reported by the marshals for prosecution but 22 were prosecuted, the penalties having been voluntarily paid in 303 cases, and in 118 cases having been remitted, thus preventing by a previous examination 421 suits." Arrests of colored freemen in the same period numbered 78, of which 27 were followed by discharge, 36 by fine or whipping, 5 by sentence to the workhouse, and 10 by remandment.

In the second year following, the slave and free negro arrests for being "out after the beating of the tattoo without tickets, fighting and rioting in the streets, following military companies, walking on the battery contrary to law, bathing horses at forbidden places, theft, or other violation of the city and state laws" advanced for some unexplained reason to an aggregate of 1424. Of those taken into custody 274 were discharged after examination, 330 were punished in the workhouse, 33 were prosecuted or delivered to warrant, 26 were fined or committed until the fines were paid, for 398 the penalties were paid by their owners or guardians, 115 were runaways who were duly returned to their masters or otherwise disposed of according to law, and the remaining 252 were delivered on their owners' orders.[50]

At an earlier period a South Carolina law had required the public whipping of negro offenders at prominent points on the city streets, but complaints of this as distressing to the inhabitants[51] had brought its discontinuance. For the punishment of misdemeanants under sentences to hard labor a treadmill was instituted in the workhouse;[52] and the ensuing substitution of labor for the lash met warm official commendation.[53]

In church affairs the two races adhered to the same faiths, but their worship tended slowly to segregate. A few negroes habitually participated with the whites in the Catholic and Episcopal rituals, or listened to the long and logical sermons of the Presbyterians. Larger numbers occupied the pews appointed for their kind in the churches of the Methodist and Baptist

[50] Official reports quoted in H. M. Henry, *The Police Control of Slaves in South Carolina*, pp. 49, 50.
[51] *Columbian Herald* (Charleston), June 26, 1788.
[52] Charleston *City Gazette*, Feb. 2, 1826.
[53] Grand jury presentments, *ibid.*, May 15, 1826.

whites, where the more ebullient exercises comported better with
their own tastes. But even here there was often a feeling of
irksome restraint. The white preacher in fear of committing
an indiscretion in the hearing of the negroes must watch his
words though that were fatal to his impromptu eloquence; the
whites in the congregation must maintain their dignity when dignity was in conflict with exaltation; the blacks must repress
their own manifestations the most severely of all, to escape re-
buke for unseemly conduct.[54] An obvious means of relief lay
in the founding of separate congregations to which the white
ministers occasionally preached and in which white laymen
often sat, but where the pulpit and pews were commonly filled
by blacks alone. There the sable exhorter might indulge his peculiar talent for " 'rousements" and the prayer leader might be-
seech the Almighty in tones to reach His ears though afar off.
There the sisters might sway and croon to the cadence of sermon and prayer, and the brethren spur the spokesman to still
greater efforts by their well timed ejaculations. There not
only would the quaint melody of the negro "spirituals" swell instead of the more sophisticated airs of the hymn book, but every
successful sermon would be a symphony and every prayer a mas-
terpiece of concerted rhythm.

In some cases the withdrawal of the blacks had the full character of secession. An example in this line had been set in
Philadelphia when some of the negroes who had been attending
white churches of various denominations were prompted by the
antipathy of the whites and by the ambition of the colored leaders to found, in 1791, an African church with a negro minister.
In the course of a few years this was divided into congregations
of the several sects. Among these the Methodists prospered to

[54] A Methodist preacher wrote of an episode at Wilmington: "On one
occasion I took a summary process with a certain black woman who in
their love-feast, with many extravagant gestures, cried out that she was
'young King Jesus.' I bade her take her seat, and then publicly read her
out of membership, stating that we would not have such wild fanatics
among us, meantime letting them all know that such expressions were
even blasphemous. Poor Aunt Katy felt it deeply, repented, and in a
month I took her back again. The effect was beneficial, and she became
a rational and consistent member of the church." Joseph Travis, *Autobiography* (Nashville, 1855), pp. 71, 72.

such degree that in 1816 they launched the African Methodist Episcopal Church, with congregations in Baltimore and other neighboring cities included within its jurisdiction.[55] Richard Allen as its first bishop soon entered into communication with Morris Brown and other colored Methodists of Charleston who were aggrieved at this time by the loss of their autonomy. In former years the several thousand colored Methodists, who outnumbered by tenfold the whites in the congregations there, had enjoyed a quarterly conference of their own, with the custody of their collections and with control over the church trials of colored members; but on the ground of abuses these privileges were cancelled in 1815. A secret agitation then ensued which led on the one hand to the increase of the negro Methodists by some two thousand souls, and on the other to the visit of two of their leaders to Philadelphia where they were formally ordained for Charleston pastorates. When affairs were thus ripened, a dispute as to the custody of one of their burial grounds precipitated their intended stroke in 1818. Nearly all the colored class leaders gave up their papers simultaneously, and more than three-quarters of their six thousand fellows withdrew their membership from the white Methodist churches. "The galleries, hitherto crowded, were almost completely deserted," wrote a contemporary, "and it was a vacancy that could be *felt*. The absence of their responses and hearty songs were really felt to be a loss to those so long accustomed to hear them. . . . The schismatics combined, and after great exertion succeeded in erecting a neat church building. . . . Their organization was called the African Church," and one of its ministers was constituted bishop. Its career, however, was to be short lived, for the city authorities promptly proceeded against them, first by arresting a number of participants at one of their meetings but dismissing them with a warning that their conduct was violative of a statute of 1800 prohibiting the assemblage of slaves and free negroes for mental instruction without the presence of white persons; next by refusing, on the grounds that both power and willingness were

[55] E. R. Turner, *The Negro in Pennsylvania* (Washington, 1911), pp. 134-136.

lacking, a plea by the colored preachers for a special dispensation; and finally by the seizure of all the attendants at another of their meetings and the sentencing of the bishop and a dozen exhorters, some to a month's imprisonment or departure from the state, others to ten lashes or ten dollars' fine. The church nevertheless continued in existence until 1822 when in consequence of the discovery of a plot for insurrection among the Charleston negroes the city government had the church building demolished. Morris Brown moved to Philadelphia, where he afterward became bishop of the African Church, and the whole Charleston project was ended.[56] The bulk of the blacks returned to the white congregations, where they soon overflowed the galleries and even the "boxes" which were assigned them at the rear on the main floors. Some of the older negroes by special privilege then took seats forward in the main body of the churches, and others not so esteemed followed their example in such numbers that the whites were cramped for room. After complaints on this score had failed for several years to bring remedy, a crisis came in Bethel Church on a Sunday in 1833 when Dr. Capers was to preach. More whites came than could be seated · the forward-sitting negroes refused to vacate their seats for them; and a committee of young white members forcibly ejected these blacks At a "love-feast" shortly afterward one of the preachers criticized the action of the committee thereby giving the younger element of the whites great umbrage. Efforts at reconciliation failing, nine of the young men were expelled from membership, whereupon a hundred and fifty others followed them into a new organization which entered affiliation with the schismatic Methodist Protestant Church.[57] Race relations in the orthodox congregations were doubtless thereafter more placid.

In most of the permanent segregations the colored preachers

[56] Charleston *Courier*, June 9, 1818; Charleston *City Gazette*, quoted in the *Louisiana Gazette* (New Orleans), July 10, 1818; J. L. E. W. Shecut, *Medical and Philosophical Essays* (Charleston, 1819), p. 34; C. F. Deems ed., *Annals of Southern Methodism for 1856* (Nashville [1857]), pp. 212-214, 232; H. M. Henry, *Police Control of the Slave in South Carolina*, p. 142.
[57] C. F. Deems ed., *Annals of Southern Methodism for 1856*, pp. 215-217.

were ordained and their congregations instituted under the patronage of the whites. At Savannah as early as 1802 the freedom of the slave Henry Francis was purchased by subscription, and he was ordained by white ministers at the African Baptist Church. After a sermon by the Reverend Jesse Peter of Augusta, the candidate "underwent a public examination respecting his faith in the leading doctrines of Christianity, his call to the sacred ministry and his ideas of church government. Giving entire satisfaction on these important points, he kneeled down, when the ordination prayer with imposition of hands was made by Andrew Bryant. The ordained ministers present then gave the right hand of fellowship to Mr. Francis, who was forthwith presented with a Bible and a solemn charge to faithfulness by Mr. Holcombe." [58] The Methodists were probably not far behind the Baptists in this policy. The Presbyterians and Episcopalians, with much smaller numbers of negro co-religionists to care for, followed the same trend in later decades. Thus the presbytery of Charleston provided in 1850, at a cost of $7,700, a separate house of worship for its negro members, the congregation to be identified officially with the Second Presbyterian Church of the city. The building had a T shape, the transepts appropriated to the use of white persons. The Sunday school of about 180 pupils had twenty or thirty white men and women as its teaching staff.[59]

Such arrangements were not free from objection, however, as the Episcopalians of Charleston learned about this time. To relieve the congestion of the negro pews in St. Michael's and St. Philip's, a separate congregation was organized with a few whites included in its membership. While it was yet occupying temporary quarters in Temperance Hall, a mob demolished Calvary Church which was being built for its accommodation. When the proprietor of Temperance Hall refused the further

[58] Henry Holcombe ed., *The Georgia Analytical Repository* (a Baptist magazine of Savannah, 1802), I, 20, 21. For further data concerning Francis and other colored Baptists of his time see the *Journal of Negro History*, I, 69-92.

[59] J. H. Thornwell, D.D., *The Rights and Duties of Masters: a sermon preached at the dedication of a church erected at Charleston, S. C., for the benefit and instruction of the colored population* (Charleston, 1850).

use of his premises the congregation dispersed. The mob's action was said to be in protest against the doings of the "bands" or burial societies among the Calvary negroes.[60]

The separate religious integration of the negroes both slave and free was obstructed by the recurrent fear of the whites that it might be perverted to insurrectionary purposes. Thus when at Richmond in 1823 ninety-two free negroes petitioned the Virginia legislature on behalf of themselves and several hundred slaves, reciting that the Baptist churches used by the whites had not enough room to permit their attendance and asł sanction for the creation of a "Baptist African Church," the legislature withheld its permission. In 1841, however, this purpose was in effect accomplished when it was found that a negro church would not be in violation of the law provided it had a white pastor. At that time the First Baptist Church of Richmond, having outgrown its quarters, erected a new building to accommodate its white members and left its old one to the negroes. The latter were thereupon organized as the African Church with a white minister and with the choice of its deacons vested in a white committee. In 1855, when this congregation had grown to three thousand members, the Ebenezer church was established as an offshoot, with a similar plan of government.[61]

At Baltimore there were in 1835 ten colored congregations, with slave and free membership intermingled, several of which had colored ministers;[62] and by 1847 the number of churches had increased to thirteen or more, ten of which were Methodist.[63] In 1860 there were two or more colored congregations at Norfolk; at Savannah three colored churches were paying salaries of $800 to $1000 to their colored ministers,[64] and in

[60] *Public Proceedings relating to Calvary Church and the Religious Instruction of Slaves* (Charleston, 1850).
[61] J. B. Earnest, *The Religious Development of the Negro in Virginia* (Charlottesville, 1914), pp. 72-83. For the similar trend of church segregation in the Northern cities see J. W. Cromwell, *The Negro in American History* (Washington, 1914), pp. 61-70.
[62] *Niles' Register*, XLIX, 72.
[63] J. R. Brackett, *The Negro in Maryland*, p. 206.
[64] D. R. Hundley, *Social Relations in our Southern States* (New York, '50), pp. 350, 351.

Atlanta a subscription was in progress for the enlargement of the negro church building to relieve its congestion.[65] By this time a visitor in virtually any Southern city might have witnessed such a scene as William H. Russell described at Montgomery: [66] "As I was walking . . . I perceived a crowd of very well-dressed negroes, men and women, in front of a plain brick building which I was informed was their Baptist meeting-house, into which white people rarely or never intrude. These were domestic servants, or persons employed in stores, and their general appearance indicated much comfort and even luxury. I doubted if they all were slaves. One of my companions went up to a woman in a straw hat, with bright red and green ribbon trimmings and artificial flowers, a gaudy Paisley shawl, and a rainbow-like gown blown out over her yellow boots by a prodigious crinoline, and asked her 'Whom do you belong to?' She replied, 'I b'long to Massa Smith, sar.' "

[65] Atlanta *Intelligencer*, July 13, 1859, editorial commending the purpose.
[66] W. H Russell, *My Diary North and South* (Boston, 1863), p. 167.

CHAPTLR XXI

FREE NEGROES

IN the colonial period slaves were freed as a rule only when generous masters rated them individually deserving of liberty or when the negroes bought themselves. Typical of the time were the will of Thomas Stanford of New Jersey in 1722 directing that upon the death of the testator's wife his negro man should have his freedom if in the opinion of three neighbors named he had behaved well,[1] and a deed signed by Robert Daniell of South Carolina in 1759 granting freedom to his slave David Wilson in consideration of his faithful service and of £600 currency in hand paid.[2] So long as this condition prevailed, in which the ethics of slaveholding were little questioned, the freed element remained extremely small.

The liberal philosophy of the Revolution, persisting thereafter in spite of reaction, not only wrought the legal disestablishment of slavery throughout the North, but prompted private manumissions far and wide.[3] Thus Philip Graham of Maryland made a deed in 1787 reciting his realization that the holding of his "fellow men in bondage and slavery is repugnant to the golden law of God and the unalienable right of mankind as well as to every principle of the late glorious revolution which has taken place in America," and converting his slaves into servants for terms, the adults to become free at the close of that year and the children as they reached maturity.[4] In the same period, upon his coming of age, Richard Randolph, brother of

[1] *New Jersey Archives,* XXIII, 438.
[2] MS. among the probate records at Charleston.
[3] These were restricted for a time in North Carolina, however, by an act of 1777 which recited the critical and alarming state of public affairs as its occasion.
[4] MS. transcript in the file of powers of attorney, I, 243, among the county records at Louisville, Ky.

the famous John, wrote to his guardian: "With regard to the division of the estate, I have only to say that I want not a single negro for any other purpose than his immediate liberation. I consider every individual thus unshackled as the source of future generations, not to say nations, of freemen; and I shudder when I think that so insignificant an animal as I am is invested with this monstrous, this horrid power."[5] The Randolph estate, however, was so cumbered with debts that the desired manumissions could not then be made. At Richard's death in 1796 he left a will of the expected tenor, providing for a wholesale freeing as promptly as it could legally be accomplished by the clearance of the mortgage.[6] In 1795 John Stratton of Norfolk, asserting his "full persuassion that freedom is the natural right of all men," set free his able-bodied slave, Peter Wakefield.[7] Robert K. Moore of Louisville mingled thrift with liberalism by setting free in 1802 two pairs of married slaves because of his conviction that involuntary servitude was wrong, and at the same time binding them by indenture to serve him for some fourteen years longer in consideration of certain small payments in advance and larger ones at the ends of their terms.[8]

Manumissions were in fact so common in the deeds and wills of the men of '76 that the number of colored freemen in the South exceeded thirty-five thousand in 1790 and was nearly doubled in each of the next two decades. The greater caution of their successors, reinforced by the rise of slave prices, then slackened the rate of increase to twenty-five and finally to ten per cent. per decade. Documents in this later period, reverting to the colonial basis, commonly recited faithful service or self purchase rather than inherent rights as the grounds for manumission. Liberations on a large scale, nevertheless, were not wholly discontinued. John Randolph's will set free nearly four hundred in 1833;[9] Monroe Edwards of Louisiana manumitted

[5] H. A. Garland, *Life of John Randolph of Roanoke* (New York, 1851), I, 63.
[6] *DeBow's Review*, XXIV, 285-290.
[7] MS. along with many similar documents among the deed files at Norfolk, Va.
[8] MSS. in the powers of attorney files, II, 118, 122, 127, at Louisville, Ky.
[9] Garland, *Life of Randolph*, II, 150, 151.

160 by deed in 1840; [10] and George W. P. Custis of Virginia liberated his two or three hundred at his death in 1857. [11]

Still other large proprietors while not bestowing immediate liberty made provisions to bring it after the lapse of years. Prominent among these were three Louisianians. Julien Poydras, who died in 1824, ordered his executors to sell his six plantations with their respective staffs under contracts to secure the manumission of each slave after twenty-five years of service to the purchaser, together with an annual pension of $25 to each of those above sixty years of age; and years afterward a nephew of the testator procured an injunction from the supreme court of the state estopping the sale of some of the slaves by one of their purchasers in such way as would hazard the fulfilment of the purpose. [12] Stephen Henderson, a Scotch immigrant who had acquired several sugar plantations, provided as follows, by will made in 1837 and upheld by the courts: ten and twenty slaves respectively were to be chosen by lot at periods five and ten years after his death to be freed and sent to Liberia, and at the end of twenty-five years the rest were to fare likewise, but any who refused to be deported were to be kept as apprentices on the plantations. [13] John McDonogh, the most thrifty citizen of New Orleans in his day, made a unique bargain with his whole force of slaves, about 1825, by which they were collectively to earn their freedom and their passage to Liberia by the overtime work of Saturday afternoons. This labor was to be done in McDonogh's own service, and he was to keep account of their earnings. They were entitled to draw upon this fund upon approved occasions; but since the contract was with the whole group of slaves as a unit, when one applied for cash the others must draw theirs *pro rata,* thereby postponing the common day of liberation. Any slaves violating the rules of good conduct were to be sold by the master, whereupon their accrued earnings would revert to the fund of the rest. The plan was carried to

[10] *Niles' Register,* LXIII, 245.
[11] *Daily True Delta* (New Orleans), Dec. 19, 1857.
[12] Poydras *vs.* Mourrain, in *Louisiana Reports,* IX, 492. The will is quoted in the decision.
[13] *Niles' Register,* LXVIII, 361. The original MS. is filed in will book no. 6 in the New Orleans court house.

completion on schedule, and after some delay in embarkation
they left America in 1842, some eighty in number, with their
late master's benediction. In concluding his public narration
in the premises McDonogh wrote: "They have now sailed for
Liberia, the land of their fathers. I can say with truth and
heartfelt satisfaction that a more virtuous people does not exist
in any country." [14]

Among more romantic liberations was that of Pierre Chastang
of Mobile who, in recognition of public services in the war of
1812 and the yellow fever epidemic of 1819 was bought and
freed by popular subscription; [15] that of Sam which was provided by a special act of the Georgia legislature in 1834 at a
cost of $1,800 in reward for his having saved the state capitol
from destruction by fire; [16] and that of Prince which was attained through the good offices of the United States government. Prince, after many years as a Mississippi slave, wrote
a letter in Arabic to the American consul at Tangier in which
he recounted his early life as a man of rank among the Timboo
people and his capture in battle and sale overseas. This led
Henry Clay on behalf of the Adams administration to inquire
at what cost he might be bought for liberation and return. His
master thereupon freed him gratuitously, and the citizens of
Natchez raised a fund for the purchase of his wife, with a surplus for a flowing Moorish costume in which Prince was
promptly arrayed. The pair then departed, in 1828, for Wash-

[14] J. T. Edwards ed., *Some Interesting Papers of John McDonogh* (Mc-
Donoghville, Md., 1898), pp. 49-58.
[15] D. W. Mitchell, *Ten Years in the United States* (London, 1862), p. 235.
[16] Georgia Senate *Journal* for 1834, p. 25. At a later period the Georgia
legislature had occasion to reward another slave, Ransom by name, who
while hired from his master by the state had heroically saved the Western
and Atlantic Railroad bridge over the Chattahoochee River from destruction by fire. Since official sentiment was now hostile to manumission, it
was resolved in 1849 that he be bought by the state and ensured a permanent home; and in 1853 a further resolution directed the chief engineer of
the state-owned railroad to pay him just wages during good behavior.
Georgia *Acts, 1849-1850*, pp. 416, 417; *1853-1854*, pp. 538, 539. Old citizens
relate that a house was built for Ransom on the Western and Atlantic right
of way in Atlanta which he continued to occupy until his death many years
after the Civil War. For these data I am indebted to Mr. J. Groves Cohen,
Secretary of the Western and Atlantic Railroad Commission, Atlanta, Ga.

ington *en route* for Morocco, Prince avowing that he would soon send back money for the liberation of their nine children.[17]

Most of the negroes who procured freedom remained in the United States, though all of those who gained it by flight and many of those manumitted had to shift their location at the time of changing their status. At least one of the fugitives, however, made known his preference for his native district in a manner which cost him his liberty. After two years in Ohio and Canada he returned to the old plantation in Georgia, where he was welcomed with a command to take up the hoe. Rejecting this implement, he proposed to buy himself if a thousand dollars would suffice. When his master, declining to negotiate, ordered him into custody he stabbed one of the negroes who seized him. At the end of the episode the returned wanderer lay in jail; but where his money was, or whether in truth he had any, is not recorded.[18] Among some of those manumitted and sent out of their original states as by law required, disappointment and homesickness were distressingly keen. A group of them who had been carried to New York in 1852 under the will of a Mr. Cresswell of Louisiana, found themselves in such misery there that they begged the executor to carry them back, saying he might keep them as slaves or sell them—that they had been happy before but were wretched now.[19]

The slaves manumitted for meritorious service and those who bought themselves formed together an element of substantial worth in the Southern free colored population. Testamentary endorsement like that which Abel P. Upshur gave on freeing his man David Rich—"I recommend him in the strongest manner to the respect, esteem and confidence of any community in which he may live" [20]—are sufficiently eloquent in the premises. Those who bought themselves were similarly endorsed in many in-

[17] "Letter from a Gentleman of Natchez to a Lady of Cincinnati," in the *Georgia Courier* (Augusta), May 22, 1828. For a similar instance in colonial Maryland see the present work, p. 31.
[18] Cassville, Ga., *Standard,* May 31, 1858, reprinted in the *Federal Union* (Milledgeville, Ga.), June 8, 1858.
[19] *DeBow's Review,* XIV, 90.
[20] William C. Nell, *The Colored Patriots of the American Revolution* (Boston, 1855), pp. 215, 216. For a similar item see Garland's *Randolph,* p. 151.

stances, and the very fact of their self purchase was usually a voucher of thrift and sobriety. Many of those freed on either of these grounds were of mixed blood; and to them were added the mulatto and quadroon children set free by their white fathers, with particular frequency in Louisiana, who by virtue oftentimes of gifts in lands, goods and moneys were in the propertied class from the time of their manumission. The recruits joining the free colored population through all of these channels tended, together with their descendants, to be industrious, well-mannered and respected members of society.

Each locality was likely to have some outstanding figure among these. In Georgia the most notable was Austin Dabney, who as a mulatto youth served in the Revolutionary army and attached himself ever afterward to the white family who saved his life when he had been wounded in battle. The Georgia legislature by special act gave him a farm; he was welcomed in the tavern circle of chatting lawyers whenever his favorite Judge Dooly held court at his home village; and once when the formality of drawing his pension carried him to Savannah the governor of the state, seeing him pass, dragged him from his horse and quartered him as a guest in his house.[21] John Eady of the South Carolina lowlands by a like service in the War for Independence earned a somewhat similar recognition which he retained throughout a very long life.[22]

Others were esteemed rather for piety and benevolence than for heroic services. "Such," wrote Bishop Capers of the Southern Methodist Church, "were my old friends Castile Selby and John Bouquet of Charleston, Will Campbell and Harry Myrick of Wilmington, York Cohen of Savannah, and others I might name. These I might call remarkable for their goodness. But I use the word in a broader sense for Henry Evans, who was confessedly the father of the Methodist church, white and black, in Fayetteville, and the best preacher of his time in that quarter." Evans, a free-born full-blooded black, as Capers went on

[21] George R. Gilmer, *Sketches of Some of the First Settlers of Upper Georgia* (New York, 1855), pp. 212-215.
[22] Diary of Thomas P. Porcher. MS. in private possession.

to relate, had been a shoemaker and licensed preacher in Virginia, but while journeying toward Charleston in search of better employment he had been so struck by the lack of religion and morality among the negroes in Fayetteville that he determined upon their conversion as his true mission in life. When the town authorities dispersed his meetings he shifted his rude pulpit into the woods outside their jurisdiction and invited surveillance by the whites to prove his lack of offence. The palpable improvement in the morals of his followers led erelong to his being invited to preach within the town again, where the white people began to be numerous among his hearers. A regular congregation comprising members of both races was organized and a church building erected. But the white attendance grew so large as to threaten the crowding out of the blacks. To provide room for these the side walls of the church were torn off and sheds built on either flank; and these were the conditions when Capers himself succeeded the aged negro in its pulpit in 1810 and found him on his own score an inspiration. Toward the ruling race, Capers records, Evans was unfailingly deferential, "never speaking to a white but with his hat under his arm; never allowing himself to be seated in their houses. . . . 'The whites are kind to me and come to hear me preach,' he would say, 'but I belong to my own sort and must not spoil them.' And yet Henry Evans was a Boanerges; and in his duty feared not the face of man." [23]

In the line of intellectual attainment and the like the principal figures lived in the eighteenth century. One of them was described in a contemporary news item which suggests that some journalists then were akin to their successors of more modern times. "There is a Mr. St. George, a Creole, son to the French governor of St. Domingo, now at Paris, who realizes all the accomplishments attributed by Boyle and others to the Admirable Creighton of the Scotch. He is so superior at the sword that there is an edict of the Parliament of Paris to make his engagement in any duel actual death. He is the first dancer (even be-

<hr>

[23] W. W. Wightman, *Life of William Capers* (Nashville, 1858), pp. 124-129.

fore the Irish Singsby) in the world. He plays upon seven instruments of music, beyond any other individual. He speaks
twenty-six languages, and maintains public thesises in each. He
walks round the various circles of science like the master of
each; and strange to be mentioned to white men, this Mr. St.
George is a mulatto, the son of an African mother." [24]   Less
happy was the career of Francis Williams of Jamaica, a play-
thing of the human gods. Born of negro parents who had
earned special privilege in the island, he was used by the Duke
of Montague in a test of negro mental capacity and given an
education in an English grammar school and at Cambridge University.   Upon his return to Jamaica his patron sought his appointment as a member of the governor's council but without
success; and he then became a schoolmaster and a poet on occasion in the island capital.   Williams described himself with some
pertinence as "a white man acting under a black skin."   His
contempt for his fellow negroes and particularly for the mulattoes made him lonely, eccentric, haughty and morose.   A Latin
panegyric which is alone available among his writings is rather
a language exercise than a poem. [25]   On the continent Benjamin
Banneker was an almanac maker and somewhat of an astrono-
mer, and Phyllis Wheatley of Boston a writer of verses.   Both
were doubtless more noted for their sable color than for their
positive qualities.   The wonder of them lay in their ambition
and enterprise, not in their eminence among scientific and literary craftsmen at large. [26]   Such careers as these had no equivalent in the nineteenth century until its closing decades when
Booker T. Washington, Paul Laurence Dunbar and W. E. B.
DuBois set new paces in their several courses of endeavor.

Of a more normal but less conspicuous type was Jehu Jones,
the colored proprietor of one of Charleston's most popular hotels
who lived in the same manner as his white patrons, accumulated

[24] News item dated Philadelphia, Mch. 28, in the *Georgia State Gazette
and Independent Register* (Augusta), May 19, 1787.
[25] Edward Long, *History of Jamaica* (London, 1774), II, 447-485; T. H.
MacDermott, "Francis Williams," in the *Journal of Negro History*, II,
147-159. The Latin poem is printed in both of these accounts.
[26] John W. Cromwell, *The Negro in American History* (Washington,
1914), pp. 77-97.

property to the value of some forty thousand dollars, and maintained a reputation for high business talent and integrity.[27] At New Orleans men of such a sort were quite numerous. Prominent among them by reason of his wealth and philanthropy was Thomy Lafon, a merchant and money lender who systematically accumulated houses and lots during a lifetime extending both before and after the Civil War and whose possessions when he died at the age of eighty-two were appraised at nearly half a million dollars.[28] Prosperity and good repute, however, did not always go hand in hand. The keeper of the one good tavern in the Louisiana village of Bayou Sara in 1831 was a colored woman of whom Anne Royall wrote: "This *nigger* or mulatto was rich, owned the tavern and several slaves, to whom she was a great tyrant. She owned other valuable property and a great deal of money, as report said; and doubtless it is true. She was very insolent, and, I think, drank. It seems one Tague [an Irishman], smitten with her charms and her property, made love to her and it was returned, and they live together as man and wife. She was the ugliest wench I ever saw, and, if possible, he was uglier, so they were well matched." [29] One might ascribe the tone of this description to the tartness of Mrs. Royall's pen were it not that she recorded just afterward that a body-servant of General Ripley who was placed at her command in St. Francisville was "certainly the most accomplished servant I ever saw." [30]

The property of colored freemen oftentimes included slaves. Such instances were quite numerous in pre-revolutionary San Domingo; and some in the British West Indies achieved notoriety through the exposure of cruelties.[31] On the continent a negro planter in St. Paul's Parish, South Carolina, was reported before the close of the eighteenth century to have two hundred

[27] W. C. Nell, *Colored Patriots*, pp. 244, 245.
[28] New Orleans *Picayune*, Dec. 23, 1893. His many charitable bequests are scheduled in the *Picayune* of a week later.
[29] Anne Royall, *Southern Tour* (Washington, 1831), pp. 87-89.
[30] *Ibid.*, p. 91.
[31] Reverend Charles Peters, *Two Sermons Preached at Dominica, with an appendix containing minutes of evidence of three trials* (London, 1802), pp. 36-49.

434 AMERICAN NEGRO SLAVERY

slaves as well as a white wife and son-in-law, and the returns of the first federal census appear to corroborate it.[32] In Louisiana colored planters on a considerable scale became fairly numerous. Among them were Cyprien Ricard who bought at a sheriff's sale in 1851 an estate in Iberville Parish along with its ninety-one slaves for nearly a quarter of a million dollars; Marie Metoyer of Natchitoches Parish had fifty-eight slaves and more than two thousand acres of land when she died in 1840; Charles Roques of the same parish died in 1854 leaving forty-seven slaves and a thousand acres; and Martin Donato of St. Landry dying in 1848 bequeathed liberty to his slave wife and her seven children and left them eighty-nine slaves and 4,500 arpents of land as well as notes and mortgages to a value of $46,000.[33] In rural Virginia and Maryland also there were free colored slaveholders in considerable numbers.[34]

Slaveholdings by colored townsmen were likewise fairly frequent. Among the 360 colored taxpayers in Charleston in 1860, for example, 130, including nine persons described as of Indian descent, were listed as possessing 390 slaves.[35] The abundance of such holdings at New Orleans is evidenced by the multiplicity of applications from colored proprietors for authority to manumit slaves, with exemption from the legal requirement that the new freedmen must leave the state.[36] A striking example of

[32] LaRochefoucauld-Liancourt, *Travels in the United States* (London, 1799), p. 602, giving the negro's name as Pindaim. The census returns of 1790 give no such name, but they list James Pendarvis in a group comprising a white man, a free colored person and 123 slaves, and also a Mrs. Persons, free colored, with 136 slaves. She may have been Pindaim's (or Pendarvis') mulatto daughter, while the white man listed in the Pendarvis item was perhaps her husband or an overseer. *Heads of Families at the First Census of the United States: South Carolina* (Washington, 1908), pp. 35, 37.

[33] For these and other data I am indebted to Professor E. P. Puckett of Central College, Fayette, Mo., who has permitted me to use his monograph, "Free Negroes in Louisiana," in manuscript. The arpent was the standard unit of area in the Creole parishes of Louisiana, the acre in the parishes of Anglo-American settlement.

[34] Calvin D. Wilson, "Black Masters," in the *North American Review*, CLXXXI, 685-698, and "Negroes who owned Slaves," in the *Popular Science Monthly*, LXXXI, 483-494; John H. Russell, "Colored Freemen as Slave Owners in Virginia," in the *Journal of Negro History*, I, 233-242.

[35] *List of the Taxpayers of Charleston for 1860* (Charleston, 1861), part 2.

such petitions was that presented in 1832 by Marie Louise
Bitaud, free woman of color, which recited that in the preceding year she had bought her daughter and grandchild at a cost
of $700; that a lawyer had now told her that in view of her lack
of free relatives to inherit her property, in case of death intes-
tate her slaves would revert to the state; that she had become
alarmed at this prospect; and she accordingly begged permission
to manumit them without their having to leave Louisiana. The
magistrates gave their consent on condition that the petitioner
furnish a bond of $500 to insure the support and education of
the grandson until his coming of age. This was duly done and
the formalities completed.[37]

Evidence of slaveholdings by colored freemen occurs also in
the bills of sale filed in various public archives. One of these
records that a citizen of Charleston sold in 1828 a man slave to
the latter's free colored sister at a price of one dollar, "provided
he is kindly treated and is never sold, he being an unfortunate
individual and requiring much attention." In the same city a
free colored man bought a slave sailmaker for $200.[38] At Sa-
vannah in 1818 Richard Richardson sold a slave woman and
child for $800 to Alex Hunter, guardian of the colored freeman
Louis Mirault, in trust for him; and in 1833 Anthony Ording-
sell, free colored, having obtained through his guardian an
order of court, sold a slave woman to the highest bidder for
$385.[39]

It is clear that aside from the practice of holding slave relatives as a means of giving them virtual freedom, an appreciable
number of colored proprietors owned slaves purely as a productive investment. It was doubtless a group of these who sent a
joint communication to a New Orleans newspaper when seces-

[36] Many of these are filed in the record books of manumissions in the
archive rooms of the New Orleans city hall. Some were denied on the
ground that proof was lacking that the slaves concerned were natives of
the state or that they would be self-supporting in freedom; others were
granted.
[37] For the use of this MS. petition with its accompanying certificates I
am indebted to Mr. J. F. Schindler of New York.
[38] MSS. in the files of slave sales in the South Carolina archives at Columbia.
[39] MSS. among the county archives at Savannah, Ga.

sion and war were impending: "The free colored population (native) of Louisiana . . . own slaves, and they are dearly attached to their native land, . . . and they are ready to shed their blood for her defence. They have no sympathy for abolitionism; no love for the North, but they have plenty for Louisiana. . . . They will fight for her in 1861 as they fought in 1814-'15. . . . If they have made no demonstration it is because they have no right to meddle with politics, but not because they are not well disposed. All they ask is to have a chance, and they will be worthy sons of Louisiana." [40] Oral testimony gathered by the present writer from old residents in various quarters of the South supports the suggestion of this letter that many of the well-to-do colored freemen tended to prize their distinctive position so strongly as to deplore any prospect of a general emancipation for fear it would submerge them in the great black mass.

The types discussed thus far were exceptional. The main body of the free negroes were those who whether in person or through their mothers had been liberated purely from sentiment and possessed no particular qualifications for self-directed careers. The former slaves of Richard Randolph who were colonized in accordance with his will as petty landed proprietors near Farmville, Virginia, proved commonly thriftless for half a century afterward; [41] and Olmsted observed of the Virginia free negroes in general that their poverty was not due to the lack of industrial opportunity. [42] Many of those in the country were tenants. George Washington found one of them unprofitable as such; [43] and Robert Carter in 1792 rented farms to several in spite of his overseer's remonstrance that they had no adequate outfit of tools and teams, and against his neighbors' protests. [44] Not a few indeed were mere squatters on waste lands. A Georgia overseer reported in 1840 that several such families

[40] Letter to the editor, signed "A large number of them," in the New Orleans *Daily Delta*, Dec. 28, 1860. Men of this element had indeed rendered service under Jackson in the defence of the city against Pakenham, as Louisianians well knew.
[41] F. N. Watkins, "The Randolph Emancipated Slaves," in *DeBow's Review*, XXIV, 285-290. [42] *Seaboard Slave States*, p. 126.
[43] S. M. Hamilton ed., *Letters to Washington*, IV, 239.
[44] Carter MSS. in the Virginia Historical Society.

had made clearings in the woods of the plantation under his charge, and proposed that rent be required of them;[45] and travellers occasionally came upon negro cabins in fields which had been abandoned by their proprietors.[46] The typical rural family appears to have tilled a few acres on its own account, and to have been willing to lend a hand to the whites for wages when they needed service. It was this readiness which made their presence in many cases welcome in a neighborhood. A memorial signed by thirty-eight citizens of Essex County, Virginia, in 1842 in behalf of a freedman might be paralleled from the records of many another community: "We would be glad if he could be permitted to remain with us and have his freedom, as he is a well disposed person and a very useful man in many respects. He is a good carpenter, a good cooper, a coarse shoemaker, a good hand at almost everything that is useful to us farmers."[47] Among the free negroes on the seaboard there was a special proclivity toward the water pursuits of boating, oystering and the like.[48] In general they found a niche in industrial society much on a level with the slaves but as free as might be from the pressure of systematic competition.

Urban freemen had on the average a somewhat higher level of attainment than their rural fellows, for among them was commonly a larger proportion of mulattoes and quadroons and of those who had demonstrated their capacity for self direction by having bought their own freedom. Recruits of some skill in the crafts, furthermore, came in from the country, because of the advantages which town industry, in sharp contrast with that of the plantations, gave to free labor. A characteristic state of affairs is shown by the official register of free persons of color in Richmond County, Georgia, wherein lay the city of Augusta, for the year 1819.[49] Of the fifty-three men listed, including a planter and a steamboat pilot, only seven were classed as common la-

[45] *Plantation and Frontier*, II, 155.
[46] *E. g.*, F. Cumming, *Tour to the West*, reprinted in Thwaites ed., *Early Western Travels*, IV, 336.
[47] J. H. Russell, *The Free Negro in Virginia*, p. 153.
[48] *Ibid.*, p. 150.
[49] *Augusta Chronicle*, Mch. 13, 1819, reprinted in *Plantation and Frontier*, II, 143-147.

borers, while all the rest had specific trades or employments. The prosperity of the group must have been but moderate, nevertheless, for virtually all its women were listed as workers at washing, sewing, cooking, spinning, weaving or market vending; and although an African church in the town had an aged sexton, its minister must have drawn most of his livelihood from some week-day trade, for no designation of a preacher appears in the list. At Charleston, likewise, according to the city census of 1848, only 19 free colored men in a total of 239 listed in manual occupations were unclassified laborers, while the great majority were engaged in the shop and building trades. The women again were very numerous in sewing and washing employments, and an appreciable number of them were domestic servants outright.[50]

In the compendium of the United States census of 1850 there are printed in parallel columns the statistics of occupations among the free colored males above fifteen years of age in the cities of New York and New Orleans. In the Northern metropolis there were 3337 enumerated, and in the Southern 1792. The former had 4 colored lawyers and 3 colored druggists while the latter had none of either; and the colored preachers and doctors were 21 to 1 and 9 to 4 in New York's favor. But New Orleans had 4 colored capitalists, 2 planters, 11 overseers, 9 brokers and 2 collectors, with none of any of these at New York; and 64 merchants, 5 jewelers and 61 clerks to New York's 3, 3 and 7 respectively, and 12 colored teachers to 8. New York had thrice New Orleans' number of colored barbers, and twice as many butchers; but her twelve carpenters and no masons were contrasted with 355 and 278 in these two trades at New Orleans, and her cigar makers, tailors, painters, coopers, blacksmiths and general mechanics were not in much better proportion. One-third of all New York's colored men, indeed, were unskilled laborers and another quarter were domestic servants, not to mention the many cooks, coachmen and other semi-domestic employees, whereas at New Orleans the unskilled were

    [50] Dawson and DeSaussure, *Census of Charleston for 1848*, summarized in the table given on p. 403 of the present work.

but a tenth part of the whole and no male domestics were listed. This showing, which on the whole is highly favorable to New Orleans, is partly attributable to the more than fourfold excess of mulattoes over the blacks in its free population, in contrast with a reversed proportion at New York; for the men of mixed blood filled all the places above the rank of artisan at New Orleans, and heavily preponderated in virtually all the classes but that of unskilled laborers. New York's poor showing as regards colored craftsmen, however, was mainly due to the greater discrimination which its white people applied against all who had a strain of negro blood.

This antipathy and its consequent industrial repression was palpably more severe at the North in general than in the South. De Tocqueville remarked that "the prejudice which repels the negroes seems to increase in proportion as they are emancipated." Fanny Kemble, in her more vehement style, wrote of the negroes in the North: "They are not slaves indeed, but they are pariahs, debarred from every fellowship save with their own despised race, scorned by the lowest white ruffian in your streets, not tolerated even by the foreign menials in your kitchen. They are free certainly, but they are also degraded, rejected, the offscum and the offscouring of the very dregs of your society. . . . All hands are extended to thrust them out, all fingers point at their dusky skin, all tongues, the most vulgar as well as the self-styled most refined, have learned to turn the very name of their race into an insult and a reproach." [51] Marshall Hall expressed himself as "utterly at a loss to imagine the source of that prejudice which subsists against him [the negro] in the Northern states, a prejudice unknown in the South, where the domestic relations between the African and the European are so much more intimate." [52] Olmsted recorded a conversation which he had with a free colored barber on a Red River steamboat who had been at school for a year at West Troy, New York: "He said that colored people could associate with whites much more easily and

[51] Frances Anne Kemble, *Journal* (London, 1863), p. 7.
[52] Marshall Hall, *The Two-fold Slavery of the United States* (London, 1854), p. 17.

comfortably at the South than at the North; this was one reason he preferred to live at the South.   He was kept at a greater distance from white people, and more insulted on account of his color, at the North than ᴍ Louisiana." [53]   And at Richmond Olmsted learned of a negro who after buying his freedom had gone to Philadelphia to join his brother, but had promptly returned.   When questioned by his former owner this man said: "Oh, I don't like dat Philadelphy, massa; an't no chance for colored folks dere.   Spec' if I'd ʋeen a runaway de wite folks dere take care o' me; but I couldn't git anythin' to do, so I jis borrow ten dollar of my broder an' cum back to old Virginny." [54]   In Ohio, John Randolph's freedmen were prevented by the populace from colonizing the tract which his executors had bought for them in Mercer County and had to be scattered elsewhere in the state; [55] in Connecticut the citizens of New Haven resolved in a public meeting in 1831 that a projected college for negroes in that place would not be tolerated, and shortly afterward the townsmen of Canterbury broke up the school which Prudence Crandall attempted to establish there for colored girls.   The legislatures of various Northern states, furthermore, excluded free immigrants as well as discriminating sharply against those who were already inhabitants.   Wherever the negroes clustered numerously, from Boston to Philadelphia and Cincinnati, they were not only browbeaten and excluded from the trades but were occasionally the victims of brutal outrage whether from mobs or individual persecutors. [56]

In the South, on the other hand, the laws were still more severe but the practice of the white people was much more kindly. Racial antipathy was there mitigated by the sympathetic tie of

[53] *Seaboard Slave States*, p. 636.
[54] *Ibid.*, p. 104.
[55] F. U. Quillin, *The Color Line in Ohio* (Ann Arbor, Mich.), p. 29; *Plantation and Frontier*, II, 143.
[56] J. P. Gordy, *Political History of the United States* (New York, 1902), II, 404, 405; John Daniels, *In Freedom's Birthplace* (Boston, 1914), pp. 25-29; E. R. Turner, *The Negro in Pennsylvania* (Washington, 1911), pp. 143-168, 195-204, containing many details; F. U. Quillin, *The Color Line in Ohio*, pp. 11-87; C. G. Woodson, "The Negroes of Cincinnati Prior to the Civil War," in the *Journal of Negro History*, I, 1-22; N. D. Harris, *Negro Slavery in Illinois* (Chicago, 1906), pp. 226-240.

slavery which promoted an attitude of amiable patronage even toward the freedmen and their descendants.[57] The tone of the memorials in which many Southern townsmen petitioned for legal exemptions to permit specified free negroes to remain in their communities [58] found no echo from the corresponding type of commonplace unromantic citizens of the North. A few Southern petitions were of a contrasting tenor, it is true, one for example presented to the city council of Atlanta in 1859: "We feel aggrieved as Southern citizens that your honorable body tolerates a negro dentist (Roderick Badger) in our midst; and in justice to ourselves and the community it ought to be abated. We, the residents of Atlanta, appeal to you for justice." [59] But it may readily be guessed that these petitioners were more moved by the interest of rival dentists than by their concern as Southern citizens. Southern protests of another class, to be discussed below, against the toleration of colored freedmen in general, were prompted by considerations of public security, not by personal dislike.

Although the free colored numbers varied greatly from state to state, their distribution on the two sides of Mason and Dixon's line maintained a remarkable equality throughout the antebellum period. The chief concentration was in the border states of either section. At the one extreme they were kept few by the chill of the climate; at the other by stringency of the law and by the high prices of slave labor which restrained the practice of manumission. Wherever they dwelt, they lived somewhat precariously upon the sufferance of the whites, and in a more or less palpable danger of losing their liberty.

Not only were escaped slaves liable to recapture anywhere within the United States, but those who were legally free might be seized on fraudulent claims and enslaved in circumvention of the law, or they might be kidnapped outright. One of those taken by fraud described his experience and predicament as follows in a letter from "Boonvill Missouria" to the governor of Georgia: "Mr. Coob Dear Sir I have Embrast this oppertuniny of Riting

[57] Cf. N. S. Shaler, *The Neighbor* (Boston, 1904), pp. 166, 186-191.
[58] *E. g.*, J. H. Russell, *The Free Negro in Virginia*, pp. 152-155.
[59] J. H. Martin, *Atlanta and its Builders* ([Atlanta,] 1902), I, 145.

a few Lines to you to inform you that I am sold as a Slave for 14 hundard dolars By the man that came to you Last may and told you a Pack of lies to get you to Sine the warrant that he Brought that warrant was a forged as I have heard them say when I was Coming on to this Countrey and Sir I thought that I would write and see if I could get you to do any thing for me in the way of Getting me my freedom Back a Gain   if I had some Papers from the Clarkes office in the City of Milledgeville and a little Good addvice in a Letter from you or any kind friend that I could get my freedom a Gain   and my name can Be found on the Books of the Clarkes office   Mr Bozal Stulers was Clarke when I was thear last   and Sir a most any man can City that I Charles Covey is lawfuley a free man . . . But at the same time I do not want you to say any thing about this to any one that may acquaint my Preseant mastear of these things as he would quickly sell me and there fore I do not want this known   and the men that came after me Carried me to Mempears tenessee and after whiping me untill my Back was Raw from my rump to the Back of my neck sent me to this Place and sold me   Pleas to ancer this as soon as you Can and Sir as soon as I can Get my time Back I will pay you all charges if you will Except of it   yours in heast Charles Covey Borned and Raized in the City of Milledgeville and a Blacksmith by trade and James Rethearfurd in the City of Macon is my Laller [lawyer?] and can tell you all about these things." [60]

In a few cases claims of ownership were resurrected after a long lapse. That of Alexander Pierre, a New Orleans negro who had always passed as free-born, was the consequence of an affray in which he had worsted another black. In revenge the defeated combatant made the fact known that Pierre was the son of a blind girl who because of her lack of market value had been left by her master many years before to shift for herself when he had sold his other slaves and gone to France. Thereupon George Heno, the heir of the departed and now deceased proprietor, laid

[60] Letter of Charles Covey to Howell Cobb, Nov. 30, 1853. MS. in the possession of Mrs. A. S. Erwin, Athens, Ga., for the use of which I am indebted to Professor R. P. Brooks of the University of Georgia. For another instance in which Cobb's aid was asked see the American Historical Association *Report* for 1911, II, 331-334.

claim to the whole Pierre group, comprising the blind mother, Alexander himself, his sister, and that sister's two children. Whether Heno's proceedings at law to procure possession succeeded or failed is not told in the available record.[61] In a kindred case not long afterward, however, the cause of liberty triumphed. About 1807 Simon Porche of Point Coupée Parish had permitted his slave Eulalie to marry his wife's illegitimate mulatto half-brother; and thereafter she and her children and grand-children dwelt in virtual freedom. After Porche's death his widow, failing in an attempt to get official sanction for the manumission of Eulalie and her offspring and desiring the effort to be renewed in case of her own death, made a nominal sale of them to a relative under pledge of emancipation. When this man proved recreant and sold the group, now numbering seventeen souls, and the purchasers undertook possession, the case was litigated as a suit for freedom. Decision was rendered for the plaintiff, after appeal to the state supreme court, on the ground of prescriptive right. This outcome was in strict accord with the law of Louisiana providing that "If a master shall suffer a slave to enjoy his liberty for ten years during his residence in this state, or for twenty years while out of it, he shall lose all right of action to recover possession of the said slave, unless said slave shall be a runaway or fugitive." [62]

Kidnappings without pretense of legal claim were done so furtively that they seldom attained record unless the victims had recourse to the courts; and this was made rare by the helplessness of childhood in some cases and in others by the fear of lashes. Indeed when complexion gave presumption of slave status, as it did, and custody gave color of ownership, the prospect of redress through the law was faint unless the services of some white friend could be enlisted. Two cases made conspicuous by the publication of elaborate narratives were those of Peter Still and Solomon Northrup. The former, kidnapped in childhood near Philadelphia, served as a slave some forty years in

[61] New Orleans *Daily Delta*, May 25, 1849.
[62] E. P. Puckett, "The Free Negro in Louisiana" (MS.), citing the New Orleans *True Delta*, Dec. 16, 1854.

Kentucky and northern Alabama, until with his own savings he bought his freedom and returned to his boyhood home. The problem which he then faced of liberating his wife and three children was taken off his hands for a time by Seth Concklin, a freelance white abolitionist who volunteered to abduct them. This daring emancipator duly went to Alabama in 1851, embarked the four negroes on a skiff and carried them down the Tennessee and up the Ohio and the Wabash until weariness at the oars drove the company to take the road for further travel. They were now captured and the slaves were escorted by their master back to the plantation; but Concklin dropped off the steamboat by night only to be drowned in the Ohio by the weight of his fetters. Adopting a safer plan, Peter now procured endorsements from leading abolitionists and made a soliciting tour of New York and New England by which he raised funds enough to buy his family's freedom. At the conclusion of the narrative of their lives Peter and his wife were domestics in a New Jersey boarding-house, one of their two sons was a blacksmith's apprentice in a neighboring town, the other had employment in a Pennsylvania village, and the daughter was at school in Philadelphia.[63]

Solomon Northrup had been a raftsman and farmer about Lake Champlain until in 1841 when on the ground of his talent with the fiddle two strangers offered him employment in a circus which they said was then at Washington. Going thither with them, he was drugged, shackled, despoiled of his free papers, and delivered to a slave trader who shipped him to New Orleans. Then followed a checkered experience as a plantation hand on the Red River, lasting for a dozen years until a letter which a friendly white carpenter had written for him brought one of his former patrons with an agent's commission from the governor of New York. With the assistance of the local authorities Northrup's identity was promptly established, his liberty pro-

---

*Kate E. R. Pickard, *The Kidnapped and the Ransomed, being the personal recollections of Peter Still and his wife Vina after forty years of slavery* (Syracuse, 1856). The dialogue in which the book abounds is, of course, fictitious, but the outlines of the narrative and the documents quoted are presumably authentic.

cured, and the journey accomplished which carried him back again to his wife and children at Saratoga.[64]

A third instance, but of merely local notoriety, was that of William Houston, who, according to his own account was a British subject who had come from Liverpool as a ship steward in 1840 and while at New Orleans had been offered passage back to England by way of New York by one Espagne de Blanc. But upon reaching Martinsville on the up-river voyage de Blanc had ordered him off the boat, set him to work in his kitchen, taken away his papers and treated him as his slave. After five years there Houston was sold to a New Orleans barkeeper who shortly sold him to a neighboring merchant, George Lynch, who hired him out. In the Mexican war Houston accompanied the American army, and upon returning to New Orleans was sold to one Richardson. But this purchaser, suspecting a fault of title, refused payment, whereupon in 1850 Richardson sold Houston at auction to J. F. Lapice, against whom the negro now brought suit under the aegis of the British consul. While the trial was yet pending a local newspaper printed his whole narrative that it might "assist the plaintiff to prove his freedom, or the defendant to prove he is a slave." [65]

Societies were established here and there for the prevention of kidnapping and other illegal practices in reducing negroes to slavery, notable among which for its long and active career was the one at Alexandria.[66] Kidnapping was, of course, a crime under the laws of the states generally; but in view of the seeming ease of its accomplishment and the potential value of the victims it may well be thought remarkable that so many thousands of free negroes were able to keep their liberty. In 1860 there were 83,942 of this class in Maryland, 58,042 in Virginia, 30,463 in North Carolina, 18,467 in Louisiana, and 250,787 in the South at large.

[64] [David Wilson ed.], *Narrative of Solomon Northrup* (New York, 1853). Though the books of this class are generally of dubious value this one has a tone which engages confidence. Its pictures of plantation life and labor are of particular interest.

[65] New Orleans *Daily Delta*, June 1, 1850.

[66] Alexandria, Va., *Advertiser*, Feb. 22, 1798, notice of the society's quarterly meeting; J. D. Paxton, *Letters on Slavery* (Lexington, Ky., 1833), p. 30, note.

A few free negroes were reduced by public authority to private servitude, whether for terms or for life, in punishment for crime. In Maryland under an act of 1858 eighty-nine were sold by the state in the following two years, four of them for life and the rest for terms, after convictions ranging from arson to petty larceny.[67] Some others were sold in various states under laws applying to negro vagrancy, illegal residence, or even to default of jail fees during imprisonment as fugitive suspects.

A few others voluntarily converted themselves into slaves. Thus Lucinda who had been manumitted under a will requiring her removal to another state petitioned the Virginia legislature in 1815 for permission, which was doubtless granted, to become the slave of the master of her slave husband "from whom the benefits and privileges of freedom, dear and flattering as they are, could not induce her to be separated."[68] On other grounds William Bass petitioned the South Carolina general assembly in 1859, reciting "That as a free negro he is preyed upon by every sharper with whom he comes in contact, and that he is very poor though an able-bodied man, and is charged with and punished for every offence, guilty or not, committed in his neighborhood; that he is without house or home, and lives a thousand times harder and in more destitution than the slaves of many planters in this district." He accordingly asked permission by special act to become the slave of Philip W. Pledger who had consented to receive him if he could lawfully do so.[69] To provide systematically for such occasions the legislatures of several states from Maryland to Texas enacted laws in the middle and late fifties authorizing free persons of color at their own instance and with the approval of magistrates in each case to enslave themselves to such masters as they might select.[70] The Virginia law, enacted at the beginning of 1856, safeguarded the claims of any credit-

[67] J. R. Brackett, *The Negro in Maryland*, pp. 231, 232.
[68] *Plantation and Frontier*, II, 161, 162.
[69] *Ibid.*, II, 163, 164.
[70] In the absence of permissive laws the self-enslavement of negroes was invalid. Texas Supreme Court *Reports*, XXIV, 560. And a negro who had deeded his services for ninety-nine years was adjudged to retain his free status, though the contract between him and his employer was not thereby voided. North Carolina Supreme Court *Reports*, LX, 434.

ors against the negro by requiring a month's notice during which protests might be entered, and it also required the prospective master to pay to the state half the negro's appraised value. Among the Virginia archives vouchers are filed for sixteen such enslavements, in widely scattered localities.[71] Most of the appraisals in these cases ranged from $300 to $1200, indicating substantial earning capacity; but the valuations of $5 for one of the women and of $10 for a man upwards of seventy years old suggest that some of these undertakings were of a charitable nature. An instance in the general premises occurred in Georgia, as late as July, 1864, when a negro freeman in dearth of livelihood sold himself for five hundred dollars, in Confederate currency of course, to be paid to his free wife.[72] Occasionally a free man of color would seek a swifter and surer escape from his tribulations by taking his own life;[73] but there appears to be no reason to believe that suicides among them were in greater ratio than among the whites.

Invitations to American free negroes to try their fortunes in other lands were not lacking. Facilities for emigration to Liberia were steadily maintained by the Colonization Society from 1819 onward;[74] the Haytian government under President Boyer offered special inducements from that republic in 1824;[75] in 1840 an immigration society in British Guiana proffered free transportation for such as would remove thither;[76] and in 1859 Hayti once more sent overtures, particularly to the French-speaking

[71] MSS. in the Virginia State Library.
[72] American Historical Association *Report* for 1904, p. 577.
[73] An instance is given in the *Louisiana Courier* (New Orleans), Aug. 26, 1830, and another in the New Orleans *Commercial Advertiser*, Oct. 25, 1831. The motives are not stated.
[74] J. H. T. McPherson, *History of Liberia* (Johns Hopkins University *Studies*, IX, no. 10).
[75] *Correspondence relative to the Emigration to Hayti of the Free People of Colour in the United States, together with the instructions to the agent sent out by President Boyer* (New York, 1824); *Plantation and Frontier*, II, 155-157.
[76] *Inducements to the Colored People of the United States to Emigrate to British Guiana*, compiled from statements and documents furnished by Mr. Edward Carberry, agent of the immigration society of British Guiana and a proprietor in that colony. By "A friend to the Colored People" (Boston, 1840); The *Liberator* (Boston), Feb. 28, 1840, advertisement.

colored people of Louisiana, promising free lands to all who would come as well as free transportation to such as could not pay their passage.[77] But these opportunities were seldom embraced. With the great bulk of those to whom they were addressed the dread of an undiscovered country from whose bourne few travellers had returned puzzled their wills, as it had done Hamlet's, and made them rather bear those ills they had than to fly to others that they knew not of.

Their caste, it is true, was discriminated against with severity. Generally at the North and wholly at the South their children were debarred from the white schools and poorly provided with schools of their own.[78] Exclusion of the adults from the militia became the general rule after the close of the war of 1812. Deprivation of the suffrage at the South, which was made complete by the action of the constitutional convention of North Carolina in 1835 and which was imposed by numerous Northern states between 1807 and 1838,[79] was a more palpable grievance against which a convention of colored freemen at Philadelphia in 1831 ineffectually protested.[80] Exclusion from the jury boxes and from giving testimony against whites was likewise not only general in the South but more or less prevalent in the North as well. Many of the Southern states, furthermore, required license and registration as a condition of residence and imposed restrictions upon movement, education and occupations; and several of them required the procurement of individual white guardians or bondsmen in security for good behavior.

These discriminations, along with the many private rebuffs and oppressions which they met, greatly complicated the problem of social adjustment which colored freemen everywhere encountered. It is not to be wondered that some of them developed

---

[77] E. P. Puckett, "The Free Negro in Louisiana" (MS.), citing the New Orleans *Picayune*, July 16, 1859, and Oct. 21 and 23, 1860.

[78] The schooling facilities are elaborately and excellently described and discussed in C. G. Woodson, *The Education of the Negro Prior to 1861* (New York, 1915).

[79] Emil Olbrich, *The Development of Sentiment for Negro Suffrage to 1860* (University of Wisconsin *Bulletin*, Historical Series, III, no. I).

[80] *Minutes and Proceedings of the First Annual Convention of the People of Colour, held in Philadelphia from the sixth to the eleventh of June*, 1831 (Philadelphia, 1831).

criminal tendencies in reaction and revolt, particularly when
white agitators made it their business to stimulate discontent.
Convictions for crimes, however, were in greatest proportionate
excess among the free negroes of the North. In 1850, for example, the colored inmates in the Southern penitentiaries, including slaves, bore a ratio to the free colored population but half as
high as did the corresponding prisoners in the North to the
similar population there. These ratios were about six and
eleven times those prevalent among the Southern and Northern
whites respectively.[81] This nevertheless does not prove an excess of actual depravity or criminal disposition in any of the
premises, for the discriminative character of the laws and the
prejudice of constables, magistrates and jurors were strong contributing factors. Many a free negro was doubtless arrested
and convicted in virtually every commonwealth under circumstances in which white men went free. The more severe industrial discrimination at the North, which drove large numbers to
an alternative of destitution or crime, was furthermore contribu-
tive to the special excess of negro criminality there.

In some instances the violence of mobs was added to the might
of the law. Such was the case at Washington in 1835 when following on the heels of a man's arrest for the crime of possessing
incendiary publications and his trial within the jail as a precaution to keep him from the mob's clutches, a new report was
spread that Beverly Snow, the free mulatto proprietor of a sa-
loon and restaurant between Brown's and Gadsby's hotels, had
spoken in slurring terms of the wives and daughters of white
mechanics as a class. "In a very short time he had more customers than both Brown and Gadsby—but the landlord was not
to be found although diligent search was made all through the
house. Next morning the house was visited by an increased
number of guests, but Snow was still absent." The mob then

---

[81] The number of convicts for every 10,000 of the respective populations
was about 2.2 for the whites and 13.0 for the free colored (with slave convicts included) at the South, and 2.5 for the whites and 28.7 for the free
colored at the North. Compendium of the Seventh Census, p. 166. See
also Southern Literary Messenger, IX, 340-352; DeBow's Review, XIV,
593-595; David Christy, Cotton Is King (Cincinnati, 1855), p. 153; E. R.
Turner, The Negro in Pennsylvania, pp. 155-158.

began to search the houses of his associates for him. In that of
James Hutton, another free mulatto, some abolition papers were
found. The mob hustled Hutton to a magistrate, returned and
wrecked Snow's establishment, and then held an organized meeting at the Center Market where an executive committee was appointed with a view to further activity. Meanwhile the city
council held session, the mayor issued a proclamation, and the
militia was ordered out. Mobs gathered that night, nevertheless,
but dispersed after burning a negro hut and breaking the windows of a negro church.[82] Such outrages appear to have been
rare in the distinctively Southern communities where the racial
subordination was more complete and the antipathy correspondingly fainter.

Since the whites everywhere held the whip hand and nowhere
greatly refrained from the use of their power, the lot of the colored freeman was one hardly to be borne without the aid of
habit and philosophy. They submitted to the régime because it
was mostly taken as a matter of course, because resistance would
surely bring harsher repression, and because there were solaces
to be found. The well-to-do quadroons and mulattoes had reason in their prosperity to cherish their own pride of place and
carry themselves with a quiet conservative dignity. The less
prosperous blacks, together with such of their mulatto confrères
as were similarly inert, had the satisfaction at least of not being
slaves; and those in the South commonly shared the humorous
lightheartedness which is characteristic of both African and
Southern negroes. The possession of sincere friends among the
whites here and there also helped them to feel that their lives lay
in fairly pleasant places; and in their lodges they had a refuge
peculiarly their own.

The benevolent secret societies of the negroes, with their special stress upon burial ceremonies, may have had a dim African
origin, but they were doubtless influenced strongly by the Ma-
sonic and other orders among the whites. Nothing but mere
glimpses may be had of the history of these institutions, for low-

[82] Washington *Globe*, about August 14, reprinted in the *North Carolina
Standard*, Aug. 27, 1835.

liness as well as secrecy screened their careers. There may well have been very many lodges among illiterate and moneyless slaves without leaving any tangible record whatever. Those in which the colored freemen mainly figured were a little more affluent, formal and conspicuous. Such organizations were a recourse at the same time for mutual aid and for the enhancement of social prestige. The founding of one of them at Charleston in 1790, the Brown Fellowship Society, with membership confined to mulattoes and quadroons, appears to have prompted the free blacks to found one of their own in emulation.[83] Among the proceedings of the former was the expulsion of George Logan in 1817 with a consequent cancelling of his claims and those of his heirs to the rights and benefits of the institution, on the ground that he had conspired to cause a free black to be sold as a slave.[84] At Baltimore in 1835 there were thirty-five or forty of these lodges, with memberships ranging from thirty-five to one hundred and fifty each.[85]

The tone and purpose of the lodges may be gathered in part from the constitution and by-laws of one of them, the Union Band Society of New Orleans, founded in 1860. Its motto was "Love, Union, Peace"; its officers were president, vice-president, secretary, treasurer, marshal, mother, and six male and twelve female stewards, and its dues fifty cents per month. Members joining the lodge were pledged to obey its laws, to be humble to its officers, to keep its secrets, to live in love and union with fellow members, "to go about once in a while and see one another in love," and to wear the society's regalia on occasion. Any member in three months' arrears of dues was to be expelled unless upon his plea of illness or poverty a subscription could be raised in meeting to meet his deficit. It was the duty of all to report illnesses in the membership, and the function of the official mother to delegate members for the nursing. The secretary was to see to the washing of the sick member's clothes and pay for the work from the lodge's funds, as well as the doctor's fees. The marshal was to have charge of funerals, with power to com-

[83] T. D. Jervey, *Robert Y. Hayne and His Times* (New York, 1909), p. 6.
[84] *Ibid.*, pp. 68, 69.
[85] *Niles' Register*, XLIX, 72.

mandeer the services of such members as might be required. He might fee the officiating minister to the extent of not more than $2.50, and draw pay for himself on a similar schedule. Negotiations with any other lodge were provided for in case of the death of a member who had fellowship also in the other for the custody of the corpse and the sharing of expense; and a provision was included that when a lodge was given the body of an outsider for burial it would furnish coffin, hearse, tomb, minister and marshal at a price of fifty dollars all told.[86] The mortuary stress in the by-laws, however, need not signify that the lodge was more funereal than festive. A negro burial was as sociable as an Irish wake.

Doubtless to some extent in their lodges, and certainly to a great degree in their daily affairs, the lives of the free colored and the slaves intermingled. Colored freemen, except in the highest of their social strata, took free or slave wives almost indifferently. Some indeed appear to have preferred the unfree, either because in such case the husband would not be responsible for the support of the family or because he might engage the protection of his wife's master in time of need.[87] On the other hand the free colored women were somewhat numerously the prostitutes, or in more favored cases the concubines, of white men. At New Orleans and thereabouts particularly, concubinage, along with the well known "quadroon balls," was a systematized practice.[88] When this had persisted for enough generations to produce children of less than octoroon infusion, some of these doubtless cut their social ties, changed their residence, and made successful though clandestine entrance into white society. The fairness of the complexions of some of those who to this day take the seats assigned to colored passengers in the street cars of New Orleans is an evidence, however, that "crossing the line" has not in all such breasts been a mastering ambition.

The Southern whites were of several minds regarding the free

[86] The By-laws and Constitution of the Union Band Society of New Orleans, organized July 22, 1860: Love, Union, Peace (Caption).
[87] J. H. Russell, The Free Negro in Virginia, pp. 130-133.
[88] Albert Phelps, Louisiana (Boston, 1905), pp. 212, 213.

colored element in their midst. Whereas laboring men were
more or less jealously disposed on the ground of their competition, the interest and inclination of citizens in the upper ranks
was commonly to look with favor upon those whose labor they
might use to advantage. On public grounds, however, these
men shared the general apprehension that in case tumult were
plotted, the freedom of movement possessed by these people
might if their services were enlisted by the slaves make the efforts of the whole more formidable. One of the Charleston
pamphleteers sought to discriminate between the mulattoes and
the blacks in the premises, censuring the indolence and vicious-
ness of the latter while praising the former for their thrift and
sobriety and contending that in case of revolt they would be
more likely to prove allies of the whites.[89] This distinction,
however, met no general adoption. The general discussion at
the South in the premises did not concern the virtues and vices
of the colored freemen on their own score so much as the
influence exerted by them upon the slaves. It is notable in this
connection that the Northern dislike of negro newcomers from
the South on the ground of their prevalent ignorance, thriftless-
ness and instability [90] was more than matched by the Southern
dread of free negroes from the North. A citizen of New Orleans
wrote characteristically as early as 1819:[91] "It is a melancholy
but incontrovertible fact that in the cities of Philadelphia, New
York and Boston, where the blacks are put on an equality with
the whites, . . . they are chiefly noted for their aversion to labor and proneness to villainy. Men of this class are peculiarly
dangerous in a community like ours; they are in general remarkable for the boldness of their manners, and some of them
possess talents to execute the most wicked and deep laid plots."

[Edwin C. Holland], *A Refutation of the Calumnies circulated against
the Southern and Western States respecting the institution and existence
of Slavery among them.* By a South Carolinian (Charleston, 1822),
pp. 84, 85.
E. R. Turner, *The Negro in Pennsylvania*, p. 158.
Letter to the editor in the *Louisiana Gazette*, Aug. 12, 1819.

CHAPTER XXII

SLAVE CRIME

THE negroes were in a strange land, coercively subjected to laws and customs far different from those of their ancestral country; and by being enslaved and set off into a separate lowly caste they were largely deprived of that incentive to conformity which under normal conditions the hope of individual advancement so strongly gives. It was quite to be expected that their conduct in general would be widely different from that of the whites who were citizens and proprietors. The natural amenability of the blacks, however, had been a decisive factor in their initial enslavement, and the reckoning which their captors and rulers made of this was on the whole well founded. Their lawbreaking had few distinctive characteristics, and gave no special concern to the public except as regards rape and revolt.

Records of offenses by slaves are scant because on the one hand they were commonly tried by somewhat informal courts whose records are scattered and often lost, and on the other hand they were generally given sentences of whipping, death or deportation, which kept their names out of the penitentiary lists. One errs, however, in assuming a dearth of serious infractions on their part and explaining it by saying, "under a strict slave régime there can scarcely be such a thing as crime";[1] for investigation reveals crime in abundance. A fairly typical record in the premises is that of Baldwin County, Georgia, in which the following trials of slaves for felonies between 1812 and 1832 are recounted: in 1812 Major was convicted of rape and sentenced to be hanged. In 1815 Fannie Micklejohn, charged with the murder of an infant was acquitted; and Tom, convicted of murdering a fellow slave was sentenced to branding on each cheek with the

---

[1] W. E. B. DuBois, in the *Annals of the Academy of Political and Social Science*, XVIII, 132.

letter M and to thirty-nine lashes on his bare back on each of three successive days, after which he was to be discharged. In 1816 John, a slave of William McGeehee, convicted of the theft of a $100 bill was sentenced to whipping in similar fashion. In 1818 Aleck was found guilty of an assault with intent to murder, and received sentence of fifty lashes on three days in succession. In 1819 Rodney was capitally sentenced for arson. In 1821 Peter, charged with murdering a slave, was convicted of manslaughter and ordered to be branded with M on the right cheek and to be given the customary three times thirty-nine lashes; and Edmund, charged with involuntary manslaughter, was dismissed on the ground that the court had no cognizance of such offense. In 1822 Davis was convicted of assault upon a white person with intent to kill, but his sentence is not recorded. In or about the same year John, a slave of William Robertson, convicted of burglary but recommended to mercy, was sentenced to be branded with T on the right cheek and to receive three times thirty-nine lashes; and on the same day the same slave was sentenced to death for assault upon a white man with intent to kill. In 1825 John Ponder's George when convicted of burglary was recommended by the jury to the mercy of the court but received sentence of death nevertheless; and Stephen was sentenced likewise for murderous assault upon a white man. In 1826 Elleck, charged with assault with intent of murder and rape, was convicted on the first part of the charge only, but received sentence of death. In 1828 Elizabeth Smith's George was acquitted of larceny from the house; and next year Caroline was likewise acquitted on a charge of maiming a white person. Finally, in 1832 Martin, upon pleading guilty to a charge of murderous assault, was given a whipping sentence of the customary thirty-nine lashes on three successive days.[2]

A few negro felonies, indeed, resulted directly from the pressure of slave circumstance. A gruesome instance occurred in

[2] "Record of the Proceedings of the Inferior Court of Baldwin County on the Trials of Slaves charged with capital Offences." MS. in the court house at Milledgeville. The record is summarized in the American Historical Association *Report* for 1903, I, 462-464, and in *Plantation and Frontier*, II, 123-125.

1864 in the same county as the foregoing. A young slave woman, Becky by name, had given pregnancy as the reason for a continued slackness in her work. Her master became skeptical and gave notice that she was to be examined and might expect the whip in case her excuse were not substantiated. Two days afterward a negro midwife announced that Becky's baby had been born; but at the same time a neighboring planter began search for a child nine months old which was missing from his quarter. This child was found in Becky's cabin, with its two teeth pulled and the tip of its navel cut off. It died; and Becky, charged with murder but convicted only of manslaughter, was sentenced to receive two hundred lashes in instalments of twenty-five at intervals of four days.[3] Some other deeds done by slaves were crimes only because the law declared them to be such when committed by persons of that class. The striking of white persons and the administering of medicine to them are examples. But in general the felonies for which they were convicted were of sorts which the law described as criminal regardless of the status of the perpetrators.

In a West Indian colony and in a Northern state glimpses of the volume of criminality, though not of its quality, may be drawn from the fact that in the years from 1792 to 1802 the Jamaican government deported 271 slave convicts at a cost of £15,538 for the compensation of their masters,[4] and that in 1816 some forty such were deported from New York to New Orleans, much to the disquiet of the Louisiana authorities.[5] As for the South, state-wide statistical views with any approach to adequacy are available for two commonwealths only. That of Louisiana is due to the fact that the laws and courts there gave sentences of imprisonment with considerable impartiality to malefactors of both races and conditions. In its penitentiary report at the end of 1860, for example, the list of inmates comprised 96 slaves along with 236 whites and 11 free colored. All

[3] *Confederate Union* (Milledgeville, Ga.), Mch. 1, 1864.
[4] *Royal Gazette* (Kingston, Jamaica), Jan. 29, 1803.
[5] Message of Governor Claiborne in the *Journal* of the Louisiana House of Representatives, 3d legislature, 1st session, p. 22. For this note I am indebted to Mr. V. A. Moody.

the slaves but fourteen were males, and all but thirteen were serving life terms.[6] Classed by crimes, 12 of them had been sentenced for arson, 3 for burglary or housebreaking, 28 for murder, 4 for manslaughter, 4 for poisoning, 5 for attempts to poison, 7 for assault with intent to kill, 2 for stabbing, 3 for shooting, 20 for striking or wounding a white person, 1 for wounding a child, 4 for attempts to rape, and 3 for insurrection.[7] This catalogue is notable for its omissions as well as for its content. While there were four white inmates of the prison who stood convicted of rape, there were no negroes who had accomplished that crime. Likewise as compared with 52 whites and 4 free negroes serving terms for larceny, there were no slave prisoners in that category. Doubtless on the one hand the negro rapists had been promptly put to death, and on the other hand the slaves committing mere theft had been let off with whippings. Furthermore there were no slaves committed for counterfeiting or forgery, horse stealing, slave stealing or aiding slaves to escape.

The uniquely full view which may be had of the trend of serious crimes among the Virginia slaves is due to the preservation of vouchers filed in pursuance of a law of that state which for many decades required appraisal and payment by the public for all slaves capitally convicted and sentenced to death or deportation. The file extends virtually from 1780 to 1864, except for a gap of three years in the late 1850's.[8] The volume of crime rose gradually decade by decade to a maximum of 242 in the 1820's, and tended to decline slowly thereafter. The gross number of convictions was 1,418, all but 91 of which were of males. For arson there were 90 slaves convicted, including 29 women.

[6] Under an act of 1854, effective at this time, the owner of any slave executed or imprisoned was to receive indemnity from the state to the extent of two-thirds of the slave's appraised value.

[7] *Report of the Board of Control of the Louisiana Penitentiary, January, 1861* (Baton Rouge, 1861). Among the 22 pardoned in 1860 were 2 slaves who had been sentenced for murder, 2 for arson, and 1 for assault with intent to kill.

[8] The MS. vouchers are among the archives in the Virginia State Library. They have been statistically analyzed by the present writer, substantially as here follows, in the *American Historical Review*, XX, 336-340.

For burglary there were 257, with but one woman among them. The highway robbers numbered 15, the horse thieves 20, and the thieves of other sorts falling within the purview of the vouchers 24, with no women in these categories. It would be interesting to know how the slaves who stole horses expected to keep them undiscovered, but this the vouchers fail to tell.

For murder there were 346, discriminated as having been committed upon the master 56, the mistress 11, the overseer 11; upon other white persons 120; upon free negroes 7; upon slaves 85, including 12 children all of whom were killed by their own mothers; and upon persons not described 60. Of the murderers 307 were men and 39 women. For poisoning and attempts to poison, including the administering of ground glass, 40 men and 16 women were convicted, and there were also convictions of one man and one woman for administering medicine to white persons. For miscellaneous assault there were 111 sentences recorded, all but eight of which were laid upon male offenders and only two of which were described as having been directed against colored victims.

For rape there were 73 convictions, and for attempts at rape 32. This total of 105 cases was quite evenly distributed in the tale of years; but the territorial distribution was notably less in the long settled Tidewater district than in the newer Piedmont and Shenandoah. The trend of slave crime of most other sorts, however, ran squarely counter to this; and its notably heavier prevalence in the lowlands gives countenance to the contemporary Southern belief that the presence of numerous free negroes among them increased the criminal proclivities of the slaves. In at least two cases the victims of rape were white children; and in two others, if one be included in which the conviction was strangely of mere "suspicion of rape," they were free mulatto women. That no slave women were mentioned among the victims is of course far from proving that these were never violated, for such offenses appear to have been left largely to the private cognizance of the masters.[9] A Delaware instance of the sort attained record through an offer of reward for the capture of a slave who had run away after being punished.

For insurrection or conspiracy 91 slaves were convicted, 36 of them in Henrico County in 1800 for participation in Gabriel's revolt, 17 in 1831, mainly in Southampton County as followers of Nat Turner, and the rest mostly scattering. Among miscellaneous and unclassified cases there was one slave convicted of forgery, another of causing the printing of anti-slavery writings, and 301 sentenced without definite specification of their crimes. Among the vouchers furthermore are incidental records of the killing of a slave in 1788 who had been proclaimed an outlaw, and of the purchase and manumission by the commonwealth of Tom and Pharaoh in 1801 for services connected with the suppression of Gabriel's revolt.

As to punishments, the vouchers of the eighteenth century are largely silent, though one of them contains the only unusual sentence to be found in the whole file. This directed that the head of a slave who had murdered a fellow slave be cut off and stuck on a pole at the forks of the road. In the nineteenth century only about one-third of the vouchers record execution. The rest give record of transportation whether under the original sentences or upon commutation by the governor, except for the cases which from 1859 to 1863 were more numerous than any others where the commutations were to labor on the public works.

The statistics of rape in Virginia, and the Georgia cases already given, refute the oft-asserted Southern tradition that negroes never violated white women before slavery was abolished. Other scattering examples may be drawn from contemporary newspapers. One of these occurred at Worcester, Massachusetts in 1768.[10] Upon conviction the negro was condemned to death, although a white man at the same time found guilty of an attempt at rape was sentenced merely to sit upon the gallows.

[9] Elkton (Md.) *Press*, July 19, 1828, advertisement, reprinted in *Plantation and Frontier*, II, 122.

[10] *Boston Chronicle*, Sept. 26, 1768, confirmed by a contemporary broadside: "*The Life and Dying Speech of Arthur, a Negro Man who was executed at Worcester, October 20, 1786, for a rape committed on the body of one Deborah Metcalfe* (Boston. 1768).

In Georgia the governor issued a proclamation in 1811 offering reward for the capture of Jess, a slave who had ravished the wife of a citizen of Jones County; [11] and in 1844 a jury in Habersham County, after testimony by the victim and others, found a slave named Dave guilty of rape upon Hester An Dobbs, "a free white female in the peace of God and state of Georgia," and the criminal was duly hanged by the sheriff.[12] In Alabama in 1827 a negro was convicted of rape at Tuscaloosa,[13] and another in Washington County confessed after capture that while a runaway he had met Miss Winnie Caller, taken her from her horse, dragged her into the woods and butchered her "with circumstances too horrible to relate"; [14] and at Mobile in 1849 a slave named Ben was sentenced to death for an attempt at rape upon a white woman.[15] In Rapides Parish, Louisiana, in 1842, a young girl was dragged into the woods, beaten and violated. Her injuries caused her death next day. The criminal had been caught when the report went to press.[16]

Other examples will show that lynchings were not altogether lacking in those days in sequel to such crimes. Near the village of Gallatin, Mississippi, in 1843, two slave men entered a farmer's house in his absence and after having gotten liquor from his wife by threats, "they forcibly took from her arms the infant babe and rudely throwing it upon the floor, they threw her down, and while one of them accomplished the fiendish design of a ravisher the other, pointing the muzzle of a loaded gun at her head, said he would blow out her brains if she resisted or made any noise." The miscreants then loaded a horse with plunder from the house and made off, but they were shortly caught by pursuing citizens and hanged. The local editor said on his own score when recounting the episode: "We have ever been and now are opposed to any kind of punishment being administered under the statutes of Judge Lynch; but . . . a due regard for

[11] Augusta *Chronicle*, Mch. 29, 1811.
[12] American Historical Association *Report* for 1904, pp. 579, 580.
[13] Charleston *Observer*, Nov. 24, 1827.
[14] *Ibid.*, Nov. 10, 1827.
[15] New Orleans *Delta*, June 23, 1849.
[16] New Orleans *Bee*, Sept. 27, 1842, reprinted in *Plantation and Frontier*, II, 121, 122.

candor and the preservation of all that is held most sacred and all that is most dear to man in the domestic circles of life impels us to acknowledge the fact that if the perpetrators of this excessively revolting crime had been burned alive, as was at first decreed, their fate would have been too good for such diabolical and inhuman wretches." [17]

An editorial in the *Sentinel* of Columbus, Georgia, described and discussed a local occurrence of August 12, 1851, in a different tone:

"Our community has just been made to witness the most high-handed and humiliating act of violence that it has ever been our duty to chronicle. . . . At the May term of the Superior Court a negro man was tried and condemned on the charge of having attempted to commit rape upon a little white girl in this county. His trial was a fair one, his counsel was the best our bar afforded, his jury was one of the most intelligent that sat upon the criminal side of our court, and on patient and honest hearing he was found guilty and sentenced to be hung on Tuesday, the 12th inst. This, by the way, was the second conviction. The negro had been tried and convicted before, but his counsel had moved and obtained a new trial, which we have seen resulted like the first in a conviction.

"Notwithstanding his conviction, it was believed by some that the negro was innocent. Those who believed him innocent, in a spirit of mercy, undertook a short time since to procure his pardon; and a petition to that effect was circulated among our citizens and, we believe, very numerously signed. This we think was a great error. . . . It is dangerous for the people to undertake to meddle with the majesty of the jury trial; and strange as it may sound to some people, we regard the unfortunate denouement of this case as but the extreme exemplification of the very principle which actuated those who originated this petition. Each proceeded from a spirit of discontent with the decisions of the authorized tribunals; the difference being that in the one case peaceful means were used for the accomplishment of mistaken mercy,

[17] Gallatin, Miss., *Signal*, Feb. 27, 1843, reprinted in the *Louisiana Courier* (New Orleans), Mch. 1, 1843.

and in the other violence was resorted to for the attainment of mistaken justice.

"The petition was sent to Governor Towns, and on Monday evening last the messenger returned with a full and free pardon to the criminal. In the meantime the people had begun to flock in from the country to witness the execution; and when it was announced that a pardon had been received, the excitement which immediately pervaded the streets was indescribable. Monday night passed without any important demonstration. Tuesday morning the crowd in the streets increased, and the excitement with it. A large and excited multitude gathered early in the morning at the market house, and after numerous violent harangues a leader was chosen, and resolutions passed to the effect that the mob should demand the prisoner at four o'clock in the afternoon, and if he should not be given up he was to be taken by force and executed. After this decision the mob dispersed, and early in the afternoon, upon the ringing of the market bell, it reassembled and proceeded to the jail. The sheriff of the county of course refused to surrender the negro, when he was overpowered, the prison doors broken open, and the unfortunate culprit dragged forth and hung.

"These are the facts, briefly and we believe accurately, stated. We do nót feel now inclined to comment upon them. We leave them to the public, praying in behalf of our injured community all the charity which can be extended to an act so outraging, so unpardonable."

A similar occurrence in Sumter County, Alabama, in 1855 was reported with no expression of regret. A negro who had raped and murdered a young girl there was brought before the superior court in regular session. "When the case was called for trial a motion for change of venue to the county of Greene was granted. This so exasperated the citizens of Sumter (many of whom were in favor of summary punishment in the outset) that a large number of them collected on the 23d. ult., took him out of prison, chained him to a stake on the very spot where the murder was committed, and in the presence of two or three thousand ne-

[22] Columbus *Sentinel,* reprinted in the Augusta *Chronicle,* Aug. 17, 1851. This item, which is notable in more than one regard, was kindly furnished by Prof. R. P. Brooks of the University of Georgia.

groes and a large number of white people,[19] burned him alive."
This mention of negroes in attendance is in sharp contrast with
their palpable absence on similar occasions in later decades.
They were present, of course, as at legal executions, by the command of their masters to receive a lesson of deterrence. The
wisdom of this policy, however, had already been gravely questioned. A Louisiana editor, for example, had written in comment upon a local hanging: "The practice of sending slaves to
witness the execution of their fellows as a terror to them has
many advocates, but we are inclined to doubt its efficacy. We
took particular pains to notice on this occasion the effects which
this horrid spectacle would produce on their minds, and our observation taught us that while a very few turned with loathing
from the scene, a large majority manifested that levity and curiosity superinduced by witnessing a monkey show." [20]

For another case of lynching, which occurred in White County,
Tennessee, in 1858, there is available merely the court record of
a suit brought by the owners of the slave to recover pecuniary
damages from those who had lynched him. It is incidentally recited, with strong reprehension by the court, that the negro was
in legal custody under a charge of rape and murder when certain citizens, part of whom had signed a written agreement to
"stand by each other," broke into the jail and hanged the prisoner.[21]

In general the slaveholding South learned of crimes by individual negroes with considerable equanimity. It was the news
or suspicion of concerted action by them which alone caused
widespread alarm and uneasiness. That actual deeds of rebellion by small groups were fairly common is suggested by the
numerous slaves convicted of murdering their masters and overseers in Virginia, as well as by chance items from other quarters. Thus in 1797 a planter in Screven County, Georgia, who
had recently bought a batch of newly imported Africans was set
upon and killed by them, and his wife's escape was made possible

---

[19] *Southern Banner* (Athens, Ga.), June 21, 1855.
[20] *Caddo Gazette*, quoted in the New Orleans *Bee*, April 5, 1845.
[21] Head's *Tennessee Reports*, I, 336. For lynchings prompted by other
crimes than rape see below, p. 474, footnote 60.

only by the loyalty of two other slaves.[22] Likewise in Bullitt
County, Kentucky, in 1844, when a Mr. Stewart threatened one
of his slaves, that one and two others turned upon him and beat
him to death;[23] and in Arkansas in 1845 an overseer who was
attacked under similar circumstances saved his life only with the
aid of several neighbors and through the use of powder and
ball.[24] Such episodes were likely to grow as the reports of them
flew over the countryside. For instance in 1856 when an unruly
slave on a plantation shortly below New Orleans upon being
threatened with punishment seized an axe and was thereupon shot
by his overseer, the rumor of an insurrection quickly ran to and
through the city.[25]

If all such rumors as this, many of which had equally slight
basis, were assembled, the catalogue would reach formidable dimensions. A large number doubtless escaped record, for the
newspapers esteemed them "a delicate subject to touch";[26] and
many of those which were recorded, we may be sure, have not
come to the investigator's notice. A survey of the revolts and
conspiracies and the rumors of such must nevertheless be attempted; for their influence upon public thought and policy, at
least from time to time, was powerful.

Early revolts were of course mainly in the West Indies, for
these were long the chief plantation colonies. No more than
twenty years after the first blacks were brought to Hispaniola a
score of Joloff negroes on the plantation of Diego Columbus
rose in 1622 and were joined by a like number from other estates, to carry death and desolation in their path until they were
all cut down or captured.[27] In the English islands precedents of
conspiracy were set before the blacks became appreciably numerous. A plot among the white indentured servants in Barbados
in 1634 was betrayed and the ringleader executed;[28] and an-

[22] *Columbian Museum and Savannah Advertiser* (Savannah, Ga.), Feb.
24, 1797.
[23] Paducah *Kentuckian*, quoted in the New Orleans *Bee*, Apr. 3, 1844.
[24] New Orleans *Bee*, Aug. 1, 1845, citing the Arkansas *Southern Shield*.
[25] New Orleans *Daily Tropic*, Feb. 16, 1846.
[26] *Federal Union* (Milledgeville, Ga.), Dec. 23, 1856, editorial.
[27] J. A. Saco, *Esclavitud en el Nuevo Mondo* (Barcelona, 1879), pp. 131-133.
[28] Maryland Historical Society *Fund Publications*, XXXV.

other on a larger scale in 1649 had a similar end.[29] Incoming negroes appear not to have taken a similar course until 1675 when a plot among them was betrayed by one of their number. The governor promptly appointed captains to raise companies, as a contemporary wrote,[30] "for repressing the rebels, which accordingly was done, and abundance taken and apprehended and since put to death, and the rest kept in a more stricter manner." This quietude continued only until 1692 when three negroes were seized on charge of conspiracy. One of these, on promise of pardon, admitted the existence of the plot and his own participation therein. The two others were condemned "to be hung in chains on a gibbet till they were starved to death, and their bodies to be burned." These endured the torture "for four days without making any confession, but then gave in and promised to confess on promise of life. One was accordingly taken down on the day following. The other did not survive." The tale as then gathered told that the slaves already pledged were enough to form six regiments, and that arrangements were on foot for the seizure of the forts and arsenal through bribery among their custodians. The governor when reporting these disclosures expressed the hope that the severe punishment of the leaders, together with a new act offering freedom as reward to future informers, would make the colony secure.[31] There seems to have been no actual revolt of serious dimensions in Barbados except in 1816 when the blacks rose in great mass and burned more than sixty plantations, as well as killing all the whites they could catch, before troops arrived from neighboring islands and suppressed them.[32]

In Jamaica a small outbreak in 1677[33] was followed by another, in Clarendon Parish, in 1690. When these latter insurgents were routed by the whites, part of them, largely Coromantees it appears, fled to the nearby mountain fastnesses where,

[29] Richard Ligon, *History of Barbados* (London, 1657).
[30] Charles Lincoln ed., *Narratives of the Indian Wars, 1675-1699* (New York, 1913), pp. 71, 72.
[31] *Calendar of State Papers, America and West Indies, 1689-1692*, pp. 732-734.
[32] *Louisiana Gazette* (New Orleans), June 17, 1816.
[33] *Calendar of State Papers, America and West Indies, 1689-1692*, p. 101.

under the chieftainship of Cudjoe, they became securely established as a community of marooned freemen. Welcoming runaway slaves and living partly from depredations, they made themselves so troublesome to the countryside that in 1733 the colonial government built forts at the mouths of the Clarendon defiles and sent expeditions against the Maroon villages. Cudjoe thereupon shifted his tribe to a new and better buttressed vale in Trelawney Parish, whither after five years more spent in forays and reprisals the Jamaican authorities sent overtures for peace. The resulting treaty, signed in 1738, gave recognition to the Maroons, assigned them lands and rights of hunting, travel and trade, pledged them to render up runaway slaves and criminals in future, and provided for the residence of an agent of the island government among the Maroons as their superintendent. Under these terms peace prevailed for more than half a century, while the Maroon population increased from 600 to 1400 souls. At length Major James, to whom these blacks were warmly attached, was replaced as superintendent by Captain Craskell whom they disliked and shortly expelled. Tumults and forays now ensued, in 1795, the effect of which upon the sentiment of the whites was made stronger by the calamitous occurrences in San Domingo. Negotiations for a fresh accommodation fell through, whereupon a conquest was undertaken by a joint force of British troops, Jamaican militia and free colored auxiliaries. The prowess of the Maroons and the ruggedness of their district held all these at bay, however, until a body of Spanish hunters with trained dogs was brought in from Cuba. The Maroons, conquered more by fright than by force, now surrendered, whereupon they were transported first to Nova Scotia and thence at the end of the century to the British protectorate in Sierra Leone.[34] Other Jamaican troubles of some note were a revolt in St. Mary's Parish in 1765,[35] and a more general one in 1832 in which property of an estimated value of $1,800,000 was destroyed before the rebellion was put down at a cost of some $700,000 more.[36] There were troubles likewise in various other

[34] R. C. Dallas, *History of the Maroons* (London, 1803).
[35] *Gentleman's Magazine*, XXXVI, 135.
[36] *Niles' Register*, XLIV, 124.

colonies, as with insurgents in Antigua in 1701 [37] and [38] 1736 and Martinique and Guadeloupe in 1752; [39] with maroons in Grenada in 1765,[40] Dominica in 1785 [41] and Demarara in [42] 1794; and with conspirators in Cuba in 1825 [43] and St. Croix [44] and Porto Rico in 1848.[45]

Everything else of such nature, however, was eclipsed by the prodigious upheaval in San Domingo consequent upon the French Revolution. Under the flag of France the western end of that island had been converted in the course of the eighteenth century from a nest of buccaneers into the most thriving of plantation colonies. By 1788 it contained some 28,000 white settlers, 22,000 free negroes and mulattoes, and 405,000 slaves. It had nearly eight hundred sugar estates, many of them on a huge scale. The soil was so fertile and the climate so favorable that on many fields the sugar-cane would grow perennially from the same roots almost without end. Exports of coffee and cotton were considerable, of sugar and molasses enormous; and the volume was still rapidly swelling by reason of the great annual importations of African slaves. The colony was by far the most valued of the French overseas possessions.

Some of the whites were descendants of the original freebooters, and retained the temperament of their forbears; others were immigrant fortune seekers. The white women were less than half as numerous as the men, and black or yellow concubines were common substitutes for wives. The colony was the French equivalent of Jamaica, but more prosperous and more self-willed and self-indulgent. Its whites were impatient of outside control, and resolute that the slaves be ruled with iron hand and that the colored freemen be kept passive.

A plentiful discontent with bureaucracy and commercial re-

[37] *Calendar of State Papers, America and West Indies, 1701*, pp. 721, 722.
[38] *South Carolina Gazette* (Charleston), Jan. 29, 1837.
[39] *Gentleman's Magazine*, XXII, 477.
[40] *Ibid.*, XXXV, 533.
[41] Charleston, S. C., *Morning Post and Daily Advertiser*, Jan. 26, 1786.
[42] Henry Bolinbroke, *Voyage to the Demerary* (Philadelphia, 1813), pp. 200-203.
[43] *Louisiana Gazette*, Oct. 12, 1825.
[44] New Orleans *Bee*, Aug. 7, 1848.
[45] *Ibid.*, Aug. 16 and Dec. 15, 1848.

straint under the old régime caused the planters to welcome the early news of reform projects in France and to demand representation in the coming States General. But the rapid progress of radical republicanism in that assembly threw most of these into a royalist reaction, though the poorer whites tended still to endorse the Revolution. But now the agitations of the *Amis des Noirs* at Paris dismayed all the white islanders, while on the other hand the National Assembly's "Declaration of the Rights of Man," together with its decrees granting political equality in somewhat ambiguous form to free persons of color, prompted risings in 1791 among the colored freemen in the northern part of the colony and among the slaves in the center and south. When reports of these reached Paris, the new Legislative Assembly revoked the former measures by a decree of September 24, 1791, transferring all control over negro status to the colonial assemblies. Upon receiving news of this the mulattoes and blacks, with the courage of despair, spread ruin in every district. The whites, driven into the few fortified places, begged succor from France; but the Jacobins, who were now in control at Paris, had a programme of their own. By a decree of April 4, 1792, the Legislative Assembly granted full political equality to colored freemen and provided for the dispatch of Republican commissioners to establish the new régime. The administration of the colony by these functionaries was a travesty. Most of the surviving whites emigrated to Cuba and the American continent, carrying such of their slaves as they could command. The free colored people, who at first welcomed the commissioners, unexpectedly turned against them because of a decree of August 29, 1793, abolishing slavery.

At this juncture Great Britain, then at war with the French Republic, intervened by sending an army to capture the colony. Most of the colored freemen and the remaining whites rallied to the flag of these invaders; but the slaves, now commanded by the famous Toussaint L'Ouverture, resisted them effectually, while yellow fever decimated their ranks and paralyzed their energies. By 1795 the two colored elements, the mulattoes who had improvised a government on a slaveholding basis in the south, and the negroes who dominated the north, each had the other alone as an active enemy; and by the close of the century the mulattoes were either destroyed or driven into exile; and Toussaint, while still acknowledging a nominal allegiance to France, was virtual monarch of San Domingo. The peace of Amiens at length permitted Bonaparte to send an army against the "Black Napoleon." Toussaint soon capitulated, and in violation of the amnesty granted him was sent to his death in a French dungeon. But pestilence again aided the blacks, and the war was still raging when the breach of the peace in Europe brought a British squadron to blockade and capture the remnant of the French army. The new black leader, Dessalines, now proclaimed the colony's independence, renaming it Hayti, and in 1804 he crowned himself emperor. In the following year any further conflict with the local whites was obviated by the systematic massacre of their small residue. In the other French islands the developments, while on a much smaller scale, were analogous.[46]

In the Northern colonies the only signal disturbances were those of 1712 and 1741 at New York, both of which were more notable for the frenzy of the public than for the formidableness of the menace. Anxiety had been recurrent among the whites, particularly since the founding of a mission school by Elias Neau in 1704 as an agent of the Society for the Propagation of the Gospel. The plot was brewed by some Coromantee and Paw Paw negroes who had procured the services of a conjuror to make them invulnerable; and it may have been joined by several Spanish or Portuguese Indians or mestizoes who had been captured at sea and unwarrantably, as they contended, reduced to slavery. The rebels to the number of twenty-three provided themselves with guns, hatchets, knives and swords, and chose the dark of the moon in the small hours of an April night to set a house afire and slaughter the citizens as they flocked thither. But their gunfire caused the governor to send soldiers from the Battery with such speed that only nine whites had been killed and several

[46] T. Lothrop Stoddard, *The French Revolution in San Domingo* (Boston, 1914).

others wounded when the plotters were routed. Six of these killed themselves to escape capture; but when the woods were beaten and the town searched next day and an emergency court sat upon the cases, more captives were capitally sentenced than the whole conspiracy had comprised. The prosecuting officer, indeed, hounded one of the prisoners through three trials, to win a final conviction after two acquittals. The maxim that no one may twice be put in jeopardy for the same offense evidently did not apply to slaves in that colony. Of those convicted one was broken on the wheel, another hanged alive in chains; nineteen more were executed on the gallows or at the stake, one of these being sentenced "to be burned with a slow fire, that he may continue in torment for eight or ten hours and continue burning in said fire until he be dead and consumed to ashes"; and several others were saved only by the royal governor's reprieve and the queen's eventual pardon. Such animosity was exhibited by the citizens toward the "catechetical school" that for some time its teacher hardly dared show himself on the streets. The furor gradually subsided, however, and Mr. Neau continued his work for a dozen years longer, and others carried it on after his death.[47]

The commotion of 1741 was a panic among the whites of high and low degree, prompted in sequel to a robbery and a series of fires by the disclosures of Mary Burton, a young white servant concerning her master John Hughson, and the confessions of Margaret Kerry, a young white woman of many aliases but most commonly called Peggy, who was an inmate of Hughson's disreputable house and a prostitute to negro slaves. When Mary testified under duress that Hughson was not only a habitual recipient of stolen goods from the negroes but was the head of a conspiracy among them which had already effected the burning of many houses and was planning a general revolt, the supreme

[47] E. B. O'Callaghan ed., *Documents Relative to the Colonial History of New York*, V, 341, 342, 346, 356, 357, 371; *New York Genealogical and Biographical Record*, XXI, 162, 163; New Orleans *Daily Delta*, April 1, 1849; J. A. Doyle, *English Colonies in America* (New York, 1907), V, pp. 258, 259.

court of the colony began a labor of some six months' duration in bringing the alleged plot to light and punishing the alleged plotters.[48] Hughson and his wife and the infamous Peggy were promptly hanged, and likewise John Ury who was convicted of being a Catholic priest as well as a conspirator; and twenty-nine negroes were sent with similar speed either to the gallows or the stake, while eighty others were deported. Some of the slaves made confessions after conviction in the hope of saving their lives; and these, dubious as they were, furnished the chief cor-roborations of detail which the increasingly fluent testimony of Mary Burton received. Some of the confessions, however, were of no avail to those who made them. Quack and Cuffee, for example, terror-stricken at the stake, made somewhat stereotyped revelations; but the desire of the officials to stay the execution with a view to definite reprieve was thwarted by their fear of tumult by the throng of resentful spectators. After a staggering number of sentences had been executed the star witness raised doubts against herself by her endless implications, "for as matters were then likely to turn out there was no guessing where or when there would be an end of impeachments."[49] At length she named as cognizant of the plot several persons "of known credit, fortune and reputations, and of religious principles superior to a suspicion of being concerned in such detestable practices; at which the judges were very much astonished."[50] This farcical extreme at length persuaded even the obsessed magistrates to stop the tragic proceedings.

In New Jersey in 1734 a slave at Raritan when jailed for drunkenness and insolence professed to reveal a plot for insur-

[48] Daniel Horsmanden, one of the magistrates who sat in these trials, published in 1744 the *Journal of the Proceedings in the Detection of the Conspiracy formed by some white people in conjunction with negro and other slaves for burning the city of New York in America, and murdering the Inhabitants;* and this, reprinted under the title, *The New York Conspiracy, or a History of the Negro Plot* (New York, 1810), is the chief source of knowledge in the premises. See also the contemporary letters of Lieutenant-Governor Clarke in E. B. O'Callaghan, ed., *Documents Relative to the Colonial History of New York,* VI, 186, 197, 198, 201-203.
[49] *Ibid.,* pp. 96-100.
[50] *Ibid.,* pp. 370-372.

rection, whereupon he and a fellow slave were capitally convicted. One of them escaped before execution, but the other was hanged.[51] In Pennsylvania as late as 1803 a negro plot at York was detected after i _arly a dozen houses had been burnt and half as many attempts had been made to cause a general conflagration. Many negroes were arrested; others outside made preparations to release them by force; and for several days a reign of terror prevailed. Upon the restoration of quiet, twenty of the prisoners were punished for arson.[52]

In the Southern colonies there were no outbreaks in the seventeenth century and but two discoveries of plots, it seems, both in Virginia. The first of these, 1663, in which indented white servants and negro slaves in Gloucester County were said to be jointly involved, was betrayed by one of the servants. The colonial assembly showed its gratification not only by freeing the informer and giving him five thousand pounds of tobacco but by resolving in commemoration of "so transcendant a favour as the preserving all we have from so utter ruin," "that the 13th. of September be annually kept holy, being the day those villains intended to put the plot in execution." [53] The other plot, of slaves alone, in the "Northern Neck" of the colony in 1687, appears to have been of no more than local concern.[54] The punishments meted out on either occasion are unknown.

The eighteenth century, with its multiplication of slaves, saw somewhat more frequent plots in its early decades. The discovery of one in Isle of Wight County, Virginia, in 1709 brought thirty-nine lashes to each of three slaves and fifty lashes to a free negro found to be cognizant, and presumably more drastic punishments to two other slaves who were held as ringleaders to await the governor's order. Still another slave who at least for the time being escaped the clutches of the law was proclaimed an outlaw.[55] The discovery of another plot in Gloucester and Middlesex Counties of the same colony in 1723 prompted the as-

[51] MS. transcript in the New York Public Library from the New York *Gazette*, Mch. 18, 1734.
[52] E. R. Turner, *The Negro in Pennsylvania*, pp. 152, 153.
[53] Hening, *Virginia Statutes at Large*, II, 204.
[54] J. C. Ballagh, *History of Slavery in Virginia* (Baltimore, 1902), p. 79.
[55] *Calendar of Virginia State Papers*, I, 129, 130.

sembly to provide for the deportation to the West Indies of seven slave participants.[56]

In South Carolina, although depredations by runaways gave acute uneasiness in 1711 and thereabouts, no conspiracy was discovered until 1720 when some of the participants were burnt, some hanged and some banished.[57] Matters were then quiet again until 1739 when on a September Sunday a score of Angola blacks with one Jonny as their leader broke open a store, supplied themselves with arms, and laid their course at once for Florida where they had been told by Spanish emissaries welcome and liberty awaited them. Marching to the beat of drums, slaughtering with ease the whites they came upon, and drawing black recruits to several times their initial number, on the Pon Pon road that day the rebels covered ten prosperous miles. But when at evening they halted to celebrate their exploits with dancing and plundered rum they were set upon by the whites whom couriers had collected. Several were killed in the onslaught, and a few more were captured on the spot. Most of the rest fled back to their cabins, but a squad of ten made their way thirty miles farther on the route to Florida and sold their lives in battle when overtaken. Of those captured on the field or in their quarters some were shot but none were tortured. The toll of lives lost numbered twenty-one whites and forty-four [58] blacks.

Following this and the New York panic of two years later, there was remarkable quiet in race relations in general for a full half century. It was not indeed until the spread of the amazing news from San Domingo and the influx thence of white refugees and their slaves that a new series of disturbances began on the continent. At Norfolk in 1792 some negroes were arrested on suspicion of conspiracy but were promptly discharged for lack

[56] *Journals of the House of Burgesses of Virginia, 1712-1726*, p. 36.
[57] Letter of June 24, 1720, among the MS. transcripts in the state capitol at Columbia of documents in the British Public Record Office.
[58] *Gentleman's Magazine*, X, 127; South Carolina Historical Society *Collections*, II, 270; Alexander Hewatt, *Historical Account of South Carolina and Georgia* (London, 1779), II, 72, 73. Joshua Coffin in his *Account of Some of the Principal Slave Insurrections* (New York, 1860) listed a revolt at Savannah, Ga., in 1728. But Savannah was not founded until 1733, and it contained virtually no negroes prior to 1750.

of evidence;[59] and close by at Portsmouth in the next year there were such savage clashes between the newly come French blacks and those of the Virginia stock that citizens were alarmed for their own safety.[60]   In Louisiana an uprising on the plantation of Julien Poydras in Pointe Coupée Parish in 1796 brought the execution of a dozen or two negroes and sentences to prison of several whites convicted as their accomplices;[61] and as late as 1811 an outbreak in St. Charles and St. James Parishes was traced in part to San Domingo slaves.[62]

Gabriel's rising in the vicinity of Richmond, however, eclipsed all other such events on the continent in this period. Although this affair was of prodigious current interest its details were largely obscured by the secrecy maintained by the court and the legislature in their dealings with it. Reports in the newspapers of the time were copious enough but were vague except as to the capture of the leading participants; and the reminiscent journalism of after years was romantic to the point of absurdity. It is fairly clear, however, that Gabriel and other slaves on Thomas H. Prosser's plantation, which lay several miles distant from Richmond, began to brew the conspiracy as early as June, 1800, and enlisted some hundreds of confederates, perhaps more than a thousand, before September 1, the date fixed for its maturity. Many of these were doubtless residents of Richmond, and some it was said lived as far away as Norfolk. The few muskets procured were supplemented by cutlasses made from scythe blades and by plantation implements of other sorts; but the plan of onslaught contemplated a speedy increase of this armament. From a rendezvous six miles from Richmond eleven hundred men in three columns under designated officers were to march upon the city simultaneously, one to seize the penitentiary which then served also as the state arsenal, another to take the powder

[59] *Calendar of Virginia State Papers*, V, 540, 541, 546.
[60] *Ibid.*, VI, 490, letter of a citizen who had just found four strange negroes hanging from the branches of a tree near his door.
[61] C. C. Robin, *Voyages* (Paris, 1806), II, 244 ff.; E. P. Puckett, "Free Negroes in Louisiana" (MS.).
[62] Puckett, *op. cit.* Le *Moniteur de la Louisiane* (New Orleans), Feb. 11, 1811, has mention of the manumission of a mulatto slave at this time on the ground of his recent valiant defence of his master's house against attacking insurgents.

magazine in another quarter of the town, and the third to begin a general slaughter with such weapons as were already at hand.

Things progressed with very little hitch until the very eve of the day set. But then two things occurred, either of which happening alone would probably have foiled the project. On the one hand a slave on Moseley Sheppard's plantation informed his master of the plot; on the other hand there fell such a deluge of rain that the swelling of the streams kept most of the conspirators from reaching the rendezvous. Meanwhile couriers had roused the city, and the rebels assembled could only disperse. Scores of them were taken, including eventually Gabriel himself who eluded pursuit for several weeks and sailed to Norfolk as a stowaway. The magistrates, of course, had busy sessions, but the number of death sentences was less than might have been expected. Those executed comprised Gabriel and five other Prosser slaves along with nineteen more belonging to other masters; and ten others, in scattered ownership, were deported. To provide for a more general riddance of suspected negroes the legislature made secret overtures to the federal government looking to the creation of a territorial reservation to receive such colonists; but for the time being this came to naught. The legislature furthermore created a permanent guard for the capitol, and it liberated at the state's expense Tom and Pharaoh, slaves of the Sheppard family, as reward for their services in helping to foil the plot.[63]

Set on edge by Gabriel's exploit, citizens far and wide were abnormally alert for some time thereafter; and perhaps the slaves here and there were unusually restive. Whether the one or the other of these conditions was most responsible, revelations and rumors were for several years conspicuously numerous. In 1802 there were capital convictions of fourteen insurgent or conspiring slaves in six scattered counties of Virginia;[64] and panicky reports of uprisings were sent out from Hartford

---

[63] T. W. Higginson, "Gabriel's Defeat," in the *Atlantic Monthly*, X, 337-345, reprinted in the same author's *Travellers and Outlaws* (Boston, 1889), pp. 185-214; J. C. Ballagh, *History of Slavery in Virginia*, p. 92; J. H. Russell, *The Free Negro in Virginia*, p. 65; MS. vouchers in the Virginia State Library recording public payments for convicted slaves.

[64] Vouchers as above.

and Bertie Counties, North Carolina.[65] In July, 1804, the mayor of Savannah received from Augusta "information highly important to the safety, peace and security" of his town, and issued appropriate orders to the local militia.[66] Among rumors flying about South Carolina in this period, one on a December day in 1805 telling of risings above and below Columbia led to the planting of cannon before the state house there and to the instruction of the night patrols to seize every negro found at large. An over-zealous patrolman thereupon shot a slave who was peacefully following his own master, and was indicted next day for murder. The peaceful passing of the night brought a subsidence of the panic with the coming of day.[67]

In Virginia, again, there were disturbing rumors at one place or another every year or two from 1809 to 1814,[68] but no occurrence of tangible character until the Boxley plot of 1816 in Spottsylvania and Louisa Counties. George Boxley, the white proprietor of a country store, was a visionary somewhat of John Brown's type. Participating in the religious gatherings of the negroes and telling them that a little white bird had brought him a holy message to deliver his fellowmen from bondage, he enlisted many blacks in his project for insurrection. But before the plot was ripe it was betrayed by a slave woman, and several negroes were arrested. Boxley thereupon marched with a dozen followers on a Quixotic errand of release, but on the road the blacks fell away, and he, after some time in hiding, surrendered himself. Six of the negroes after conviction were hanged and a like number transported; but Boxley himself broke jail and escaped.[69]

In the lower South a plot at Camden, South Carolina, in

[65] Augusta, Ga., *Chronicle*, June 26, 1802.
[66] Thomas Gamble, Jr., *History of the City Government of Savannah* [Savannah, 1900], p. 68.
[67] "Diary of Edward Hooker," in the American Historical Association *Report* for 1896, pp. 881, 882.
[68] *Calendar of Virginia State Papers*, X, 62, 63, 97, 368.
[69] *Ibid.*, X, 433-436; *Louisiana Gazette* (New Orleans), Apr. 18 and 24 (Reprinting a report from the *Virginia Herald* of Mch. 9), and July 12, 1816; MS. Vouchers in the Virginia State Library recording public payments for convicted slaves.

1816 [70] and another at Augusta, Georgia,[71] three years afterward had like plans of setting houses afire at night and then attacking other quarters of the respective towns when the white men had left their homes defenceless. Both plots were betrayed, and several participants in each were executed. These conspiracies were eclipsed in turn by the elaborate Vesey plot at Charleston in 1822, which, for the variety of the negro types involved, the methods of persuasion used by the leading spirits and the sobriety of the whites on the occasion is one of the most notable of such episodes on record.

Denmark Vesey, brought from Africa in his youth, had bought his freedom with part of a $1500 prize drawn by him in a lottery, and was in this period an independent artisan. Harboring a deep resentment against the whites, however, he began to plan his plot some four years before its maturity. He familiarized himself with the Bible account of the deliverance of the children of Israel, and collected pamphlet and newspaper material on anti-slavery sentiment in England and the North and on occurrences in San Domingo, with all of which on fit occasions he regaled the blacks with whom he came into touch. Arguments based on such data brought concurrence of negroes of the more intelligent sort, prominent among whom were certain functionaries of the African Church who were already nursing grievances on the score of the suppression of their ecclesiastical project by the Charleston authorities.[72] The chief minister of that church, Morris Brown, however, was carefully left out of the conspiracy. In appealing to the more ignorant and superstitious element, on the other hand, the services of Gullah Jack, so called because of his Angola origin, were enlisted, for as a recognized conjuror he could bewitch the recalcitrant and bestow charmed crabs' claws upon those joining the plot to make

---

[70] [Edwin C. Holland], *A Refutation of the Calumnies circulated against the Southern and Western States, with historical notes of insurrections* (Charleston, 1822), pp. 75-77; H. T. Cook, *Life and Legacy of David R. Williams*, p. 131; H. M. Henry, *Police Control of the Slave in South Carolina*, pp. 151, 152.
[71] News item from Augusta in the *Louisiana Courier* (New Orleans), June 15, 1819.
[72] See above, p. 421.

them invulnerable. In the spring of 1822 things were put in train for the outbreak. The Angolas, the Eboes and the Carolina-born were separately organized under appropriate commanders; arrangements were made looking to the support of the plantation slaves within marching distance of the city; and letters were even sent by the negro cook on a vessel bound for San Domingo with view apparently both to getting assistance from that island and to securing a haven there in case the revolt should prove only successful enough to permit the seizure of the ships in Charleston harbor. Meanwhile the coachmen and draymen in the plot were told off to mobilize the horses in their charge, pikes were manufactured, the hardware stores and other shops containing arms were listed for special attention, and plans were laid for the capture of the city's two arsenals as the first stroke in the revolt. This was scheduled for midnight on Sunday, June 16.

On May 30 George, the body-servant of Mr. Wilson, told his master that Mr. Paul's William had invited him to join a society which was to make a stroke for freedom. William upon being seized and questioned by the city council made something of a confession incriminating two other slaves, Mingo Harth and Peter Poyas; but these were so staunch in their denials that they were discharged, with confidential slaves appointed to watch them. William was held for a week of solitary confinement, at the end of which he revealed the extensive character of the plot and the date set for its maturity. The city guard was thereupon strengthened; but the lapse of several days in quiet was about to make the authorities incredulous, when another citizen brought them word from another slave of information precisely like that which had first set them on the *qui vive*. This caused the local militia to be called out to stiffen the patrol. Then as soon as the appointed Sunday night had passed, which brought no outbreak, the city council created a special court as by law provided, comprising two magistrates together with five citizens carefully selected for their substantial character and distinguished position. These were William Drayton, Nathaniel Heyward, James R. Pringle, James Legaré and Robert J. Turnbull. More saga-

cious and responsible men could certainly not have been found.
A committee of vigilance was also appointed to assist the court.
This court having first made its own rules that no negro was
to be tried except in the presence of his master or attorney, that
everyone on trial should be heard in his own defense, and that
no one should be capitally sentenced on the bare testimony of a
single witness, proceeded to the trial of Peter Poyas, Denmark
Vesey and others against whom charges had then been lodged.
By eavesdropping those who were now convicted and confront-
ing them with their own words, confessions were procured implicating many others who in turn were put on trial, including
Gullah Jack whose necromancy could not save him.   In all 130
negroes were arrested, including nine colored freemen. Of the
whole number, twenty-five were discharged by the committee of
vigilance and 27 others by the court. Nine more were acquitted
with recommendations with which their masters readily complied, that they be transported. Of those convicted, 34 were deported by public authority and 35 were hanged. In addition
four white men indicted for complicity, comprising a German
peddler, a Scotchman, a Spaniard and a Charlestonian,[73] were
tried by a regular court having jurisdiction óver whites and sentenced to prison terms ranging from three to twelve months.
    A number of Charleston citizens promptly memorialized the
state assembly recommending that all free negroes be expelled,
that the penalties applicable to whites conspiring with negroes
be made more severe, and that the control over the blacks be
generally stiffened.[74]   The legislature complied except as to the
proposal for expulsion. Charlestonians also organized an association for the prevention of negro disturbances; but by 1825

[73] *An Account of the late intended Insurrection among a portion of the
Blacks of this City. Published by the Authority of the Corporation of
Charleston* (Charleston, 1822); Lionel H. Kennedy and Thomas Parker
(the presiding magistrates of the special court), *An Official Report of
the Trials of sundry Negroes charged with an attempt to raise an insurrection, with a report of the trials of four white persons on indictments for
attempting to excite the slaves to insurrection* (Charleston, 1822); T. D.
Jervey, *Robert Y. Hayne and His Times* (New York, 1909), pp. 130-136.
    [74] *Memorial of the Citizens of Charleston to the Senate and House of
Representatives of the State of South Carolina* (Charleston, 1822), reprinted in *Plantation and Frontier*, II, 103-116.

the public seems to have begun to lose its ardor in the premises.[75]

The next salient occurrence in the series was the outbreak which brought fame to Nat Turner and the devoted Virginia county of Southampton. Nat, a slave who by the custom of the country had acquired the surname of his first master, was the foreman of a small plantation, a Baptist exhorter capable of reading the Bible, and a pronounced mystic. For some years, as he told afterward when in custody, he had heard voices from the heavens commanding him to carry on the work of Christ to make the last to be first and the first last; and he took the sun's eclipse in February, 1831, as a sign that the time was come. He then enlisted a few of his fellows in his project, but proceeded to spend his leisure for several months in prayer and brooding instead of in mundane preparation. When at length on Sunday night, August 21, he began his revolt he had but a petty squad of companions, with merely a hatchet and a broad-axe as weapons, and no definite plan of campaign. First murdering his master's household and seizing some additional equipment, he took the road and repeated the process at whatever farmhouses he came upon. Several more negroes joined the squad as it proceeded, though in at least one instance a slave resisted them in defense of his master's family at the cost of his own life. The absence of many whites from the neighborhood by reason of their attendance at a camp-meeting across the nearby North Carolina line reduced the number of victims, and on the other hand made the rally of the citizens less expeditious and formidable when the alarm had been spread. By sunrise the rebels numbered fifteen, part of whom were mounted, and their outfit comprised a few firearms. Throughout the morning they continued their somewhat aimless roving, slaughtering such white households as they reached, enlisting recruits by persuasion or coercion, and heightening their courage by draughts upon the apple-brandy in which the county, by virtue of its many orchards and stills, abounded. By noon there were some sixty in the straggling ranks, but when shortly afterward they met a

[75] Address of the association, in the Charleston *City Gazette*, Aug. 5, 1825.

squad of eighteen rallying whites, armed like themselves mainly
with fowling pieces with birdshot ammunition, they fled at the
first fire, and all but a score dispersed. The courage of these
whites, however, was so outweighed by their caution that Nat
and his fellows were able to continue their marauding course in
a new direction, gradually swelling their numbers to forty again.
That night, however, a false alarm stampeded their bivouac and
again dispersed all the faint-hearted. Nat with his remaining
squad then attacked a homestead just before daybreak on Tuesday, but upon repulse by the five white men and boys with several slave auxiliaries who were guarding it they retreated only to
meet a militia force which completed the dispersal. All were
promptly killed or taken except Nat who secreted himself near
his late master's home until his capture was accomplished six
weeks afterward. The whites slain by the rebels numbered ten
men, fourteen women and thirty-one children.

The militia in scouring the countryside were prompted by the
panic and its vindictive reaction to shoot down a certain number
of innocent blacks along with the guilty and to make display of
some of their severed heads. The magistrates were less impulsive. They promptly organized a court comprising all the justices of the peace in the county and assigned attorneys for the
defense of the prisoners while the public prosecutor performed
his appointed task. Forty-seven negroes all told were brought before the court. As to the five free blacks included in this number the magistrates, who had only preliminary jurisdiction in
their cases, discharged one and remanded four for trial by a
higher court. Of the slaves four, and perhaps a fifth regarding
whom the record is blank, were discharged without trial, and
thirteen more were acquitted. Of those convicted seven were
sentenced to deportation, and seventeen with the ringleader among
them, to death by hanging. In addition there were several slaves
convicted of complicity in neighboring counties.[76]

[76] W. S. Drewry, *Slave Insurrections in Virginia, 1830-1865* (Washington, 1900), recounts this revolt in great detail, and gives a bibliography.
The vouchers in the Virginia archives record only eleven executions and
four deportations of Southampton slaves in this period. It may be that
the rest of those convicted were pardoned.

This extraordinary event, occurring as it did after a century's lapse since last an appreciable number of whites on the continent had lost their lives in such an outbreak, set nerves on edge throughout the South, and promptly brought an unusually bountiful crop of local rumors. In North Carolina early in September it was reported at Raleigh that the blacks of Wilmington had burnt the town and slaughtered the whites, and that several thousand of them were marching upon Raleigh itself.[77] This and similarly alarming rumors from Edenton were followed at once by authentic news telling merely that conspiracies had been discovered in Duplin and Sampson Counties and also in the neighborhood of Edenton, with several convictions resulting in each locality.[78]

At Milledgeville, the village capital of Georgia where in the preceding year the newspapers and the town authorities had been fluttered by the discovery of incendiary pamphlets in a citizen's possession,[79] a rumor spread on October 4, 1831, that a large number of slaves had risen a dozen miles away and were marching upon the town to seize the weapons in the state arsenal there. Three slaves within the town, and a free mulatto preacher as well, were seized on suspicion of conspiracy but were promptly discharged for lack of evidence, and the city council soon had occasion, because there had been "considerable danger in the late excitement . . . by persons carrying arms that were intoxicated" to order the marshal and patrols to take weapons away from irresponsible persons and enforce the ordinance against the firing of guns in the streets.[80] Upon the first coming of the alarm the governor had appointed Captain J. A. Cuthbert, editor of the *Federal Union,* to the military command of the town; and Cuthbert, uniformed and armed to the teeth, dashed about the town all day on his charger, distributing weap-

[77] News item dated Warrenton, N. C., Sept. 15, 1831, in the New Orleans *Mercantile Advertiser,* Oct. 4, 1831.
[78] *Federal Union* (Milledgeville, Ga.), Oct. 6, 1831, citing the Fayetteville, N. C. *Observer* of Sept. 14; *Niles' Register,* XLI, 266.
[79] *Federal Union,* Aug. 7, 1830; American Historical Association *Report* for 1904, I, 469.
[80] American Historical Association *Report* for 1904, pp. 469, 470.

ons and stationing guards. Upon the passing of the baseless panic Seaton Grantland, customarily cool and sardonic, ridiculed Cuthbert in the *Southern Recorder* of which he was editor. Cuthbert retorted in his own columns that Grantland's conduct in the emergency had proved him a skulking coward.[81] No blood was shed, even among the editors.

There were doubtless episodes of such a sort in many other localities.[82] It was evidently to this period that the reminiscences afterward collected by Olmsted applied. " 'Where I used to live,' " a backwoodsman formerly of Alabama told the traveller, " 'I remember when I was a boy—must ha' been about twenty years ago—folks was dreadful frightened about the niggers. I remember they built pens in the woods where they could hide, and Christmas time they went and got into the pens, 'fraid the niggers was risin'.' 'I remember the same time where we were in South Carolina,' said his wife, 'we had all our things put up in bags, so we could tote 'em if we heerd they was comin' our way.' "[83]

Another sort of sequel to the Southampton revolt was of course a plenitude of public discussion and of repressive legislation. In Virginia a flood of memorials poured upon the legislature. Petitions signed by 1,188 citizens in twelve counties asked for provision for the expulsion of colored freemen; others with 398 signatures from six counties proposed an amendment to the United States Constitution empowering Congress to aid Virginia to rid herself of all the blacks; others from two colonization societies and 366 citizens in four counties proposed the removal first of the free negroes and then of slaves to be emancipated by private or public procedure; 27 men of Buckingham and Loudon Counties and others in Albemarle, together with the Society of Friends in Hanover and 347 women, prayed for the abolition of slavery, some on the *post nati* plan and others

[81] *Federal Union*, Oct. 6 and 13 and Dec. 1, 1831.
[82] The discovery of a plot at Shelbyville, Tennessee, was reported at the end of 1832. *Niles' Register*, XLI, 340.
[83] F. L. Olmsted, *A Journey in the Back Country* (New York, 1863), p. 203.

without specification of details.[84] The House of Delegates responded by devoting most of its session of that winter to an extraordinarily outspoken and wide-ranging debate on the many phases of the negro problem, reflecting and elaborating all the sentiments expressed in the petitions together with others more or less original with the members themselves. The Richmond press reported the debate in great detail, and many of the speeches were given a pamphlet circulation in addition.[85] The only tangible outcome there and elsewhere, however, was in the form of added legal restrictions upon the colored population, slave and free. But when the fright and fervor of the year had passed, conditions normal to the community returned. On the one hand the warnings of wiseacres impressed upon the would-be problem solvers the maxim of the golden quality of silence, particularly while the attacks of the Northern abolitionists upon the general Southern régime were so active. On the other hand the new severities of the law were promptly relegated, as the old ones had been, to the limbo of things laid away, like pistols, for emergency use, out of sight and out of mind in the daily routine of peaceful industry.

In the remaining ante-bellum decades, though the actual outbreaks were negligible except for John Brown's raid, the discoveries, true or false, and the rumors, mostly unwarranted, were somewhat more frequent than before. Revelations in Madison County, Mississippi, in 1835 shortly before July 4, told of a conspiracy of whites and blacks scheduled for that day as a ramification of the general plot of the Murrell gang recently exposed.[86] A mass meeting thereupon appointed an investigating committee of thirteen citizens with power to apply capital pun-

[84] *The Letter of Appomattox to the People of Virginia: Exhibiting a connected view of the recent proceedings in the House of Delegates on the subject of the abolition of slavery and a succinct account of the doctrines broached by the friends of abolition in debate, and the mischievous tendency of those proceedings and doctrines* (Richmond, 1832). These letters were first published in the Richmond *Enquirer*, February 4, 1832 et seqq.
[85] The debate is summarized in Henry Wilson, *History of the Rise and Fall of the Slave Power in America* (Boston, 1872), I, 190-207.
[86] See above, pp. 381, 382.

ishment; and several whites together with ten or fifteen blacks were promptly put to death.[87]

Widespread rumors at the beginning of the following December that a general uprising was in preparation for the coming holiday season caused the summons of citizens in various Georgia counties to mass meetings which with one accord recommended special precautions by masters, patrols and militia, and appointed committees of vigilance. In this series the resolutions adopted in Washington County are notable especially for the tone of their preamble. Mentioning the method recently followed in Mississippi only to disapprove it, this preamble ran: "We would fain hope that the soil of Georgia may never be reddened or her people disgraced by the arbitrary shedding of human blood; for if the people allow themselves but one participation in such lawless proceedings, no human sagacity can foretell where the overwhelming deluge will be staid or what portions of our state may feel its desolating ruin. This course of protection unhinges every tie of social and civil society, dissolves those guards which the laws throw around property and life, and leaves every individual, no matter how innocent, at the sport of popular passion, the probable object of popular indignation, and liable to an ignominious death. Therefore we would recommend to our fellow-citizens that if any facts should be elicited implicating either white men or negroes in any insurrectionary or abolition movements, that they be apprehended and delivered over to the legal tribunals of the country for full and fair judicial trial." [88] At Clarksville, Tennessee, uneasiness among the citizens on the score of the negroes employed in the iron works thereabout was such that they procured a shipment of arms from

[87] *The Liberator* (Boston, Mass.), Aug. 8, 1835, quoting the Clinton, Miss., *Gazette* of July 11.
[88] *Federal Union* (Milledgeville, Ga.), Dec. 11, 1835. At Darien on the Georgia coast Edwin C. Roberts, an Englishman by birth, was committed for trial in the following August for having told slaves they ought to be free and that half of the American people were in favor of their freedom. The local editor remarked when reporting the occurrence: "Mr. Roberts should thank his stars that he did not commence his crusade in some quarters where Judge Lynch presides. Here the majesty of the law is too highly respected to tolerate the jurisdiction of this despotic dignitary." Darien *Telegraph*, Aug. 30, quoted in the *Federal Union*, Sept. 6, 1836.

the state capital in preparation for special guard at the Christmas season.[89]

In various parts of Louisiana in this period there was a succession of plots discovered. The first of these, betrayed on Christmas Eve, 1835, involved two white men, one of them a plantation overseer, along with forty slaves or more. The whites were promptly hanged, and doubtless some of the blacks likewise.[90] The next, exposed in the fall of 1837, was in the neighborhood of Alexandria. Nine slaves and three free negroes were hanged in punishment,[91] and the negro Lewis who had betrayed the conspiracy was liberated at state expense and was voted $500 to provide for his security in some distant community.[92] The third was in Lafayette and St. Landry Parishes, betrayed in August, 1840, by a slave woman named Lecide who was freed by her master in reward. Nine negroes were hanged. Four white men who were implicated, but who could not be convicted under the laws which debarred slave testimony against whites, were severely flogged under a lynch-law sentence and ordered to leave the state.[93] Rumors of other plots were spread in West Feliciana Parish in the summer of 1841,[94] in several parishes opposite and above Natchez in the fall of 1842,[95] and at Donaldsonville at the beginning of 1843;[96] but each of these in turn was found to be virtually baseless. Meanwhile at Augusta, Georgia, several negroes were arrested in February, 1841, and at least one of them was sentenced to death. A petition was circulated for his respite as an inducement for confession; but other citizens, disquieted by the testimony already given, prepared a counter petition asking the governor to let the law take its course. The plot as described contemplated the seizure of

[89] MS. petition with endorsement noting the despatch of arms, in the state archives at Nashville.
[90] *Niles' Register*, XLIX, 331.
[91] *Ibid.*, LIII, 129.
[92] Louisiana, *Acts* of 1838, p. 118.
[93] *Niles' Register*, LXIX, 39, 88; E. P. Puckett, "Free Negroes in Louisiana" (MS.).
[94] New Orleans *Bee*, July 23, 29 and 31, 1841.
[95] *Niles' Register*, LXIII, 212.
[96] *Louisiana Courier* (New Orleans), Jan. 27 and Feb. 17, 1843.

the arsenal and the firing of the city in facilitation of massacre.[97]

The rest of the 'forties and the first half of the 'fifties were a period of comparative quiet; but in 1855 there were rumors in Dorchester and Talbot Counties, Maryland,[98] and the autumn of 1856 brought widespread disturbances which the Southern whites did not fail to associate with the rise of the Republican Party. In the latter part of that year there were rumors afloat from Williamsburg, Virginia, and Montgomery County in the same state, from various quarters of Tennessee, Arkansas and Texas, from New Orleans, and from Atlanta and Cassville, Georgia.[99] A typical episode in the period was described by a schoolmaster from Michigan then sojourning in Mississippi. One night about Christmas of 1858 when the plantation homestead at which he was staying was filled with house guests, a courier came in the dead of night bringing news that the blacks in the eastern part of the county had risen in a furious band and were laying their murderous course in this direction. The head of the house after scanning the bulletin, calmly told his family and guests that they might get their guns and prepare for defense, but if they would excuse him he would retire again until the crisis came. The coolness of the host sent the guests back to bed except for one who stood sentry. "The negroes never came." [100]

The shiver which John Brown's raid sent over the South was diminished by the failure of the blacks to join him, and it was largely overcome by the wave of fierce resentment against the abolitionists who, it was said, had at last shown their true colors. The final disturbance on the score of conspiracy among the negroes themselves was in the summer of 1860 at Dallas, Texas, where in the preceding year an abolitionist preacher had

[97] Letter of Mrs. S. A. Lamar, Augusta, Ga., Feb. 25, 1841, to John B. Lamar at Macon. MS. in the possession of Mrs. A. S. Erwin, Athens, Ga.
[98] J. R. Brackett, *The Negro in Maryland*, p. 97.
[99] *Southern Watchman* (Athens, Ga.), Dec. 18 and 25, 1856. Some details of the Texas disturbance, which brought death to several negroes, is given in documents printed in F. L. Olmsted, *Journey through Texas*, pp. 503. 504.
[100] A. DePuy Van Buren, *Jottings of a Sojourn in the South* (Battle Creek, Mich., 1859), pp. 121, 122.

been whipped and driven away. Ten or more fires which occurred in one day and laid much of the town in ruins prompted the seizure of many blacks and the raising of a committee of safety. This committee reported to a public meeting on July 24 that three ringleaders in the plot were to be hanged that afternoon. Thereupon Judge Buford of the district court addressed the gathering. "He stated in the outset that in any ordinary case he would be as far from counselling mob law as any other man, but in the present instance the people had a clear right to take the law in their own hands. He counselled moderation, and insisted that the committee should execute the fewest number compatible with the public safety." [101]

On the whole it is hardly possible to gauge precisely the degree of popular apprehension in the premises. John Randolph was doubtless more picturesque than accurate when he said, "the night bell never tolls for fire in Richmond that the mother does not hug the infant more closely to her bosom." [102] The general trend of public expressions laid emphasis upon the need of safeguards but showed confidence that no great disasters were to be feared. The revolts which occurred and the plots which were discovered were sufficiently serious to produce a very palpable disquiet from time to time, and the rumors were frequent enough to maintain a fairly constant undertone of uneasiness. The net effect of this was to restrain that progress of liberalism which the consideration of economic interest, the doctrines of human rights and the spirit of kindliness all tended to promote.

[101] *Federal Union* (Milledgeville, Ga.), Aug. 21, 1860, quoting the Nashville *Union.*
[102] H. A. Garland, *Life of John Randolph,* I, 295.

CHAPTER XXIII

THE FORCE OF THE LAW

IN many lawyers' briefs and court decisions it has been said that slavery could exist only by force of positive legislation.[1] This is not historically valid, for in virtually every American community where it existed at all, the institution was first established by custom alone and was merely recognized by statutes when these came to be enacted. Indeed the chief purpose of the laws was to give sanction and assurance to the racial and industrial adjustments already operative.

As a rule each slaveholding colony or state adopted early in its career a series of laws of limited scope to meet definite issues as they were successively encountered. Then when accumulated experience had shown a community that it had a general prob-

[1] The source of this error lies doubtless in Lord Mansfield's famous but fallacious decision of 1772 in the Somerset case, which is recorded in Howell's *State Trials*, XX, § 548. That decision is well criticized in T. R. R. Cobb, *An Inquiry into the Law of Negro Slavery in the United States of America* (vol. I, all published, Philadelphia and Savannah, 1858), pp. 163-175.

Cobb's treatise, though dealing with slaves as persons only and not as property, is the best of the general analyses of the legal phase of the slaveholding régime. A briefer survey is in the *Cyclopedia of Law and Procedure*, William Mack ed., XXXVI (New York, 1910), 465-495. The works of G. M. Stroud, *A Sketch of the Laws Relating to Slavery in the Several States* (Philadelphia, 1827), and William Goodell, *The American Slave Code in Theory and Practice* (New York, 1853), are somewhat vitiated by the animus of their authors.

The many statutes concerning slavery enacted in the several colonies, territories and states are listed and many of them summarized in J. C. Hurd, *The Law of Freedom and Bondage in the United States* (Boston, 1858), I, 228-311; II, 1-218. Some hundreds of court decisions in the premises are given in J. D. Wheeler, *A Practical Treatise on the Law of Slavery* (New York and New Orleans, 1837); and all the thousands of decisions of published record are briefly digested in *The Century Edition of the American Digest*, XLIV (St. Paul, 1903), 853-1152.

The development of the slave code in Virginia is traced in J. C. Ballagh, *A History of Slavery in Virginia* (Baltimore, 1902), supplemented by J. H. Russell, *The Free Negro in Virginia* (Baltimore, 1913); and the legal régime of slavery in South Carolina at the middle of the nineteenth century is described by Judge J. B. O'Neall in *The Industrial Resources of the Southern and Western States*, J. B. D. DeBow ed., II (New Orleans, 1853), 269-292.

lem of regulation on its hands its legislature commonly passed an act of many clauses to define the status of slaves, to provide the machinery of their police, and to prescribe legal procedure in cases concerning them whether as property or as persons. Thereafter the recourse was again to specific enactments from time to time to supplement this general or basic statute as the rise of new circumstances or policies gave occasion. The likeness of conditions in the several communities and the difficulty of devising laws to comply with intricate custom and at the same time to guard against apprehended ills led to much intercolonial and interstate borrowing of statutes. A perfect chain of this sort, with each link a basic police law for slaves in a separate colony or state, extended from Barbados through the southeastern trio of commonwealths on the continent. The island of Barbados, as we have seen, was the earliest of the permanent English settlements in the tropics and one of the first anywhere to attain a definite régime of plantations with negro labor. This made its assembly perforce a pioneer in slave legislation. After a dozen minor laws had been enacted, beginning in 1644, for the control of negroes along with white servants and for the recapture of runaways, the culmination in a general statute came in 1688. Its occasion, as recited in the preamble, was the dependence of plantation industry upon great numbers of negro slaves whose "barbarous, wild and savage nature . . . renders them wholly unqualified to be governed by the laws, customs and practices of our nation," and the "absolutely necessary consequence that such other constitutions, laws and orders should be in this island framed and enacted for the good regulating and ordering of them as may . . . restrain the disorders, rapines and inhumanities to which they are naturally prone and inclined, with such encouragements and allowances as are fit and needful for their support, that . . . this island through the blessing of God thereon may be preserved, His Majesty's subjects in their lives and fortunes secured, and the negroes and other slaves be well provided for and guarded against the cruelties and insolences of themselves or other ill-tempered people or owners."

The statute itself met the purposes of the preamble unevenly.

The slaves were assured merely in annual suits of clothing, and the masters were given claim for pecuniary compensation for slaves inveigled away or illegally killed by other freemen; but the main concern of the statute was with routine control and the punishment of slave malfeasances. No slaves were to leave their masters' premises at any time unless in company with whites or when wearing servants' livery or carrying written passes, and offenders in this might be whipped and taken into custody by any white persons encountering them. No slaves were to blow horns or beat drums; and masters were to have their negro houses searched at frequent intervals for such instruments, as well as for weapons, runaway slaves and stolen goods. Runaways when caught were to be impounded, advertised and restored to their masters upon payment of captors' and custodians' fees. Trading with slaves was restricted for fear of encouraging theft. A negro striking a white person, except in lawful defense of his master's person, family or goods, was criminally punishable, though merely with lashes for a first offense; and thefts to the value of more than a shilling, along with all other serious infractions, were capital crimes. Negro transgressors were to be tried summarily by courts comprising two justices of the peace and three freeholders nearest the crime and were to be punished immediately upon conviction. To dissuade masters from concealing the crimes of their negroes the magistrates were to appraise each capitally convicted slave, within a limit of £25, and to estimate also the damage to the person or property injured by the commission of the crime. The colonial treasurer was then to take the amount of the slave's appraisal from the public funds and after making reimbursement for the injury done, pay the overplus, if any, to the criminal's owner. If it appeared to the magistrates, however, that the crime had been prompted by the master's neglect and the slave's consequent necessity for sustenance, the treasurer was to pay the master nothing. A master killing his own slave wantonly was to be fined £15, and any other person killing a slave illegally was to pay the master double the slave's value, to be fined £25, and to give bond for subsequent good behavior. If a slave were killed by accident the slayer was liable only to suit by the owner. The destruction of a slave's life or limb in the course of punishment by his master constituted no legal offense, nor did the killing of one by any person, when found stealing or attempting a theft by night. Ascertained hiding places of runaway slaves were to be raided by constables and posses, and these were to be rewarded for taking the runaways alive or dead.[2] This act was thenceforward the basic law in the premises as long as slavery survived in the island.

South Carolina, in a sense the daughter of Barbados and in frequent communication with her, had enacted a series of specific laws of her own devising, when the growth of her slave population prompted the adoption of a general statute for negro police. Thereupon in 1712 her assembly copied virtually verbatim the preamble and some of the ensuing clauses of the Barbadian act of 1688, and added further provisions drawn from other sources or devised for the occasion. This served as her basic law until the shock of the Stono revolt in 1739 prompted the legislature to give the statute a greater elaboration in the following year. The new clauses, aside from one limiting the work which might be required by masters to fourteen and fifteen hours per day in winter and summer respectively, and another forbidding all but servants in livery to wear any but coarse clothing, were concerned with the restraint of slaves, mainly with a view to the prevention of revolt. No slaves were to be sold liquors without their masters' approval; none were to be taught to write; no more than seven men in a group were to travel on the high roads unless in company with white persons; no houses or lands were to be rented to slaves, and no slaves were to be kept on any plantation where no white person was resident.[3]

This act, supplemented by curfew and patrol laws and variously amended in after years, as by the enhancement of penalties for negroes convicted of striking white persons and by the requirement that masters provide adequate food as well as cloth-

[2] Richard Hall ed., *Acts Passed in the Island of Barbados from 1643 to 1762 inclusive* (London, 1764), pp. 112-121.
[3] Cooper and McCord, *Statutes at Large of South Carolina*, VII, 408 ff.

ing, was never repealed so long as slavery continued to exist in South Carolina. Though its sumptuary clauses, along with various others, were from first to last of no effect, the statute as a whole so commended itself to the thought of slaveholding communities that in 1770 Georgia made it the groundwork of her own slave police; Florida in turn, by acts of 1822 and 1828, adopted the substance of the Georgia law as revised to that period; and in lesser degree still other states gave evidence of the same influence. Complementary legislation in all these jurisdictions meanwhile recognized slaves as property, usually of chattel character and with children always following the mother's condition, debarred negro testimony in court in all cases where white persons were involved, and declared the juridical incapacity of slaves in general except when they were suing for freedom. Contemporaneously and by similar methods, a parallel chain of laws, largely analogous to those here noted, was extended from Virginia, herself a pioneer in slave legislation, to Maryland, Delaware and North Carolina and in a fan-spread to the west as far as Missouri and Texas.[4]

Louisiana alone in all the Union, because of her origin and formative experience as a Latin colony, had a scheme of law largely peculiar to herself. The foundation of this lay in the *Code Noir* decreed by Louis XV for that colony in 1724. In it slaves were declared to be chattels, but those of working age were not to be sold in execution of debt apart from the lands on which they worked, and neither husbands and wives nor mothers and young children were to be sold into separate ownership under any circumstances. All slaves, furthermore, were to be baptized into the Catholic church, and were to be exempt from field work on Sundays and holidays; and their marriages were to be legally recognized. Children, of course, were to follow the status and ownership of their mothers. All slaves were to be adequately clothed and fed, under penalty of confiscation, and the superannuated were to be maintained on the same basis as the able-bodied. Slaves might make business contracts under their

[4] The beginning of Virginia's pioneer slave code has been sketched in chapter IV above; and the slave legislation of the Northern colonies and states in chapters VI and VII.

masters' approval, but could not sue or be sued or give evidence against whites, except in cases of necessity and where the white testimony was in default. They might acquire property legally recognized as their own when their masters expressly permitted them to work or trade on their personal accounts, though not otherwise. Manumission was restricted only by the requirement of court approval; and slaves employed by their masters in tutorial capacity were declared *ipso facto* free. In police regards, the travel and assemblage of slaves were restrained, and no one was allowed to trade with them without their masters' leave; slaves were forbidden to have weapons except when commissioned by their masters to hunt; fugitives were made liable to severe punishments, and free negroes likewise for harboring them. Negroes whether slave or free, however, were to be tried by the same courts and by the same procedure as white persons; and though masters were authorized to apply shackles and lashes for disciplinary purpose, the killing of slaves by them was declared criminal even to the degree of murder.[5]

Nearly all the provisions of this relatively liberal code were adopted afresh when Louisiana became a territory and then a state of the Union. In assimilation to Anglo-American practice, however, such recognition as had been given to slave *peculium* was now withdrawn, though on the other hand slaves were granted by implication a legal power to enter contracts for self-purchase. Slave marriages, furthermore, were declared void of all civil effect; and jurisdiction over slave crimes was transferred to courts of inferior grade and informal procedure. By way of reciprocation the state of Alabama when framing a new slave code in 1852 borrowed in a weakened form the Louisiana prohibition of the separate sale of mothers and their children below ten years of age. This provision met the praise of citizens elsewhere when mention of it chanced to be published; but no other commonwealth appears to have adopted it.[6]

[5] This decree is printed in *Le Code Noir* (Paris, 1742), pp. 318-358, and in the Louisiana Historical Society *Collections*, IV, 75-90. The prior decree of 1685 establishing a slave code for the French West Indies, upon which this for Louisiana was modeled, may be consulted in L. Peytraud, *L'Esclavage aux Antilles Françaises* (Paris, 1897), pp. 158-166.
[6] *E. g.*, Atlanta *Intelligencer*, Feb. 27, 1856.

The severity of the slave laws in the commonwealths of English origin, as compared with the mildness of the Louisiana code, was largely due to the historic possession by their citizens of the power of local self-government. A distant autocrat might calmly decree such regulations as his ministers deemed proper, undisturbed by the wishes and apprehensions of the colonial whites; but assemblymen locally elected and responsive to the fears as well as the hopes of their constituents necessarily reflected more fully the desire of social control, and preferred to err on the side of safety. If this should involve severity of legislative repression for the blacks, that might be thought regrettable and yet be done without a moment's qualm. On the eve of the American Revolution a West Indian writer explained the régime. "Self preservation," said he, "that first and ruling principle of human nature, alarming our fears, has made us jealous and perhaps severe in our *threats* against delinquents. Besides, if we attend to the nistory of our penal laws relating to slaves, I believe we shall generally find that they took their rise from some very atrocious attempts made by the negroes on the property of their masters or after some insurrection or commotion which struck at the very being of the colonies. Under these circumstances it may very justly be supposed that our legislatures when convened were a good deal inflamed, and might be induced for the preservation of their persons and properties to pass severe laws which they might hold over their heads to terrify and restrain them." [7] In the next generation an American citizen wrote in similar strain and with like truthfulness: "The laws of the slaveholding states do not furnish a criterion for the character of their present white population or the condition of the slaves. Those laws were enacted for the most part in seasons of particular alarm produced by attempts at insurrection, or when the black inhabitants were doubly formidable by reason of the greater proportion which they bore to the whites in number and the savage state and unhappy mood in which they arrived from Africa. The real measure of danger was not un-

[7] *Slavery Not Forbidden by Scripture, or a Defence of the West India Planters.* By a West Indian (Philadelphia, 1773), p. 18, note.

derstood but after long experience, and in the interval the precautions taken were naturally of the most jealous and rigorous aspect. That these have not all been repealed, or that some of them should be still enforced, is not inconsistent with an improved spirit of legislation, since the evils against which they were intended to guard are yet the subject of just apprehension." [8]

Wherever colonial statutes were silent the laws of the mother country filled the gap. It was under the common law of England, for example, that the slaves Mark and Phillis were tried in Massachusetts in 1755 for the poisoning of their master, duly convicted of petit treason, and executed—the woman as the principal in the crime by being burned at the stake, the man as an accessory by being hanged and his body thereafter left for years hanging in chains on Charlestown common.[9] The severity of Anglo-American legislation in the seventeenth and eighteenth centuries, furthermore, was in full accord with the tone of contemporary English criminal law. It is not clear, however, that the great mitigation which benefit of clergy gave in English criminal administration [10] was commensurately applied in the colonies when slave crimes were concerned. Even in England, indeed, servants were debarred in various regards, that of petit treason, for example, from this avenue of relief. On the other hand many American slaves were saved from death at the hands of the law by the tolerant spirit of citizens toward them and by the consideration of the pecuniary loss to be suffered through their execution. A Jamaican statute of 1684 went so far as to prescribe that when several slaves were jointly involved in a capital crime one only was to be executed as an example and the loss caused by his death was to be apportioned among the owners of the several.[11] More commonly the mitigation lay not

[8] Robert Walsh, Jr., *An Appeal from the Judgments of Great Britain respecting the United States of America* (Philadelphia, 1819), p. 405.
[9] A. C. Goodell, Jr., *The Trial and Execution for Petit Treason of Mark and Phillis* (Cambridge, 1883), reprinted from the Massachusetts Historical Society *Proceedings*, XX, 132-157.
[10] A. L. Cross, "Benefit of Clergy," in the *American Historical Review*, XXII, 544-565.
[11] *Abridgement of the Laws in Force in Her Majesty's Plantations* (London, 1704), pp. 104-108.

in the laws themselves but in the general disposition to leave to the discipline of the masters such slave misdeeds as were not regarded as particularly heinous nor menacing to the public security.

Burnings at the stake, breakings on the wheel and other ferocious methods of execution which were occasionally inflicted by the colonial courts were almost universally discontinued soon after the beginning of the nineteenth century. The general trend of moderation discernible at that time, however, was hampered then and thereafter by the series of untoward events beginning with the San Domingo upheaval and ending with John Brown's raid. In particular the rise of the Garrisonian agitation and the quickly ensuing Nat Turner's revolt occasioned together a wave of reactionary legislation the whole South over, prohibiting the literary instruction of negroes, stiffening the patrol system, restricting manumissions, and diminishing the already limited liberties of free negroes. The temper of administration, however, was not appreciably affected, for this clearly appears to have grown milder as the decades passed.

The police ordinances of the several cities and other local jurisdictions were in keeping with the state laws which they supplemented and in some degree duplicated. At New Orleans an ordinance adopted in 1817 and little changed thereafter forbade slaves to live off their masters' premises without written permission, to make any clamorous noise, to show disrespect to any white persons, to walk with canes on the streets unless on account of infirmity, or to congregate except at church, at funerals, and at such dances and other amusements as were permitted for them on Sundays alone and in public places. Each offender was to be tried by the mayor or a justice of the peace after due notice to his master, and upon conviction was to be punished within a limit of twenty-five lashes unless his master paid a fine for him instead.[12]

At Richmond an ordinance effective in 1859 had provisions much like those of New Orleans regarding residence, clamor,

[12] D. Augustin, *A General Digest of the Ordinances and Resolutions of the Corporation of New Orleans* ([New Orleans], 1831), pp. 133-137.

canes, assemblage and demeanor, and also debarred slaves from
the capitol square and other specified public enclosures unless in
attendance on white persons or on proper errands, forbade them
to ride in public hacks without the written consent of their masters, or to administer medicine to any persons except at their
masters' residences and with the masters' consent. It further
forbade all negroes, whether bond or free, to possess offensive
weapons or ammunition, to form secret societies, or to loiter on
the streets near their churches more than half an hour after the
conclusion of services; and it required them when meeting, over-
taking or being overtaken by white persons on the sidewalks to
pass on the outside, stepping off the walk if necessary to allow
the whites to pass. It also forbade all free persons to hire slaves
to themselves, to rent houses, rooms or grounds to them, to sell
them liquors by retail, or drugs without written permits from
their masters, or to furnish offensive weapons to negroes whether
bond or free. Finally, it forbade anyone to beat a slave unlawfully, under fine of not more than twenty dollars if a white person, or of lashes or fine at the magistrate's discretion in case the
offender were a free person of color.[13]

Of rural ordinances, one adopted by the parish of West Baton
Rouge, Louisiana, in 1828 was concerned only with the organization and functions of the citizens' patrol. As many chiefs of
patrol were to be appointed as the parish authorities might think
proper, each to be in charge of a specified district, with duties of
listing all citizens liable to patrol service, dividing them into
proper details and appointing a commander for each squad.
Every commander in his turn, upon receiving notice from his
chief, was to cover the local beat on the night appointed, search-
ing slave quarters, though with as little disturbance as possible to
the inmates, arresting any free negroes or strange whites found
where they had no proper authority or business to be, whipping
slaves encountered at large without passes or unless on the way
to or from the distant homes of their wives, and seizing any

[13] *The Charters and Ordinances of the City of Richmond* (Richmond, 1859), pp. 193-200.

arms and any runaway slaves discovered.[14] The police code of
the neighboring parish of East Feliciana in 1859 went on further to prescribe trials and penalties for slaves insulting or abus-
ing white persons, to restrict their carrying of guns, and their
assemblage, to forbid all slaves but wagoners to keep dogs, to restrict citizens in their trading with slaves, to require the seizure
of self-styled free negroes not possessing certificates, and to prescribe that all negroes or mulattoes found on the railroad without written permits be deemed runaway slaves and dealt with as
the law regarding such directed.[15]

In general, the letter of the law in slaveholding states at the
middle of the nineteenth century presumed all persons with a
palpable strain of negro blood to be slaves unless they could
prove the contrary, and regarded the possession of them by masters as presumptive evidence of legal ownership. Property in
slaves, though by some of the statutes assimilated to real estate
for certain technical purposes, was usually considered as of chattel character. Its use and control, however, were hedged about
with various restraints and obligations. In some states masters
were forbidden to hire slaves to themselves or to leave them in
any unusual way to their self-direction; and everywhere they
were required to maintain their slaves in full sustenance whether
young or old, able-bodied or incapacitated. The manumission
of the disabled was on grounds of public thrift nowhere permitted unless accompanied with provision for their maintenance,
and that of slaves of all sorts was restricted in a great variety
of ways. Generally no consent by the slave was required in
manumission, though in some commonwealths he might lawfully reject freedom in the form bestowed.[16] Masters might
vest powers of agency in their slaves, but when so doing the masters themselves became liable for any injuries or derelictions en-

[14] Police Regulations of the Parish of West Baton Rouge (La.), passed
at a regular meeting held at the Court House of said Parish on the second and third days of June, A. D. 1828 (Baton Rouge, 1828), pp. 8-11.
For a copy of this pamphlet I am indebted to Professor W. L. Fleming
of Louisiana State University.
[15] D. B. Sanford, Police Jury Code of the Parish of East Feliciana, Louisiana (Clinton, La., 1859), pp. 98-101.
[16] E. g., Jones, North Carolina Supreme Court Reports, VI, 272.

suing. In criminal prosecutions, on the other hand, slaves were considered as responsible persons on their own score and punishable under the laws applicable to them. Where a crime was committed at the master's express command, the master was liable and in some cases the slave also. Slave offenders were commonly tried summarily by special inferior courts, though for serious crimes in some states by the superior courts by regular process. Since the slaves commonly had no funds with which to pay fines, and no liberty of which to be deprived, the penalties imposed upon them for crimes and misdemeanors were usually death, deportation or lashes. Frequently in Louisiana, however, and more seldom elsewhere, convicted slaves were given prison sentences. By the intent of the law their punishments were generally more severe than those applied to white persons for the same offenses. In civil transactions slaves had no standing as persons in court except for the one purpose of making claim of freedom; and even this must usually be done through some friendly citizen as a self-appointed guardian bringing suit for trespass in the nature of ravishment of ward. The activities of slaves were elaborately restricted; any property they might acquire was considered as belonging to their masters; their marriages were without legal recognition; and although the wilful killing of slaves was generally held to be murder, the violation of their women was without criminal penalty. Under the law as it generally stood no slave might raise his hand against a white person even in self-defense unless his life or limb were endangered, nor might he in his own person apply to the courts for the redress of injuries, nor generally give evidence except where negroes alone were involved. All white persons on the other hand were permitted, and in some regards required, to exercise police power over the slaves; and their masters in particular were vested with full disciplinary power over them in all routine concerns. If they should flee from their masters' dominion, the force of the state and of other states into which they might escape, and of the United States if necessary, might be employed for their capture and resubjection; and any suspected of being fugitives, though professing to be free, might be held for long periods in custody and in the end, in default of proofs of freedom and of masters' claims, be sold by the authorities at public auction. Finally, affecting slaves and colored freemen somewhat alike, and regardless as usual of any distinction of mulattoes or quadroons from the full-blood negroes, there were manifold restraints of a social character buttressing the predominance and the distinctive privileges of the Caucasian caste.

It may fairly be said that these laws for the securing of slave property and the police of the colored population were as thorough and stringent as their framers could make them, and that they left an almost irreducible minimum of rights and privileges to those whose function and place were declared to be service and subordination. But in fairness it must also be said that in adopting this legislation the Southern community largely belied itself, for whereas the laws were systematically drastic the citizens in whose interest they were made and in whose hands their enforcement lay were in practice quite otherwise. It would have required a European bureaucracy to keep such laws fully effective; the individualistic South was incapable of the task. If the regulations were seldom relaxed in the letter they were as rarely enforced in the spirit. The citizens were too fond of their own liberties to serve willingly as martinets in the routine administration of their own laws;[17] and in consequence the marchings of the patrol squads were almost as futile and farcical as the musters of the militia. The magistrates and constables tended toward a similar slackness;[18] while on the other hand the masters, easy-going as they might be in other concerns, were jealous of any infringements of their own dominion or any abuse of their slaves whether by private persons or public functionaries. When in 1787, for example, a slave boy in Maryland reported to his master that two strangers by the name of Maddox had whipped him for killing a dog while Mr. Samuel Bishop had stood by and let them do it, the master, who presumably had no means of reaching the two strangers, wrote Bishop demanding an explanation of his conduct and intimating that if this were

[17] *E. g.*, Letter of "a citizen" in the Charleston *City Gazette*, Aug. 17, 1825.
[18] *E. g.*, *L'Abeille* (New Orleans), Aug. 15, 1841, editorial.

not satisfactorily forthcoming by the next session of court, proceedings would be begun against him.[19] While this complainant might not have been able to procure a judgment against a merely acquiescent bystander, the courts were quite ready to punish actual transgressors. In sustaining the indictment of a private citizen for such offense the chief-justice of North Carolina said in 1823: "For all purposes necessary to enforce the obedience of the slave and render him useful as property the law secures to the master a complete authority over him, and it will not lightly interfere with the relation thus established. It is a more effectual guarantee of his right of property when the slave is protected from wanton abuse by those who have no power over him, for it cannot be disputed that a slave is rendered less capable of performing his master's service when he finds himself exposed by law to the capricious violence of every turbulent man in the community. Mitigated as slavery is by the humanity of our laws, the refinement of manners, and by public opinion which revolts at every instance of cruelty towards them, it would be an anomaly in the system of police which affects them if the offense stated in the verdict [the striking of a slave] were not indictable." [20] Likewise the South Carolina Court of Appeals in 1850 endorsed the fining of a public patrol which had whipped the slaves at a quilting party despite their possession of written permission from their several masters. The Court said of the quilting party: "The occasion was a perfectly innocent one, even meritorious. . . . It would simply seem ridiculous to suppose that the safety of the state or any of its inhabitants was implicated in such an assemblage as this." And of the patrol's limitations: "A judicious freedom in the administration of our police laws for the lower order must always have respect for the confidence which the law reposes in the discretion of the master." [21]

[19] Letter signed "R. T.," Port Tobacco, Md., Aug. 19, 1787. MS. in the Library of Congress.
[20] The State v. Hale, in Hawks, *North Carolina Reports*, V, 582. See similarly Munford, *Virginia Reports*, I, 288.
[21] The State v. Boozer *et al.*, in Strobhart, *South Carolina Law Reports*, V, 21. This is quoted at some length in H. M. Henry, *Police Control of the Slave in South Carolina*, pp. 146-148.

The masters were on their private score, however, prone to disregard the law where it restrained their own prerogatives. They hired slaves to the slaves themselves whether legally permitted or not; they sent them on responsible errands to markets dozens of miles away, often without providing them with passes; they sanctioned and encouraged assemblies under conditions prohibited by law; they taught their slaves at will to read and write, and used them freely in forbidden employments. Such practices as these were often noted and occasionally complained of in the press, but they were seldom obstructed. When outside parties took legal steps to interfere in the master's routine administration, indeed, they were prompted probably as often by personal animosity as by devotion to the law. An episode of the sort, where the complainants were envious poorer neighbors, was related with sarcasm and some philosophical moralizing by W. B. Hodgson, of whose plantation something has been previously said, in a letter to Senator Hammond: "I am somewhat 'riled' with Burke. The benevolent neighbors have lately had me in court under indictment for cruel treatment of my fat, lazy, rollicking sambos. For fifty years they have eaten their own meat and massa's too; but inasmuch as rich massa did not *buy* meat, the *poor Benevolens* indicted him. So was my friend Thomas Foreman, executor of Governor Troup. My suit was withdrawn; he was acquitted. I have some crude notions about that thing slavery in the end. Its tendency, as with landed accumulations in England, or Aaron's rod, is to swallow up other small rods, and inevitably to attract the benevolence of the smaller ones. You may have two thousand ac.es of land in a body. That is unfeeling—land is. But a body of a thousand negroes appeals to the finer sentiments of the heart. The agrarian battle is hard to fight. But *'les amis des noirs'* in our midst have the vantage ground, particularly when rejected overseers come in as spies. *C'est un peu dégoutant, mon cher ami;* but I can stand the racket." [22]

[22] Letter of W. B. Hodgson, Savannah, Ga., June 19, 1859, to J. H. Hammond. MS. among the Hammond papers in the Library of Congress. "Burke" is the county in which Hodgson's plantation lay.

The courts exercising jurisdiction over slaves were of two sorts, those of inferior grade and amateurish character which dealt with them as persons, and those of superior rank and genuine magisterial quality which handled them as property and sometimes, on appeal, as persons as well. These lower courts for the trial of slave crimes had vices in plenty. They were informal and largely ignorant of the law, and they were so quickly convened after the discovery of a crime that the shock of the deed had no time to wane. Such virtues as they sometimes had lay merely in their personnel. The slaveholders of the vicinage who commonly comprised the court were intimately and more or less tolerantly acquainted with negro nature in general, and usually doubtless with the prisoner on trial. Their judgment was therefore likely to be that of informed and interested neighbors, not of jurors carefully selected for ignorance and indifference, a judgment guided more by homely common sense than by the particularities of the law. Their task was difficult, as anyone acquainted with the rambling, mumbling, confused and baffling character of plantation negro testimony will easily believe; and the convictions and acquittals were of course oftentimes erroneous. The remodeling of the system was one of the reforms called for by Southerners of the time but never accomplished. Mistaken acquittals by these courts were beyond correction, for in the South slaves like freemen could not be twice put in jeopardy for the same offense. Their convictions, on the other hand, were sometimes set aside by higher courts on appeal, or their sentences estopped from execution by the governor's pardon.[23] The thoroughness with which some of the charges against negroes were considered is illustrated in two cases tried before the county court at Newbern, North Carolina, in 1826. In one of these a negro boy was acquitted of highway robbery after the jury's deliberation of several hours; in the other the jury on the case of a free negro woman charged with infanticide had been

<hr>

[23] The working of these courts and the current criticisms of them are illustrated in H. M. Henry *The Police Control of the Slave in South Carolina*, pp. 58-65.

out for forty-six hours without reaching a verdict when the
newspaper dispatch was written.[24]

The circuit and supreme courts of the several states, though
the slave cases which they tried were for the most part concerned only with such dry questions as detinue, trover, bailment,
leases, inheritance and reversions, in which the personal quality
of the negroes was largely ignored, occasionally rendered decisions of vivid human interest even where matters of mere
property were nominally involved. An example occurred in
the case of Rhame *vs.* Ferguson and Dangerfield, decided by the
South Carolina Court of Appeals in 1839 in connection with a
statute enacted by the legislature of that state in 1800 restricting
manumissions and prescribing that any slaves illegally set free
might be seized by any person as derelicts. George Broad of St.
John's Parish, Berkeley County, had died without blood relatives in 1836, bequeathing fourteen slaves and their progeny to
his neighbor Dangerfield "in trust nevertheless and for this purpose only that the said John R. Dangerfield, his executors and
assigns do permit and suffer the said slaves . . . to apply and
appropriate their time and labor to their own proper use and be-
hoof, without the intermeddling or interference of any person or
persons whomsoever further than may be necessary for their
protection under the laws of this state"; and bequeathing also to
Dangerfield all his other property in trust for the use of these
negroes and their descendants forever. These provisions were
being duly followed when on a December morning in 1837 Rebecca Rhame, the remarried widow of Broad's late brother-in-
law, descended upon the Broad plantation in a buggy with John
J. Singletary whom she had employed for the occasion under
power of attorney. Finding no white person at the residence,
Singletary ordered the negroes into the yard and told them they
were seized in Mrs. Rhame's behalf and must go with him to
Charleston. At this juncture Dangerfield, the trustee, came up
and demanded Singletary's authority, whereupon the latter
showed him his power of attorney and read him the laws under

[24] News item from Newbern, N. C., in the Charleston *City Gazette,* May
9, 1826.

which he was proceeding. Dangerfield, seeking delay, said it would be a pity to drag the negroes through the mud, and sent a boy to bring his own wagon for them. While this vehicle was being awaited Colonel James Ferguson, a dignitary of the neighborhood who had evidently been secretly sent for by Dangerfield, galloped up, glanced over the power of attorney, branded the whole affair as a cheat, and told Dangerfield to order Singletary off the premises, driving him away with a whip if necessary, and to shoot if the conspirators should bring reinforcements. "After giving this advice, which he did apparently under great excitement, Ferguson rode off." Singletary then said that for his part he had not come to take or lose life; and he and his employer departed. Mrs. Rhame then sued Ferguson and Dangerfield to procure possession of the negroes, claiming that she had legally seized them on the occasion described. At the trial in the circuit court, Singletary rehearsed the seizure and testified further that Dangerfield had left the negroes customarily to themselves in virtually complete freedom. In rebuttal, Dr. Theodore Gaillard testified that the negroes, whom he described as orderly by habit, were kept under control by the trustee and made to work. The verdict of the jury, deciding the questions of fact in pursuance of the judge's charge as to the law, was in favor of the defendants; and Mrs. Rhame entered a motion for a new trial. This was in due course denied by the Court of Appeals on the ground that Broad's will had clearly vested title to the slaves in Dangerfield, who after Broad's death was empowered to do with them as he pleased. If he, who was by the will merely trustee but by law the full owner, had given up the practical dominion over the slaves and left them to their own self-government they were liable to seizure under the law of 1800. This question of fact, the court concluded, had properly been put to the jury along with the issue as to the effectiveness of the plaintiff's seizure of the slaves; and the verdict for the defendants was declared conclusive.[26]

This is the melodrama which the sober court record recites.

[26] Rebecca Rhame vs. James Ferguson and John R. Dangerfield, in Rice, *Law Reports of South Carolina*, I, 196-203.

The female villain of the piece and her craven henchman were foiled by the sturdy but wily trustee and the doughty Carolina colonel who, in headlong, aristocratic championship of those threatened with oppression against the moral sense of the community, charged upon the scene and counseled slaughter if necessary in defense of negroes who were none of his. And in the end the magistrates and jurors, proving second Daniels come to judgment, endorsed the victory of benevolence over avarice and assured the so-called slaves their thinly veiled freedom. Curiously, however, the decision in this case was instanced by a contemporary traveller to prove that negroes freed by will in South Carolina might be legally enslaved by any person seizing them, and that the bequest of slaves in trust to an executor as a merely nominal master was contrary to law; [26] and in later times a historian has instanced the traveller's account in support of his own statement that "Persons who had been set free for years and had no reason to suppose that they were anything else might be seized upon for defects in the legal process of manumission." [27]

Now according to the letter of certain statutes at certain times, these assertions were severally more or less true; but if this particular case and its outcome have any palpable meaning, it is that the courts connived at thwarting such provisions by sanctioning, as a proprietorship valid against the claim of a captor, what was in obvious fact a merely nominal dominion.

Another striking case in which the severity of the law was overridden by the court in sanction of lenient custom was that of Jones vs. Allen, decided on appeal by the Supreme Court of Tennessee in 1858. In the fall of the preceding year Jones had called in his neighbors and their slaves to a corn husking and had sent Allen a message asking him to send help. Some twenty-five white men and seventy-five slaves gathered on the appointed night, among them Allen's slave Isaac. After supper, about midnight, Jones told the negroes to go home; but Isaac stayed a while with some others wrestling in the back yard, during which, while Jones was not present, a white man named

[26] J. S. Buckingham, *Slave States in America*, II, 32, 33.
[27] A. B. Hart, *Slavery and Abolition* (New York, 1906), p. 88.

Hager stabbed Isaac to death. Allen thereupon sued Jones for damages on the ground that the latter had knowingly and unlawfully suffered Isaac, without the legally required authorization, to come with other slaves upon his premises, where he had been slain to his owner's loss. The testimony showed that Allen had not received Jones' message and had given Isaac no permission to go, but that Jones had not questioned Isaac in this regard; that Jones had given spirituous liquors to the slaves while at work, Isaac included, but that no one there was intoxicated except Hager who had come drunk and without invitation. In the trial court, in Rutherford County where the tragedy had occurred, the judge excluded evidence that such corn huskings were the custom of the country without the requirement of written permission for the slaves attending, and he charged the jury that Jones' employment of Isaac and Isaac's death on his premises made him liable to Allen for the value of the slave. But on Jones' appeal the Supreme Court overruled this, asserting that "under our modified form of slavery slaves are not mere chattels but are regarded in the two-fold character of persons and property; that as persons they are considered by our law as accountable moral agents; . . . that certain rights have been conferred upon them by positive law and judicial determination, and other privileges and indulgences have been conceded to them by the universal consent of their owners. By uniform and universal usage they are constituted the agents of their owners and sent on business without written authority. And in like manner they are sent to perform those neighborly good offices common in every community. . . . The simple truth is, such indulgences have been so long and so uniformly tolerated, the public sentiment upon the subject has acquired almost the force of positive law." The judgment of the lower court was accordingly reversed and Jones was relieved of liability for his laxness.[28]

There were sharp limits, nevertheless, to the lenity of the courts. Thus when one Brazeale of Mississippi carried with him to Ohio and there set free a slave woman of his and a son whom he had begotten of her, and then after taking them home

[28] Head's *Tennessee Reports*, I, 627-639.

again died bequeathing all his property to the mulatto boy, the supreme court of the state, in 1838, declared the manumission void under the laws and awarded the mother and son along with all the rest of Brazeale's estate to his legitimate heirs who had brought the suit.[29]   In so deciding the court may have been moved by its repugnance toward concubinage as well as by its respect for the statutes.

The killing or injury of a slave except under circumstances justified by law rendered the offender liable both to the master's claim for damages and to criminal prosecution; and the master's suit might be sustained even where the evidence was weak, for as was said in a Louisiana decision, the deed was "one rarely committed in presence of witnesses, and the most that can be expected in cases of this kind are the presumptions that result from circumstances." [30]   The requirement of positive proof from white witnesses in criminal cases caused many indictments to fail.[31]   A realization of this hindrance in the law deprived convicted offenders of some of the tolerance which their crimes might otherwise have met.   When in 1775, for example, William Pitman was found guilty and sentenced by the Virginia General Court to be hanged for the beating of his slave to death, the *Virginia Gazette* said: "This man has justly incurred the penalties of the law and we hear will certainly suffer, which ought to be a warning to others to treat their slaves with more moderation." [32]   In the nineteenth century the laws generally held the maiming or murder of slaves to be felonies in the same degree and with the same penalties as in cases where the victims were whites; and when the statutes were silent in the premises the courts felt themselves free to remedy the defect.[33]

Despite the ferocity of the statutes and the courts, the fewness and the laxity of officials was such that from time to time other agencies were called into play.   For example the maraudings of

[29] Howard's *Mississippi Reports*, II, 837-844.
[30] Martin, *Louisiana Reports*, XV, 142.
[31] H. M. Henry, *Police Control of the Slave in South Carolina*, pp. 69-79.
[32] *Virginia Gazette*, Apr. 21, 1775, reprinted in the *William and Mary College Quarterly*, VIII, 36.
[33] The State *vs.* Jones, in Walker, *Mississippi Reports*, p. 83, reprinted in J. D. Wheeler, *The Law of Slavery*, pp. 252-254.

runaway slaves camped in Belle Isle swamp, a score of miles above Savannah, became so serious and lasting that their haven had to be several times destroyed by the Georgia militia. On one of these occasions, in 1786, a small force first employed was obliged to withdraw in the face of the blacks, and reinforcements merely succeeded in burning the huts and towing off the canoes, while the negroes themselves were safely in hiding. Not long afterward, however, the gang was broken up, partly through the services of Creek and Catawba Indians who hunted the maroons for the prices on their heads.[34] The Seminoles, on the other hand, gave asylum to such numbers of runaways as to prompt invasions of their country by the United States army both before and after the Florida purchase.[35] On lesser occasions raids were made by citizen volunteers. The swamps of the lower Santee River, for example, were searched by several squads in 1819, with the killing of two negroes, the capture of several others and the wounding of one of the whites as the result.[36]

More frequent occasions for the creation of vigilance committees were the rumors of plots among the blacks and the reports of mischievous doings by whites. In the same Santee district of the Carolina lowlands, for instance, a public meeting at Black Oak Church on January 3, 1860, appointed three committees of five members each to look out for and dispose of any suspicious characters who might be "prowling about the parish." Of the sequel nothing is recorded by the local diarist of the time except the following, under date of October 25: "Went out with a party of men to take a fellow by the name of Andrews, who lived at Cantey's Hill and traded with the negroes. He had been warned of our approach and run off. We went on and broke up the trading establishment."[37]

[34] *Georgia Colonial Records*, XII, 325, 326; *Georgia Gazette* (Savannah), Oct. 19, 1786; *Massachusetts Sentinel* (Boston), June 13, 1787; *Georgia State Gazette and Independent Register* (Augusta), June 16, 1787.
[35] Joshua R. Giddings, *The Exiles of Florida* (Columbus, Ohio, 1858).
[36] Diary of Dr. Henry Ravenel, Jr., of St. John's Parish, Berkeley County, S. C. MS. in private possession.
[37] Diary of Thomas P. Ravenel, which is virtually a continuation of the Diary just cited. MS. in private possession.

Such transactions were those of the most responsible and sub-stantial citizens, laboring to maintain social order in the face of the law's desuetude. A mere step further in that direction, how-ever, lay outright lynch law. Lynchings, indeed, while far from habitual, were frequent enough to link the South with the fron-tier West of the time. The victims were not only rapists [38] but negro malefactors of sundry sorts, and occasionally white of-fenders as well. In some cases fairly full accounts of such epi-sodes are available, but more commonly the record extant is la-conic. Thus the Virginia archives have under date of 1791 an affidavit reciting that "Ralph Singo and James Richards had in January last, in Accomac County, been hung by a band of dis-guised men, numbering from six to fifteen"; [39] and a Georgia newspaper in 1860 the following: "It is reported that Mr. William Smith was killed by a negro on Saturday evening at Bowling Green, in Oglethorpe County. He was stabbed sixteen times. The negro made his escape but was arrested on Sunday, and on Monday morning a number of citizens who had investigated the case burnt him at the stake." [40]   In at least one well-known in-stance the mob's violence was directed against an abuser of slaves. This was at New Orleans in 1834 when a rumor spread that Madame Lalaurie, a wealthy resident, was torturing her ne-groes. A great crowd collected after nightfall, stormed her door, found seven slaves chained and bearing marks of inhuman treatment, and gutted the house. The woman herself had fled at the first alarm, and made her way eventually to Paris.[41] Had she been brought before a modern court it may be doubted whether she would have been committed to a penitentiary or to a lunatic asylum. At the hands of the mob, however, her shrift would presumably have been short and sure.

The violence of city mobs is a thing peculiar to no time or

[38] For examples of these see above, pp. 460-463.
[39] Calendar of Virginia State Papers, V, 328.
[40] Southern Banner (Athens, Ga.), June 14, 1860. Other instances, gleaned mostly from Niles' Register and the Liberator, are given in J. E. Cutler, Lynch Law (New York, 1905), pp. 90-136.
[41] Harriett Martineau, Retrospect of Western Travel (London, 1838), I, 262-267; V. Debouchel, Histoire de la Louisiane (New Orleans, 1841), p. 155; Alcée Fortier, History of Louisiana, III, 223.

place. Rural Southern lynch law in that period, however, was in large part a special product of the sparseness of population and the resulting weakness of legal machinery, for as Olmsted justly remarked in the middle 'fifties, the whole South was virtually still in a frontier condition.[42] In *post bellum* decades, on the other hand, an increase of racial antipathy has offset the effect of the densification of settlement and has abnormally prolonged the liability to the lynching impulse.

While the records have no parallel for Madame Lalaurie in her systematic and wholesale torture of slaves, there were thousands of masters and mistresses as tolerant and kindly as she was fiendish; and these were virtually without restraint of public authority in their benevolent rule. Lawmakers and magistrates by personal status in their own plantation provinces, they ruled with a large degree of consent and coöperation by the governed, for indeed no other course was feasible in the long run by men and women of normal type. Concessions and friendly services beyond the countenance and contemplation of the statutes were habitual with those whose name was legion. The law, for example, conceded no property rights to the slaves, and some statutes forbade specifically their possession of horses, but the following characteristic letter of a South Carolina mistress to an influential citizen tells an opposite story: "I hope you will pardon the liberty I take in addressing you on the subject of John, the slave of Professor Henry, Susy his wife, and the orphan children of my faithful servant Pompey, the first husband of Susy. In the first instance, Pompey owned a horse which he exchanged for a mare, which mare I permitted Susy to use after her marriage with John, but told them both I would sell it and the young colt and give Susy a third of the money, reserving the other two thirds for her children. Before I could do so, however, the mare and the colt were exchanged and sent out of my way by this dishonest couple. I then hoped at least to secure forty-five dollars for which another colt was sold to Mr. Haskell, and sent my message to him to say that Susy had no claim on the colt and that the money was to be paid to me for the children of

[42] F. L. Olmsted, *Journey in the Back Country*, p. 413.

Pompey. A few days since I sent to Mr. Haskell again who informed me that he had paid for the colt, and referred me to you. I do assure you that whatever Susy may affirm, she has no right to the money. It is not my intention to meddle with the law on the occasion, and I infinitely prefer relying on you to do justice to the parties. My manager, who will deliver this to you, is perfectly acquainted with all the circumstances; and [if] after having a conversation with him you should decide in favor of the children I shall be much gratified." [43]

Likewise where the family affairs of slaves were concerned the silence and passiveness of the law gave masters occasion for eloquence and activity. Thus a Georgian wrote to a neighbor: "I have a girl Amanda that has your servant Phil for a husband. I should be very glad indeed if you would purchase her. She is a very good seamstress, an excellent cook—makes cake and preserves beautifully—and washes and irons very nicely, and cannot be excelled in cleaning up a house. Her disposition is very amiable. I have had her for years and I assure you that I have not exaggerated as regards her worth. . . . I will send her down to see you at any time." [44] That offers of purchase were no less likely than those of sale to be prompted by such considerations is suggested by another Georgia letter: "I have made every attempt to get the boy Frank, the son of James Nixon; and in order to gratify James have offered as far as five hundred dollars for him—more than I would pay for any negro child in Georgia were it not James' son." [45] It was therefore not wholly in idyllic strain that a South Carolinian after long magisterial service remarked: "Experience and observation fully satisfy me that the first law of slavery is that of kindness from the master to the slave. With that . . . slavery becomes a family relation, next in its attachments to that of parent and child." [46]

[43] Letter of Caroline Raoul, Belleville, S. C., Dec. 26, 1829, to James H. Hammond. MS. among the Hammond papers in the Library of Congress.
[44] Letter of E. N. Thompson, Vineville, Ga. (a suburb of Macon), to J. B. Lamar at Macon, Ga., Aug. 7, 1854. MS. in the possession of Mrs. A. S. Erwin, Athens, Ga.
[45] Letter of Henry Jackson, Jan. 11, 1837, to Howell Cobb. MS. in the possession of Mrs. A. S. Erwin, Athens, Ga.
[46] J. B. O'Neall in J. B. D. DeBow ed., *Industrial Resources of the South and West*, II (New Orleans, 1852), 278.

On the whole, the several sorts of documents emanating from the Old South have a character of true depiction inversely proportioned to their abundance and accessibility. The statutes, copious and easily available, describe a hypothetical régime, not an actual one. The court records are on the one hand plentiful only for the higher tribunals, whither questions of human adjustments rarely penetrated, and on the other hand the decisions were themselves largely controlled by the statutes, perverse for ordinary practical purposes as these often were. It is therefore to the letters, journals and miscellaneous records of private persons dwelling in the régime and by their practices molding it more powerfully than legislatures and courts combined, that the main recourse for intimate knowledge must be had. Regrettably fugitive and fragmentary as these are, enough it may be hoped have been found and used herein to show the true nature of the living order.

The government of slaves was for the ninety and nine by men, and only for the hundredth by laws. There were injustice, oppression, brutality and heartburning in the régime,—but where in the struggling world are these absent? There were also gentleness, kind-hearted friendship and mutual loyalty to a degree hard for him to believe who regards the system with a theorist's eye and a partisan squint. For him on the other hand who has known the considerate and cordial, courteous and charming men and women, white and black, which that picturesque life in its best phases produced, it is impossible to agree that its basis and its operation were wholly evil, the law and the prophets to the contrary notwithstanding.

INDEX

Acklen, Joseph A. S., plantation home of, 239, 240.
  rules of, for overseers, 262-273.
Africa, West, *see* Guinea.
Agriculture, *see* cotton, indigo, rice, sugar and tobacco culture.
Aiken, William, rice plantation of, 251-253.
Aime, Valcour, sugar plantation of, 242-244.
Amissa, enslaved and restored to Africa, 32.
Angolas, tribal traits of, 44.
  revolt of, 473.
Antipathy, racial, Jefferson's views on, 123.
  in Massachusetts, 119.
  in North and South compared, 439-441.
  Northern spokesmen of, 131.
Arabs, in the Guinea trade, 9.
Asiento, 17-19, 22, 23, 30.
Azurara, Gomez E., 1, 2.

Baltimore, negro churches in, 423.
Barbados, emigration from, to Carolina, 85, 86.
  to Jamaica, 49.
  founding of, 46, 47.
  planters' committee of, 48.
  slave laws of, 490-492.
  sugar culture in, 46-49.
Belmead plantation, 230-232.
Benin, 6, 32.

Black codes, 75-77, 103-112, 489-514.
  administration of, 501-509.
  attitude of citizens toward, 503, 512-514.
  local ordinances, 497-499.
  origin of, in Barbados, 490-492.
  in the Northern colonies, 103-112.
  in Louisiana, 493, 494.
  in South Carolina, 492, 493.
  in Virginia, 75-77.
  tenor of, in the North, 103-112.
  in the South, 499-501.
Bobolinks, in rice fields, 90.
Bonny, 32, 34.
Boré, Etienne de, sugar planter, 164.
Bosman, William, in the Guinea trade, 25, 34, 44.
Branding of slaves, 26, 63, 304, 328, 454, 555.
Bristol, citizens of, in the slave trade, 32.
Burial societies, negro, 450-452.
Burnside, John, merchant and sugar planter, 246.
Butler, Pierce, 129.
  the younger, 251.
  slaves of, sold, 374.

Cain, Elisha, overseer, 234-238.
Cairnes, J. E., views of, on slavery, 354-357.
Calabar, 2, 44.
  New, 32.